BY THE SAME AUTHOR

The International Nomads

The Golden Oases

THE LAST
PRIMA DONNAS

THE LAST PRIMA DONNAS

LANFRANCO RASPONI

LIMELIGHT EDITIONS
NEW YORK 1985

First Limelight Edition, March 1985
Copyright © 1975, 1976, 1977, 1978, 1979, 1980, 1981, 1982
by Lanfranco Rasponi

All rights reserved under International and Pan-American Copyright Conventions.
Published in the United States by Proscenium Publishers Inc., New York, and
simultaneously in Canada by Fitzhenry & Whiteside, Limited, Toronto.
Originally published by Alfred A. Knopf.

The following interviews are reprinted by permission of OPERA NEWS,
a publication of the Metropolitan Opera Guild, 1865 Broadway, New York, N.Y. 10023:
Maria Caniglia, Gina Cigna, Denise Duval, Mafalda Favero, Germaine Lubin,
Ester Mazzoleni, Toti dal Monte, Augusta Oltrabella, Iva Pacetti, Lina Pagliughi,
Gianna Pederzini, Gilda dalla Rizza, Sara Scuderi, Giulietta Simionato,
Bianca Stagno Bellincioni, Renata Tebaldi, Giulia Tess.

Library of Congress Cataloging in Publication Data
Rasponi, Lanfranco.
The last prima donnas.
Originally published: New York: Knopf, 1982.
Includes index.
1. Women singers—Interviews. I. Title.
[ML400.R37   1985]   782.1′092′2 [B]   84-26129
ISBN 0-87910-040-0

Manufactured in the United States of America

To Robert Jacobson

CONTENTS

Contents

ACKNOWLEDGMENTS

I wish to express my warmest thanks to all the people who helped to make this volume possible, and in particular to Robert Gottlieb, Karen Latuchie, Patricia Myrer, Julie Fallowfield, Peter Gravina, Gerald Fitzgerald, Genna Smakov, Mary Jane Matz, Wally Toscanini, Jarmila Novotna, Gianna Pederzini, Rita Streich, Claire Watson, Iride Reggiani, Maria Lucia Godoy, Mario Caldas, Ferdinando Markan, Pasquale de Antoniis, Adonido Gadotti, Paolo Queiroz, Luigi Barzini, and Wilton Wynn.

Prima donnas in my father's day were, as the words indicate, the first ladies among the women singers, because of their vocal gifts and the considerable sacrifices they made for their profession and the art they served. These qualities gave them an intangible glamour. Today they no longer exist, for they have become traveling robots, interested mainly in making money, their personality squashed by stage directors.

WALLY TOSCANINI

INTRODUCTION

This volume consists of conversations I have had with some great prima donnas of the past, some now dead and others still very much alive. The earliest of these encounters dates back to the 1930s; the last of them took place in 1980. It is a book full of nostalgia, for the divas as I knew them are members of an extinct race. There are today some capable younger singers, but none of them have that intangible magic that gave to the past ones a very marked personality and glamour. It is Renata Tebaldi's opinion that when Joan Sutherland, Leonie Rysanek, and Leontyne Price (all past fifty-five), Christa Ludwig (fifty-four), Birgit Nilsson (sixty-four), and Magda Olivero (seventy) retire, there will only be one prima donna left: Montserrat Caballé. The explanations as to why prima donnas no longer exist are manifold. As we will hear from those interviewed, the main factors are the constant traveling, the wish to earn money quickly, the lack of connoisseurs at the head of opera houses, and the concentrated effort on the part of conductors and stage directors to quash the individuality of artists. Curiously, the same phenomenon has occurred in the motion picture industry: there are no more glamorous film stars.

The prima donnas I have selected—and it was not an easy task, since there are still so many important ones in retirement—either excelled in a certain repertoire or in a certain style of singing, or achieved a position of pre-eminence for a number of different reasons. Alas, some, such as Maria Jeritza and Rosa Ponselle (who have since died), were too ill by the time I asked to see them. Others have been overlooked deliberately because they are still very much in evidence: divas such as Licia Albanese, Eleanor Steber, Risë Stevens, and Beverly Sills. I thought it more interesting to talk, in some cases, to those about whom less is known, since this collection of talks and reminiscences is meant as a reference for the future.

In many cases, it took some real detective work to locate these former celebrities, for most of them disappeared and left no trace. My actual encounters with these past glories of the lyric stage were numerous, and somewhere along the line nearly every prima donna of this century or the last is at least mentioned. In a curious way, it is like a closed circle, for there is constant interconnection among them. It is fascinating to note that many of the same episodes and stories (such as the one concerning Lotte Lehmann and Viorica Ursuleac) are told so differently that one must wonder where the truth lies. There are roles such as Gutrune, Chrysothemis, Lakmé, Donna Elvira, Donna Anna, the Marschallin, Lady Macbeth, and even Tosca and Eva that are either loved or hated. And some great operatic figures— Richard Strauss, Toscanini, Karajan, Lauri-Volpi, Gigli, among many others —are seen in entirely different lights by these former divas, especially as colleagues rather than as artists.

Retirement is always difficult for a singer, and I have often been reminded of an ambassador who reaches the end of the road. From being the center of much attention and admiration, with every facility at his disposal, economically and in so many other ways, suddenly there is nothing left but memories. In certain countries an ambassador is retired at age sixty, in others at sixty-five, and in Spain, for instance, at seventy; but his working life lasts much longer. Usually he can obtain some sort of job on a board of directors of a bank or with an important industrial company, or he can become the president of some cultural society. But all a prima donna can hope for is to become a teacher. Most of the prestigious ones, as we will see, have taken this direction (alas, there are too many to mention) and others give courses in interpretation (such as Elisabeth Schwarzkopf, who has also staged a *Rosenkavalier* in Brussels). Some went into management, and at one point Emma Carelli became the very successful director of the Rome Opera with her husband, Walter Mocchi. The famous mezzo Maria Gay and her husband, tenor Giovanni Zenatello, did the same at the Arena in Verona; Mary Garden for a short time managed the Chicago Opera; Maria Llacer, the Royal Opera House in Madrid; and Flagstad, the Oslo Lyric Theatre. Though she has not completely retired, Beverly Sills is now head of the New York City Opera.

The best teachers have not necessarily been those who were most admired as singers. A certain involvement is necessary of which some of the great stars are incapable; others simply do not have the gift of communication. So much too depends on the human material they have at their disposal, for it is not every day that a Sembrich has taught a Dusolina Giannini, a Calvé a Cigna, a Carmen Melis a Tebaldi, a Giuseppina Baldassare Tedeschi an Albanese, a Berger a Streich, a Maria Ivogün a Schwarzkopf, or an Adami Corradetti a Katia Ricciarelli. Florence Page Kimball, never a very celebrated concert singer herself, had the God-given ability to impart her knowledge and total dedication: among her many rewards was Leontyne Price.

It is distressing to realize how few of the former divas have enough income to live on comfortably. So many causes explain their plight. The period during which they made money was relatively short; and a certain luxurious life style was necessary to establish their status. Then there was the destruction of so much property during the Second World War, and the galloping inflation. And above all, most of these artists were not commercially minded.

Although I took notes of the dialogues with the former stars—the tape recorder froze them—and I have done an enormous amount of checking, there are undoubtedly some dates and facts that are not exact. Most of the divas confessed to not having kept diaries or files, and no doubt people will discover inaccuracies. I have used the birth dates they gave me; often these do not correspond to the dates in musical dictionaries. Many records have been lost: many opera archives are either closed or in a chaotic state.

In nearly all the prima donnas there was a sly humor which never failed to surprise me, and anecdotes about their wit abound. Way back, when Giulio Gatti-Casazza, long-time general manager of New York's Metropolitan Opera, was discussing a contract with the lovely Lina Cavalieri and, trying to reduce the fee she asked, covered her with compliments, she replied: "Those are very sweet words, but they will not help to pay for the chauffeur." On a radio interview Maggie Teyte was asked by Peter Gravina why she thought *Pelléas et Mélisande* had never become popular in the United States; she replied, "You Americans don't know your Maeterlinck." And to someone who asked her about Mary Garden, her great rival as the Debussy heroine, Teyte said, "Mary is lecturing, but I still sing." Licia Albanese once told a soprano with limited vocal resources who planned to sing Butterfly at the Met, "You have the voice and the figure, but my advice is to hide a microphone in the obi."

Nevertheless, except in the case of singers I interviewed while they were still active, the leitmotiv of these interviews is melancholy, not only because the divas' raison d'être has ceased to be, but also because of their well-founded fears for the future of opera, to which they had dedicated their lives with passion. They discussed ever-growing signs of disintegration in the entire operatic structure. Opera, as a result of factors such as the absurd demands of unions, is becoming such a luxury that the singers all wonder how much longer the structure can stay on its feet. All but Sena Jurinac and Rita Streich have retired, and the curtain will soon be coming down on them.

It is easier to sing well than to have to explain why you didn't.

LICIA ALBANESE

Audiences today have become so used to bad singing that they applaud frantically when a high note is taken off-key. We would have been hissed and booed and received rotten tomatoes!

MARIA CANIGLIA

A prima donna was expected to dress with care and elegance, buy her own costumes, stay in the best hotels. Our salaries were ridiculous compared with those paid out today, but we were artists, and finances appeared unimportant. This is why so many of us have ended up in the poorhouse while today's top singers have fat bank accounts.

GILDA DALLA RIZZA

I should like to say over and over again that I used my voice the same way a painter uses his brush. He throws the color he wants on the canvas. I threw color into my roles in the different tones that I sang.

MARY GARDEN

To become a sensation overnight is the greatest plight that can befall a young singer, for the responsibilities ahead are tremendous. I know because it happened to me.

ESTER MAZZOLENI

A prima donna dies no less than three times: First go her looks, that is death number one; then her voice, that is number two; and finally the death she shares with the others.

LILLIAN NORDICA

Modern composers are trying to create a new register for the voice which does not exist.

MAGGIE TEYTE

The singer is at the service of the audience and not vice versa. I always try to give them my all. I feel the same duties toward the public whether it is La Scala or Newark.

MAGDA OLIVERO

When voice students ask me to be their teacher, they run away after I tell them that I will keep them on scales for four years. But I know that this is the secret of why I was able to sing well for over four decades.

AUGUSTA OLTRABELLA

I have never understood why so many colleagues do not realize their own limitations. I always knew mine. My voice was like a flute, and I always stuck to the coloratura repertoire, which was the only right one for me.

LILY PONS

Anyone with good common sense should realize that most stage directors today respect neither the wishes nor the instructions of librettists and composers. If this system is to go on, we will be faced with a complete travesty of the operatic repertoire.

HILDEGARD RANCZAK

All the orchestras today are tuned to a diapason that augments constantly. Should this continue, there won't be any voices left. We singers are not like violinists, who tune their violins. Our instrument is our throat.

RENATA TEBALDI

When we performed, conductors were our best friends. They advised and protected us. Today they hate singers and go out of their way to destroy them.

GIULIA TESS

THE LAST
PRIMA DONNAS

VOICES AND REPERTOIRE

For those who may be only partially immersed in the lyric theatre or relatively new to it, the following pages are meant to clarify the different types of female vocal instruments and a few of the different roles in the repertoire. The problems that exist today—there have been many changes in the undertaking of certain roles in the last two decades, and they are increasing daily—are far from easy to comprehend. For, in fact, an exception seems possible for almost every assignment in the chaotic conditions of the opera houses today, partly as a consequence of the disappearance of certain types of voices, such as the dramatic soprano and the contralto. My observations are the result of over fifty years of assiduous operagoing, from the time my mother took me to the Pergola Theatre in Florence to a matinee of *Falstaff* with the incomparable Mariano Stabile in the lead, which opened the enchanted gates of what was to become a hobby and a passion, to the present, when so much is third-rate and so little magic remains.

As we shall see, the differences in the types of female voices are not as pronounced as one might think, with continual exceptions to the established rules, particularly since some voices become darker or grow in size with the passing of time.

Basically, there are five types of soprano: dramatic (divided into two categories—those with agility and those without), lirico spinto, lyric, leggero, and coloratura. (In Germany the dramatic soprano is called a *hochdramatischer Sopran* and the spinto a *jugendlicher dramatischer Sopran*.) The first three types encompass more or less the same register or range but are differentiated by their coloration, timbre, and volume. When a part is written for dramatic soprano, considerable amplitude of sound is necessary to break through the heavier orchestration.

It is generally agreed that there are three registers, or divisions, to all types of female voices: the bottom, the middle, and the top (where the high notes, or *acuti,* occur). Dramatic sopranos should be able to employ a certain type of chest tone to give emphasis to particular phrases in the bottom register, but this should be handled in such a way as never to give the impression of "shifting gears." The middle voice should be rich and the top generous, but all three registers should appear to be invisibly sewn together.

Mezzo-sopranos can be divided into four groups: the ones with agility, the lyric, the spinto, and the dramatic. But again, this classification does not always work on a practical basis. Giulietta Simionato and now Marilyn Horne have had no difficulty switching from one to another but have kept away from the heavy Wagner and Strauss roles. And lyric and spinto mezzos, depending on the timbre and coloration of the voice, can share some of the same roles too. Contraltos generally have far less flexibility than mezzos, since they are always displaying their lower register; usually a contralto need not go above an F. Then there are voices that are neither true sopranos nor true mezzos, for they can reach neither the first notes of the mezzo's low range nor the higher range of the soprano. The French call them "falcon" after Marie-Cornélie Falcon, a famous singer of the Paris Opéra in its heyday in the 1830s.

"Verismo" and "realismo" are terms used to describe a certain type of opera, but they also imply the sort of voice necessary to their performance. According to the *Oxford Dictionary of Music,* verismo is the tendency in (chiefly Italian) composers of the late nineteenth and early twentieth centuries to take subjects filled with naturalism (in the sense of strong realism) in the manner of writers such as Zola and Verga. "Verismo" derives from the Italian word *"vero,"* meaning true; and, in theory at least, all operas that concern the representation of realistic situations and characters belong to this school. There are some operas that are accepted by all as being pure verismo —*Cavalleria rusticana* is one—and others about which no definitive conclusion can be drawn. Everyone seems to agree that diction and phrasing are essential to verismo, for text and music are inseparably bound. One of the theories so often expressed in my various conversations is that to succeed, verismo operas need forceful personalities, great acting ability, and a particular type of expressive vocalism. The reason that so many of them have fallen by the wayside since the Second World War is the lack of interpreters to give them the vital charge they demand.

On the subject of verismo opera, Gian Carlo Menotti once told me: "There is total confusion among musicologists on this term. It is, in my opinion, photographic lyric theatre, a reality with no moral lessons. Many experts confuse contemporary operas with verismo. This is incorrect. My operas, for instance, do not belong to this school at all, whatever people may say. Mine are all symbolic. Behind a drama that may appear realistic, there is always a suggestion of something else. For instance, *The Medium* is a battle between faith and doubt, a metaphysical sort of anguish. *The Saint of Bleecker Street* is a representation of faith versus nonfaith. Britten's *Albert Herring* is pure verismo, but his *The Turn of the Screw,* dealing with the supernatural, is not. People are always confusing the human aspects of the libretto with verismo. As far as Berg, Schoenberg, and company are concerned, I would call their scores 'espressionismo.' Today there is no more verismo music being written, for dissonance and verismo don't mix." All the singers with whom I discussed verismo—and they include many not represented here—consider the operas of Mascagni, Giordano, Catalani, Zandonai, Leoncavallo, Wolf-Ferrari, Montemezzi, Cilea, and Alfano *verista* in spirit and practice. Puccini, in their opinion, is also very much a member of this group. Although *Turandot* deals with a fairy tale written by Gozzi in the eighteenth century, everyone claims it is eminently *verista* because of its gripping emotions.

Sopranos who specialize in the Wagnerian or verismo repertoires need not have much agility, unlike those who take on the baroque heroines of Handel or Vivaldi and the bel canto roles of Mozart, Cherubini, Rossini, Bellini, and Donizetti—and some of the Verdi roles as well. The heavier the voice, the more difficult it is to achieve agility: to float a high note is infinitely more difficult for a dramatic soprano than for a spinto or a lyric. Much depends on the quality of the voice and the solidity of a carefully constructed technique. The latter is rapidly fading into oblivion.

Some spintos are able, in special cases, to take on dramatic roles, and some lyrics can go on to the spinto repertoire. While *La forza del destino* and *Aida,* for instance, can be sung by both dramatic sopranos and spintos, Leonora in *Il trovatore* requires—particularly in the fourth act—an extension in the lower reaches that most spintos find hard to manage. There are roles, such as Desdemona in *Otello,* that should really be sung only by spintos or dramatic sopranos; despite many passages comfortable for a lyric, she cannot do justice to the big third-act concertato. Still, most lyric sopranos sing it anyhow.

A high C comes easily enough to most lyrics but is more difficult for spintos and dramatic sopranos, whose comfortable top often ends at a high A or B-flat. Elsa in *Lohengrin* and Sieglinde in *Die Walküre* are both fairly sparing of the high register—Elsa need reach only one, rapid high B-natural in the course of the opera. And because of the lighter orchestration, Elsa can be sung successfully by a lyric soprano (in fact, in Italy Albanese did very well by it). But Sieglinde belongs to either a spinto or a dramatic soprano, not only because of the heavier scoring but because much of the music lies in the center of the voice, which carries less easily than the top. To the untrained ear, both of the Verdi Leonoras—in *Trovatore* and in *Forza*—sound about the same in range. But the *Forza* Leonora never goes beyond a B-natural, while her *Trovatore* namesake must sing not only several high B-flats but also high Cs and D-flats. (Often the D-flat in the last act is lowered to B-flat.) This is why Renata Tebaldi, who often sang *Forza*, never went near *Trovatore* except on records, where short "takes" and the lack of performance pressure often enable a singer to achieve effects unheard in an opera house. Some spintos and dramatic sopranos avoid *Aida* because of the translucent high C in "O patria mia," which is difficult to transpose. Both Rosa Ponselle and Tebaldi sang Aida in the early parts of their careers to much acclaim and then dropped it after unfortunate experiences with this note, which is terribly exposed. And many Wagnerian dramatic sopranos shy away from the *Siegfried* Brünnhilde, for the range is much higher than that of the other two Brünnhildes, in *Die Walküre* and *Götterdämmerung:* in the one hour that she is onstage, she is faced with B-flats and B-naturals galore, as well as two high Cs. And apart from these notes, the entire tessitura stays high, which makes reaching for the top notes inevitably more difficult, since the voice is already tired.

If a dramatic soprano is an able enough technician, she can reduce the scale of her instrument if a score so demands and even in certain instances take on such lyric roles as Mimi, or Eva in *Die Meistersinger*. In fact, the latter was sung by two of the great dramatic sopranos in the early 1900s, Johanna Gadski and Emmy Destinn. Over the years there have been voices that have become stronger on reaching maturity and have been able to go on to a heavier repertoire. But in so doing some of them, like Sena Jurinac's, have lost their facility at the top. This Yugoslav soprano, for instance, used to sing the role of Marzelline in *Fidelio*, making an unforgettable impression. Later, when she took on the heroic role of Leonore, it was obvious to all that despite her authority and winning personality, she had misjudged the growth of her vocal accomplishments. (Unwisely, she then went on to *Forza*.) More recently her path has been followed by Gundula Janowitz, a lyric who also undertook Leonore, with questionable results. Conductors today pay little attention, for if Klemperer and Mehta accepted Jurinac, it was Bernstein who conducted *Fidelio* for Janowitz.

Since dramatic and spinto sopranos are becoming rarer and rarer, lyrics are constantly encouraged by conductors and managers to assume the heavier roles, with the usual result that they force their voices and in a short time finish their careers. The momentary (it is hoped) disappearance of the dramatic soprano is puzzling everyone. From time to time a great discovery is announced, but one hope after another has been dashed. Do these singers tackle the repertoire too soon, without the necessary preparation? Or are their instruments not really of the range and expansiveness needed for the roles? I shall mention two among the many who have been the greatest disappointments. When the Greek-Argentinian Elena Suliotis exploded onto the international scene in the mid-sixties, many critics were sure another Callas had been discovered. Immediately she allowed herself to be cast as Abigaille in *Nabucco* and Norma and Minnie in *La fanciulla del West;* the feast was soon over. Then, a few years ago, a young and attractive Hungarian soprano, Sylvia Sass, arrived in London, preceded by a considerable reputation at home. (It must be remembered that though there are some superb voices behind the Iron Curtain, the training there leaves much to be desired.) Her debut at Covent Garden was hailed as sensational. Then one hope after another was dashed, and once more a great promise went unfulfilled.

Recently a young Argentinian soprano, Adelaide Negri, has been in the news. She made her debut at the Metropolitan in February 1982 in *Norma,* and her recklessness is already a matter of public record, for she goes from coloratura assignments such as the Queen of the Night and *Semiramide* to dramatic ones such as Elisabetta in *Don Carlo* and Giulia in *La vestale.* May she turn out to be another Marcella Sembrich, whose brilliant career lasted thirty-two years and whose astonishing vocal technique was such that she was able to go from the Queen of the Night and Rosina to Elsa and Elvira in *Ernani*!

In her own inimitable way, Ester Mazzoleni stopped me from using the term dramatic soprano when speaking of current singers: "Today we, the old-timers, call them the screaming sopranos. Now they not only give all, they also give what they haven't got."

It is absurd, for example, to assume that because a soprano is black she can sing Aida as superbly as Leontyne Price and Martina Arroyo have. Yet this seems to have been the destiny of several gifted lyrics: Gloria Davy, Felicia Weathers, and others allowed themselves to be persuaded into taking on more than they could handle.

It is interesting that in the current invasion of Oriental musicians, few of the singers have really established themselves in the front rank of the international market. There doesn't seem to be a mezzo among them—the timbre is usually that of a light lyric. And they are stereotyped as Butterfly or as Mascagni's Iris, even when their voices are really suited to neither. Teachers claim that these students are wonderfully prepared musically but that their voices are small and lacking in expression. The most established of them, Yasuko Hayashi, whom I heard sing an excellent Anne Truelove in *The Rake's Progress,* does not seem to know exactly where she is heading. Much in demand because of her musicianship, at one moment she takes on a leggero role like Adina in *L'elisir d'amore,* at another a spinto role like Maria Stuarda, and at still other times a dramatic role such as Donna Anna. In the winter of 1982, a new comet appeared on the Italian horizon in the person of a very comely coloratura named Masako Deguci. With Tebaldi's blessings, she has been greeted as a revelation by critics and public alike.

Before Japan had such an industry of singers there were two—Tamaki Miura and Tapales Isang—who left a very definite mark. Both of them were superb singing actresses, and if neither had an important voice, they both possessed a certain sorcery which made them great interpreters. Miura was even asked by André Messager to sing the Chicago premiere of his charming opera *Madame Chrysanthème* in 1920. I recall hearing Isang sing *Butterfly* on two different occasions during my youth, and she managed, exquisitely and effectively, with a limited but beautifully produced instrument, to convey the nuances of the score. Miura sang even more dramatic parts such as Santuzza.

There exists, particularly among the spintos and the dramatics, the phe-nomenon called by the Italians *voci corte*—short voices—which actually means that they have a short top, or, to be more precise, have difficulty going beyond high A. As Gina Cigna explains so well in her interview, finding the top is for a singer a matter of hit-or-miss. Some are born with it, and others have to struggle to obtain it. There are those who never find the key and must learn to get along without it. This happens particularly with heavy voices. The apparent trick is to be sparing with the middle, for the more you push it, the shorter the upper register becomes. Among some of the famous sopranos who either started with this handicap or became victims of it were Giuseppina Cobelli, Lotte Lehmann, Ponselle, Tebaldi, Victoria de los Angeles, Régine Crespin, Jurinac, Irmgard Seefried, and Pia Tassinari. In the case of Ponselle, the situation remained much the same over the years, but with Tebaldi it got considerably worse. Among the mezzos with a short top and a glorious middle are Jean Madeira, Rita Gorr, Cloë Elmo, and Fedora Barbieri, who, after a career of forty-two years, is still very active in Italian character roles. Then there are those who go slowly from lyric to spinto and then on to dramatic: Maria Caniglia is a good example. This darkening of the voice happens, in certain instances, after childbirth, and it is seemingly very dangerous to begin singing too soon thereafter. At least four months should elapse, and then there must be a long period of vocalizing before a singer resumes her career. Failure to observe this rule was apparently one factor that ended the career of the exceptionally gifted Onelia Fineschi, who undertook the dramatic *Trovatore* Leonora at La Scala in 1948, when she was essentially a lyric; the double strain was too much for her and she was forced to quit.

The leggero is a light lyric with an innate agility; actually, she is halfway between a lyric and a coloratura. She is usually assigned soubrette roles along with the ingenues and the very youthful heroines. Among them are Giulietta in *I Capuleti ed i Montecchi,* Amor in *Orfeo ed Euridice,* Marzelline, Zerlina in *Don Giovanni,* Susanna in *Le nozze di Figaro,* Blondchen in *Die Entführung aus dem Serail,* Despina in *Così fan tutte,* Zerlina in *Fra Diavolo,* Adina in *Elisir,* Norina in *Don Pasquale,* Oscar in *Un ballo in maschera,* Juliette in *Roméo et Juliette,* Elvira in *L'italiana in Algeri,* Gretel, Nannetta in *Falstaff,* and many others.

Musetta in *La Bohème* in recent times has become a free-for-all sort of part, and one has seen spintos such as Ljuba Welitsch, Maralin Niska, Brenda Lewis, and Josephine Barstow sing it, along with mezzos such as Marilyn Horne (in the early part of her career) and Elena Zilio. The latter has also sung Amor in Chicago, thus making transposition imperative. Even Renata Scotto, who now calls herself a dramatic soprano, tackles Musetta. In the past, it was always sung by a lyric or a leggero.

Since the coloratura repertoire is limited, some of these singers take on leggero roles too, provided that their middle is resistant enough. Lily Pons never did, nor did Amelita Galli-Curci. Pons had the mad scene of *Lucia* transposed upward so she could show off her Fs and Gs above the staff.

The most-performed standard coloratura fare consists, besides *Lucia di Lammermoor,* and Gilda in *Rigoletto,* of Rosina in *Il barbiere di Siviglia, Linda di Chamounix, Lakmé, Dinorah,* Leila in *Les Pêcheurs de perles,* the Queen in *Le Coq d'or,* Philine in *Mignon,* Olympia in *The Tales of Hoffmann, Le Rossignol,* and often enough *La traviata.* Marguerite in *Les Huguenots* is sometimes undertaken by a coloratura, provided her middle is strong enough. Sophie in *Der Rosenkavalier* is a toss-up between leggeros and coloraturas too; but while it has some difficult duets and trios, it does not have any aria such as the "O beau pays" in the Meyerbeer opera, which puts the fear of God into those who must sing it.

There are some roles written for coloratura that demand so special a technique in trill and staccato that even the most renowned ladies belonging to this breed do not attempt them. The Queen of the Night in *Die Zauberflöte* (which Mozart wrote for his sister-in-law, Josefa Hofer, who had from all accounts an exceptional upper range) is considered the most treacherous of all scores written for this type of voice. Apart from the cruel stratospheric top notes—there are five high Fs—it demands a voice able to convey the Queen's anguish and her tempestuous nature. Joan Sutherland attempted it (transposed downward) but dropped it from her repertoire soon afterward. Lina Pagliughi undertook it successfully, but Toti dal Monte and Lily Pons never went near it. Roberta Peters, with her limited means, tackled the fiendish tessitura but was unable to bring to the role any dramatic expression.

Zerbinetta in *Ariadne auf Naxos* is also a fiendish coloratura part, but one requiring a smaller instrument than the Queen of the Night, thus making it easier to find singers who can handle the role. But it also requires great musicianship—Reri Grist and Patricia Wise, for instance, are two very successful Zerbinettas who have not attempted the Mozart queen. Erika Köth for years made it her own. Maria Nemeth, the Vienna Staatsoper's reigning dramatic soprano in the twenties and thirties, and Felicie Hüni-Mihacsek, the reigning spinto at the Munich Opera during more or less the same period, were considered phenomena, as they were both able to do ample justice to the role of Pamina's mother. Then there were two who became institutions of a sort, for, miraculously, they went on for years coping successfully with the role's difficulties—Erna Berger and her pupil Rita Streich, who were also delicate Gildas and charming Sophies in *Der Rosenkavalier*. Now it is Zdislawa Donat and Edita Gruberovà who most often sing the Queen.

There is another role in the coloratura range that can baffle the uninitiated with its series of high E-flats: Elvira in *I puritani*. Maria Barrientos, Galli-Curci, Mercedes Capsir, and Pagliughi, as far as I have been able to ascertain, sang it in the original key. After a long period of being put away in cold storage—the tenor's tessitura is no joke either—this opera thrived again in the 1970s, with Beverly Sills, Cristina Deutekom, and Sutherland all much in demand for the role. Then came a great dearth of coloraturas, but now suddenly there are five emerging with tremendous promise: the Americans Ashley Putnam and Gianna Rolandi, the Italians Luciana Serra and Mariella Devia, and also the Lebanese Sona Ghazarian.

Marie in *La Fille du régiment,* a favorite of such coloraturas as Pons, Sutherland, Sills, and Anna Moffo (when she was a coloratura), found a successful interpreter some years ago in Mirella Freni, a lyric, for the very simple reason that the fireworks had been cut. But this is usually true of operas that are not in the everyday repertoire; the public does not expect the D, E-flat, or E at certain moments, as it does in *Rigoletto*, *Lucia*, *Sonnambula*, or other established favorites.

The Mozart repertoire has been subjected to perhaps the greatest number of modifications in the last hundred years. Konstanze in *Entführung*, Fiordiligi in *Così fan tutte*, Elettra in *Idomeneo*, and Donna Anna in *Don Giovanni* were written for small theatres and orchestras—the only kind in existence at that time. While the other roles that Mozart wrote for sopranos (with the exception of the Queen of the Night) did not demand a dramatic with agility, all of these do. Not only was it much easier in times gone by to find agility in medium-size voices of a fairly darkish color, but today the big opera houses and vast orchestras have changed the problem completely, with the result that often these four parts are assigned to sopranos who are not dramatics, very much changing Mozart's conception, for there simply no longer exist dramatic sopranos who can take on these tessituras. Coloraturas like Sylvia Geszty, Edita Gruberovà, and Gianna Rolandi now sing Konstanze, and lyrics like Ileana Cotrubas, not very successfully. But we are a long way from the times when Lilli Lehmann could sing her brilliantly along with the Queen of the Night and the Brünnhildes. Ponselle sang Donna Anna, but the second aria was lowered a whole tone (Dusolina Giannini told me that when she took on this role at the Metropolitan, she too had to sing it transposed, as there was not the time to readapt the orchestra score to the original). Today, many compromises have to be reached if these operas are to be given. Yet for those who heard and admired Elisabeth Schwarzkopf's Fiordiligi for years, it must come as quite a surprise to listen today to Margaret Price in this part, which she has made her own. While Schwarzkopf gave an enchanting performance, Price—a spinto—is, with her big voice and amazing agility, much more what Mozart had in mind. Lyrics like Helene Döse, Rita Talarico, and Edda Moser appear as Donna Anna, but they cannot begin to do justice to this score, as Price can when she sings the role.

The dramatic Wagnerian repertoire is the most taxing of all, along with some of the Strauss operas *(Salome, Elektra, Die Frau ohne Schatten)*, and yet previously, when orchestras were smaller, the diapason lower, and conductors more considerate, the prima donnas lasted longer. That Wagner did not want the sound to be so immense as it has become today is proved by the fact that at Bayreuth he had the orchestra covered. Actually, perhaps because they alternated more with operas of other composers and had not become so specialized, or simply because more consideration was shown them and orchestras were smaller, the great Wagnerian sopranos such as Nanny Larsen-Todsen, Margarete Matzenauer, Félia Litvinne, Gertrud Kappel, Marta Fuchs, Elisabeth Ohms, Frida Leider, Anny and Hilde Konetzni, and Anny Helm had much longer careers than those who followed them. Flagstad sang way beyond her fifty-fifth birthday, but she entered the Wagnerian repertoire only after she was thirty-five, while Helen Traubel, who retired at fifty-two, had a long concert career before concentrating on opera at the age of forty.

Birgit Nilsson also did not attempt the heavy Wagnerian heroines in the early days—her first big international success was at the Glyndebourne Festival as Elettra in *Idomeneo* in 1951—and even after she started being singled out for the dramatic German repertoire, she went on singing Italian roles for many years. Outstanding as Lady Macbeth and Turandot, she was less successful (particularly in the United States, where audiences are accustomed to a more Italianate sound) as Amelia, Aida, and Tosca. She sang fewer of the Wagnerian roles at the Met, her home for so many years, than Flagstad had, never going near Elsa, Senta, or Kundry.

Astrid Varnay went right into the heavy Wagnerian dramatic heroines and then on to the German mezzo repertoire, and she now sings character roles such as Martha in *Faust*. She has been in the business since 1941, when she substituted for Lotte Lehmann as Sieglinde at the Met, where she remained until the early fifties, returning for the Kostelnička in 1974. Margaret Harshaw took on the Wagnerian ladies (never Strauss) only after she had changed from a mezzo to a dramatic soprano. And after a decade of Kundrys and a few Brünnhildes in *Walküre*, where she had considerable trouble with the high B-natural at the end of the "Ho-yo-to-ho," Régine Crespin moved away from Wagner. But then what happened to Ludmila Dvořaková, Klara Barlow, Anita Välkki, Ursula Schröder-Feinen, and so many others?

Ortrud in *Lohengrin*, Kundry in *Parsifal*, and Venus in *Tannhäuser* are, in the Wagnerian repertoire, the most equivocal roles, since despite the vehement complexities of these characters, they are written in a range that is comfortable enough for a very darkish-timbred dramatic soprano as well as for a high mezzo. The three Gertruds, Kappel, Rünger, and Grob-Prandl, dramatic sopranos, all appeared as Ortrud, as did Marjorie Lawrence. The last sang both Elisabeth (often performed by a spinto) and Venus in *Tannhäuser;* other sopranos who have appeared in both roles include Elisabeth Ohms, Birgit Nilsson, Daniza Mastilović, and Gwyneth Jones. Flagstad sang

Kundry but never abandoned Elsa or Elisabeth for Ortrud or Venus. Martha Mödl, Astrid Varnay, and Marianne Schech all successfully took on both Ortrud and Kundry, and among the mezzos who did so were Kerstin Thorborg, Karin Branzell, Elisabeth Höngen, Irene Dalis, Christa Ludwig, and more recently Eva Randova. From time to time even Isolde has attracted mezzos, since there are many pages that lie comfortably enough in the mezzo range. One who did splendidly by it was Margarete Matzenauer. In more recent times a very fine Brangäne, Irene Dalis, went on to Isolde in San Francisco, but she did not feel comfortable with its tessitura and never sang it again. Many of her admirers often wondered whether her decline, which followed not much later, was due to the great effort her vocal cords had made. As we will see, several divas learned Isolde and then got cold feet, choosing not to appear in this role.

In the verismo repertoire, again we find operas in which the leading lady can be assigned to either a dramatic soprano or a mezzo; the tessitura lies mainly in the middle and does not remain high for more than a phrase or two. Typical of these heroines is Santuzza in *Cavalleria.* Among the memorable sopranos who have succeeded in this part one recalls Gemma Bellincioni (who created it), Lina Bruna Rasa, Gina Cigna, Iva Pacetti, Zinka Milanov, Maria Caniglia, Dusolina Giannini, and the magnificent Eileen Farrell; among the mezzos—apart from Simionato, the greatest of them all —Ebe Stignani, Fiorenza Cossotto, and Tatiana Troyanos. On the other hand, both Cloë Elmo in 1947 and Fedora Barbieri in 1953 tried it at the Met without success. *Fedora* is another opera that has been a vehicle for sopranos—such as Gemma Bellincioni (who created this role too), Lina Cavalieri, Maria Jeritza, Maria Callas, Iris Adami Corradetti, and Maria Caniglia—as well as mezzos—Gianna Pederzini, Elena Nicolai, and recently Viorica Cortez.

Likewise, both Cassandra and Dido in Berlioz's *Les Troyens* (which has been rediscovered everywhere with the most enormous success) have a tessitura that suits either a soprano or a mezzo. In recent productions we have been treated to sopranos Régine Crespin and Shirley Verrett (in both roles) and Evelyn Lear, and to mezzos such as Josephine Veasey, Nadine Denize, Christa Ludwig, and Marilyn Horne. Marguerite in the same composer's *La Damnation de Faust* is another toss-up between sopranos and mezzos, but the role is infinitely more effective when sung by a mezzo, since most sopranos cannot do full justice to the important lower range.

Recently, Debussy's Mélisande, which has always been the property of lyric sopranos, from Mary Garden and Maggie Teyte to Elisabeth Söderström and Judith Blegen, is being taken over by mezzos, with Frederica von Stade, Maria Ewing, and Anne Howells prominent among them. In my opinion, a lower voice greatly detracts from the childish and eerie quality of Debussy's magical creature. Denise Duval claims that since orchestras are becoming larger and the role lies in the middle of the voice, many lyrics can no longer be heard; she deplores this betrayal of Debussy's wishes. Teresa Stratas is one who went from the youngster Yniold to the lead.

Actually, it is the French composers who most frequently wrote these interchangeable roles. Operas such as *Carmen, Mignon,* and *Werther* were written originally for the Opéra-Comique, a relatively small theatre, which therefore necessitated a relatively limited orchestra. Carmen, Mignon, and Charlotte in *Werther* were written with the accent on the middle voice. And while I feel that all three gain by being sung by a mezzo (as a contrast to the three secondary heroines—Micaëla in *Carmen,* and Sophie in *Werther,* lyrics, and Philine in *Mignon,* a coloratura), musically there is nothing to prevent a soprano with a strong and velvety middle range from undertaking them. Actually, it is very strange that every prima donna longs to take a crack at Carmen, for it is one of the most ungrateful roles ever written. No one is ever right for the critics or the public; she is either too much a slut or too much a lady. And the audience's big applause is always reserved for the three other characters, Micaëla, Don José, and Escamillo, whose single arias inevitably bring down the house. Carmen, on the other hand, with her four solos—the Habanera, Séguedille, "Là-bas," and card scene, none of which ends on a high note—has to work hard to receive the applause so easily won by the others.

Bizet chose Célestine Galli-Marié, a mezzo, to create Carmen, but this has not stopped an avalanche of sopranos—Lilli Lehmann, Emma Calvé, Mary Garden, Geraldine Farrar, Marjorie Lawrence, Florence Easton, Ninon Vallin, Maria Jeritza, Lily Djanel, and more recently Régine Crespin, Victoria de los Angeles, and now Evelyn Lear—from essaying it. Callas, Leontyne Price, and Moffo have recorded the part without appearing in it on the stage. Contraltos (now an extinguished species) such as Rosette Anday, Aurora Buades, Fanny Anitua, Gertrud Wettergren, Maria Olczewska, Bruna Castagna, Maria Gay, and Margarete Klose have all sung it with great success. And every mezzo you can think of—Conchita Supervia (notwithstanding her tiny voice), Gabriella Besanzoni, Gianna Pederzini, Ebe Stignani (despite her figure), Giulietta Simionato, Elisabeth Höngen, Jennie Tourel, Gladys Swarthout, Risë Stevens, and, today, Marilyn Horne, Shirley Verrett, Viorica Cortez, and Grace Bumbry—has become identified with the cigarette girl. Now even Teresa Berganza, with her small instrument, has succumbed to it, like her late compatriot Supervia.

(This opera curiously helped deprive the musical world of one of its greatest divas. Rosa Ponselle retired when she was still an idol, angered and hurt by the notice she had received from the leading New York critic for her performance as Carmen in 1935. Anyone who has read Olin Downes's evaluation of her interpretation of the gypsy girl in *The New York Times* can only be shocked at the vulgarity of the vicious attack on so exalted an artist still at the height of her vocal powers. Having known Downes well later on, I was surprised that this seemingly benign and civilized person could have been so cruel to so superb an artist. General Manager Edward Johnson's refusal to give her a new production of *Adriana* also played its part in her withdrawal.)

Mignon, so popular until the Second World War, is much the same. Again Galli-Marié had the honor of creating a role at the Opéra-Comique, so Thomas, like Bizet, surely intended that a mezzo undertake the part. Yet there have been several soprano Mignons—Ninon Vallin at the Opéra-Comique, for example, and Maggie Teyte—and two coloraturas—Maria Ivogün, who made it her own in Berlin, and the American Marie van Zandt. At the Metropolitan, it was for years the exclusive property of Lucrezia Bori. Then, after Bori's retirement, it went to three mezzos: Gladys Swarthout, Jennie Tourel, and Risë Stevens. Since the departure of Edward Johnson in 1950 it has never been revived by the Met, but elsewhere in the United States it has been performed as a vehicle for Marilyn Horne.

Charlotte in *Werther* is far more dramatic and touching when sung by a mezzo; the letter scene in particular needs sumptuous vocal equipment. But it has been sung by a variety of sopranos, including Eames, Farrar, Garden, dalla Rizza, Vallin, Caniglia, Maria Carbone, Mafalda Favero, Crespin, and Heather Harper. Among the mezzos who have made a great impression in this role were Elena Gerhardt—who eventually became the most distinguished lieder interpreter of her time—and later Gianna Pederzini, Simionato, Dame Janet Baker, Frederica von Stade, and Ludwig. More recently Brigitte Fassbänder has sung it in Munich.

Gounod's Juliette has attracted lyrics, leggeros, and coloraturas. For the famous waltz, the composer scored two different versions, one in F and one in G, so that the interpreter could choose which suited her best. There are many passages that demand a certain agility, but since the orchestration is not heavy, a coloratura whose instrument is not too birdlike can easily attempt it. In fact we have had sopranos who were between the lyric and spinto, like Eames and Farrar, who made a great success of it, along with such coloraturas as Patti, Galli-Curci, and Patrice Munsel, and leggeros like Vina Bovy, Eidé Norena, Bidú Sayão, and Christiane Eda-Pierre. Lyrics who have sung Juliette include Lucrezia Bori, Grace Moore, Dorothy Kirsten, Janine Micheau, Favero, Rosanna Carteri, Jeannette Pilou, and Mirella Freni. Anna Moffo sang it too, but it is difficult to classify her, for she started out as a coloratura, then became a lyric, and now goes in for spinto parts.

Thaïs, the Massenet heroine, is another part that has tempted all sorts of sopranos. Its range is considerable—from A below middle C to a high D (except, of course, when transposed)—and it affords great displays of both acting ability and a beautiful figure (if such is there to be displayed). Long forgotten on the shelf, Thaïs has now been resurrected with a vengeance, and all over the world the penitent courtesan is very much alive again. Sybil Sanderson, Cavalieri, Garden, Farrar (who confessed that she disliked the role intensely), and Bianca Stagno Bellincioni, great singing actresses, made it their own. Dramatics such as Maria Jeritza and Marjorie Lawrence, along with lyrics of the caliber of Geneviève Vix, Fanny Heldy, the lovely Helen Jepson, Favero, and Duval, all sang Thaïs. Leontyne Price, a spinto, essayed it at the Chicago Lyric but never sang it again, for it did not prove a success. In the 1970s we had Carol Neblett (since she is prone to sing everything and anything, it is difficult to pinpoint just what kind of soprano she is), who delighted the public by baring her breasts; Beverly Sills, a coloratura; Anna Moffo, a former coloratura; and Elena Mauti Nunziata, a lyric.

Charpentier's Louise is one of the most vocally gratifying roles ever written by a French composer, and it can be handled by a spinto as well as by a warm-timbred lyric. *Louise* has usually been a vehicle for non-French singers with voices that are somewhat steely and a little harsh, for the score really demands an Italianate sound. With the exception of Ninon Vallin and Fanny Heldy (a Belgian), it has had as its most famous interpreters Mary Garden, the Scottish diva, whose extraordinary personality made up for the deficiencies in her instrument, Salomea Krusceniski, Lucrezia Bori, and four Americans—Geraldine Farrar, Grace Moore, Dorothy Kirsten, and, more recently, Arlene Saunders, the American who is established so firmly in Germany. A spinto who was vocally magnificent as the Parisian girl torn by her love for Julien and the bourgeois family traditions was New Zealander Frances Alda, whom Toscanini chose to be the first interpreter of the role at La Scala. (After a successful European career, Alda became a member of the Metropolitan Opera and remained there until she retired in 1930.)

Among the Italians who had successes in this part were Juanita Caracciolo, dalla Rizza, Favero, and Oltrabella. Both Ileana Cotrubas and Beverly Sills, in quick succession, recorded it.

A Mozart role that we have always taken for granted should be sung by a soubrette type of leggero is Zerlina, and we have had the unforgettable creations of Graziella Pareto, Elisabeth Schumann, Sayão, Favero, Nadine Conner, and Roberta Peters. Then suddenly mezzos began being assigned the part—Jane Berbié, Rosalind Elias, Huguette Tourangeau, Maria Ewing, and Anne Howells come to mind—and one cannot help but wonder why.

Dorabella in *Così* is another part usually sung by agile mezzos, and yet sopranos such as Frances Peralta, a dramatic, and Editha Fleischer, Suzanne Danco, and Sena Jurinac, lyrics, have undertaken it. Again, the musical balance is thrown off, since Fiordiligi must be sung by a spinto—also agile—and Despina by a leggero. As we will see, there is a difference of opinion as to whether Donna Anna in *Don Giovanni* is more dramatic than Donna Elvira. A number of sopranos have graduated from the latter to the former, and some did or do continue to sing both. Among them one recalls Elisabeth Rethberg, Eleanor Steber, Sena Jurinac, and Lisa della Casa, and more recently Hildegard Hillebrecht, Judith Beckmann, Edda Moser, Luisa Bosabalian, and Antigone Sgourda.

In *Le nozze di Figaro* several sopranos (including Jurinac, Hilde Gueden, and Evelyn Lear) have sung both the Countess Almaviva and Cherubino. Cherubino, and Octavian in *Der Rosenkavalier* (called "trouser roles," because a woman sings the part of a teen-aged boy), are written very much for the middle of the voice, so that both sopranos and mezzos tackle them. But there is a big difference between the two roles, since the Strauss orchestration is much heavier and the singer must make a far greater effort to be heard above it. Actually, many prima donnas (including Lotte Lehmann, Elisabeth Söderström, and Lisa della Casa) have started as Sophie—a leggero role—graduated to Octavian, and then taken on the Marschallin.

The balance of the voices is far more effective when Octavian is sung by a mezzo or a falcon, since the Marschallin and Sophie are sopranos—or were, until the chaos of present-day opera. But there is no doubt that this is one of the strangest scores ever written. When Strauss composed it—its premiere was in 1911—the orchestration was considered absolutely staggering, for it required 114 instruments, 17 of which are for a separate orchestra on the stage. Anachronisms abound—such as the waltz, not existing in the eighteenth century, in which the opera is set—so that when it was first performed it created, quite rightly, a tremendous ruckus.

These three women, one of whom plays the part of a boy who then dresses as a chambermaid, have been sung by such varied types of voices that one can only conclude that this charming score is very pliable. The Marschallin's music does not lie very high, and it has been sung successfully by sopranos like Traubel, Crespin, and of course Lotte Lehmann, all of whom had a short top. On the other hand, for its creation in Dresden, Strauss himself chose Margarethe Siems, a singer gifted with an extraordinary extension, for she could sing seemingly with equal ease all the coloratura roles—including Zerbinetta, which she created—and then also turn to Amelia, Aida, and Isolde. Strauss always claimed that she was ideal as the Marschallin. Over the years we have seen dramatics such as Marta Fuchs, Frida Leider, Astrid Varnay, Anny Konetzni, and Mercedes Llopart make good, along with such spintos as Hilde Konetzni, Maria Reining, Leonie Rysanek, Viorica Ursuleac, Montserrat Caballé, and Teresa Zylis-Gara, and the lyrics Felicie Hüni-Mihacsek, Gabrielle Ritter-Ciampi, Elisabeth Schwarzkopf, Evelyn Lear, and now Kiri Te Kanawa.

It is the same story with Octavian, for it was successful when interpreted by Lucrezia Bori, Delia Reinhardt, Bianca Stagno Bellincioni, Irmgard Seefried, and Jarmila Novotna, all lyrics; its creator, Marie Gutheil-Schoder, Hildegard Ranczak, Gilda dalla Rizza, Tiana Lemnitz, and Josephine Barstow, spintos; Maria Jeritza, a dramatic; and a huge batch of mezzos that includes, among the better known, Giulietta Simionato, Gianna Pederzini, Risë Stevens, Hertha Töpper, and, currently, Brigitte Fassbänder, Tatiana Troyanos, Anne Howells, Yvonne Minton, and Ilse Gramatzki. There is also a small group who started with Octavian and then moved to the Marschallin, or continued to sing them both. Among them are Germaine Lubin, Elisabeth Grümmer, Jurinac, and Ludwig. There were also those who, instead, went straight from Sophie to the Marschallin; these include Clara Ebers and Eleanor Steber. Curiously, Elisabeth Rethberg, who made her Met debut as Aida and sang mainly spinto roles, stuck to Sophie.

Cherubino is a far shorter role than Octavian, and the Mozart scoring is infinitely lighter. Memorable sopranos who became very much identified with the character were Farrar, Jurinac, Novotna, and Olivera Miljakovic; and among the most admired mezzos one recalls Supervia, Simionato, and, more recently, Berganza, von Stade, and Ewing.

A third important trouser role is the Composer in Strauss's *Ariadne auf Naxos*—another toss-up between spinto and mezzo. It is a charming part but also a real booby trap, for it lies too low for a soprano and too high for a mezzo. Sopranos of the stature of Lotte Lehmann, Jurinac, Lear, Helga

Pilarczyk, Irmgard Seefried, and Teresa Stratas have had a try at it, as well as such mezzos as Kerstin Meyer, Christa Ludwig, Hertha Töpper, and Tatiana Troyanos.

Violetta in *La traviata* is mystifying in the extreme, for all types of sopranos sing this beautiful role, and none of them can possibly do it complete justice. Lyrics, spintos, and dramatics encounter their share of difficulties in the perplexing agility demanded by the first act, and coloraturas begin having their troubles in the second act, which demands much emotional impact—plenty of voice is needed for "Amami, Alfredo." Name almost any soprano, and you will find that at a certain point this role, like Carmen, has proved irresistible. Needless to say, many of them must have the first-act scena lowered by a half-tone or an entire tone, and even then the "Sempre libera" is a holy terror. From Gemma Bellincioni to Tetrazzini, from Sembrich to Mazzoleni, from Farrar to Garden (who tells in her autobiography that she never sang it outside France and Belgium because the audiences in other countries expected her to take a high E-flat at the end of the first act, a note she simply did not have), from Lilli Lehmann to Galli-Curci, from Muzio to Bori, from Ponselle to Toti dal Monte and dalla Rizza, from Mercedes Capsir to Ines Alfani Tellini and Adelaide Saraceni, from Sayão and Favero to Albanese and Gueden, from Oltrabella to Olivero, from Steber to Stella, Caniglia, Novotna, Callas, Sutherland, and more recently Maria Chiara, Pilar Lorengar, Adriana Maliponte, Katia Ricciarelli, and Te Kanawa—all have essayed Violetta.

Renata Tebaldi and Mirella Freni both had stormy nights at La Scala with it. (Tebaldi, by lowering the first act, did well by it later at the San Carlo in Naples and at the Metropolitan.)

In the huge Verdi repertoire there are two roles that are sung by either a heavy mezzo or a dramatic soprano: Lady Macbeth (who must reach a D-flat) and Eboli in *Don Carlo*. The range of these two formidable ladies allows for both types of voices, provided the soprano's hue is dark enough. In the 1930s the Tasmanian soprano Margherita Grandi was considered the greatest Lady; she did a great deal to reintroduce this opera into the repertoire. Then, in the same period, the Argentinian Hina Spani—who reigned at the Colón in Buenos Aires but was also a great favorite in Italy—was a Lady Macbeth short in size but vocally splendid. Regina Resnik (when she was still a soprano), Astrid Varnay, Gina Cigna, Amy Shuard, Elisabeth Höngen, Vera Schwarz, and Martina Arroyo also had various opportunities to come to grips with this tigress. Like Turandot, it is an Italian role that usually finds its major exponents in non-Italian singers. Birgit Nilsson, Inge

Borkh, and Maria Callas have triumphed in the part; far less successful was Leonie Rysanek, whose middle voice was not strong enough or sufficiently in focus. Among the mezzos now very much identified with Lady Macbeth are Grace Bumbry and Shirley Verrett. For years in Central Europe it was Elisabeth Höngen who was considered the most exciting after Sigrid Onegin went into retirement. Recently even Galina Vishnevskaya has taken it on, and her vibrant, metallic, often harsh tones probably would have pleased Verdi, who made it very clear in all his letters that he did not wish a beautiful-sounding soprano in the part.

Eboli, on the other hand, was the daily fare of such dramatic sopranos as Giuseppina Cobelli and Caterina Mancini, who were much in demand for the role. Among the mezzos (who must have a certain amount of agility for the Veil Song), Stignani and Simionato have left a mark, along with Onegin, Fedora Barbieri, Grace Hoffman, and Irene Dalis. Christa Ludwig fled from the Karajan production in Salzburg after the first performance, having cracked conspicuously on the last high note of "O don fatale." Other modern exponents are Verrett and Bumbry, along with Mignon Dunn, Elena Obraztsova, and Fiorenza Cossotto.

Gilda in *Rigoletto* was written originally for an agile lyric, but with the passage of time higher notes were interpolated, and it has become the custom for coloraturas to sing the role. "Caro nome" should finish in a trill on an E-natural, but sometimes the more brilliant ones go to high E by a succession of trills. In German, Scandinavian, and English opera houses a lyric is acceptable (for years in Vienna it belonged almost exclusively to Hilde Gueden), but as Mirella Freni well knows after her very unwelcome reception at La Scala, if the "Caro nome" does not end at least with the E-flat, the public is vociferous in its disapproval. The Metropolitan in its new production recently used a lyric, Ileana Cotrubas, and while she was accepted politely, she did not bring down the house as Pons and Peters did, and in Geneva the same happened with the excellent British soprano Valerie Masterson. Milanov sang the last act in an NBC broadcast with Toscanini, but this part of the score demands no particular agility. Among the lyrics who sang it at the Met have been Edith Mason and Queena Mario.

Perhaps the most curious of all roles ever written is that of Prince Orlofsky in Johann Strauss's *Die Fledermaus*. This short but effective role is scored in such a way that the most disparate voices can assume it. In fact, it has been performed by sopranos, mezzos, contraltos (when they are available), and, more recently, by tenors and baritones as well.

There is one opera, *The Tales of Hoffmann,* that requires a coloratura in the first act, the doll Olympia; a spinto, dramatic, or mezzo for the second, the courtesan Giulietta; and a lyric for the last, the unhappy Antonia. A number of sopranos have had the temerity—much to the opera house directors' delight—to assume all three parts. It goes without saying that even at best, one of the three is somewhat sacrificed—usually Giulietta, which lies in the middle of the voice and has the very effective Barcarolle. Among those who have taken on this formidable assignment were Eidé Norena, Jarmila Novotna, Fanny Heldy, Vina Bovy, Virginia Zeani, Anja Silja (in her early years), the Swiss soprano Colette Lorand, Anna Moffo, Sutherland, and now Ursula Koszut and Edda Moser. Lucrezia Bori often took on Giulietta and Antonia on the same night, but she never attempted Olympia. Christiane Eda-Pierre, formerly a coloratura, sang Olympia beautifully, and now that she has moved on to lyric roles, she performs Antonia with great pathos.

Britten's *The Rape of Lucretia* is another opera written in such a way that both sopranos and mezzos can take it on. In fact, Jarmila Novotna and Regina Resnik (as a soprano), Kathleen Ferrier and Dame Janet Baker all lent distinction to this heroine. Sir William Walton wrote Cressida in *Troilus and Cressida* for soprano; Magda Laszlo created the part in Great Britain, and Dorothy Kirsten in San Francisco in 1955. But Walton rescored it for mezzo so that Dame Janet Baker would appear in it when it was revived at Covent Garden in 1976.

A short but effective role is Marina in *Boris Godunov*. The leading female in this opera dominated by male voices, Marina can be sung by either a spinto or a mezzo. And we have seen it tossed around among such mezzos as Louise Homer, Thorborg, Stevens, Thebom, and Dunn and such sopranos as Jurinac, Vishnevskaya, Janis Martin, and Crespin.

Rosina in *Il barbiere di Siviglia* was written by Rossini for a coloratura mezzo, and he had his reasons, for this sort of voice brought a warmth to the character that is lost when a coloratura or leggero soprano takes it over. This habit began only a few years after its premiere in Rome in 1811; Maria Malibran seems to have been the first. Since Rossini did not protest—he admired this singer very much—this practice has gone on for so long that one cannot really call it an offense to tradition. It has proved a great vehicle for such coloraturas and leggeros as Patti, Sembrich, Tetrazzini, and Melba, and later for Elvira de Hidalgo, Graziella Pareto, Capsir, Galli-Curci, Toti dal Monte, Pons, Sayão, Renata Scotto, and Roberta Peters. Callas had one of her few defeats in this part at La Scala and never went near it again. Beverly Sills had a try at it in Boston under the motherly guidance of Sarah

Caldwell (and later in New York), but so far Joan Sutherland has not approached it, though Montserrat Caballé recently has in Nice. Since coloratura mezzos appear to be far more abundant today than their colleagues in the soprano range, they are increasingly taking over the role. Conchita Supervia's remains the definitive interpretation, but now we have Marilyn Horne, Teresa Berganza, Frederica von Stade, Maria Ewing, Jane Berbié, and Lucia Valentini.

Puccini's *La fanciulla del West,* which had its premiere in 1910, swept through every opera house in the world shortly before the First World War; after a long period when it was performed only in Italy, it has now again become the rage. Minnie, its heroine, is considered by some musicians to be the equivalent of a dramatic Wagnerian heroine. The orchestration is in fact very heavy; and unlike the Wagnerian dramas, which develop slowly, *Fanciulla* is a crescendo of passions that can easily carry an emotional soprano right off balance. For decades it was the property of the superdramatic sopranos; but now, with the very worrying and increasing lack of this type of voice, lyric sopranos are attempting it. Emmy Destinn (who created the role), Eugenia Burzio, Gilda dalla Rizza, Tina Poli-Randaccio, Carmen Melis, Giulia Tess, and Maria Jeritza were among its famous early interpreters. Later came Iva Pacetti, Maria Caniglia, Elisabetta Barbato, Maria Carbone, and Franca Somigli. Tebaldi sang it, but only in the United States (she also recorded it). Since then, the divas who have appeared in this meaty part have managed, in some cases, to create a believable character, but rarely with sufficient vocal resources.

Leontyne Price had to stop singing for a while after being lured by Sir Rudolf Bing to open the season at the Metropolitan in this work, because the strain became evident in her voice. After a few months all was well, but naturally she never sang Minnie again. It proved heavy for Eleanor Steber and Antonietta Stella. Dorothy Kirsten, a lyric, but older when she first assumed the part and of a cooler nature, managed the hurdles with sagacity and knew how to save herself for the climaxes. Even Callas—who sang everything, including Turandot—never went near Minnie, the difference being that the Chinese princess appears for two acts only, and never with the emotional impact of the American country girl in love with the bandit.

Turandot demands a dramatic with a very special tessitura and is considered another "killer." Ever since its world premiere in 1926, it has been the vehicle almost exclusively for non-Italian prima donnas. It is nearly impossible to find a dramatic in Italy with the required bite, the capacity of the instrument to overcome a heavy orchestration (the three enigmas in the second act are a frightening crescendo), the brilliance at the top, and the glacial timbre to express the character of the cruel princess, who does not break down and become human until the end. Rosa Raisa, who created it at La Scala, was Polish, and Jeritza, who sang it first at the Metropolitan, was Czech. With the exception of Bianca Scacciati, Muzio (who sang it rarely), Pacetti, and Germana di Giulio—very great Turandots—all the others have been non-Italian, in some instances specialists in Wagner or Strauss. Now, amazingly enough, Montserrat Caballé and Carol Neblett have entered the arena (is there anything they will not try?), and Joan Sutherland and Katia Ricciarelli have recorded it, but neither has sung it on the stage. The outstanding Turandot today is the Bulgarian Ghena Dimitrova, one of the rare dramatics in existence today.

Norma, an opera that will turn up constantly in this volume, used to be considered holy ground for dramatic sopranos of great agility, and it was approached with a sense of enormous reverence. In the twenties and thirties there were very few indeed who dared to challenge it; among the successful were Raisa, Muzio, Scacciati, Pacetti, Ponselle, Vera Amerighi Rutili, and Cigna, who was the last to undertake it at the Metropolitan before Milanov assumed the sacred mantle, with less than brilliant results. The magnificent voice was all there to do the role full justice, but there was not quite the feline intensity that Bellini intended. Since the war Maria Callas, despite her lack of vocal purity, was most impressive in the role for several years, and then came Anita Cerquetti, considered by Ester Mazzoleni (a legendary interpreter in the early 1900s) to have been the last to know what the role required. Since then Sutherland, Caballé, and Margaret Price have assumed it, but with question marks on the part of critics and public alike: the first for her bad diction, lack of temperament, and insufficient incisiveness; the second for being obliged to force somewhat her splendid instrument and, like Sutherland, the lack of a lower register to cope with some of the important phrases; and the third for insufficient temperament and being too Mozartian.

For a few years after the war, the role was sung decorously by Maria Pedrini and the American Lucille Udovick, both somewhat lacking in personality, and by Germana di Giulio, who sang the opera in Italy with great dignity. But since then it has been a free-for-all. From the Turk Leyla Gencer to the American Nancy Tatum and the Dutch Cristina Deutekom, from the Yugoslav Radmila Bakocevic to the Italians Maria Luisa Cioni and Renata Scotto, from the two mezzos Bumbry and Verrett to the coloraturas Sills and Deutekom—all were or are giving their own very limited versions of what many consider to be one of the most beautiful operas ever written. Much of the same is happening to the very lovely role of Adalgisa. While tradition demanded a mezzo with agility and a large voice, now just about anyone sings it, including light sopranos, such as Margherita Rinaldi.

A mezzo with agility is needed for most of the Rossini operas (Rosina in *Il barbiere di Siviglia*, *La Cenerentola*, *L'italiana in Algeri*, Arsace in *Semiramide*, *Tancredi*, Neocle in *L'assedio di Corinto*, Isolier in *Le Comte Ory*, Malcolm in *La donna del lago*); Mozart (Sesto in *La clemenza di Tito*); Romeo in Bellini's *I Capuleti ed i Montecchi*; many of the operas by Monteverdi, Handel, Lully, and Rameau; and Adalgisa in *Norma*. The last is often sung, however, by other types of mezzos possessing a certain amount of flexibility. For instance, Fiorenza Cossotto, who in the early days could sing *Barbiere* quite comfortably, gave it up long ago but still sings Adalgisa. Teresa Berganza, a coloratura mezzo, has always limited herself to a very few operas, since her voice is small and could not possibly cope with such scores as *Tancredi* and *Semiramide*, where the fioritura must be handled by a much larger instrument.

The mezzo repertoire often shared by the lyric and spinto includes Neris in Cherubini's *Medea*, Urbain in *Les Huguenots*, Fidalma in Cimarosa's *Il matrimonio segreto*, Preziosilla in *La forza del destino*, Maddalena in *Rigoletto*, Hansel, Mallika in *Lakmé*, Nancy in *Martha*, and Countess Geschwitz in *Lulu*. And then there are those roles that, as we have already seen, are shared at times by sopranos. Spintos with a certain agility can take on Leonora in Donizetti's *La favorita*. Also at the disposal of spinto mezzos are Amneris in *Aida*, Dalila, Laura in *La Gioconda*, Dulcinée in Massenet's *Don Quichotte*, Jocasta in Stravinsky's *Oedipus Rex*, and those parts previously discussed that are often undertaken also by sopranos. The dramatic mezzos, who often spread out into the spinto territory, sing such parts as the Countess in *The Queen of Spades*, the High Priestess in Spontini's *La vestale*, the Mother in *Louise*, Marfa in *Khovanshchina*, Azucena in *Il trovatore*, Fidès in *Le Prophète*, the Wagnerian ladies Ortrud, Venus, Brangäne, Fricka, and Waltraute, the Principessa di Bouillon in *Adriana Lecouvreur*, the Old Prioress in *Les Dialogues des carmélites*, and Madame Flora in *The Medium*. Actually, such assignments as Quickly in *Falstaff*, Ulrica in *Un ballo in maschera*, Erda in *Siegfried*, Klytämnestra in *Elektra*, and Herodias in *Salome* belong to the contralto range, which today appears no longer to exist (we will see in the Tebaldi interview why this is taking place). So today these roles are taken over by dramatic mezzos, who do not have those necessary dark tones and develop artificial chest tones to compensate.

Gluck's Orfeo is another role that should be sung either by a contralto or by a mezzo with an unusually strong lower register. It is one of the most demanding parts ever written, for during three acts the protagonist is onstage all the time, and the other two roles, Euridice and Amor, though effective, are brief. One recalls only a few who did full justice to the part after the First World War: Dame Clara Butt, Fanny Anitua, Sigrid Onegin, Margarete Klose, Gabriella Besanzoni, and Ebe Stignani. After the Second World War Kathleen Ferrier, Giulietta Simionato, and Elisabeth Höngen come to mind. Risë Stevens attempted it, but her instrument was not really imposing enough; nor was Kerstin Meyer's. More recent Orfeos, like Julia Hamari and Yvonne Minton, cannot begin to give sufficient depth and pathos to this noble character with their pretty but limited voices.

Today the revolution among mezzos is even more pronounced than among sopranos. A very special case is that of Dame Janet Baker, who, with the necessary transpositions, managed to take on soprano roles such as Maria Stuarda and Alceste with much success. The excellent Greek coloratura Agnes Baltsa, whose instrument delicately conveys Dorabella's amorous problems and the agile demands of Bellini's Romeo, sang Herodias under Karajan in his Salzburg production of *Salome*. It is an ungrateful role which encourages a lot of yelling and which lately has become strongly identified with Astrid Varnay, whose instrument is frayed after forty-one years of wear and tear. She has also sung Eboli, which is far too heavy for her current voice.

When previously mezzos turned into dramatic sopranos (or vice versa) because they felt that their top was increasing (or diminishing), they never looked back; certainly they never took on roles in both repertoires at once. The progress is usually safer when a soprano becomes a mezzo, for it always remains a big question whether the middle tones will suffer when the voice is moved up. It is one matter to hit the top notes with facility, as many mezzos can manage, and another to sing an entire score in an upper key. Elsa Alsen made the switch in 1923 and remained a dramatic soprano until she retired. There was the much-loved Rose Bampton, who gave up a very successful career as a mezzo to become a hollow-sounding soprano, and this despite her unfailing musicality. Her friendship with Toscanini led her to be chosen as Leonore for his NBC broadcast of *Fidelio*, but her appearances at the Metropolitan as Donna Anna, Sieglinde, Elsa, Alceste, Kundry, and Aida have left no significant trace. Margaret Harshaw did much better, but she never really achieved the distinction as a dramatic soprano that she had previously won as a mezzo. As for her Donna Anna, however, the results were very questionable. Janis Martin appears thus far to be more successful in her change of status. The unusually intelligent Regina Resnik, on the other hand, who always had problems with the high register when she sang dramatic roles, became a very successful low mezzo, creating a marvelous Dame Quickly and a stirring Klytämnestra. At the Met one recalls no divas other than Resnik and Bampton to sing both Aida and Amneris: Resnik went from Aida to Amneris, and Bampton from Amneris to Aida.

Conversely, a fine mezzo who then developed into a spectacular dramatic soprano was Giannina Arangi-Lombardi, who had one of the most celebrated high Cs of her era and was the greatest Lucrezia Borgia between the two world wars. Another who made a spectacular change was Marta Fuchs, who at first sang Orfeo and Azucena and then became one of the great Wagnerian and Straussian dramatic sopranos—and who also sang a very fine Donna Anna.

In recent years three famous mezzos—Christa Ludwig, Grace Bumbry, and Shirley Verrett—have attempted the transition but seem unwilling entirely to abandon their original repertoire. It is generally agreed that all three committed a big error. Ludwig, who now has reverted to mezzo roles, sticks to the Marschallin though she was an unforgettable Octavian. When Bumbry appears as Tosca, Salome, Gioconda, Medea, Sélika, Abigaille, or Norma, she is obviously not at home despite her dramatic flair, and after a while there are obvious signs of strain.

Verrett, who was an admirable Adalgisa, has now—like Bumbry—taken on Norma, and to a newcomer to the world of opera the fact that both she and Sills sing this most difficult of roles ever written for soprano (Lilli Lehmann used to say she would have preferred to sing two *Götterdämmerung* Brünnhildes in succession rather than one Norma) is confusing to a degree. Her Norma at the Met was not favorably received. When she played Amelia in *Un ballo in maschera* at La Scala in 1978, her lack of central notes elicited considerable booing. But, again, she cannot make up her mind: in 1977 she was still singing Azucena; in 1978, Leonora in *La favorita;* and in 1981, Dalila at Covent Garden, and in 1982 Leonore in *Fidelio* at the Met. In order to celebrate Marian Anderson's eightieth birthday, Bumbry and Verrett, who have had delightful little public quarrels in the past, gave a concert together, to the joy of New Yorkers, in the winter of 1982. They alternated, in their solos and duets, soprano and mezzo parts, and many in the audience were understandably very confused. A famous old diva, who wishes to remain anonymous, remarked to me: "They all think they can do like Margarete Matzenauer, who kept on singing two repertoires, the mezzo and the dramatic. But she was a freak in a way, for she really had two voices, although the mezzo range was exceptionally beautiful, and the dramatic satisfactory but not in the same class. However, she could go with ease from Brangäne to Isolde, from Orfeo to Countess Almaviva, from Fricka to Brünnhilde in *Die Walküre.*"

There is a definite repertoire for the "falcon" voice as well. Falcon, the original Valentine in *Les Huguenots* and Rachel in *La Juive,* lost her voice after only six years, but she left behind her a trail of glory, despite the fact that her beautiful instrument could not go beyond a B-flat. And she did not have a sufficient low register to be a mezzo. Victoria de los Angeles (who sang soprano roles but was always in trouble with the high notes) is, in my opinion, an example of a typical falcon. Her somewhat understated stage personality did not help matters. She managed to get through some of the Puccini roles and Eva in *Meistersinger* because of the beauty of her middle voice, but she was totally defeated at the Metropolitan by Martha, a role in which such brilliant lyrics with agility as Christine Nilsson, Adelina Patti, Marcella Sembrich, Frieda Hempel, and Frances Alda had emerged. Even Maria Barrientos and Margherita Carosio, both coloraturas, made a hit in it. If the Flotow opera finished de los Angeles's Metropolitan schedules (they wanted her to sing Donna Anna, but she sang it in San Francisco instead), it did not end her appearances as a recitalist, as which she had few peers. But if she had sung *Werther, Mignon,* and other operas in that range, many experts think, she would have had a far more enduring operatic career.

Singers who undertake contemporary scores often have stated how most of them are damaging to the vocal cords. Evelyn Lear told me she stopped just in the nick of time or her instrument would have been hopelessly damaged. Having made an enormous hit in Berg's *Lulu* in Central Europe, she was sought after by every house, not only for this excruciating score but for many other modern works. She often sang Marie in *Wozzeck,* and she created Lavinia in Marvin David Levy's *Mourning Becomes Electra* at the Metropolitan in 1967. This opera, which was a great success, with eleven performances, has never been revived. She stopped singing for a while, gave her voice a rest, and then began taking lessons. The result was beyond even her hopes, for she is now again an exquisite Mozart singer and has become one of the finest Marschallins on the international scene, having sung the role even at La Scala under the demanding Carlos Kleiber. Anja Silja is another soprano with marvelous looks, much individuality, and a serviceable voice, who, because of her affectionate friendship with Wieland Wagner, was thrown into heavy Wagnerian parts much too early and then, after his death, plunged recklessly into modern scores. The voice has lost its color, but she still undertakes operas by Schoenberg, Berg, and Janáček, in which the various breaks in her vocal organ are not so noticeable.

It is difficult for young singers, eager for opportunities, to refuse opera companies offering them world premieres that will get extensive press coverage and bring them to the attention of the public. The wise ones get out before the harm is done. When composers like Gian Carlo Menotti, who writes melodious arias and ensembles gratifying to the voice, present new operas, they are torn to bits by the critics for being old hat. But a lot of water has passed under the operatic bridge, and Mascagni, Zandonai, Giordano, Montemezzi, Pizzetti, and Respighi, who seemed revolutionary at the time, appear antiquated compared with Einem, Henze, Nono, and Berio. The twelve-tone and electronic operas simply do not attract audiences, despite the theatre managements' attempts to force them down their throats. Even subscribers don't go and can't find friends to whom to give their tickets. After the world premiere in March 1982 at La Scala of Berio's *Storia*, which laid a big egg, I could not help recalling the witty remark of Sir Rudolf Bing in his autobiography: "I am always being told that opera will die unless the new works are performed. It seems to me that these days a better case can be made for the proposition that opera will never die unless the new works are performed."

In Europe today, part of the problem is the strong connection between politically oriented composers and managers who are usually appointed not for their musical knowledge but to serve as an extension of one of the political parties. Typical of this is what happened in Florence on March 10, 1982, when opera made headlines on the political front. The communist mayor and council resigned. They had wanted Mario Casalini, a Florentine publisher, to succeed Massimo Bogianckino—who had been called by the French socialists to direct the Paris Opéra—as general manager of the opera house. The socialists, however, backed by several other parties, elected their own man, Francesco Romano, a jurist.

Janáček, suddenly in the repertoire of many opera houses, did not write gratefully for the voice. Hildegard Ranczak expressed her concern for all the young singers taking on assignments in the heavy roles of *Jenůfa, Kátá Kabanová, From the House of the Dead,* and other of his operas. "I just wonder," she said, "what will happen to their vocal cords in a few years. He was practically a contemporary of Mahler, but what a difference between them, for Mahler knew how to write superbly for the voice." Another role that is very harmful to the vocal cords is Renata in Prokofiev's *The Fiery Angel*. I recall a lovely-looking Italian soprano, Floriana Cavalli, who made a big splash in this opera, and unwisely (the work suddenly became very fashionable) agreed to sing it in many opera houses. She joined those who quietly slipped into oblivion.

Usually, the singers who start out in these contemporary works are unable to sing anything else after a while. The Swiss soprano Cristel Goltz is an example. Much in demand, she created Orff's *Antigonae* and Liebermann's *Penelope* and was very successful as Salome, Elektra, and Marie in *Wozzeck*, but she really could not do justice to any nonmodern score. Patricia Neway is another singer who lost her top by specializing in so many modern operas, and it is a pity, for hers was a very great talent.

There are small voices that are produced in so expert a manner that they are heard even in very large theatres over large orchestras. The Italians have an expression for this phenomenon—*voci che corrono* (voices that run). Bidú Sayão had the good fortune that her mini-instrument could always be counted on to cut through and reach the farthest seat in the house. Rita Streich is another who managed this trick, but Reri Grist is exactly the opposite. This delicious soprano's tiny voice at times simply cannot pierce through the barrier of sound, but she has the intelligence not to force it and to wait for quieter passages. The reason that Albanese with her small voice was able to sing Butterfly so often over thirty years is that she wisely never tried to produce sounds that would endanger her instrument in the heavy orchestral sections. If the conductor covered her, she accepted it. She was also, along with Magda Olivero and Mafalda Favero, a mistress of what Italians call *l'accento,* the articulation of the words, which in many instances can well substitute for lack of vocal power. When the dramatic passages demand a bigger sound, intelligent and able phrasing can work miracles in creating the needed atmosphere of a crescendo. This art was developed when the verismo and realismo operas became fashionable.

THE HUGE VOICES

EBE STIGNANI

ELENA NICOLAI

EVA TURNER

GERTRUD GROB-PRANDL

Preceding Birgit Nilsson, the only current singer with a truly huge voice, were four singers—two mezzo-sopranos and two dramatic sopranos—who filled the opera houses and outdoor arenas with oceans of sound, and the source seemed inexhaustible, for theirs were unusually long careers. All four of them told me that the basic volume of their instruments was there from the beginning, but that with the passing of time and the gaining of experience, their vocal cords became increasingly stronger and the outpouring of such cascades of sound, which stunned the public, became absolutely natural to them.

I heard all of them. Ebe Stignani, an Italian, had a timbre that was beauty personified and an astounding technique. Apart from the colossal size of her voice, she was a phenomenon for her miraculous breath control and the unequaled facility of her legato. With the exception of Flagstad, in this last half-century no one but Stignani went from one register to another with such complete smoothness, and it was my privilege to attend many of her performances. Elena Nicolai, a Bulgarian, and Dame Eva Turner, an Englishwoman, both possessed a tremendous passion which, combined with their enormous instruments, was totally mesmerizing. The first I heard as Amneris and Carmen, the second as Sieglinde and Leonore in *Fidelio*. I never had the opportunity to evaluate Gertrud Grob-Prandl, an Austrian, in the heroic Wagnerian repertoire which brought her such fame, but her Turandot was astounding, not only for the tremendous volume, which cut through the vast orchestra like steel, but also for the facility with which she negotiated the infernally high tessitura. Needless to say, even today, when all such passions should be spent, I could surmise in various conversations with other singers a probably subconscious, subtle resentment of these four for their God-given abundance of volume.

EBE STIGNANI

I met Ebe Stignani for the first time when, accompanied by her husband, she walked into my Manhattan office in 1948—I recall vividly it was a brisk autumn day—to discuss my firm's doing publicity for her forthcoming Carnegie Hall recital. I had heard her in Florence many times in the late twenties and thirties and had been, like everyone else, totally awed by the voice, which was usually referred to as the miracle of the century. She was a short woman, not exactly stout, but with a big bosom and a short neck, and looked far less large in person than she did on the stage. Her manner was impersonal but cordial; and had I not known that she was, at the time, forty-four years old, I would have been unable to state her age: she might have been thirty-five or fifty. Of all the great prima donnas I have known, she was the one with the least personality and the greatest dignity. She always spoke of herself as if she were talking about another person— "Stignani" here and "Stignani" there; it was never "I." In a certain way, this was tremendously effective, for one felt one could discuss everything freely, as if one were speaking of someone else. Her husband, an engineer, was quiet, unassuming, gentle; and one could feel there was a perfect rapport between them.

She came straight to the point. She had been told that never having sung at the Metropolitan (Edward Johnson had engaged her for the famous 1939–40 season, when all Italian artists were impeded by the fascist government from leaving the country so as not to deprive the Italian opera houses of their glories), she needed some press buildup, and asked what we could do about it. I began asking her questions, and she replied candidly. "I can give you the facts of my life and career, but there is nothing colorful about me. As a matter of fact, the only color I possess is in my voice, and it has always been my throat which has been my passport. I am not an interesting woman in any way. I was given a magnificent gift, and in a way I am like a priestess, for I feel that it is my responsibility to keep this flame lit in the best possible manner. It is not that I believe in reincarnation, really, for I

35

Ebe Stignani as Ulrica in *Un ballo in maschera*.

am too much of a good Catholic, and yet it is almost as if this blessing had been passed on to me in a mysterious way by someone who came before me. I am Stignani because of my voice. I often wonder who I could have been otherwise. Anyhow, the question has ceased to torment me, for I have been too busy ever since I started. It has been an avalanche, and I am very fortunate that I am a healthy, strong woman who has been able to take on these immense endeavors. I have been singing for twenty-five years, and if my calculations are correct, I still have ten good years ahead of me.

"I do not think of what will happen when I stop," she went on, "because I have always been philosophical and am convinced that things fall into place. But as I have never rested ever since I first began, I believe that I will simply disappear. One is important while one is, and when you are no more, you have the luxury of being what you have never had the chance of ever being. Therefore, I don't look at retirement, as so many of my colleagues do, as a calamity, but rather as the inevitable parable. After all, one is born, one lives, one dies. And the voice is born and dies too, you know. There is no way out, so why not accept it resolutely and philosophically? Most singers consider their careers as a profession, and of course they are right. But somehow for me it has always had another dimension too, and this is perhaps the reason why I have always been at peace with myself. You cannot invent jealousies, envies, or rows where I am concerned. I have only been able to relate to jealousy while singing, for that was imposed by the music and the text. That is why, perhaps, I have always loved Orfeo more than any other role, for it suits my placid and slightly melancholic nature. For me, it is undoubtedly the most heavenly music ever written. When I sing 'Che puro ciel,' I feel transported. I have sung many more Amnerises—a staple of the repertoire one cannot get away from—and this characterization, underlined by violent jealousy, is so tremendous one cannot not express it. But it has never been the real me, if you can understand what I want to say. One does not conquer jealousy, one is simply born without it, and I was among these blessed mortals. I have always been happy at the success of my colleagues; and anyhow, quite frankly, during all these years—all modesty apart—there really has been no competition in my wing to speak of. There have been and are some great mezzos, but none have been blessed with my particular sort of voice."

The Carnegie Hall recital was a triumph that those who attended will never forget. This simple woman walked out on that bare stage and all she had to do was to open her golden mouth to leave everyone astounded at the beauty of the timbre, the enormous control, the stunning facility with which she went up and down the scale, and the purity of the vocal line. And, supposedly, she was not a recital singer. At least she did not think she was, having sung, until then, few concerts. Actually, she was a natural, for she could reveal the extraordinary gamut of her styles; and the lack of personality of which she had been so conscious could not have mattered less. And there, in a way, was her form of sorcery. As she had so correctly diagnosed, it was the voice and voice alone that mattered. But what she had not counted on was that the blasé and sophisticated New Yorkers, used to the glamorous divas—that was the beginning of the end of that era—were overcome by the utter modesty and simplicity of her approach. Once she left the stage, one almost forgot what she looked like; and yet when she was on it, there she was, and what she had stated—"I am Stignani"—was so true. A peculiar charm was there, a smile that went straight to the heart.

She was true to her prophecy. When she retired in 1958, she vanished into a bourgeois apartment in Imola, in Romagna, and no one heard of her again until she died in 1975 at the age of seventy-one. She was, as far as I know, never seen attending any performance and led the most retiring of lives. When asked why she had lost all contact with the world of which she had been queen, she very simply replied, "I do not understand what goes on today. In the space of fifteen years everything has changed. Voices come and go. There is no continuity left. Everyone is singing what he or she should not. It is beyond me." And when asked if she thought this was because with the facility of air travel everyone who had become a leader in the profession sang too much, she replied, "Up to a point. I do not believe the trouble lies really there, although it does have its influence. I sang a great deal, as did the wonderful Gina Cigna, and she, Scacciati, and Arangi-Lombardi were the three exceptional dramatic sopranos of my day, but we never strayed from what was right for our voices, and we had conductors who knew their scores. We were protected. That, I believe, is the main difference."

After her sensational Carnegie concert, everyone had been sure that the Metropolitan would immediately make an important offer. It did not. Mr. Bing was about to take over, and he had very little interest in old-timers; he engaged Fedora Barbieri instead. It was the only major theatre she did not sing in, and if it hurt, she never showed it. During the next ten years (her last role was Azucena in *Il trovatore* in London in 1958, after thirty-three years in the theatre) she had a tremendously busy career, always with La Scala as her base, and sang often with Maria Callas. She was a very busy recording artist, and her list is most impressive, including two recordings of *Norma,* one with Cigna and the other with Callas. There are many who think that her recording of Verdi's Requiem, under the direction of Serafin, with Gigli, Pinza, and Caniglia, has never been equaled. She first sang in the United States in San Francisco in 1938—Santuzza in *Cavalleria*—and after the war she sang there, among other roles, Dame Quickly, Laura in *La Gioconda,* and again Santuzza. In Chicago she appeared as Venus in Monteverdi's *Il ballo delle ingrate,* Azucena, and Santuzza.

"I was born in Naples," she related, as I was busily taking notes on her biography, "and I always knew that my interest lay in music. Before studying voice, I began with the piano, and for five years, at the Conservatory of San Pietro di Maiella (Caniglia was there too, but she was younger —one of the most charming ladies I know), I studied with Agostino Roche. It was he who put me on guard about remaining a mezzo-contralto, for I could sing easily both these repertoires when they were considered different, and not moving into the soprano spheres. 'They will all try to talk you into it,' he kept warning me, and how right he was. 'And the battle is not over yet. But while you will be able to sing short dramatic soprano roles like Santuzza, the color of your instrument is that of a mezzo, and leave it that way or you will suddenly find yourself in no man's land.' I had confidence in him and never strayed from his advice. I was even talked into studying Norma and actually could sing it with ease. But then I began to realize how different it was to sing it with a piano accompaniment, as compared with singing it with full orchestra in a large theatre. And I stuck to Adalgisa. I have sung 'Casta diva' on record and many times in concerts, but that is less than five minutes of the whole. Although Roche kept me for five years on scales and solfège, he insisted I study choir music too, and harmony. I have diplomas in all these various musical studies.

"People are always surprised that I do not look or act like a Neapolitan, that I do not have the quick temperament of these darling people, but the fact is that my having been born in Naples and raised there does not mean that I am Neapolitan. In fact, since my family came from Imola, I have always considered myself *una romagnola*. I feel certain that having spent my childhood and youth in Naples influenced me in certain ways, for these people have music in their veins and hearts. However ignorant, they are innately musical.

"I don't know whether it was because of the climate or what, but my voice was already pretty well placed when I began studying, and it did not take long before I could go with ease from low F to high C. My breathing had to be improved upon, and although the basic agility was there, it had to be worked upon and enlarged. In fact, I sang many coloratura mezzo roles later, but never went near some of the Rossini heroines, for I was aware that I did not have the proper figure to do them justice. There was the adorable Conchita Supervia then, and she was perfection itself as Rosina, Isabella in *L'italiana in Algeri,* and Cenerentola. She had the charm and humor that went with these roles, along with a dazzling technique despite a small voice. I knew I could not possibly compete with her. But I did sing Arsace in *Semiramide,* with all its pyrotechnics.

"When I first started my career, I had the know-how to tackle many operas, but I practically had no repertoire at my disposal. Roche always was of the opinion that this was not so important and would come with time. I started at the very top, for at the age of twenty-one I appeared as Amneris in a production of *Aida* at the San Carlo in Naples in 1925. It all went so fast, it is difficult for me to recall the order, but I do know that Toscanini, who had spies in every corner of the world, heard about my beginnings, called me for an audition, and had me sing Meg in his famous production of *Falstaff* in Verdi's birthplace, Busseto. I graduated to Dame Quickly later, for in those days it was almost the exclusive property of the inimitable Elvira Casazza. Today's singers tend to underevaluate the difficulties of *Falstaff,* one of the trickiest musical scores ever conceived and written. But then they do tend to underevaluate everything. Meg is certainly the least important of the four ladies in the opera, and yet if she misses a comma or a split second, she can ruin the performance. It is all a question of timing, and if you are not musical, God save you.

"Anyhow," she said with a knowing smile, "I passed my test, for he engaged me for the 1926–27 season at La Scala for three operas, *La Gioconda, Der Freischütz,* and *Götterdämmerung.* I was amazed that he should assign me Ännchen, since it is scored for a soprano, but the role is short. And to have me go from that to the deeper and stupendous regions of Waltraute— another brief part, but terribly important—was proof of great confidence." She continued to sing at La Scala for twenty-seven years, though during some of the war years the theatre did not function.

"As I have sung with all the greatest conductors, I am naturally very spoiled. Is Toscanini the greatest? Perhaps. What he had was a prodigious way of imposing his will and yet allowing you to be yourself. When I first started rehearsing with him, despite the fact that my instrument was very large, I was afraid that I might be drowned. Not at all. If this happened at the rehearsals sometimes, never did I have this experience at the perform- ances. On the contrary, he was consideration itself. I found Victor de Sabata very great too, and on an equal scale I would place Antonio Guarnieri,

Tullio Serafin, Franco Ghione, Vittorio Gui, Ettore Panizza, Gino Marinuzzi. Each one had his way, and one had to learn how to adapt oneself to their batons. Serafin, in some ways, was the most elastic, and Guarnieri the most impenetrable. His Wagner was out of this world. I sang a lot of Wagner. Ortrud and Brangäne were often thrown at me, and I loved the latter in particular. The warning from the tower is one of the most haunting pieces of music ever written. But then I am versatile, for I go from Adalgisa to Azucena, from Fidalma in *Il matrimonio segreto* to Marina in *Boris,* from the Witch in *Hansel and Gretel* to Ulrica in *Un ballo in maschera,* from Dalila to Carmen, from the High Priestess in *La vestale* to Laura in *La Gioconda* and Preziosilla in *Forza.* In the years preceding the Second World War, Preziosilla was considered a very prominent part, and I simply cannot understand why it is now assigned to almost anyone. It throws the entire work off balance. It is immensely difficult, for it requires a lot of agility and the orchestration is very heavy.

"I had the privilege of singing in *La vestale* with Rosa Ponselle in her only Italian appearance, at the Maggio Musicale Fiorentino. It was one of the loveliest voices in the world, short on top, but the quality was superb, pure Renaissance velvet. I stood in the wings every time to listen to her delivery of 'Tu che invoco,' one of the great emotions I have received in my life. I had just left the stage and she had remained alone. It was a heavenly sound—earthy and at the same time disembodied. There lay the miracle of Ponselle, fire and spirit at the same time. Cigna was wonderful too, but there it was different—all fire. But she gave me tremendous emotions too. When she stood there, in the second act of *Norma,* and realized that I was her rival, I was frozen. The scene was hers, and that's all there was to it. No one could compete with her. There was no point even in trying. Anyhow, I was never, and never will be, a great actress. Each and every one of us has his limitations.

"There were two roles which became very much identified with me," she went on. "Leonora in *La favorita* and Eboli in *Don Carlo.* If Donizetti had written *La favorita* for me, it could not have been more ideal for me. Not only did it never present any difficulties, but I always almost wished there had been more. Eboli will always remain connected with one of the most nerve-racking evenings of my career—I who claim to have no nerves. I had studied it and knew it inside out, but when I was called the morning of the performance at La Scala to substitute for the ailing Giuseppina Cobelli, I was in a panic. First of all, Cobelli was a beautiful woman—and there never was a kinder one either—a tremendous favorite, and had made the role her own despite the fact that she was a soprano. Antonino Votto, the conductor, told me he would take all the responsibilities: 'You have to sing it sooner or later. It is much better this way, as you will have little time to worry,' he told me very convincingly. But I was far from convinced. Little Stignani, short in size and plump, taking on Cobelli. Merciful heavens! Thus far my notices had been splendid, but I had gone on as myself. Here I was taking someone else's place, and it is difficult to imagine today —she only died a short time ago—what her position was then. Well, I won my battle, and it was, in a way, a great lesson, for I knew then that I could depend on my voice and that the rest, in my case, did not matter.

"I have sung a lot in South America, in Argentina and Brazil, was engaged various times at Covent Garden, the San Carlo in Lisbon (what a beautiful theatre!—I am going back there next year), and then in Germany too, in Munich and Berlin. Last year I had the great satisfaction of singing in Paris in *Trovatore* and *Favorita,* and I do not recall such ovations even in South America, where, heaven knows, if they like you, they tear you to pieces with their admiration. When I took the high C at the end of the concertato in the second act of the Donizetti opera, I thought the audience would go mad. And I thought of Roche's advice. A high C, the kind God gave me, amazes people in a mezzo, while it would have been taken for granted in a dramatic soprano.

"I think it is a great luxury to have favorites," she continued, "and I never could afford this. I liked to vary and found every role interesting per se. I never sang much in the modern-score department, for I find it very detrimental to the organ. Too disconnected, dissonant, unbecoming to the organ. Respighi and Pizzetti were different, for they knew how to write for the voice. But many of the others I turned down. The satisfaction of having established your reputation is not in saying yes but in saying no. I was always in the fortunate position of being able to choose what I wanted to do, and if I did not, it was only to favor someone who had been particularly kind to me on a certain occasion.

"I adored Gigli, for instance, it was always thrilling for me to be able to sing with him, and if he really insisted on having me as a partner, I would often give in. I don't know whether he was the greatest tenor I ever sang with, but I think he is the one who satisfied me the most.

"I always protect my health, never go out much, do absolutely limit myself to the essentials. I have always loved going to the theatre and the cinema; it is the greatest form of escape for me. Parties, receptions, dinners are not, as they represent a considerable effort. They expect to meet an extraordinary person, all these people who clamor for an introduction, but there is nothing extraordinary about me except the voice, and that they must come to the theatre to hear. I find exposure useless and at times even dangerous. Let them see the artist from a distance, greater than life—it is more impressive, less disappointing. I believe a lot in decorum, for people must respect the artists, even if we have to renounce a lot to warrant it. But then it is a sort of mission. It is like bringing a sort of gospel—the message of the great composers. We are honoring them, and this we must never forget. It is not they who are honoring us. If I had not married and had a son, who is the joy of my life, I would almost say that I lived the existence of a nun.

"This is where I think changes are coming in. I see already colleagues who want to live it up. But one cannot, if one is serious about what one is doing. I have always admired temperament in others, but have been scared by it, for I have seen that it often shortens the career. If you allow yourself to get carried away with a part, the voice suffers. That is why there are certain roles, like Santuzza and Azucena, which I accept only from time to time."

I asked her what was her favorite aria.

"How can I answer that when there are so many that are so intrinsically beautiful? Also, the words are so indissoluble from the music. Certain arias seem more glorious than others because of the text, and I always give a great deal of importance to the meaning of the lines. For instance, can anything be more sublime than the words 'Mon coeur s'ouvre à ta voix'? Every time I have agreed to sing Dalila, it is because of this very aria. What is more wonderful than a heart which opens up to the sound of a voice that is dear? I cannot think of anything. And I would like to imagine that the hearts of the people who listen to me experience just this very sensation. If I am able to do this, then I am content, for then my small mission in this tormented world we live in is done.

"Do you see how difficult it will be to do publicity for someone so normal, so sensitive, like me? You are not publicizing a person but a voice, and how do you do that?"

ELENA NICOLAI

Elena Nicolai emerged as an outstanding dramatic mezzo-soprano at La Scala in 1938, when Stignani and Pederzini were already well entrenched there, and rapidly began sharing the repertoire with them. A tall, handsome, immensely dynamic woman in her early seventies when I spoke with her in 1977, she is one of the most articulate and clear-thinking opera stars I have ever interviewed. As a matter of fact, she had so much of interest to say that I went back to see her a second time that winter. She lives in Milan in a spacious, oddly furnished apartment which is in character with the various facets of her strong personality.

Born in Bulgaria—she was named Stianca Nikolova—she came to Milan at the age of nineteen and for five years studied at the conservatory, first with Vincenzo Pintorno and then with Ettore Pozzoli. She made her debut as Annina in *Der Rosenkavalier* at the San Carlo in Naples just to get the feeling of her voice on the stage, but that was the only minor role she ever sang. She made what she considers her official debut as Laura in *La Gioconda* under Franco Ghione in Noto. This appearance in Sicily led immediately to repetition of the same part in Cremona—Ponchielli's birthplace—with Cigna and Gigli, under Tullio Serafin. She then went on to sing, with the same three artists, Ponchielli's *Il figliuol prodigo.* Then immediately the doors of La Scala opened for her to sing the Principessa di Bouillon in *Adriana,* and a short time later she was asked to replace Stignani, who had engagements elsewhere, in some repeat performances of Boito's *Nerone* under Marinuzzi.

"My goodness, what a responsibility, to sing Rubria," she declared, "and step into the shoes of Stignani, who was then a goddess. Her fame was justified, for she had one of those fabulous instruments which come once a century. She was no great shakes as an actress, but then one cannot have everything—and she had a technique which was utterly spectacular. She opened her mouth and one was mesmerized by the richness and evenness of her timbre. I really was thrown to the wolves, but then, being part wolf

44

myself, I put up a tremendous battle and won. This is no Stignani, the critics said, but this is Nicolai, a name to be watched. I had never laid eyes on Marinuzzi until that evening and had had no rehearsals with Pertile, the king of tenors at La Scala; Maria Carena, a great dramatic soprano with a marvelously rich voice; and Alexander Sved.

"It all seemed like a dream. Night after night, as a student, I used to go to La Scala and sit in the last row of the top balcony to imbue myself with all types of operatic music, and I kept wondering whether I would ever have the opportunity to sing there at least once. How could I ever have imagined that it would become my second home? In those days I fell under the spell of Toscanini's favorite contralto, Elvira Casazza. She was already on the wane, but when I think of her, shivers go down my spine. The voice was far from beautiful, but the expression and the color she gave to the words have always been my inspiration.

"I was born stubborn, and I have had to live with it. Marinuzzi was so enthusiastic about me that he immediately wanted me for La Zia Principessa in *Suor Angelica* and the Witch in *Hansel and Gretel,* and I refused point blank. 'At the end of my career, perhaps; now certainly not,' I said. 'You are very presumptuous,' he replied, 'and you will never sing with me again.' Fate willed it otherwise, and we became intimate friends later. I was engaged in Trieste to sing *Lohengrin* under the baton of Hermann Scherchen, and, curiously, they were also giving the same opera at La Scala with Marinuzzi at the helm. Stignani fell ill, and every mezzo who knew the part was contacted. None was available. So, in despair, the management of La Scala called Trieste to beg the favor of rearranging the schedule so that I could commute and sing Ortrud in both theatres. If it had not been for the personal satisfaction of winning the skirmish with Marinuzzi I don't believe I would have accepted, for in those days the train journey—there were no planes—between Trieste and Milan was a long one, and it meant singing Ortrud almost every night. But, somehow, the triumph I had in the holy of holies (that is what we called La Scala in those days) made Ortrud practically my exclusive property for one quarter of a century. I had the temperament, the dark color in my voice, and the arrogance the part demands. I grew quite fond of this terrible bitch, for she never failed to bring in ecstatic reviews. Marinuzzi, who was very temperamental, was basically a kind man and had a sense of humor. One night after the performance he said to me, 'When I offered you the Witch, which you refused so categorically, I had no idea how marvelous you would be in that part,' and I replied, 'One witch is enough for now, Maestro.'

Elena Nicolai as Dalila in *Samson et Dalila*.

"It was when I was in Trieste again," she went on, "where I was appearing as Amneris, that the Arena in Verona called in despair for me to commute there and sing Ortrud, replacing Maria Benedetti, a good singer but with little temperament, who was ailing and had to cancel all of the performances. My success there was such that for two decades I sang during the spectacular summer season.

"Pia Tassinari was, in my opinion, the finest Elsa I ever sang with, and there were several dozens. She had such a smooth way of phrasing, and she could be ethereal and the sound traveled great distances. Tebaldi was also a stunning Elsa, and I recorded this opera with her. I never understood why, after a certain period, she abandoned this opera, for it was one of her greatest achievements.

"It was in Verona that I was called upon to sing Laura in *La Gioconda* in 1947, and it came as a surprise for all of us to learn that the title role had been assigned to an unknown Greek, Maria Callas. Little did I know that for the next fifteen years I was to be her constant partner. When I saw her for the first time, I must confess that I was stunned at her dimensions, for not even Lina Pagliughi, the nightingale in the body of a tank, had seemed quite so huge. And if the truth must be known, let me tell you that when I first heard her vocalize in the hotel—we had adjoining rooms—I had very mixed impressions. For if the top seemed brilliant, the center simply did not exist. Yet there was a flame burning in that voice, a musicality that had something very special. When we first met—somehow I sensed that she was a tigress—I said to her laughingly, 'In Bulgaria, they say that if a Greek and a wolf both knock at the door of a house at the same time, one had better leave the Greek out and let the wolf in.' And she replied as quick as lightning, 'In my country, instead, they say that when God met a Bulgarian he said to him that while he always gave a Greek one gift, he gave his neighbor two, for he needed them.' But I had the final word: 'Yes, I know the story, but you have left out what the Bulgarian answered God —"Take out one of my two eyes, for I can manage very well with one." ' This established a special relationship between us, and we never had a quarrel —and goodness knows, she had many.

"Anyhow, to get back to that historical *La Gioconda*, Maria was not in the least fabulous, as so often has been said; but Serafin, who was a regular magician, understood her latent capacities and possibilities. And it is he who worked with her and made her what she became—helped, naturally, by her burning ambition and willpower. The voice ceased to wobble and the center was restored.

"Almost immediately after, I sang Brangäne in Genoa to her Isolde. She was not a Wagnerian soprano, and being intelligent, she knew it. She did sing Brünnhilde, a few times, and Kundry, but then withdrew from the Wagnerian wing. The voice was too uneven, and for Wagner one needs very firm legato for those interminably long phrases. She made an interesting character out of the Irish princess, but the middle register was just not strong enough, and she had to force. Then I sang Amneris to her Aida, and Adalgisa with her in *Norma,* at La Scala and later practically in every theatre in Italy.

"I first sang Adalgisa in Piacenza with the very remarkable soprano Vera Amerighi Rutili, also of huge dimensions, but with a nobility that left one in awe. I shall ever be grateful to her, for she took me aside at the dress rehearsal and said to me, 'You are a very young woman, and I wonder if I could offer you some advice, being an old-timer.' 'Indeed, I would be most grateful,' I replied. 'When you make your entry in the first act,' she said, 'even if it *is* to meet your lover, do not rush in as if you were going to a marvelous party. Remember that you are a priestess, and project this image to the public the moment you enter.'

"When I asked her to tell me more, she said something I have never forgotten. It made so much sense, it was so obvious, and yet no one had ever told me before. 'The entrance in an opera is of the greatest importance, for you must let the audience know who you are right away. How you walk, hold yourself, the kind of light your eyes give out—this you must never fail to put across the footlights, and this will make it easier for you. It is like introducing yourself, letting them know who you are. If they don't notice you when you come in, it will take a long time for them to do so later.' I treasured her words always.

"Of all the Normas I sang with, and there were so many, Pacetti was the most sublime. Unlike Callas, she sang to her children as if she really had been their mother. With Maria, this never came across. There was something sterile about her, and one felt that she had none of her own. No real warmth. With Pacetti, at the beginning of the third act, I was myself torn apart every time. Scacciati, much admired by Toscanini, was great, but the voice never poured out the way it did with Pacetti or Cigna. The latter, of course, was quite extraordinary, for one had the impression that she was burning long before she walked into the flames of the fire that was going to kill her. Her eyes were fantastic—like stars. And her 'Casta diva' was sung as a prayer, the way it should be, not as an aria. From the wings, I always listened to her, and I felt each time that she had been transported elsewhere while singing it. Maria Pedrini and Anita Cerquetti in particular were, later, also very fine in this part.

"In Rio de Janeiro I sang *Norma* with Antonietta Stella, a ravishing Aida and Elisabetta di Valois (I recorded *Don Carlo* with her), but she had no business doing this Bellini role. The conductor Franco Ghione used to say, 'One learns Norma with one's lungs and muscles.' Well, Antonietta did not follow this advice, but spent all her time listening to the recordings of Cigna and Callas. It was all terribly impersonal and just was not right. As far as I know, she never sang it again.

"In Trieste—you will think that I was permanently there—I sang in *Norma* again with Maria, and we had by then appeared in this opera many times, for after La Scala there had also been Venice and Palermo, among other cities. She was very nervous that night, and I began sensing it from the very beginning. In the second act, when she put her arm around me, she pulled so strongly that my wig was in considerable danger. I managed to get away from her and place myself at a certain distance. But she followed me and repeated the same overaffectionate gesture in even a more marked manner. This time it was touch and go whether the wig would come off. Again I miraculously escaped from her, and this time I had learned my lesson —I just kept moving. There were no explanations afterward. I did not ask for any, and she said nothing. Did she do it on purpose? Was it an accident? I shall never know, as my relations remained very cordial with her until the end. I even recorded *Forza del destino* with her and Richard Tucker, whom I admired so much, and she was impeccably polite. A strange, unhappy, discontented human being, but one who undoubtedly brought a certain magic to all her interpretations, even if she was not a vocal purist. Alas, others tried to do the same and it was a disaster."

What had Callas's Aida been like?

"Good enough, but it was not one of her best creations, for there was not that purity of line required. Where, in my opinion, she was supreme was in *I vespri siciliani,* and as Medea and Lady Macbeth.

"I sang with so many Aidas, and among the finest I would put Tebaldi, when she was at her peak; Adriana Guerrini, who never received the international acclaim that she deserved; and Carla Castellani. The latter's Nile scene was unforgettable, a texture of silk and divinity. You know, 'O cieli azzurri' is one of the most difficult arias Verdi ever wrote, and Carla made it seem as if it were the easiest thing in the world. Why she too did not go further I shall never know. But that is the way the lyric theatre is, full of impenetrable mysteries; and even when you are in it the way I was, up to my ears, there are so many imponderables that are difficult to weigh. Some singers need a ringmaster, and Callas was immensely fortunate in finding Serafin, and Sutherland in meeting and marrying Bonynge. Would they have gone so far if they had not had that fortune? I do not believe so.

"I was particularly happy in roles such as Azucena and Eboli, although I felt very much at home as Carmen and Dalila. Eboli has a far more difficult scoring than most people realize. In the *canzone del velo* not only is there much agility but an A-natural, and in 'O don fatale' a B-natural. The reason this is so tough is that the aria lies in the middle of the voice. If one wants to sing Azucena the way it is written—and that is the only way I ever sang it, but, of course, today practically no one does—one must overcome many tricky passages, and a B-flat at the end which arrives when one has already given all. I had the figure and temperament for Carmen and Dalila, so I was called to perform them often, and for many seasons my partner was invariably Ramón Vinay, whose voice was opaque and strangely veiled but who always brought out a living character. I also sang all the roles which lie in no man's land, as I call them, for they can be undertaken by both a soprano with a very low register and a mezzo with a very good top. So I was often Fedora, which again suited my good figure, and I remember Gigli and Giacinto Prandelli as being the most affecting of the many Lorises I sang it with. In *Fedora* the rapport between the princess and her beau is particularly essential, more so than in many other operas. While Gigli created the character with his amazing instrument, so tender and passionate, Prandelli was one of the most aristocratic tenors, perhaps the most so, that I have ever appeared with. He did what Amerighi Rutili had spoken about—he established who he was as he walked on the stage. I sang the Giordano heroine a lot, even outside Italy, including Mexico City, the Liceo of Barcelona, and Bilbao, where the quality of the performances has always been very high.

"The *Walküre* Brünnhilde does have a C in the 'Ho-yo-to-ho,' which was no problem for me, as it came naturally. So to oblige the Arena in Verona, which was my summer home, I sang it there; and then, as it had gone very well indeed, I repeated it in other theatres. But I was careful not to accept too many engagements for this part, as I lived in terror that it might affect my middle and lower registers. So it was like walking on eggs. The mise-en-scène was so spectacular in Verona that emotionally it affected me deeply. For when I was put to sleep there was real fire on every side, and the effect was unbelievable. Just look at what they do today and tell me. There is a red light—sometimes—and that is all. Of course, despite interminable pleas from conductors and managements, I never went near the other two Brünnhildes. The one in *Siegfried* is scored for a much higher voice, and the one in *Götterdämmerung*, which is the most beautiful of all, was too long for me to expose myself to its dangers. Santuzza sat well with me—I even recorded that role, with the superb Mario del Monaco—and I enjoyed it fully, but, again, no more than a certain number of performances a year. I could have started singing Amneris and Ortrud a second time on the same day, but the Mascagni opera never. Those twenty minutes are totally draining in a way which someone who has not sung it can never understand.

"At my first performance of *Carmen* at the Arena of Pola, I had a charming Micaëla, and I remember saying, 'That small voice will go very far,' and I was right. It was Licia Albanese. I lost track of her, for she moved to the United States, and I never sang there. The reason is absurd, but then we live in an absurd world. After the Allies took over Italy, my name appeared among the artists who had sung for the Germans, and that precluded any possibility of a visa. And of course it was true. But how could I say no? Poor Marinuzzi was sick with worry and anxiety because he had a son on the Russian front, and the news was more and more terrible each day. He wanted to try again—he had made many attempts—to get him out of that hell before it was too late, so he decided to conduct a concert for the German troops and asked me to be his soloist. I simply could not refuse him, but in life one often pays bitterly for kind actions. Anyhow, like in *Carmen,* it is all in the cards. What must be will be. Later, when everything was finally cleared up, it was too late. There were other mezzos firmly entrenched at the Metropolitan, and my opportunity had been lost. Anyhow, by then I was happily married to Dr. Andrea Maggio, a very able nose-and-throat specialist and a most charming man. We had a daughter together, and he did a lot to keep my vocal cords in shape. He died in 1963, and so a very special curtain descended on that very important chapter of my life."

I asked her about a famous episode when she made front-page news by supposedly slapping the face of Franco Abbiati, then the prestigious critic of *Il Corriere della Sera.*

"It is not true!" she replied, and in a marvelous mixture of Lady Macbeth and Dame Quickly attitudes and comments she proceeded to tell the tale. "But I shall have to start from the beginning. In the summer of 1948 I was singing Carmen and Amneris at the Arena of Verona when Oldani of La Scala rang me up asking me to give up my September holiday—I tried to always give myself a month off a year—to come and sing at La Scala, where they were planning an extra, early-fall season. He told me they needed me desperately and that I must not let them down. So my much, much needed vacation went to hell, and instead I sang Amneris again and Laura in *La Gioconda.*

"This entire project had been organized at Toscanini's prodding, to introduce his Italo-American protégée, Herva Nelli, to the Italian public. This soprano may have been great under the inimitable maestro's baton—so many were, for he had a sort of witchcraft—but without him she was nothing to write home about. I could not understand what all the fuss was about, nor did anyone else. In fact, as far as I can recall, I do not believe that her mediocre appearances led her on to other theatres in Italy.

"Abbiati wrote that at the first performance I sounded tired and out of sorts, which surprised me very much. Since he had always praised me, this hurt. Again, another kind action that turned against me, because an early-fall season at La Scala meant nothing to me when it was my permanent home. So when I ran into him at one of the other performances—he was standing with a group of people in the big hall—I went right up to him, wishing to explain the circumstances that had led me to accept the engagement despite the fact that I knew myself I needed a rest. But with the intention of taking him away from the others and talking to him privately, I grabbed his arm, and I have a firm grip. I raised my voice in order to be heard in the confusion that always reigns during intermissions. Somehow my quick gesture was interpreted by people at a distance as something more than it was, and the silly story of the slap reached the press rooms with the rapidity of a supersonic plane.

"Next day I was astonished to see this absurd tale splashed across the front pages, and I then called my agent to arrange a press conference for me so that I could explain what had really happened. 'Are you totally mad?' he asked me, with a very happy tone in his voice. 'I was about to ring you. Do you know that within this past hour more than ten theatres have called up to ask for your services! You are the most celebrated singer in Europe at the moment, and everyone wants you. This kind of publicity is worth more than gold ingots.' He was right, for offers kept pouring in like an avalanche. And I was not in trouble with the La Scala management, for they were well aware that I had done no such thing. I am a Bulgarian and half wolf"—again she laughed as only she can—"but I do know my p's and q's.

"As a matter of fact, not long afterward I sang at La Scala the fiendish part of Klytämnestra in *Elektra* with Mitropoulos—a great conductor, but who had absolutely no consideration for the human voice. As a person, I found him enchanting and so good—but alas, not to the vocal cords. All he wanted was an ocean of sound—alas, how many have followed in this catastrophic attitude!—and we, the fish, had to put up an immense battle not to be drowned. He paid me a considerable compliment, for he told me I was the only mezzo he knew who did not have to scream out the part, and he wanted to have me in other theatres for the same assignment. But I never went, always finding excuses not to sing with him again. You will appreciate my tact, I hope!" And she laughed heartily again.

"Oddly enough, my goodbye to the stage came in 1963 at La Scala as the Witch in *Hansel and Gretel,* and I was true to my promise to Marinuzzi, long since dead, that I would only take on this role at the end, and not at the beginning as he had wished. It was a dignified occasion, for the production was delightful, and there could not have been a more adorable couple singing the leads, Fiorenza Cossotto and Renata Scotto. How well they sang then, with such refinement and style! It was the year of my dear husband's death, and I felt down and dispirited, so had no incentive to go on. But the voice was still in good shape."

And with this she sang me a phrase of a Bulgarian folk song, with a remarkable richness of sound. And the memories returned of when she had made such an indelible impression on me as Carmen, giving to the card scene a finality I have never heard since, and to the last act a tragic dimension of Greek classical stature.

"Then, by a fluke, I went into the movies." She laughed again. "I was quietly sitting at home one day and the telephone rang. It was my good friend and fan, Vittorio de Sica, suggesting the role of a very rich woman in a film he was about to make called *Il boom.* 'Oh, how sweet of you!' I replied. 'I would adore to be rich, even if it is only on the screen!' So I accepted, and this led to various comedy roles, and I enjoyed them. But my heart had always been in music, and there it remained.

"Of course, I am outraged at what is happening today. The other night I had Cigna and the Prandellis for dinner, and we discussed the ecology that conductors and metteurs-en-scène have brought to the world we loved so much until the early hours of the morning. Let me give you an example. I was hired to appear as Marfa in *Khovanshchina* at the San Carlo in Naples with Antonio Guarnieri, who, like Serafin, was a real genius, even if a quieter and less dynamic one. He had an argument with the stage director —the trend was beginning already—at the very first rehearsal, for he wanted to bring innovations to the libretto. 'Be kind enough to reread the text tonight,' the maestro said very quietly (but we all heard him), 'and come back tomorrow giving me your opinion if you really think Mussorgsky and Stassov'—they wrote the libretto together—'would have approved.' The next day the following conversation ensued. 'I still think,' the director said with enormous presumption, 'that my ideas would improve the action.' 'I am afraid I do not agree with you,' Guarnieri answered him, again very calmly, 'since I do think the people who wrote it knew what they wanted. Why don't you write a libretto, find a composer, and then we shall discuss it? I am sure you are full of talent, but the answer is no and again no and once again no.' That was the way then—deep respect and veneration.

"Guarnieri never used a stick. His gestures were infinitesimal, but marvelously set the palette of the orchestra's colors. He really conducted with his eyes, which always seemed to me like very strong candles in a darkened room. He always conducted seated, and only got up when he wished to obtain the effect of a fortissimo or pianissimo. I sang Ortrud with him many times, and I do not believe any other conductor obtained such effects as he did in *Lohengrin*. It was like a transparent tapestry. Today I cannot believe my eyes when I see these young conductors waving frenetically, and I always fear they are going to land in the pit. What are they trying to prove?

"There is no more ensemble today, everyone rushing in and out to catch planes and then sit endlessly in airports because of strikes. Serves them right. When I hear that a singer is stuck in some airport, I laugh and say aloud to myself, 'Will this teach him a lesson?' And then I know that it won't. I never accepted an engagement for the money it could bring me, but for the glory and satisfaction it could offer me. I would rather have sung with Guarnieri for a hundred lire than with—" and she stopped in her tracks— "for a hundred thousand.

"The unity is gone, and with it the entire structure. Voices do not and cannot last in these conditions. Also, no one loves them anymore, especially the critics. Typical of this is the review of *Tristan und Isolde* at La Scala the other day in *Il Corriere della Sera*. Two long columns for Carlos Kleiber, and I am not quite sure if seven or eight lines for the singers. The critic said Ruza Baldani was a 'pale' Brangäne and that is all. But don't you think that this good artist has a right to be told why she was 'pale'? I do—I really do. The Isolde got a line and a half, Kurwenal a mention. A great satisfaction nowadays to wear yourself out all evening and just be mentioned!

"I adored my profession and hope that I served it with honor. Anyhow, even in the midst of this cyclone we are passing through, I have memories that no one can take away from me. With Eboli, I can repeat in a different meaning—she was speaking of her beauty and I of my instrument—that when God singled me out with this blessing, it was a *don fatale*—a fatal gift. Eboli was, with Ortrud, mine for so long that I came to understand her completely, and I do think 'O don fatale' is the greatest aria ever written for a mezzo."

DAME EVA TURNER

It is indeed rare to meet a truly happy person, but after spending a couple of hours with Dame Eva Turner, I knew I had enjoyed that unusual privilege. When I met her in the fall of 1978, she was eighty-six years old —she was born in Oldham, England, in 1892—and living in a comfortable London flat, on a spacious ground floor. I had the impression that this great prima donna was marvelously adjusted to her past and present, enjoying anything and everything that came her way. There was gratitude for all that her wonderful career had given her and all that had followed as a result. I had in front of me a very positive person, who had accepted the acclaim not because she felt it was her due, but because she knew she had worked hard and earned it. And after the curtain had been rung down on a career of thirty-two years, she remained active in the world of music, teaching singing and obviously loving the increasing challenge of it.

She sacrificed everything to her art and does not regret it. "I never married," she explained to me, speaking as if she had always known me and immediately establishing a cozy contact. "And the reason is that I discovered at an early age that I was the sort of person who could not divide herself in half. I admire colleagues who can combine a full private life with a full career. I never could, for in order to have a successful public one, I had to work every minute of the day and not allow anything else to distract me. The competition in those days was staggering, and I could not be satisfied to trail behind. I knew, from the very beginning, that I must get in the front line and stay there. The latter part is the most difficult in the game of opera I was involved with, for there are always new, exciting talents coming along, and you must keep getting better all the time. There must be total concentration, you know, and above all the sacred fire. I had it all the way and loved every minute of it. In fact, I was unhappy away from the stage, which was right in my nostrils and became a part of me. Actually, I shall let you in on a secret. I still have it burning within me. The ovations I usually received at each one of my appearances never went to my head, for

Eva Turner in the title role of *Turandot*.

I knew that next time I must be even better. To sit on one's laurels is fatal.

"One learns one's lessons as one goes along," she laughed, "and never to take anything for granted. I had appeared at Covent Garden many times, but it took the wide recognition of all the leading Italian opera houses to have the London public receive me as a revelation in *Turandot* in 1928 when I appeared there in the spring international season. I had made progress, but not that much. It was only when it became known that all the leading Italian lyric theatres were actually fighting for my services that my compatriots became interested. This is an old story which has happened to so many others, but when it happens to you, then you know what it really means. I shall have forever a deep-seated affection for Italy and the Italians, for I owe them everything. They took me in, totally unknown, and turned me into a star."

She then burst forth in the best Italian I have ever heard spoken by a foreigner, each word pronounced as an actor would on the stage, and she continued the dialogue in Dante's tongue. When I complimented her, she smiled. "My German is equally good," she said, "for in my opinion clear diction is a must in a reputable singer. What are the notes without the words, will you please tell me? Today, alas, there is much mumbling on the proscenium, but opera must be either a drama or a comedy sung and not a garbled series of sounds.

"But you have asked me for my story, and here it is. My father was an engineer who played the piano well, and I began to sing with him. When I was ten years old we left Oldham, where I was born—it is a rather ugly town near Manchester—as he was transferred to Bristol, and this is where I heard my first opera performed, by the Carl Rosa touring company, which was later to become the focal point of my life. I came home that night announcing to the family that I was going to be an opera star, and the vocation was born, irrevocably. Not only were there no protests from my parents, but, on the contrary, they were delighted, and when my voice began to develop they sent me to study with Don Rootham, who had taught the celebrated Dame Clara Butt. At sixteen I was in London on a special grant to continue my studies at the Royal Academy of Music. Edgardo Levi, famous for writing all the cadenzas for standard songs and arias, and his wife, Gigia, took an interest in me, and I owe them a tremendous debt. In the British capital I also went on with my piano studies, took courses in harmony, and much time was spent in learning diction.

"My beginnings were far from glamorous, but I cannot help but think that they were most useful. When I left the Royal Academy, I joined the

Carl Rosa company chorus. We toured England and Ireland from one end to the other, and I got used to the routine and learned a lot watching the principals. Slowly I began to emerge with bit parts such as the Shepherd in *Tannhäuser* and Kate Pinkerton in *Butterfly*. Suddenly it was the turn of Micaëla and Musetta. In my early days I was paid four pounds a week, and my first appearance in London was in 1917, when we spent some weeks at the Garrick Theatre. Slowly, I worked my way into becoming the leading soprano of the company, and because of war conditions, traveling was most difficult. We came to Covent Garden for a month in 1920, and my first appearance came as Santuzza, followed by Musetta, Leonora in *Il trovatore*, Butterfly, Antonia in *The Tales of Hoffmann,* and Venus in *Tannhäuser,* a diversified group of ladies. I continued to study daily with Albert Richards Broad, who had been a singer and was then in a managerial capacity with the company. He developed my voice, which increased enormously in volume. In 1924 I was handed Leonore in *Fidelio,* which had not been performed in London since Sir Thomas Beecham had conducted it in 1910; therefore, it became an important event.

"Ettore Panizza, the distinguished conductor, happened to be in the British capital and heard me as both Butterfly and Leonore, which was to become one of the roles most identified with me. He came backstage at the end of the Puccini opera, politely introduced himself, and told me I must immediately go to La Scala and audition for Toscanini. I thought he was joking. I did not know one single aria in Italian except 'Ritorna vincitor,' for with the Rosa company we sang everything, alas, in English. I was very honest with him when I realized that he was serious. *'Ma questo non importa,'* he replied, *'l'italiano verrà più tardi'*—this does not matter, the Italian will come later.

"I did not see that I had anything to lose, and perhaps everything to gain, so I took off with my coach for Milan. I had never sung for a great conductor before, and, to my surprise, I was not half as scared as I had anticipated. He was very cordial and immediately offered me a contract for the 1924–25 season. I managed to take four months off and concentrate on learning roles in Italian, including the two I was to start with: Freia in *Das Rheingold* and Sieglinde. The first one was under Vittorio Gui, who became one of my best friends with his adorable family, and the second under Ettore Panizza. In both operas I had Nazzareno de Angelis as Wotan, and I really did not know what a true basso was meant to sound like until I heard him. The success was instantaneous. In the meantime I had actually sung Sieglinde in Turin under Fritz Busch's inspired direction, and this was lucky, as I had the opportunity to try out this part in Italian before joining La Scala. With the Rosa company I had sung Brünnhilde in both *Die Walküre* and *Siegfried*, but never Sieglinde, which was to become one of the roles I was called upon to do the most often.

"Then everything happened all at once. I was on call everywhere and was invited by several German opera houses for the Italian repertoire. Gui had me sing Sieglinde and *Fidelio* at the Maggio Musicale Fiorentino, which in those days rivaled Salzburg. I had a particular triumph in Genoa, and it was in Brescia that I sang my first Turandot, and for the rest of my career I became particularly identified with this very taxing score. Alfano, who had finished the opera after Puccini's death, had been heard to declare that I was ideal for the part, and I could not accept all the engagements that were offered to me—also because I think it is an opera which one must not oversing. A limited number of performances a year is enough, for it is terribly demanding and exhausting because of its mercilessly high tessitura. I would have sung it at its premiere in London in 1927 had it not been for a particular circumstance. The request to do Turandot in London—this was in 1927—came too late, as I had already accepted an engagement for Buenos Aires, and Bianca Scacciati—also very great as the Chinese princess—got the job instead.

"Buenos Aires gave me immense satisfactions, and as I look back I simply cannot believe what a company of exceptional singers had been gathered. We all sailed together, and what fun we had! In the group were Toti dal Monte, Isabel Marengo, Miguel Fleta, Tito Schipa, Marcel Journet, Ezio Pinza, Benvenuto Franci, Giacomo Lauri-Volpi, Ebe Stignani—just to mention a few—and Claudia Muzio. As for the latter, she is perhaps the artist who made the most unforgettable impression on me of all. The way she said 'È tardi' in *La traviata* still haunts me, for it simply dissolved the audience in tears. She was a wonderful person and spoke English beautifully. She had been sent to a Catholic school in Hammersmith in 1912 when her father was stage manager at Covent Garden. We talked for hours over the years, as if we had grown up together, and never once was I in the vicinity that I did not send her some Parma violets when she sang Violetta. We met often, and her untimely death was not only a great blow to the world of opera but a personal loss for me. She rehearsed more than anyone I ever knew—often alone, to get the feeling of a particular stage and the dimensions of a particular house. It was quite a challenge in those days to sing *Aida* and *Trovatore,* for there were three Amnerises and Azucenas to contend with who were absolutely terrific. Aurora Buades, the Spanish contralto, Irene

Minghini-Cattaneo, and Ebe Stignani all, in their own personal way, were absolutely superb, and I could not possibly make a choice among them. Of course, the voice of Stignani was a miracle per se—the timbre, the intonation, the perfection of the three registers—but she did not have the temperament of the other two. Buades was more earthy, and Minghini-Cattaneo aristocratic. I loved singing with all three of them, but I knew, on each occasion, that each one of them could steal the show if I was not very careful.

"An opera that I added in those years was *La fanciulla del West,* and Minnie suited my temperament. I believe that the first time I ever sang it was in the lovely San Carlos opera house in Lisbon. Somehow, I lost Butterfly in the interim, for many lyric sopranos could sing it in Italy, and I was always being assigned dramatic roles. Actually, Butterfly can be sung by both, for the orchestration is very rich. When I returned home for the Covent Garden season in 1928, *Turandot* was repeated for me, and I had the wonderful satisfaction of having my own people give me the recognition they had not afforded me earlier. I also appeared as Santuzza and Aida.

"That same year marked my American debut, and I sang twenty performances at the Chicago Opera, which at that particular time was as important as the Metropolitan. My debut could not have been made in more auspicious circumstances, for I sang Sieglinde in *Die Walküre* with the glorious Brünnhilde of Frida Leider, the magnificent Fricka of Maria Olczewska, and the impressive Wotan of Alexander Kipnis. I felt I was flying high among giants, and I was.

"There existed such courtesy in those days. I recall I was in my dressing room taking off my makeup after having sung Amelia when there was a discreet knock at the door, and the wardrobe mistress went to see who it was, for I had left word I did not want to be disturbed. It was Madame Galli-Curci, very much a grande dame, all dressed in black. She came in with great assurance and complimented me, making so many intelligent remarks about the way I had tackled certain phrases and taken certain notes. There was no condescension on her part, only a sense of comradeship—and she was then the reigning prima donna. Those were the days when Chicago was dominated by two divas: Mary Garden, a tremendous showwoman, and Rosa Raisa, who made an unforgettable impression on me as Rachel in *La Juive.* I returned there the following year, when they had moved to the Civic Opera House, and that time I added Elisabeth to the other roles.

"In the meantime I had done my first *Forza del destino* in Naples and my first *Turandot* at La Scala with the wonderful Georges Thill. Another role, which I undertook at Mascagni's own request and repeated often under his direction, was Isabeau, which I performed with him even at the Arena in Verona and at the Opera in Rome. It is a killer, believe me, but I could handle it. In this period I had acquired a house in Lugano, which is just across the border from Italy, and which can be reached from Milan in one hour. It is there that I retired, when time permitted it, to study new scores.

"In the meantime, practically every year I was called back for the international season at Covent Garden in the spring, and then had the opportunity to get to know and appreciate Beecham's great qualities. I made extensive tours with him and the London Philharmonic Orchestra as soloist. With Sir Henry Wood I sang at the gala concert for the King and Queen at the Albert Hall on May 11, 1934, and had as my companions the adorable Conchita Supervia and the inimitable Richard Tauber. Naturally, I drowned them with my 'Dich teure Halle' and 'In questa reggia,' but that was not my fault, for my voice was getting larger and larger. I had the pleasure of doing the Verdi Requiem too, with the London Symphony Orchestra, under Sir Adrian Boult. Then at Covent Garden I sang both Sieglinde and Brünnhilde, some very delightful performances of *Ballo* with Dino Borgioli, and a revival of *Freischütz*.

"It was during a performance of this opera that my beloved father died suddenly in the stalls. He had not been well for some time, and in fact I had canceled my debut as Norma in Italy to be with him. Strangely, the chance to sing it again never came, as the war approached and eventually broke out. I was not told of my father's demise until after the performance, and Beecham broke the news ever so gently.

"Goodness, there is so much to recall! Apart from La Scala, Turin was my second Italian home, and it was here that I sang my first Italian Brünnhilde in both *Walküre* and *Siegfried* and also *La Wally*. My partner in *Don Giovanni* was Carlo Galeffi, who was an ideal protagonist. And do you know who the Zerlina was? Magda Olivero. She is still singing, and I say bravo. She always had a very special quality of her own, not really a beautiful voice, but a magnetic quality on the stage that few possess. In 1937 with dear Giovanni Martinelli I sang at the coronation season at Covent Garden in *Turandot* and *Aida*, and that fall I took on Isolde with Albert Coates conducting. I loved this part more than I can ever say, and I am only sorry that with the outbreak of the war a short time later I sang it so few times. There were three superb Isoldes in my day, and I would not dare say which one I preferred, whether Leider, Flagstad, or Lubin. Each one gave her own interpretation, and each one was immensely moving and valid. Then Chicago invited me again for Turandot—the Calaf on this occasion was Galliano Masini, and on his good nights he was not to be equaled—Aida, and Sieglinde. When war broke out, I had to leave Italy—my last performances were in *Turandot* in Bologna—and settled in London, and despite the fact that my flat went up in smoke in 1943 with everything in it—many memorabilia that can never be replaced—I refused to move. I was invited over and over again to go to the United States, but I knew where my duty lay and stuck it out. I sang a lot at Promenade concerts and on the BBC, as well as hundreds of recitals for men and women in uniform. It made me sick to have Italy on the other side, but man proposes and God disposes. When the war was over, I did return to Italy and sang Turandot again there. They had not forgotten 'la Turner,' as they called me. And then I returned to Covent Garden, of course, and sang until 1948. My high Cs were still ringing, and yet at fifty-six I thought it was better to stop. No farewells. I just slipped away.

"You asked me a pertinent question, and I shall try to answer it. I am firmly convinced that singing the Italian repertoire does not in the least preclude taking on the Wagnerian one too. We have many examples in the past, and even in my time there were Florence Easton, Maria Müller, Elisabeth Rethberg, Margarete Matzenauer, Maria Jeritza, and Maria Caniglia, just to name a few who come to mind, who were at ease in both. Giuseppina Cobelli was superb as Isolde and at the same time thrilling as Tosca and Eboli. But with the passing of time, strong voices have become rarer and rarer, and opera houses, once they latch on to them, do not let go, and use them only in Wagner and Strauss. Flagstad always spoke to me of how she longed to go back to Italian roles, but no one would let her. I do believe that I was the last to go from one to the other all through my career with total facility. Nilsson did for a while, but then she stayed mainly with the German roles. I never sang *Götterdämmerung* except in excerpts, for despite the fact that I had turned from a lyric into a spinto and later a dramatic—I went the whole way—Brünnhilde in the last opera of the *Ring* is very long, and I was afraid it would tire my vocal cords in the long run. I did not attempt Kundry, for it lies very much in the center, and in fact many mezzos and contraltos undertake it.

"You are quite right when you say that today it is mainly the Wagner and Strauss sopranos who sing Turandot, but this was not true previously. Among many, look at Rosa Raisa, who created it, Gina Cigna, Maria Nemeth, Anna Roselle, Germana di Giulio, and Maria Pedrini, to name some who all belonged to the Italian repertoire. I think this is because there are no true dramatic sopranos left. Caballé is singing it now, but with all my enormous admiration for her this is surely not for her. For the Chinese princess you need a bite in the instrument, very special breadth of voice, and if you don't have the right vocal cords, it can knock you out you, I know. I sang well over two hundred performances of it, and I think I can speak out of experience. The more you sing it, the more you realize where the obstacles are and where you can relax a tiny bit.

"There are no set regulations for anyone. Look at Nilsson with her tremendous voice. She always refused Senta, and intelligent as she is, she must have known why it was not for her. Instinctively I knew that Strauss was not quite right for me, and I kept refusing *Elektra* and *Salome*. The rules and the standards have changed. In my day you never would have agreed to record an opera that was not in your repertoire. Today they all do it, knowing perfectly well that on the stage they could not sustain it.

"Then why do it? Money, money, money is the answer. But you have heard this from all the others. None of us were out for the pot of gold. In fact, here I am at eighty-six still teaching, not only because I enjoy it but also because I must meet the everyday demands. I taught for eight years at the University of Oklahoma, where I was very happy, and then in 1959 I left to take on a professorship at the Royal Academy, where I came from in the first place. The cycle completed itself. I left in 1966 and now only take private pupils. Amy Shuard was one of them, and others have been Jeannette Coster, Linda Esther Gray, and Roberta Knie, who followed me to England from Oklahoma. She is very gifted, you know, but forces too much, like all the others. I worry for her future. While it is true that there are many splendid young British singers today, let us not forget how great some of the past ones have been. Just think, for instance, of Florence Easton, Mary Garden, and Maggie Teyte. The latter's Butterfly and Hansel were enchantment itself."

I asked her what she considered her finest achievements.

"It is difficult to answer," she concluded, "for I loved all my roles and was totally absorbed by them. But from what emerges in articles and from letters, my name is most closely remembered for *Turandot* and *Fidelio*, which is interesting, since it proves that if your technique is really secure, you can sing verismo along with bel canto. I recall going once from Donna Anna to Isabeau without the slightest problem.

"But the most thrilling moments I spent in my career were during the last acts of *Die Walküre* and *Siegfried*. In the first they occurred when I was being put to sleep surrounded by the magic fire, and in the second when I woke up, after twenty years, still surrounded by flames. There is an enchantment about this music that is overwhelming, and I recall that when I sat up on the rock and began to sing 'Heil dir, Sonne! Heil dir, Licht! Heil dir, Leuchtender Tag!' [Hail to thee, Sun! Hail to thee, Light! Hail to thee, Shining Day!], despite my steady nerves and sense of discipline, I was absolutely carried away by the ecstasy of those phrases. And when, toward the end, I sang 'Er ist mir ewig, ist mir immer' [He is eternally mine, he is mine forever], I had goose flesh all over me. It is probably the most overwhelming love scene ever written or conceived, for it is the process of a goddess turning into a woman. The many hours Brünnhilde must wait in that opera before coming on—she only appears in the final scene—were well worth the glorious duet ahead."

KAMMERSÄNGERIN GERTRUD GROB-PRANDL

When I walked into the lovely garden of a house in Glanzing, near Vienna, on a very warm afternoon in June 1979, I had the impression of England. This feeling was only enhanced by the appearance of Gertrud Grob-Prandl, accompanied by her British husband, Charles King; she looks like an English matron of excellent background. However, this celebrated *hochdramatisch* soprano—whose instrument, many have claimed, was even larger than Eva Turner's or Birgit Nilsson's—is Viennese born and educated, and this second marriage dates from not long ago. Her family name was Grob, and she added the Prandl when she married in 1947. Her first husband died in 1965, and for several years she remained a widow. Her career, which lasted thirty-two years, had very firm roots in Vienna. Only now and then a trace of a foreign accent is noticeable in her admirable English. Along with a highly developed sense of humor, she has the exquisite manners of an old-fashioned lady. After spending two hours with her, I was conscious that she had created an atmosphere of an old acquaintance renewing past encounters. She talked with good sense and clarity about the high points of her distinguished career.

"I had made up my mind," she confessed, "that I would stop singing the day I discovered that it was no longer an immense pleasure, to which I always looked forward with great anticipation, but an effort. And perhaps it was a mistake to stop in 1972, for I have missed my work more than I could ever imagine—it may have been a temporary sense of fatigue. Birgit Nilsson is still continuing, and there is barely six months' difference in our ages. When I appeared as Venus in *Tannhäuser,* in the Paris production, at my home base, the Vienna Staatsoper, it just happened that my contract was up on January 1, 1972, the date of this performance, and had to be renegotiated and renewed. It was then that I decided I would not sign a new one, which would have meant three more years, and that I would consider it my local farewell. I had, if I may say so, never sung this role better than on that night. I still had many engagements to fulfill in France and Germany, but when they were done with, I closed the chapter that had been the reason

Gertrud Grob-Prandl in the title role of *Elektra*.

for my life and to which I had dedicated all of myself. I had always said to my husband and friends that I would never consider an official goodbye performance, as to me it would have seemed like singing at my own funeral. People learned of my retirement not through any press statement but by word of mouth.

"I started to take on *Elektra,*" she continued, "toward the end, as everyone had always put the fear of God into me about the perils of tackling this score, giving me ample proof of how many colleagues' voices had started going rapidly downhill after essaying it. But my reaction was different. I certainly would never advise a young singer to undertake it, but if you are experienced, there are ways of getting around some of the difficulties. What is very tiring is that she must move constantly, much like a wild animal in a cage, and sing those arduous phrases at the same time. But once I had got the action worked out, I did not feel uncomfortable in it.

"Of all the roles I sang (and the number is pretty staggering—in the early years I was given just about every score in sight to perform), the *Götterdämmerung* Brünnhilde, which incidentally was my favorite, is the most demanding of all, for she never has a moment of respite, and it is highly dramatic from start to finish. Isolde is far less so, for there are long stretches in the second act which are essentially lyrical, and a great part of the third act belongs to the tenor. I have not kept count of how many times I undertook these two roles, but it runs into several hundreds. In fact, in the second half of my active career, Ortrud and Leonore in *Fidelio,* the *Ring* and *Tristan und Isolde,* were practically my daily bread.

"Leonore never presented any problems, for I was born with perfect pitch, and the 'Abscheulicher,' which is a treacherous aria mainly because of the constant accompaniment of the horns, never gave me the jitters. One night in 1969 a bunch of fifty superb roses appeared in my dressing room at the Vienna Staatsoper 'with the gratitude of the management,' and I could not figure out this unusual homage. So I asked what it was all about, and the reply was very simple. That night marked my fiftieth appearance in this opera in that theatre—a lot considering it is not a staple of the repertoire. The opening of the reconstructed Vienna opera house, as you know, took place on November 5, 1955, with *Fidelio,* and Martha Mödl got the assignment. I was not upset, for I opened the rebuilt Berlin Staatsoper a month later in the same opera. Actually, it was all very fascinating, for Mödl, a great artist and a German, got the assignment in Vienna, my hometown, and I received it in her own country. That is how the chips fall in the operatic world of which I was a part.

"Having sung every role in the Wagnerian repertoire—for, apart from those mentioned, I undertook often Eva, Elsa, Elisabeth, Senta, and Irene in *Rienzi*—I always kept away from Kundry. Somehow, I never felt it was right for me. She is a mysterious character, and I can understand Karajan's having used two different singers for this role. I have always found it necessary, on a professional level, to comprehend the text as well as the music, and Kundry remains a puzzle. Ortrud, which I sang very often, in my estimation should always be sung by a dramatic soprano and not a mezzo, for the tessitura lies quite high; but now the tendency is in the other direction. There is a reason for this, and that is the disappearance of dramatic sopranos today, an unexplainable mystery. I realized the demands made by the scoring of Ortrud when in the first part of my operatic activities I sang so many Elsas, and in the second act, during the superb scene of the confrontation of the two women, I assisted at the sad spectacle of so many mezzos strangling on the top notes.

"As I was in great demand for the heavy Wagnerian wing all over Europe, I sang often in France and Italy. In the latter, a country I came to love intensely and where I felt totally at home, I sang Isolde and *Götterdämmerung* at La Scala and the *Ring* all over, including Rome, Palermo, Naples, and Bologna. For Reggio Emilia I even relearned Ortrud in Italian.

"When in Italy they discovered that *Turandot* was in my repertoire in Vienna—I first sang it in German there, then switched to Italian later—I was constantly asked to sing it everywhere, including in the open-air spaces of the Arena of Verona, the Boboli Gardens in Florence, and the Caracalla Baths in Rome. I often had Lauri-Volpi as my Calaf, and it was such fun competing with him, holding on to the high notes in the last duet, even if it was in bad taste. When he realized that he could not beat me on that score—my breath control was my glory—we became close friends. He was the most intelligent person I ever talked to about voice, and how cleverly he judged his colleagues! I even learned *Turandot* in English for some performances at Covent Garden in 1951 with Sir John Barbirolli. I never thought I looked much like a delicate Chinese princess, but then my consolation came from the fact that none of the other sopranos did either.

"The tenor who played the most vital part in my life was Max Lorenz. Although he was my senior by many years, when he partnered me as Siegmund for my first *Walküre*, my first *Siegfried* (in Barcelona of all places), and my first *Tristan*, he behaved like a brother and assisted me at every step. I learned so much from him, for he insisted on coming to every rehearsal to help me and remained for a long time after it was over to impart to me all his precious knowledge and how to get over some difficult passages.

"But to go back to the early days, my father felt that I must learn a profession, having experienced during the First World War what could happen to one's savings. And since I was musically inclined, he sent me to the conservatory to study the piano, with the idea of my earning a diploma so that I could teach. When I was sixteen, the school was preparing to give an amateur performance of Beethoven's Ninth Symphony, and more voices were needed to complete the chorus. So we were all auditioned, and when my turn came, the various professors were stunned by the size of my instrument. And it was immediately decided that I should join a singing class. The course lasted four years, but before the fourth year was over, I had already been signed by the Volksoper. Most of my training was accomplished with Papier Singer-Burian, assistant to the famous retired mezzo Rosa Baumgarten. I made my debut as Santuzza, and then came many other Italian roles, all sung in German, Leonore in *Fidelio,* and a new production of *Ariadne auf Naxos* with Richard Strauss present, who was very anxious for me to appear, under his baton, in *Die ägyptische Helena*—a project, alas, which, thanks to the increasing nightmare of the war, never took place. It had been obvious to all, from the very beginning, that I was a real *hoch-dramatisch* soprano, because of not only the volume but the darkish sound of my timbre.

"It was in January 1944 that I was invited to join the Staatsoper, where I remained for twenty-eight years, and made my debut there as Elsa. But in September of that year the opera house was forced to close because of a decree called 'Total Krieg Einsatz'—everything for the war—and we were all assigned jobs for the defense. Mine was to proof gas masks but the difficulty I faced was the lack of filters. I had, when the opera house closed, prepared the Marschallin for a series of performances which, naturally, never materialized. And then later it never came my way. In the prewar days this beautiful part was always assigned to either a dramatic or a spinto, but then later when this type of instrument became more and more hard to find, it was given to lyrics like Elisabeth Schwarzkopf and Lisa della Casa. Opera started again at the Volksoper in May 1945 as, in the meantime, our beloved Staatsoper on March 12, 1945, was flattened to the ground by Allied bombs. So many sets and costumes had been destroyed in the blitz that the management had to prepare a repertoire based on what was available. I found myself singing Rosalinda in *Die Fledermaus* for a total of thirty-five performances, and this delicious score was never offered to me again, much for the same reason that I told you about the Marschallin. With the dearth of dramatics, Rosalinda became the property of lighter voices, and I was used for the other roles which demanded my heavy instrument.

"I sang my first Brünnhilde in *Die Walküre* in 1949, under Clemens Krauss, with his wife, Viorica Ursuleac, as Sieglinde. What a lovely, secure, large top she had! Krauss was, as far as I am concerned, Conductor Number One. No one has ever been able to approach him. He was a very *grand seigneur,* and he possessed the unique combination of being imaginative and yet giving the singer a sense of total security. He knew voices and brought the best out of them. Anny Konetzni was approaching the end of her important career, and this is why I was assigned the heroic Wagnerian ladies. Hers had been a most beautiful instrument, although, personally, I always preferred her sister, Hilde, a more sensitive and aristocratic interpreter. When I first sang Elsa in 1944, Anny was my Ortrud. She was a very jealous woman, and not only of me, but even of her own sister, whom she prevented from singing Isolde and other roles which, I believe, she could have done very well. Hilde sang with me Sieglinde and Gutrune many times, even at La Scala, and she was wonderfully pliable and intelligent. She was a fine colleague, as her sister was not.

"I have never been envious," she laughed, "for it is simply not part of my nature. It makes no sense. How is opera to continue if there is only one singer for certain roles? As soon as I heard Nilsson—she sang Elsa to my Ortrud and Sieglinde to my Brünnhilde—I knew that fortunately we had another superb voice. But when she stops—already she has eliminated many roles—I don't really know what will happen. There seems to be a blank on the horizon.

"Karl Böhm was the head of the Staatsoper only for one year, from 1954 to 1955, and had to resign following tremendous criticism for his continual absences abroad. Then came Karajan until he left in a huff in 1964. I always respected him and had a pleasant relationship with him, and I recall with particular pleasure performances of Brünnhilde and Senta. Böhm conducted my debut at the Colón in Buenos Aires in *Die Walküre* in 1950, which was particularly interesting for the presence of two great artists, Tiana Lemnitz and Margarete Klose. They were no longer at the height of their vocal bloom, but my goodness! what style and presence!"

"And when did you first take on Isolde?" I inquired.

"I was assigned this part when the Staatsoper was still performing at the Theater an der Wien, as sort of a dress rehearsal before the entire company went to Brussels, and there the success was so great that, upon my return to Vienna, I was immediately made a Kammersängerin. In 1951 in Italy I first sang it in Naples and at La Scala under de Sabata's direction, an experience I treasure. His reading of the score was so light and poetical, with a very particular flavor which most conductors are unable to obtain from an orchestra. I should have sung again with him *Götterdämmerung* in 1954, but then at the last minute he got ill and was replaced by Heinz Tietjen, who for so many years had been the brilliant Intendant of both the Berlin Städtische Oper and the Bayreuth Festival. He knew the Wagnerian tradition inside out, and it was very interesting to work with him. Winifred Wagner came for this occasion and brought the original score."

I inquired about Bayreuth.

"No, I never appeared there," she said. "I was approached a couple of times, but I already had engagements in South America, and later they had Varnay and Mödl. As for North America, I appeared only in San Francisco, and turned up there in the early fall of 1953, when everyone was terribly upset over the very recent death of its director, Gaetano Merola. There, if memory serves me, I sang in *Tristan, Die Walküre,* and *Un ballo in maschera.* In New York they had Nilsson, so they certainly did not need me."

When I asked her whom she considered the greatest artist at the Vienna Opera during her tenure there, her answer coincided with so many others. "It is a hard question to answer, for there were many, but perhaps Elisabeth Höngen was the most special. There was a quality about her which is hard to define, for every time, in an important assignment or a smaller one, she had a magnetism that came, I believe, from the utter and total concentration she was able to give to her role."

"And what is your life today?" I asked her.

"I enjoy my freedom to the fullest," she replied, terminating our talk, "and that is why I have always refused teaching propositions. We live here in the country a great part of the year, but we also have a flat in Vienna. I do not really have friends among my ex-colleagues, whom I usually run into at funerals—which, alas, become more and more frequent. I never mixed my private life with my professional one, for I always wanted to keep out of all the intrigues which existed—and I am sure still exist—in this opera house. Perhaps it was a mistake, but I never fought for certain assignments such as Ariadne, which I loved and, like the Marschallin and Rosalinda, was handed over increasingly to lyrics and spintos. I was so in demand that I had to keep refusing engagements, for I always limited my appearances to somewhere between sixty and seventy a season and insisted on taking holidays every year to give my voice a rest, since my repertoire was the heaviest there is."

THE WAGNERIAN ENCHANTRESSES

KIRSTEN FLAGSTAD

GERMAINE LUBIN

HILDE KONETZNI

ELISABETH GRÜMMER

Although each of these four extraordinary sopranos sang a large number of operas very successfully, it was their interpretation of Wagnerian heroines that led them to world fame. Both Kirsten Flagstad and Germaine Lubin often sang the so-called *jugendlich dramatisch* heroines to great acclaim, but it was their assumption of the heroic roles that stunned the audiences and critics. Hilde Konetzni and Elisabeth Grümmer always remained in the more lyrical repertoire, attaining tremendous prestige.

Curiously enough, both Flagstad, who was Norwegian, and Lubin, who was French, underwent tremendous battles to prove that they were not Nazi sympathizers. Flagstad was given a clean bill of health by her own country, but attacked unmercifully by some Americans; Lubin was given a very rough time by her own compatriots. Grümmer, who also suffered greatly from the Second World War, losing her husband and all her property, had to make a success of her career in order to survive.

KIRSTEN FLAGSTAD

When I went to see Kirsten Flagstad in her hotel suite in New York City to interview her for *The New York Times* in 1940, she was the greatest box-office draw in the United States. At a time when the old Metropolitan Opera House rarely displayed the Standing Room Only sign, any appearance by the Norwegian soprano immediately sold out. Her position was unique, for not only did she triumphantly bring back the popularity of the Wagnerian repertoire, with Lauritz Melchior as her frequent partner, but at a time when Lily Pons, Grace Moore, Gladys Swarthout, Nino Martini, Lawrence Tibbett, and several others had created a very special brand of operatic motion-picture glamour, she shunned publicity and refused to play the game. It had not been easy, in fact, to persuade her to see me, and the fact that the newspaper for which I was requesting our interview was the most important in the United States did not appear to impress her in the least. She simply could not have cared less.

But once I was in her presence, she was graciousness personified, articulate and easy to talk to. There was a delightful reticence about her of the kind that only truly great persons possess, and, unlike so many other prima donnas, there was a total absence of egotism on Flagstad's part. If she was conscious that she had the United States at her feet at that particular moment, this never was evident in our conversation. There were traces of real humor when she discussed her age and the strangeness of becoming a sensation overnight after a career that had already spanned well over two decades. Her debut had taken place in 1913, when she was eighteen (she was born in the town of Hamar in 1895).

As is well known, when she made her debut as Sieglinde in 1935 at the Metropolitan, she had no real reputation to speak of except in her homeland. In fact, she was toying with the idea of retiring in 1933 when an offer came to sing at Bayreuth. It had come through the bass Alexander Kipnis, who had sung King Marke to her Isolde in Norway when at the eleventh hour she replaced the famous Nanny Larsen-Todsen.

Kirsten Flagstad as Brünnhilde in *Die Walküre*.

That first year in Bayreuth she appeared as Ortlinde in *Die Walküre* and the Third Norn in *Götterdämmerung*. The following year she was moved to Sieglinde and Gutrune, and this is where the Metropolitan came in. It seems that Otto Kahn had heard her in Norway in 1929 as Tosca and had been impressed enough to mention her to Gatti-Casazza, the general manager. There had been an effort to get in touch with her, but she did not reply; she had just remarried and did not want to leave her husband. But in 1934 a Wagnerian soprano was needed desperately at the Met, as Frida Leider was not returning and Anny Konetzni had been able to accept only a few performances, since she had a long-standing contract with the Vienna Staatsoper, where she was a big star. So it was arranged for Flagstad to leave Bayreuth between performances and audition in Switzerland for the conductor Artur Bodanzky and Gatti-Casazza. She made a favorable impression, but the heavily draped and walled hotel room in which she was made to sing did not really give her the opportunity to show the amazing dimensions of her instrument. Although the enthusiasm had not been overwhelming, she was hired, for it was already very late, and no other really valid sopranos had turned up in the interim.

Gatti-Casazza was convinced that Konetzni would be the more successful of the two, but he was mistaken. The Leider fans were in a stew, as rumors were rife that if Gatti-Casazza had made a bigger effort, he could have retained her services. Still, the unknown lady from the frozen north made a big success as Sieglinde on her debut on February 2. But it was on the 6th, four days later, that as Isolde she created a furor that will never be forgotten by those who were present. With the addition that season of two Brünnhildes, in *Walküre* and in *Götterdämmerung*, which were new to her, she established herself as the greatest soprano of her time. The critics could not find enough words to praise her, the public began to idolize her, and she became a legendary figure.

She sang in public until 1955, except during the war, when she was able to return to Norway to be with her husband (who was later accused of collaboration with the Nazis). But when I saw her in 1940, she told me she would have already retired had it not been for the war. "Now I don't know," she said in her quietly modulated voice. "There is no real reason for me to stop until I can find the way to go home. I miss my husband and family terribly, more than anyone can possibly understand, but it is all very difficult with Norway occupied by the Germans.

"I feel very strongly that artists should stop when they are on top," she declared, "when the flame is still burning intensely. There is nothing sadder than twilight. I do not believe Wagner ever wrote more heavenly music than the four so-called Wesendonck lieder, two of which were studies for *Tristan*. Of course for me he was a very great poet too, and I don't think there is anything more beautiful than that phrase in his 'Schmerzen': 'Und gebieret Tod nur Leben,/Geben Schmerzen Wonnen nur;/O Wie dank' ich, dass gegeben/Solche Schmerzen mir Natur' [And, if only death gives birth to life, if only sorrow brings bliss; Oh, how thankful I am that Nature has given me such sorrows]. You know, when I sing this particular stanza, I always feel I almost cannot bear it, for my heart is ever full of all the mindless thousands of people, innocent and brave, who are dying in this useless, monstrous war. One must believe that death regenerates life somehow or one goes crazy. I am very attached to my own country, passionately so really, and I love the winters there when no light transpires and the summers when darkness does not exist. And I want to be able to spend my remaining years quietly on the North Sea, ever so dramatic and mysterious, even terrifying at times, always hauntingly beautiful. But you perhaps may not be able to understand this. I am afraid of man, never of nature." But this wish never really came true; she worked until shortly before her death in 1962, and even served as director of the Norwegian National Opera.

Although she was not beautiful, I was impressed by Flagstad's distinction and bearing. Tall and well proportioned, she wore her blond hair parted in the middle. Her eyes had a soft, indefinite tonality of gray, and her perfectly oval face was quite regular. There was not a trace of makeup, and her skin had the appearance of someone's who spent many hours in the fresh air. She conveyed a sense of health which disappeared on the stage when she undertook the romantic heroines. From time to time she giggled like a child, particularly when looking for a difficult word in English. There was no coyness in her conversation, for everything she stated was firm and decisive. She talked fast, but the ring of sincerity was so complete I knew that she meant every word she said.

How had she managed to take on so many engagements and never appear out of sorts? She replied placidly: "I have a serene nature, and that is why I can manage to do so much. I am rarely nervous. When I happen to be, the critics and the public say that I am tired. But they are wrong: I am never tired of singing. God gave me the strength and the willpower. It is perfectly true that I usually sing full voice at all the rehearsals and that I don't spare it. Most singers cannot do this, I know, but I was born with this particular ability. When the Metropolitan asked me—to save a very particular situation for which they could not find an alternative—to sing three nights in succession, and all Wagnerian roles, I accepted, not only to be helpful but because I knew I could do it without any harm to my instrument. I can rehearse two operas in succession, always giving out my all, and suffer no ill effects from it. I was also blessed with the facility of learning new scores very rapidly. The first year I was at the Metropolitan I took on two Brünnhildes (the *Walküre* and *Götterdämmerung* ones), digesting them in very little time.

"I was born with a voice already placed," she continued, "but of course there was a lot I had to learn about breathing and control. First my mother gave me lessons, and then Ellen Schytte-Jacobsen. At thirteen I had already studied and knew Elsa by heart; and at fourteen, Aida. But actually I did not begin my training until I was sixteen, and all of this came naturally, for my father was a conductor and my mother, if I may be so immodest to say, the best singers' coach in Norway. My oldest brother became a conductor and my youngest a pianist. And it is not finished yet; my sister dedicated herself to the cello. So you see? I was bathed in music from the beginning, and I cannot conceive of life without it. I was made to study the piano, and this is, in my opinion, a must for all singers. Counterpoint, harmony, and theory bored me, but I got my share of them too.

"On December 12, 1913, I made my first public appearance, as Nuri in d'Albert's *Tiefland,* as a last-minute replacement for a soprano who got sick. Actually, I think it is a good way to begin, for you simply do not have the agony of a debut ahead of you. You are suddenly on the stage and you must deliver. Because of my facility in taking on new assignments, I believe that sixty-eight of them came my way, including operettas and revues. Actually there was very little Wagner except Eva, for which perhaps my voice is a little too heavy now, but I went from Handel's *Rodelinda* to Agathe in *Freischütz,* from Nedda in *Pagliacci* to Mimi in *La Bohème,* from Micaëla in *Carmen* to Amelia in *Ballo in maschera* and Desdemona in *Otello.* I even sang Marguerite in *Faust,* in a revival of *Euryanthe,* and Minnie in *La fanciulla del West.*

"Don't ask me anything about voice production," she stated, laughing, "for I simply don't know. There is only one right way to sing, and that's it. But we are all different and each one of us must find his own way. It is very much like what the Bible preaches, I feel: everyone must work out his own salvation. I went on studying and I still do.

"I am sure one should not approach Wagner too soon, and I probably would not be where I am today if I had done so. It was instinct that guided me, nothing else. In 1928, I was hired by the opera house in Göteborg, and it is there that, after some time, I tackled his heroines, although only a handful of them at the beginning. So, do you see, it was almost fifteen years after my debut before I started in his repertoire, and by then I was ready. But after Eva, I went on to Elsa and Elisabeth, and then eventually Isolde.

"People have often asked me how it is that I have a strong lower register which does not seem to interfere with the fact that the central and high ones are also on a par. This is difficult to answer. I recall that as a young student I spent a year studying Schubert's lieder on my own, for I have always had a passion for him, before I realized that the score was for contralto. And even then I was able to sing them in that key without straining. Perhaps it is a privilege which nature has favored me with, and there lies the answer.

"It is too bad that I was born without ambition. Do you know that when I was asked to go to St. Moritz for the Metropolitan audition I did not want to, and it was my husband, Henry Johansen, who pushed me to do so? He is a wealthy man—now with the occupation I hate to think what has happened—so it was certainly not the money which he considered in such an engagement, but he felt that I should have an international career. I could not have cared less. At the same time, when I am on the stage I want to do the best I can. The moment I walk out before an audience I am determined to win it over. I have tried to understand this split in my personality, if such you want to call it, and I cannot. I have never known envy or jealousy, for they are completely lacking in my temperament."

What did it feel like being the number-one diva in the world?

"Basically, nothing has changed," she replied. "I still feel shy, and I never feel that I deserve all these ovations. Success has not changed me in the least. I don't have a secretary or maid, for I hate people fussing around me. I answer all the letters I receive myself, and this perhaps comes from the way I was brought up. To receive a typed letter which you know has been dictated is so impersonal and cold. I do not have a social life for two reasons: first of all, I am not interested in it, and secondly, I simply don't have the time. I study constantly, for I leave nothing to chance, not even with those roles that I know are well ingrained in my throat. I go over the score time and time again, page by page, and every time I notice a detail that had escaped me. That is why I can sing one hundred Isoldes in a year and never be bored. Imperceptibly, I never repeat myself.

"When I was given Kundry to perform, I had exactly two weeks' time to learn it. I well knew this was a very different type of heroine and a very complex one, and while I memorized the score very rapidly, it took a long time for me to really get my teeth into her character, which is so mysterious and fascinating. While everywhere—at the Vienna Staatsoper, in London at Covent Garden, and of course in every American city—I am now so identified with Wagner that this is all I sing, with the exception of *Fidelio*, I still would like people to hear me in a different type of repertoire. But I am not one to impose myself, and I don't like bargaining. I may have delusions, but I think I can do the Italian parts well. But no one wants me and I'm not one to beg. Now really the situation has reached absurd proportions, for whether in recital or on the air I am always asked for the 'Ho-yo-to-ho' and the Liebestod. It is utterly grotesque to sing these pieces without an orchestra, but the public grumbles until I have sung them. It is a great pity that Wagner did not write more songs; how I could have used them!

"I love to do lieder recitals, and I keep adding new songs, including many American ones which I find very expressive and beautiful. If my heart really belongs to Schubert, Brahms, and Schumann, I am always intrigued by Bach and Handel, which are an endless fountain of beauty. Being Scandinavian, I adore Grieg too—I don't believe people realize what a glorious composition the *Haugtussa* cycle is—and in recent years I have taken a great liking to Mahler. As for Sibelius, I feel that all his songs are part of me. It sends shivers down my spine every time I perform it. At every Carnegie Hall recital I always like to present a new program, but I will not use a notebook with the texts of the songs the way so many of my colleagues do. So this means memorizing about twenty-five new pieces each time. Incredibly enough, the critics never seem to like my American group. I always read the critics, for I find that one can always learn something from each and every one of them. I am against any form of translation and refuse to sing Wagner in any other language but German. The loveliness of the text is such that any change would harm the score. I have sung Italian roles in Norwegian, for then I was not in a position to argue, but I knew all along how wrong it was.

"It is not true that I knit in my dressing room!" She giggled when I asked her this question. "Whoever started that rumor does not seem to know that I spend every available moment looking at the score I am involved with on that particular occasion. But I do admit that sometimes I play patience during that long third act of *Tristan* while I am waiting to be called onstage, after his endless monologue, to close the opera with the Liebestod. This, however, does not mean I do not knit, but this takes place when I am listening to music either on a gramophone or on the radio. I would like to take it along when I attend some concerts, but that would be impolite toward my fellow artists. It is absolutely correct that I like to dress myself and change costumes without anyone's help. As I told you before, I hate someone roaming around me, and particularly during a performance, when I must concentrate on what I am about to sing. I also put on my own makeup, for I believe that after all these years I do know what suits me. I loathe discussing money—this is true too—and always leave that to others.

"I don't really have favorites," she went on, prodded by my curiosity, "but perhaps the *Götterdämmerung* Brünnhilde is the one which moves me the most. Leonore in *Fidelio* is also very close to me, despite the difficulties it presents, not only vocally but in appearance. But every role, the more you scratch, becomes an ocean of discoveries. Senta, at first hand, seems like quite a simple girl snapped in a whirlwind, but there is more to her than just that.

"Opera is, of course, far more tiring than concerts. The costumes, the wigs, the tension of the entrances and exits, the uncertainty of what one's colleagues may do or not do, the keeping in contact with stage and orchestra at the same time—it is far more exhausting than being alone on the platform and dealing with each problem yourself, even if this means singing more.

"You asked me what was the most exciting event of my American career, and you will be surprised at my reply—it will prove to you what a simple human being I am. Recently a train was held forty minutes for me in Detroit so that I could catch it after a broadcast, and this did not really impress me much. But having a rose named after me at a flower show in that same city pleased me more than anything else I can think of. It is not only because I have always loved flowers, but it is the knowledge that long after I will be gone into another world and my voice will be forgotten, my name will be remembered because of this rose. It is a poetic thought, and I adore poetry. Singing is an ephemeral art. What does one leave behind? But a rose, if the species endures, is something, and one hundred years hence horticulturists will ask: 'Who was Flagstad?' "

Somehow she managed to return to her husband in Norway in 1941, and during the war years she sang only in Zurich, where in 1942 she appeared as Rezia in *Oberon*, Leonore, and Alceste. When hostilities ended she had to begin earning a living once more, since her husband had died in 1946 and his assets had been frozen, while inflation had done away with her savings. She returned to Covent Garden for several seasons, sang the *Ring* cycle under Furtwängler's direction in Milan, and appeared in various other European capitals, going from triumph to triumph. But when she came back to the United States, there were unbelievable protests everywhere she sang because she had been accused of being sympathetic to the Nazi regime. Her strength lay in total belief in her own innocence, and she went on, with tremendous courage and serenity, facing hostile crowds outside the concert halls and delirious audiences inside. Rudolf Bing, a Jew himself, was so convinced she had never collaborated with the Nazis but had simply gone home to be with her family that he re-engaged her for the Metropolitan; and those present that evening in 1951 when she returned, after a ten-year absence, as Isolde will never forget the wave of emotion that engulfed the public as the diva once more poured out her glorious golden tones. That season she also sang *Götterdämmerung, Siegfried,* and *Fidelio.* The following year her appearance as Alceste revealed another facet of her sensibility and art, for she demonstrated that she was not only bel canto personified, but an actress of true stature. Those lucky enough to hear her in London at the Mermaid Theatre as Purcell's Dido will hold on to that privileged memory for the rest of their lives. She retired—with many recordings to her credit, and still more to come—in 1955, at the age of sixty. Had she wished, she could have continued, for apart from diminished high notes her voice was still in perfect shape.

In my opinion, she was way over and above any other singer I have ever heard. Her voice was unique in its grandeur and flexibility. After a heroic phrase she could utter one of shattering delicacy, almost as if the thread to which it was attached might break off at any second. It never did. Her diction was magnificent, and she possessed a musicality that is impossible to describe. For me she was also an extraordinary actress: again, the greatest ever. With few gestures and the stateliness of a regal figure of ancient times, she dominated the stage and made everyone else around her disappear. As she said to me in the interview, "I don't think of acting; I only remember to express the words of the text."

In the last years of her career, she became a superb interpreter of Richard Strauss's lieder; and on May 2, 1950, several months after Strauss's death, she had the supreme privilege of singing the premiere of the Four Last Songs —the last compositions he ever wrote, and perhaps the most soul-searching of all—under Furtwängler's direction in London. It was a historic occasion, a great triumph. It was indeed most miraculous how Flagstad managed to reduce her huge vocal organ and give these heartrending songs an intimate reading, setting an example for all the interpreters who followed her. Despite her immense modesty, she must have been pleased that, along with the special rose, her name would forever be connected with Strauss's last and in many ways most touching work.

GERMAINE LUBIN

I visited Germaine Lubin in 1978, when she was eighty-eight years old. This extraordinary woman had not learned to live with the injustices she felt she had been subjected to; and, like Hecuba, she could not find peace. I was enormously struck by the parallel between her and the grandly tragic Greek queen.

When I walked into the extremely sophisticated and very personal apartment of the former diva on the Quai Voltaire, which had one of the most extraordinary views Paris has to offer—the Louvre, the Seine, the Tuileries, and all the rest—I was totally unprepared for the highly emotional and yet perfectly rational dialogue I was to experience. And when she appeared, slightly bent by an incurable form of arthritis and a little lame ("I fall all the time," she said, "but I never break anything"), I tried to imagine what she had been like when she was considered one of Europe's most beautiful women, and the greatest female singer France had had since Calvé. She possessed not only a superb timbre, always immediately recognizable, but also a unique sense of style which permitted her to excel in all repertoires and made her the object of the passion of many important men. With her white hair immaculately groomed, her famous pale-blue eyes alight like sparks and emphasized by a smart bright-blue suit, she seemed extraordinarily small and fragile. But there was nothing fragile in the way she evoked the agonizing drama that had cut off her career at the end of the Second World War, and the numerous humiliations she had suffered.

"Like Amfortas," she declared calmly but ever so bitterly, "my wounds are destined to remain open. The Greeks had a saying that he whom the gods love dies young. But I can add another one: He whom the gods favor will be sent to hell and burn there. I am still burning, and despite the fact that the years have proved my innocence, I will not find peace until I die, and perhaps not even then. The envy, jealousy, meanness, cruelty, and savagery of the human race is frightening; but only when one has been subjected to it in full, the way I was, does one fully realize the impact of its absurdity and terror. I always try to remember the words of Félia Litvinne, of whom I shall speak later: 'To sing Isolde is worth all the sorrow of living.' Certainly, her statement was prophetic in my case.

"It all started innocently enough," she explained, "with Lauritz Melchior, who sang an unforgettable Parsifal to my Kundry at the Paris Opéra. He was so impressed with my performance that as soon as he returned to appear at the Berlin Opera he spoke about me to the Intendant, Heinz Tietjen. An emissary arrived while I was doing a series of *Fidelios* to invite me to sing Sieglinde in the German capital, and although it was never one of my favorite Wagnerian roles (she is a victim, and instinctively I have always disliked victims—and how right I was, as the future proved!), I accepted. The Berlin Staatsoper had the reputation of being the best in Europe, blessed with all the great conductors like Furtwängler, Clemens Krauss, and Richard Strauss, and the top artists. Hitler was there too, but I lived for my art, and politics never interested me.

"I had to relearn the role in German, and at my debut, on February 20, 1938, the success was overwhelming. The French ambassador, François Poncet, brought a monumental man to my dressing room strapped into a uniform with his chest covered with medals. 'This is Marshal Göring,' he said. '*Wunderbar!*' the visitor repeated three times, kissing my hand and squeezing it until it hurt. They had barely left when Tietjen walked in to offer me Kundry at the next Bayreuth Festival. It had always been my dream to appear in the Wagnerian temple, and he had no difficulty in persuading me. The following day the German critics hailed me as a sensational discovery and the French dailies had banner headlines that no French singer had ever had such a fantastic reception in Germany.

"When I reported to Bayreuth the following summer, Winifred Wagner received me like a queen, and we became close friends—a bond that the horrors of the future were never to destroy. One night she had a party at Wahnfried to which Hitler came with his staff. He complimented me by saying, '*Sie sind eine Verführerin*'—you are a seductress—and he asked me to sit next to him, which upset the protocol no end. He never said anything interesting really, a series of banalities, and accustomed as I was to stimulating French political figures, I was amazed that a chief of state would not have a more sophisticated conversation. He seemed ill at ease, and, if this is possible, shy, at least with me. But then I recalled that he had started as a house painter. Göbbels, who was present, gave me the creeps, but Hitler did not. And I simply could not understand what people meant when they said he had charisma. The next day a huge bunch of flowers came from him

Germaine Lubin as Elsa in *Lohengrin*.

with a signed photograph in a silver frame. The dedication read, 'with sincere admiration and gratitude.'

"It was only in Bayreuth that the persecution of the Jews came to my attention, for I read diatribes against them on the walls. But never did I hear of the existence of concentration camps, either then or later, during the occupation of France. And I am firmly convinced that many Germans told the truth when they protested that they did not know. All I heard at the time was that the financial power of the Jews had become too great and must be curtailed. But within my circle there were no signs of it. I was confronted all the time with the Jewish husband of Frida Leider, whose glorious career was coming to an end, and the Jewish wife of Franz von Hösslin, who conducted me in *Parsifal* and later in *Tristan*. Karajan's wife at the time, Anita, was supposedly Jewish too.

"Anyhow, I was re-engaged to sing in Berlin the following winter; again Sieglinde and Kundry, plus Ariadne under Strauss's own direction. We had been friends for a long time, ever since I had sung the same opera with him at the Vienna Staatsoper, and he again tried to persuade me to undertake *Salome* under his baton. But again I told him I was a devoted Christian, and the idea of prancing around with the head of St. John the Baptist on a platter revolted me. He then suggested I sing Marie in his new opera, *Friedenstag* (I still have a letter from him regarding this project), and I promised him to look at the score. But events precipitated and the opportunity never came. Ursuleac got the job instead.

"Then Tietjen offered me Isolde for the next Bayreuth Festival, with a fabulous cast consisting of Margarete Klose, Max Lorenz, Josef von Mano-warda, Jaro Prohaska, and this seemed to me to be the pinnacle—a dream come true. So I signed the contract. The occupation of Czechoslovakia came next, and like everyone else I was terribly upset. In fact, despite the irresistible desire to sing Isolde in Bayreuth, I considered canceling, finding some doctor to write me a false medical certificate. I talked it over with some of my intimates, and none of them encouraged me to do so. 'France has not cut off diplomatic relations,' they argued, 'so why should you take such a firm stand?' I even talked it over with officials of the Quai d'Orsay. 'Go, by all means,' they said. 'We need an ambassador of your prestige in the domain of art.'

"I was hailed by the press as the greatest Isolde of all time, but I explained to Winifred Wagner that I could not attend her supper, for I did not wish to meet Hitler again. She understood, but was not prepared when, at the end of the performance, she told him I was too tired to come to Wahnfried, and he announced that he would come to compliment me in my dressing room. There was no way she could stop him, and there he was. He kissed my hand and said, '*Ich habe in meinen ganzen Leben eine solche Isolde niemals gesehen und gehört*'—I have never seen or heard an Isolde like you in my entire life. 'Really?' I asked with a pronounced question mark. 'Really,' echoed Winifred.

"I never saw Hitler again, despite many reports to the contrary. The next day Tietjen told me that at the Führer's instigation, he was told to negotiate any sort of contract with the Berlin Staatsoper that would be agreeable to me and to meet any financial demands I might make. I replied that this was impossible, since I had a longstanding contract with the Paris Opéra, which only permitted me some guest appearances in other lyric theatres.

"It was part of the binding agreement with Bayreuth that no artist could leave the town without a specifically signed permission. And as there were a few days between the next-to-the-last and the final performance of *Tristan*, I asked Tietjen for permission to go to the Auvergne for three days to see my daughter. It was granted. Just as I was about to enter the car that was to take me back to Germany, the news came over the air that war had been declared. I was overwhelmed by the turn of events, and having seen the might of the German army at close range during my Berlin stay, I had dark forebodings. Later, via Switzerland, arrived a letter from Winifred expressing her regret that I had been unable to return to sing the last Isolde. After a curiously ominous, quiet winter, like in a nightmare, the Germans broke down all resistance, and soon it was all over. I had fled to Auvergne, but Jacques Rouché, the head man of the Paris Opéra, to whom I owed a great deal and who combined great efficiency with fantasy and imagination, begged me to return, for it had been decided to reopen the opera house so as not to run the risk that it be taken over too by the Nazis. My loyalty to him was total, and after much indecision I decided to go back and help him. This turned out to be the greatest possible error I ever made. For the next five years I sang at the Opéra regularly.

"My son Claude, who was in the army," she proceeded, her voice becoming tighter and tauter, "became a prisoner, and I managed to get him freed. But he was not the only one. A never-ending number of people came to me with their problems—and many testified later in my defense—and I did everything I could to help. Not only was I able to arrange that some war prisoners be freed, but I got people out of jail, hid people in my castle, was able to get many out into the unoccupied zone. Although I was accused later of being in constant touch with Nazi leaders, most of my efforts were made through Winifred Wagner, and let it be known once and for all that she never faltered and made every effort to have these wretched people released. She sent Captain Hans Joachim Lange to see me, a most civilized human being, who took great risks in lending me a helping hand. So much so that in the end the Nazis arrested him for having saved a group of Jews. I was invited over and over again to sing in Germany, and they always accepted my very simple answer: 'There is no way that, as a Frenchwoman, I can accept such an offer.' When *Fidelio* was revived, there was an interminable ovation after the 'Abscheulicher,' whose text is a hymn of defiance toward injustice. With so many Germans in the audience, I did not want to create an incident and refused to take my usual solo bow. Despite the insistence of the public, I held firm to my decision, and I do not believe I have ever sung that monstrously difficult and sublime aria with more emotion, deeply realizing all the implications of Leonore's state of mind.

"An offer suddenly came for me to go and sing in the United States and, full of hope, I asked for an exit visa. Abetz, the German ambassador to France, refused point blank to issue me a passport, claiming my presence was essential to the Opéra. Naturally, I had mentioned some neutral nation and not the U.S.A., as I knew that the answer would have been a resounding no, since it was considered the number-one enemy. Alas, I was too well known to try and disappear, crossing into unoccupied France either with falsified papers or on foot. The frontier was patrolled at every inch.

"I took on the Marschallin in 1941, instead of Octavian, which I had sung so often, and I still treasure a sonnet Henri Sauguet sent me after the performance. I had no idea this delicious composer could write such elegant poetry. Karajan came to conduct *Tristan* with the Berlin Staatsoper and with all the same cast I had sung with in Bayreuth. I had no choice but to appear as Isolde. I saw a lot of the Karajans and can assure you that despite all that has been written, they were not Nazis. My old friend Jean Cocteau was so entranced with my Irish princess he wrote me a letter that brought tears to my eyes, for he well understood the rapture that enveloped me, a sort of sublimation that set me on fire and yet drained me.

"When the much-awaited liberation came," she proceeded, the voice changing color again, "an avalanche of anonymous letters poured in non-stop. France had never been so divided since the time of the Huguenot wars. Those who had managed to leave could not forgive those who had remained, and all personal quarrels and hatred came to the fore with a frightening violence. I was aware that two prima donnas—everyone knows their names, but I will not stoop so low as to mention them—had always loathed me for being the reigning diva and getting all the plum parts. They saw the opportunity to destroy me, and they succeeded. I kept being arrested and then released again, for the accusations—so outrageous that in other circumstances they would have been hilarious—always proved groundless. Except for having eaten the flesh of children, there is nothing I was not accused of. Everyone who knew me was fully aware that, alas, I was not a sexual woman. I fell in love, but always on a spiritual plane, and sex never interested me. It took me a long time to realize that the men I really loved were Tristan, Siegfried, Lohengrin, Tannhäuser, and heroes of that sort. But when the war was over, suddenly it turned out that I had been the mistress of everyone from Ribbentrop to Admiral Dönitz (I had never even met him!) and Hitler, who supposedly was impotent. I was also unquestionably godmother to Göring's children. Just how this would have been possible, since I never returned to Germany after the declaration of war, was a little difficult to explain. Much was said about a visit I paid to the German embassy in Paris, for this immediately revealed I was a spy. It was later proved that I had gone to plead for my great friend Maurice Franck's liberation. The deluge of recriminations and horrors never stopped, and every new anonymous letter brought new interrogations.

"It did emerge," she continued, "that I managed to have not only my son Claude liberated from being a war prisoner, but many others too. I had hidden several people in my chateau near Tours and had gotten several persons, including some Jewish friends, out of jail. But all these testimonies took time to organize, for a lot of these people had moved or could not be immediately located. Their names and declarations are all there for anyone to peruse at the Justice Department.

"After over thirty years' faithful service I was dismissed by the Opéra— along with several others, including Rouché—with no right to any kind of pension. As if that were not enough, I was condemned to 'national degradation' for five years, and a certain part of my money was confiscated. No musical conservatory was allowed to take me on as a teacher, and I was denied a passport to go sing outside of France. Geneva had sent me a contract to sing *Tannhäuser* there. I was refused permission to go. There were many others—Sacha Guitry, Alfred Cortot, Serge Lifar (he managed to vanish for a long time)—who were also persecuted. Poor Janine Micheau was suspended for a year, since she had agreed to sing in Strauss's *Ariadne* on the French radio.

"My husband, Paul Géraldy, was absolutely marvelous throughout all my trials and tribulations, stuck to me valiantly, fought like a tiger to establish my innocence. But in the meantime, it was a losing battle for me—one against time, for I knew that the bloom in my voice could not last much longer. An engineer, a doctor, a painter, can start again after a five-year interruption. But a singer at my age was fighting against the pitiless deterioration of the vocal cords. Finally, on March 29, 1950, I held a recital and insisted on including some lieder. I have always considered that art was apart from politics, and anyhow it is inconceivable that Schumann, Brahms, Wagner, or Strauss had any connection with the horrors perpetrated by the Nazis. In France we too had some monsters, like Marat, Robespierre, and Danton, and what have their terrible deeds got to do with the music of Rameau, Lully, or Gounod? Should one not perform Prokofiev or Shostakovich because of the hundreds of thousands of people done away with by Lenin and Stalin? Anyhow, despite the alarming condition of my nerves, I had a triumph, and the public would not leave the hall. I went to Zurich and Geneva for more recitals and gave more in Paris.

"Then my son Claude committed suicide, and I never sang again. I was frozen into such a state of shock that suddenly nothing mattered anymore. That his mother's vicissitudes had affected him—he was a withdrawn and sensitive person—there is no doubt, but had they influenced him in the end toward this act of total desperation? I shall never know, and the doubt will always linger. Fate willed it that I was able to save him from prison, where he might easily have died the way so many others did, but I could not save him from himself.

"Slowly, very slowly," she went on, the voice now almost a whisper, "life began again, and I began coaching many artists. Régine Crespin came to me to learn the Marschallin, and Suzanne Sarroca, Octavian, and I keep taking on students. Now I have a very talented one, Jocelyne Taillon, who recently sang a very effective Geneviève in the new production of *Pelléas* at the Opéra, where I go quite often. The other night my seat was deep down the aisle, and evidently as I was pushing my way in, someone recognized me and mentioned my name. A spontaneous ovation greeted me from the people around me, and I was struck by the fact that it meant absolutely nothing to me. When it would have held some importance, it did not come. Now it is too late."

I asked her to trace quickly the high points of her prestigious career, and in a mixture of French, German, English, and Italian—she speaks all of them with great facility—switching from one to another whenever she wished to use certain expressions typical of that language, she said she always thought the very special quality of the timbre of her voice was due to the blend of races running in her veins: French, Alsatian, and Kabyle, a race which has been settled in Algeria for centuries. "It was a strange mixture," she went on to explain, "of a crystalline sound emitted by a highly emotional person. So the clarity was always present, and behind it the strength, which grew enormously over the years, which usually does not exist with that type of instrument. Until the very last day, I never stopped studying and experimenting, and my technique was very secure. In fact I could go from Mozart, Weber, Gluck, and Gounod to the heavy heroines of Wagner and Strauss without the slightest worry.

"But let us begin in order," she started recollecting, "since I too had a father and a mother. He was a doctor, and shortly after my birth we moved to French Guiana, where he was employed. He was a gifted pianist and started me off at the age of four. My mother used to take my brother and me back to Paris from time to time, and eventually at the age of fifteen I joined the Conservatoire. Here I had a marvelous teacher, de Martini, who fell in love with my voice, which at that time consisted of only one octave. Slowly, carefully, and patiently, he built it up, until I could take a D above high C with ease. He taught me the basics so well, and the D"—and in saying this she walked over to the Steinway piano and hit the note several times with one finger—"remained with me always, despite the very taxing roles I undertook in the second part of my career. From the very beginning, everyone agreed I was a dramatic soprano, but it was decided it would be wiser to start with lyric roles and move on to the heavier ones later.

"Gabriel Fauré, at the time head of the Conservatoire, singled me out and taught me most of his songs himself. They have become part of me and never left me." She pointed to various volumes piled up on the piano. "I never ceased singing them, even when I became a lieder recitalist, for to me they are immensely tender, evocative, and will find a very important and permanent place in our song literature. Strangely, Hofmannsthal did not appreciate them. I recall sitting at the piano in his house in Austria and playing them as I sang them. He began yawning. 'What is the matter, Hugo?' I asked. 'Do sing some Schubert instead,' he replied. 'These are so boring.' I was speechless that a man of his sensitivity and taste did not appreciate them.

"I won first prizes, and both the Opéra and the Comique offered me contracts. It appeared to my mentors that the latter would be a better starting-off point until I found my whereabouts, and I made my first appearance there as Antonia in *Les Contes d'Hoffmann*. Two years later I moved to the Opéra, and there I began with Marguerite in *Faust*. At first, I was a little shy and did not let myself go enough. My diction was far from

perfect, and I was not a born actress, but that one over there"—she pointed
to the photograph of a woman in a silver frame—"helped me tremendously.
She was Félia Litvinne, who was born in Russia but made most of her career
in France, and had one of the most beautiful voices in the world. I had heard
her when I was a student as Alceste, and she took my breath away. I took
lessons from her for ten years, and if I became a real actress and my diction
proved exemplary, I owe it all to her.

"But I never stopped studying. Jean de Reszke, I feel, did not add much
to my knowledge, but Lilli Lehmann did a lot for me. For many years I
used to go to Salzburg in the summer to work with her, and her classes were
veritable killers. She was terribly demanding and severe, and after several
sessions with her I used to be utterly worn out. I originally went to her to
prepare Donna Anna when Bruno Walter asked me to sing this part in
Salzburg, and I always thought it was best to go to whoever had been the
best in a certain role. And she did teach me how to lighten my voice in the
most remarkable way—so much so that she insisted I sing Konstanze. But
the opportunity never arose. The Paris Opéra did not have *Entführung* in
its repertoire, and so many other offers poured in. For Octavian I went to
Marie Gutheil-Schoder, who had created the role.

"I first sang *Rosenkavalier* in the delicious opera house in Monte Carlo,"
she related, "under the direction of Victor de Sabata, one of the greatest
conductors in my opinion, and with Gabrielle Ritter-Ciampi as a great
Marschallin. Her breathing was a miracle, for one simply could not see
where it came from, and her phrasing was exquisite. I don't really believe
there has been a Donna Elvira like her. She sang it with me under Walter's
direction at the Paris Opéra, and I was enraptured. When *Rosenkavalier* first
appeared on the boards of the Paris Opéra in 1927, I insisted with the
management that Gutheil-Schoder be in charge—but I am rushing ahead of
myself.

"At first I did many roles of the French repertoire, such as Gounod's
Juliette, Thaïs (which I even sang at a gala evening in Madrid before the
king and queen of Spain), Rameau's *Castor et Pollux,* and then later the
horribly long and difficult *Ariane et Barbe-Bleue* by Dukas. I made excursions
into the Italian repertoire and sang many Aidas and Toscas. The way the
Opéra was run in those days, certain roles were assigned to the same artists
—they used to call them *les titulaires*—and it was difficult for a newcomer
to get a chance at them without stirring up endless controversies and
jealousies. So, as I had a great facility to learn new roles and was beautiful
—or at least that is what everyone said—many new operas were thrown

at me, including Vincent d'Indy's *La Légende de Saint Christophe,* a work which did not hold the public's interest. But he was a sweet man and a great friend of mine and my husband's, for in 1913 I had married Paul Géraldy, without a doubt the most charming man in the entire world, and an exquisite poet and writer. Did you ever read his *Toi et Moi?* 'Moi' was me, you know. During the First World War, I was sent to sing for the soldiers at the front, and it was there that Marshal Pétain met me and fell in love with me. Little did I know what troubles this infatuation on his part would bring me! He was a very nice man, but there was no possible way for me to consider his propositions. I was very much taken with my husband, and that was that. In this period I also sang Fauré's *Pénélope,* which suffers from a poor libretto.

"In 1921 my first really great big chance came," she recalled, her light-blue eyes flashing, "for the management decided to let bygones be bygones and reintroduced Wagner, barred by war, into the repertoire. I was assigned Sieglinde, and it was a triumph. The doors were thus open for me to enter the Wagnerian repertoire. When I sang Elsa in May 1922, the success was so astounding that suddenly I was the number one star at the Opéra. Eva followed the following year.

"Echoes of my terrific notices as Elsa reached Vienna, and I was invited to make my debut there in this role under Clemens Krauss's direction. I had to relearn the part in German, but the reviews were ecstatic there too. My husband and I became great friends with Hofmannsthal and Richard Strauss, not to speak of Helene Thimig, the great Austrian actress, and her husband, Max Reinhardt—Thimig acted in my husband's play *Aimer* at the Josefstadt theatre. And I was reinvited to sing *Ariadne auf Naxos* the following year with Strauss conducting. Again another triumph, and the participation of Elisabeth Schumann as one of the nymphs was unforgettable.

"Another great step forward in my career was when the Paris Opéra presented me as Alceste in 1926 with Georges Thill as my partner and Madame Nijinska as choreographer. It was a sort of apotheosis, and the opera remained in the repertoire for a long time. I went on happily to the Brünnhildes, Elisabeth, and Kundry, along with *Fidelio.* I always kept away from Senta, for I did not feel it suited my voice. But Isolde proved my ideal, and so did Elektra, choreographed by Serge Lifar. Cassandra in *Les Troyens* also entered my life, and in Amsterdam I took on the beautiful score of *Iphigénie en Tauride* for the first time.

"As I told you before, emotionally I was a complicated woman. I fell in love spiritually with men, and they with my body. Sex never meant anything to me, and I kept hoping I might be awakened along these lines. The greatest mistake I ever made was to insist on a separation from my husband when I thought I had fallen in love with another man. And I was so straitlaced that I did not become his mistress until I had left Paul. It continued—it had to, too much had been involved in this decision—but it was a disaster. I never found in him what I was stupid enough to think I could, and he was deeply disappointed in my lack of response. The malediction was that I looked sexy and actually was not."

I asked her how she compared herself with Kirsten Flagstad.

"Each and every one is different," she replied. "Comparisons are impossible. We first met before the Second World War, at a Zurich Wagnerian festival, and while she was appearing in *Tristan,* I was Sieglinde and also doing the Wesendonck lieder under Furtwängler's baton. I was overwhelmed by the volume of her instrument, the beauty of the timbre, the dignity and the simplicity. What a wonderful woman, so friendly and gentle. I often thought of her later when the Americans crucified her despite the fact that her countrymen had not. She was Nordic and I Latin—that tells the story. My upper register was, in my estimation, more vibrant and clear. I heard her again in Milan in the early fifties under Furtwängler's direction, and despite the years creeping on, she was still splendid. Furtwängler too, who had done so much to protect Jews in the Berlin Philharmonic, had a hell of a time. But then, although I am a devout Christian, I have learned that justice is not of this world. And I have not reached as yet the state where I can forget—and I am not so sure that I can forgive either."

When Germaine Lubin died in 1980, the French press gave her a tremendous sendoff. After all, she had been one of France's glories.

KAMMERSÄNGERIN
HILDE KONETZNI

There was a time when the Vienna Staatsoper was dominated by the overwhelming personalities of two prima donnas who happened to be sisters and equally esteemed as artists: Anny and Hilde Konetzni. Anny (who died in 1968, fifteen years after a stroke had paralyzed her) was a *hochdramatisch* soprano, celebrated for her heroic Wagnerian roles, the three Brünnhildes and Isolde in particular. Hilde was instead a *jugendlich dramatisch* or spinto, and although her repertoire was vast, it was in the less strenuous and more romantic Wagnerian roles that she built her immortality. Her Sieglinde, Elsa, Elisabeth, and Senta were considered magical, and she also managed to make a great success of Wagner's least sympathetic female character, Gutrune. Even today her name is revered in Austrian and German musical circles, and there are sundry experts who claim that her Sieglinde was even greater than Lotte Lehmann's, who was considered the supreme interpreters of this role. I recall her Elvira and Chrysothemis at the Salzburg Festival and her Leonore in *Fidelio* in Vienna as being exceptional for the beauty of the timbre and the facility with which she made each role stand out and yet remain part of an ensemble. With what immense ease she tackled the "Abscheulicher," one of the most fiendish arias ever written—the best I ever heard after Flagstad's.

When I called on her in June 1979—she died the following year—in her large apartment in the heart of Vienna, she greeted me ceremoniously, like a lady from the distant past, with the natural assurance of someone who still reigned over a vanished empire. Assisted by her charming daughter, who spoke excellent English (my German is somewhat sketchy), she slowly answered my questions, after offering me an elaborate snack and drinks. A born diplomat, she had the perfect manners of someone who did not wish to offend either the living or the dead, but who recalled very vividly both the kindnesses and the discourtesies of the past. In her middle seventies—she was born in 1905 in Vienna from a family of Czech origin—she looked every inch the prima donna she used to be. Although it was often said that

Anny was a difficult person and envious of her sister's success—she discouraged Hilde from singing "her" roles—Hilde made no reference to family rivalry. She admitted, however, that the only roles they had shared were Leonore in *Fidelio* and the Marschallin. "It was better that way," she declared. "Otherwise the public would get the two of us mixed up, and this would not have been right. 'To each her own' was my motto."

Both sisters had been record-breaking swimmers in their youth, and in Hilde's opinion this helped them later in the technique of breathing when singing. In fact, the breath control of the lady I had before me was celebrated. When I mentioned this to her, she did not indulge in self-praise. "The very base of singing is just that," she said, "and the trouble today is that all these girls have the mania of remaining thin, so they do not have a body that allows them to have the proper diaphragm. I am up against it every day at the conservatory where I teach. This is not the only problem, but the smallness of the voices seems to be related to the muscular frame, which seems to be practically nonexistent." She then stopped and asked me if I had heard a young soprano who is now enjoying an important career and currently much in favor with Karajan. "If she would put on some weight, I dare say that she might be able to sing with the dividends of her instrument instead of using the capital. For a voice exists there, and quite a pretty one."

"Do you give her long?" I asked.

"No, I don't. What is right is right and what is wrong is wrong even in this age of technical miracles. The laws of nature are stronger than the individual's, but try and tell these young people. Wasted time. But I go on wasting it, for I feel it is my duty if something is to remain out of the present shambles. The other day one of them answered me that if she put on some pounds, they would not accept her for a certain operatic assignment on television, and I replied that despite their bulk both Caballé and Pavarotti were televised constantly. And I added, 'It is because they are among the best singers we have today, and the public adores them despite all their extra flesh.' She shrugged her shoulders and said, 'But they have already arrived.' I did not get discouraged and answered, 'Yes, but you will never get there unless you have a structure that permits you to take long breaths.' In my opera studio we have been able to locate only one mezzo, and not a single contralto—an extinct species, like the dinosaurs."

With humor and grace she told me the story of her beginnings. "I did not study voice very long," she explained, "at the New Vienna Conservatory. I went to visit Anny, three years older than me and already singing

Hilde Konetzni as Senta in *Der fliegende Holländer*.

at the opera house in Chemnitz for two seasons. Chemnitz, as you probably know, is not a very large town in what is now East Germany, but it had a very respectable lyric theatre. The director came to visit Anny, and upon being told I was a voice student, insisted on hearing me. Immediately he proposed that I assume the role of Sieglinde three days later. He confessed that he was in a fix and needed one desperately. Because of my youth, and perhaps also to show off to Anny that I too could be appreciated, I took on the challenge, learned the role that later was to become so identified with me, and with tremendous courage went on. Although I was offered a contract, I did not accept it, for I knew that I needed more schooling, and returned to Vienna to study for another year and a half. I then was hired by the small but first-class opera house in Gablonz, Czechoslovakia, a very musical town. Then they heard about me in Prague, and, unknown to me, I was auditioned during one of my performances. I was immediately signed by the German Opera there and remained for four years. It is there that I really got the experience that was to prove invaluable later on. I repeated the same roles I had undertaken in Gablonz, plus many others, including *Kreidekreis* by Zemlinsky, Schoenberg's teacher and brother-in-law. I sang all the Italian parts in German.

"The Vienna Staatsoper, where my sister had just been engaged, came along with a very tempting offer, and then for one year I divided my time between the two cities. After my success in my native city—I made my debut there as Elisabeth in 1935—the insistence on the part of the management of the Staatsoper was such that, in order to dedicate most of my time to Vienna, I did not renew my contract with Prague, which was due for renegotiation. In a way I was sorry to cut my ties with Prague, one of the most beautiful cities in the world, and where so many wonderful opportunities had come my way. But I was Viennese and loved my family and friends, and I knew the theatre so well—as a young girl I had spent all my allowance to go and listen to all the great singers. One of my great favorites—a sort of idol for me—was Maria Nemeth, whose Turandot was equally as great as her Queen of the Night. She was a phenomenon, for unlike Callas she sang so incredibly diversified a repertoire without changing registers. There was no switching there, just a formidable technique, accompanied by one of those haunting voices such as the Hungarians used to have.

"From Vienna I began to spread my wings. Bruno Walter took me with him to Paris in May 1936, to appear as Elvira in a memorable *Don Giovanni* he conducted with Pinza as the Don and the unforgettable Elisabeth Rethberg as Donna Anna. It was as Elvira that I made my debut at the Salzburg

Festival that same year, and I was engaged there over and over again until 1961. I had the chance to sing the First Lady in the famous Toscanini *Zauberflöte* in 1937 with a God-sent cast—Novotna, Rosvaenge, Kipnis, Domgraf-Fassbänder, Thorborg. I also scored as Chrysothemis that same year in an unforgettable *Elektra* conducted by Knappertsbusch, and with Rose Pauly; she was the most demoniacal Elektra I can remember. Then came the turn of the Marschallin.

"As far as Mozart is concerned, Donna Elvira was my door opener on so many occasions, and this is the reason, perhaps, that I have always had a particular affection for her. It is not an ungrateful role in my opinion, as has been stated so often, for there is always something happening when she is on the stage, and she has some of the most lovely music to sing in the opera. But Donna Anna, which I also took on later, is a bore. She is static, except in the very opening scene, and it is not very clear whether she has been subjected to the Don's sexual attack or not. I always like to understand a character, know what makes her tick, and with Donna Anna one is never sure. I did not have the agility for either Konstanze or Fiordiligi, but I sang Countess Almaviva often enough.

"I have often found I was not in agreement with some of my colleagues about roles. I adored Gutrune, for instance, and so many other sopranos hated taking her on. Perhaps the reason I became so fond of her is that she is not liked by anyone, and I feel sorry for people like her. And it was a great challenge to be appreciated by the audiences in this role. She knows what she wants from the beginning. In my opinion she is on a par with Brünnhilde all the way. I agreed to sing her even at Covent Garden and La Scala. And I loved Chrysothemis, which many sopranos do not enjoy singing, for they feel that most of the success goes to the other two, Elektra and Klytämnestra. When I sang it, I gave it my all, and I received as many ovations as the others, probably because I have always been a fighter and enjoyed any sort of challenge onstage.

"Although I am well aware that I am far better known for my Wagnerian interpretations—and this is easily explainable, for I was called upon to sing his heroines so often on the international circuit—actually I sang a great deal of Verdi too. Sieglinde and Elisabeth are the roles I sang the greatest number of times, followed by Leonore in *Fidelio,* the Marschallin, and Elvira, but I appeared in ever so many Verdi operas, from Desdemona to the two Leonoras in *Trovatore* and *Forza* to Elisabetta in *Don Carlo* (how many times I sang this opera under Bruno Walter's magic wand!) and Amelia in *Un ballo in maschera.* I always turned down *Aida,* for I knew I was not right for it. The third act's tessitura was uncomfortable for me. Although I recorded a lot of Puccini, I never sang his works onstage, for verismo did not suit my vocal production, and I knew that my temperament would get the best of me. I also kept away from *Jenůfa* for the same reason. I studied it at length and then decided against it. Although the Marschallin and Chrysothemis were staples of my career until the end, I kept away from most of the other Richard Strauss operas except *Die Frau ohne Schatten,* which I feel one must avoid until one is terribly experienced, for it is full of dangers. I loved Strauss himself, as a person and as a conductor, and I think he is really the last of the giants in the composition of operas, with the possible exception of Poulenc.

"My sister sang a heroic Leonore in *Fidelio;* mine was far more lyrical and less opulent. But the part suited me, for despite its arduous tessitura the 'Abscheulicher' never held any terrors for me. But it is hard to explain why what proves very difficult for one is not for another, even if one belongs to the same type of voice. I believe it is really a question of certain passages."

I questioned her about Wagner.

"He knew, like Verdi, how to write for the voice," she explained, "in the most fabulous way. With the stamina and the right balance between the center and the top, the roles I sang presented no difficulties and were to me immensely inspiring. After I sang Elsa and Elisabeth, in particular, I felt so totally cleansed and purified. Senta is the most interesting character of all, almost Freudian, and what heavenly music she is allotted! But she must remain a mysterious figure and not a pivot of the action, as so many of the new directors interpret her today. This for me is all wrong. I never went near Eva despite many offers. She did not interest me, and so I never sang the beautiful quintet. Somehow, Sieglinde suited me for thirty years, as I felt that even after three decades I could do justice to this marvelous creature of Wagner's.

"As for the tenors, you asked me about who I felt really did justice to Wagner. I would name three: Set Svanholm, Max Lorenz, and more recently Jon Vickers.

"Perhaps the most incredible experience I ever had was in London in 1938, when I was engaged to sing at Covent Garden, and it made me internationally famous overnight. I was due to make my debut as Chrysothemis and had gone to the theatre by myself very inconspicuously the night before to hear *Der Rosenkavalier* with Lotte Lehmann as the Marschallin. Suddenly she stopped in the middle of the act and walked out. There was pandemonium and the curtain came down. She simply announced she did not feel in good form and could not continue. Someone remembered that I had asked for a ticket so I must be in the house. I had been very successful in this part even in Salzburg. My name was called out, and I left my seat to see what was wanted. Somehow, it all happened so fast that I did not even have the time to think that they were going to ask me to replace her. But they did.

"As I told you before, I have always enjoyed challenges, and this was the greatest ever. Lehmann's Marschallin was considered, right or wrong, the greatest, and no one in London knew me. I accepted. But there were no costumes. Lehmann had left the theatre in a tearing hurry and, amazingly enough, had carried them off with her. But that was Lotte! She only thought of herself. So while the public patiently waited, having been told that a replacement had been found, the management was desperately looking for something that I could wear. I cannot recall where the dressing gown for the first act was located, but I do remember that I told them that I had seen a woman sweeping in, at the entrance, in a lovely evening cape. They spent the entire second act trying to find her, and it was with her wrap that I made my entrance in the third act. (As you know, the Marschallin does not appear in the second.) Somehow they also found a white wig for the final scene. You cannot believe the triumph I had. I thought they would never allow me to go home and have a good sleep before the *Elektra* the next night. When I awoke late in the morning, I had to move out of my room and take another one, for there were literally dozens and dozens of bouquets and baskets of flowers, including a bunch of roses from Lehmann herself. And all the critics had raved.

"After my performances in London, I returned to Vienna to appear as Milada in Smetana's beautiful *Dalibor,* another opera that has vanished; it is one of the roles I have treasured most. Suddenly there was an urgent telephone call from London. Could I get on the first train leaving for the British capital? Lehmann had just canceled Sieglinde for the following night. I got there just in time, having received the permission of the Staatsoper, which was flattered that I was so needed. And then the next year I sang several roles at Covent Garden. I returned there after the war to appear in *Fidelio* with the entire Vienna company, and then later, with Anny as the Brünnhilde, as Sieglinde and Gutrune.

"In 1938 I made my one and only concert tour of the United States. Then I was engaged for the Chicago Opera in 1946, but there was a big financial mess. I only know that it never took place. But I did go to the Colón in Buenos Aires, where I appeared as Donna Anna and the Dyer's Wife in *Die Frau ohne Schatten.*"

I asked her about conductors.

"For me there were three whom I worshiped above all," she stated. "Bruno Walter was one of the most gentle and sensitive human beings I have ever come across. He would say tenderly to me, '*Schatz*, would you sing this once again for me?' I would have been ready to jump from a fourth floor for him! I recall rehearsing *Dalibor* at the piano with him and Theodor Mazarof, a Bulgarian tenor who made a brief splash. Suddenly the tenor and I found ourselves dissolved in tears—one of those magical experiences that are never repeated. The way he prepared us was so unbelievably beautiful, and what he made of the music so heavenly, we both had the same instant reaction.

"Knappertsbusch was unique. He did not believe in rehearsals with singers, for he wanted spontaneity at all costs, and yet with those eyes of his like fires in the night fixed on you, you simply could not go wrong. I sang my first Sieglinde with him in Vienna, and when I was called by him, there was not even a piano in the room. In a few words he explained what he wanted from me—and he got it. He always did.

"As for Furtwängler, he was also a giant, but in his case the great trick was never to look at him, for as far as singers were concerned his baton was confusing. But he was such a musician, and as he never varied the tempos, once one became accustomed to his ways, one could navigate smoothly."

"And what about Karl Böhm?" I asked.

"He is not a nice person, almost sadistic at times with us singers," she replied, and did not go any further. (This opinion was shared by many of her colleagues.)

"And Erich Kleiber?" I timidly inquired.

"Tremendous," she stated, "and such a considerate person. It was he who was conducting the London orchestra in *Der Rosenkavalier* when Lotte left everyone in the lurch. His kindness to me that evening, when I think back, was that of an angel, if such a being exists."

Married to a Yugoslav, Mirko Urbanic, since 1940 (he was a colonel in the Austrian army), she gave her last performance in 1974—on January 28, to be exact.

"You know, we did not speak of the war," she explained, "for we are here to talk about music. But everything was swept away: the savings, the properties; and with the devaluation, all was lost. We also went hungry for a long time. I had to start all over again. I simply could not afford to retire, and when I did, it was because of a heart attack. And if I go on teaching, it is because I still need to earn money. Although it helps, it is certainly not the pension that permits us to live. So I went on to mezzo roles, then smaller, cameo parts at the Volksoper, where Ljuba Welitsch is still doing pretty much what I did. It is no shame there in Vienna to go on making a living, you know. Actually, my last appearance was in *Der Zigeunerbaron,* which is a charming operetta. I was even called to other theatres—for instance, Zurich, where I appeared in works like *Der Bettelstudent.*

"Now they are pulling out old recordings, and one is about to come out of my lieder—I sang many recitals, but not as many as I would have liked, for the offers came pouring in to sing in so many theatres. I also created a very extraordinary opera in Zurich, written for only one person—*Niobe* by Sutermeister—in 1946, and in Hamburg in 1949, *Königin Elisabeth* by Fred Walter. But I was always leery about modern scores, and carefully considered the harm they might do to the voice, which is unique, a gift from God, and which I would not have exchanged for all the gold in the world."

Three hours had elapsed, and it was time to go. "Goodbye," she said. "I have enjoyed our chat, for you have made me talk of cherished memories, and they are, along with my family, all I have left."

KAMMERSÄNGERIN
ELISABETH GRÜMMER

Anyone who has heard Elisabeth Grümmer sing "Selig, wie die Sonne meines Glückes lacht"—the opening passage of the *Meistersinger* quintet— or "Einsam in trüben Tagen" and "Euch Lüften die mein Klagen" in *Lohengrin* cannot have forgotten how the lovely voice, both ethereal and vibrant, soared effortlessly and made this Wagnerian music an unforgettable, exalting experience. No one else, in many critics' estimation, has ever attained so delicate a spirituality and at the same time so romantic an approach as this soprano, who for thirty years was considered the greatest Eva and Elsa of her time.

We met in Paris in the fall of 1978, in one of the rehearsal studios on the sixth floor of the Opéra-Comique, where she was then engaged as a teacher. During our talk, which lasted two and a half hours, I quickly realized that this exceptional interpreter of a certain repertoire—she always knew what suited her, and never budged from it—though she would have succeeded in anything else she might have undertaken.

So warm is her personality, so sensible her point of view, so serene her outlook, and so well-balanced her attitude toward life, that one feels privileged to be in her presence. Smallness, pettiness, pride, and jealousy do not appear to exist in her makeup, and one realizes how absolutely exceptional her talent must have been for her to achieve the position she held for three decades without resorting to intrigues of any sort. Her colleagues had spoken to me about how she remained a total stranger to the machinations that went on in the various opera houses. In a curious way, as our talk developed, I came to realize that it was undoubtedly her philosophy of life that she could not escape her fate.

"Nothing that happened to me," she told me with a warm, luminous smile, "ever seemed to be in the cards, and yet, of course, it all was. But everything always came to me in a roundabout way, never directly. My maiden name was Schilz, and I was born in Alsace-Lorraine in 1911. If I had been born a few years later, I would have been French, but, again, destiny

Elisabeth Grümmer as Elisabeth in *Tannhäuser*.

willed it that at the end of my life I should end up in France. As a child, my family moved to Meiningen in Thuringia—my father was transferred there for his job—and it used to be one of the most charming towns in the world. It was tremendously theatrically minded, and even every school had its own theatre, and amateur performances went on all the time. So I became continually involved with them. I also began to study the piano, not because I was particularly attracted to it, but because it was my parents' wish. They thought—and how right they were, as it turned out later—that it was an important part of one's upbringing.

"That I had a pretty voice," she continued, totally relaxed, "soon became evident, because I would be asked to sing more and more often at amateur affairs. One day a girl friend of mine and I were asked to prepare a song-and-dance act in rococo costumes and white wigs for an officers' ball, and my parents had no reason to object, but on the contrary were rather proud that out of so many girls at school I had been chosen. It so happened that the director of the local state theatre came to the ball; and after our number, which was warmly applauded, he came up to me, introduced himself, and asked me if I wanted to become an actress. I thought he was joking and pulling my leg. I refused point blank, but he insisted and said, 'Should you ever change your mind, my offer remains open, and all you have to do is come and see me.'

"I did not give it another thought until three months later. My father, who was employed at a motorcycle factory, was moved to another city, and I could not bear the thought of leaving Meiningen, where I had so many interests and friends—including a little romance. So I recalled the proposal made to me, and I went to see the Herr Direktor. He had not changed his mind and offered me a three-year contract, which had to be signed by my father as I was a minor. And so I began, to my amazement, with fairly important assignments.

"My parents did not believe that I would continue, for I did not appear to have any real ambition. But instead I stayed on. What kept amazing me was my lack of fear. I just walked out before the audience and delivered my lines; not a trace of anxiety. I was immensely fortunate to play opposite some great actors, such as Max Grube, and it has always been my conviction that other people's greatness does rub off on one's own shoulders. Much later, in fact, when I became an established singer, what interested me most was to know who would be appearing along with me, for you give your best when you are with the best. Whenever it was necessary for an actress to sing because the assignment demanded it, I was always given the part, and I began to realize—for some of the music allotted to me was far from easy—that my voice was naturally placed.

"But after some years my life took another turn. One afternoon, as I left a rehearsal, I walked by the Symphony Hall, where they too were rehearsing, and it was the Beethoven Violin Concerto. Somehow the sound coming out of the instrument of the violin soloist enthralled me, and I slipped into the hall and sat down, drinking in the music like nectar. I learned that it was Grümmer, the first violinist of the orchestra. But I was shy, did not go to congratulate him, and left as silently as I had come in. However, it was meant that destiny should bring us together very soon afterward. I met him at a party a few days later, and we fell desperately in love. Marriage followed, and almost immediately he was offered the post of kapellmeister in the opera house in Aachen, which at that time had Karajan as a conductor. The offer was too tempting, and he accepted. So I gave up my job, followed him, settled in Aachen, and had a daughter.

"I never gave the theatre another thought, and music instead became part of the household. I got more and more interested in singing, so I began taking lessons, but never with the idea of a career. I sang for my own pleasure, and occasionally for friends. So unselfconscious was I, with no fear or nervousness, that one night when Karajan was at a dinner we were attending, I was asked to sing and did. I recall, he did not compliment me, but I was not in the least offended, for I attached so little importance to what for me was simply a pleasure. But some weeks later I answered the telephone and it was the maestro. I naturally thought he wanted to speak to my husband, so after greeting Karajan, I said I was sorry that he was out and would have him call upon his return.

" 'But it is to *you* I want to speak,' he said. 'I shall explain in a minute the favor you must do me. The first performance of *Parsifal* is on Good Friday'—as I can so well remember, it was less than a week away—'and I am very dissatisfied with one of the Flower Maidens. Will you oblige me, come right over, and take it on?' I was absolutely thunderstruck, and realized I could not say no, since my husband was so deeply involved with him. But I had heard *Parsifal* many times and knew how tricky that scene was, with one Maiden coming in after the other, all a question of split seconds, in many ways far more complicated than taking on a leading assignment. I was not afraid for myself, but for my husband if I was not equal to the task. It would have created a difficult situation. My husband thought it all very funny when he came home, but I did not.

"Anyhow, I rehearsed and rehearsed," she recalled, laughing, "and I must say that even in those early days, Karajan had a wonderful and easy beat. You must realize that I had never been on any operatic stage before and I was really being thrown to the wolves, floating around in those somewhat ridiculous veils. Somehow I lived through the experiment, and the dissatisfaction of the maestro with that particular soprano again entirely changed the course of my life. And the die was cast. Again, I don't recall Karajan complimenting me or even thanking me. But that is not his style.

"If I was stunned by his first telephone call, I was even more so by the second one, when he asked me to appear in *Der Wildschütz,* as Alice in *Falstaff,* and as Octavian in *Der Rosenkavalier.* My husband again was highly amused and told me I could not refuse. Believe it or not, as I learned later, my being given Octavian was entirely due to my legs, because Karajan always had a great sense of the character looking just right, and he felt that my legs, in knee breeches, would fit correctly into the picture. Little did he realize that this would be, for many years, a staple of my repertoire, for along with the Marschallin, which I took on later, it was one of the roles I was called upon to sing everywhere. As we all know, Octavian is an ambiguous role, not only the libretto, but vocally, for it can be sung by both sopranos and mezzos. It never goes very high and remains a lot of time in the middle. But I never had difficulties with it, for I simply refused to darken my voice to suit its needs.

"Actually, when eventually, many years later, I was offered the Marschallin to sing, I accepted, for I knew I was ready for it, but I never went back to Octavian. There are many artists—Lisa della Casa was one of them and did them both superbly—who went from one to the other. But I simply could not. Before taking on the Marschallin, I stopped singing Octavian for eighteen months, as I felt I needed to get as far away from it as I could. I had to study the opera all over again, with a different outlook, sensitivity, and maturity. I had to get Octavian out of my system, and it was very difficult, for he was deeply ingrained within me.

"In those days Karajan was married to Elmy Holgerlöf, his first wife, and I have only the fondest memories of her. What a superb artist she was in her repertoire, which was operetta. Very few have ever equaled her, for she had grace, style, and musicality. I can never forget Karajan, although in recent years I have seen little of him, for he was really responsible for my career. Without him I would have just remained the wife of a violinist. But, again, fate sometimes is kind, or at least, when you look at it from a detached point of view, tries to replace what has been lost forever.

"Actually, my husband, who was happy at my success, taught me a lesson that I believe is responsible for my being able to sing as well and long as I did. He always said that the reason so many singers' careers went astray was the lack of continuation of study. And I never stopped until the end, not only vocalizing every day but taking lessons with the best teachers who were available. There is a lot you can do yourself, but no matter how strong the discipline, there must be someone else who follows and hears what sometimes you do not. It is like having your checkups with good doctors. You can never have enough of them. Voices have a way of taking on bad habits, and if these are not caught in time, then it can become too late.

"Anyhow, Duisburg came along and offered me an advantageous contract, and as Aachen was not far away, I accepted, but also continued to sing in what had become our hometown. In the meantime the ghastly war had come upon us, and it was in 1943, when I was appearing with the Duisburg Opera in Dresden, that I received a telegram from Aachen informing me that our house had been completely destroyed. This grisly message did not mention my husband, who had not signed it. This gave me a terrible jolt. A few hours later, as I was preparing to go home—the company had immediately granted me leave—another telegram followed: my husband's body had been found buried under the debris.

"It is difficult, even after all these years, to describe what one feels when one realizes one's entire world has gone forever. I still had my daughter—thank God, she was visiting her grandparents at the time—and it is she who saved me from going crazy. I had to continue because of her; there was no other way out. Needless to say, all we owned had been destroyed, and now I had to earn a living to keep us both alive.

"Somehow, after the funeral I staggered back to Dresden to finish my performances. And there, in that delicious rococo opera house—perhaps the most beautiful the world has ever known—not long before it was destroyed forever by Allied bombs, we gave a performance of Der Rosenkavalier that will remain in my memory as the definitive one. I cannot begin to tell you what marvelous acoustics that theatre had, and what an incomparable Marschallin Margarete Teschemacher was, and how enchanting Maria Cebotari was as Sophie. They were both to die, unhappily, very young. And Kurt Böhme was the best Ochs ever.

"I threw myself into my work," she said firmly, "for I knew it was my only salvation, and there is no doubt in my mind that the terrible experiences I had lived through had an effect on my voice. At least I was told by so many people that it had become more mellow and introspective. After Duisburg, I was hired by the Berlin Städtische Oper [later the Deutsche

Oper] when it reopened in 1946, and there I stayed twenty-five years, until 1971, when I thought the time had come for me to retire. I was then sixty, and until the end I went on singing leading roles, for my instrument was really unimpaired. What was the cause of this, I am not quite sure. The fact that I began late certainly had something to do with it, for it saved me the wear and tear of the first years. But I think that always keeping in vocal shape, never allowing one moment of distraction or taking anything for granted, had a lot to do with it, along with the fact that I never allowed myself to overbook my calendar. I was also very firm with managers, Intendants, and conductors, and never took on scores that I thought might be unsuited to my voice.

"I sang a great deal of Mozart, and this, I believe, is a singer's salvation, for it helps one to stay on the right path. The Countess in *Le nozze di Figaro* is the role I sang the most often, along with Eva and Elsa, but Pamina, Fiordiligi, both Ilia and Elettra in *Idomeneo,* and also Susanna were daily fare. I took on Donna Anna often and sang it, along with several other operas, at the Salzburg Festival for several years. It is, in my opinion, essentially a lyric role, despite the fact that for so many years dramatic sopranos had the habit of undertaking it. Now, of course, this breed does not seem to exist anymore. Anyhow, with the exception of 'Or sai chi l'onore,' which demands some dramatic effects, Anna requires a lot of agility, and it suited me. Even Elettra in *Idomeneo* is in the lyric range. Certainly, it requires more volume than Ilia, and dramatic expression, but if you look at the score well, there is no demand for a dark-colored or heavy voice.

"Agathe in *Freischütz* also became very much identified with me, for I had the long, sustained breaths for 'Leise, leise,' one of the most beautiful arias ever conceived. Eva introduced me for the first time outside Germany, at Covent Garden in 1951, under Sir Thomas Beecham, who was a first-rate conductor. He had a particular sensitivity with singers. Actually, with the exception of Toscanini and Bruno Walter, I sang with all the top conductors, and in my estimation, on an operatic level, the most satisfactory was Erich Kleiber. One felt not only inspired by him, but protected. He was never concerned with himself, the way so many are today, but tried incessantly to make one give the best of oneself.

"When I first began my career, the competition was tremendous, for there were still many superb singers around. But I soon discovered that there is always room for another one, provided she has solid qualities to offer. Mercifully, I never had to fight my way to the top. It just came naturally.

I never went after any opera house or performance, for this type of aggressiveness simply is not in harmony with my character. I was not a Verdian soprano, although both Desdemona and Alice suited me very well, and I sang them often. But I did not have the necessary bite in my voice for his other heroines. I also kept away from Puccini, for my voice did not have the sensuous quality his operas demanded, with the exception of Mimi, which I was called upon to perform often. I was tempted by *Madama Butterfly,* but having been an actress, I was very conscious of the importance of the physical identification with a part, and I knew I was too tall for the ex-geisha. I appeared many times as Elisabeth, which with Elsa and Eva seemed to have been written for me. But I never went near Sieglinde, despite many entreaties. It simply did not suit me. I also kept away from many of the Strauss operas, for I thought them dangerous for my instrument. But the Countess in *Capriccio* was perfect for me, and I had a particular affinity with both its music and text. This opera is not for everyone, but for an elite, and must be given in a small theatre where every word can come over the footlights.

"From Berlin I branched out, and I believe I sang in all the most important theatres in the world—including the Metropolitan, which came very late in my career. I was often at the Bayreuth Festival too, and also at Glyndebourne. I recorded many operas, but is one ever satisfied with one's performance when faced with it there in the playback? One of the most curious is the *Hänsel und Gretel* I recorded with Elisabeth Schwarzkopf and in which I took on the part of the boy. I think that our voices blended quite well together.

"I was fortunate to begin my career when ensembles still existed. Now they have been destroyed, and of course this is one of the most obvious illnesses that affect the lyric theatre everywhere. The conception of casting has also totally changed. Singing a role does not mean doing well by it. And this is another obstacle to the way opera is conceived today. Of course every prima donna prefers to sing Carmen and Leonore in *Fidelio* to Micaëla and Marzelline, for they are more interesting and arresting. But one must have the necessary goods at one's disposal. I was asked repeatedly to take on Leonore, but I always stuck to Marzelline, for I knew that this was where I belonged. And I sang many, many Micaëlas, as it would have been absurd for me to tackle the gypsy. Of course, if you have a good technique, you can sing almost everything—but can you do real justice to what the composer had in mind? This is the point every artist seems to forget today. It is the dimension that the role requires that a singer must keep in mind. I knew I could have sung Brünnhilde in *Siegfried,* for it is fairly short, and I had the high notes that are so important in the scene of her awakening. My voice, despite its purity, could ride easily over any orchestra, but it simply did not have the heroic ring that Wotan's daughter must have.

"Conductors are very responsible today for the miscasting, as they simply don't care about what happens to voices anymore, and singers no longer have the musical education and good sense to know where they belong. I recall Leo Blech insisting that I sing Salome and getting so cross with me for refusing him that he did not speak to me for one year. I would never sing Arabella either, as much as I loved her, for the scoring is very heavy. One hears sopranos today say that Eva and Elsa, for instance, are bores. I simply cannot believe my ears. Have they not read the beautiful texts? How can they be so indifferent to the immense poetry with which these heroines are imbued?"

I asked her whom she admired the most of all the women singers she had heard in her lifetime. "Tiana Lemnitz was one of them," she replied, "and what I considered the greatest compliment after performances of *Die Zauber-flöte* was when people would say that I reminded them of her, for her Pamina was out of this world. Erna Berger was one of the greatest techni-cians I ever came across, and Frida Leider moved me perhaps more than anyone else. Schwarzkopf, before she became so mannered, was a tremen-dous artist. For five seasons in Salzburg she sang Elvira to my Anna in *Don Giovanni,* and it is one of the most complete impersonations of a role I have ever met with. She *was* Elvira, that's all. What greater compliment can one give an artist? And Furtwängler, who conducted us, was of the same opinion.

"It is difficult, perhaps impossible, to judge singers today. Eventually, perhaps sooner than we think, it will become evident that they are destroy-ing themselves. And then there will have to be a very complete reversal.

"I have been teaching now ever since my retirement, for I feel it is my duty to pass on whatever I know. I give courses in Lucerne in the summer, and now here in Paris. My problem is that, incredibly enough, I do not speak French! But it is never too late to learn. That has always been my attitude and always will be. And I try to tell my students—of course there is always an interpreter—that they must take a lot of time off to themselves, learn to think and feel. For I am convinced that talent is formed in silence."

THE GREAT CREATORS

GILDA DALLA RIZZA

VIORICA URSULEAC

DENISE DUVAL

Although many of the prima donnas whose conversations appear in this volume created a number of contemporary works, the three most important, in my opinion, were Gilda dalla Rizza, Viorica Ursuleac, and Denise Duval. The first one's name will forever be linked with Puccini, Mascagni, and Zandonai; the second's with Richard Strauss; and the third's with Francis Poulenc.

My interview with dalla Rizza was not as protracted as I would have liked, because of the already very precarious condition of her health, which she faced with such gallantry and which was to lead a short time later to her death. But the other two generously gave me several hours each.

They could not have been more different: dalla Rizza, an Italian, was passionate in her opinions and immensely preoccupied with the decline of what had been her profession. Ursuleac, a Rumanian, revealed a certain detachment and a delightful form of almost black humor. Duval, a French-woman, was far more of a *femme du monde;* she would have been totally at ease even in a different type of background and created a very sophisticated atmosphere around her, answering my questions with keen perception.

GILDA DALLA RIZZA

In April 1975, in Room 7 at the infirmary of Milan's Casa Verdi, the celebrated home for aged and retired musicians, Gilda dalla Rizza—aged eighty-three—was convalescing from a broken hip. She sat propped up on her bed in a pale-blue woolen *liseuse,* her widely spaced eyes flashing with temperament and humor, and her white hair immaculately groomed. Here was the legendary soprano whom Puccini chose for the world premiere of *La rondine* and the European premiere of *Suor Angelica* and *Gianni Schicchi.* For Mascagni she created *Il piccolo Marat;* for Zandonai, *Giulietta e Romeo;* for Vittadini, *Anima allegra*—and the list goes on and on. Puccini never ceased declaring not only that she was the greatest of Minnies, but that she had a special way of infusing magic into all his operas. Zandonai considered her the finest of all Francescas, and Giordano was equally enthusiastic about the way she interpreted Fedora and Maddalena in *Andrea Chenier.*

"I am a relic of another age," she said in a strong, resonant voice, "and my world is dead and buried. I deplore the conditions surrounding the lyric theatre, and I am convinced every opera house will have to close down for a while and make a fresh start. The theatre has become a temple full of revolting merchants, and this is in strict contradiction to the artistic ideals it represents. All the theatres are in deep financial trouble everywhere, and worst of all in Italy, where the interest on the debts is piling up into tens of billions. But how can they meet the demands of the unions?

"Take La Scala. The opera season lasts only six months, and there are three, at most four, performances a week, but the chorus members receive six hundred thousand lire a month [approximately $800] year round, the orchestra players exactly double that, and the stagehands at least a million and a half. Still they want more. One strike after the other, and productions are continually delayed, some canceled. Don't tell me these people love opera. They are doing their best to kill it off.

"I went to a dress rehearsal not long ago, and while the unfortunate mezzo-soprano was in the middle of an aria the conductor stopped and the

Gilda dalla Rizza in the title role of *Francesca da Rimini*.

orchestra walked out. 'What is happening?' I asked, not believing my eyes. 'Every hour they have the right to a twenty-minute break,' they answered me. Is that art, I ask you? When Toscanini conducted at Bayreuth he refused to accept payment, because he declared it would desecrate the memory of Wagner. And when he was music director at La Scala he insisted that they subtract from his salary the equivalent of the days he spent away from Milan. Now that is dedication to art, as I knew it and practiced it myself. We never spoke of singers, only of artists. Today there are only singers, no more artists. They all have villas in Switzerland and Swiss bank accounts. They will sing anywhere and anything for a good fee. You will not find the great names of today in thirty years' time here at the Casa Verdi, where I and many distinguished colleagues live quietly, for we cannot afford anything else. These people sell their voices the way a salesman sells shirts or ties.

"In my day," she continued, "we gave everything of ourselves for art's sake, because we believed in what we were doing. Puccini could ask me to go anywhere to sing for him at a low fee, and I would accept. There are great voices today, to be sure—some just as great as, perhaps even greater than in my own time. But they give nothing of themselves. I often ask myself, What have they done with their heart? Were they born without it? How can one sing so beautifully such divine music and put nothing into it? Then I reason with myself and know the answer: These singers are living in a different world, where there are no more ideals, where patriotism is laughed at, where family ties have disintegrated, and passion no longer exists."

She paused for a moment and added, "I should make an exception— Magda Olivero. I don't know how old she is, but she is well over sixty. It does not matter. She is the only one I would walk a long distance in the cold and rain to hear today. We will not speak of the voice—it is what it is—but this woman knows what art is all about. I was so moved by her Adriana that I thought, God has helped Magda keep going so people can still know what it was like when singing was art.

"There used to be many artists I would walk in the cold and the rain to hear," she continued with enthusiasm. "Caruso, with whom I sang many times, not only had heartbreak in his voice, but his emotional impact on his colleagues was shattering. Goodness, how many wonderful tenors I sang with! Hipolito Lazaro in *Il piccolo Marat* was a volcano of fire and passion. And Schipetta—Tito Schipa—his voice was pure gold. And Gigli, Aureliano Pertile, Antonio Paoli—his Otello was extraordinary. I could go on and on. Chaliapin, with whom I sang *Mefistofele* in Genoa, was an animal of such magnetic power that shivers went down the spine of the whole audience. Titta Ruffo was also unique. Toti dal Monte's mad scene in *Lucia* left one numb—it was no bird singing, but an agonizing, beautiful experience. Giuseppina Cobelli's Katiusha in *Risurrezione,* Fiora in *L'amore dei tre re,* and Eboli, just to mention a few of her magical performances, were all heartbreaking. Claudia Muzio had a fragility in her voice, despite its strength, that was ever so deeply moving. Giulia Tess's Salome was so extraordinary that when Richard Strauss asked me to sing it I refused. I knew I could never equal her, and I decided at the very beginning of my career that I would never be second, only on a par. But with Strauss I did sing Octavian, a role that turned up many times in my life, and Arabella. The latter I had to take over from a German soprano in Genoa. She got ill, and I had ten days to prepare it. Singing with Strauss was a real privilege. He was so calm, collected, and gentle. He did not appear to fall off the podium when he conducted his own music, the way so many do today. He knew what he was doing, and even the very tricky *Arabella* seemed easy under his expert hands.

"Now you want to know something about me," she went on as I prodded her with questions. "It's really not very interesting. I was fortunate all the way. I had a voice that could fit in so many different types of scores, and though I am not very good at mathematics, I think I sang eighty-eight roles. My career was fabulous, and I had a happy personal life with my husband, Tino Capuzzo, a very gifted tenor, who scored heavily in the Mascagni operas then very much performed. We fell in love while singing *Francesca da Rimini* in Trieste, and instead of the five planned performances there were fifteen: people in the audience knew right away those love scenes were for real. I never fell out of love with him, and when he died much of the flavor of life went with him.

"I was born in Verona, and after a big success in school delivering a song at the age of eleven I knew I wanted to be an opera singer. I was finishing my studies in Bologna—I was exactly twenty—when the impresario of the Teatro Verdi turned up one day in my teacher's studio. He could not find the right person to sing Charlotte in *Werther,* a role that lies a little low for sopranos and a little high for mezzos. He heard me and insisted I prepare the part. I had to learn it in a hurry, and with the courage of youth I went on. It was a success, and engagements kept pouring in for the next thirty years nonstop. Before I knew it I was engaged for *La forza del destino* in Alessandria, Mascagni's *Isabeau* and Puccini's *Fanciulla* in Florence. I never considered myself a dramatic soprano, yet I was eminently successful in dramatic verismo roles. I learned how to use my instrument so as never to force it, and to utilize what we Italians call *l'accento* instead of resorting to chest tones."

I asked why verismo operas have gone out of the repertoire.

"Simply because there are no artists today who can perform them," she replied. "There are some magical operas in that group, but you require passion, heart, and imagination to put them over. You need great personalities. Where are they?

"Puccini heard me early in my career, and I became his 'Gildina.' He considered my voice suitable for all his operas, and if I had not been very firm I would have sung only his works. I sang them all, including the title role of *Turandot*—at the opera house in Monte Carlo, for it is a small jewel, and I knew that there I would not have to force. My relationship with him was marvelous, and I have so many wonderful letters from him. He chose me for the world premiere of *La rondine* in Monte Carlo in 1917, with Schipa in the tenor role, and I have never known an opera to have so much in its favor and to have had such bad luck in later years. While I was singing in Europe and South America, and Bori in the United States, it was performed quite often, but then there were some poor performances, with the wrong assumption on the part of opera houses that it was more an operetta than a real opera. Nothing could be further from the truth. Magda is a most difficult assignment, for it is very light at moments, very intense and emotional at others. I loved it all the way.

"Puccini not only insisted that I create *Suor Angelica* at the European premiere of *Il trittico* in Rome in 1918, but also that I sing Lauretta in *Gianni Schicchi*. 'That is impossible, Maestro,' I replied. 'How can I, with just a few minutes' intermission, go from the agonizing tragedy of the nun to the gaiety of the Florentine girl?' 'You can do anything,' he stated, with terrifying finality, 'and you will do it for me.' I adored him and therefore accepted this considerable challenge. I went on singing *Suor Angelica* until the very end; my last appearance before the public, in 1942, was in this opera, exactly thirty years after my debut in Bologna. All of his operas (with the exception of *Turandot*, which I sang only once, on a special occasion) were to be part of my yearly fare, and *Butterfly* is the one I sang most often. There are letters from 1921, when Puccini was composing *Turandot*, that attest to the fact that he wanted me as Liù. But he ended up writing the role for a lyric, and my voice was too heavy by the time the opera received its world premiere in 1926.

"It was very stupid of me not to have written down all of Puccini's instructions about how he wanted his heroines to be interpreted, and now it is too late. He had very definite ideas about all of them. He gave great importance to the first appearance of the heroine in an opera. In fact, so much did he ingrain in me of this very intelligent and wise approach that I ended by following it, after much reflection, in all my other operas. If one is a good actress, *Fanciulla* is the easiest, for she enters while there is a row among the miners and separates them before she begins singing. So she can project the type of young woman she is: determined and accepting no nonsense. The maestro used to tell me that her femininity must develop slowly during the first act and really comes to the fore when she dances for the first time. He considered Butterfly's entrance the most difficult of all. She has to be heard always a little more strongly as she approaches the bridge, unseen, and there is a passage which he considered essential to the understanding of the entire opera. How many times we went over it! It goes 'Al richiamo d'amor, d'amor venni alle soglie ove s'accoglie il bene di chi vive e chi muor' [At the call of love, I have come to the portals of love where is gathered the happiness of those who live and those who die]. He wanted that phrase to stand out in particular, in the midst of all the rejoicing, for in it is the key to the impending tragedy. Of course, he was right. It took much time and patience—the voice must suddenly change color when the 'di chi vive' is pronounced and then darken very gently and melancholically for the 'e chi muor.' The overwhelming obstacle here is that Cio-Cio-San is still unseen. As for *Tosca*, again, when she is first heard, offstage, he wanted the first two 'Mario's to sound natural, since he kept repeating to me that she is a religious woman and would not shout in church. Then the other three 'Mario's—very hard to put over—he wanted more impatient, but not hysterical, as so many sopranos make her sound.

"In *Manon Lescaut*, when she answers des Grieux's question as to who she is—'Manon Lescaut mi chiamo'—her voice, heard for the first time, must not sound too demure. In Puccini's opinion, it is really false modesty, and one must etch her character right away with the manner in which she introduces herself. 'Sound girlish but firm,' he used to tell me. When we were rehearsing in Rome for the European premiere of *Gianni Schicchi*, what he demanded of me was logical but so difficult to put over. After coming in and standing silent for a while, Lauretta must quickly establish her character in the midst of the confusion, with the members of Buoso Donati's family running around. She is no coy or modest well-brought-up Florentine girl, but a determined young woman. Her first phrase— 'Rinuccio, non lasciarmi'—Puccini wanted fairly loud so that it would be heard distinctly over the din of the action, but not overly so. To find just the right volume caused me much worry. 'You must let them know that you know what you want with that first sentence,' Puccini kept saying.

"My debut at La Scala was in 1916, in *Andrea Chenier,* right in the midst of the First World War, and this was followed immediately by *Isabeau.* In both operas my tenor was Edward Johnson—or Eduardo di Giovanni, as he was called in Italy. He was to be my Rinuccio in the first *Schicchi* in Rome and again in Mascagni's terrifying *Parisina* at the Costanzi, when Lina Pasini-Vitale gave out and Emma Carelli pushed me into this opera with twenty-four hours' notice. I had heard two performances of it and thought it a masterpiece. This was in 1914, when the opera was being given for the first time in the Italian capital immediately following its triumph in Milan, where twelve performances had been given instead of four, establishing Tina Poli-Randaccio as one of the major singing actresses of the century. The kindness and camaraderie of Johnson will never be forgotten, for if I came through it, much of the credit is his. What is infernal about this superb score is that the first two acts lie in the center of the voice, and then in the third the tessitura goes very high. I also had Maestro Edoardo Vitale trying to sabotage me, for he was furious at Carelli for not postponing the performance, being very much infatuated with his wife. I can only call it the rash daring of youth.

"Because of the war and then postwar conditions, La Scala remained closed for five years. When I returned there, Toscanini chose me, to my great surprise, to sing *La traviata.* I was scared to death, but I accepted the challenge. It will make me or break me, I thought. All my colleagues were there that night of November 28, 1923, with their guns pointed at me. 'Gildina is marvelous in verismo roles,' they were all saying, 'but how can she possibly tackle the first act? She is absolutely reckless.' But what they did not know was that ever since my debut in 1912, I had kept up my agility with daily scales. I escaladed Everest with no trouble, and it was a huge surprise to everyone. We did fourteen performances—a very large number in those days—and Violetta became a role deeply identified with me. That I was able to lighten my voice kept amazing people. And yet I always was very successful as Suzel in *L'amico Fritz* and as Massenet's *Manon.*

"The following year Toscanini asked me to appear as Alice in *Falstaff* and Louise. At rehearsals of the Charpentier opera I nearly died of fright. He took 'Depuis le jour,' already very tough because of the endless legatos, so slowly that I kept wondering whether my voice would give out. I could not understand it, for the maestro usually had the opposite tendency—to

hurry tempos and go quite fast. But when I performed it I realized why
he was doing this. All hell would break loose after this aria, and there was
always an interruption of several minutes of thunderous applause. The effect
of this aria was stunning, for this slow, rapturous cry of love underlined an
enchanted dream on the top of Montmartre after all the confusion of the
city."

"Did you ever sing Wagner?" I asked.

"Yes, but none of his roles interested me from a dramatic point of view,
and the vocal aspects of a role were never quite enough for me. The Wagner
heroines have to stand around for hours doing nothing. I did sing Elsa,
because Gigli insisted I appear with him, and he sang Lohengrin like a god.
I also agreed to do Eva in *Die Meistersinger,* because I fell in love with the
quintet, but after that caprice was satisfied I dropped her, because she is a
nice but dull girl. That's why I always refused to do Micaëla, another insipid
character. Carmen was more tempting, but Gabriella Besanzoni was around
in those days, and no one could equal the velvet in her voice and the verve
of her personality.

"I often sang with Mascagni, who was a remarkable conductor, apart
from being in my opinion a great composer. I sang all his operas, including
Iris. I even took on Santuzza, but not for long. Again I felt I was not on
the same level in this role as Lina Bruna Rasa, who was so much more suited
to the wretched Sicilian girl than I was. In the French repertory I loved
Thaïs, and *La Damnation de Faust,* and I immensely enjoyed singing Falla's
La vida breve and Granados's *Goyescas.* But of all the roles I undertook the
one closest to me was Francesca da Rimini. I loved it because of the very
romantic libretto: the words of d'Annunzio are simply divine, and how right
the music is in underlining every nuance and thought! Then the part gave
me great satisfaction on an acting level. I loved the other Zandonai works
too, particularly *Giulietta e Romeo.* What a delightful man he was—how
considerate when he conducted!

"Conductors nowadays want to dominate everything. They have enlarged the orchestras; they insist on a spotlight on themselves and do their
best to drown out the voices. And thank goodness we did not have stage
directors in my day like those of today, who impose on the singers how
they must act and move! It was all so much more personal and real. We
all had to figure out what was right for us, and that is how the personality
was born. We had our own costumes—very expensive, you know—and
perhaps that is why we are all in the poorhouse. But I developed my own
style. I knew what colors were becoming, what wigs did well by me and

what suited me. With all the admiration I had for Muzio and Gina Cigna, what was right for them would have been wrong for me. Now it is all a factory. Like animals in a circus, they all must obey the whims of directors —often so untalented, not even very knowledgeable about the libretto and the score—and of the costume maker, who lies awake nights thinking up ways to make the singers look ridiculous. The composer and librettist left every indication as to how they wanted the operas performed, and the one who is now the most betrayed is Wagner.

"I spent part of every year appearing in South America, in Buenos Aires, Rosario, Santa Fé, Santiago, São Paulo, and Rio de Janeiro. All the top casts and conductors assembled there. In Italy every small provincial town had the best season possible, with all the stars, and we were happy to appear there. There were no bankrupt theatres, but then we did it *con amore,* all of us— chorus, orchestra, stagehands. The winter season in Monte Carlo was superb, and we did many interesting things there.

"After I retired, for many years I gave classes in Venice at the conservatory. Interesting, but so disheartening. No discipline, you know—no dedication. After a little while friends of the pupils say 'Brava, brava!' and off they go, convinced it is that easy. It is a disaster of epic proportions."

A month later, on May 7, 1975, Gilda dalla Rizza closed her eyes forever.

KAMMERSÄNGERIN VIORICA URSULEAC

In many ways, Viorica Ursuleac is the most legendary of all the former divas I interviewed; she became Richard Strauss's favorite soprano and created four of his operas. But it was particularly difficult to track her down; she now lives in a mountain village some miles outside Munich and has completely retired from the world. No, she did not want to talk about the past, she told me on the telephone; all she wanted was to be forgotten and live in close contact with nature. "I was born in 1894," she said, "so what has been has been, and let us forget the past."

But chance willed that in June 1979, while in Vienna, I heard that she was in town for a concert commemorating the twenty-fifth anniversary of the death of her husband, the conductor Clemens Krauss, who had died suddenly in 1954 while engaged in Mexico City. I was able to locate her in the hotel where she was staying and presented myself, unannounced, at nine o'clock in the morning. At the desk I was informed that she was having breakfast in the dining room, and I rushed there, calling out loudly, "Frau Kammersängerin Krauss!" An old lady made a sign and I went to introduce myself. Again the answer was negative, for the reasons she had explained on the telephone. I then knelt in front of her and told her that since she was so important a part of musical history, she had no right to refuse me. She burst out laughing and then, after a moment, she said, "No one has paid me such a gallant homage since I was a young girl. You win. Come back and meet me here tomorrow at eight in the morning. I am an early riser and have a full day." She had conquered me immediately. Despite the heat, she was dressed in a tweed suit, and with her snow-white hair, blue eyes of a vibrant hue, and irresistible smile, there was little trace of the celebrated prima donna who had dominated the Central European operatic world.

Naturally, the next day I was prompt for the rendezvous, fearing that it would be a brief encounter. But, as so often happens, once she began to open up—and with enormous frankness and charm—time came to a stop for both of us, and when I finally looked at my watch, it was twelve-thirty. "Goodness," she said, "I was counting on this morning to do some shopping!"

I had only heard her once, in Florence's Boboli Gardens in June 1938, as Sieglinde in *Die Walküre,* conducted by Karl Elmendorff, but I recalled that a very definite enchantment had emanated from her. "I loved this part," she told me, as I reminded her of this particular occàsion, "but unfortunately it did not come my way very often. As you probably know, it is not a role that requires a brilliant top, and this is what made my fame. Almost until the end I could hit a high D with facility."

Then, in meticulous detail, she described the unfolding of her musical life. "I was born in 1894 in Czernowitz, Bukovina, where both German and Rumanian were spoken, and I was one of six children. My father, a Greek Orthodox archdeacon, had a superb tenor instrument which he trained for years in order to impart vocal lessons to young priests. My mother too had a lovely voice, and I was brought up in a highly active musical home. Inevitably I was sent to Vienna, where I remained at the Academy for five years, to be trained for a singing career.

"I went to Zagreb to visit some friends, and one afternoon I was singing with the window open. The Intendant of the opera house happened to walk by, heard me, and was struck by the particular color of my instrument, which always had a very definite sound of its own. He inquired who I was, came to see me, and offered me a contract. After four weeks of rehearsals, I started out as Charlotte in *Werther,* and followed this assignment with Micaëla, Mimi, and Marie in *The Bartered Bride.* Then I had to learn some Croatian operas, but a Croatian doctor came into my life; I fell in love with him and got married. He would not hear of my continuing, and I dropped my career after the birth of a daughter. I soon realized that I had made a serious mistake, and in my letters to the family I told them of my unhappiness. My brother wrote me that our father was gravely ill and I must rush to his side. So, taking Naditza with me, I went to Czernowitz only to learn that it had all been a ruse to get me away, for my father was in perfect health. It sounds made up, but I assure you it is all true!

"Rudolph Bella, a friend of my parents' who was a very good composer and conductor, asked me shortly after my arrival to learn Brahms's Alto Rhapsody in forty-eight hours, since the contralto he had engaged was ill. All my protests were in vain. At that time I was a lyric, later turning into a spinto, and singing such a low score seemed madness to me. But my lower register was much stronger than I had reason to believe, and the success at this concert led to an engagement in the local opera house with a salary that was sufficient to buy a few postage stamps. I made my debut there as

Viorica Ursuleac as Marie in Richard Strauss's *Friedenstag*.

Eudoxie in *La Juive,* written for a leggero-coloratura, and then moved on to many roles, including Butterfly. It was then that in order to support myself and my child—I never went back to my husband, whom I later divorced—I began to give lieder recitals, which were always to continue to be part of my musical activity. When I became famous, I was lucky enough to have Clemens Krauss as my superb accompanist.

"The opera house in my native town had been run as a German one, but after the First World War Czernowitz became part of Rumania, so all the operas were given in Rumanian. I was engaged for a concert in Bucharest, attended by Marie, the beautiful and imaginative queen, and to my eternal shame, I fell asleep at the hotel, arriving at the Athénée concert hall half an hour late. I was greeted icily, and quite rightly so. How dare I, a nobody, keep Her Majesty waiting, always punctuality itself, and the public? I went out onto the stage in a terrible state of nerves, but, worse still, I noticed that the accompanist literally was trembling all over. Miracles do happen—or at least they did—for my first number, the exceedingly difficult 'Come scoglio' from *Così,* was applauded enthusiastically by the kind queen, who in the meantime had been informed of what had happened to me. The public naturally followed her, and the evening ended with Her Majesty inviting me to the palace the next day. She was not only one of the great beauties of her time, but her know-how with people was fantastic and her musical culture considerable. As I had become one of her subjects, she said, she was very interested in me and talked seriously about my having an international career.

"She wasted no time, and a short time later I was called to audition for Felix Weingartner, who at that time was musical director of the Vienna Volksoper. He accepted me, and in 1922 I began my activities there, first in smaller roles, and then graduating to Marguerite in *Faust,* Elsa, Elisabeth, Charlotte, and Butterfly. But my initial huge success came with *Louise,* which had never been previously performed in Vienna. It became the hit of the season. My Julien was the superb Rumanian tenor Trajan Grosavescu, who later made unfortunate international news when his wife—sick with jealousy because he did not want her to accompany him to Berlin, where he had to fulfill some engagements—shot him dead. A great loss to the operatic world! Clemens Krauss had left his post as assistant at the Vienna Staatsoper to take on the direction of the Frankfurt opera house and was looking for a soprano. Twice I was suggested to him for an audition and he refused to hear me, claiming he suffered a very strong allergy to artists who came from the Balkans—he said they were too temperamental and unreliable. But I would not be defeated, and with the connivance of others I sang for him under an assumed name.

"He did not get angry, as I feared, when I told him the truth, but was amused by the joke I had played on him. But then he was a wonderful human being, as I was to discover later, and little could I imagine then that I would someday become his wife. The old saying that when it rains it pours was experienced by me at that time. For just at the moment that he said he would sign me, the Nuremberg Opera came along and offered me almost double the salary he had proposed. But I considered the privilege of singing with him so great that I said to hell with the money. But that was the way we were then—artists, and not commercial robots. The contract with Frankfurt was for six years, and when Krauss returned to Vienna later I began doing many guest performances in Dresden, where Fritz Busch was the artistic director, and at the Vienna Staatsoper. In the latter theatre I went on the first time substituting for Lehmann in *Manon Lescaut*. It was during that period that everyone decided that I had the ideal voice for the Strauss scores, and I was assigned the Empress in *Die Frau ohne Schatten* and *Die ägyptische Helena*. I was later to create four of his operas. I have masses of letters from Richard Strauss with very specific indications as to how he wanted them performed, and they are the only treasure I have left. I sang all his works with the exception of *Intermezzo, Die schweigsame Frau,* and *Salome,* which I never felt was suited to my instrument. The Composer and then also Ariadne, the Marschallin, and Chrysothemis were part of my daily fare. Strauss was a very modest man in some ways. In connection with Chrysothemis, the first time he heard me in this role he came to my dressing room and said, 'Thank you for proving to me that I did not make any mistakes when writing this part. I have often been tormented by doubts, but the way you handle the parlando revealed to me that it can be done the way I wrote it. None of the others do.'

"*Arabella,* which I created in Dresden in 1933 with Krauss in the pit, and which we repeated with the same cast at Covent Garden the following year, has, in my estimation, one of the loveliest scores he ever conceived. If one has the extension and the floating top, it is not one of his most difficult operas to sing, nor is the Countess in *Capriccio,* which I created in Munich in 1942, again under Krauss's direction. The latter is a delicate, highly sophisticated, introspective work that is a masterpiece of understatement, and yet ever so profound, with witty dialogue. The libretto, written by Krauss, is as fine as any of those of von Hofmannsthal.

"But *Friedenstag,* which first saw the light in Munich in 1938, as ever with

Krauss conducting, and which Strauss dedicated to me, is a horse of a different color. The composer claimed there were twenty high Cs, but I never counted them. He always used to say that it was after conducting me —he had a very definite gift with the baton—as Chrysothemis that he had decided I was the only soprano who could tackle that fiendish tessitura. While I loved performing Elektra's gentle sister, who brings a little sunshine into the tremendous tragedy, I must confess that despite some stunning pages I was never really sold on *Friedenstag*. It is so difficult that in fact it is never given. In 1944 I sang in Salzburg at the dress rehearsal for an invited audience of *Die Liebe der Danae*—I can still recall that the date was August 14— which was scheduled to have its world premiere two days later. But war conditions became so ghastly within forty-eight hours that all theatres were closed by a government decree. It had to wait until 1952 to be given in public. It is not a stirring work, but it reminded me in some ways of some of the lyrical pages in *Ariadne,* and there are some very beautiful moments. It needs a very poetic staging, and again it has those high incandescent tones so typically Straussian.

"*Arabella* became the great favorite of Hitler, and he came to hear me sing it in Berlin ten times. He was Austrian, of course, and perhaps this eminently Viennese atmosphere made him somewhat nostalgic. I met him on several occasions, and cut down to life size, he was a strangely timid man in his contacts—at least with us artists. He never talked politics, but always asked questions about singing problems. I never was aware of Eva Braun at that time, and she never accompanied him to the opera house.

"The reason I went to the Berlin Staatsoper in 1934 with a ten-year contract, although I did make guest appearances in other leading theatres, was that, having obtained a fabulous success there as a guest, Furtwängler, who was then music director and whom I highly respected, offered me a wonderful contract. He was unsurpassed as an orchestral conductor, but in opera it was a different story. I never learned how to follow his baton one hundred percent. When I sang Chrysothemis with him for the first time, I was highly embarrassed by various errors that I made, but there was no time to apologize to him, for it was he who came to me, immediately after the curtain calls, to excuse himself. And he asked me as a favor to explain to him how Krauss, whom he greatly admired and was jealous of at the same time, dealt with certain passages. But what he did that night implied real humility and heart. For a man in his position to apologize revealed to me his greatness. He also conducted the Berlin premiere of *Arabella* for me. In Vienna, instead, it was Lotte Lehmann who sang the first performance."

Here I stopped her, for I had always been told that Lehmann had detested Ursuleac. To my surprise, she was perfectly willing to discuss this *cause célèbre*.

"I always loved Lehmann for her intensity and fire on the stage," she replied in a detached manner. "But, alas, it was not reciprocal. As I have a philosophical attitude, I never look back, and I forgive her for all the harm she caused me. I believe her hatred for me originated when I exploded on the Viennese horizon with my easy top register just when she was beginning to have a very difficult time with hers. One must remember that at that time, with Jeritza in the United States, she considered herself to be the undisputed queen, and in many ways she was.

"I will only speak briefly of all the miseries she subjected me to at the Salzburg Festival, where I was engaged for the Countess in *The Marriage of Figaro* and she for the Marschallin, which I was to sing later for a total of a hundred and fifty-two performances.

"At that time I had never sung *Der Rosenkavalier* and was asked to learn the role in a hurry, for Lehmann would not sing one of the performances scheduled. I forget now the reason, but it was a valid one. But when she learned that I was the one chosen to replace her, she changed her plans and insisted on being available that night so that I should not sing it. She started loathing me when Strauss began to single me out for certain assignments, as she considered him her personal property.

"But this is a trifle compared with the trouble she made for me on a political level. Göring heard Lehmann in Germany and was very impressed with her; and as he was anxious to make the Berlin Staatsoper the most important in Europe, he contacted her to offer her a highly lucrative engagement. She rushed to Berlin to discuss this with him, but made it a condition that Chrysothemis, Arabella, and Sieglinde be sung only by her. It so happened that my contract was already in operation and that among the roles assigned to me were those she asked for. I did not have exclusive rights to them, but they were on my list. She had a fit of hysteria when she heard this, walked out of his office, and returned to Vienna. From then on she did nothing but spread stories that I was a dedicated Nazi. Nothing could have been further from the truth. I never meddled in politics and minded my own business. That I was proud to be a member of the Berlin Staatsoper there is no doubt, but only because it was by far the finest ensemble in the world. Ask anyone and they will confirm this. She then left for the United States, and I remained to honor my contracts in Berlin and do guest performances in other cities.

"Lehmann had hated Jeritza too, and the stories of her rages in Vienna when the Hungarian soprano began to prove her talent are endless. But Jeritza was a different type of person—temperamental, yes, but never an *intriguante*. I was full of admiration for her too, and consider her Elisabeth in *Tannhäuser* unsurpassed. When she walked into the hall of song before beginning 'Dich teure Halle,' she was an unforgettable vision. I sang Sieglinde to her Brünnhilde and always found her very pleasant to work with. I remember that way back when I heard her at the very beginning as Micaëla, I sensed hers to be a great talent.

"Anyhow, the war came with all its horrors, and my homes and savings went up in smoke. Lehmann became a valiant anti-Nazi heroine, and I paid dearly for my lack of political judgment. But I was not the only one—I was in very good company!"

I asked her more questions about Strauss and his friendship with Clemens Krauss, who became her husband during the war. "Strauss heard him conduct the *Ring*," she explained, "in Frankfurt way back in the twenties, and realized what a fabulous conductor he was. They came to a complete understanding with the passing of time, and I think the reason is that while Strauss was a very introspective person, rather closed in on himself, Krauss understood his reticence and was able to draw him out. He was a passionate admirer of all his music and kept predicting that he would become one of the giants of all time. Somehow they formed a perfect team."

"And what about Frau Strauss?" I inquired.

"Her husband used to say that Pauline was always acting, and I believe he was right. She was a real character, and musically very prepared and on her toes. Few people remember that she had been an exquisite lieder singer, and had even made a big success singing in *Tannhäuser* at the Bayreuth Festival. She was very commercially minded, and we owe it to her that he kept turning out so many scores. Domineering and efficient, she had by far the stronger character of the two."

Had she herself ever sung at the Bayreuth Festival?

"Never, but in those days one could not be everywhere at once. Now they are ubiquitous, one night here and the next there. We stayed where we were. I always appeared at the Munich summer festival and for some years at the one in Salzburg. For my epoch I sang a lot, for I calculate roughly that in the thirty-five years of my career I sang over three thousand operatic performances, which averages, if I am not mistaken, about eighty-five per year—and this does not count all the recitals and concerts I participated in with the symphony orchestras.

"As the voice developed, my repertoire increased accordingly, and I was very strong in the Italian wing too. But in Italy, where I appeared often, I sang only the German operas. I recall a *Frau ohne Schatten* in Rome with Rose Pauly, a fantastic Dyer's Wife, in 1938—it was the first performance ever of this work, *una novità,* as the Italians called it, for the Eternal City —and we had a lot of trouble with it, for we had to relearn it in Italian, and Marinuzzi, a great conductor, fell ill. Strauss came for the premiere, and the next afternoon Pauly and I went for a walk on the old Appian Way to see the sights and enjoy the fresh air. Suddenly, to our astonishment, we saw Strauss seated on a crumbling wall, in total meditation. He looked transfigured by the beauty of the surroundings, but not to the extent of not seeing us. He got up, came toward us, and, pointing to two columns nearby, he opened his arms and embraced us, an unheard-of thing for him to do. 'The two of you are my saviors, solid as those pillars. You have achieved miracles.' I like to remember him the way he was on that glorious afternoon, on the eve of the terrible conflict that engulfed humanity.

"At La Scala, along with *Die Frau,* I also sang Fiordiligi, Chrysothemis, and Sieglinde on different occasions. I sang a lot of Mozart—the Countess, Donna Elvira, Pamina, and Fiordiligi—many Leonores in *Fidelio*—Leonora in *Forza del destino* over a hundred and fifty times, along with numerous *Otello*s and *Ballo*s, and of Puccini many Toscas and Minnies. Of the Wagnerian ladies the one I was called upon to sing the most frequently was Senta. Krauss had been assistant conductor in Vienna when Puccini went to prepare Jeritza for *Fanciulla del West,* and he is the one who taught me this wonderful part, remembering in detail all of Puccini's instructions. I found Tosca and Minnie more difficult dramatically than vocally, as the action never ceases and the tension mounts into a veritable frenzy. I even had Gigli as my Cavaradossi, and no one ever has caressed this part the way he did— or ever will. I insist on the word 'caress.' His was a heavenly instrument, incapable of producing one ugly note. Turandot I found difficult for the opposite reason, for there are long periods when she must be hieratic and stand practically still while pouring out a big volume of voice. Erna Berger often sang Liù with me, and she was exquisite, in some ways the most fragile and effective of the many I have heard in this part. I never undertook Aida or Santuzza, because I knew instinctively they were not suited to my vocal cords.

"After the war," she observed, "none of us were allowed to sing for a certain period of time—we were guilty of having sung during the Nazi regime. And then, finally, it did occur to the authorities that we had not had much choice to do otherwise! My career took off again on wings. My last performances in Vienna were in 1952, but my final performance came as the Marschallin the following year in Wiesbaden. I taught for a while, even at the Salzburg summer courses during the Festival, and prepared certain singers for their assignments. Now I just remain in my Alpine cottage and pursue a very friendly contact with different types of birds—much nicer, I assure you, than many human beings."

I inquired from her whether she ever attended the opera in Munich.

"No, no more," she concluded, her smile suddenly disappearing. "The last time I went was when they resurrected *Die ägyptische Helena,* for which I had a warm affection and, may I add, deep nostalgia. It was a shocking experience. The metteurs-en-scène want to change everything today, and I feel deeply sorry for them and the public. Their ignorance is so obvious, their pretensions so great. And the audience, which has not heard the operas as they really are, is cheated all along the line. It is a horrible travesty. I will not be here to see it, but eventually, if opera is to continue, there must be a violent reaction. It could never be too violent, in my humble opinion."

DENISE DUVAL

Denise Duval, born in 1921, sang for only twenty-two years, from 1943 until 1965; but in that span she won a unique position for herself as the supreme interpreter of Poulenc's three operas. She created both *Les Mamelles de Tirésias* and *La Voix humaine* and was Paris's first Blanche in *Les Dialogues des carmélites,* which she sang over two hundred times after the French premiere at the Opéra on June 21, 1957. She has not kept track of how often she sang the other two, but she thinks that she performed the one-act *La Voix humaine* to Cocteau's text—a forty-five-minute solo turn—well over three hundred times in the six years after its unveiling at the Opéra-Comique on February 6, 1959.

"Poulenc, like Wagner, wrote out his instructions very clearly," she declared to me during a visit I paid her in Paris in the fall of 1976, "and those who do not want to follow them are in deep trouble. For it is only by observing them very closely that one can do his operas the full justice they deserve. For *La Voix humaine* he states in the preface that the protagonist must be young and elegant, for this is not an aging woman who has been left by her lover. It is the interpretation of the text on the part of the singer upon which depends the length of the *points d'orgue* which are so important in this score. The conductor should discuss this in detail, in advance, with the singer. All the unaccompanied passages of singing are very free in tempo in function of the mise-en-scène. One must be able to go from a state of anguish to one of calmness and vice versa. The entire work must be bathed in a total orchestral sensuality.

"Even for *Les Dialogues,* whose libretto originates from the masterful play of Bernanos, despite the tremendous drama that develops and unfolds, Poulenc wanted restraint. For it is through this that inexorably one can reach the total sublimation of the 'Salve Regina' of the last act when the blade of the guillotine falls with harsh sounds which should not be all the same. Actually, when it is Blanche's turn, it is no longer the 'Salve Regina' that she intones, but the four last verses of the 'Veni Creator.' In the final 'in saeculorum'—she does not finish with the word, for the axe falls on her—the difficulty of singing Blanche is overwhelming, for it must remain within a total purity of line, almost a transparency, and one must be made of stone if one is not overcome by the emotion. This transparency already exists in the previous magnificent duet between Blanche and Constance when they discuss the meaning of death and its implications. How difficult it is to sing it the way Poulenc wanted, making it important and at the same time not overly so. It is the sort of scene the public must remember later, but not be particularly struck by while it is taking place. When Blanche sings 'La mort d'une autre?' there is the germ of what will happen at the end.

"Poulenc wanted the interludes that unite the various episodic scenes to sound full and symphonic, but he was so attached to the beautiful text that he wanted the orchestra to be ever so light, so every word sung could be heard. At one point he was so shocked to find the production had disintegrated in this respect that he withdrew it from the boards."

Blanche was the last role Miss Duval performed, at the Teatro Colón in Buenos Aires, having collapsed from an overdose of cortisone erroneously prescribed by her doctor. It almost killed her, and she was hospitalized for two years. "Despite many tempting offers," she declared, "I decided not to resume my career when I was finally cured. I suddenly realized that everything was changing at a terrific speed, that the seriousness I was used to in the musical world no longer existed. I knew I had had the best and couldn't see the point of facing a series of disappointments and mishaps."

As we talked, I noticed there was not a line on her wonderfully alert face. She is petite and svelte, her hair short and exquisitely groomed with a sort of rare elegance, yet very contemporary.

"Though I was born in Paris," she went on, "I left when I was two weeks old. My father was in the army, and I was whisked away to follow him and my mother to Indochina and Senegal before going on to China, where he commanded the French troops in Tientsim. Later, when he was stationed in Bordeaux, I studied both voice and acting at the conservatory there. At the end of my three-year course I won the first prize, and with it automatically came a contract with the Bordeaux Opera. There I got lots of experience and sang all the repertory, from Marguerite in *Faust* to Massenet's *La Navarraise,* from Micaëla to Mimi and Butterfly, from *L'Heure espagnole* to Henri Büsser's charming *Le Carrosse du Saint-Sacrament, The Love for Three Oranges,* and Thaïs, which along with the Poulenc heroines and Mélisande

Denise Duval as Elle in *La Voix humaine*.

became the role I was most identified with. Strange as it may seem, I even undertook Santuzza, but the theatre was small.

"The pay was so little in Bordeaux at that time that I took a few days off between performances and went to Paris for an audition at the Opéra. There were dozens of singers who sang one after the other, and I felt like a sheep in a herd. They offered me a chance to appear in *L'Aiglon* by Honegger the following season, but that was a long way off, so I decided to go home and continue my career in Bordeaux. But fate willed otherwise: Max Ruppat, Maurice Chevalier's impresario, who happened to be a great friend of some friends of mine, immediately arranged for me to audition for Paul Derval and the directors of the Folies-Bergère. They were enthusiastic and offered me a very juicy contract for one year, which I accepted. I sang the aria from *Madama Butterfly* in costume, then a Chopin song in a crinoline with romantic curls down my back. When the news reached Bordeaux, everyone was very angry, for no one could conceive of anyone performing in that sort of theatre without appearing naked! My poor parents were thunderstruck, and my teacher nearly had a stroke. Then the opportunity came for me to audition again at the Opéra, but this time I was the only one to sing for the administrator, Georges Hirsch. I was given a contract that was to begin after the Folies-Bergère.

"I made my debut in *Hérodiade* at the big house and in *Madama Butterfly* at the Comique in a new production by Max de Reveux. At a rehearsal of the latter I was advised to sing out and make a particular effort, as important people were to be in the auditorium. I had no idea who they were, and naturally was consumed with curiosity. Suddenly, after a few bars, a voice rang out from the darkness: 'That's the soprano I need!' It was Francis Poulenc, and a few minutes later I was introduced to him. What a delightful, warm-hearted, direct, simple human being! They don't make the likes of him anymore. It was to be a very close friendship until his death. He explained to me that he wanted me to create his one-act opera *Les Mamelles de Tirésias* at the Comique, that he had lost three prima donnas one after the other—they all had gotten pregnant. 'No danger of you being in that condition?' he asked. 'No,' I replied, quite startled. 'I'm not even married.'

"You cannot imagine what happened at the premiere. Presented after *Tosca*—it was a long evening, even by Bayreuth standards—we were booed, insulted, and hissed. In fact, it was a theme far too advanced for those times. I had to wear not only trousers but a beard, and I had to act like a man while my husband sat at home, produced babies, and attended to household chores. But the directors of the Comique persevered, and the performances went on. The public began to accept the opera and find ravishing moments in the score. In connection with this opera, which has Apollinaire's play as its setting, Poulenc wrote, 'If my music succeeds in producing laughter, while still allowing to be felt through it some moments of tenderness, and real lyricism, my aim will have been fully attained, since thus I shall not be false to the poem of Apollinaire, where the most violent buffoonery alternates at times with melancholy.' I recall one of Thérèse's phrases, which got more and more laughs with every performance and was so hard to put over. It goes something like this: 'Ah, dear freedom, I have won you at last! But first let's buy a newspaper to learn what's been happening!' And along with the opera, people in Paris talked a lot about me.

"Poulenc happened to be an intimate friend of Christian Dior, and it was just at this time that Dior was beginning to attain his fame. He took a liking to me and offered to dress me *en exclusivité*. Since I had a good figure, it was great fun and an unhoped-for privilege for me. It also created a lot of attention for my career, which got off to a good start. I became much in demand for contemporary scores and sang in the premiere of Germaine Tailleferre's *Petit Naviré* and also Milhaud's *Pauvre Matelot*.

"When Cocteau was signed to design a new *Pelléas et Mélisande*, I was asked by Henri Gui to take on the Debussy heroine. Immediately I refused, as I didn't feel I could do justice to her. I admired the music, tinted by magic, but the character of the young woman eluded me: I'm a very positive person and always know who I am, where I am, and what time it is, while Mélisande lives in a cloud of uncertainty and elusiveness. I found it very difficult to identify myself with someone who sings, 'Je ne sais pas ce que je dis. Je ne sais pas ce que je sais. Je ne dis plus ce que je veux. Je ne sais pas' [I don't know what I am saying. I don't know what I know. I no longer say what I want. I don't know]. She is never quite real and immensely delicate.

"There are women like her, of course, but I cannot understand them. But so much pressure was put on me by Gui and the directors of the opera house that I finally gave in. I shall never quite understand what happened that opening night. Perhaps I made such a desperate attempt to become Mélisande that I achieved it. Anyhow, it was a triumph, and the critics raved. So every theatre wanted me for the part, and I became very much involved with this opera. This experience helped me to gain a lot of confidence in myself, for only I knew what a battle it had been to identify with this strange creature. I recall asking Fanny Heldy, who had been a great interpreter of Mélisande, to give me some advice. She refused point blank, not even offering any excuse, and she died without my having ever met her. Great interpreters of a role have, I feel, the duty to pass on their knowledge.

"Poulenc had been commissioned by Ricordi to compose *Les Dialogues des carmélites* for La Scala. But for seven long years it looked as if it never would be finished. There was a serious nervous breakdown, and it really was a miracle Poulenc finally snapped out of it. During that period he worked only in fits and starts. At last it was ready, and anyone who heard him play the score could tell that it was a masterpiece. The premiere in Milan in 1957, with Virginia Zeani as Blanche, was an overwhelming success. Paris heard it for the first time that same year, under Pierre Dervaux. The rehearsals were very painstaking, and Poulenc never missed one. He sang all the roles, somewhat off key—but what an enchanting pianist he was! Actually, if he had not been so lazy, he could have been a great pianist. I sang Blanche, Régine Crespin was Madame Lidoine, and Denise Scharley was Madame de Croissy. When the last curtain came down, everyone was in tears, both in the audience and onstage. For me Blanche meant a deep emotional experience every time I undertook the role; and as time wore on and I sang it over and over again, I was always deeply disturbed by this gentle, noble creature. Poulenc wrote very trickily, as every soprano knows who has sung his music. In *Dialogues* Blanche goes from the scene of the ragoût, where the tessitura lies very high, to the final one of the guillotine, which instead is very low. *La Voix humaine* is a killer, not only because you have the stage to yourself for its entire length, but because the phrasing—sometimes long, sometimes short, always in a low key, half singing, half parlando—is a tour de force of no mean order. It lies better really for a darker voice, à la Charlotte in *Werther,* but that sort of instrument cannot quite produce the hysterical impression that is so essential. I sang *La Voix humaine* in every corner of the globe, including the Glyndebourne Festival, for I never could refuse Poulenc, and he felt I was just right for it. But I couldn't take on any other opera while I was doing it, for it would have been too much of a stress. Musically speaking, in my opinion, *Les Mamelles* is the most imaginative of the Poulenc operas, *Dialogues* the most touching, and *La Voix humaine* the most compelling."

Singing, even after all these years, remains somewhat of a mystery to her, she candidly asserted. "Technique is the base of everything, but there is nobody left, at least in France, to teach it. Breathing is everything, and you know there are not thirty-six ways to breathe. So what is the answer? Some of the most difficult roles represented no problem for me, but the reverse was true as well—*Manon,* for instance, defeated me. After three performances at the Comique, I swore I would never sing it again, and I never did. Actually, it is an easier score than many others, but it created a psychological block within me. And I had spent a fortune on the costumes! But Rameau's *Les Indes galantes,* infinitely more difficult, was smooth sailing. Nowadays, though, every opera must be reconsidered and revalued. When I sang Butterfly it was no problem for a lyric soprano. Today it is, because the orchestras have increased enormously, and so many of the new opera houses are like big barns. I can understand perfectly why mezzo-sopranos are asked now to sing Mélisande; the part lies low, and a lyric soprano cannot possibly be heard over an orchestra of a hundred instruments or more."

As far as her appearances in the United States are concerned, Duval has fond memories of the Poulenc works she sang in concert form and of a *Thaïs* in Dallas with Zeffirelli as director and designer. "I was brought in on a platter by two Nubian slaves, and the effect was startling. Franco managed to keep the style of this old warhorse and yet inject a lot of new life into it. That is what should be done by young directors and, alas, is not. They call it 'experimenting.' I'm depressed by what I see around me and happy in many ways to be out of the rat race. Poulenc was, in my estimation, the last of the great modern composers of opera, and I'm proud that my name will always be connected with his. I owe a lot to him, and I find it impossible to evaluate what I would have become without him."

THE GREAT COLORATURAS

AMELITA GALLI-CURCI

TOTI DAL MONTE

LINA PAGLIUGHI

MARGHERITA CAROSIO

In the period between World War I and the post–World War II 1940s, the reigning coloraturas were Amelita Galli-Curci, Toti dal Monte, Lina Pagliughi, Margherita Carosio, and Lily Pons (who will be covered in another chapter). Curiously, although Galli-Curci's, dal Monte's, and Carosio's voices were very different—the first had a metallic sound of an incredible brilliance, the second an almost mezzo timbre despite its fantastic agility, and the third a birdlike quality—they all shared the ability, rare in a coloratura, to bring a deep emotion to their roles. Galli-Curci and Carosio had to exercise diligence to acquire this ability, but with dal Monte it was more of a natural gift: she developed an unsuspected upper register from what had appeared at first to be a different type of instrument. As for Pagliughi and Pons, both had a marvelous precision and refinement, but not the expressive delivery that the other three achieved.

AMELITA GALLI-CURCI

When Amelita Galli-Curci received me in her drawing room in a Central Park South hotel in New York in the fall of 1936, she had just returned from an unsuccessful attempt at a comeback, singing Mimi in *La Bohème* in Chicago, the scene of her earlier American triumphs. It was the first time she had sung in public following a major goiter operation and a long period of rest. No surgeon had wanted to operate until the specific moment when this delicate intervention was most likely to succeed, and the long wait had been the cause of a nervous condition which she discussed very frankly. As the operation had apparently been successful, she could not understand why her voice had not regained its previous splendor. She explained that she had chosen Mimi—a lyric role—in order not to expose herself too much on so important an occasion. She was crestfallen that her comeback had been unsuccessful, and my heart immediately went out to her. She seemed determined to overcome this obstacle, which she insisted was temporary; and I realized that her purpose in granting me an interview was to declare publicly her intention to re-educate her voice and rebuild its resilience and agility. How sad it was that all her efforts were in vain. A famous specialist with whom I discussed her case was of the opinion that at her age—she was then fifty-four years old—the vocal cords are no longer able to regain their lost suppleness, particularly after so long a period of inactivity and so great a trauma.

Galli-Curci's most ardent admirers and devoted fans had admitted to me that her intonation, which even at the height of her glory had been her weakest point, deteriorated rapidly with the advancement of the goiter in the late twenties. In fact, in 1930 the Metropolitan, where she had reigned as a queen, had not renewed her contract. She did continue to give recitals for a while, but this undoubtedly did not help her vocal cords, which had once been considered a miracle of elasticity and brilliance. Now I had before me a small, pathetic creature, bereft of her one and only treasure, who felt the need—even with me, whom she had never met—to discuss her anguish

Amelita Galli-Curci as Violetta in *La Traviata*.

and disillusion. Very much a lady in her appearance and manner, she had the narrow face of a Modigliani model, dominated by an aquiline nose and a pair of tormented, almond-shaped eyes. She reminded me of a frail bird, the very long neck and the sloping shoulders adding a strange dimension to her figure. It was difficult to think of her as a diva, and I simply could not imagine how, onstage, she had given the illusion of being beautiful. But obviously I was wrong, for I was told by many people, including some of her ex-colleagues, that when she emerged from the wings she had so extraordinary a presence that she projected a mysterious sort of loveliness. There have always been, as the French say, *des belles laides* and *des laides belles,* and she obviously belonged to this latter category.

I had been so strongly warned of her arrogance that I was surprised at the cordiality with which she greeted me. But even in the midst of this painful defeat—the newspapers had been full of the disaster—she retained the assurance of the days when she had been idolized. She spoke softly, without that metallic sound which is instantly recognizable in her recordings. Her Italian was that of a cultivated and refined woman, the choice of words absolutely correct and at times even poetic. During our very long meeting she never spoke ill of other singers; she simply ignored them. It was as if she had been all alone on an island; her lack of interest in others was complete. Nothing seemed to be of any importance to her except the personal drama she was undergoing.

Slowly I managed to bring the subject back to her past and asked her questions about her luminous career.

"When I was fifteen," she told me, "I was the source of envy and jealousy of every mother in Milan, the city in which I was born and brought up. Having come out of the conservatory with every possible prize, I was the treasured pupil of the famous maestro Vincenzo Appiani. My technique as a pianist was already so perfected that I was much in demand for recitals in the homes of the rich Milanese. It was a godsend, for my father had undertaken some business affairs that had gone sour, and in this manner I was able to earn my living without having to be a burden to the family.

"I often went to La Scala for my own pleasure and then played on my piano the scores of the operas I had heard, often singing along in some of the passages. It became known that I was also gifted vocally, and one evening, after dinner, in the apartment of some friends, I was invited to sit at the piano and sing. Fortunately, no one had told me that Pietro Mascagni was among the guests, for in this case wild horses could not have dragged me to the piano. Instead, he came over, introduced himself, and paid me all sorts of compliments. He had been under the impression that I had under-taken a singing course, for he asked me how many years I had studied. And he was amazed when I told him the truth.

"He encouraged me to pursue a singing career and then said the following words, which are etched in my heart: 'You have a unique timbre, and this is a very rare gift. I would recognize your voice twenty years from now anywhere, and this is something so many others would give anything to possess. Remember that there are many gifted pianists, but not singers.'

"A few days later, while attending a concert of Busoni, who was then considered one of the greatest living pianists, I kept looking at his hands and then at mine. And I said to myself, How can I with my tiny hands hope for a great career? A mediocre one; but a fabulous one, no. But then in life everything is dominated by chance. Just as I was considering taking Mas-cagni's advice and switching to singing, I found myself one night again in the home of acquaintances and accompanied myself warbling 'Caro nome.' Two minutes later a man asked to meet me, explained excitedly that he was organizing an operatic season in the adorable town of Trani in Puglie and contemplating a series of *Rigolettos*. There was little money that he could offer me, but he would be happy to have me as Gilda. I accepted immedi-ately, for I knew I had nothing to lose. Trani was very distant from Milan, and if I had not scored, no one in my hometown would have been aware of it.

"How I dared present myself in this tremendously difficult role without ever having studied, I will never know. But this happened in 1912, and I was twenty-four years old. You see me now after this ghastly experience in Chicago, and you have in front of you a scared woman. But previously I never knew what fear meant. In Trani my assurance was a source of marvel to me, particularly since my success had been extraordinary, and instead of six performances we gave ten. On the return journey to Milan I stopped in Rome, and without an introduction of any sort I asked to see the director of the Teatro Costanzi. The secretary stared at me incredulously. I wanted an audition? Was I mad? The Intendant only arranged auditions weeks in advance and only heard people recommended by either conductors or agents in whom he had confidence. But she did not know my willpower. I waited until he came out of his office and told him I had a great proposition to make him. 'I am simply wonderful,' I told him, 'and if you hire me now, you can get me very reasonably.' He was amused and so taken aback by my freshness that he agreed to give me a hearing the following day.

"When I presented myself alone on the stage, he asked, 'But where is your accompanist?' 'I need no one,' I replied, and started 'Caro nome' seated at the piano. He was impressed enough to have a pianist come over right away because, he said, he wanted to see how I moved on the stage. He hired me immediately for a series of *Rigolettos* and for *Don Procopio* by Bizet. Gilda has always been my good-luck piece. All my first battles I won with her. This wretched, unfortunate girl put me on the map, and in no time I had Rome at my feet. Everyone was enthusiastic, and the Eternal City launched me."

As she spoke, I remembered what Giacomo Lauri-Volpi had declared about her performance as Rigoletto's daughter: "It is as if Verdi had written this part for her. Pure crystal, and at the same time an emotional force that vibrates and haunts one."

"In Italy I sang everywhere except at La Scala," she continued. "They offered me Lisa in *La sonnambula,* and I replied, 'It is either Amina or nothing. Amelita never enters by the service door.' And as I never go back on my decisions, even later, when they begged me over and over again, my answer was always no. My enormous success in Spain led me to Havana, where the opera seasons were first-class and the top artists in the world engaged. Again fate intervened. My husband, the Marchese Curci—yes, in the interim I had married—and I had decided to return to Europe via New York, which as yet we had never visited. I made no effort to contact the Metropolitan, for at that time they had a very important coloratura, Maria Barrientos, in the company, and usually there is no room for more than one, given the limited repertoire for this type of voice. On Fifth Avenue—and goodness only knows what a busy thoroughfare this is!—we heard a voice yelling from the other side of the street, 'Amelita, Amelita!' It turned out to be a Sicilian who had been so very hospitable to us in Catania, where the preceding season I had undertaken, at the beautiful Teatro Bellini, Elvira in *I puritani.* He insisted we have lunch with him that very day, as he had as his guest Cleofonte Campanini, one of the great conductors of his era, who was at that time the director of the Chicago Opera House. He had conducted the world premiere of *Madama Butterfly* at La Scala in 1904. It turned out he knew all about me and asked to hear me. After the audition, he gave me a contract to sing Gilda in the Windy City in November 1916. Once more the hunchback's daughter—I could never get away from her!

"Again, fate had willed that the management of the Victor company, at that time in full expansion, had heard of me after my triumphs in South America and signed me to a long contract. My first record with them, the Bell Song from *Lakmé* and the 'Ach, ich fühl's' from *Die Zauberflöte,* became the greatest best-seller on their list. The sales continued to grow so that it was way ahead of those of Caruso, then the most successful of all recording artists. By the time I arrived in Chicago I was already a great celebrity, and my debut there, if I may be so immodest, was one of the greatest triumphs ever to take place in that important musical center.

"From one day to the next I became the highest-paid prima donna in the United States, and offers poured in. The Manhattan Opera Company, in those days the great rival of the Metropolitan, followed in 1918, and again it was pure hysteria on the part of the public, which in those days exploded like a bunch of firecrackers. Finally, the demand of the audience for my participation in the seasons of the Metropolitan was such that Gatti-Casazza was obliged to offer me a contract. But Caruso died suddenly the summer before my opening night there, and Gatti-Casazza, who was Mr. Wisdom himself, knew that his greatest draw had gone. He begged me to change all my engagements, which I recall as a veritable nightmare, so that I could open the season with *La traviata,* and offered me double the number of the few performances originally signed for. I accepted, but I was very tough with him: the condition was that he pay me exactly double. One does not remain in the corridors for nothing, does one? That same season Jeritza came along and made a big splash in her repertoire. With his dry wit Gatti-Casazza asserted, 'God in his infinite mercy has sent me a pair of precious shoes: in one he put Galli-Curci; in the other, Jeritza.'

"At the Metropolitan, until 1930, I was the sovereign, and my name was sufficient to sell every ticket in the house. The role I sang the most often was Rosina. Lucia, which was never my favorite, however, was the most in demand everywhere. The music is not first-rate, and in the mad scene it took a gigantic effort for as small a woman as me to fill those immense stages with all those cadenzas and trills. But somehow it never failed to create pandemonium in the house, and as a showpiece it was irresistible. I made it far more emotional, despite the way it is written, than the coloraturas who had preceded me, and I came out of it transfigured.

"The two heroines closest to my heart were Violetta and Juliette in the Gounod opera. Unfortunately, the latter—except for the waltz in the first act—does not demand much agility, and it is agility that the public wanted to hear from me. As for *La traviata,* it is a masterpiece from beginning to end. It has everything: tenderness, sensuality, humanity, despair, and the most beautiful death scene ever composed. I was always much in demand for *Lakmé,* as the public demanded I appear in those operas that showed off my high register; but, between us, I always found it very second-class music.

Except for the hazardous tessitura, it is more like an operetta than an opera. I always directed my efforts to the same goal: to place emotion in a type of voice that is unsuited to it. I have studied this problem a lot, and I hope that long after I have disappeared I shall be remembered for this contribution I have made to the lyric theatre. What was always more important than anything else was to give palpitations of the heart to the sort of instrument that is almost an abstraction. With *La sonnambula* and *I puritani* the expression lies entirely in the music. If the public is not deaf or insensitive, how can one fail to move it when one sings Amina or Elvira? But with Meyerbeer's *Dinorah,* one of the eight operas I sang at the Metropolitan, one must work hard to squeeze out the humanity. It is the destiny of the coloratura to be like an acrobat on a steel wire. The public waits anxiously to see if you are going to crack on a certain note or be unable to finish a certain difficult filatura, just like the public in a circus follows attentively to see if the poor wretch is going to miss a jump and fall below.

"A coloratura must possess, at all times, a total serenity not to fall into the traps the music offers her, and I have always preferred to sacrifice some of the purity of tone to find a more human expression. And the result has been, undoubtedly, that a more metallic type of production has come into being. This is why I have always preferred recitals to opera, for they offer many more escapes and a greater sense of responsibility, which has always been a challenge to me. In an opera one depends on five hundred other people: the designers, costumers, stagehands, orchestra, chorus, conductor, colleagues, and several others. On the concert stage you win your battle—or lose it—alone. Far more satisfactory! One also has the opportunity to show more facets of one's musicality. In my case, I always had to include some compositions by Handel and Mozart with cadenzas to satisfy the audience, which has paid a high price to hear me, but then I always slipped in some Monteverdi, Paisiello, Scarlatti, and Pergolesi, to name a few of my favorite Italian composers. They prove difficult because of their apparent simplicity, which is an illusion. After a group of lieder I usually wind up with a group of Spanish songs, which are very suited to the timbre of my voice, and which always prove successful.

"But the composer closest to my heart has always been Debussy. I always include some of his songs whenever possible, but I cannot sing 'La Chevelure' or 'Beau Soir,' to mention a couple of them, in a hall that is very big. Debussy needs intimacy, for with him the nuances are everything—it is the things that are barely sketched that really count with him. My adoration for him began when I was a pianist, for to me he is the only composer who is also a painter. Many have tried to imitate him; no one has succeeded. My greatest ambition has always been to sing Mélisande, but it lies very much in the middle of the voice, and I always hoped I might be able to undertake it at the end of my career. But what do I have ahead of me?"

Suddenly the tone of her voice changed. It had become ever so fragile, and she seemed on the verge of tears. "I am deeply concerned," she said, "about the evolution of music. I do go to the avant-garde concerts, and I leave them with a sense of total anguish. I have the impression that they have been written by machines. And this word 'dissonance'! What does it mean? Is it the total destruction of music and the end of all that it stands for?"

What would Amelita Galli-Curci think today? I have often wondered. She died in California on November 26, 1963, at the age of eighty-one, and I have never forgotten our conversation of forty-six years ago. It could have been yesterday. But in the world of memories, finally, the element of time does not count.

TOTI DAL MONTE

Two weeks before she died in January 1975, I went to call on Toti dal Monte at the ancient hospital of Santa Maria Nova in Florence, where she was being treated for faulty circulation in her right leg. She claimed she was much better and was making arrangements to return to her home in Pieve di Soligo in a few days. She did go back to her villa there, and shortly afterward she passed away, her agile mind intact.

The news of her death made the front pages of every newspaper in Italy, for she had been one of its most beloved stars. Whenever she attended a performance, the audience invariably recognized her and gave her a rousing welcome. She had, in fact, changed relatively little from the time she had reigned supreme in European opera houses and concert halls. Small and solidly built, she was still graceful and feminine in her movements; her huge eyes were wonderfully alert in her very mobile face.

I recall her in various operas in the 1930s, but the performance that I will always remember as an overwhelming experience was a matinee of *Lucia* at the Comunale in Bologna. Her voice had the fantastic agility of a coloratura, but its sound was darkish, sensuous, and quite large. Her mad scene was not the usual exercise in fluted high tones but a tremendously dramatic experience. Her Gilda too was a fountain of sound; and her "Tutte le feste" in particular was heartbreaking.

"I always had very high blood pressure," she told me, "and in fact I retired because of it. Otherwise I could have gone on singing, for my voice was still in good shape. My last operatic appearance was in Catania during the war as Norina in *Don Pasquale,* and then I went on giving recitals for a few more years. The reason my voice was still fresh is that I turned down many tempting offers all through my career and accepted only a limited number of engagements every year. I never subjected my instrument to the wear and tear of too much use. For many years I went every summer to South America, as I had engagements in Buenos Aires and Rio, and in those long ocean trips one had the opportunity to study new scores and fill one's lungs with fresh air."

Toti dal Monte as Rosina in *Il barbiere di Siviglia.*

Why had she sung only one season at the Metropolitan? I asked her.

"You are opening up an old wound," she replied with a luminous smile. "I made my debut in 1924 as Lucia and also sang Gilda. The success was, if I may say so, enormous, and for the only time in my career it proved to be my downfall. When I went to see Gatti-Casazza before my return to Europe, in order to discuss the following year's contract, he offered me half the fee I had been paid that first season. He claimed that this was for economy's sake—too many great stars under contract—but those in the know informed me there was another reason. At that time there was a reigning coloratura soprano at the Metropolitan, and she had bitterly resented my reception. And she had given the management an ultimatum: The little new Italian must go. I have never resented anyone, as I feel that there is always room for singers of quality. Anyhow, I naturally refused Gatti-Casazza's offer, and that was that. A few years later, that prima donna's career came to a sudden halt; but then there was the big recession, and, anyhow, I was solidly booked." (Although dal Monte never mentioned the name of the prima donna, it was easy to guess that she was referring to Galli-Curci—at that time an enormous attraction at the Met.)

"I did return to the United States, however, for many satisfactory performances at the Chicago Opera. Rosa Raisa was then the number-one star there, and for a very good reason. She was simply magical.

"I was born in Magliano Veneto in 1893," she said, "and my mother died when I was seven. My father, a schoolteacher, brought me up with an overwhelming passion for music. He taught me how to play the piano and also to sing with him duets by Schumann and Mendelssohn. When he was transferred to Venice, he made arrangements for me to continue my piano studies at the conservatory. For five years I played eight hours every day. Although I had a certain facility, my hands were far too small for me to become a concert pianist. Then one day my right hand developed a terrible cramp. My father quickly decided I must study voice and through a friend made arrangements for me to audition for Barbara Marchisio, Rossini's favorite contralto, for whom the great composer wrote the Petite Messe Solennelle. She had been unsurpassed in *Semiramide, La Cenerentola,* and *L'italiana in Algeri.* With her sister Carlotta, who had also been a great singer, she lived in a villa in Mira, near Venice, and held classes there. I sang the Jewel Song from *Faust*—warning her, however, that I did not have the B-flat. 'The voice for now is small,' she said, 'and there is not much natural agility. But all of this can be remedied, for the voice is essentially very pretty, and the child is not devoid of talent. But she must stop the piano right away, for it is much too fatiguing for her. Look how tiny she is! I want her to breathe all the fresh air she can for one year, and in the meantime the voice will have a chance to mature. In twelve months' time we shall begin to work.'

"And the following year I began," she continued. "And for five years I took the steamer every day from Venice over to Mira. My lessons were gratis. My voice was somewhat dark in timbre, almost a mezzo, and yet Marchisio not only uncannily built up a solid upper register but developed an astonishing coloratura. I owe her everything, a debt I was never able to repay.

"One day, very casually, she told me I was ready and packed me off to audition for the directors of La Scala in the Casa Ricordi in Milan. I was hired for three months at ten lire a day. The year was 1914. It was decided that I would make my debut as Biancofiore in Zandonai's *Francesca da Rimini,* which was to have its Scala premiere with Raisa, Pertile, and Giuseppe Danise in the leads. Gino Marinuzzi, the conductor, advised me to change my name, which was Antonietta Meneghel. 'Too difficult,' he said, 'to write and pronounce.' I suggested my grandmother's, dal Monte, and he approved of it. As everyone called me Toti instead of Antonietta, I suggested that for a first name. He repeated it several times. 'Yes, that is a name one remembers,' he declared.

"After many performances of *Francesca* I sang Franck's *Les Béatitudes.* Then no other role appeared to be forthcoming. One day I heard people gossiping backstage that in the forthcoming *Cavalleria rusticana,* to be conducted by Mascagni himself and with the celebrated Hariclea Darclée as Santuzza, the part of Lola had not been assigned as yet. I learned it overnight and proposed myself for it. 'It is written for a mezzo,' I was informed. 'It's not for you.' 'But I know it and I can darken my voice,' I insisted. I was auditioned and given the assignment.

"Then came a series of Gildas opposite the great Battistini in a provincial tour of *Rigoletto.* This led to an engagement in the same role at the Costanzi in Rome, and the critics all wrote that a new prima donna had been born. I also sang *Lodoletta* there in the season of 1921–22, with Mascagni himself coaching me in the lovely role. When he came to congratulate me after opening night, he wept. I knew then I had won my battle—not easy following in the footsteps of Rosina Storchio and Bianca Stagno Bellincioni. Walter Mocchi, a real operatic tsar, came along and gave me a two-year contract, taking me to Buenos Aires and Rio, where I had the opportunity, for the first and only time in my career, to sing

Musetta in *La Bohème,* with Gilda dalla Rizza and Beniamino Gigli.

"Then a cable arrived from La Scala offering me Gilda in a series of *Rigolettos* to be conducted by Toscanini. As luck would have it, when I had been singing this part in Rome, Signora Carla Toscanini—on her way from Milan to Naples, where her husband was going to land from an American stay—had stopped in Rome and by chance had heard me. When the maestro decided to do *Rigoletto,* she suggested me to him.

"I was naturally most flattered, but everyone told me that Mocchi would never let me out of the contract. I did not listen to my colleagues and, cable in hand and tears in my eyes, went to see him in his office. He stormed and fumed, and I wept and wept. Suddenly he went to a cabinet, took out my contract, and tore it up. 'I have no right to stand in your way, but next year you will sign another agreement with me,' he said. And of course I did.

"Gilda opened the big doors of La Scala for me, and it became my principal home. I sang many, many operas there, and I cannot remember them all. But some of them are *La sonnambula, Lucia, Barbiere di Siviglia, Linda di Chamounix, Don Pasquale, Lodoletta,* and *Daughter of the Regiment. La sonnambula* was always the closest to my heart, and I do not know of more heavenly music ever written for a soprano. It is the opera that brings back the tenderest of memories and the greatest inner satisfactions. But the two operas with which I became the most closely identified were *Lucia* and *Madama Butterfly.* I even sang the Donizetti heroine with Toscanini in Berlin and Vienna."

"Do you have any regrets?" I asked her.

"Ever so many!" she answered. "Incredibly enough, I never sang any of the Mozart operas. Somehow in the period between the two wars they were performed far less often, and the opportunities never came. I have sung so much Mozart in recitals and orchestral concerts that I know I could have done justice to Konstanze, Fiordiligi, and the Contessa. Then I would have loved to sing *Lakmé,* but in Italy and South America it is never given. I never sang *I puritani.* Serafin asked me to sing it with him in Florence and requested a rapid answer. I looked at the score and became frightened by all those E-flats. I refused and only later realized that most sopranos transposed it. And again the opportunity never came again. I had the E-flat, and I sang it in Gomes's *Lo schiavo,* but that was very difficult, and Bellini wrote several. I did sing, however, Stravinsky's *Le Rossignol* and enjoyed it immensely.

"In the second half of my career, I took on heavier roles such as Butterfly, Mimi in *La Bohème,* Manon, and *La traviata.* I had misgivings about all four of them and tried them out in provincial theatres to gauge the results. Butterfly became so identified with me that I could have sung nothing else, so many were the requests, and it is strangely enough the only full opera I ever recorded. But the other three all became favorites too. It was not the vocal aspects of La traviata that worried me, but the fact that I knew I did not have the right glamorous figure for the consumptive heroine. Although I had been hailed all along as a singing actress, I still had grave doubts. But the initial reception in a secondary theatre was such that I undertook to sing it at the San Carlo in Naples, and the premiere there proved I had won a considerable victory. Gradually I sang less and less the coloratura repertoire.

"Maestro Guarnieri, who taught me all the nuances in La sonnambula, used to say, 'Toti sings in the interest of her voice.' And it is true. I always held back, following the advice of Barbara Marchisio, who every day for five years said, 'You may need the reserve later.' And until the end, that was the only way for me."

Toti dal Monte married the tenor Enzo de Muro Lomanto in 1928 and lived happily with him until his death some twenty years ago. They often sang together, and retired to live in a villa at Pieve di Soligo in the Veneto. Their only daughter, Marina Dolfin, has become a well-known actress and recently played the important role of Dolly in the RAI series of Anna Karenina. After her retirement from singing, Toti dal Monte herself made several appearances in motion pictures and also played some of the Goldoni comedies to sold-out houses, putting her charming Venetian accent to good use.

"But now the curtain has fallen on that activity too," she said, and as I think back on her parting words an uncanny sensation pervades me. "I was offered teaching jobs," she said, "all over the world, including one at the conservatory in Moscow. I refused, for I no longer believe in the musical life of today. The method is lost, the will to study nonexistent. Artists are no longer sheltered; they are thrown into the arena to the lions, and much of the fault lies with today's conductors and directors of opera houses. Voices are like the juice of a fruit—they squeeze it and then throw it away.

"I had a natural talent, but it was Marchisio's genius and firm discipline, combined with my patience and modesty, that eventually brought me fame and satisfaction. But I never took a step longer than half of my foot. I am glad that my life is coming to an end and that I shall no longer be present to watch helplessly the total disintegration of all the musical values I have treasured and in which I completely believe."

After the news of her death, I rang up Wally Toscanini in Milan and asked her for an evaluation of this great prima donna.

"She not only had a hauntingly beautiful voice," she replied, "but she was a consummate musician and a great actress. One believed in every gesture she made and in every word she uttered. Her diction was a joy, and her coloratura was not an exercise, unlike most of the others; it was a deeply felt human expression."

LINA PAGLIUGHI

In the early 1930s I was overcome by the coloratura soprano Lina Pagliughi, whom I first heard in *I puritani* and later as Gilda and Lucia. Hers was truly the voice of an angel. The fact that her weight was four times that of most other prima donnas did not disturb me in the least, so enchanted was I with the purity of her tone and the astounding ease with which she tackled all kinds of ornamentation. I had no idea then that she was an American, born in 1907 near Mulberry Street in New York City of Italian immigrant parents, and that at the age of one and a half she had moved to San Francisco. Nor did I know that Luisa Tetrazzini had wanted to adopt her, after hearing Pagliughi sing in California when she was seven years old: a child prodigy already singing in public. "This is my successor," Tetrazzini had declared.

Although known to Americans through her many recordings, Pagliughi sang little in her home country. Her one concert tour, under Sol Hurok's aegis, was interrupted at the start of the Second World War when she rejoined her husband, who was trapped in Italy.

When I went to converse with her in the little Adriatic resort of Gatteo, I was unprepared for the fact that she is now so heavy that I do not believe there exists a scale that could possibly do her justice. But her charm, her brio, her good common sense and humor, made me immediately forget her appearance. I was carried away by the simplicity, wisdom, generosity, and gentle firmness of this very, very special spirit inhabiting so many mountains of flesh.

Pagliughi has lived in Italy ever since she was fifteen years old. In her numerous appearances all over the world, she sang in all the great opera houses except the Metropolitan. In the two hours I spent with her, she never once mentioned the Met: it was as if that house did not exist for her. But never in my long talk with her did I sense any kind of bitterness, envy, or jealousy on her part. It did not take me long to realize that this is a person who was wise enough to take life as it came and to enjoy it thoroughly.

"We were very poor people," she declared with disarming honesty, "and my adorable father, who had come from Genoa, was an upholsterer. I was born singing, so it could not be helped that people should start immediately taking notice of this baby nightingale. At the age of seven I was already giving recitals and attending all the operas and concerts that I could possibly afford. There was no question in my mind, even at that age, that God had made me in order that I dedicate my life to singing. The fact that Luisa Tetrazzini heard me and was full of praise did not go to my head. I knew there never could be anyone like her. She wanted to adopt me, and my parents—my mother was a strong-willed Bolognese—answered, 'Thank you very much—never!' But she did become my second mother. When my father took me to Milan to perfect my musical education with Maestro Manlio Bavagnoli (the father of Gaetano, who made a very brilliant career as a conductor), she took me entirely under her wing, and we became very close.

"When I heard that she had suffered a stroke, I was singing the Queen of the Night in *The Magic Flute* in a memorable production at the Maggio Musicale Fiorentino, with Vittorio Gui conducting; Tancredi Pasero singing Sarastro; Mafalda Favero, Pamina; Mariano Stabile, Papageno; and Ferruccio Tagliavini, Tamino (he was very young then, and a flawless singer already). I rushed to Milan between performances. I was heartbroken. Her speech had been affected, and when she embraced me, trying in vain to speak, she never stopped weeping. What a tragic ending for someone who had one of the most beautiful voices in the world! It was the last time I saw her, for, mercifully, a short time later she closed her eyes forever.

"Apart from being a unique singer—for never there was or will be another voice like hers—she was an astonishing human being. Until the very end, she could tackle Es and E-flats with a security and a roundness that left me gasping. There was nothing she could not do with that instrument of hers! She kept insisting that I learn to use my chest tones the way she did. But I was always pulling out excuses, for I was well aware that while she could use them fearlessly, I never would be able to do the same and that I risked injuring my vocal cords. She was the most marvelously kind and humane person, and everyone who knew her could not help but respect and love her deeply. In fact, her home was always full of young people, not only asking for advice—they still did in those days—but also enjoying the pleasure of her good company.

"I thought so much of her when Maria Callas died suddenly, alone and lonely. Everyone had admired her on the stage, for she had very special attributes, but no one loved her in life. How could one? She repaid kindnesses with acid, and she ended up walled inside her expensive Parisian apartment. It is lucky, in many ways, that she was spared having to face old

Lina Pagliughi in the title role of *Lucia di Lammermoor*.

age, for she was already ever so sarcastic and bitter when she was on top and could afford being generous. How very sad, don't you think? What is living if not being surrounded by human warmth?

"Tetrazzini took her retirement with philosophy and wisdom and never stopped helping people of all stations. I learned a great lesson from her. When my time came to bid farewell, no regrets—only deep thankfulness for what has been. Privileges do not last forever. They are given and then taken away, and one must know instinctively when the time for the swan song has come.

"I was most fortunate, for my voice was naturally placed, even in every scale, with all the topmost notes firm and round and the picchiettati solid. As a child I already had a tremendous breath control, untaught ... you know, a gift from nature. In fact it was decided in San Francisco that since I already sang effortlessly, it was wise for me to take up the piano, which I did, since that would help my musical knowledge. And I graduated from the conservatory before taking off for Italy to learn repertoire and get going.

"I started at barely seventeen with Gilda at the Nazionale in Milan, and I was soon replacing Toti dal Monte in extra performances of this same role, with Carlo Galeffi in the lead, at La Scala. Although I idolized Toti, who was a very great star, I was not in the least nervous. As a matter of fact, I never knew what fear was when facing a public and never vocalized before a performance. Toti [in the corner of the piano I noticed a photograph of dal Monte with the dedication "To Lina, the purest of singers"] later was to teach me a very helpful lesson about what not to do. She took on in the second phase of her career lyric roles like Violetta, Butterfly, Manon, and Mimi, and did them beautifully, of course, with that sensitivity which so characterized her. But somehow her coloratura was never the same. Following in her footsteps intrigued me, but my radar told me to watch out.

"I agreed to sing Mimi in Pontedera, a provincial town, to see what would happen. The role appealed to me tremendously, and I knew that my voice was robust enough to undertake it. But I never sang it again, and any offer that came to sing a lyric part was turned down by me very firmly. It is hard to explain. I knew that the experiment had not been good for me, and it was a matter of several weeks before I felt that my coloratura was again the way it should be. And believe me, despite what everyone is doing now, everyone must stick to his own yard. It is most foolish for all these ladies and gentlemen today to switch from one repertoire to the other. It simply does not work, for the vocal cords have their limitations.

"Provided it was coloratura, I never found any score difficult. I cannot in all honesty, as some people have said, declare that *I puritani* is more difficult than *Lucia,* or that Stravinsky's *Le Rossignol,* which I sang in every opera house, was harder than Respighi's *La campana sommersa* [there is a photograph of Respighi with the inscription "To Signora Pagliughi, the Rautendelein of my dreams"] or Giordano's *Il re* [a photo of Giordano has the dedication "Your performance was magical"]. As long as the role was within my vocal boundaries, I never encountered problems.

"Style is another matter. That is something one must grasp and develop and feel. I sang a lot of Mozart, from Konstanze to Fiordiligi, from the Queen of the Night to whatever her name is in *L'impresario.* And it was as much a part of me as Rossini and Donizetti. But the approach is all different, for they all have their own way of saying things. Perhaps Amina, ever so elegiac, gave me the greatest satisfaction. Somehow this part fitted me like a glove. I recall in Florence some young people took a carriage, and when I came out of the theatre, they pushed me on it and dragged me all the way to the Hotel Savoia. They had disposed of the horses and wanted to pay me this honor. And then, there in the square, people who had followed from the opera house kept shouting 'Brava, brava!' until I wept from the emotion. Those were exciting times. I sang Violetta until the end of my career, and although the second act was heavier than the others, it was still eminently suited to my voice.

"I was never envious. On the contrary, I admired other coloraturas with a passion. There has never been a Rosina like Elvira de Hidalgo, and I know that, unconsciously, I copied her, or tried to. When I first heard Amelita Galli-Curci way back in my little-girl days, I was so overwhelmed I went home and announced that I had changed my mind and never wanted to sing again. She was like a flute—ethereal, evanescent, superb. Then when I heard her in Sydney—I went with all my colleagues; we were all on tour there —in a recital in 1932, I left the hall crying. She was a shadow of herself; nothing came out of what had been a heavenly throat, and despite the long scarf around her neck, one could see so well the goiter that had destroyed her. What a cruel fate she suffered, and I felt so deeply sorry for her! Did she have to continue? She must have needed to go on earning her living.

"Those were the days of glorious voices. Now there is no soprano leggero —or if there is, I have not heard of it. There was Renata Scotto, who was enchanting, and now, after all those heavy parts she has undertaken, she screams—goodness how she screams! And look what happened to the very gifted Sills for the same reason.

"It is not true that coloraturas need have a short existence. When I went back to La Scala after the war to sing *Lucia* with Gigli, I had been singing well over twenty years, and the condition of my voice had never been better. [In another corner there was a photograph of Gigli: "To my beloved Lucia, whose vocal qualities are truly magical—Yours lovingly, Edgardo Beniamino."] And now just listen for a moment." With the greatest facility, she let out a G-sharp that left me speechless. "If one is careful with one's vocal cords, the freshness stays along with the agility. The trick is not to misuse it and know what is right for one. I stopped singing not because my voice was worn, but because I began to see advancing very rapidly the signs of disintegration that have brought opera where it is today.

"The two arias of the Queen of the Night are reputed to be impossible to sing. They are not if you have the notes. Difficult yes, impossible no. I once sang a whole series of performances of *The Magic Flute* sitting down. The costumes were so heavy and it was too late to change them, and I felt so terribly impeded in them that I decided to sing the two arias comfortably seated and managed very well. Actually, the first is the hardest, for there is a long stretch in the center before the fireworks begin going up to F. I am all in favor of the pyrotechnics' beginning at once, as in the second aria. Actually, they are great fun. I use them now as vocalizing exercises for some of my students." And she demonstrated just that a few minutes later with a British student, Tania Croft Murray, who sang as Pagliughi sat at the piano and played exquisitely, from memory, the royal arias. "These British girls are very serious, thank heavens. One of them, Elizabeth Harwood, has gone out into the world and made quite a name for herself. It could not have happened to a nicer person.

"What was delightful about Italy—an Italy that is no more—was the quantity of delicious provincial opera houses, all vying with one another to give the best performances. We were not interested in money in those days, for we loved our trade above all. I recall one season at the Ponchielli in Cremona—I was there for *La sonnambula*, Cigna was singing *La Gioconda*, Lina Bruna Rasa (I still tremble when I think of her Santuzza), *Cavalleria,* and Caniglia, in her youthful vocal splendor, *Tosca.* Those were the times when contraltos reigned, and Minghini-Cattaneo, Anitua, Buades, Stignani, and Besanzoni were formidable. I feel sorry for young people today, who cannot possibly have an idea what a real contralto sounded like. Besanzoni was later to be the impresaria of the Municipal in Rio de Janeiro, and I had a marvelous time there with her as well as at the Municipal in São Paulo. She was a divine human being—warm, understanding, and so able. It was in Brazil that I tackled for the first time not only the stunning role of Cecilia in Gomes's lovely opera *Guarany* (later at La Scala, when I sang the duet with Gigli, there was such a revolution up front that— unheard of for that theatre—we were obliged to repeat it) but also Micaëla, a last-minute replacement to save the performance. And in Buenos Aires I sang my first Violetta and first Rosina.

"Why do I live in Gatteo? I really don't know, except that my husband, the tenor Primo Montanari, came from Gatteo al Monte, a village near here. I sold the property there after his death, for it has become impossible to cope with farms in Italy. And I bought this little house here on the sea, where the winters are mild and everything, so far, is on the quiet side. I gave up my flat in Milan ten years ago, and all my students followed me here. I have over twenty of them, and it is most enjoyable, you know. I feel it is my duty to impart what I know before I leave this earth. Anyhow, since my husband, whom I adored, died—it was love at first sight way back in 1927, and we never had a cloud between us—I would have been lonely without this burning interest. I think it is a great privilege to give."

"Any regrets?" I asked her.

"Not important ones," she replied, "except for the fact that all the original tapes of those marvelous Rossini operas such as *Le Comte Ory* and *La gazza ladra,* which I had put my soul into at the time of the recordings, were destroyed in the bombing of Turin. However, enough records remain so that people in the years to come will know what my voice was like. Now RCA has reissued its *Rigoletto,* because it was the very first electric record-ing. My Duke of Mantua in this was Aurora Buades's husband, the tenor Roberto d'Alessio—the Rudolph Valentino of opera—and the Sparafucile, interestingly enough, was Salvatore Baccaloni, before he became a basso buffo. So there are two recordings of my Gilda—the other one is on Cetra. And this is heartwarming, for it is the jester's daughter who proved to be the key of entry into the doors of all the fabulous opera houses, and also the door to my husband's heart. He heard me during those early beginnings in Milan, asked to meet me through Gaetano Bavagnoli, whose father had been my coach, and we knew then and there that we were made for each other. And" —pointing to a portrait of the very handsome Montanari in his costume as the Duke of Mantua, a role he sang often—"he was the most important of all, for he gave me great happiness."

Lina Pagliughi died in 1980, three years after my meeting with her.

MARGHERITA CAROSIO

When I saw Margherita Carosio in 1980, after a break of thirty years, I simply could not believe that this woman, past seventy, could look so incredibly young and sprightly. I came right out and asked her for her secret. For there she stood in front of me, still ravishing, her black hair glistening, her eyes scintillating, her figure svelte and elegant, and with the same delicious smile that had won her millions of fans. "Don't you know that nightingales don't get old?" she laughed. "One day they just turn over and die. They don't lose their voices either. Sustaining long phrases is something else, but I can still hit a high F with no effort. Robins and wrens get old, but my breed does not. It's not as good as it may seem, for there is an age and a time for everything. It is difficult to look what you no longer really are, but the pretense must go on."

This very great artist, who for over thirty years had opera audiences eating out of her hand and then continued to delight the public with her exquisite recitals, always had a reputation in the musical world as being someone very special. Delicate, sensitive, moody, impractical and beguiling, poetical and subtle, Carosio was a law unto herself. A professional to her fingertips, she never allowed herself to become complacent in her work. Her repertoire was infinitely more varied and musically interesting than those of dal Monte, Pagliughi, and Galli-Curci. There never was another Adina in *L'elisir d'amore* like her, brittle, witty, utterly charming; or a more tragic Lucia di Lammermoor, whose mad scene really appeared crazed, her fluted tones unearthly, yet utterly tragic and heartbreaking. She did not have the most beautiful voice in the world, but she had a combination that so many other singers never had: a humor that was irresistible and a pathos that tore one apart. She could turn easily from comic opera to tragic because she had, in her own métier, a form of genius that escaped even the most acute observers. No one really ever penetrated her secret. Was it mainly instinct, paired with great technical vocal skill, or was what looked so spontaneous and natural all worked out to the minutest detail? After several conversations

Margherita Carosio as Elvira in *I puritani*.

with her, I came to the conclusion that she was simply blessed with an imaginative sensitivity that is totally out of the ordinary.

Although I am told that, indifferent to money, she made poor investments and is in financial straits, one would never know it. When I met her in her native Genoa, she was dressed in an old-fashioned but elegant manner. A consummate actress on the stage, she is one in real life too, and refuses to acknowledge difficulties. Is it pride or consideration for others, not wanting pity in any form? Hard to answer, but the bravery is all there in this fragile woman, whose career I wanted to reconstruct, since relatively little has been written about her. She was always publicity shy, and she performed in a period when not much written attention was given to any one singer, as there were so many extraordinary ones.

She was born into a musical family, and her father was a celebrated singing teacher. "Everything I became," she told me, "I owe to him. I used to say to him, 'I am good wool, but you are an extraordinary weaver.' " He was the general director of singing in all of the Genoese schools, and he started his daughter very early. At fourteen years of age she was already singing in public in costumed excerpts from operas—even taking on dramatic parts—and at sixteen she received her diploma from the conservatory to teach singing. Her official debut came in Novi Ligure with *Lucia,* but she continued to study piano, violin, and ballet. It was an engagement in Brescia as Musetta in *La Bohème* with Rosetta Pampanini and Angelo Minghetti that brought her immediately to Covent Garden in 1928. Margaret Sheridan, the Irish soprano so beloved by Toscanini, heard her and suggested her to the management, and she appeared there with Sheridan as Mimi and Pertile as Rodolfo. Because of her slim figure, she was asked to sing the role of Boris's son in *Boris Godunov,* one of those minor roles that stand out, and she accepted for the opportunity to sing with Chaliapin. "It was a tremendous experience," she told me, "for he made me realize what it meant not to take on a role but to become it. The entire horizon of opera changed for me." (Live tapes of these performances were made and have recently been reissued.)

In those days in Italy there were several outstanding coloratura sopranos —each with a very loyal public. And so it was not easy for Carosio to make her way, particularly since coloratura roles are relatively few. Because of her extraordinary modesty, she never pushed, asked for favors, or stooped to any intrigues. "I am grateful for the tremendous competition of those days," she told me, "for one had to be first-rate and walk up the ladder step by step. One can judge by the results today. Singers are catapulted into prominence much too soon and quickly vanish into oblivion. The attitude is so totally different today, I am at a loss to understand it and cannot even begin to discuss it. It is very much like those Catholic priests who want to serve Mass, dress as civilians, enter politics, and marry. For me it is total dedication to God or nothing. It was much the same with my profession. I was totally absorbed by our métier, and in many ways it was like taking the veil. One had to make untold sacrifices in order to arrive and then stay on top. It never occurred to me that any form of compromise could exist.

"That is why my marriage was a failure, for I soon realized that it was impossible for me to lead a double life: the disciplined artist and the dutiful, practical wife. Art won, and there are, as always, compensations. I think I became a valid artist because success, when it came suddenly and exploded, never went to my head. My father brought me up repeating over and over that one good notice today does not mean one tomorrow. It became part of my credo. The public will forgive you once, but rarely twice, and never a third time. And audiences are, whatever people say, always right. You pay to have a decent meal, and you do not return to a restaurant where the food has been unsatisfactory. An expensive ticket gives one the right to listen to a first-rate singer and not a mediocre one. I never quarreled with the public, for in my opinion it was usually ninety-eight percent right."

I asked her about style, for which she became so celebrated.

"That is something," she replied, "that one develops with blood, sweat, and tears. But you must be sensitive to begin with. It is like planting jasmine in a carrot field: the results will be totally negative. Some singers cannot become stylists, for despite superior vocal cords and an assured technique they do not have the necessary radar. Pergolesi is not Handel, Haydn is not Mozart, Rossini is not Donizetti, Bellini is not Verdi, and so forth. The approach must be different, not only in the throat, but also in the mind and the heart. This comes not just from study but from a very particular sense of introspection and an elasticity of the senses. I even took on hellish contemporary scores such as Stravinsky's *Le Rossignol* and Giordano's much-underrated *Il re,* for I felt that every experience enriched me; but I accepted only a few occasional performances of these works. Curiously, Stravinsky's strange arpeggios made me understand those of Bellini even better. Can you follow me? It's like how the shock of a distorted face by Picasso makes you realize better what Bronzino's or Lorenzo Lotto's portraits were all about. Style is in a way a sense of measure, of knowing the shades, not mixing up Schiaparelli's shocking pink with rose pink, and the smells too. A song, in my opinion, is perfumed in its own particular way, and the scent must be delivered even if the public is not aware of it. It's a comma here, a period there, a question mark somewhere else. When Amina in *La sonnambula* sings 'Come per me sereno,' it is a picture she paints with her own eyes and spirit, difficult because it is the quintessence of innocence, and to deliver this you must know what it means and feels like. When you are confronted with 'Qui la voce sua soave' in *I puritani,* Bellini's most difficult score, the ecstasy is crystallized, and the great difficulty lies in the fact that you must convey limpidity. The voice must have no body, it must float, and yet it must create a very definite emotion. Bellini, in my estimation, is more difficult than Mozart, for the latter is eighteenth century, and his characterizations are always framed in some way or another with a well-established character; Bellini's are not. Fiordiligi and Konstanze, which I sang often, are both difficult vocally, but their essence was easier to fulfill than Amina's or Elvira's, who are incredibly romantic and yet contained."

Actually, Carosio's debut at La Scala, where she was to become a reigning favorite for well over two decades, came suddenly. Ines Maria Ferraris, the scheduled Oscar, took ill just as *Un ballo in maschera* (with the formidable cast of Arangi-Lombardi, Minghini-Cattaneo, Pertile, and Galeffi, and Gabriele Santini on the podium) was about to have its premiere. Carosio did not know Oscar, but when she was approached to audition the next morning, she stayed up all night studying the score and was immediately rushed into the tricky part. This led to Philine in *Mignon,* a role that put her on the map, and from then on everything was offered her at Italy's holy of holies. But the real consecration came when she appeared in the world premiere of Mascagni's *Nerone* in 1935 as Egloge. She stole all the notices.

"As usual, chance played a big part," she told me. "I had never met Mascagni, nor would he ever have thought of me. But he was in Pesaro conducting some performances of *Il barbiere di Siviglia,* in his own very slow but assured manner, and the prima donna scheduled for Rosina fell ill. I was rushed there, and the dress rehearsal took place at one-thirty a.m. He was a vigorous, energetic man, and very kind—totally underestimated, from my point of view. He asked me to go to Rome and audition for him, as he was casting his new opera, for which there was much expectation. When I turned up at the Hotel Plaza, where he made his headquarters, and sight-read the score with him, he could not believe that I had not been able, somehow, to snatch a copy—it was not even published at the time—and learn the role. I got the job instantly. The critics did not care for the opera, but the public adored it, and every city in Italy demanded it. Then there were more offers than I could honor."

Metro-Goldwyn-Mayer, heavily involved in musical films, offered her a seven-year contract at this time: she was so very photogenic. But it meant giving up, at least temporarily, her operatic career, and, as usual, the money did not tempt her. She did appear in several Italian motion pictures, including one entitled *Regina della Scala* and *Sarasate,* in which she played Adelina Patti. She also made a film of *L'elisir d'amore* (an opera she recorded for HMV), and her voice was dubbed into a number of films in which she did not appear. She never sang in the United States, but appeared often at the Colón in Buenos Aires (Rosina, Philine, Gretel, Gilda, and the Queen in *Le Coq d'or*), in Germany, and all over Europe. She returned to Covent Garden after the war for *La traviata.*

"I did not go near Violetta for a long time," she explained, "as I wanted to have it very firmly in my throat and be able to dedicate all my attention to the acting. But when I started singing it, there was an avalanche of requests, and it is one of the operas that I performed the most often. The Strehler production at La Scala in 1947—his debut in this opera house— was the finest I appeared in of this work. In the third act, he had a balcony where guests sat at gaming tables and gambled. Although only half seen by the audience, they were present when the confrontation scene occurs. Alfredo throws the money at Violetta, and suddenly all the gamblers arose at once to watch what went on downstairs. It was a wonderfully effective bit of theatre instead of, as usual, having the chorus rush in from the outside. Violetta became another Gilda for me, as until then Rigoletto's daughter had been so identified with me that for years I simply could not escape her. I tried to limit my appearances in the open air—as you know, in Italy opera thrives in the summer breezes, which are so harmful to the vocal cords— but the Arena in Verona was fairly well protected with those high walls, and there I did consent to appear as Gilda, Adina, Oscar, Ines in *L'africana,* and several other parts. Wide-open spaces are very hard for a coloratura, but mine traveled with ease, including the high E.

"Mezze voci and messe di voce, in my time, were the sine qua non of a good singer. Now they no longer exist. What you listen to is a form of ventriloquism, fascinating in some respects, but not based on breathing. It is a sound that distresses me, for it is not natural, and I know that eventually it can only end in disaster. I believe that the reason I was able to sing for almost forty years is that I always took rests in the summer and did not go near the lyric repertoire until the end. My first Mimi at La Scala, with de Sabata, came only in 1950, and as it made a big splash, I was deluged with offers. But I was careful not to sing too many *Bohèmes,* for Mimi demands far more strength in the middle of the voice than usually thought. Massenet's *Manon,* which I first sang in Trieste with di Stefano, is lighter, and so is the delicious *Martha.*"

I asked her if she could recollect high points in her career.

"There are too many to mention," she replied, "but appearing as Pamina with Klemperer was a superlative experience, for he made this part, which until then I had found beautiful vocally but dull dramatically, come to life for me; and being so hypersensitive, I was overcome by the emotion he infused into this character. But perhaps the most thrilling moment of my professional life came when, after a performance of *La traviata* in Rome, a handsome old lady came into my dressing room and said, 'You are wonderful! You are the only one coming after me who knows how to die in this opera. They all fall to the floor—too ridiculous, with all those men and Annina around! Your death was thrilling, for it was totally real.' I looked at her. Who was she? She must have guessed my curiosity: 'Sorry I did not introduce myself. I am Gemma Bellincioni.' My throat became paralyzed, and I could not utter a word. So I fell on my knees and kissed her hand. She had been, after all, the greatest Violetta of them all!" Some years ago, Giorgio Strehler told me that Carosio's *Traviata* had been one of his great operatic experiences and that her sensibility was a unique phenomenon.

"Of course, I always admired temperament," she confessed. "And even in my own repertoire, within limitations, it always came to the fore. But I envied Ersilde Cervi Cairoli, Augusta Concato, Maria Zamboni, who had the power to evoke my tears, and I think that to be able to create emotion in an audience is a privilege given to very few. I never suffered from a sense of rivalry, for I do not believe that one can compare basically either singers or artists. As you see, I purposely speak of both, for I always divided my colleagues between the first class and the second. The artist is he who makes significant what at first glance is not, and who communicates from the inside. It is not the note or the gesture but what lies behind that really matters. I enjoyed different challenges, and that is why I loved going from the sparkling Zerlina in *Fra Diavolo* by Auber to Menotti's *Amelia al ballo,* which I created at La Scala in 1954, or going from the scheming Norina in *Don Pasquale* to a new, strange opera by Guido Pannain based on the tragic heroine Beatrice Cenci and the very difficult and witty Aminta in Richard Strauss's *Die schweigsame Frau.*

"My career was interrupted twice: once by a terrible automobile accident in Egypt when I was singing *Traviata* and *La sonnambula* in Alexandria and

Cairo; and then I stopped during the last period of the war. I narrowly missed getting killed while rehearsing *Così fan tutte* in Florence at the Comunale when the theatre received a direct hit and all the men in the orchestra lost their instruments. I also was sent to give recitals in Germany, and the train that I had been booked on to go to Düsseldorf was bombed and everyone died. But there had been a switch at the very last minute when my recital in Berlin's Beethoven Hall started very late because of the alarms.

"I shall never forget those concerts in Germany, attended only by women, as the men were all at the front. In one of the stations I saw men returning from the Russian front, and some were blind, armless, legless, or just ghosts. I was literally ill and could not continue. One cannot sing unless one's nerves are steady. Mine were always fragile to start with, so you can imagine how these shocks affected me. I always needed a certain amount of solitude and was never gregarious, despite my affection for some of my fellow artists. What I had to give was saved for performances, which took their toll, for mine was an expressive agility—not just scales and notes put together—and virtuosity per se never interested me. I admired it in others, but it did not go with my nature. You pay for your need to be alone later, of course, but then there is a price for everything. Art for me always came first, and I do not regret the consequences.

"I cannot answer which was the most enthusiastic public," she said, in answer to my question. "At the Liceo of Barcelona I recall that after a *Linda di Chamounix* the applause went on for so long that the electricians left one by one, and the last time I came out on the stage it was practically pitch dark. In Johannesburg I was booked for one recital and had to give five. In Nice during *Martha* there was pandemonium after 'The Last Rose of Summer,' and I simply could not understand why, as it is not that difficult to sing. But again I go back to what I told you before. One critic wrote that the scent of the rose was all over the theatre—a compliment that I treasured, for it was in my nostrils as I sang it. People are usually very tough, but suddenly—it is like a miracle—they can also be immensely perceptive. And this is what one must try to remember about them, even in this immensely troubled world we live in. American GIs were incredibly prodigal with applause. Right after the war, in 1945, I sang a stream of performances at the San Carlo in Naples, and it was then that I learned what Margherita is in English: Margaret. At the end of an aria they would scream 'Brava Margaret!' No marguerite has ever been named after me, but a camellia has."

I like to remember Margherita Carosio at a benefit recital (she shared the program with Giovanni Martinelli) in Venice in the summer of 1938, with all the public dressed to kill and the crown princess presiding. When the soprano walked out in a black crinoline-like dress, with her tiny waist, her raven-black hair pulled back by a string of diamonds, she was a vision I still treasure today. And then, when she started to sing, it was really like hearing a nightingale. The extreme decorum and grace that impressed me so much then are still intact.

THE GREAT DRAMATICS

ESTER MAZZOLENI

IVA PACETTI

GINA CIGNA

ZINKA MILANOV

Between the debut of Ester Mazzoleni in 1906 and the retirement of Zinka Milanov in 1966 runs a period of exactly sixty years. During this time there were several great dramatic sopranos, some of whom I will discuss later; but many, unfortunately, have since died. I was fortunate to meet and talk with four of the most celebrated: Mazzoleni, Iva Pacetti, Gina Cigna, and Milanov.

Mazzoleni's career lasted exactly two decades, ending with her marriage in 1926. Never having heard her except on technically poor recordings, I can only repeat what the old connoisseurs who did hear her live told me. Her voice, rich with a very personal timbre and exceedingly expressive, apparently was not large, but it was so expertly handled that it rose impressively over orchestras; and though she was not a particularly gifted actress, she had a tremendous presence. In bel canto operas such as *La vestale* and *Lucrezia Borgia,* she was seemingly peerless; and in *I vespri siciliani,* her virtuosity was astonishing.

Iva Pacetti, who began her career in 1920, retired in 1947 for reasons of health. For two decades her career coincided with that of Gina Cigna, and they shared much of the same repertoire, although Pacetti was by far the more versatile. In the years preceding the Second World War I heard Pacetti often, and although she was known to have nights when her pitch was imperfect, I was never present on such occasions. She was beautiful and distinguished looking and had a marvelous dramatic flair, and her instrument, ample and sensual, had a strong emotional impact.

Cigna, who had to abandon her profession after twenty years because of a serious heart attack, was of Italian parentage but born, raised, and trained (by Emma Calvé) in France. (The first years she sang at La Scala her name appeared as Sens, that of her first husband.) Her large, darkish instrument had the slightly metallic tinge shared by so many French-schooled voices. An imposing figure onstage, she had tremendous authority and was a thrilling performer. I recall her imperious Abigaille, her stupendous Donna Elvira, her regal Norma, and her amazing Turandot of many faces, whose voice melted and became very sensual in the love duet.

Milanov, whom I heard at least thirty times at the Metropolitan, was among the last of the great sopranos in this range. She lasted far longer than the others—nearly forty years after her debut in 1927, one of the longest careers on record for this type of instrument. Never an actress, she nevertheless walked through her parts with much panache; and despite a long period of faulty intonation, which she later was able to correct, hers was the most beautiful instrument of all, with pianissimos that have become legendary.

ESTER MAZZOLENI

When my interest in opera first was aroused, in the late 1920s and early 1930s, I would speak enthusiastically of Arangi-Lombardi, Ponselle, Cigna, Scacciati, and Pacetti as the great dramatic sopranos. But the old-timers would always say, "Ah, but you never heard Ester Mazzoleni!" So when I walked into the famous prima donna's apartment in Palermo during the winter of 1977, I wondered what sort of lady I would find. There she was, the woman who had shaken people to their depths with her dramatic fire, sitting in a huge armchair, a majestic woman with short snow-white hair, an aristocratic profile, and a knowing smile, her legs covered by a pretty cashmere shawl. At ninety-four years of age, she is a living legend.

"How did you ever discover that I am still alive?" she asked. "You know, I am the only one left of my generation, the only one to be forgotten by our Maker. Did you see the *Jesus of Nazareth* by Franco Zeffirelli on television? Isn't it great that there still exists such a sensitive human being? It made me very happy, for I cannot begin to tell you how upset I was at the *Norma* they showed on television from La Scala, with decor consisting of crates that looked as if they had come right off a ship. That they should dare to do this to my *Norma* is a sacrilege!" Thus the sprightly conversation began.

"Does my story interest you?" she inquired incredulously. "I shall try to be brief. I was born in 1882 in Sebenico in Dalmatia, which at the time, thank goodness, belonged to civilized Austria. It was an adorable city with strong cultural interests. My ancestors had settled there, but originally they came from Bergamo, and they still felt very attached to Italy, so much so that eventually I was sent to the Santa Anna school in Pisa and then to Notre Dame de Sion in Trieste. Naturally I spoke German, and as a child I learned French too. My family was very well off, but their greatest wealth was their love for the arts. I grew up in a cultivated atmosphere, and my father, Paolo, who had spent a lot of time in Milan, knew very well the Countess Maffei, Verdi's patroness and friend; the librettists Felice Romani, Antonio Ghislan-

Ester Mazzoleni as Giulia in *La vestale*.

zoni, and Francesco Piave, as well as Niccolò Tommaseo, who had been born in Sebenico; and last but not least Italy's most admired writer, Manzoni. My uncle Francesco was a celebrated tenor who made his debut in 1857 at La Scala in *I lombardi.* In fact, he became so famous that the opera house in Sebenico, the Teatro Sociale, was renamed Mazzoleni. All the best singers came there, and I lived in a musical atmosphere from the start, studying the piano, and singing at parties with my brother, who later became a lawyer. I began to study singing with Maestro Ravasio in Zara, but with no intention of becoming a professional.

"As a matter of fact, I was all set to become a painter, and in early 1906 I went with my father to Milan to find lodgings so as to take courses at the art academy. At the Pensione Pace, where we were staying, we met Maestro Rodolfo Ferrari, a well-known conductor at the Rome Opera. He heard me sing one day and was so enthusiastic that he persuaded my father to accompany me to Rome for an audition with the management of the opera house, then called the Teatro Costanzi. I didn't take any of this seriously until they listened to me and offered a contract to begin right away. My father and I were overwhelmed. In a matter of days I learned Leonora in *Il trovatore.* Amelia Pinto, who was celebrated at La Scala for her Isolde and Brünnhilde and had also created in that theatre Ricke in Franchetti's *Germania,* with Caruso, all under Toscanini, was engaged in Rome at the time and took me under her wing, giving me very valuable advice: 'You are pushing too hard in the very dramatic first scene of the last act. Whatever the conductor may say, don't force, even at the cost of being covered by the orchestra. Always give less than you have and then you will preserve intact your cords.' The diva who had sung the initial performances of Leonora had left because of another engagement, and I was to take her place. So there I was, not quite twenty-three, making my debut in opera, without having had the time to realize what was happening to me.

"The public was enthusiastic, but the next morning when my father came into my room with a bunch of newspapers under his arm and an anguished expression on his face, I began to cry. 'So they have torn me to shreds!' I wailed in tears. 'No,' he replied, 'it is far worse. They all say they haven't heard so stunning a voice in ages.' 'But then,' I asked, bewildered, 'why do you look so worried?' 'Because,' he answered, with his customary good sense, 'don't you realize, little dumbbell, what this means? You now have to live up to this explosion of praise, and you must work, work, work! You became a celebrity overnight, and this is far more dangerous than being a flop. Now you are in the soup and you must drink it.' He was perfectly right, of course, for I had been born with a gift God bestowed on me, but I had no experience. However, God was kind to me all the way, for he also provided me with an unfailing instinct that always protected me.

"In Rome I was hurriedly given Freia in *Das Rheingold,* then Rachel in *La Juive,* which then was a great drawing card. Offers began to pour in from all over Italy, and when I was in Bari appearing as Stephana in Giordano's *Siberia,* a telegram came from the great impresario Lusardi in Milan, asking me to travel there right away, as Toscanini wanted to hear me. This was barely a year and a half after my Roman debut. 'I'm not ready yet,' I said to my father. 'I couldn't possibly face the great maestro now. Anyhow, we have a good excuse. I am engaged here and I can't leave.' 'Nonsense,' replied my father. 'This is too good an opportunity to miss. You were born under a lucky star, and we have time to get there and back before your next performance, which is three days away.'

"I was very obedient then, and off we went next morning to Milan, a very long trip in those days. I was usually not affected by nerves, but when I had to appear before Toscanini and sing 'Pace, pace' I was overcome. He said nothing for a while, then ordered me to sing another aria. Then, without making a single remark to me, he turned to one of his assistants and said, 'I want this girl engaged for a period of three years, not a day less.' 'Will you trust your father from now on?' was the remark my parent made, with a big grin on his face, as we went to discuss what could be done about the engagements I was contracted for. La Scala could do anything it wanted at that time, and the other theatres released me."

Then everything began to happen rapidly, she explained. "It all seems like a dream. I made my debut at La Scala on January 18, 1907, under Toscanini, in a beautiful but very taxing role, Queen Isabella of Spain in Franchetti's *Cristoforo Colombo,* with a cast that included Pasquale Amato in the title role, Nazzareno de Angelis (the most formidable basso of my generation), and Luisa Garibaldi, at that time the reigning mezzo in the house. It was such a smash that we did sixteen performances. What has happened to this exciting work? In limbo to make room for Berio and Nono, no doubt. Then I sang a series of *Loreleys,* an eminently romantic opera that remained very close to my heart, at the Regio of Parma, under the direction of the unforgettable Cleofonte Campanini, and then *Tosca* with Riccardo Stracciari, a very effective Scarpia, and *Un ballo in maschera* in Trieste.

"Next came one of my most unforgettable experiences, which taught me a significant lesson. Toscanini was in the midst of rehearsing *La forza del destino* at La Scala, and the Leonora was the leading prima donna of that period, Eugenia Burzio. She was a tigress onstage as well as in private life.

Somehow a terrible quarrel erupted between her and 'God,' as we called him, and I was called back to Milan in haste. With the greatest of ease, the maestro announced to me that I would replace Burzio, as he had fired her. Despite being young and strong, I thought I would faint. The premiere was only a short time away; I barely knew the role—one of the most demanding in the entire Verdi repertoire; and I would be the victim of the legions of Burzio fans. One cannot imagine the following she had. People were hysterical about her. It all seemed sheer madness. I explained that La Scala had granted me the permission to sing guest performances elsewhere. 'Nonsense,' God replied. 'We shall attend to that problem. You will be Leonora, and that's that!' Later I learned to say no.

"You cannot imagine what happened on that opening night, March 19, 1908. All hell broke loose in the house after the tenor started 'O tu che in seno agli angeli' too soon and off key. The poor man, Icilio Calleja, a Spaniard, had been brought in at the last minute to replace Ignacio Dygas, a Pole, and he was frightened to death. As is often the case when the audience gets worked up, it vented its anger in all directions; and before we had the time to realize it, the civilized atmosphere had turned to that of a bullring. Amato and Garibaldi, two singers then very much in favor, were booed and hissed mercilessly. I cannot begin to describe to you the state I was in, for until the final scene the only ones who had been saved from the furies were de Angelis and myself. But I still had 'Pace, pace' before me, and I went onstage convinced that my turn had come for the storm to sweep me under. Miraculously, at the end, as I almost crumbled, there was a standing ovation. Later Toscanini, with his eyes blazing, appeared in my dressing room to announce that he had canceled further performances of this opera. 'Brava, bravissima,' he added, 'but don't let this success go to your head.' I crossed my heart and he walked out."

Ester Mazzoleni did not sleep that night; she tossed around mulling everything over. "It was true," she commented, "that Garibaldi had not been at her very best, and that Amato, a superb artist whom Toscanini adored, was not a Verdian baritone in the real sense of the word—he was a superb Barnaba, Nelusko, and Jack Rance, for instance, but the timbre did not have the warmth the Verdi characters need. But both of them were revered figures, and they had been exposed to a crushing humiliation. I learned at their expense that any singer, no matter how famous, is only as good as his last performance, and that any public can suddenly become thirsty for blood. Toscanini's words stayed with me from then on, and that evening was never forgotten.

"I spoke before about my instinct guiding and protecting me. I never accepted a role without looking at the score very thoroughly and singing it. Though I was very happy with Isolde, reaching the end without the slightest fatigue, I never accepted Brünnhilde. All singers come across certain passages that are ungrateful to their voices, and there were stretches in her music that did not suit mine.

"No one understood why I always refused to take on Butterfly—everyone sings it. It was not because of my height—many tall sopranos have gotten away with it—but because in my estimation it is one of the leading voice killers, for the orchestration is heavy, and if one wants to follow Puccini's directions, there are infinite nuances that must cut across. I sang instead Tosca, Suor Angelica, and Mimi. The theory that any dramatic soprano, or lyric or coloratura, can sing all the operas written for her type of instrument is folly. You must have the courage to face what is right for you and what is not. I sang Giordano's *Siberia* often, but never his *Fedora,* a very glamorous part, for it lies in the middle of the voice all the time, and then what happens to you after a few performances? Norma is an immensely demanding role, but I knew after going over the opera carefully that with some further work on my breath control it would be just right for me. After my first *Norma* in Bologna in 1910, this opera became one of my treasured properties. It stayed with me until the end, and it is with the Druid priestess that I drew the curtain on my career, in Naples in 1926.

"At that time there were three exceptional Normas: Giannina Russ, Celestina Boninsegna, and myself. Russ was a superb virtuosa but a little cold; Boninsegna's tone was utterly ravishing but a little too sweet. Mazzoleni, the critics claimed, combined the bel canto art with much fire. It became one of the roles I was asked to perform most frequently, along with Lucrezia Borgia, Aida, and La Gioconda. The last was tricky, for in order to produce the drama one must press on the middle. I learned how to get around that by putting emphasis on the phrasing and not on the vocal cords. Technique never worried me, for my voice was even in the three registers, and I had agility and facility on top. With concentration and study, I could overcome all the difficulties, provided the tessitura was right for me.

"I simply cannot understand what is happening now. They all sing Norma today—the coloraturas, like Sutherland, Deutekom, and Sills; the lyrics, like Maria Luisa Cioni and Scotto; the spintos, like Caballé, whom I admire in certain roles very much. But how can they do justice to this terrifying score? It is an utter travesty of what Bellini wrote, and the audience takes a lot of punishment. The last great Norma for me was Anita Cerquetti. Now mezzos, I am told, in the United States are also about to jump into this free-for-all.

"An opera I took time to undertake was *La traviata*, for I wanted to ensure that I could make my voice brilliant enough for the first act. The role suited my temperament and became a staple of my operatic wardrobe, along with more Verdi: *Aida, I vespri siciliani, Forza, Trovatore, Ballo,* and *Don Carlo.* When Giovanni Zenatello had the clever idea of turning the Arena of Verona into an open-air summer opera—the acoustics are marvelous—he insisted that I inaugurate the first season in 1913 as Aida, and though I always used to take the summer months off at my villa near Abbazia, I accepted. It was a thrilling experience, and later I even sang Norma there."

The soprano retraced her steps back to La Scala, where after her success in *Forza* a series of extraordinary challenges was thrown at her. Among them was *I vespri siciliani*, missing from the roster since 1875, with a fantastic cast (Amedeo Bassi, Stracciari, de Angelis). This really established her as a Verdi soprano and a big star. Spontini's *La vestale* had not been performed there since 1825, and La Scala had waited for the right person to tackle that sublime score, a real test of bel canto. It went so well that instead of the five performances scheduled there were sixteen, and when La Scala went to Paris the following year, 1909, it was one of the operas chosen. There too the enthusiasm was tremendous. This revival gave new life to this opera, with every theatre demanding it, including the Colón in Buenos Aires, which Mazzoleni found a "noble" theatre.

She continued: "The extraordinary reception given to the Spontini masterpiece gave the Scala management the encouragement to present Cherubini's *Medea*, which strangely enough had never been performed in Italy before. The composer was a Florentine who had moved first to England, then to France, where Marie Antoinette helped to launch him on his way to fame. He remained on, through the revolution, and after the triumph of *Lodoïska*, an opera that was performed two hundred times in one year, he brought out *Medea* in 1797. What is so fascinating about him is that he started out as a writer of comic operas. *Medea* is, undoubtedly, one of the most advanced operas ever written, and one of the most shattering. When I started rehearsing it, I was overwhelmed with panic. I knew I could do justice to the music, but when I studied the immensely demanding score, I was so enthused by the music that I had not fully realized the demands it made dramatically. The role needs a Rachel or a Bernhardt, and though I had been establishing a reputation as a singing actress, the combination of bel canto personified and the bedevilment of the character in its various displays of tenderness and then fury confounded me. This was a woman whose temperament flared from the moment she came on the stage until the end. How to create a crescendo? I learned more about coloring my voice from this opera than from any other. I remembered my days as a painter and tried to apply what I had learned from the palette.

"If I dwell so long on this undertaking, it is because I consider it the most important event in my career. Interest in this revival was immense, and people came from all over. Even Puccini was in the audience, and when he came back to see me after the ordeal was over, he told me he had rarely been so moved. I recall that every time I reached, at the end, the 'Atre Furie, volate a me! La man a piombar già s'appresta. Figli miei, ch'io v'uccida!' [Black Furies, come to my aid. Already my hand hurries to the deed. My children, I must slay you], I was almost in a state of hypnotic trance. It is in my opinion one of the greatest dramatic scenes ever written. I find it inconceivable that this opera was shelved until 1953, when it was brought back as a vehicle for Callas. I had to laugh then—with all due respect for the Greek artist—at how the eleven performances we gave in the 1909–10 season were forgotten and it was all made to sound as if hers had been the Italian premiere!

"In 1916 La Scala threw at me another forgotten and fine Spontini opera, *Fernando Cortez,* which had never been performed there, with Panizza conducting and Giuseppe Danise as Montezuma. But unlike *La vestale,* this did not enthrall the audience, and it was only performed five times. My role, Amazily, was madly difficult—that much I can recall. At La Scala I had also brought back *L'africana,* absent since 1888, and it has never been given there since. In this production I had Viglione Borghese as Nelusko, one of the great baritones of my era, but the one who was unique in this part, Titta Ruffo, created sparks. This is the only way I can describe him. Today's public has no conception of what a real baritone used to sound like.

"As for *Lucrezia Borgia,*" she related, laughing, "its resurrection came— the last time it had been given was in 1893 with the Rumanian soprano Elena Teodorini—because of Alessandro Bonci's wish to sing Gennaro. Since the protagonist is a hellish role, they thought of me right away. I read the score and fell madly in love with it. So the favor to Bonci turned into a veritable bonanza for me, as I became so identified with the Donizetti heroine after La Scala, I sang it absolutely everywhere. The aria 'Com'è bello' demands real bravura and at the same time a highly emotional charge. In my opinion it is one of the most formidable challenges, not only vocally but from an interpretative standpoint. Bonci was an exquisite tenor, immensely refined and stylish, and I recall singing with him ever so many *Ballos.* There has never been another tenor who sang 'È scherzo od è follia' like him, with a natural laugh built into the music. His was an ethereal sound that seemed to travel to the moon and back. There was no limit to his breath control, and I listened to him transfigured.

"Strange things happen to a singer, for which there seems to be no explanation. At the San Carlo in Naples I sang for the first time Valentine in *Les Huguenots,* for the part appealed to me, but I thought of it as an ensemble opera—there are many characters, including roles for two other prima donnas, the Queen and the page Urbain, who have lovely arias. Despite a most distinguished cast, I received the longest ovation of my career. I was embarrassed because of my excellent colleagues, and simply could not understand the fuss.

"In those days one could learn a lot from the critics, who loved us singers and took infinite pains to describe our merits or faults. They knew a lot about voices, and I simply cannot understand what has transpired. Today's critics hate singers and consider them of no importance. They write five thousand words to destroy divine scores like *Lucrezia Borgia* or *Anna Bolena* and then fifty words about the cast. In my case, how they worried when I took over verismo roles, as they were afraid these might impair my voice. But I knew what I was doing and chose those which I knew could not harm me. Of Catalani, apart from *Loreley* I appeared only in *Dejanice,* which I treasured, but never *La Wally.*"

Ester Mazzoleni's decision to retire was very sudden. "In Palermo," she explained, "I had met and fallen in love with a pearl of a man, a notary, who refused to be a diva's husband and follow her around. He had his profession and made it very clear that he would not abandon it. My voice was still in excellent shape, and I could have gone on for several more years, but did I have a right to renounce personal happiness when I had already been blessed with every possible success? So I made up my mind, said goodbye to the stage, and never regretted it. First of all, I had chosen a wonderful human being, and we had two daughters who have been my pride and joy. My husband died soon after the Second World War. With the advent of communism in Yugoslavia, the many buildings and farms I had inherited there were confiscated. My delightful villa was taken away from me too. As an artist I always lived exceedingly well, but I never became money-mad the way singers are today. With the various inflations and what was wiped out by the war, not much is left. However, I cannot complain, and since an automobile accident immobilized me, I never leave this apartment. But friends keep me abreast of all the gossip. I taught at the conservatory until I was seventy and then retired. It was also my pleasure to give courses at the Accademia Chigiana in Siena when Count Chigi, a unique patron of the arts, was still alive.

"Singing, alas, remains only on records, and those I made don't give the palest notion of what my voice was really like. The other day a recording arrived of my duets with Zenatello, Francesco Vignas—the greatest Lohengrin and Tristan imaginable—and Pasquale Amato, released in Austria. It made me realize that my great colleagues and I have not been totally forgotten."

In the spring of 1982, this great artist celebrated her one hundredth birthday in Palermo.

IVA PACETTI

Among the great dramatic sopranos Italy produced in the 1920s and 1930s, Iva Pacetti stood out, her name synonymous with considerable personal beauty, enormous temperament, and a strong, velvety voice able to tackle a wide-ranging, demanding repertory. When she greeted me in her luxurious apartment—with its immense drawing rooms, valuable seventeenth-century paintings, and fine baroque furniture—in the fashionable Parioli section of Rome, I was confronted with a still stunning-looking woman, elegant in a black frock with two pearl necklaces, soft ash-blond hair, and an overall air of royalty. During our two-hour talk, what impressed me most were the utter dignity of the former diva, her assurance and honesty, underlined by the modesty of one who has known what greatness means. She viewed the past as if it were a tapestry, the sequence of events not always in accordance with dates. Born around the end of the last century, she made her debut in 1920.

"I am very detached from the past," she began quietly, almost sotto voce. "It all seems to have happened in another existence. The present is so ugly and uncertain, the revolution of values so distressing. Yet I am so grateful for what has been. All this"—she pointed around, with her lovely hands, to her possessions—"can be taken away, but no one can pocket the marvelous experiences and satisfactions I had.

"I came from literally nothing, and mine was a very simple family. My father was the head operator in a textile factory in Prato, where I was born, and of course today Prato is almost a part of Florence. It has always been a highly industrious town, of serious people, whose merchant traditions go back to the Middle Ages. My mother was an expert at embroidery, another lost art, and I spent many hours mastering the difficult skill as a youngster. It taught me the ability to concentrate—which came in very handy later.

"The flame of singing has burned within me ever since I can remember, and at the age of thirteen my voice was already formed. I began going to

Iva Pacetti as Leonora in *Il trovatore*.

Florence for singing lessons. At first it was decided I was a mezzo-soprano, but by the time I was sixteen everyone had concluded I was a dramatic soprano. My name, Iva, has no precedents in the family, just as there was nobody musical at home.

"I was waiting for a chance to begin—not so easy in those days with such a wealth of good voices around. And when it came, there was no time to assess what was happening. The carnival season—every provincial town in Italy used to have operatic seasons in that period, another tradition that has been lost—was on in the delightful Teatro Metastasio in my hometown, and La Rossini, who was to have sung Aida, fell ill. At eleven in the morning I was put through an orchestra rehearsal—in that period unions did not exist —and that night I went on without a single stage rehearsal. Folly, of course; but I was fortunate. Though I was never satisfied with anything I did, because of an inborn, maddening sense of agonizing responsibility, I never had nerves or stage fright. Once I was on the stage, there were no inhibitions or indecisions. The reappraisal came afterward. Anyhow, on that night it seemed perfectly natural to be in love with Radames, to meet my father, Amonasro, after such a long separation, to want to be buried alive with my beloved—it all fell into place.

"This was in 1920, and my success made the front pages. An immediate engagement followed to sing Aida and Tosca in Florence, and then many other theatres followed. In 1922, less than two years after my debut, I was called by La Scala to appear as Elena in *Mefistofele* with a fabulous cast: Juanita Caracciolo was Margherita; Nazzareno de Angelis, the protagonist; and Pertile, Faust.

"Toscanini conducted, and despite the unhappy experiences I had with him, I admired and respected him tremendously. He became annoyed at the very beginning when I turned up at the first piano rehearsal chaperoned by my mother. We were simple people, and provincial; that was our way. The maestro, after all, had picked me out from many applicants at an audition in the offices of the celebrated impresario Lusardi. As I was very thin then, every effort was made to teach me how to look more sensuous—was I not to represent the most beautiful woman in the world, for whom the Trojan War had been fought?—and to teach me how to walk like a queen. I was in seventh heaven, for the next day all the critics wrote that a great new dramatic soprano had been born. Elena is a short role, but ever so grateful. Her apostrophe 'La luna immobile innonda l'etere' [The motionless moon floods the firmament], her recollection of the destruction of Troy, and then the love duet with Faust, 'Ah! amore! misterio celeste' [Ah! love! celestial mystery], are all wonderfully melodious, offering the opportunity to show off the roundness of one's tones.

"But after the fourth performance Scandiani, who ran La Scala, came to see me and apologized profusely, explaining that Toscanini did not like me and wanted me to be replaced. Never had I seen a man so embarrassed. Where I found the nerve I shall never be certain—since I was totally unsophisticated then and did not know the rules of the theatre—'After four performances and the superb notices,' I replied, holding back the tears, 'he has no right to protest against me, and I shall go on singing Elena as contracted.' I then ran to Lusardi, who backed me up, and the result was that I sang the remaining eight performances. We also had a gala night attended by King Vittorio Emanuele.

"In the meantime, all the opera houses were after me. I sang Elena again in Padua with Serafin, who then chose me for Amelia in *Ballo* at the San Carlo in Naples, with Bonci, then well over fifty, whose Riccardo has never been equaled, and Stracciari, an overwhelming Renato. I succeeded to such an extent that six operas followed the same season, and I was re-engaged there for many years. It was at the San Carlo that I sang my first Wagnerian role, Elisabeth in *Tannhäuser*. Emma Carelli, whose flair for casting was unparalleled, signed me to open the 1925–26 season at the Rome Opera, which she managed, with *Francesca da Rimini*, and again it was a triumph —so much so that Carelli insisted that I sing Brünnhilde in *Die Walküre*. And then came the Roman premiere of Giordano's *La cena delle beffe* (the role of Ginevra is one of the most sensuous I have ever undertaken), *Otello*, *Aida*, *Andrea Chenier*, and *Turandot* right after the premiere. You know that Carelli, herself a great singing actress, was responsible for creating all the wonderful dramatic effects of Tosca's finale of the second act. These effects have become the standard interpretation. I was absolutely fearless in those days.

"And then," she smiled, "we must return to Toscanini and another incredible chapter in my book. He was determined to conduct Dukas's *Ariane et Barbe-Bleue* on a text by Maurice Maeterlinck—we were now in 1927 —an opera that has never encountered real success since its premiere in Paris in 1907. And the leading soprano part, terrifying in its length and vocal hurdles, was hard to cast. He listened to thirty-one sopranos (at least so I was told at the time) and then in despair asked for me. I had by then established the fact that I was very versatile and could be equally successful in both the Verdian and Wagnerian repertoires along with verismo and realismo scores. Naturally, this was a source of immense satisfaction, but one should never fall victim to pride. It goes without saying that since Toscanini was the music director of La Scala, I had never been invited back since the *Mefistofele* days. The rehearsals began, and immediately he berated me for producing a score with many phrases underlined by the coach with whom I had learned this incredible part. '*Che cosa è questa porcheria?*' [What is this mess?] he shouted, throwing the score across the room. At one of the piano sessions, where Ariane has a thirty-five-minute monologue, he stopped and said, 'Now we will take a break.' Idiot that I was, instead of shutting up I remarked, 'Thank you, Maestro, I'm utterly worn out.' He made no comments at the time, but we rehearsed that scene every day for hours, until I was ready to drop dead. And no question ever of a break.

"At the first stage rehearsal—I shall never forget this as long as I live—when all of Bluebeard's wives are lined up, he screamed at me, 'You are a sheep! For this role a lioness is needed!' The critics had always commented on my fiery temperament, and that day it blossomed in full. No one, not even the sublime Toscanini, had the right to insult me in front of everyone. With all eyes staring at me, I marched out of La Scala and began walking. 'Pacetti, Pacetti!' I heard a voice cry out in back of me. It was the metteur-en-scène Gioacchino Forzano. 'Are you insane? This can mean the end of your career.' 'Perhaps,' I replied, 'but no one is going to call me what he did!' And I walked away. By the time I had reached home on foot, Scandiani was already there. The question was very simple: either I continued or the production would have to be canceled. So much pressure was put on me that I returned to the next rehearsal. Toscanini was icy but correct, and I sang the various performances. But to show his distaste, the great man never came out to take a bow with me, and that was that. Again, the opera was not a hit. It is a mixture of Wagner, Debussy, and Mussorgsky, an allegory that would not please the feminists of today, for five out of the six wives prefer slavery with a man to freedom without him. The scene where Ariane breaks the glass door is a killer, but then so is all the rest. She is on stage incessantly.

"My career did not suffer one bit," she continued. "On the contrary, everyone in the business said I had guts. I remained an admirer of Toscanini's genius, but we never met again. He was a strange man with his friends too. In 1922, the year of my *Mefistofele* at La Scala, there was the most terrific to-do over the fact that he had refused to conduct the local premiere of *Il trittico* and had handed over the assignment to Panizza. In the same period Toscanini was conducting *Rigoletto* and *Boris* there. Puccini had been enormously hurt and complained to everyone about it. And while Toscanini in those days conducted for three seasons *Debora e Jaele* by his friend Pizzetti, when it came to *Turandot*—which, as everyone knows, was given its world premiere at La Scala in 1926, after Puccini's death—Toscanini led only the first three performances and then handed over the others to Panizza. This again created a storm of gossip, since after the *Trittico* drama Puccini and the maestro had been on friendly terms again. As far as I know, he never went near *Turandot* again. The contradictions in this exceptional man were many. Between 1924 and 1928 he conducted four different productions of *Nerone* by Boito, which never really got off its feet; no one could figure out why.

"I was not called back to La Scala until the maestro left," she reminisced, "and then it was for good. My return there was in January 1930 in *La forza del destino*. I, who worshiped Muzio, absolutely trembled at the decrescendo, crescendo, and then decrescendo again in 'Pace, pace,' at which she excelled. But I learned how to handle the obstacles, and it became one of my best roles. The following year Bruno Walter chose me to sing Donna Anna with him, and this was a delightful experience. No temperament there—all kindness and consideration. In all the years I sang at La Scala I appeared, if memory serves me correctly, in eighteen different operas, including the world premiere of Porrino's *Gli Orazi* and the first local performance of Cherubini's *Le due giornate*. But the most important musically was the Milan premiere of Strauss's *Die Frau ohne Schatten,* in which I undertook the Dyer's Wife. The tessitura kept me on my toes—so many high Cs!—but the part was spellbinding, and I am sorry I never had the chance to sing it again. Instead, I appeared many times as the Marschallin.

"At La Scala I went from the Verdi heroines to Tosca and Manon Lescaut, from *Fidelio* to verismo operas such as *Fedora* and *Cavalleria,* where I had quite an *histoire* with Mascagni, who was conducting . . . but let the dead lie. Santuzza is a role I sang often and which eventually I was able to control, for it can wear you out. At La Scala in 1939 there were rehearsals going on for the revival of Pizzetti's *Fedra,* which had not been given since 1914, when the celebrated Florica Cristoforeanu had created this rather over-whelming part. Cobelli, who was due to appear as the protagonist, fell ill three days before its first performance. They begged me to take over, and I accepted—madness, for it was a cruel assignment, and there was no time to really get my teeth into it. But it turned into a memorable personal success and I could see why both Rosa Raisa [in 1915] and Ponselle [at Covent Garden in 1931] had been attracted to this intensely tragic character.

"I was gifted with a memory that was a blessing, and I even learned Elsa in less than a week, replacing my idol Muzio, who was indisposed, at the

Rome Opera, with Pertile as Lohengrin. To please Edoardo Vitale, who was one of our best Wagnerian conductors, I even learned and sang both Kundry and Isolde. I never would undertake too much Wagner, for I feared that my agility might become impaired, but from time to time it was a joy to plunge into that inspiring repertoire. I didn't approach *La traviata*—in which so many of my colleagues, including the divine Muzio, sang 'Sempre libera' a tone under—until I could handle it in the original key, and I worked very hard at it. The role was right for me, and I sang it a lot. But *Butterfly*, which I adored, was not appropriate; I was too tall and statuesque to create the illusion, and as I believed fervently in looking the part, I discarded it. *La fanciulla del West,* on the other hand, became my very own, and I dipped with relish and gusto into the verismo ladies, appearing often as Francesca da Rimini, Adriana Lecouvreur, and Fedora. I remained, however, always a Verdian soprano, often undertaking—besides the roles already mentioned—Maria in *Boccanegra,* Elvira in *Ernani,* Alice in *Falstaff,* Elisabetta in *Don Carlo,* and even Abigaille in *Nabucco,* which is most risky because of its almost acrobatic jumps in tessitura. It certainly is not a role one can afford to sing often. But one must learn how to fence and give one's vocal cords time to recover from certain assignments, sometimes a period of several weeks. This is what is missing today.

"Norma became one of my most frequent roles, and perhaps, as I look back, it is the one that afforded me the greatest satisfactions. I sang it even at the Colón in Buenos Aires, where many extra performances had to be added. I also loved *Il pirata,* which was revived in Rome in 1935, in the centenary of Bellini's death, in an admirable production conducted by Serafin, and with Gigli and Mario Basiola as my partners. No wonder Giulia Grisi always insisted on singing it, as does Caballé today. Imogene's mad scene is a sublime page out of Bellini's genius and the precursor of the other great mad scenes in *Lucia, Anna Bolena,* and Thomas's *Hamlet,* for *Il pirata* dates back to 1827. There is also a moment that reminds one of 'Casta diva,' when the melody is sustained in F major. For me nothing is more divine than the 'Deh! tu innocente per me l'implora' [Oh, you who are innocent, plead with him for me], when suddenly, in her deranged state of mind, she recognizes her son, who has been brought to her. Even more so than *Norma,* this demands a dramatic coloratura, but, thank heavens, I was able to do justice to the roulades and agilities which are marked in the score *con gran forza* [with great strength] and *modo lacerante* [excruciating manner]. Unfortunately, after the revivals with Callas and Caballé it has fallen again into oblivion. But it is not an opera that can be handed to a mediocre interpreter."

In the United States Pacetti sang in Chicago in *Aida, Tosca,* and *Andrea Chenier,* and she was re-engaged there for the following season. "Then the crash came," she commented, "and there was none. I did sing in South America almost every year. It was at Covent Garden that I heard and greatly admired Rosa Ponselle, who was appearing in *Forza* when I was in *Tosca.* I returned to the hotel one day at three in the afternoon and found a frantic message to ring up Covent Garden immediately. Ponselle was ill; would I replace her as a big favor? Having heard the production of *Forza* a few nights before, I accepted on one condition—that the first-act aria be reinstated. Ponselle, whose instrument was superb but a little short on top, had it cut out.

"I always went to hear other singers, for there was much to learn. While singing in *Don Giovanni* at the Maggio Musicale Fiorentino, I was so fascinated with Mafalda Favero's Zerlina that I stayed in the wings, an unheard-of thing for me, to watch her. I adored Ersilde Cervi Cairoli's Adriana, and everything Carmen Melis did, despite a limited voice—what a tremendous artist! Galeffi was the greatest of the baritones, and his Posa in *Don Carlo* destroyed me in the death scene, so tender and spiritual was his farewell.

"The tenors I sang with constantly were Gigli, Lauri-Volpi, Masini, and Pertile. If Lauri-Volpi had a good evening, he topped everyone. I remember an *Aida* we sang together in Barcelona as one of the most nerve-racking experiences of my life. He ended 'Celeste Aida' in falsetto, and the hissing that went on was frightening. This put the fear of God in all of us, as it meant it was one of those bloodthirsty audiences. Then in the great concertato of the second act he was astonishing, and in the third act he was so inspired he made me cry, which is never good while one is singing.

"With Gigli, whose timbre was beauty personified, one knew exactly where one stood. My goodness, how many *Manon Lescauts, Toscas, Forzas,* and *Aidas* I sang with him, entirely relaxed! I recorded *Pagliacci* with him, but actually I never sang Nedda in the theatre. Masini was much like Lauri-Volpi; when in form he sang like an angel. Pertile was the greatest of them all—a man with no personality offstage, but who had the genius of becoming one hundred percent the character he represented in each opera. It was like osmosis. He could go from Walther in *Meistersinger* to Otello, and it was difficult to believe it was the same man. I sang with Martinelli when he was no longer in his prime, but he made a deep impression on me.

"My career came to an end very suddenly in 1947, after a performance of *Turandot.* I woke up the next morning riddled with arthritis. I went through two years of hell and finally was cured. I was itching to start again, but my second husband, the late Gaetano Turilli, would not hear of it. He had been anxious for a long time that I retire. Perhaps it was for the best. The parting with the raison d'être of one's life is perhaps less painful in this way, and I console myself with the wise phrase of the Marschallin: 'Such' dir den Schnee vom vergangenen Jahr' [Seek the snows of yesteryear]."

Iva Pacetti died in the winter of 1981.

GINA CIGNA

It was with great anticipation that I called on Gina Cigna in her stately apartment in Milan; she had sent shivers down my spine during my youth in Florence, where she sang year after year in a variety of roles. Could this extremely attractive, relatively small, but erect and dynamic woman be almost eighty? (She was born in Paris in 1900.) I did not expect anyone so animated, down-to-earth, and totally honest, full of that particular form of witchcraft called charm. Her features, which appeared rather imperious onstage, are actually those of a willful but refined lady. Within a matter of minutes I felt as if I had always known her; her eyes, which her colleague Elena Nicolai had described as "fantastic—like stars," spoke as expressively as her words.

For many years a distinguished singing teacher, she held posts at the conservatories in Genoa, Toronto, and Palermo—where she became a friend of Ester Mazzoleni—and spent her summers at the Accademia Chigiana in Siena. Now she has returned to the city that made her famous and is teaching on her own. Her involvement with pupils such as Elena Mauti Nunziata, Maria Parazzini, Celestina Casapietra, and Cristina Angelhokova—who are all now much in demand in leading theatres—keeps her very much in touch with what goes on in the lyric theatre, and she is deeply concerned about what is happening.

"Actually, when I look back," she explained rapidly, but with a caressing voice, "I am amazed at how much I crowded into twenty years. That is all my career lasted. I am the victim of the adage 'The show must go on.' I was driving to Vicenza for a repeat performance of *Tosca*—Milan is quite nearby—and was the victim of a violent automobile accident. It happened at five in the afternoon, and the performance was to begin at nine. Apart from all the bruises, I felt absolutely wretched, but I went on, so as not to let the management down with a sold-out house. Those were the difficult years after the war when private managers risked everything to keep opera alive. I never sang again—I had suffered a very serious heart attack and not realized it. I was put into intensive care for several months. But there was no question of my being able to sing again. Every doctor—and I saw many —agreed that any effort would be fatal. I was deeply shaken, for opera was my life, and I could not conceive of living without it. But there was no way out. All my savings and properties had been swept away by the Second World War, so I had to start again as a teacher.

"But to go back to the beginning," she continued, "I was born in the French capital, and the fact that I had an Italian-sounding surname—my first name was Geneviève—is due to the fact that an Italian ancestor of mine followed Napoleon to France, married a French girl, and settled in Paris. My father took all the courses in the famous military academy of St. Cyr and lost his life at the front in the First World War.

"My ambition was to be a pianist, so I went to the Paris Conservatoire, where I had the unhoped-for opportunity to study with Alfred Cortot. I have always kept up the piano, and I accompany all my students. I enjoyed singing for the pleasure of my friends, and when I was eighteen I sang at a party one evening. Unknown to me, Emma Calvé was there—if I had been aware that so legendary an ex-diva was present, I never would have opened my mouth. And in all probability I never would have become Cigna, the soprano.

"Calvé talked to my mother and told her she thought I had the potential to become an important singer. Mother was stunned, and so was I. For seven years I studied with Calvé. She was an exceedingly severe person, and the breathing exercises she put me through are not to be believed. She insisted I change the air in my lungs the way the yogis do. Calvé was sure that I was a mezzo, and in fact I had no high notes. But I was immensely stubborn and did not wish to be a mezzo—all the roles that attracted me belonged to the soprano repertoire. So I tried and tried, and, miraculously, one day my throat finally opened up and I produced an F-sharp. It was like a padlocked door that suddenly had opened. From then on I began to consolidate what I had gained, and the other notes came until I finally reached high C. You cannot imagine my exaltation, or the surprise of Madame Calvé, who simply could not believe her ears. I advise young singers to keep trying. Somehow the stairs leading to the top are there, but the problem is to find them. Some voices are born perfectly placed, and the high register is there, free and easy. But some need very strong willpower and discipline to find it.

"Calvé saw my future in Italian opera and felt I could do much better in Italy than in France. So when she finally felt that I was ready, she got

Gina Cigna in the title role of *Norma*.

in touch with an old agent she knew in Milan and sent me there. Within a matter of days, he arranged an audition with Toscanini and his assistants, including the important so-called secretary, Anita Colombo. To their amazement, I sat down at the piano and accompanied myself. I so well recall the selections Madame Calvé had made so that I could show off my volume and technique—'D'amor sull'ali rosee,' 'O cieli azzurri,' and—please believe it—'Una voce poco fa.' I was engaged on the spot and made my debut at La Scala—my first appearance on any stage—as Freia in *Das Rheingold* with Ettore Panizza conducting on January 23, 1927. A very short time later Toscanini quarreled with the theatre and left for the United States to take on the leadership of the New York Philharmonic.

"My first big successes at La Scala came with Donna Elvira and Elisabeth in *Tannhäuser,* the only other Wagner role I ever undertook. The *Don Giovanni* was memorable both at La Scala and at the Maggio Musicale Fiorentino, with Guarnieri conducting in Milan and Bruno Walter in Florence with formidable casts. At La Scala the Donna Anna was Giannina Arangi-Lombardi, who had started out as a mezzo and then had made the change into dramatic soprano brilliantly. Her Mozart was an unforgettable lesson in style. Her technique was formidable, but she reminds me, thinking back, of Sutherland—and she was not Australian! Her diction was hazy. But then I always preferred temperament and interpretation to voice alone. In a certain sense"—and she laughed—"one could understand why Stabile, the Don, had such a hell of a time seducing her. . . . For me Callas could not touch Muzio. With Muzio you suffered agonies with her heroines, with Callas never. I am not taking away from the Greek that she had *beaucoup de chien* [great presence], but, goodness, she sang with three voices!

"Ebe Stignani had a superb instrument, but among mezzos I much preferred Elena Nicolai. They both sang Adalgisa with me innumerable times. In the second and third acts, when Nicolai was my partner, there existed a current of electricity impossible to explain. With Stignani it was heavenly singing—that's all. No other mezzo has aroused me as Eboli and Ortrud as Nicolai did. Gianna Pederzini's instrument could in no way compare to the other two, but when she was onstage she never missed. Sparks flew in every direction, and I watched her absolutely mesmerized. With a thread of a voice she held the audience spellbound. That is art. Even as Amneris, she made her judgment scene vital and interesting, despite the lack of vocal equipment."

Cigna's first *Norma* was in Vigevano in 1931. "It was trial ballooning before taking on the enormous responsibility in the leading houses, and then from Palermo to Florence and Paris, from Catania to London (where I sang in four different seasons), from Buenos Aires to Rio de Janeiro, from Chicago to the Metropolitan. I sang it everywhere, and it always remained" —she pointed to her heart—"right here. Every time I sang 'Casta diva' I felt transfigured, as if I had been transported away from everyone and everything—a curious sensation I never had with any other aria. It was a tremendous privilege, a sort of special blessing bestowed on me. I often wondered if other sopranos had the same feeling. And I recall that every time the invocation to the goddess of the moon was over and I had to return to reality, intoning the difficult 'Ah! bello a me ritorna'—which is really a form of allegro, in contrast to the fluent measures and the endless legatos of the prayer—I had to take hold of myself to break away from the enchantment I had been bathed in a few moments earlier.

"While I was enthralled with the hair-raising challenges of Abigaille, which I first sang at the Maggio Musicale Fiorentino in 1933 and repeated at La Scala the following year with the same admirable cast (the superb Carlo Galeffi was a Nabucco born to the purple), I intensely disliked Lady Macbeth. She is a fiendish woman, and the score as cruel as she is. Verdi wanted an ugly, strident voice for it, and he was absolutely right. Everyone always refers to the difficulties of the sleepwalking scene—'Una macchia è qui tuttora' [A spot is still here]—but what about the second-act scene, 'La luce langue' [The light is fading]? It was written for the Paris version of this opera in 1865, in place of another aria heard in Florence at the premiere, and the intensity, plus the strange tessitura, is shattering. But as I made a big hit with it, every theatre demanded this opera.

"Another opera they threw at me over and over again was *Tosca,* and I refused it as often as feasible. Curious that I should have closed my career with it. It's exhausting because of the permanent nervous tension, and vocally it is most unsatisfactory. 'Vissi d'arte' is badly placed, following the murderous duet with Scarpia, particularly since it is in the form of a prayer and requires smooth legato. Why all these sopranos want so desperately to sing it remains a mystery to me. But *Francesca da Rimini,* which in Anglo-Saxon countries has never been recognized as the masterpiece it is, has an exquisite score and offers a tremendous scope for a singing actress. There are no arias, but what does it matter? All the duets are so rewarding, and is there anything more poetic than the 'Benvenuto, signore mio cognato' [Welcome, my lord brother-in-law]? Both productions I sang at La Scala, in 1936 and 1942, had Carmelo Maugeri as an admirable Gianciotto."

Who had taught her the acting for which she was so renowned?

"I never went to drama school," she replied, "but I did study certain roles with some of their famous interpreters. When I had to prepare *La traviata*, which I sang for the first time at La Scala in 1935 with Schipa as Alfredo, I went to Rosina Storchio, and I learned a lot from her, particularly about facial expression. It was amazing to watch her change expressions to the sound of the music. Then I went to Hariclea Darclée for *Tosca*, which she had created along with *Iris* and *La Wally*. She had a gigantic personality —no wonder Puccini, Mascagni, and Catalani had been sufficiently impressed with her to hand over their treasures to be judged by the public for the first time—and she taught me a lesson in stage deportment I shall never forget.

"For *Norma* I went to Giannina Russ, who, with Ester Mazzoleni, had been one of its leading exponents. I recall as if it were today what she said to me, and it made so much sense: 'It is not easy to put oneself in the shoes of the Druid priestess, for what kind of shoes did she wear? But I came to the conclusion that, Druid or not, a priestess must behave like one, and that dignity is totally essential, even when Bellini demands certain emotional outbursts. Norma must therefore always be a little larger than life, but not overly so. There you have the key: to demand and obtain respect, and at the same time project to the public that you are a distressed human being.' I remembered her words and applied them successfully to my interpretation.

"I was also enamored of another Bellini opera, *La straniera*. It has a silly libretto, but the score is so glorious it transcends all the nonsense. I sang it at La Scala in a deluxe revival—it had been performed last in 1842—with Marinuzzi conducting and a cast that included Pederzini, Mario Basiola, and Francesco Merli. With Merli I had a duet, sustained by a slow, long-breathed melody, that is Bellini at his summit. There is a passage sung by Alaide, my role—'Io nacqui per penar, per fare altrui soffrir' [I was born to suffer, to make others suffer]—that is in some ways so ahead of the composer's period that I was astounded."

The soprano had married Maurice Sens, a native of Bordeaux, back in 1921, six years before her debut, and he died in Paris the day of her first appearance as Catalani's Loreley. "The show must go on," she repeated tersely. "But you can imagine the condition I was in that evening. When I think of it, the nightmare returns. The marriage produced a son, and Canada gave me a daughter-in-law. I am the blessed grandmother of four. Later I married Mario Ferrari, with whom I have been very happy.

"Perhaps the most significant honor bestowed on me was to be chosen by Respighi to create his *Maria Egiziaca* under the worthy baton of Bernardino Molinari in Rome, and then for the first performance of his *La fiamma* at La Scala on February 9, 1935, with the astonishing Elvira Casazza, close to fifty, who was to stay on at La Scala until 1941, and Stignani, then thirty-one—two mezzos who for half a century dominated this theatre. It was the first and last time I appeared with the two of them, a historical occasion of sorts. That *La fiamma* could be totally forgotten—I even sang it in Budapest, in a production designed by Gustave de Olah, undoubtedly the most beautiful mise-en-scène I have ever seen—leaves me speechless. It has everything—a marvelous score, terrific libretto, and ideal possibilities for decor, since the setting is Byzantine. As for *Maria Egiziaca,* it is far more static, but it has such a holy, mystical score and a wonderful text by Guastalla —it is really more like an ancient mystery play–oratorio—that, again, I feel strongly it will eventually find its right place in the repertoire. It deals with the redemption of a young sinner who retired in the desert to do penance for forty-seven years and was found dying by a monk who buries her with the help of a lion. I wish there were more lions like him today. Guastalla based it all on a famous legend of the sixth century, originally written in ancient Greek.

"My list of offbeat roles is very long. In Brazil I sang in *Lo schiavo* by Carlos Gomes, their greatest operatic composer, even in Campinas, his birthplace. As I was always most particular about my costumes—I had my own and would never accept engagements if there was ever any question about this—I made inquiries about the opera, and the answer was 'Senhora, bracelets and necklaces, and that is all.' I managed somehow to follow these instructions. In Rio de Janeiro and São Paulo I also appeared in Gomes's *Maria Tudor*—not superior music by any means, a potpourri of sundry other composers; but this Brazilian composer had a great sense of the theatre, and there never was a dull moment.

"A most hazardous assignment was the Italian premiere at La Scala of Richard Strauss's *Daphne,* in an Italian translation, in 1942. Considering this a high honor, I accepted it right away, impulsively, sight unseen, and that was a gigantic mistake. Though I admired Strauss passionately, when I looked at the score I was flabbergasted by its tessitura. You kill yourself, and in the end you have absolutely nothing. But I could not extricate myself from this assignment, so vivid had been my enthusiasm when I was offered this opportunity. Even the incomparable Gino Marinuzzi, who was conducting, felt totally baffled by it and complained that too few rehearsals had been arranged for such a work. Finally, one day, he moaned to me, 'You can swim for yourself, and I am not going to worry about you. I must concentrate on all the other members of the cast, who are in deep, treacherous waters. Just do as you please. It will be all right.' Despite all our good will, it did not prove a success; only two performances were given. I adored the Marschallin—as grateful a part as Daphne is not—and I shall always recall with infinite pleasure appearing in *Rosenkavalier* at the Rome Opera with Pederzini, who made an unforgettable Octavian.

"I was very partial to the two Catalani operas, *Loreley* and *La Wally,* permanent fixtures in my repertoire. I was less fond of Mascagni, I must admit—particularly *Isabeau,* though it holds the stage admirably. I sang it in 1934 under the composer's direction at La Scala, and I recall a sumptuous production at the Baths of Caracalla in Rome. To my immense surprise—this was not an opera for which people ordinarily queued up for tickets—the public went wild every night, and despite the size of the al fresco auditorium it was impossible to find a seat. Most open-air audiences go to see a spectacle, not for the music, but in this case we were called out over and over again with shouts of approval, as if we had sung the most beautiful score in the world. This made me realize how theatrical this work is, with much of the merit going to Illica's libretto—he had a real knack for the lyric medium. He rarely missed, and he wrote in all, I believe, eighty operatic scripts. I also sang Santuzza, of course, and more times than I wish to remember.

"In 1939 it was of great interest to be assigned, at La Scala, Asteria in Boito's *Nerone,* the posthumous opera of this strange man, who had been one of the great loves of Eleonora Duse and the superb librettist for *Otello* and *Falstaff,* but who had written the music for only one other opera, *Mefistofele.* He had died in 1918, and Toscanini, who premiered the opera in 1924, conducted it in four different productions in the short interim before he moved to America, hailing it as a great work of art. I was most disappointed in it. Everyone told me that the opera really stood on the shoulders of Pertile, and he did not appear in it with me. I am not quite sure what happened, but this tenor, who was Mr. La Scala, did not sing there between 1937 and 1943—one of those unfathomable mysteries of the lyric theatre.

"As much as I enjoyed my excursions into verismo, it was the classical roles that held me spellbound: Gluck's *Alceste,* Monteverdi's *L'incoronazione di Poppea,* and Rossini's *Mosè.* The revival of *Mosè* at La Scala in 1937, after a nineteen-year absence, was the kind of feast dreams are made of. It had Pagliughi as Sinaide, Pasero in the title role, Armando Borgioli as the Pharaoh, and Marinuzzi in the pit. It was thrilling for me to be singing

Anaide, which in the 1918 production had been interpreted by Giannina Russ, the fabulous diva who had instructed me in *Norma.*

"Apart from the Verdi heroines, who were my daily fare, the three operas I was called upon to sing the most often were *La Gioconda,* which at La Scala I sang in five different productions, *Turandot,* and *Norma.* In 1935 I took part in the triumphant revival of Ponchielli's *Il figliuol prodigo,* whose score is almost as thrilling as *Gioconda,* and which had been last heard in 1892. De Sabata gave the most exciting reading of it, and I was certain that we had resurrected a work that would become part of the repertoire. I could not have been more mistaken. Whenever some theatre asked me for *Gioconda,* I suggested this opera instead—absolutely to no avail. No one was interested.

"I was a great favorite in Buenos Aires, and it is because I was appearing there when the war broke out that I was unable to return to the Metropolitan, where I had been received so warmly during two seasons, 1937 and 1938, in six different operas, including *Norma,* taking up where the great Ponselle had left off. Since my mother and son were back in Italy, I rushed home, intending to take them with me to the United States. But the gates closed, and none of us were allowed to leave. In Gibraltar, on the way back from Argentina, the ship I was on got stopped by the British for eleven days, and this should have given me a clear cue of what was to come. Anyhow, there was not much else I could have done, because my duties as a daughter and mother came first. My very good friend Maria Caniglia (despite reports, we were never rivals; she had not even started undertaking dramatic roles—that came much later), Favero, Masini, Stignani, and others found themselves in my situation. Supposedly the government loved us so much they could not part with us.

"We did not have the mentality of today's singers, who want to sing everything and, alas, are allowed to do so. We were brought up with a deep reverence for the composer and the librettist. Some years ago I was invited to talk in the intermission at the televised *Norma* from La Scala. I never should have accepted, because I always say what I think. It did not sit well with anyone when I announced that what I was hearing was not Bellini's *Norma.* We will not even discuss the sets—crates here and there, like in a storage house, the Druids all packed up to go where?—or the poetry of the text, which was ignored. But the singing? Caballé has a God-given, beautiful lyric instrument, but she was forced to force all the time, and I use the same verb twice on purpose. How can a great artist like her agree to be part of such a shambles? Leyla Gencer, who had sung a few Normas at La Scala some years earlier, was also an invited guest. Before we went on in front of the cameras, she asked me casually whether I had ever sung *Norma*. It is true that she is Turkish, but she has been around Italy for a long, long time, and my recordings of this opera are still in the music shops and continue to sell amazingly well. So I replied very politely, 'Yes, Madame—only over five hundred times.'

"When I sang Elisabetta di Valois in *Don Carlo* at Covent Garden with Sir Thomas Beecham, that wise man eliminated the Fontainebleau act, feeling it added little of interest to the score and protracted the evening too much. After hearing it recently at La Scala under Claudio Abbado's baton, I completely agreed. Not even *Parsifal* has ever seemed so long. *Don Carlo* is very close to my heart, and it made me very ill to see what Luca Ronconi was capable of doing to it at La Scala, which should be aware of the traditions it should uphold. If this is rejuvenation, innovation, and a new interpretation of a work of art, God help us in His infinite mercy. I have decided to stay away from opera houses during this concerted effort to destroy everything, or I will have another heart attack, and this will be the final one.

"My pupil Elena Mauti Nunziata, who started off so well in *I puritani* —I arranged for her to sing it in Palermo, and she was a revelation—told me she is considering *Aida,* because two conductors have approached her to sing it. She will not study it with me! I have given my very blood to these students, and it is most discouraging to realize that it all has been in vain, for the very people who should guide and assist them are out to destroy them. But when I think of 'Casta diva,' I know I was blessed."

ZINKA MILANOV

When Zinka Milanov made her farewell appearance at the Metropolitan Opera House on April 13, 1966, as Maddalena di Coigny in *Andrea Chenier* after a career that had spanned nearly forty years, there was a definite impression among the audience that an era had closed forever. Apart from having had—and preserved—one of the most beautiful voices of the century, she had always been every inch a prima donna in the grand, old-fashioned manner. From the first moment she walked onto the stage there was an imperiousness, an absolute assurance, that were hers and hers alone. Although she rarely delved deeply into the characters she portrayed (her personality was much too strong to adapt to the various heroines in her repertoire), she dominated the roles at all times by a sort of majesty that few of her colleagues possessed. Some people were critical of this lack of involvement, but everyone respected her, for in her throat was a golden sound that no one else had displayed since Ponselle. And she had what Ponselle lacked: a resplendent top. In the first years she tended toward sharpness, but later she corrected this defect with strenuous work and discipline. If none of her characterizations had real depth, the luster of her instrument was more than ample compensation.

When I went to talk to her in April 1979 in her apartment in New York, she fit me in between two lessons, since she is deeply involved in this new phase of activity. I found her somewhat bigger than I remembered her being, but for a woman in her middle seventies (she was born in 1906) she looked wonderful. Her inborn arrogance is as delightful as ever. It is not an arrogance that annoys, for it is totally spontaneous; and if anyone has a right to it, it is she, for never was there anyone else like her. The conversation jumped around like a frog in a large pond, because she is deeply curious and interested in everything. So many were the questions she asked me that at times I found it difficult to insert my own.

Milanov's is an encyclopedic knowledge of the art of singing. Her observations on singers past and present were positively scintillating and provocative, always right on the mark. Her strength and energy do not permit her to be discouraged by the turn of current musical events. She did not say, as so many of her colleagues had, that all is ended, but, instead, "We must start again in every direction, with no time to lose."

Milanov's career was unusual: although she was always active, she did not really come into her own until its second half. She is that phenomenon of a singer who improves enormously with time; she was gifted with reserves that were nothing if not prodigious.

Born in Zagreb, she started to study early with the legendary Wagnerian soprano Milka Ternina, the first Tosca at Covent Garden and the Metropolitan. "She was a most demanding teacher—scales, scales, and then again more scales, until I could cry. But my instinct—even then when I was so ignorant of this art—told me she was right. This is what developed my voice and gave it elasticity. I was not allowed to touch any score until breathing had become second nature to me. She waited to concede me the signal to begin until it all had become a part of my subconscious system. Never for one moment did she encourage me to specialize in Wagner, for she thought my tone was too velvety and clear.

"She was shy, reserved, and difficult," she went on, "but intelligent, and I feel that those years were the best investment I ever made. Our relationship came to a sudden end when one day she got angry at me and slapped me. This I could not tolerate, even from the idolized Ternina, and I refused to go back. Actually, I started out as a mezzo, but she foresaw right away that I would become a soprano. In fact, the high C came along in no time. The lower register had to be made larger, but the passage notes—F and F-sharp —which so many singers have trouble with, fortunately did not represent a problem for me, since they were there all the time. I was also born with a pianissimo in my throat.

"I made my debut as Leonora in *Il trovatore* in 1927 in Zagreb, and then for the next years I divided my time between Zagreb and Liubiana, singing everything in Croatian. This period was not particularly rewarding, but it did teach me repertoire, which included some of the lighter Wagner and Strauss operas. My first real chance came when I was called to Dresden to appear in *Aida* with Tino Pattiera, a celebrated tenor at that time. This led to an engagement in Prague, where they wanted to sign me up almost exclusively for the Wagnerian wing. Bojdar Kunç, my brother and adviser, a very fine musician, stopped me from accepting, claiming—and rightly so —that my voice was too Italianate in sound and production.

"Then I was brought to Vienna to substitute for an ailing soprano, for

Zinka Milanov as Santuzza in *Cavalleria rusticana*.

Aida again, and my unhoped-for fortune was that Bruno Walter was in the pit. He took a liking to me, and this was a tremendous break. It was very difficult at that time to establish an identity, for there were ever so many fine spintos and dramatics already in the key positions. It was Walter, a kind and considerate man, who suggested me to Toscanini for the Verdi Requiem in Salzburg in 1936, as he knew Toscanini was looking for a soprano soloist with my kind of voice. He arranged an audition for me, and to my delight the 'King' accepted me right away after I had intoned the 'Libera me.'

"At this time I always sang under the name of Zinka Kunç, my real one, and eminently satisfactory as far as I was concerned. In Zagreb and Liubiana I was singing, among other roles, Sieglinde, Elsa, Marguerite in *Faust*, Leonore in *Fidelio*, Tosca, Manon Lescaut, Minnie in *La fanciulla del West*, and Turandot, all of them in Croatian. This same language was used by me when I sang in Prague at the National Opera, while all the others sang in Czech; but when I appeared at the German Opera House in the Czech capital I was obliged to use German. It was all very nerve-racking! Then later I had to relearn all of my roles in Italian, a real marathon.

"Obviously, in all our lives, things are meant to be. When I heard in Zagreb that they were planning a production of *La forza del destino*, I simply could not understand why I had not been asked to be Leonora. Of the sopranos in the company, I was by far, in my opinion, the most qualified. So I went to protest to the director of the opera house, and he told me rudely that if I was not pleased he could dispense with my services. And I left, just like that.

"It turned out to be the best thing I ever did, for with the hideous war in the cards, I would have undoubtedly been prevented from leaving Yugoslavia. While in Vienna I had made a big success as a guest in *Tosca*, but no offer of an engagement on a permanent basis came. In the meantime Edward Johnson, Maestro Artur Bodanzky, and Edward Ziegler came to Prague to hold some auditions, which I missed, for I was singing in Bratislava. When I returned, they were about to leave, but it was suggested that I make immediately a special audition for them. I had sung the night before, but I said what the hell, and the Nile scene impressed them sufficiently so they gave me a contract."

It was with Leonora in *Il trovatore*, the role of her debut in Zagreb, that Milanov presented herself for the first time to a Metropolitan Opera House audience, on December 17, 1937. This time she sang in Italian and under the new name of Milanov, for Johnson did not feel that Kunç was glamorous enough. With Ponselle having suddenly retired that year and the star of

Rethberg on the decline (because of emotional disturbances), a dramatic soprano was very much needed. At first the critics were not enthusiastic, noting her pitch troubles and her lack of sophistication as an actress, but everyone recognized the potential of her superb voice. She went to the Colón in Buenos Aires, the Municipal in Rio de Janeiro, and the Bellas Artes in Mexico City, and her reputation began to grow. Toscanini used her on several occasions, and her appearances with him in the Verdi Requiem, the Beethoven Missa Solemnis, and the famous broadcast of the last act of *Rigoletto* gave her an added prestige. The way she held the B-flat in the "Libera me" in Verdi's sacred score—with a purity of emission that recalled the young Rethberg—did more than any operatic aria for her reputation in the United States.

Her repertoire at the Metropolitan was mainly Verdi, but she was also assigned Donna Anna, Tosca, Santuzza, Maddalena in *Chenier,* La Gioconda (in which she excelled), and Norma (in which she did not). It seems incredible that in all her years at the Thirty-ninth Street house (twenty-six in all, with a total of 421 performances, including 123 on tour) Milanov sang a total of only thirteen roles—eight for the first time during the Johnson regime, an additional five during Bing's. The opera she sang most often was *Aida,* with a total of seventy-eight performances, and the one she sang least was *Ernani,* with eight in all. One wonders why she did not press for more assignments. She claims that she did not want to push and ask for more diversification, but given her temperament and iron willpower, that seems unlikely. (In her nineteen years at the Metropolitan, Ponselle sang twenty-two different operas, and Rethberg in her two decades at the theatre sang thirty. Even Leontyne Price, who has sung very sparingly there since her Met debut in 1961, preferring the very high fees she receives in concerts, has appeared in sixteen different leading roles.)

"The reason I left the Metropolitan in 1947," Milanov explained, "was not only that I had married General Lubomir Ilic (he was Tito's ambassador to various countries, including Norway, Denmark, Mexico, and Switzerland), but also that Edward Johnson and I simply did not get on. When I first started I was paid one hundred and twenty-five dollars a week, and ten years later I received three hundred, which was totally ridiculous. I considered it insulting, but every time I talked to him about this untenable situation, he smiled—he was very good at that—and repeated that he could not afford more. So I packed up and went abroad, making my Scala debut in 1950 in *Tosca.* Then, when in that year Rudolf Bing took over, he arranged for me to sing *Ballo in maschera* in Hartford, for he had never heard me and wanted to do so in a theatre. And then I was back . . . with a big bang."

There is no doubt that when she returned to the Metropolitan, she was an infinitely better artist and a far more precise singer, and the Milanov legend began at this time. But she did not become an international commuter, and stayed pretty much in the United States, appearing with several American companies but adding no new roles to her repertoire.

"I think I went on as long as I did—and actually I could have gone on longer, for I was still in excellent shape—because I only sang what was right for me and limited my number of performances. I never allowed myself to sign too many contracts and spread myself too thin. I never would touch *Fanciulla* or *Turandot* after the early days in smaller theatres. The size of a house is very important, and, unfortunately, today they are all big. You can sing Turandot in a small one; you must shout it in a large one. I am happy in many ways that I closed my career in the old Metropolitan—it was the last year of its existence—and did not have to readapt myself to the new one. The new one does not have the warmth or the distinction of the old. My best singing did come after my fortieth birthday, but this is the way it should be. Today it is the other way around. Most singers begin having their disturbances at the age of thirty-five, because their foundations are not right. While the bloom of youth is still in the vocal cords, the sun shines. Then the problems begin to pile up, and very fast. Look around, please, and it's pretty much of a disaster. Some voices are born with a vibrato; others get it by singing incorrectly. The wobble—so prevalent today—comes from forcing, and this means that the vocal cords are irritated; to make it more explicit, they are swollen. Vibrato, which is actually a fluctuation of pitch, is inevitable when the lower register is improperly placed. Every aria and duet must be prepared with extreme calculation—when to give out and when to save yourself and then to soften the phrase.

"Mezze voci and pianos are a must. How can you get to the end of a Verdi aria if you don't employ them? You find that you are totally worn out. If you have developed the pianos—one must find them; they exist, believe me, in every voice—then you must learn to fence with them vis-à-vis the passages which, according to the score, must be loud. You will notice that when a singer can no longer handle a piano, the top is already crumbling. It is the unfailing alarm signal. Verdi's pianos are everywhere: on top, in the middle, and in the lower regions. I forbid my pupils to go near Verdi until they have mastered this absolute must. If the voice is not large enough for the second-act concertato in *Aida* and you must force, how can you sing correctly, a few minutes later, the melting phrases of the love duet in the third? This is why Caballé, whom I admire so much in Donizetti —she really has a piano—should not sing Aida.

"The color of the sound is what made me, and it is with it that I imbued life into all my heroines. Acting is all very well, but it does not take the place of the voice. When they say 'a great actress,' beware. It usually means that there is not much voice there. Of course, many instruments are manufactured; but mine was not—it was all there from the very beginning. It needed to be fortified and disciplined. Today the confusion is utterly bewildering, for there are so many singers who cross over, like in a ferry, between soprano and mezzo roles. They simply don't seem to know what they are. If they have a limited top, they become inclined to sing mezzo roles; and if mezzos have a top, instead they take on soprano parts. But a mezzo with a dazzling top is one thing, and carrying on throughout the opera the tessitura of a soprano is another. Most lyrics today take on dramatic parts, and either you cannot hear them or they shout. A dog is a dog and remains a dog even if he wishes he were a cat. The laws of nature cannot be changed. You are what you are.

"But we must cut it short—another student is about to arrive. I admit that I loathed retiring—Mr. Bing would have liked me to do so earlier, to make room for others—for the theatre was my life, and continues to be, on a different scale, through my pupils and the established singers who come to me when they are in trouble. You would be amazed at how many they are, and it is no wonder, with the schedules they try to keep and all the wrong assignments they accept. I give classes here, in my villa in Abbazia, and in Belgrade, depending on where I am. Fatiguing, yes; rewarding, no. Then why do I do it? Because the hope that some of my knowledge can survive is stronger than me."

THE GREAT SPINTOS

HILDEGARD RANCZAK

MARIA CANIGLIA

RENATA TEBALDI

These three sopranos, one Czech-German and the other two Italian, left behind them trails of glory that turned into legends. The pattern of each of their careers is different, as is the character of each singer. Hildegard Ranczak never had an international career, except for guest appearances here and there; but for thirty years she was among the most admired artists in Central Europe, at a time when competition was very stiff. She told me that there were so many engagements to fulfill in both Austria and Germany that she was never able to branch out abroad. She was equally versatile in the Richard Strauss repertoire—with which her name will always be identified —and the Verdi and Puccini operas, but she was neither a Mozart nor a Wagner singer of note. Her sex appeal was famous, and she imbued her characterizations with deep psychological insight.

Maria Caniglia and Renata Tebaldi, possessors of two of the most beautiful voices of this century, had several points in common, and yet their careers were totally different. Tebaldi came into prominence in 1946, at the age of twenty-four, sixteen years after Caniglia had established herself as one of the most beloved and sought-after sopranos of that era. During those sixteen years Caniglia had already sung thirty-two leading roles at La Scala. Far more versatile than Tebaldi, Caniglia had a much wider repertoire and went from lyric to spinto and finally to dramatic roles. Tebaldi was more reticent; from the very beginning she drastically limited her choice of roles, and she discarded several (Marguerite, Eva, Elsa) after the early days.

Though gifted with divine instruments, both Caniglia and Tebaldi were hampered by a relatively short top. While Caniglia managed, through a firmer technique, to have a longer operatic career—despite the enormous number of engagements she accepted—Tebaldi, who sang far less often, started much earlier to have trouble with the upper register. Mario del Monaco told me that the Aida she sang with him in 1950 at the San Francisco Opera was the most beautiful rendition of the Verdi heroine he had ever heard, and that vocally her Tosca had no equals. But in the spring of 1959, when she sang Aida with Karajan in Vienna, she had such a difficult time with "O patria mia" that she refused to take a bow at the end of the third act. And as far as I know, she then put the Ethiopian slave on the shelf.

There is no doubt that Tebaldi's vocal problems would have brought an even earlier end to her career had a love affair not developed between her and her audiences. The public loved her with an almost religious devotion; and even during her last years onstage, when so many of the high notes were hit-or-miss affairs, she was still Tebaldi, and the public adored her all the same.

KAMMERSÄNGERIN HILDEGARD RANCZAK

One of Richard Strauss's most beloved interpreters, Hildegard Ranczak (born in 1895) was for two decades the number-one attraction at the Munich Nationaltheater. Not only was she beautiful, but she was gifted with a remarkable theatrical sense. I never heard her in person, but it is common knowledge that she possessed that hard-to-define quality called magnetism, combined with a strong, resonant, well-placed voice that climbed with ease and never had a hard edge.

Petite, chic, with large, inquisitive, naughty eyes and her snow-white hair softly waved, she bounced into the hall of the Bayerischer Hof Hotel on a June morning in 1979 with the nimbleness of a young woman. She surprised me with her somewhat tough American accent—acquired in Pittsburgh, where she lived with her parents from the age of two until she was sixteen. Her father was Czech, her mother of German extraction, and she herself was born in Mahr-Ostrau, which at the time was under Austrian domination, but later became Czech. It came as a shock to the directors of St. Mary's School in Pittsburgh when, at the age of sixteen, she announced that she would not be returning the following year: she had decided to go to Vienna to be trained as a singer.

"My parents were indeed inspired," she declared, "to send me, during my American years, to a ballet school. This was to help me vastly to move with grace on the stage. In Vienna I began immediately to study with Professor Schleman Ambrose, a former concert singer of note, and remained with him for seven years. Not knowing one word of German, I had to learn it rapidly. In those days voice lessons were a serious matter, for technique had to become so ingrained that one could sing even over a cold. This accounts for the fact that there were fewer cancellations then. Ambrose used to make me sight-read for hours, and this was to prove very helpful in learning new scores quickly. He warned me that although he had no doubts that I was a *jugendlich dramatisch*, I should not undertake anything but lyrical roles at first, until I had found my way, and I obeyed him.

227

Hildegard Ranczak as the Dyer's Wife in *Die Frau ohne Schatten*.

"My start came in 1919 in Düsseldorf as Pamina, and she was followed by such light roles as Marzelline in *Fidelio,* Susanna in *Le nozze di Figaro,* and Marie in *The Bartered Bride.* I received a solid basic training there, remaining for four years. My assumption of Butterfly proved an eye opener to the management, for it revealed that my instrument was far larger than suspected. Many operas came my way, including a very attractive contemporary one: *Sheherazade* by Bernhard Seklis. My first Strauss endeavor was Sophie in *Der Rosenkavalier;* little did I expect that this composer would play such a major part in my life. My Marschallin was Felicie Hüni-Mihacsek, and I would like to mention her, for I learned more from her than from any other woman singer, so valid was her technique, and effortless. This Hungarian, who had the most lovely and soothing timbre, was unforgettable as Fiordiligi, the Countess, and Desdemona. Later she shifted to dramatic roles, and, tragic to say, that heavenly voice went to pieces. Even in those days, although far less frequently than today, such misjudgments occurred.

"Then Otto Klemperer came along and invited me to follow him to Cologne, where he ran the opera house. He was a very striking conductor and excelled in the contemporary scores. In those days he was married to Johanna Geisler, and those who did not hear her Rosalinda in *Die Fledermaus* cannot possibly imagine the wonders she accomplished with that role. Klemperer became a Catholic, but this did not help him when later the insane Hitlerian campaign against the Jews progressed. It was all utterly inexplicable, for certain artists or their mates were not considered Hebrews. Göring was heard to say one day, 'I decide who is a Jew.' I found myself eventually in the midst of it all, but in the musical world one was far less aware of it because of the various exceptions made.

"Anyhow, to go back, Klemperer assigned me to my first Tosca, Marta in *Tiefland,* and another lovely opera by d'Albert, entitled *Toten Augen,* unjustly now put on the shelf. Then he insisted I take on Salome, and I spent sleepless nights wondering whether this score would wreck my voice. It turned out to be the triumph of my career, an opera I could never get away from and which I sang until the end, having learned how to come to terms with this stupendous but dangerous work. My guardian angel helped me, for early in the game I had the chance to sing it under the direction of Strauss himself, and this made all the difference, for he gave me invaluable advice. If I was able to succeed in this part and protect my instrument, I owe it entirely to him. Actually, the music is so rousing most sopranos are tempted to give all from the very beginning. Instead, it must be kept in close check, and one builds the tension slowly until the big finale, reaching the crescendo by stages.

"The first time I rehearsed it with him, as Salome enters, at the phrase 'Ich will nicht bleiben' [I will not stay] he said, 'Once more,' and I went on repeating it until I was able to cut down my instrument to the exact size he wanted. But when, at the end, she has to sing, 'Warum schreit er nicht, der Mann?' [Why does he not cry out, this man?] he called out and remarked, 'Too loud.' While the *professori* in the orchestra sat there with a look of total disbelief at this nobody who dared contradict God himself, I argued with him. 'If this is not approaching the climax—when she is waiting, becoming hysterical because he has not been beheaded yet—then tell me when to expect it?' I asked. He was a very reasonable man and agreed. 'If you think this is where she should begin to let out her fury, it's all right with me. I can sense you have a feeling for the part; do it your way,' he said. He always respected me after this episode, and until his death in 1948 not only did he use my professional services all the time but we became close friends. What I learned from him—I was to sing Salome with him ever so many times—was that in order to save my vocal cords, I must never be emphatic, but learn to use my voice to cut through the orchestral texture like a knife. I used his teaching always when performing this opera with others. 'If you sing loud,' Strauss told me, 'conductors will instinctively increase the sound of the orchestra.' And he was one hundred percent right.

"When from Munich, much later, a group of us had to go to his villa in Garmisch for piano rehearsals, his wife, Pauline—who was stinginess personified—made us all take off our shoes before entering the house so as not to spoil the carpets. He only came to Munich for orchestral rehearsals, but he could always do as he pleased. . . . Do you know the story of how they got married?"

I confessed that I did not.

"It's absolutely delightful," she chuckled. "In the early days he was a conductor at the Mannheim opera house and she was a soprano in the company. One day, at a rehearsal, she was at fault, and he remonstrated with her. She got very angry with him and threw the score at him from the stage. 'Sing the damned passage yourself' she supposedly yelled at him. He adored her ever after, and inevitably a wedding followed. Some men enjoy being mishandled. But actually she was very good for him. Because of her lust for money, she imposed herself and made him compose. Otherwise, being a gentle and slightly lazy man, he would have worked far less.

"I sang with Strauss so often that I knew that clear beat of his inside out.

It is because he was so tremendous a composer that one forgets what a first-rate conductor he was. He always wanted me for Zdenka in *Arabella,* for he thought I looked well in trousers, although my voice was not quite light enough for it.

"During the war we were performing, under his baton, his *Die ägyptische Helena,* and not only did the lights go out but we remained in darkness for the rest of the performance. So we all took our places in front of the stage and sang it in concert form, with the orchestra helped by whatever candles were available. The obvious solution would have been to cancel, but Pauline Strauss would not allow it because of the mightily handsome remuneration he received. This opera never became really popular, but I do not think the last word is said—just consider the tremendous re-evaluation of *Die Frau ohne Schatten* these last few years—for it is rich in lyricism and lovely orchestral sonorities. The essay Hugo von Hofmannsthal wrote way back in 1928 explains a lot about the libretto. If I recall correctly, he called it 'a mythological opera, the truest of all forms.' It has a different dimension from the other Strauss operas, and the staging must be classical, handsome, and timeless. The instructions must be followed to the letter or the work simply does not function. These smart-aleck directors had better keep hands off.

"After Cologne, I moved for three years to Stuttgart's opera house, one of the most important in Germany. Here I added most of the Puccini scores, and Carmen—which, with Salome, became one of my most often performed parts. My interpretation was considered very different, for I did not conceive her as a bitch, but as a woman with her own special code of morals. Then an invitation came to become a member of the Munich National-theater, and there I remained for twenty years, never moving again. Knappertsbusch assigned me for the first time to Octavian, and this I sang too at the drop of a hat. In Munich I was given more and more Verdi heroines, those of *Il trovatore, Ballo in maschera,* and *Forza* included. Amelia, along with Tosca, I sang also with Marinuzzi, and I was enthralled by his more hurried Italian tempos, which increased the tension and drama. I was called upon to sing Aida frequently in Berlin, first under Leo Blech's direction and then de Sabata's. The latter kept repeating that my voice was totally Italianate in timbre and production and that Italy needed an artist like me, suggesting that I go to Milan, where he would have me engaged at La Scala. Other musicians had told me this very thing, and some who remembered Emmy Destinn, a Czech, who also specialized in Italian parts, claimed I sounded like her. But I was tied down to numerous engagements, and it appeared like a major, risky move. It would have meant building up a reputation in another country, and as events were to prove, with the disastrous advent of the war, it was a wise decision.

"My first Aida, actually, took place under Clemens Krauss, a giant among conductors. I would have turned somersaults for him. The way he used to say 'Piano, piano' still echoes in my ears. He was a master at obtaining an iron discipline, but along with it came to the fore always his perfect manners and gentleness. I would never place Knappertsbusch, despite his fanatic admirers, in the same class. He had his qualities, but, goodness, how noisy he was! I recall many Aidas with him too, and the love duet of the third act invariably represented a strain. This is romantic music, and there are soft passages he ignored. For him it was heroic from start to finish. But my relations with him were excellent, and when he moved to Vienna, he invited me frequently as a guest. For a long time I was allowed by the Munich Opera a certain amount of time off to do regular appearances in Berlin, which at that time had a very impressive list of singers.

"I never went near Wagner, for my instrument was too bright in color. Instead, Krauss's wife, Viorica Ursuleac, was equally ideal for some of the Wagner and Strauss roles. Although she had a lovely, facile top, I was constantly amazed at the two hours' vocalizing she went through before each performance. Hers was, in my opinion, a marvelously constructed, not really natural voice which she used with uncanny intelligence. It is very difficult for people to understand how often the same type of voice is faced with entirely different difficulties.

"Krauss chose me to create Clairon in the world premiere of *Capriccio* in Munich on October 28, 1943, so I had plenty of opportunities to watch Ursuleac mold the enchanting role of the Countess, and she was a perfectionist. Singing with her was a joy, for she was totally secure and never tried to steal scenes from others. Actually Clairon is written for a mezzo, but Krauss thought I was just right for this part. And I had such confidence in his judgment that I accepted with closed eyes. The text, written by Krauss himself, is delightful, but it is an ensemble opera for which there is never enough rehearsing. The music and the libretto are like an invisible chain, and one must be on the alert at all times. Coming in one second earlier or later can ruin an entire scene.

"Actually, my relationship with Krauss and Ursuleac spanned a very long period. In 1937 I had sung *Salome* under his direction in Paris, along with Octavian to Ursuleac's Marschallin. With Ursuleac I sang many Zdenkas to her Arabella, Aithra to her Ägyptische Helena, and the Dyer's Wife with all those high Cs to her ravishing Empress in *Die Frau ohne Schatten.* I never went near *Elektra,* and as for *Salome,* I always insisted on a three-day break between performances. After the initial stages, I no longer sang the Mozartian repertoire."

I asked her what she thought of Maria Cebotari's controversial Salome.

"She was a most sensitive, appealing artist," she replied, "but Herod's stepdaughter was not right for her. The instrument was too fragile, and she had to force.

"Somehow, I knew instinctively what I could take on after reading a score and singing it out. When they offered me Minnie, I took my time and then decided in the affirmative. As in the case of Salome, I knew that with the proper balance on phrasing and building the anxiety up slowly, I could reach the end safely. It became literally my property after the first time I sang it in Munich in 1932. The poker scene is one of the most effective pieces of stagecraft ever invented, and I brought down the house every time. When Krauss came to direct the Munich Opera in 1937, he decided to leave it in the repertoire, for he thought it was one of the best productions in the theatre. Again Knappertsbusch was my first conductor in this opera, for which he had a veritable passion. In many ways I found *Tosca,* never my favorite heroine, tougher than *Fanciulla,* and yet many sopranos do not agree with me. Minnie is marked by a slower rise to the climax than the Roman prima donna, who is already in a state of acute restlessness the moment she walks into the church. In the third act Minnie can relax, but Tosca cannot. If one is not extra careful, it's easy to let Tosca carry one away, and I have seen some of my colleagues become slightly ridiculous. Both these works depend a lot on the conductor. He must be pliable and not indulge in overemphasis, for the drama is already there in the music.

"When the Nazis came to power, I married a German, in order to have a name that did not sound foreign, for one risked being thrown out of the country. Perhaps it would have been better, but every singer is haunted by the pension he is to receive after twenty-five years' uninterrupted work. We were expected to live in grand style, have expensive clothes, look like stars. All this cost money, and there was not much saving possible. Anyhow, as events proved, all bank accounts were wiped out. Later I divorced and remarried, but my private life was unexciting. Now I have been a widow for twenty years. Apart from losing everything with the war, all of us who had sung under the Hitlerian regime were deprived of our right to make a living between 1945 and 1947. We had to be investigated. The clever ones, such as Hans Hotter, Julius Patzak, and Ludwig Weber, went to Vienna, where this rule somehow did not apply. But those of us who remained all received the same treatment. Did it never occur to the occupying forces that we had no other choice, since we had to go on making a living to eat? I certainly did not have the stuff martyrs are made of, so I went on doing the only thing I was trained for: sing. For this we were punished, only later to receive ever so many apologies, be reinstated, and eventually given our full pensions. I began again in 1947, and then in 1950 quit as Carmen at the Munich Opera, for I was fifty-five years old.

"I could have gone on doing character parts, as so many others did, but this was not my style. I had been a leading diva and could not bear to come to terms with the idea of becoming a comprimaria. Vanity? No doubt. As my pension was insufficient, I sold my only possession, a house, to help meet the bills, which augment every day. Anyhow, time ahead is short, and the apocalypse on its way. I forgot to tell you the greatest irony of all. When we were deprived of our right to sing, I was invited to become a member of East Berlin's opera house. But I did not like the atmosphere and declined. During those two years I came to know who my friends were. They came forward, generously keeping me alive and giving me back trust in human nature, which I had lost.

"No, I don't teach, and it is a matter of pride, for I am very aware of the position I held and the name I carry. Today students will not take seven years off, the way I did, to approach humbly what is awaiting them, and I do not wish to have failures on my hands. All the time I hear some of these young singers, in no way prepared, boast that they have studied with one of my former colleagues, and then actually I discover they only spent a few months with them. I stay away from opera houses, for I know only too well that they cannot begin to function properly again until ensembles are formed as in old times. Are there happy endings? I don't think so . . . just the hope to fade away gently, with the memory of over eighty heroines to whom I once gave life and all my being."

MARIA CANIGLIA

On April 16, 1979, Maria Caniglia died in Rome after a brief illness. I was fortunate to have seen her on two different occasions in the late spring of 1978; one visit proved insufficient to cover the territory of her crowded schedules and listen to her instructive appraisal of the unhappy conditions of today's operatic world. A simple, direct, humorous Neapolitan by birth, she received me in her comfortable flat, near the Piazza Ungheria in Rome, with the manner of someone completely at home with a stranger. She wore glasses—"like a professor"—but otherwise her celebrated classical face was not much changed. Her remarkable authority was accompanied by a rebellious sort of resignation to her inability to combat the declining state of the operatic world.

"I belong to the group of singers," she asserted, "who gave too much of themselves. But I identified myself with the various roles I was called upon to interpret so much that during the twenty-nine years of my professional life, until the very last day, it was a losing battle against myself to control and save my forces. But to donate of oneself, whether onstage or in life, means living intensely; and without sorrow nobody can be a complete human being. I suffered a great deal in the theatre, for every time I conferred all my heart and soul. If toward the end my vocal resources were no longer what they had been, the public respected and loved me, because instinctively it recognized I did not spare one ounce of my being."

Daughter of a family that originated in the Abruzzi province, Maria Caniglia was born in Naples on May 5, 1906. It was considered a blessing when she was accepted by Agostino Roche as his student, since he had been responsible for the amazing technique of Ebe Stignani. "She was two years older than me," Caniglia reminisced, "and made her debut five years ahead of mine. From the very first time I heard her I was astounded by her, and little could I have foreseen that we were destined to sing together constantly. There did not exist a nicer person; her dedication to her art was like a boulder of granite. Roche claimed, from the very beginning, that I was a

Maria Caniglia as Amelia in *Un ballo in maschera*.

spinto, since my instrument was large and exuberant. It was a gift from God that it had a very characteristic timbre of its own, a tremendously significant introduction into musical circles. Roche did not believe in half measures, and in 1929 he sent me to La Scala to audition for three major conductors: Gino Marinuzzi, Ettore Panizza, and Giuseppe del Campo. They were unanimous in wanting to hear me again in six months' time in a group of more lyrical arias. Auditions can be very tricky, for the singer is nervous, the house empty, and there is no orchestra. Anyhow, when they did listen to me again, I received far more spinto assignments from them than lyric, and I was to remain at La Scala for twenty-one years.

"In the meantime, I had been engaged to make my first public appearance in 1930 at the Regio in Turin; and the role, unluckily, was an ungrateful one: Chrysothemis in *Elektra*. Despite the vast effort it entails, the applause always goes to the heroine and Klytämnestra. Giulia Tess was simply astounding in the title role, and her identification with Agamemnon's daughter was so complete that at the end, she fell in a terrifying faint and was never in a condition to go out and greet the thunderous applause. I felt so embarrassed, taking a curtain call without her; but it was all part of the experience Roche had talked so much about.

"When I went to La Scala at the beginning of 1931, I had been engaged only to sing Maria in the local premiere of *Lo straniero* under the baton of its composer, Ildebrando Pizzetti, one of Toscanini's closest friends and much admired by him. He was not the best conductor by any means, but at that time it was the fashion for composers to lead their own scores. To my astonishment, I was booked for the remaining months of the season.

"The next assignment consisted of the international baptism of *La notte di Zoraima* under the leadership of its composer, Italo Montemezzi. Oddly, this opera, which was so enthusiastically received that it was repeated the following season by popular demand, has disappeared, like the other very valid Montemezzi work *Giovanni Gallurese*, which was repeated seventeen times the same season when first performed in Turin. These are the unsurmountable mysteries of this world, which even my very expert and intelligent husband, Pino Donati—we married in 1939—was unable to explain to me, and he was in a position to know, for at different times he was the Intendant of the Arena in Verona, the Comunale in Bologna, and later the Chicago Opera.

"Anyhow, to *Zoraima* I owe the invaluable friendship of its protagonist, Giuseppina Cobelli. She was a most exceptional person, both as an artist and as a woman, and took me under her protection. Whenever she could, she came to my performances, made notes, and the next day telephoned me to pass on her impressions, both positive and negative. They were invaluable to me, for no one had a greater sense of the theatre than she had. Her courage was immense, for she became increasingly deaf, but such was her innate musicality that she never missed an entrance. Her unforgettable Isolde was the barrier that precluded me from ever accepting this divine role when, at the end, I took on dramatic parts. Like Muzio, who was my idol, she died at an age when she still had so much to bestow on us all.

"At La Scala in those enchanted days, productions followed one another at a pulsating rhythm. Every leading Italian theatre, by law, had to produce a new contemporary work every year, and while some were decidedly not worth the effort, there were enough that were, and I was very much in favor of this. It produced lots of new composers, who had a sense of friendly rivalry, and it gave them the opportunity actually to see their works on the stage. Some remarkable scores came to the fore.

"In the meantime, during my first season, Mascagni's lovely *Le maschere*, which had not been performed in this theatre since its premiere in 1901, conducted by Toscanini, was in rehearsal, and again the composer was on the podium. Bianca Scacciati was Rosaura; Mafalda Favero, Colombina; and Angelo Minghetti, a tenor who was so handsome that he stirred up storms of passions, the Florindo. Then thunder struck. Scacciati's mother died, suddenly, and there was no possibility that poor Bianca could go on, since she was in a state of total shock. This happened exactly two days before the dress rehearsal, and in those days La Scala would not even consider postponing a performance. I was rushed to audition for Mascagni, vaguely aware of what might be happening to me. He very politely listened to me, and then came the *pronunciamento*: 'I think she will do.'

"There was not an instant to lose. I was put in the hands of an able coach and studied the role night and day. Because of the frequent ensemble work, it was full of pitfalls. During my long career, this is the one instance when I was overcome by a sense of total panic. No one today can possibly realize the prestigious positions held by Mascagni and Scacciati in their respective domains. He was one of the world's leading operatic composers, and with enormous influence in Italian musical circles. As for Scacciati, she was one of La Scala's reigning sovereigns, worshiped by an adoring public, and I was a nobody. Mercifully, I came out of this nightmare with flying colors.

"But my stress was to continue unabated. *Der fliegende Holländer* was also in rehearsal, and the first performance was ten days away. The diva booked for Senta withdrew for very valid health reasons, and Maestro Panizza implored me to substitute for her. Senta, as you know, is halfway between a spinto and a dramatic. Her ballad 'Johohoe! Johohohoe! Traft ihr das Schiff im Meere an, blutrot die Segel, schwarz der Mast? [Have you met the ship upon the sea, bood-red the sails, black the mast?] is beautiful, haunting, and treacherous vocally, for it goes from moments of extreme lyricism to others of febrile exaltation. It is a crescendo, and must establish right away this visionary, romantic character who is exceedingly abnormal. The opera had not been performed at La Scala since 1893, so it was for many a first hearing. It has interested me very much to see, during the course of my life, how increasingly popular it has become, and I think that the great development of interest in the supernatural has had a lot to do with it. And in some ways Senta is bent on her own self-destruction—something that has become quite usual nowadays. It was a great challenge for me, for I proved to all that I could really enter into a character so remote from my own, since she is the most neurotic of all of Wagner's heroines.

"Again the battle was won, and this was a major one. The management was very grateful, and Wagner was to come my way often, for I sang Elsa, Eva, and Elisabeth. I did not have the restraint for these quietly passionate creatures, but the scores were ideal for my voice, which was always at its best in the middle register. And with time the mysticism of Elisabeth conquered me completely. Later I even took on Sieglinde, closer to my impulsive nature. How marvelously Wagner wrote for the voice! But a lot of breath control is needed for the legatos and the poetical phrasing.

"At this time Wagner was performed constantly in our opera houses, as much as Verdi and Puccini, by a formidable group of Italian singers and a few foreigners living in Italy. It infuriates me to realize that by 1950 there was nobody left, and that if Wagner is to be performed in Italy, the only solution is to bring in foreigners. When *Lohengrin* came back to La Scala with Karajan in 1953, he had Mödl, Schwarzkopf, Windgassen, and an all-German cast. When they brought it back in 1957 with del Monaco, it was a fiasco, for this very great tenor had no idea of how to approach the lyricism of the role. The result is that today Wagner has almost vanished from our stages. I find this absolutely scandalous, not because I am against non-Italians—music must be universal—but because it shows how our local stock of voices has become nonexistent.

"When I came to La Scala, some of the world's outstanding prima donnas were there—roughly twenty, I would say, I would classify as deluxe. There was plenty of work for each and every one of them, with a repertoire that varied between twenty and twenty-four productions a year, with first-rate casts always taking over from the original ones if the opera was repeated often—not like today, when the second casts are made up of fifth-rate elements. Now there is Freni, then Freni, and again Freni. Has it become a monopoly, or must we reach the conclusion that there is nobody else? In my era, my colleagues, no matter how great their fame, were all civil and polite. I do not recall one unpleasant word, and none of them seemed to resent my somewhat spectacular entry into the ranks, for I was entrusted with more and more responsibilities. Cigna and Pederzini are still among my closest friends. We were stimulated by each other's performances, we wanted to do better as a result of the examples set by the others; but there was no envy. There was fun too. Pederzini used to say, 'Oh, if I only could have Stignani's vocal cords,' and Stignani would moan, 'Oh, if only I could have Pederzini's pep and figure.'

"We never raised the question of who received which assignment, because we knew that the great conductors—de Sabata, Santini, Marinuzzi, Panizza, Serafin, Gui, Ghione, Guarnieri—and the others who were in charge understood the scores and voices inside out and had the instinct to choose the right singer for the right role. It was also very much a question of balance with the other instruments, a principal element now ignored. Freni and Domingo together would have been unthinkable in our day. There were no favorites; each got his due, and all rivalry was eliminated. It is difficult to describe the total harmony that existed then, thanks to a combination of mutual respect, understanding, and good manners. I shall never forget that Scacciati, when I took over her role at short notice in the Mascagni opera, took the time to write me an affectionate letter of thanks. I never heard of a jealousy such as the one that existed, for instance, between Melba and Tetrazzini."

Not being acquainted with this particular story, I asked about it.

"I was told while singing in London in 1937," she said, laughing, "that Melba was most unhappy at the triumph Tetrazzini had received at Covent Garden, her home ground, and had made some pointed remarks which were immediately repeated to the Italian diva. The latter one day happened to pass by the suite in the Savoy Hotel where Melba was practicing. Tetrazzini turned to the Savoy's manager, who was accompanying her, and asked, 'How many cats have you in your lovely hotel?' After the war I was to know bitchery with the newcomers in Milan, and not as amusing as Tetrazzini's. But I shall not speak about it . . . water under the bridge." (Caniglia left La Scala in 1951—she felt that all the choice roles were going to Tebaldi and Callas—and moved permanently to the Rome Opera, where she had been a frequent guest and was given carte blanche. In Rome she became as big an attraction at the Opera as the Sistine Chapel was at the Vatican. If her memory served her correctly, she appeared in thirty-three different operas in Rome and thirty-six at La Scala. Although she did not speak unkindly of either Tebaldi or Callas, I could sense that no love was lost on them.)

"Conductors took a loving interest in us," she recalled. "Serafin advised me never to undertake either *Butterfly* or *Ernani*. He explained why: 'For *Butterfly* you are too emotional. This opera would destroy you in no time, for you will always be unable to control your feelings. You have a top, but it is not your glory, and for Elvira in *Ernani* the upper range must be exceptional or it does not come off. You could manage it, but with the hundreds of roles at your disposal, why not concentrate on what you can do best?' Needless to say, I accepted his verdict unconditionally and never went near either of them.

"From lyric roles I moved more and more into spinto repertoire, and in the last decade of my working years I took on dramatic roles, although I never considered myself a dramatic soprano. I was forced into it to help the opera houses. Maria Carena and Clara Jacobo had retired, poor Bruna Rasa was shut up in an insane asylum, and Pacetti, along with Cigna, had fallen by the wayside for reasons of health. There just weren't enough dramatic sopranos to meet the demands, and the various managements were in despair. '*Signora, signora, per favore, lo prego,*' and so forth all day long. Because of the actual famine for this type of voice—which has now reached the starvation stages—I went on to the terrifying classical bel canto operas first, such as *Norma, La vestale,* and *Poliuto*. Then, when I had learned enough tricks to get around some of the difficulties in their cruel tessitura, in the last years, when I knew little harm could come to me, I added *Nabucco, La Gioconda,* and *La fanciulla del West,* whose finale of the second act gave me a new lease on life. There were never fewer than fifteen curtain calls.

"Actually, some voices expand and grow darker, so that a spinto can turn into a dramatic. Sometimes it happens after childbirth, and this is true in my case. In fact, after the birth of my son my vocal cords got stronger, and I was very conscious of this when singing the Verdi repertoire, which I never abandoned until the end. But as far as I am concerned, the upper range did not expand in proportion to the middle. When one hears that Freni and Scotto have turned from lyrics into dramatic sopranos, one realizes the total ignorance that reigns today—alas, among the critics too. These excellent singers are singing dramatic roles, yes; but their voices have not expanded into that range. They are still singing with their lyric voices, giving out often what is simply not there. Freni's voice, although far harder than it was, appears to have suffered less, but she has also attempted less strenuous scores.

"To go back to Verdi, the last role of his I added to my already long list of his operas was Leonora in *Oberto,* a splendid, strangely forgotten score, in 1951, the year I packed my trunks and left La Scala, never to return.

"At La Scala the discipline was spartan. When I was going to sing *La traviata,* which I did several seasons, my contract was very explicit about the operas I must not sing anywhere in the preceding three months. While I was a permanent member, I was allowed time off to appear elsewhere. What I sang later did not matter; it is what I did beforehand that counted. And this made a lot of sense. Then everything changed, and, alas, for the worse. I remember Callas singing *Iphigénie en Tauride,* the lovely but heavy Gluck score, and then two or three weeks later *La sonnambula,* which requires incredible agility—and this at La Scala! No one can do this and not pay a heavy price for it later. In my epoch there, if we made a mistake, the conductor never called us to task but rather reprimanded the assistant who had prepared us: 'Why didn't Signorina Caniglia hold that breath five seconds longer?' or something of the sort. We rehearsed for weeks, but it was all so well organized it never seemed like an effort. Everyone was there . . . and on time. When you went on, the score was firmly embedded in your throat.

"Some operas needed more rehearsals than others, *Falstaff* being one of them because of all the ensemble work. Once de Sabata got annoyed with one of the violinists, who did not come in at the right time, and he turned in his direction to make him a sign. Just at that moment came the ladies' entrance, and de Sabata's eyes were not on us. We all missed our cue, and what a time we had getting back on the track! Most of the audience did not realize the mess, but the connoisseurs did. I sang in this opera with Toscanini at the Salzburg Festival, and it was my first time with him, since by the time I joined La Scala he had already left for the United States.

"Once La Scala announced you for a new role in the forthcoming season, there came an avalanche of requests to repeat it in other theatres. This is a proof of the immense prestige La Scala used to have. If I was treated like a queen at Covent Garden, the Liceo in Barcelona, the San Carlos in Lisbon, the Municipals in Rio de Janeiro and São Paulo, the Colón in Buenos Aires, and many other distinguished opera houses, it was all due to the fame La Scala had conferred on me. At the Metropolitan I appeared only in the 1938–39 season, for a total of twelve performances, which included *Tosca, Otello, Aida, Falstaff,* and *Boccanegra.* The following year I was unable to return, since the passports of the most notable Italian singers were all withdrawn because of the war. Looking back at it now, it is amusing to think that we were considered national treasures, but at the time it was far from being a joke. But, wherever I went, I was always happy to return to La Scala and its discipline, which affected everyone alike.

"We were never allowed to go onstage," she recalled with a smile, "without a complete inspection. Even our hands were inspected to make sure we were not wearing personal rings. Can you imagine such a thing today, when tradition is so ignored that at a production of *Turandot* at the Maggio Musicale Fiorentino the Chinese crowds were garbed in black— a color that does not exist in China—and here in Rome in the Samaritani production of *La traviata* Violetta dies in a hospital ward? In every act the fog pours in from every window. I asked what it meant, and the answer was 'to express loneliness.' And so you know what I replied? 'I thought instead it was to explain why she developed tuberculosis!'

"We all had to provide our own costumes—a huge expense, but a sensible one, for what becomes one person turns into a disaster for the next. I was able to buy the entire collection of the lovely costumes belonging to Luisa Tetrazzini's sister, Eva, which were then adapted for me. They had to belong to the style of the period of the action, and on this point there was no discussion.

"Because of my sensuous and warm timbre, I accepted many verismo operas: *La Wally, Cavalleria, Guglielmo Ratcliff,* Cilea's *Gloria, Francesca da Rimini, Fedora, Chenier,* and the fascinating *Parisina* by Mascagni, one of the most murderous scores ever written. But too many verismo roles, thrilling as they are for an interpreter, are dangerous, for they usually lie very much in the middle of the voice, where one must push a lot to obtain the needed effects.

"D'Annunzio never could be called an author of the verismo school, for he is emphatic, ponderous and, at times, very poetic. Yet his *Parisina,* as set to Mascagni's music, is a *verista* opera. Despite the lofty and aristocratic positions of the characters, they all are deeply imbued with life's tribulations, as seen in a modern key, and the score is vibrant, underlining each word with enormous detail.

"Because of my flair for contemporary scores, I had the privilege of being the first to interpret Respighi's *Maria Egiziaca* and later his *Lucrezia,* two beautiful scores too soon forgotten. Some colleagues of mine don't consider Respighi *verista.* Although his librettos have a supernatural or heroic or religious theme, from the very first day that I began to interpret him—I have been so closely identified with his work—I always thought his way of writing for the voice was pure *verista*. An instrument that is not sensuous cannot do justice to his music, and what is this if not proof of verismo?

"At La Scala one often had surprises, but there were always solid reasons for them. When in my fourth season I was assigned Charlotte in *Werther*, a role that seemed not quite right for my voice (it is often done by a mezzo or a dramatic soprano, and in fact Pederzini and Cristoforeanu had preceded me at La Scala), the reason turned out to be that Schipa was the protagonist, and since his instrument was so very light, they did not want, for the vocal equilibrium, a voice that was too heavy. It was a joy to appear with him, and I had the pleasure of repeating this lovely role with him often. (To give you another example of how conductors then noticed every nuance, Guarnieri, who led the Massenet opera, took me aside at the dress rehearsal and whispered, 'Signorina Caniglia, Charlotte is not a femme fatale—why not diminish your eyebrows somewhat, for from the front they make you look like a vamp.' Naturally, I thanked him and proceeded to do as told.) I was not a Mozartian, and the Countess I sang at La Scala did not suit me. Gluck was instead my cup of tea, and I loved singing *Iphigénie en Tauride* in 1936 with de Sabata.

"As modest and cozy as Schipa was, the same cannot be said of Gigli, with whom I sang over five hundred times and recorded various operas. He did not speak to me for two years. Then suddenly his anger was spent, and he invited me and my husband to dinner as if nothing had ever happened. '*Cara Maria*' and all of that! You can imagine how convincing our love scenes were during those twenty-four months when, offstage, he cut me dead. The rage was sparked by a performance of *Tosca* in Rome with Tito Gobbi as our Scarpia. After 'Vissi d'arte' I received an endless ovation. Although there were insistent demands for a repeat, I did not grant the encore. But at the end of the second act, when I was invited by the Intendant to take a curtain call alone, Gigli declared that if I acceded to this request, he would not continue to sing, accusing me of having a claque. To this I replied, 'Then, my dear Beniamino, you are implying that I bought every seat in the house!'

"Now allow me to be a little catty. Despite the glory of his instrument, the marvelous security and the perfection of his technique, Gigli did not have the pianos of Schipa or Pertile. He sang in falsetto—well camouflaged, but falsetto nevertheless. Now they all use it. Pianos do not exist anymore, with the exception of Caballé, who is the last exponent of this lost art.

"Speaking of encores, do you know what happened to poor Maestro Ghione in 1934? I was present at La Scala at an all-star performance of *Il barbiere di Siviglia* with Toti dal Monte, Schipa, Franci, and Chaliapin. After

'La calunnia,' which the Russian bass sang in his own inimitable manner, the public roared and demanded a *bis*. Chaliapin advanced to the front of the stage and made a gesture to Ghione in the pit, and the wretched conductor was so totally taken aback that he gave in to the request. Pandemonium followed, with the management suspending Ghione for two seasons, since he was considered the culprit for breaking a long-standing tradition. He was in charge of the opera and therefore responsible.

"I always believed in going to the source for advice. When I prepared *Manon Lescaut* I went to Carmen Melis, and for *Fanciulla* to Gilda dalla Rizza, since they had been exceptional interpreters of these two Puccini operas. Another artist who influenced me a lot was Ersilde Cervi Cairoli in *Adriana*. When she sang at the end, 'Io volo, io volo, come una bianca colomba' [I fly, I fly, like a white dove], I was mesmerized, for her face took on the pallor of death.

"But all this is finished. There are no more emotions to be had in the lyric theatre. All the wrong people are assigned to the wrong roles; and this, I have decided, is not due to ignorance: it has simply become a must. Either they cannot be heard or, like Elena Obraztsova, they shout as if they were calling for help from another planet. When La Scala was rebuilt and the old-timers replaced by a very rich merchant who had done a lot to help in the reconstruction, intrigues and favoritism exploded. And the enchantment was finished. Anyhow, the singer no longer matters now, and, what is worse, neither does the composer. Now critics speak of Ponnelle's *Cenerentola*, Ronconi's *Nabucco,* or Strehler's *Don Carlo*. In a way they are right, for these men change everything to suit themselves, and the original work is left in shambles."

While discussing the Verdi heroines, for which she had been so famous, I asked her if there was one aria in particular that had most affected her.

"Not an aria," she replied, "but the duet 'La Vergine degli angeli' with the bass, later joined by the chorus, in *Forza*. I don't believe Verdi ever wrote a more inspired and mystical page than this, not even in the Requiem. The setting too, with all the monks carrying candles, is so awe-inspiring. I was never able to sing it without weeping. Since my husband passed away, I have thought increasingly about death, and just a short time ago I was thinking how wonderful it would be to go into the beyond to the tune of that music, praising the Holy Virgin."

When I read about Caniglia's death in 1979, I vividly recalled her wish. I only hope it came true, for no one deserved to enter the gates of heaven the way she wished more than she did, whose warm voice gave so much pleasure to mankind.

RENATA TEBALDI

In 1979 Renata Tebaldi opened the door of her cozy apartment in Milan, and I could not believe my eyes. If I had not known that she was born in 1921 or 1922, I would have believed her to be fifteen years younger. Never had she appeared more relaxed and glamorous, her ingratiating smile as natural and impulsive as ever. She had always had definite opinions, but now she had become particularly articulate about her feelings and beliefs, and she looked back on her long career with a stimulating mixture of detachment and passion.

"Young singers today," she declared sadly, "think of what was my profession in a manner that to us of the preceding generation is totally incomprehensible. Discipline was our credo, and the everyday preoccupation was not to sing roles that might force our instruments. Our ambition was to be able to sing for a period of at least thirty years. It was a question of deep pride and also a profound attachment to our art. Those who have taken our place are victims of a form of recklessness that is very close to madness. Does life hold no promises for them? Do they wish to burn their vocal cords in a short period? They begin, take on engagements, and then suddenly disappear. They will sing anything and everything. Responsibilities, truthfully, must be shared by the directors of the opera houses, who are not only incapable but in some ways sadistic. A coloratura wants to sing *Norma*? It's all right. A mezzo wishes to sing the Druid priestess? Just fine. We have examples before our very eyes that make one shudder. Everything is allowed, and the chaos reigning everywhere is harrowing. Young conductors simply don't know their profession. Alas, even with the most celebrated, we witness the results. In my era they spent years as assistants, an invaluable apprenticeship. Each one knew how to play several instruments, and the conductor was our spiritual confessor and adviser. Now they have the pretension to put on operatic performances without the proper singers. It can only end disastrously.

"These conductors rush the tempos so, it is impossible to follow them. What happens to the breathing apparatus if they don't allow the time for it to function? They want the score to proceed always faster. With all the cuts that had been reinstated, *Il trovatore,* conducted by Riccardo Muti not long ago in Florence, lasted far less time than usual. I was filled with admiration for Gilda Cruz-Romo, the Leonora. What a monstrous effort for her to sing the fourth act, which presents considerable difficulties, at that infernal gallop—and what is more, she managed it! This mania to hurry the tempos—just look at the scores and they are always clearly indicated—against the composer's wishes! Supposedly it is meant to increase the dramatic tension. There is also the craze on the part of conductors and metteurs-en-scène to crush the personality of the artist. The sad truth is that in a short period of time they have almost completely succeeded. Tell me—with the exception of Caballé and Domingo, who is there? Montserrat is the last prima donna, capricious at times, but she obtains what she wants because she knows what is right for her. Placido too is one who will not allow anyone to step on his toes. He has his ideas—I know him well—and, thankfully, he imposes them, for he knows how to render his characters human.

"It is much easier to make sheep out of people. Look at young people the world over. They are all dressed alike; blue jeans are their uniforms. How can a young soprano realize that Violetta is not Tosca, that Tatiana is not Elsa? They don't know how to wear costumes, and there is no one to teach them. Béjart has rewritten *La traviata* with Violetta turned into a sculptress, Germont singing 'Di Provenza' surrounded by his family, Violetta arriving at Flora's reception in a coffin, and so forth and so on. So one can only reach the conclusion that everything is possible and nothing impossible. What can young people make out of such a *Traviata*? That Verdi, Piave, and Dumas *fils* were all mad?

"I have had my experiences. I was obliged to engage in veritable battles at the Metropolitan over the costumes. I am a tall woman, and by long experience I know what I must not wear. The designer had decided that Violetta must be a giantess. At a certain moment I asked Mr. Bing who was more important to the new production of this opera—the designer or Tebaldi. And he gave in, because he knew that all the performances were sold out—and there were many—not because of the designer, but because of me. But with Mr. Bing, despite the fact that he was a dictator, one could always come to terms. Often I make an examination of my conscience and ask myself whether I was a fool, in consideration of all that I see happening around me. And then I say, Renata, you were right, because you served your profession honestly. You have been, like Adriana Lecouvreur (a role I adore), 'l'umile ancella' of the geniuses who wrote so much wonderful music.

Renata Tebaldi in the title role of *Adriana Lecouvreur*.

"I ask myself what goes on in the heads of the delicious Mirella Freni and the ever so talented Renata Scotto—she sang an enchanting Walter, a trouser role, with me in *La Wally* at La Scala in 1954—who are both lyric sopranos, with voices infinitely smaller than mine. The first one sings not only Elisabetta di Valois at La Scala but Aida in the big auditorium in Salzburg. And the second appears not only in *I vespri siciliani, Il trovatore, Un ballo in maschera, Don Carlo,* and *Norma,* but in *La Gioconda, Macbeth, Nabucco,* and goodness knows what else. And I, a spinto, recorded *Don Carlo, Ballo,* and *Trovatore,* but never dared sing them in a theatre, for these operas are written for dramatic sopranos and only they can really honor the scores. Mirella is intelligent, and she comes out of *Don Carlo* passably. *Ma chi glie lo fa fare?* [But who makes her do it?] She is totally out of her element, while she is incomparable as Susanna and the Gounod Juliette, to mention two of the parts that truly suit her. And Scotto can only force her instrument out of all proportion. Serafin begged me to take six months off and prepare Norma with him. And I replied, 'But there is Callas, who does it so well.' 'It does not matter,' he answered. 'You will sing it with your voice. It will be your Norma, and I can guarantee you it will be a huge success.' But not even Serafin, whose judgment about voices was unsurpassed, made me budge from my decision.

"Where are the big voices today? There are only tiny mosquitoes flying around. And we—Milanov, Nilsson, del Monaco, Corelli, and others—lost three and four kilos at each performance, so tremendous was the tension we gave to our assignments! It was our blood we gave to the audiences. How could we have been such fools?

"What worries me more and more—this problem had already started when I was still singing—is that today singers are all confronted with a diapason that is much too high. It should not go over 440, but there are many orchestras that start at 443 and arrive even as high as 450. Conductors will do anything to obtain a more brilliant sonority. The orchestra in Florence, as far as Italy is concerned, has the highest diapason of all. The late Dimitri Mitropoulos imposed it when he conducted *Elektra* there. This is the reason why real contraltos and bassos no longer exist: because of the enormous increase in the diapason, all the voices are pulled up. To go back to *Il trovatore* in Florence, there was a pompous announcement that Carlo Cossutta would sing 'Di quella pira' in the original key written by Verdi and not the higher version that has become traditional with all tenors. The truth is that the one Verdi composed has become a tone higher!

"The sensuousness that prevailed in all of Wagner's works no longer exists. Why did this composer write so many F-sharps at the beginning of his scores? He knew very well the effect he wished to obtain. Those who play instruments these days no longer know how to extricate themselves from so many problems; the gongs, the bells, all the special musical instruments, all have had to be readjusted or made over. The diapason should be the same everywhere, and Serafin, who saw ahead very clearly, did his best to impose this point of view at a congress held in Great Britain. But it continues to vary from one orchestra to the next. How are voices going to resist? Every day we see promising singers who destroy themselves in no time. This is a period of strikes; why don't all the singers get organized, refuse to open their mouths, and say *basta*? It does not take great intelligence to predict that a big step backward will have to be taken. It will all come to a stop, and then there must be a new, fresh start."

Then, briefly, she told me her story. Born in Pesaro, she went to live with her mother and her maternal grandparents in Langhirano, a small town near Parma. Her parents had separated before her birth, and for a long time she thought that her father, a cellist by profession, was dead. There was later a reconciliation, but it did not last long, and her father returned to Pesaro. A very sensitive child, Tebaldi suffered from this situation and became enormously attached to her mother, Giuseppina. At the age of three Tebaldi was stricken with polio, but this is a part of her life she prefers to forget. Eventually, although her right hip continued to give her some trouble, she began to study piano in Parma, and her teacher discovered that she had a voice. She auditioned for the conservatory in Parma and was accepted, pretending to be eighteen, the age of admittance, when she was really only sixteen.

She had studied there for two years when she went to Pesaro to spend Christmastime with her uncle Valentino, her father's brother. As destiny would have it, he owned a small cafe where the famous former diva Carmen Melis came to buy pastries. She was then a teacher at the conservatory in Pesaro, the most celebrated in Italy. He talked to her about his niece, and she consented to listen to Tebaldi in her hotel suite. Still a true prima donna in her ways, she terrified Tebaldi, who was a simple country girl. But, although Melis criticized her manner of singing, she agreed that the voice had a lovely timbre. The next day, and for the rest of her holiday, she went to Melis for certain readjustments, particularly in connection with vowels, and when she returned to Parma no one could believe it was the same voice, so drastic had been the improvement.

It was then that Tebaldi decided to move to Pesaro permanently to study with Melis. In Pesaro she lived with her father's family and took classes with Melis both at the conservatory and privately. Then the war came, and because of the frequent bombings, the conservatory had to close. Melis moved to Como, and Renata, with her mother, evacuated to the countryside, where she continued to vocalize on her own.

"La Signora Melis and I kept in touch as best we could," she told me, "and in 1944 she let me know that she had arranged for me to make my debut as Elena in *Mefistofele* in Rovigo, under the very well-known conductor Giuseppe del Campo. I went to meet Melis ten days before the performance to study the role—a short one, but very effective—and she was perfectly marvelous; she never left me, even in the wings of the theatre, until the curtain went up. There I was on the couch, terrified. But la Signora was pleased with the results."

For the next two years not much happened, because of the disastrous conditions the country was in, but Tebaldi did manage to sing a few performances here and there. The great test came in 1946 when she appeared as Desdemona in Trieste with two famous interpreters, Merli and Biasini. The news spread like wildfire that a wonderful new voice had appeared on the horizon.

"Immediately," she said, "all the theatres opened their doors to me, and it was thrilling for me that all the sacrifices my mother had made for me —she always would have preferred to see me married and settled—had not been in vain. Desdemona, until the end of my career, remained my favorite heroine: innocent, good-natured, the victim of love and jealousy, which know no laws.

"In three decades I had some exceptional partners as the Moor. Merli was close to the end of his professional life—he was fifty-nine years old at the time—and he was marvelous: tender, anguished, tormented, and with a stupendous diction. No other tenor—in this role as well as in many others —had the vocal splendor and the irresistible strength of Mario del Monaco. What perhaps was missing a tiny bit was the humanity. Ramón Vinay was a superb singing actor, but the voice was somewhat veiled. Jon Vickers's approach is the most intellectual, and it is a miracle how suddenly he is able to produce some immensely delicate phrases. James McCracken is formidable in his own way: impetuous, passionate, almost brutal.

"It is a role that poses many question marks, for the tessitura lies almost always in the middle, and the orchestration is heavy. Any tenor who becomes entangled with this tempting part is apt to lose some of the freedom in the upper register. It is the decision that Domingo must make now. He is admirable in this opera, but will he be able to continue to appear in *Rigoletto* and *Ballo*? Del Monaco had to reduce his repertoire drastically, for he was so in demand for the Moor everywhere that he ended by accepting most of the offers. Corelli, I know, has been tempted, but has never decided. Martinelli, perhaps wisely, only began to sing it in his last years."

After this parenthesis, she continued: "I was in Brescia appearing with Giacinto Prandelli in *L'amico Fritz* when I was called to go to La Scala for an audition with Toscanini, who had just returned to Italy from the United States and wished to hear the new voices in the lyric market. I was stunned when he chose me right away to appear at the gala reopening concert of the reconstructed Scala. Apart from the beautiful prayer of Rossini's *Mosè*, in partnership with the unforgettable Tancredi Pasero, I don't really recall much of anything that went on that evening, with the entire audience in tears—and so were we, the singers. The stage was not ready yet, and so performances were given in the Palazzo dello Sport. I really started my Scala operatic career there, first as Margherita and Elena too in *Mefistofele* and then in *Lohengrin* in the summer of 1946. The following year I appeared in *La Bohème* and as Eva in *Meistersinger* in La Scala's first season after its reconstruction. June 26, 1950, was another important date, for Toscanini again chose me, for the Verdi Requiem, which was preceded by the same composer's Te Deum. At one of the rehearsals the maestro decided that I should sing the E-natural in the Te Deum, which comes after the trumpet has taken it and must be in the same timbre. This is an important detail, for it created a legend around me that is not true, and this is what happened. Toscanini decided that this one note I sang must sound as if it came from heaven, and for this reason he had me placed way over above the chorus. The story got around—and persists still today—that the maestro had declared that I had the voice of an angel.

"Anyhow, it is a party I attended on another occasion, where I was seated next to the maestro, that led me to undertake *Aida*. Toscanini asked me about my repertoire and if I sang *Aida*. I replied that I did not, as I felt it belonged to the dramatic soprano wing. He explained that he felt I could, taking certain precautions, and said he would show me. And he did in his studio. He was absolutely extraordinary, for he sang the entire part himself, giving me precious advice. So I did agree to sing it at La Scala in 1950, and, amusingly enough, when I left because of other commitments, it was Maria Callas who took over, making her debut in Milan.

"At the Maggio Musicale Fiorentino, I was offered the revival of a forgotten opera by Rossini, *L'assedio di Corinto*, and I accepted. Actually, the genius from Pesaro wrote it first as *Maometto II* for the San Carlo in Naples, with his wife, Isabella Colbran, in the lead. Then he rewrote it for the Paris Opéra under the title *Le Siège de Corinthe,* where it received a triumphant baptism in 1826 with the famous Laure Cinti-Damoreau. It then was performed everywhere, and in London it was Giuditta Grisi who sang it, having already performed it in Italy. After 1860 it disappeared from the repertoires, and for me this was quite a challenge. The reason I accepted it was that Rossini, fed up with all the ornamentations the various divas requested, had written a different type of score from his usual ones. Gabriele Santini conducted, and the success was so great that we repeated it in other cities.

"When La Scala revived it"—she laughed—"in 1969, with Thomas Schippers conducting (later the Metropolitan imported the production for the debut of Beverly Sills), for me it was like listening to another score, so much had they fiddled around with it, putting in all the fioriture. It was impressive singing, but we go back to where we started: there is no more respect for anyone or anything. After all, Rossini must have known what he wanted.

"During those first years I also often sang the last opera Rossini ever composed: *Guglielmo Tell.* It is a work, alas, that has more or less vanished, for the vocal extension of the tenor role is such that there is no one today who can cope with it. A few have tried, but without success. Lauri-Volpi has written, most interestingly, about his experiences when he sang in its one hundredth anniversary at La Scala—and if *he* found it difficult, God save the others! In my epoch there was Mario Filippeschi, who could cope with it very adroitly. With Rossini it is most difficult to cheat, for his orchestrations are very light and the singer is therefore very exposed.

"My debuts at both Covent Garden and the San Francisco Opera came in 1950. The directors of the War Memorial Opera House had heard my Aida at La Scala and requested that I start my American career with the Ethiopian slave. But because of endless complications in my engagements, I was only able to start at the Metropolitan Opera in 1955. Desdemona introduced me to that marvelous audience which I love with all my heart. I shall never forget the sympathy, so affectionate and deeply felt, of the entire operatic public when my mother died suddenly in Manhattan and I canceled the entire season. I was destroyed by her loss—we were so terribly close; she had sacrificed her entire life for me. It took me a long time to overcome this shock. And when I returned the following season, the ovation that greeted me was absolutely overwhelming. I knew that everyone in that theatre loved me, and it is wonderful to know there can be such deep affection from strangers.

"I ended by singing less and less in Europe, for so little time was left after the Metropolitan, the Chicago Opera, and the enormous amount of recording I did of entire operas and single recitals. I did return always to sing at the San Carlo in Naples, for that was my second spiritual home, the first being New York. Neapolitans are marvelously warm people, and it is in this city that I had the opportunity to sing for the first time Verdi's sublime and neglected opera *Giovanna d'Arco,* which has a somewhat foolish libretto, but such heavenly music."

I did not ask her about her relations with La Scala, which had deteriorated because of Antonio Ghiringhelli's subservience to Callas: she must be served first. I knew it was a subject she preferred not to discuss; she may have been deeply hurt, but she never showed it. After *Forza* in 1955, she returned to La Scala from time to time, in 1959 for *Tosca* and then in 1960 for *Chenier.* She spoke admiringly of Callas and never mentioned the widely reported origin of the Callas-Tebaldi rivalry. It happened in Rio de Janeiro in 1951 when both of them were appearing at the Municipal: the Greek diva's Tosca was booed, and she accused Tebaldi of having organized a cabal against her. But in Milan people remember that even in 1950 Callas's resentment toward the then-reigning prima donna had already begun; and when Tebaldi failed to make a success of her first *Traviata* in Milan (she was to be vindicated later with a triumph in this opera in Naples), Callas went around saying to everyone, "Poor thing, I feel so sorry for her." There was certainly plenty of room for both of them at La Scala, but the wily Greek edged out Tebaldi, who was not a fighter and was never malicious. Strong willed and stubborn, yes, but never unkind. During the three decades I have known her, never once have I heard her admit that there had been a feud, although she was fully conscious that the attendant publicity would be fantastic. "Callas is flamboyant and thrives on this sort of thing," Tebaldi said to me at the height of the press reports. "I am not, and I don't feel I need any of this. I can stand on my accomplishments. I have my public and she has hers. There is enough space for both of us—to each her own."

She talked about Callas with utter serenity and a pity that I could feel was totally sincere. "Maria did mark an era—no one can take that away from her. She insisted on singing everything and did. Now everyone wants to do likewise, and, alas, it is not working out.

"I had never seen her again after she lost all that weight—mind you, I insist on repeating that no unpleasant words ever passed between us—and then one night she came to the Metropolitan when I was singing Adriana.

No one dared tell me that she was in the audience, fearing that this would upset me. Why should it? Then, suddenly, after the performance was over and I had returned to my dressing room, the door opened and there she was with Mr. Bing—and the photographers, naturally. She threw herself in my arms and was flattering to a degree about my interpretation. Curiously, she, who sang everything, never got around to the Cilea opera. I remember so well her words: 'I am so happy to have been present at your great success.' It was a tragic moment in her life, for she had been abandoned by Onassis, for whom she gave up her career. I never saw her again, and then, suddenly, the news of her death gave me a veritable chill. How much that proud woman, left all alone, must have suffered! I often wonder what happened to her two dogs, who belonged to the same breed as mine. I am happy she came that night, for it tore down a wall that as far as I am concerned never existed.

"I owe an immense debt of gratitude to the United States," she affirmed with moving sincerity, "where I lost many complexes I had. I learned to become more sure of myself, to dress, to take better care of my appearance, and, above all, to think differently. At the Metropolitan, where I stayed until 1972, I sang more than two hundred fifty performances: *Aida, Forza, Traviata, Tosca, Chenier, Bohème, Falstaff, Adriana, Manon Lescaut, Boccanegra, Fanciulla,* and *Butterfly*. After I sang this last for the first time in Barcelona, every theatre demanded it. Mr. Bing thought I was too tall for the former geisha, but after reading the rave reviews from Naples and Rome he gave in. Much later, in 1966, in the first year of the new house in Lincoln Center, after my voice had become much darker—I had to stop singing for almost a year because of total exhaustion—I took on *La Gioconda* in an unforgettable production of Beni Montresor and under the direction of Margherita Wallmann, who talks of me with such true affection in her charming autobiography, *Balconies from the Sky*. I sang over thirty performances of this opera at the Metropolitan and then again in Naples. Mr. Bing wanted me for Tatiana in *Onegin,* a role I sang at La Scala and which was just right for my voice and personality; but I never felt that my English was sufficiently advanced, and at the Metropolitan this Russian opera was given in English.

"Diction, as far as I am concerned, is of capital importance. That is why I never appeared in any of my Wagnerian roles in the United States, as, quite rightly so, these operas are done in German. In Italy I appeared often as Eva, Elisabeth, and Elsa, another part that suited my instrument and nature, but I never felt I was equal to them in German, for my diction in that language leaves much to be desired. In fact, even in the hundreds of recitals I gave

—an activity I followed with enormous satisfaction after I left opera—I never dared make excursions into lieder."

(She made no reference to the debacle of her first Adrianas at the Metropolitan in 1963; her voice was simply in terrible shape in a role that does not require a high range. Wisely, she stopped singing for a year and went through an extensive reappraisal of her vocal technique. When she reappeared a year later in *La Bohème,* the middle of her instrument was as gorgeous as ever and the upper register somewhat mended, but there was still a hard edge to the top that remained with her until the end.)

"I laugh when I read some critics call the Metropolitan in my era an opera house ruled by routine. Can one speak of routine when in the space of ten days *Tosca* was performed once with Milanov, once with Nilsson, and once —all modesty forgotten—with me? Competition is the healthiest thing there can be in the singing profession. For the public, it is more interesting when different interpreters follow one another in repertory works. One may love *La Bohème,* but one does not always want to listen to the same Mimi. But today who is there? When I think of who was before the public when I started, I realize where we have fallen. Think of Caniglia, Carosio, Favero, Nicolai, Barbieri, Stignani, Cigna, Pacetti, Bechi, Pasero, Andrea Mongelli, and Tagliavini, to name a few, and then later Simionato, Milanov, Sutherland, del Monaco, di Stefano, Bastianini, Corelli, Siepi, Tucker, Warren— my goodness! there was excitement then; they were all superb. I shall never get over the death of Leonard Warren onstage while I was appearing with him in *Forza.* He was a wonderful colleague, and what a voice! Now the same little group sings everywhere, rushing from one theatre to the other, with no rehearsals, no sense of responsibility toward the public, asking always for higher and higher fees. How can you arrive by plane at four o'clock in the afternoon and then sing at eight? They must all have nerves of steel. Not only did I always go to bed early the night before a performance, but I never spoke to anyone on the telephone, unless it was an emergency, for twenty-four hours before. I shall never become a singing teacher, for I do not have the patience to put up with the total lack of discipline existing today. My admiration for Pagliughi, Saraceni, Cigna, Carbone, and all the others who give their all to these students is boundless, but I am not a martyr. Fortunately, I made many recordings, and the royalties do continue. For singing as much as I did in the United States meant paying very high taxes, and not so much remains. *Ma pazienza—* despite all the sacrifices, it was all wonderful."

THE GREAT LYRICS

INES ALFANI TELLINI

ADELAIDE SARACENI

MARIA LAURENTI

DOROTHY KIRSTEN

A choice had to be made—a difficult one—as to which of the prestigious sopranos of the lyric repertoire I would interview. There are lyric sopranos to be found in other chapters, where some particular characteristics have placed them. But the reason for selecting these four will, I hope, become clear.

Alfani Tellini, an aristocrat to her fingertips, was one of the greatest stylists of this century, as her several recordings attest. Saraceni, who started as a coloratura and then became a lyric, created several important new works and was outstanding for her versatility and intelligence. Laurenti represents the typical Italian lyric; her instrument—I recall it vividly—evoked infinite pathos and sentiment, and with her good sense she never left the right path. Kirsten is the outstanding American lyric; and with her wonderful instinct for knowing just what was right for her, she lasted longer than any of the others.

INES ALFANI TELLINI

Toscanini used to say that when he conducted Gluck's *Orfeo* at La Scala with Ines Alfani Tellini as Euridice, the public understood what the opera was all about. She was so beautiful that people sympathized fully with Orpheus's superhuman efforts to win his wife back from the dead. Her voice was pure, crystalline, and exquisitely modulated.

"Ines was never ambitious," Wally Toscanini explained to me before my appointment with the former diva. "She was much too much of a lady to push herself forward or she would have become a great international star. She was the closest we had in Italy to Lucrezia Bori. The moment she walked on the stage, you knew she was an aristocrat. Immense charm, innate taste, and a great sense of style distinguished her from so many of her colleagues. My father always thought highly of her and used her many times as Nannetta in *Falstaff*, even in the celebrated production that he took to Berlin and Vienna. She also sang an enchanting Pamina under his direction, and one immediately believed that she was a queen's daughter."

One can only surmise Ines Alfani Tellini's age, since she was married and already the mother of two children when she first appeared with Toscanini in 1921 at La Scala. But as she greeted me in 1976 at the door of her daughter's penthouse apartment in the heart of old Milan (her own was undergoing repairs at the time), wearing a smart pink Chanel suit, her ash-blond hair delicately arranged, she appeared not only ageless, but charged with a sort of femininity that seemed to belong to another time.

"I was born an Alfani," she explained, "and Tellini was my husband's name. We were both from Florence, where my family had been comforta-bly established for centuries, and he was many years older. I had studied the piano for years at the conservatory in Florence, and even after my marriage continued to play for my own pleasure. And often I would delve into the lieder literature and sing along. I had never given any thought to a singing career, but Amedeo Bassi, the great tenor who sang Parsifal and Siegmund under Toscanini, happened to hear me by chance and put the bug into me.

Ines Alfani Tellini as Marguerite in *Faust*.

He simply would not believe that I had not studied. I had a hard time convincing him that I was entirely self-trained. He claimed that all I had to do was to study a few roles and that I would have no trouble getting engagements. I was so bored at home—my husband and I had nothing in common—that I took him at his word. My husband was so convinced that Bassi was joking that after a while he consented that I go to Milan to undertake some auditions. I did, and to my own amazement an offer came immediately for me to sing Nedda in *Pagliacci* at the Teatro dal Verme in Milan, where the standard of performances was highly respectable.

"La Scala heard of my promising debut—all the critics had raved—and an audition was arranged for Toscanini. While he sat in the auditorium in total darkness, I was on the well-lit stage in a state of shock. I started off with 'Connais-tu le pays?'—which of course was most unwise, since it is written for mezzo-soprano. 'Now something else, lighter if possible, to show off the other side of the voice,' I heard the great man say. So I plunged into Leila's aria from *The Pearl Fishers*. Then he asked for a third selection. Absurdly convinced he wished me to continue because he did not like me, I murmured, 'But if the maestro is not pleased, I do not wish to waste his time.' 'Don't you realize, you silly fool, that if I were not interested in you, I would not ask you to go on?' he thundered. Shaking, I went on. When he had enough, I was taken down some steps into the theatre to meet him. As Angelo Scandiani, the director of La Scala, ushered me out, he said, 'We will let you have an answer within two or three weeks.' Three days later I was given a contract for three years.

"And La Scala became my home for many years," she continued, "and Toscanini my God. He never once got angry with me, and never made the kind of remarks that drove some of my colleagues to tears. Only once, like the tenderest of fathers, he said, 'You know that I never expect the slightest mistake from you.' And he was totally right, for I had come in a fraction of a second too late. I sang Nannetta with many other conductors after he left, including the admirable Panizza, but *Falstaff* could never quite be the same without him.

"In those days there were four fabulous Alices: Mercedes Llopart, Gilda dalla Rizza, Rosa Raisa, and Maria Labia. But there was only one Falstaff: Mariano Stabile. He was unique, for apart from being a magnificent actor, he had the voice and the style. To me, then as today, style is everything. I sacrificed everything to it, and I would not change if I had to start all over again. Alas, it is a vanishing trait. Style for me means not to change an iota of the score or libretto for the sake of longer applause or a better notice.

"I became quite versatile," she explained, "and built up a larger repertoire. At La Scala I went from Micaëla and Marzelline to Paisiello's *Nina, o sia La pazza per amore,* and Rabaud's *Marouf,* among others. A role that came my way often was Gretel, and it packed Italian opera houses. Now it has disappeared in Italy, and the current generation does not know of its existence. The most precious Hansel of all was Conchita Supervia, adorable in trouser roles. Loving lieder as I did, I built up a concert career and spent several months a year concertizing. In 1934 I was the first Italian to be asked to do a series of recitals in Russia, and I returned there regularly until the war. I also sang *La traviata* there, one of the operas most closely identified with my career, but it is not an experience I recall with pleasure. The standards of my colleagues were appalling, and style was a state of grace sadly neglected and ignored. I have been very spoiled, for I only sang with the top conductors and the best artists. Needless to say, my marriage went on the rocks, but until his death my husband and I remained good friends. He simply could not accept my success, while for me music was my reason for living—that, and my deep affection for my children.

"I became a Mozart specialist," she went on, "and I was called upon constantly to sing—in addition to Pamina—Zerlina, Susanna, and Despina. I also became very fond of *L'oca del Cairo,* which Mozart had begun in 1783 but never finished. Virgilio Mortari assembled it, and it was delicious, like a light cream on a cake. The sets of Nicola Benois at La Scala were enchanting; in my opinion he was the number-one stage designer of that time. This little work was performed quite often here and there, and then disappeared. One of the parts I sang often was Marguerite in *Faust,* and later I added the one in *Mefistofele.* It was in Parma that I sang the Gounod opera for the first time, and Ezio Pinza, the protagonist, spoiled me for those who came later. When I sang *Faust* in Rome, I had Giacomo Lauri-Volpi in the title role, and my row with him became public knowledge. At the first performance, in the garden scene, he held on to a high note way beyond the point of decency. Since he had not included this extra dividend at the dress rehearsal, I was caught off guard and did not hold on to mine. But at the second performance, although it was very much against my principles, I did, as I knew that if I didn't, the public would think I did not have the stamina. He got absolutely furious and was very rude. Since I have never put up with bad manners, I refused ever to appear with him again. On the Scala tour with Toscanini in 1929 to Vienna and Berlin, in which I participated, he sang in *Il trovatore* with the maestro and repeated his usual trick at the end of 'Di quella pira.' Toscanini berated him in no uncertain terms, but to no avail. At the second performance he did it again, and then the maestro's ire knew no limits—a reaction that was totally warranted in my opinion. To give you an idea of what a different type of man Pertile was, the first of the many times I sang with him in *Lohengrin* I was naturally worried about the love duet in the third act, for his was a very big voice and mine extremely lyrical. He automatically cut his voice down to size, and when I thanked him for his consideration he replied, 'Signora, it is only natural, for two voices must sound well together.'

"I have never sung a note that was not marked in the score," she said with determination, "and always refused any sort of compromise. If a single note had to be transposed to suit my voice, I simply did not accept the assignment. Whatever I sang was always in the original key, and I would never accept embellishments, which I could do with facility and which are so customary these days. I remember when I appeared in *I Capuleti ed i Montecchi* in Catania for the first time, at a very important Bellini celebration, with the great Marinuzzi conducting, we found ourselves in agreement on this important point.

"I loved Bellini's Giulietta, and it became a role very much identified with me. It is a very difficult assignment, for it calls for a total purity of tone, agility, and at the same time one must express real pathos. I do not think Bellini ever wrote a more heavenly aria than 'Oh! quante volte, oh quante.' But the legato, the holding together of the words and the phrases, needs a very strong vocal technique, and no trickery saves you here. What I adore about this score is that, though less showy than other Bellini works, it goes way deep into the recesses of the heart. The second aria, 'Morte io non temo' [Death I do not fear you], is perhaps more effective, but a little less difficult, for the text per se is so infinitely moving, and the words have always been a great help to a singer. I am thrilled that this opera is being rediscovered and that I see it turning up again in various theatres.

"I also sang many Desdemonas, and although the concertato in the third act was a little heavy for the timbre of my very lyrical instrument, I found the way to cut through over the large ensemble. This is a vocal problem that some colleagues never solved, but I did and always managed never to force. For me forcing was always taboo. Perhaps the opera I sang most often was Massenet's *Manon*. Unfortunately, I never kept a score card, but it must have been well over three hundred times. I also went on in later years, when my voice got darker, to Puccini's *Manon Lescaut,* and it was with this role, in Brussels, that I brought down the curtain on my career. That night I no longer felt restrained. I had always feared the heavy orchestration of the last two acts. But that night I sang out 'Sola, perduta, abbandonata' as I had always wanted to.

"Puccini was never quite right for me, at least in my estimation, for my voice did not have that sort of sensuousness which most of his heroines require. I did sing Liù often, and Mimi, a role that made me famous at the Colón in Buenos Aires. Everyone tried to push me into singing Butterfly and Tosca, but I always said no.

"In between engagements I recorded several operas for Columbia, and most of them are still available. Recording sessions were far slower in those days, and much more time was necessary. Among the roles I recorded were Norina in *Don Pasquale* and Adina in *L'elisir d'amore,* both with the tenor Christy Solari; Micaëla in *Carmen,* with Pertile as an exceptional Don José and Aurora Buades a fiery protagonist; and Nannetta in *Falstaff,* with Giacomo Rimini in the title role. His was an important voice, but his interpretation could not touch Stabile's.

"After my foolish retirement, my energies had to be channeled. I say 'foolish' because actually I was still in top form. But I was so afraid of not doing it in time, before those unfailing signs of wear and tear I had noticed in some of my colleagues caught up with me. So I began teaching, and for twelve years I had a most interesting time as director of the opera workshop at the Accademia Chigiana in Siena, where we did many dazzling revivals. Count Guido Chigi had total faith in me, and I had a free hand. It is I who called my cousin Franco Zeffirelli, then a very young man, to do the sets and costumes for the delightful productions of eighteenth-century operas such as Traetta's *Le serve rivali,* Orlandini's *Il marito giogatore,* Fioravanti's *Le cantatrici villane,* Rinaldo di Capua's *La zingara,* and the delicious *Betly* by Donizetti. It became a sort of festival, and people came from everywhere. The late queen mother of Belgium, Elizabeth, who was an excellent musician and played the violin quite well even at her advanced age, came and stayed with Count Chigi every summer and often would turn up at my classes and rehearsals. At first she intimidated me, but later I got quite used to her, and we became good friends. I also taught at the conservatories in Naples, Palermo, Bolzano, and Rome.

"I go on teaching voice, but it becomes more difficult every day, for I simply cannot find students who have the flame burning. And in this profession, believe me, it is a must. Discipline and dedication are important, but one must have a willpower of iron, and they simply don't have it anymore. I am well aware that they are disoriented, and with good reason. How can you interpret an opera today when the text is no longer respected?

After all, the music is written around the text, and these directors—who have completely taken over the theatres—simply ignore it. They do what they please with it, and if Norma sings about the moon, it is invisible, and the mistletoe she is supposed to cut is not there either, because the tree does not exist from which she is supposed to cut it. I go to La Scala from time to time, but less and less often, for it is all falling apart. A really pleasant experience recently was listening to Alfredo Kraus singing *Werther* there. He is one of the rare artists today who know what style is all about. But, alas, he is not a young man. Most of the big names before the public today do not have any idea what style means."

She concluded her rendezvous with me, jangling her many pretty bracelets and pushing back a lock of hair. "As a mother," she said, "I have been very lucky. You have now met my daughter, who is a darling; and my son, Piero, who lives in Rome, has given me many proud moments. He is very gifted as a film writer, and you have undoubtedly seen many of his films —*Quattro passi nelle nuvole, L'onorevole Angelina* with Anna Magnani, and *Vivere in pace,* among many others. I am a very lucky woman, for they never resented their mother's frequent absences from home, and they remember many points about my career that I have forgotten. To me, at this time of my life, it's all strangely and inexplicably unimportant. The only thing that matters is the knowledge that I never betrayed any of my beloved composers, who so enriched my life, and that I gave every ounce of my spiritual being to the muse of music."

ADELAIDE SARACENI

One of the most aristocratic figures ever to have graced the Italian lyric theatre was Adelaide Saraceni; and my recollections of her Violetta and Gilda at the Maggio Musicale Fiorentino during the thirties are very vivid. She moved onstage with infinite allure, her delicate features strengthened by an aquiline nose of great distinction; and she sang with the ease of a nightingale, and exquisite, almost transparent pearly notes. None of her recordings give an idea of the delicious color of her effortless voice or the wonderful facility of her coloratura.

When I met her in her comfortable apartment in Milan, where for thirty years she has been teaching and coaching, I told her that I recalled her voice sounding like a violin.

"It is strange you should say that," she said, sitting very erect on a stiff chair, her soft white hair framing her Renaissance face, "because I studied the violin for eight years. And always, when I sang, I thought of the instrument that I had deeply loved and worked at with ever so much concentration and love. That was very long ago. But I make no mystery of my age. I am now over eighty, and I began in earnest with the fiddle when I was seven years of age.

"I was born of Italian parents in Rosario, Argentina, in 1895. I came to Italy for the first time with my father, who wanted me to audition to see whether my voice was worth training. I was just fifteen. The husband of my violin teacher was a singing coach; he had heard me do some solos in church with the other children, and he kept telling my family that I should study. My father, who was a realist, wanted other opinions too. The verdict was favorable, and I spent seven years in Pesaro dedicating all my time and energies to scales and arpeggios under the very capable direction of Edvige Ghibaudo. Did you ever hear of her? She had been very celebrated at one time, and Cilea chose her to create the role of the Principessa di Bouillon in *Adriana Lecouvreur*. Whatever I became I owe to her, for she was sensible, and taught me not only a solid technique, but discipline.

"When she felt I was ready, she sent me to Milan for some auditions. And

—can you believe it?—I only knew one aria: 'Qui la voce' from *I puritani*. 'But what must I do if they ask me for something else?' I asked, petrified. 'They won't,' she replied very firmly. 'When they hear how you sing it, they will not need to ask for anything more. It is one of the most treacherous arias written, and you do it full justice. The only thing I ask you is not to audition if you do not feel in perfect condition.' And as she predicted, I was hired immediately on the strength of that heavenly Bellini aria.

"My debut as Rosina in *Il barbiere di Siviglia* in the adorable opera house of Lugo di Romagna went off so well that a string of offers followed, and I built up my repertoire in the provincial theatres, which in those days were first-class. For ten years I was re-engaged every year at the opera house in La Valletta on the island of Malta, where there was a very good operatic tradition and all the best artists came for guest performances. I started as a coloratura of substance, and then, with the passage of time, I became a lyric, but with my agility unimpaired. In fact, I continued to sing Gilda until the very end of my career.

"When I came to the fore," she admitted candidly, "the competition in the coloratura section was simply ferocious. Elvira de Hidalgo was still very much around, and her Rosina was fabulous. And then there were Toti dal Monte, Lina Pagliughi, and Mercedes Capsir, to name the big stars, and all three were fantastic. And they were soon joined by Margherita Carosio. Don't ask me for comparisons. I have never compared singers, for they are all different. From my point of view, although my admiration for all three was boundless, Pagliughi's voice was the most beautiful, and in certain passages unequaled. If Lina had a different figure—she was enormous, because, I believe, of some dysfunction of her glands—she would have been number one. Toti was a scintillating person, and everything came alive onstage with her. Hers was a dark-colored kind of coloratura, and her technique was astounding. Mercedes had a typically Spanish instrument, slightly metallic and hard in certain areas—but how she used it! Listen to all her complete recordings, in particular *La traviata*, and you will know what I mean. I adored her Amina and Rosina too, for they had body and yet the notes floated like clouds. Margherita was very special: there was a deep meaning to every phrase. And how versatile she was!

"With this sort of competition I did not sing *Lucia* often, for I could not equal them in any way. *Rigoletto, La traviata, Elisir d'amore, Sadko, Martha, Manon, Faust, Le nozze di Figaro* (I sang Susanna), Liù in *Turandot* —these became my daily fare, with later ever so many Adrianas and Alices in *Falstaff*.

"It was as Susanna that I nervously entered the portals of La Scala in 1928,

Adelaide Saraceni as Volkhova in *Sadko*.

in a historic production with Stabile as an incomparable Figaro and Richard Strauss in the pit. He was a man of few words and gestures, but he was precision and clarity personified. I immediately felt secure with him, and he was a most considerate gentleman. I sang the role again at La Scala in another production, conducted by my compatriot Ettore Panizza. I recall two adorable Cherubinos, Conchita Supervia and Gianna Pederzini, and I really would not know to which one to hand the palm. But I preferred Giannina Arangi-Lombardi's stunningly sung Countess to that of the Spanish soprano Mercedes Llopart, who had personality, but less security in the bel canto area.

"Along with Violetta and Liù, the role I sang the most often was Gilda. It is a most ungrateful and thankless part, an ingenue whose every phrase is a vocal trap, sandwiched in between two vibrant real males. As I look back, it is difficult to imagine the number of superb Rigolettos available at that time. Where have the baritones gone today? Milnes, Bruson, Cappuccilli—not enough. While Galeffi's was the most superbly sung—I remember the electricity in the air when I sang with him in this opera at La Scala—it was Viglione Borghese's that gave me the greatest emotion. In the third-act finale, his fury against the Duke mixed with tenderness toward me was so overwhelming that I was invariably overcome. Riccardo Stracciari was very great too, although it was as Germont that he was terrifying as a partner. To sing Violetta with him was suicide, because in the second-act duet he absolutely stole the show every time. Franci was a marvelously theatrical jester, and Tagliabue came a close second. Bechi was also magnificent, although it is his Iago that has never been surpassed. Armando Borgioli and Mario Basiola were also Rigolettos of great quality, and each and every one had his own brand of characterization.

"I was the Liù in the second production of *Turandot* at La Scala, replacing Maria Zamboni, and the first in Naples, with the spectacular Bianca Scacciati as the princess in Bologna and Genoa. I closed my career in this part, with Gina Cigna as my partner, in Genoa, because of an Allied bombardment that destroyed the theatre. After the hair-raising panic of that night, I swore that I would never sing this part again, and I never did, despite the innumerable offers to change my decision. My nerves simply gave out, and I still tremble when I think of it.

"I was prepared to tackle my first Desdemona in Turin when that opera house was razed to the ground by another massive bombardment, and so I never had the satisfaction of portraying the wretched Venetian noblewoman. Francesco Merli, who died only the other day, was to have been

my Otello, and if Pertile had not reigned supreme, Francesco would have
had an even more brilliant career than he had.

"At La Scala I had all sorts of memorable moments. I sang a long series
of *Elisirs* with Schipa, whose Nemorino was utterly irresistible. Then Wolf-
Ferrari chose me to create Rosaura in his *La vedova scaltra,* a witty, sizzling
score with Goldoni's wonderful text, and it proved such a success that I
repeated it in most of the important Italian opera houses. Then I had the
luck to be singled out by Respighi to sing in the Italian premiere of his
La campana sommersa the role of Rautendelein, which the great Elisabeth
Rethberg introduced to the Metropolitan. It was such an enormous hit that
the following season the Scala management decided to bring it back for
opening night. While Martinelli sang Heinrich in New York, Pertile was
my companion at La Scala and, as usual, was the greatest artist of all.

"Speaking of tenors, there was never a finer or less selfish colleague than
Gigli. As I sailed off to sing *Manon* opposite him at the Colón in Buenos
Aires, two hours after the ship had sailed Maestro Tullio Serafin came and
knocked at my stateroom door. He calmly announced that for a series of
reasons which I have now totally forgotten, the Colón's management had
switched the Massenet opera to the Puccini one. 'You must be joking!' I said.
'What I am doing on this boat? Where is the port where I can get off?' 'You
will do nothing so foolish,' he proceeded, with his usual calm. 'You will
sing *Manon Lescaut.*' 'But how?' I cried in despair. 'I am not a spinto! I have
never studied it! It would be total, utter madness!' 'But I will be there,' he
said, taking my hand, with that authority which distinguished him. And I
shall never forget the infinitely paternal expression on his face when he said
so tenderly, 'But I will be there.' In ten days' time, he had taught me the
score so well that I had memorized every word and phrase.

"When we arrived in Buenos Aires and I saw the size of the Colón, I
almost fainted dead away. But Serafin was right there to comfort me again.
Gigli arrived only for the dress rehearsal, as was his custom, but another
tenor had gone through all the rehearsals with me. On opening night, scared
out of my wits, I went onstage in a state of terror. But in the second act
I became so enchanted with Gigli's singing, I forgot myself to such a point
that he whispered to me, 'You idiot, it's your turn.' He had so hypnotized
me that my stage fright had left me.

"At the curtain call after the second act, the house roared its approval,
and before I knew what was going on, Gigli had pushed me ahead of him
and run off the stage. And the applause continued, deafening. When I joined
him again in the wings, I said, 'But why did you do that? You are the

elephant and I am the fly.' 'Well,' he replied facetiously, 'I wish all flies were as good as you. You deserved your curtain call alone, and I wanted to prove to you that the public was impressed with your own merits.'

"Well, that was the way he was. And on every occasion I appeared with him—I sang many *Marthas* and *Fausts* with him—he always turned out to be the most adorable colleague possible. As for *Manon Lescaut,* it remained in my repertoire, but I was always most careful of where I sang it and with whom.

"I was always apprehensive about Puccini, and although I sang Mimi and Butterfly on many occasions, particularly with Butterfly I accepted only engagements with maestros I knew would be considerate of my type of voice.

"Apart from the many Susannas, the other Mozart part I sang was Elvira, which suited me well. I sang a series of performances under Serafin's direction at the Rome Opera, and I was astonished that Galeffi, the Don, who had the most Verdian of all baritone voices, could reduce his huge instrument and be a real Mozartian.

"In Rome I sang often, including the premiere of Lualdi's *Il diavolo nel campanile,* which was greeted with endless boos. But in those days the public was well educated and made a very definite distinction between the score it had hated and the artists. I well recall that I did not want to go out and take a solo bow after all those noises in the audience. The management insisted, and with a heavy heart I did as I was told. When I came out, I received the kind of ovation I would have had after singing Violetta or Cio-Cio-San.

"In Rome I had the usual experiences every soprano had when appearing with Lauri-Volpi. I sang Ginevra in Giordano's *La cena delle beffe* with him as the impetuous Giannetto, and there never was a performance at which I did not have to be on the alert, for sometimes he would hold on to the high C in the big duet and sometimes not at all. I had already sung with him in a very remarkable production of *Les Huguenots* at the Arena in Verona, with a great cast that included Raisa, Rimini, Pasero, and Pederzini. As Marguerite de Valois, I had a very tricky duet with the tenor, and unlike at the dress rehearsal, on opening night he held on to the high C as if his life depended on it. I was not ready for this and felt mortified. But I said nothing, and at the next performance, having worked a lot on my breathing in the meantime, I too held on until the bitter end, which was not appreciated. But he was magnificent, and this is what counts. And where is magnificence today?

"Mascagni was a very dear man, although his conducting was like a whistle-stop train, and I was most fortunate to fall into his good graces. He used me often for the gentle and melodious part of Suzel in *L'amico Fritz,* and also as Silvia in *Zanetto,* with Pederzini, in trousers, as the compelling protagonist. When I sang with this great composer—in my estimation shockingly neglected nowadays—I took extra time to work on my breathing, for I knew what was lying in store for me."

What other prima donnas and their roles did she find memorable?

She did not stop a second to think. "Cervi Cairoli's Adriana, dalla Rizza's Francesca, Cobelli's Sieglinde, Muzio's Violetta—all had another dimension. And what an immensely brave woman Cobelli was, as deaf as a post, using a hearing aid and never missing a beat! She was music itself. And the only word to describe Muzio is sublime. When we first appeared in the same theatre at the same time, at the Massimo in Palermo, she was doing *Traviata* and I *Adriana.* There could not have been a more considerate and gentle person. Incapable of an unkind thought. As far as conductors go, perhaps the one I enjoyed working with the most was Gaetano Bavagnoli. He made everything seem so simple, and from the podium one felt total protection.

"I never married"—she answered my question—"but I loved a man intensely for forty-seven years. He had a wife and children, and I respected his family so much I never would have accepted his leaving them. So there was no way out. Sometimes life is like that. One is trapped and one must make the best of it. He died four years ago, soon followed by his wife. For me it was never a sin, because when love is the kind I experienced, one is transfigured. His son understood this so well that when this year I did not turn up at the cemetery on the anniversary of his death, my arms full of flowers, he telephoned me to find out what had happened and seemed much concerned. I explained that a high fever had kept me glued to my bed and made the journey impossible.

"As for the lyric theatre of today, I am even more concerned than some of my great colleagues, because since I teach, I am deeply involved—to my neck. So far I have put on the stage seventy-two students, actually led them on by the hand. With the exception of some American and Japanese pupils who have a sense of duty, most of the others have none, and it is an exhausting uphill battle I am engaged in every day. They do not listen to advice, and once they learn how to fly a little they are convinced their wings will carry them far away. I have seen, with much distress, some of my students start off well and then ride to a fall. They don't concentrate anymore, and make no effort to understand the text."

She then gave the most amazing demonstration of what she can still do. She sang out "Gioir" from *La traviata* on the most perfect pitch, and a shiver went down my spine. "Do you see? This word actually means everything. It's so brief, and yet it encompasses enjoyment, passion, physical and spiritual love. 'Gioir' at that moment characterizes Violetta more than anything else that has happened in the opera. But most of them sing it as if they were saying *'Buona sera.'* But I have had a few satisfactory students, and among them is the American Lella Cuberli, who has acquired a real knowledge about bel canto.

"Alas, the men in charge of our opera houses are all political appointees, and knowing nothing of voices, they make the most appalling mistakes. In my day impresarios assembled the singers first and then, depending on who was available, built the repertoire accordingly. Now they decide on the operas and then assign them to whatever singer they can get hold of. I am tired—there are days when I work ten hours—but above all disconcerted, with great forebodings for the future. The only consolation is that the time ahead gets shorter and shorter. Every day I read of some beloved colleague who has departed into the beyond.

"All I will leave behind is a few recordings, and I only wish that I had been able to do more. Still available are my *Don Pasquale* with Schipa and *Pagliacci* with Apollo Granforte, a superb Tonio, released by His Master's Voice."

As I left, I looked at the huge number of photographs, with warm, affectionate phrases from operatic celebrities past and present. But I was unable to detect one of an artist of whom she had spoken so glowingly. "And why is she not here?" I asked.

"She was put away in a drawer. I have never been involved in politics, and I loathe those who are attuned to that sort of thing only to follow the wind and reap some benefits. This particular one offered the fascist salute from the stage, when no one asked her, and then on the day of the liberation I saw her with my own eyes riding in an open car here in Milan giving the fist salute of the communists. My respect for her vocal accomplishments never wavered, but my respect for her as a woman was finished. And here in this room, I want to be surrounded only by people I love and admire, not only as artists but as human beings."

MARIA LAURENTI

As I sat in her stylish and pretty apartment in Palermo in 1978 during the two and a half hours Maria Laurenti granted me, I could not help thinking of the title of one of Pirandello's great plays, *Il piacere dell'onestà*—The Pleasure of Honesty—for here was a former prima donna whose total honesty was so complete and refreshing that I found myself deriving enormous pleasure from it. Recalling her as the most touching Liù in *Turandot* and Mariella in *Il piccolo Marat* of my youth, I found before me a small, well-dressed woman in her middle seventies, her intelligent and kind face lit by two enormous, inquiring, expressive eyes.

"I sang for twenty-eight years," she explained in answer to my questions, "and then for sixteen years taught at the conservatory here in Palermo. Now I continue giving lessons at home . . . but we will discuss that later.

"Recently, I celebrated the fiftieth anniversary of my marriage to Silvio Costa Lo Giudice, whom you will recall as one of the outstanding tenors of his day, but you will not see him today. He is beginning to suffer from arteriosclerosis, and this is not a good day. His brother, Franco Lo Giudice, was also a famous tenor and excelled in verismo parts, but he lives in Catania. The Lo Giudices are Sicilians, and that is why we came to live here after our retirement.

"There never was a cloud in my marriage, which is all the more extraordinary since I had no intention of tying myself down. After a few years in the profession, I had come to the conclusion that it was hard to mix the ingredients of career woman and dutiful wife. But from the day he first saw me, with typical Sicilian tenacity, Silvio never gave me a moment's peace. We met in Florence, where we were appearing in *Turandot* together. I was sitting with my aunt—I was always sent everywhere with a chaperone— in my dressing room, and the door was opened. He stuck his head in and used the familiar *tu*. 'How dare you?' I asked him, annoyed at his familiar manner. 'I am going to give you *tu* for the rest of your life, as someday you will become my wife,' he answered me, walking away. My aunt and

I looked at each other and laughed. But the fact is that a year later he had won the battle, and I have never regretted it.

"The Turandot in that performance, and in many others I would sing, was an astonishing Englishwoman, Eva Turner. She opened her mouth and a flood of sound came out, mesmerizing in its size and accuracy. I often studied her vocal production and simply could not understand how she could unleash so tremendous a flow of notes. And she was a thoroughly nice, kind, and generous woman.

"After studying for six years in Rome (where I was born in 1904) with Elvira Cerasoli, I was sent to Milan to learn repertoire with the celebrated Giuseppe Fatù. What had actually persuaded my parents to let me enter the singing profession was an audition that was arranged for me in Rome, where I sang for Giacomo Lauri-Volpi, who had just been discovered by Emma Carelli and had made a big impression at the Rome Opera. He was most enthusiastic and predicted a good future for me. In Milan Fatù was a close friend of the great Rosina Storchio (she had created *Butterfly, Zazà, Lodoletta, Siberia,* Leoncavallo's *La Bohème,* and many other operas), who had been one of La Scala's reigning divas until 1918, and he persuaded her to teach me Mimi and Massenet's Manon. She did this sort of thing on occasion, but one had to be highly recommended to her.

"I shall always consider this one of the greatest privileges life gave me, for she was a woman of another era. She was grace, femininity, and courtesy personified. And how many crafty and shrewd bits of stage business she taught me, small details that seemed so unimportant and yet added so much to an overall interpretation. I so well recall that at the same time Rosina Torri was also under her tutelage, to whom she was imparting her magical knowledge of *Butterfly.* I was awaiting my turn and watched. Suddenly, at the end of the lesson, in a burst of spontaneity, Rosina—who was to become a very great Cio-Cio-San herself—fell on her knees and kissed Storchio's hands. 'How will I ever dare take on this assignment?' Rosina asked in tears. It was an eye opener for me too, and I bided my time before taking on *Butterfly,* which became one of the operas I sang the most often.

"Curiously, despite my being a lyric, this score never fatigued me, and I treasured my first teacher's advice: 'If your vocal cords are tired after singing a certain role, eliminate it immediately. It simply means it is not right for you. Sometimes one miscalculates reading a score, for one cannot visualize the entire work from an orchestral point of view.' She had another theory which I always respected and which, after over half a century, I still think is eminently valid and can save a lot of voices. Only choose those

Maria Laurenti as Eva in *Die Meistersinger*.

assignments, she used to say, where you feel that you do not have to give out all you possess. Choose those that allow you to maintain a considerable amount of reserve. I was a lyric with a big voice, and I could have easily taken on some heavier parts. But I never did, remembering her words, which were proved to me every day by listening to my colleagues.

"If I talk so much about the production of my voice, it is because I get very upset at how casual it has become today. I was made to study the piano, harmony, solfeggio, and every day I realized more and more how important this knowledge was. The singers of my generation were taught how to produce their instruments naturally. Now this art is lost. Do you think Freni or Scotto sings naturally? Not in my opinion. Sometimes it is remarkable, but never spontaneous.

"My debut took place at the Teatro Carcano in Milan, an opera house then where all the great stars appeared when not engaged at La Scala, and the vehicle was *Bohème*. It went very well, and then many doors opened. We were fortunate in those days, for we had the provincial theatres where we could learn and measure our strength. Now in Italy they have been destroyed, and we have experimental centers, which are not the same thing. One must have the opportunity to sing in a house filled with people, not in the empty hall of an institute.

"My next chance came to sing Desdemona to Renato Zanelli's celebrated Otello, although at La Scala he was particularly famous for his Tristan. Then Margherita in *Mefistofele* in several cities with three phenomenal bassos: Pinza, de Angelis, and Pasero. De Angelis was Mephisto in life too; he was the devil incarnate. What a terrifying, glorious performance! And like Eva Turner, it was an ocean of sound.

"After my marriage my husband and I were often engaged together, and I also sang many times with my brother-in-law. We often found ourselves hired for the same season, all three of us, but singing separately. I remember one weekend in Bologna when I sang in *Otello,* my husband in *Risurrezione* with the unforgettable Giuseppina Cobelli, and my brother-in-law in *La fanciulla del West.* Franco was outstanding in the contemporary repertoire, and at La Scala he became famous for his Giannetto in *La cena delle beffe,* Gosta in *I cavalieri di Ekebù,* the *Nerone*s of both Boito and Mascagni, and the two Montemezzi works *L'amore dei tre re* and *La notte di Zoraima.* He was also terrific as Calaf, a role my husband—more of a spinto than a dramatic tenor—also sang often. The heaviest part Silvio undertook was Enzo, in a memorable performance of *La Gioconda* at La Scala with Cigna and Stignani.

"It was an era when many of my female colleagues were married to members of the same profession. Tenors seemed to be favored, and Toti dal Monte had one too, Enzo de Muro Lomanto. He had a very light instrument, and quite agreeable, but when he was nervous he unnerved everyone who sang with him. I shall tell you a little story which is very revealing of how the mood of a public can change in a matter of minutes. We always used to say that the Spanish public that went to the opera house was the same one that attended the bullrings, and with the same reactions. I was singing *Manon* with de Muro Lomanto as my des Grieux in Madrid, and during the first-act duet, 'Nous vivrons à Paris,' he began to stray from pitch, and we finished in the midst of catcalls and protests. But it was not over. In the second act, just before he was to begin the exquisite 'La rêve,' he went off again, and this time it was pandemonium. I waited and waited, and then, making a gesture to the conductor to go on, I uttered my little sentence, 'Hélas! qui ne fait pas de rêve?' Poor Enzo then had no choice but to go on and start the aria. Somehow, despite the fact that he was literally trembling, he sang it like an angel, with style and feeling. The same audience that had been ready to kill him gave him an ovation that virtually never seemed to stop!

"Naturally, in many of these marriages, one of the two was superior to the other. But we were fortunate, for my husband and I enjoyed the same professional standing, which facilitated life and also helped artistically, since four ears are better than two and we could give one another helpful advice.

"After the birth of our son, Gino, my professional activities had to be geared differently. In those days the only ocean travel was by ship, and if one was hired for seasons in either North or South America it meant an absence of several months. This I was never able to do, as I refused to leave my child more than a few weeks at a time. So I went often to Lisbon's San Carlo, to Madrid (it is there that I portrayed my first Butterfly), to Barcelona (where I appeared in a memorable *Turandot* before the king and queen), and in several German cities. But I preferred to sing in Italy to be on call if Gino needed me.

"In those days La Scala was considered a temple—alas, it is no longer— and one was hired after a decade of experience. In fact, I first went there in 1935 and made my debut as Elisetta in *Il matrimonio segreto,* conducted by Marinuzzi, with a dream cast of Favero, Tess, Schipa, and Baccaloni. I sang with Schipa often in Cilea's *L'arlesiana,* also at La Scala, and among the many things I don't understand about what is happening today is the disappearance of this very valid opera from the repertoire. Before the Second World War it was performed as often as *Adriana Lecouvreur.*

"Schipa and Pertile were the two greatest tenors, along interpretative lines, I ever sang with. Pertile was not handsome, nor was the timbre of his instrument impressive. But after a few minutes one was mesmerized—both onstage and in the audience—by his ability to become the character. I sang with him often in *Lohengrin*—if I remember correctly, the first time was at the enchanting Royal Opera House in Cairo, later destroyed by fire— and every time he appeared in the first act he *was* the knight of the Holy Grail. *Lohengrin* used to be as popular as *Aida* or *Trovatore* in Italy, and now it is very rarely performed.

"How we rehearsed in those days! And no wonder we were all well prepared. When I sang Eva in *Die Meistersinger* at La Scala under the great Guarnieri, he always called the five of us who took part in the diabolically difficult quintet into his dressing room before the third act and had us go over it once again. When I sang the first Roman performance of Respighi's *Belfagor,* the composer unfortunately was already dead. But his indomitable widow, Donna Elsa, was there at every rehearsal, score in hand, and knew the inflection she wanted for every phrase and sound. Stabile, who had created the title role at La Scala, repeated it in Rome, and his interpretation was as fabulous as his Falstaff.

"When I read today of what the various theatres offer the public, I am astounded at the enormous number of works I used to sing that have vanished. In the case of some of them, I can understand, such as the enchant- ing works of Wolf-Ferrari—they need a top-notch ensemble and a great number of rehearsals, which nowadays are no longer possible. Nothing could be more adorable than *Il campiello,* which I sang at La Scala under Gavazzeni's airy baton and with Mafalda Favero as Lucieta, but it is not a work that can be put on unless a great ensemble can be gathered, with the proper amount of rehearsal. The same applies to his *La vedova scaltra, Le donne curiose,* and *La dama boba.* Other delightful operas that have fallen by the wayside are those by Zandonai. My brother-in-law and I created his *Giuliano,* and I appeared often in *La farsa amorosa,* both airy and charming.

"Another splendid opera that is eminently theatrical and appealing, Mas- cagni's *Il piccolo Marat,* which I sang innumerable times, was a staple of every Italian opera house; and when Hipolito Lazaro sang the lead, there was standing room only. Forzano's libretto is excellent, and in my opinion it contains some of the best pages Mascagni ever wrote. He honored me by thinking that I was just right for Mariella, both vocally and histrionically, and chose me over and over again for the role. Now the new generation does not even know of its existence. By the time I came onto the stage, Lazaro had already been singing a long time, and yet as Marat he looked the eighteen-year-old he was supposed to be. His voice was huge . . . but then, let us discuss this matter for a while, as neither I nor many of my former colleagues can find an explanation for this phenomenon.

"Why are there no big instruments today? When one recalls the trumpet-like sounds of Maugeri, Franci, de Angelis, Mongelli, Lauri-Volpi, Grob-Prandl, Llacer, Stignani, Cigna, and Turner, and more recently del Monaco and even Tebaldi, which not only filled a hall but could be heard several blocks away, one wonders why there are none now. In my fourteen years at the conservatory in Palermo I never came across one, and it gives food for thought. One can develop the vocal cords with study and perseverance and make them bigger, but the basic potential must be there. It is a problem that fascinates me, for there must be a reason.

"My retirement in 1953 was not planned. My voice was in good shape, and there was no such plan in my mind. I was in Brescia, where I sang almost every year at the Teatro Grande, then one of the best in Italy, waiting in the office of the general manager to discuss a contract for the following year. Suddenly, from another room, I heard two voices discussing me. 'Laurenti is still valid, but you should have heard her twenty years ago,' one of them said. All at once something snapped inside of me. It was a hard decision to make, but no one could dissuade me from quitting. I honored my commitments, but I made no more. No one knew of my planned retirement except my husband. My last performances were as Nedda in Genoa opposite Gigli, and in a way I was sorry, for it was a part I was called upon to perform constantly, but one which, like Micaëla, I was never able to get attached to. I felt I must tell Gigli, who was a great friend and with whom I had sung Mimi everywhere. He would not believe it or accept this *colpo di testa,* as he called it. He begged me to reconsider. 'The lyric theatre still needs an artist like you,' he kept saying. 'My voice is not what it was twenty years ago either, and I have no intention of giving up.'

"He was a kind colleague and a considerate one. As far as timbre is concerned, for me no one ever matched Gigli's facility and loveliness of sound. With him it was like sailing on a smooth sea.

"I think there is a time for every artist to take stock and know when to retreat gracefully. There are rare exceptions such as Magda Olivero. She is a phenomenon apart. Once when she was delivering some pianissimos that were out of some other world, I asked her where they came from, for the thought crossed my mind that they were head tones. Not at all. She took my hand and put it over her diaphragm, and it was more solid than a rock. No one knows her exact age, but I don't think it matters. What does is the fact that with the thread of a shattered voice, she can still hold an audience in the palm of her hand. That is art.

"Naturally, when you have given your life to an ideal, it is distressing to see a solid construction disintegrate. I have been close to it because of my teaching responsibilities. The elimination of agencies in this country has been pure folly. One goes to a shop to buy merchandise, and one calls upon an agent when looking for a singer. Agents were our advisers and benefactors. They knew voices and did not allow one to make mistakes. Where would I have been without one? Now no one knows where to turn, neither the young singers nor the managements. So they hold auditions in some of the theatres, but these young voices have had no opportunity to measure their possibilities anywhere. The size of the voice is so important, and to go from a small room in a conservatory onto a large stage is totally unrealistic. Most of my students, and many of them totally dedicated, have had to take jobs as teachers.

"They keep saying that Italy no longer produces singers, but why is this? Take Renato Bruson, who in everyone's opinion has the most beautiful baritone voice we have today. Just ask him how many years he knocked at doors that would not open, how no one took any interest in him. He is sturdy and strong and did not give up, thank goodness, but others don't have the same toughness. I have a young tenor, a local boy, Gianni Bevaglio, with a very fine tenor voice. He was finally engaged by Riccardo Muti to take over Manrico from Carlo Cossutta in *Il trovatore* in Florence when Cossutta had to leave for other engagements, and he sang three very good performances. That was almost two years ago, and even with the paucity of tenors he is still waiting for another chance. Figure it out. I cannot. If we did not make it in our time, it meant we were not up to it, for the chances were there and every door opened.

"Now, of course, many of the theatres do not function anymore, and those that do have the same small group of singers who rush from one to the other. Impresarios risked everything to put on an opera season, for they had to fork the money out of their own pockets. Now everything must be controlled by the region and is run on a political basis. When I think of the salaries we received, I just laugh—five thousand lire per performance was considered a lot. Now the theatres that do function are saddled with a tremendous bureaucracy. How can all this work out economically? It cannot, and the theatres are all bankrupt. People are now paid all year, hundreds of them, for seasons that last a few months. Recording companies have come in and control, they assure me, the engagement of their own stars. My husband and I recorded a lot for Columbia. All out of print! *Pazienza.*"

DOROTHY KIRSTEN

Dorothy Kirsten's career followed a very special pattern; she stands alone, and for many reasons. First of all, with the exception of a year spent in Italy she is entirely American-trained. She had a very distinguished career and won international fame, and yet only twice did she appear outside the United States: on a tour that included performances in Moscow, Leningrad, Tiflis, Riga, and Stockholm; and with her home company, the Metropolitan Opera, in Tokyo in *La Bohème*. She sang, I believe, for more consecutive seasons than any other leading soprano at the Met—thirty years—and built her tremendous following with relatively few roles. But she always knew how to husband her resources with keen intelligence and shrewdness, and she never overstepped the bounds of her ability. Kirsten retired officially at the age of fifty-eight, after a gala farewell *Tosca* at the Metropolitan on December 31, 1975; but since then she has returned to the stage there and elsewhere when desperately needed to replace an indisposed colleague. In 1979 she came to the rescue of *Tosca* at the Met, flying in from California at the eleventh hour to replace Leonie Rysanek, who had suddenly canceled.

Illness has never plagued Kirsten, for from the very beginning she knew how to look after herself, limiting her engagements and leading a healthy outdoor life in California and Hawaii. The performances she canceled during her long career were so few that she earned the eternal gratitude of American impresarios.

When one converses with her, one realizes how much good sense she possesses, and how she quietly maintained her position by becoming indispensable in certain operas. Although at first she seemed to specialize in the French repertoire—Manon, Gounod's Juliette, Marguerite, and Louise—during the last decade of her career she sang only Puccini roles: Butterfly, Mimi, Tosca, Manon Lescaut, and Minnie. At one time she appeared as Violetta in *La traviata,* and she became renowned for her Fiora in *L'amore dei tre re.* If the Metropolitan was her permanent home, the San Francisco Opera (where she sang in almost as many seasons as in New York) gave her not only several opening-night performances, but the opportunity to sing in the American premieres of Poulenc's *Les Dialogues des carmélites* and Walton's *Troilus and Cressida*.

Kirsten knew the commercial importance of the Metropolitan. She needed its name for her recitals, which always brought her a much higher income than her operatic fare. She was a good recitalist in the grand old tradition. People expected a diva and they got one, always in an effective, becoming gown, properly bejeweled and impeccably groomed. She never looked like a waif, as Victoria de los Angeles did, or a hausfrau, like Christa Ludwig. She gave the audiences far from highbrow programs, but neither did she sing down to them. She always managed to find a happy medium, and the public adored her. Her many radio and, later, television appearances helped her build a name throughout the United States. She never played important parts in movies, but she benefited enormously from the publicity of those she did do. She could have done more in the movies, but Rudolf Bing did not much approve of that sort of thing.

Actually, it was a radio program on which she sang that opened up her horizons. Grace Moore happened to hear Kirsten and arranged for her to go to Italy to further her studies with Maestro Astolfo Pescia. But while Moore started right at the top, making her operatic debut as Mimi at the Metropolitan, Kirsten began with a comprimario part in Massenet's *Manon* in Chicago. Later, in the same city, she sang Musetta to Moore's Mimi, and then moved on to the City Center in New York, where she first established her reputation.

"It all came slowly but surely," she reminisced with me, looking wonderfully glamorous and healthy for a woman past sixty. "But in life you are either a person to whom success comes easily or one who has to work hard for it. I belong to this second group, and I do not regret it. My foundations were so secure that they served me over a much longer period of time than I could have hoped for. I was always ambitious, but never greedy, and I knew instinctively that there is always room for someone who is a serious professional. I have seen during my life so many shooting stars: a huge success and then nothing. You have to learn your own limitations and then work within their frame.

"In New Jersey my father, George Kirsten, was a builder, and my mother an organist. In Montclair, where I was born in 1917, I studied voice with the idea of going on Broadway. I also took classes in 'aesthetic dancing' with one of the original Mary Wigman dancers. My year with Pescia in Italy was not a success, for he wanted to turn me into a dramatic soprano, and

Dorothy Kirsten as Fiora in *L'amore dei tre re*.

despite the fact that he had been one of Gigli's teachers and had a lot of experience, I knew my own voice better than he did. Later I went to Ludwig Fabri and took classes with him until he died at the age of ninety-three. He used to say, 'Every good forte is based on a piano tone,' and of course he was totally right. With him I sang Mozart over and over again, although I never did on the stage, for I didn't have the type of instrument needed for his music. But his arias and songs were my training ground. I discovered that a singer is much like an automobile: if you drive in town a lot and shift gears constantly, your car will last far less time than if you drive it mainly in the country. If you jump from one repertoire to the other, the way most singers do today, the voices inevitably suffer, like the gears. And if you sing forte a lot, there comes a point when a pianissimo becomes impossible to obtain.

"Puccini is very tough if you allow his emotional heroines to get the best of you. I managed to remain in control at all times, and it took a lot of discipline to convey the drama and not be carried away by it. All my Italian colleagues told me I was insane to undertake Minnie, particularly at that stage of my career, for they all warned me that it is a killer—they call it, in fact, Puccini's Brünnhilde. And they were right. But I never permitted that second act, which builds from one thrilling climax to another, to wear me out. I may not have been as intense as some of the Italian divas, but I was able to project Minnie's anguish within my own means. It was really very amusing at the Metropolitan, for they kept giving the part to other sopranos terribly eager to take it on, and then, inevitably, one by one, they fell by the wayside—one had to stop singing for six months. And then there was Dorothy willing to put on her boots and go on. I never resented this, because in the end, who won? That's what counts.

"When I first went into opera, my voice was lighter and therefore more flexible. That's why I could handle the fioriture of Violetta, Manon, and Marguerite with ease. Actually, it was in *La traviata* that I made my debut at the City Center and received the rave notices that eventually led to my Metropolitan engagement. I never enjoyed Massenet's Manon as much as I did Puccini's, which is so much more emotional, so Italian in its sensuousness and warmth. I don't believe that Puccini ever wrote anything as heartbreaking as 'Sola, perduta, abbandonata' in the last act. Here is a woman who wants desperately to live because of the love she carries for her lover and yet knows that the end is near. It's a crescendo of despair. But I don't think that it should be sung in concert form, like 'Un bel dì' or 'Vissi d'arte.'

"Of course, the Massenet opera is probably closer to the spirit of the Abbé

Prévost's heroine. The Cours-la-Reine scene, so often omitted, is difficult to sing, for it demands real coloratura, and then comes the St. Sulpice scene, which by Massenet's standards is a wave of rapture and intensity. It's practically impossible for the same voice to do full justice to both these scenes, and that is why so often the first one is cut out. In the Puccini opera, the second act is the trickiest, for there are some high notes that must not be screamed out, as most sopranos sing them, for they're part of the context. Actually Cesira Ferrani, who was chosen by Puccini to create the role in Turin, was a lyric soprano who sang Micaëla and later Mélisande. So I don't believe that Puccini wanted his Manon to take on such heavy, dramatic connotations or he would have chosen another singer. But so many spintos have sung it now that the public is apt to expect a big voice. There is a difference. Minnie does demand a larger voice; in fact, Puccini entrusted its premiere to Emmy Destinn, the great dramatic soprano of that period. The orchestration is almost Wagnerian in scope, and although there are no real arias, in some ways it's more demanding than Salome, for you have to cut through a solid instrumentation and yet sound tender and loving at first and then ready to go to any limit for the bandit Minnie has fallen for so desperately. Salome is a hysterical girl, but no real emotion is needed. I learned how to tackle my many Minnies by using a sort of computer system. Save now, Dorothy, I would say to myself; use phrasing instead, or the voice will simply give out. I was also faced with being an American singer taking on a highly disturbed (as psychiatrists would say today) young American woman as visualized by an Italian. It would have been pretty easy to look ridiculous. For an Italian or a Latin to rant is accepted by the public with greater facility than for Dorothy from New Jersey.

"One of my most interesting experiences was studying *Louise* with old Charpentier himself. He was charm personified and was used to having English and American girls coming and begging for his advice. First Mary Garden, then Grace Moore, and finally Dorothy. *Louise* was never meant, he told me, despite its many characters, to be performed in a large theatre. He wrote it, in fact, for the Opéra-Comique. In fact, neither Rioton, who sang in its world premiere in 1900, nor Mary Garden had a large voice. At the Metropolitan both Farrar and Bori, essentially lyric both of them, made it their own until Grace came along. Naturally, when it's presented in a large house, the chorus and orchestra are bigger, and everything takes on totally different proportions. It suited my voice perfectly and I loved it from start to finish. I simply cannot understand why it has now become fashionable for the critics and the intelligentsia to discard it as old hat and unworthy of its fame. Toscanini considered it a work of art and introduced it at La Scala in 1906 with Frances Alda, who had not yet come to America. Between 1922 and 1925 he conducted three revivals in Milan, and the opera stayed in the repertoire of La Scala. In Paris it was performed over a thousand times in a period of seventy-five years, so it stands to reason that it's damn good. Now they have made two complete recordings of it, so perhaps it will pick up again. But we all know how off-course the critics have been and can be. Just recall that when *Tosca* was performed in New York for the first time it was described by the *Times* as 'repulsive,' and the celebrated critic Henry Krehbiel stated it was 'hideous.' They were not very much with it, were they?

"Mr. Bing would not hear of reviving *Louise,*" she sighed, throwing up her arms in the air, "but ever so generously offered me Marie in *Wozzeck.* Being a good sport, I told him I would look at the score. It did not take long for me to make up my mind. 'Thank you for thinking of me.' I told him 'The answer is no.' What would have happened to me after screaming that cruel, dissonant music? He also wanted me to do Lisa in *The Queen of Spades,* which I had performed in San Francisco. But he didn't know that after the four performances I sang there I had regretted the assignment. It's one of the few times in my life that I miscalculated the orchestration, which is very heavy—a dramatic soprano is really needed. Mr. Bing kept trying, I must admit. He also offered me Elisabetta in *Don Carlo* and the title role of Samuel Barber's *Vanessa,* and after deep consideration I knew neither of them was right for me. The two really need either a strong spinto or a dramatic. There were two roles I would have undertaken gladly, Desdemona and Leoncavallo's Zazà, but they never came my way.

"When I was hired by the Metropolitan, Edward Johnson was the general manager, and having been an excellent, sensitive singer himself—everyone told me his Pelléas was unsurpassed—he knew voices and rarely made a mistake. With Mr. Bing it was another story. I was asked to go to La Scala and appear as Minnie on three different occasions, but the offers always came too late—you know how the Italians are—and there was no way I could get a release from my American contracts. So I missed out on the excitement of an international career. But then, time was limited, for I always insisted on having several months free a year to be with my husband, Dr. John French, a well-known neurologist, whose base was in California. There I could lead a normal and healthy life, play golf and take long walks. You can't imagine how helpful this is for building up stamina and keeping the vocal cords in shape.

290 THE GREAT LYRICS

"But you know, looking back, I have been very spoiled. Tagliavini was my first Cavaradossi, Bjoerling my first des Grieux in the Massenet opera and del Monaco in the Puccini one, Jan Peerce my first Rodolfo, and Charles Kullman and Richard Tucker among my first Pinkertons. But somehow the tenor who produced the most sparks for me was Corelli. He sings with the heart, and when we were together he always looked at me and never at the conductor. He always produced a sense of total reality on the stage, and some of our appearances together in *Fanciulla* were fabulous. I don't think that either the critics or the public were ever aware of this man's search for perfection. He was never satisfied with what he had done, and this, for me, is a sign of greatness. There was never that Cheshire-cat smile on his face —on the contrary, he showed a deep self-examination of where he could have done better."

She had a lot to say about her appearances in musical comedies. "Let us not call them musicals," she laughed, "for nowadays no voice is needed for them. On the contrary, they seem to choose people who simply cannot sing. The ones I appeared in are better called operettas and were written ever so wisely for the singer. In fact, today many opera companies are producing works like *The Merry Widow* and *Naughty Marietta,* for voices of operatic caliber are needed. I particularly enjoyed appearing in *The New Moon, The Great Waltz, Countess Maritza,* and *The Merry Widow,* but these were always limited appearances because of other commitments, and also not to tire the voice, for singing every night takes a toll. I also recorded some with Gordon Macrae, which turned out very satisfactorily. Our voices somehow blended well together."

When I asked her about future plans, she was very explicit.

"I am interested in remaining in the world of opera, which is the one I know best, and have already started directing several productions. Teaching is not for me—these young people are too much in a hurry. In a hurry for what? To have to give up five years later. Vocal cords must be given the chance to develop and the diaphragm time to become strong. Without it, where are you? It's wonderful that there is so much enthusiasm for opera among the young and that so many new opera companies are sprouting up all over the place. But in my estimation some of them are too ambitious. How can you give *Fidelio* or *Macbeth* with student casts? What I have noticed with dismay is the total disregard today for blending the right kind of voices together. You cannot have a spinto Rodolfo and a very lyrical Mimi, or vice versa. Not only does it not sound right, but it obliges the lighter voice, particularly at the beginning, when there is not yet much experience, to keep up with the stronger one in order to be heard. It then becomes a competition, and opera is not a sport. When these young people ask me about repertoire, I compare it to buying a dress off the rack. If the voice is too big, you can always alter it and you will be more comfortable in it. But if it's too small, forget it, for it will never do."

Dusolina Giannini once told me a story that emphatically shows that Dorothy Kirsten had the stuff of which prima donnas are made. The New York City Opera was in its infancy and had planned a program in which young, relatively unknown American singers could perform and gain experience. Giannini and Jennie Tourel had agreed to sing at token fees in order to help the company attract more customers. A press conference had been called, and the singers had to pose in various costumes for the photographers. Dorothy, coming in with a retinue of people, was to don the gown she would wear for the first act of her debut in *La traviata*. Immediately, and with enormous assurance, she asked, "Where is my dressing room?" "I am afraid," Giannini replied, "that you do not realize that nothing is organized here as yet, and we have all had to share the same one." To which Dorothy said: "I would think that if anyone had the right to a private dressing room it would be me." "I had a feeling right away that this girl would go places," Giannini told me. "She was at the very beginning of her career, but she behaved like someone who had already arrived."

THE GREAT ARTISTS

GIANNA PEDERZINI

ELISABETH HÖNGEN

JARMILA NOVOTNA

LISA DELLA CASA

Outstanding personalities are becoming increasingly rare in all fields of endeavor, and this leveling has not, unfortunately, failed to reach the lyric theatre. Much of it, rightly, is blamed on stage directors and conductors; but young people today no longer seem to have the ambition to be different from one another. They seem content with looking and dressing alike and using a vocabulary that every year becomes poorer in words and expressions. Some of the finest singers today simply do not stand out, either onstage or off. They go through the motions the way they are told, but nothing happens. Characterizations—so essential a part of opera—rarely come forth. Even a big star like Mirella Freni is faceless onstage, looking demure even when rage or passion should be devouring her. Not one shiver of emotion goes through the audience when she appears. Fiorenza Cossotto may have lost the sheen in her upper register, but when she is onstage, everyone knows it.

But this general facelessness was not always the rule. The four artists whose profiles follow are, in the opinion of many, the last of the great operatic personalities. Not only were they singers of impeccable musicianship, but their characterizations were gripping. On- and offstage they were outstanding individuals. Singers, conductors, critics, and discriminating operagoers constantly cited these four names: mezzo-sopranos Gianna Pederzini and Elisabeth Höngen and sopranos Jarmila Novotna and Lisa della Casa.

Neither Pederzini nor Höngen had an outstanding voice, but their musicality was such that leading conductors vied for their services, and their stage presence was so electrifying that many contemporary scores would have failed without them. Pederzini, though not beautiful, was voluptuousness personified, and in operas like *Carmen, Conchita,* and *Samson et Dalila* she drove the public into a veritable frenzy of excitement. After Besanzoni retired, Pederzini's Carmen was considered by all to be the most thrilling and provocative. But, sexy artist that she was, she took on character roles too, bringing to them a fierce and stimulating intensity. (Tito Gobbi raves about her in his autobiography, claiming that "when she sang the role of the mother in *L'arlesiana* and began 'Esser madre è un inferno' [to be a mother is hell], a sort of shiver would run through the house and the whole audience would go tense. She was also a superb Fedora—so much so that Giordano transposed the role for her—and for as long as she was on the operatic stage hardly anyone else even attempted the role.") Höngen was very aristocratic and delicate looking, but her strength and stamina left people speechless.

Pederzini and Höngen were both born in 1906. Pederzini began her career in 1925 and retired in 1961. Höngen began later, in 1933, when she was twenty-seven, and retired in 1971. Although they shared many of the same roles, Pederzini became famous for her verismo repertoire and Höngen for her Wagner and Strauss. They are not in the least alike: the Italian is still all fire and pep, while her German counterpart is quiet, reserved, and slightly melancholic.

Jarmila Novotna, born in 1907, started singing at eighteen and retired three decades later. She was a legendary beauty with an uncanny gift for the stage. In her seventies she is still a treat for the eyes. She made a spectacular career despite a voice that was not prepossessing; so remarkable were her musical skill, her knowledge of her vocal boundaries, her irresistible charm, natural glamour, and superb showmanship, that she won over all the most outstanding conductors and metteurs-en-scène. She was human, unmalicious, generous, adored by everyone in all walks of her life, for she was a prima donna in looks and distinction but not in character. She brought a radiance to every role she undertook: her every entrance was like a burst of sunshine.

Lisa della Casa was also a great beauty and possessed the best voice of the four, an effortless instrument of good size and quality, though slightly inexpressive at the top. Like Novotna, she created an atmosphere on the stage that was captivating and tremendously feminine. Her Arabella was pure enchantment, and her Countess Almaviva the best one could ever hope for.

I was fortunate to hear all four of them on many, many occasions, and there was one role—Octavian—that I heard sung by all of them. They were, each one along a different line, exceptionally gifted artists who make their successors seem like shadows on a Chinese screen.

GIANNA PEDERZINI

As I entered Gianna Pederzini's large, intensely lived-in Roman drawing room in 1979, I was greeted by a group of large photographs in silver frames, crowded together on an immense bookcase. In rapid succession I saw Tullio Serafin's inscription ("To Gianna, whose name signifies art"), Umberto Giordano's ("To the superb and fascinating Fedora"), Victor de Sabata's ("With infinite admiration and profound friendship"), Ildebrando Pizzetti's ("To the most remarkable of interpreters"), Vittorio Gui's ("To one of the greatest artists of this century"), Giacomo Lauri-Volpi's ("From the greatest of her fans"), Francis Poulenc's ("Pederzini, you're a genius. I will never be able to say enough about your interpretative powers. You shall always be Madame de Croissy"), and Gian Carlo Menotti's ("To the marvelous artist who has made the composer fall into a trance"). And the prima donnas range from Maria Callas ("With infinite affection") to Renata Tebaldi ("To the great Gianna").

One could converse with Pederzini for hours. Her career lasted from 1922 until 1961, and her memory is agile, her observations sensible, her wisdom profound, and her kindness totally impulsive. There is a marked nostalgia for the high standards to which she was accustomed, and an angry refusal to watch the collapse of an art to which she had dedicated her every ounce of living. It is easy to see why this woman conquered her audiences, not only with her dynamism, but with her sensuality. Born in 1906, she is still arresting looking: her huge eyes are pools of a variety of emotions; her sensuous mouth opens to reveal dazzlingly white teeth; her mane of black hair is brushed back like a sibyl's in a fresco by Michelangelo. The feline agility of her movements gives her body, though no longer as shapely as in the past, a strong electric charge.

"I was born in Avio, in the hills near Verona, and my father was a businessman with a splendid voice who sang for his own pleasure. He died when I was ten. When the First World War burst upon us, we lived very close to the front, and my mother decided it was her duty to take us three

Gianna Pederzini in the title role of *Conchita*.

children to a safer location. Because of a series of circumstances too long and uninteresting to explain, she chose Naples, which was then a wonderful city. As I grew up there, a singing teacher who lived in the same apartment house heard me and was impressed. After giving me some lessons, he decided that I had enough possibilities to audition for the great tenor Fernando de Lucia, who had retired and was accepting pupils. He had been famous for his bel canto interpretations of Bellini and Rossini, and he also had created several operas for Mascagni—*L'amico Fritz, Silvano, I Rantzau*—so he had a knowledge of verismo too. By some miracle he accepted me, and I shall be in his debt forever. He taught me not only what singing was all about, but impeccable diction, which he claimed—and how right he was!—made the difference between a singer and an artist. When he sang to illustrate a passage, his tones were still pure gold. I studied with him for five years, so in all I had seven years of intensive training.

"There had never been a doubt that I was a light mezzo, with extreme facility in the upper register. It never was a large instrument, and de Lucia begged me to build up my repertoire slowly until I could measure my possibilities. I made my debut in Messina as Preziosilla in *La forza del destino*, a role that pursued me through the years and which I heartily detested, as she is called in only to break the gloom of this lovely work. Its tessitura is high, and her two big scenes demand a lot of energy to shed a little pep onto the proceedings. The next roles on my agenda were La Cieca in *La Gioconda* and Pierotto in *Linda di Chamounix*. This was my first trouser role, and many, many were to follow, for I had the figure for them—don't look at me now—and onstage I always looked very young. It was difficult to get away from Preziosilla at first, for the rumor got around that I was just right for it. I was the only singer, as far as I know, who took the trouble to learn how to play the drums for the 'Rataplan,' a cruel piece of vocalism, for it keeps going up and down. As it invariably brought down the house and I had really a thin waist then, impresarios kept raising their fees until I simply could not refuse to take on this gypsy girl who follows the army around and is crazy enough to sing an aria 'Evviva la guerra'—long live war.

"The big breakthrough came in Rome, when this opera house was on a par with La Scala. Again because of my figure, Marinuzzi chose me to appear as Cherubino in *Le nozze di Figaro* with a fabulous cast, and from then on there were more offers than I could take care of, since the critics had claimed I was a revelation. Trouser roles were assigned to me nonstop, and I shall mention a few of them for which I felt great affection: Octavian,

Isolier in *Le Comte Ory,* Urbain in *Les Huguenots* (I remember a memorable production at the Arena of Verona with Raisa, Saraceni, and Lauri-Volpi), Hansel, the lead in Mascagni's enchanting one-act opera *Zanetto,* and Maffeo Orsini in *Lucrezia Borgia.* The revival of this opera, which had been shelved since the days of Mazzoleni, at the Maggio Musicale Fiorentino, with Arangi-Lombardi and Gigli as mother and son, proved a spectacular success, and we artists could not get over the waves of applause that engulfed us. Orsini has one important aria, the drinking song 'Il segreto,' which comes in the last act and is really full of irony, for it foreshadows a gripping scene where everyone is murdered. It is full of pitfalls, demanding a lot of agility, but is a real show stopper. Sigrid Onegin always sang it at her recitals, and now Marilyn Horne. Cherubino stayed with me for many years, and with the exception of a few Dorabellas it remained, unfortunately, my only excursion into Mozart.

"I was soon in a position to choose what suited me, and while I enjoyed being on my toes, I never saw any reason to take on assignments that I knew would cause me worries. For instance, Laura in *La Gioconda* and Eboli were eliminated after a few performances, for they did not suit my sort of instrument. Actually, I took on Eboli after long reflection, at the Rome Opera, following the constant requests of the management, for I loved the music and the character. On opening night I had such a triumph after 'O don fatale' that my esteemed colleague Iva Pacetti burst into my dressing room during the intermission and embraced me. 'I have never heard such an ovation!' she said. 'And you who were so afraid! Gianna, believe me, this will be one of your greatest roles.' But I sensed it was detrimental to my vocal cords. Don't let anyone tell you differently—it is really written for a dramatic soprano with a good low range. The tessitura is very tricky, and in fact no one was more superb than Cobelli, who was a dramatic soprano. Charlotte in *Werther* soon became one of my preferred heroines, along with Mignon. Charlotte, whom I sang in four different productions at La Scala, was fortunate in being loved by such tenors as Schipa and Tagliavini, both outstanding in this lovely Massenet score. I sang *Mignon* everywhere, and in the thirties it was one of the most popular operas in the repertoire. Now it has mysteriously disappeared, probably because the régisseurs cannot find some message in it that they can twist out of shape. I love it so much that perhaps it is better this way than to have it distorted. I could go on and on about Schipa. Never did a man receive from the muse of song so few means and yet manage, every time, to achieve miracles with them. He was a blessed artist and human being.

"When my Carmen was introduced at La Scala"—she smiled with obvious satisfaction—"it exploded like fireworks. I had already tried it out in Brescia and Palermo, but Milan was something else. After the divine Besanzoni (I never heard her, but socially she was the most *simpatica* person one could meet), the great Giuseppina Zinetti, and Cristoforeanu, it was quite a card I dared play at the gaming table. I was totally different from all the others. I interpreted it as a work of true verismo, which it is. I read a great deal about Galli-Marié, the creator of this opera, and the way Bizet really wanted it. He wrote it for a small theatre, the Opéra-Comique, and it was never meant to become the huge spectacle that it has turned into today. I followed this original conception: sexy, intimate, snakelike. I never sang to the public, only to the characters on the stage. Not only did I win a smashing victory, but it became my warhorse. Actually, the requests poured in so fast and furious that I could have eliminated all the other operas and sung only Carmen. But I played hard to get, and I was too ambitious artistically to settle down even with this fascinating creature. A wave of nostalgia surrounds me when I begin thinking of all the Don Josés who appeared with me, from Gigli to Lauri-Volpi, Merli to Masini, Vinay to Corelli, all giants. Vinay's instrument was what it was, always slightly veiled, but his intensity was galvanizing, and I enjoyed very much appearing with him as Dalila too.

"The success of my Carmen brought Zandonai to my door begging me to appear in his *Conchita*, written for a soprano. He was an irresistibly charming man, gentle and imaginative, and we talked and discussed a lot, looking at the score inch by inch. I liked the part, but the tessitura just was not right. He agreed to make all the changes I demanded, and there exists at Ricordi's a Pederzini edition of this score. To my amazement, it became another *Carmen*. Every theatre demanded it. Guarnieri conducted it at La Scala, Serafin in Rome, Panizza at the Colón in Buenos Aires . . . I could continue ad infinitum. It is another delightful opera that is now, absurdly, abandoned.

"My friendship with Zandonai led me on to appear as the Comandante in his *I cavalieri di Ekebù*, based on Selma Lagerlöf's powerful novel *Gösta Berling*. Toscanini had conducted the world premiere in 1925, with the stupendous Elvira Casazza in the lead, and had found it such an interesting work that he brought it back for a second time before he left for the United States. Now it too is forgotten, but believe me, it holds the audience spellbound, and my part was absolutely riveting. If Zandonai had not died in 1944, I would have appeared as his Francesca da Rimini, for as in *Conchita* he had started to make the necessary changes in the tessitura so that I could sing it. I often thought about it later, but I never dared ask anyone else to undertake the transpositions. That is the way we were in those days. With the blessing of the composer, fine. Otherwise it is disrespectful—or at least so it was. Now they will do anything. At a recent production of *Carmen* here in Rome, all the gypsies wore miniskirts, and believe me, it was not an edifying sight.

"Because of my agility and sense of comedy, I became the era's most famous specialist among the Italians in the Rossini mezzo repertoire. *Il barbiere, L'italiana in Algeri,* and *Cenerentola* became my daily fare after Supervia's sad death. Among the many wonderful Figaros I sang with, I would put Gino Bechi ahead of all the others. His verve, his rapidity of phrasing and action, his sense of timing, were all absolutely riveting. Vocally, I don't believe there is anything I tackled that is more exhausting than the rondo in *Cenerentola,* for it comes on at the very end, and the florid passages succeed one another with a vengeance—exceedingly difficult, but always within my possibilities.

"I sang Adalgisa, and some of the Verdi roles, although I never thought that my instrument, with a few rare exceptions, was of the timbre to do justice to his scores. Amneris came and went in my career—I appeared in two productions of *Aida* at La Scala—and it is amazing what one can do dramatically with the judgment scene. Toward the end of my career, just for a lark, I undertook Quickly. But one of the great surprises of my professional life came with Azucena. Although I was fascinated by this other gypsy—how many I already had up my sleeve!—and deeply attracted to her, I knew it was meant for either a very low mezzo or a contralto, and I wavered and wavered. Finally, when my lower register had become darker, I took the plunge at the Rome Opera, with Santini conducting and Lauri-Volpi as Manrico. To my astonishment, an ovation—undoubtedly the longest I ever received—greeted my 'Condotta ell'era in ceppi.' There simply was no way the conductor could start again. And I went on singing it until the end of my career with equal success.

"Unknown to me, at the premiere in Rome, Carmine Gallone, at that time one of the most important film directors in Italy, was present with a group of colleagues. At the end of the performance he came backstage and introduced himself. 'I was planning to make a motion picture of *Forza,* but I have changed my mind. Your performance is so extraordinary it must be put on the screen.' I thought he was joking, but the next day he came to my apartment with a very tempting contract. If I may be so immodest, I think it turned out to be one of the best operatic films ever made, and, in fact, it keeps turning up on television. It was very clever of Gallone to turn back the clock while Azucena tells her horrifying tale and show her as she looked twenty-five years before, when the events took place—a very affecting and effective idea. I never interpreted her as an old hag, the way so many do—after all, gypsies start early in life with their exploits—but as the action proves, she is still very strong and vital. It is one of the most vibrant characters I ever portrayed.

"I was very wary of contemporary scores, for I watched many fine voices of dear colleagues absolutely wrecked by taking on these wretched tessituras. But after much consideration and deliberation I did accept a few. Among the operas I created, Pizzetti's *Vanna lupa,* which inaugurated the Maggio Musicale Fiorentino in 1949, was the most interesting of all. But goodness gracious me! what a complicated opera, and how expensive to produce! It requires no fewer than twenty-eight able singers. I also found Honegger's *Judith* worth my while, and with the splendid Boris Christoff as my Holofernes I had a great success with it at the Sagra Musicale Umbra in Perugia. Two more parts I thought about for a long time before undertaking were Bloch's Lady Macbeth and the Kostelnička in *Jenůfa.* Then *The Medium* came along, and I resisted it for a long time. It seemed too theatrical and Grand Guignol. She seemed like such a cruel and sadistic woman, but Menotti, who is an irresistible charmer, convinced me to try it at least once. Again I had been wrong. The role became so associated with me that I sang it with more than twenty opera companies, including the huge Colón in Buenos Aires, which was quite an effort—the work was really written for an intimate theatre. And it was as the wicked Madame Flora that I gave my farewell performance at the Rome Opera in 1961.

"I had the great honor to sing at La Scala in the world premiere of Poulenc's *Les Dialogues des carmélites* on January 26, 1957, in the part of Madame de Croissy, the Old Prioress. I was enthralled with my assignment, and consider this the greatest opera written since the Second World War. I became very friendly with the composer during the many rehearsals, a sensitive man and with a great sense of humor. He knew the limitations of the human voice, unlike all his contemporaries, and I adore his songs too. His death in 1965 was a very personal loss for me; since our first meeting we had always kept in touch.

"As a mezzo with an extended upper register, I was able to take on with facility Santuzza, Katiusha in *Risurrezione,* and Fedora, all roles that belong to verismo and afford unlimited acting possibilities. I loved all three of them, but I was careful not to accept too many engagements of these works, so as not to lose the flexibility that was essential for the bel canto repertoire. I also felt very comfortable in the shoes of the Principessa di Bouillon in *Adriana Lecouvreur*—what a marvelous second act she has!—and, amazingly, I took part in the first performance of this opera at La Scala, on April 24, 1932. The premiere had taken place in 1902 in Milan, but at the Teatro Lirico, with a cast that included none other than Caruso as Maurizio and Giuseppe de Luca as Michonnet. How and why this melodious and popular work had never been given in Milan's holy of holies remains a mystery. But the success was so overwhelming that in the next twenty-five years La Scala presented it in nine different seasons. Cobelli was the protagonist, and her magic will never be equaled, despite a peculiar voice and a short top.

"What Cilea had done to La Scala to receive such shabby treatment is a puzzle. His superb *L'arlesiana,* perhaps in some ways even more valid than the popular *Adriana,* had received its world premiere at the Teatro Lirico in 1897, again with Caruso. It did not reach La Scala until April 11, 1936, and again I was afforded the opportunity to sing a leading role—Rosa, a tremendously affecting and dramatic figure. I had as my colleagues Schipa, Laurenti, and Basiola—another evening to remember. It proved once more that I was really born for verismo, and it became one of the operas I sang over and over again.

"My career never became really international, although I did sing for several seasons at the Colón in Buenos Aires, both before and after the Second World War, at the Liceo in Barcelona, and at the Deutsches Opernhaus in Berlin. In London I sang only one role at Covent Garden—guess what—Preziosilla! I was busy between La Scala, the Rome Opera, and other leading Italian theatres, and then in the summer the Carro di Tespi, a marvelously organized traveling opera company with all the top artists, which played to huge crowds in the open air in all the provincial cities. It was a spectacular achievement really, for it moved like a circus, and the productions were top-notch. This sort of thing kept the interest in opera alive everywhere, and the prices were very reasonable. It was a far less agitated life then, and a far more satisfactory one. There was time to rehearse; and with so many fabulous singers, the competition was healthy and stimulating. The public had the opportunity to compare the artists— not like today, when there are only a few who appear over and over again. Singing with third-class casts is the worst thing that can happen to a good singer, for he loses his sense of standards. In Rome for ten extraordinary years we had Serafin as the musical director, and what he accomplished was nothing short of miraculous. At the Colón the quality of the performances was impeccable, and what a public! Never have I received more affectionate and touching a welcome as when I returned there after the war. At my entrance as Mignon the entire audience stood up and shouted my name in unison.

"I made many recordings before the war, and all the original tapes were destroyed when the offices of La Voce del Padrone were razed to the ground during the bombardments in Milan. . . . After the war there were several offers to go to the United States, but none of the proposals seemed right for so important a debut.

"My greatest regret in not having been born a soprano is that I was unable to sing Puccini, as he really ignored the mezzo except in small parts. As a favor to Vincenzo Bellezza, a marvelous operatic conductor, I accepted La Zia Principessa in *Suor Angelica,* but except for the duet she has little to do. In the lighter vein, I was called upon to perform in Offenbach's *La Belle Hélène* and the title role in the adorable *Boccaccio* by Suppé. The Carro di Tespi put on a lovely production of this, and I was very doubtful that it would work al fresco before ten thousand people. But again I miscalculated; it was the great hit of the season.

"I was born with a knack for getting along with conductors. Everyone had told me how difficult and demanding Artur Rodzinski was, but when I sang under his baton in *The Queen of Spades* at the Maggio Musicale Fiorentino, I got on with him like a house on fire.

"Today I go on giving courses in interpretation here at the Academy of Santa Cecilia . . . when it is possible; there are strikes all the time. I do it out of stubbornness, because these ignorant and pretentious young people are obliged, when they are kind enough to attend, to listen to the voice of experience. In my era ours was a total dedication; today it has become like learning how to type. Now, after a few months they are on the stage, cheating the public and themselves. Above all they are ruining their chances of a good career. But what is there to do? I get very angry and then calm down, for I know they are all victims of an infernal machine bent on destroying everything. The Italian public will learn how to live without opera, for it isn't possible to continue with ignorant politicians running the opera houses. There is a limit to how far this absurd situation can go, with every opera turned into a political message of sorts. Music is music. There is no message except that which touches the heart."

KAMMERSÄNGERIN
ELISABETH HÖNGEN

In the Viennese musical world no one is more deeply regarded and respected than Elisabeth Höngen, who retired in 1971 after a career spanning thirty-eight years of uninterrupted and intense activity. "One of the greatest artists I ever sang with," Ljuba Welitsch declared to me. "Her intelligence and musicality were absolutely mesmerizing." "I sang *Orfeo* with her at the Salzburg Festival," Jarmila Novotna said, "and she was a magnificent singing actress." The late Baron Erwein Gecmen Waldek, an old friend of Karajan's and for fifty years an assiduous and discriminate habitué of the Vienna Staatsoper, said to me, "I don't believe there ever was a more versatile artist. There were more beautiful voices, but none more expressive, and she could handle Amneris, Carmen, Brangäne, the Countess in *The Queen of Spades,* or Eboli, just to name a few, with a stunning intensity and a sense of characterization that made her unique. And what a marvelous lieder singer too, so truly distinguished on the stage—a '*Künstlerin*' all the way."

"It is no secret," the former prima donna asserted while discussing her career in 1978 in her little, doll-like house lost in the Vienna woods, "that I am over seventy, having been born in 1906. I sang until I was sixty-five not only because I was still very much in demand but because there were some roles I felt I could still handle with dignity." In front of me sat a handsome, thin—almost frail—very refined-looking woman, in a superbly cut brown suit. Her large green eyes emerged from a finely chiseled, highly sensitive face. "It is one of life's inevitable paradoxes that in the last years, when I had so much experience and less vocal stamina, I took on less important parts, while in the first two years of my career, at Wuppertal, the entire mezzo repertoire was thrown at me, including Verdi's Lady Macbeth and all of the *Ring.* But I never thought of a role as big or small. I got engrossed in creating a character and that was that. In German opera houses, as you know, however, this is more normal. For instance, I gladly accepted Karajan's offer to sing Marcellina in *Le nozze di Figaro* at the Salzburg Festival with a fabulous cast that included Schwarzkopf, Seefried, and other big names, and later I even made a recording of it. She is an amusing person and a lot can be done with her. In many productions her aria, charming and difficult, is cut out simply because the artist engaged for the role is not equal to it.

"I was also most happy to appear as Geneviève in *Pelléas* at the Vienna Staatsoper with Karajan, and then later at La Scala under Serge Baudo and with Hilde Gueden as Mélisande. It is a brief role and yet totally absorbing. She is in many ways the key to the entire Maeterlinck text. And she is the only one who has a long passage to deliver. One does not know what to call it, for it is not exactly an aria—Debussy's music is too impressionistic for this—and yet almost. She reads to her father-in-law, Arkel, her son Golaud's letter to her other son, Pelléas, his half-brother, in which he explains meeting Mélisande and marrying her. His words are so poetic, so tender and revealing. For he describes his bride: 'Je ne sais ni son âge, ni qui elle est, ni d'où elle vient, et je n'ose pas l'interroger . . . ' [I know neither her age, nor who she is, nor from where she comes, and I do not dare to question her], and it is through Geneviève's reading that the anguish and the mystery must come through. She is the interpreter, so to speak, of the drama that will follow. At the end of the scene with Arkel, when he agrees to accept the new wife of his grandson, who has asked that a lamp be lit on top of the tower to make it known to him that she is welcome or he will never return home, Geneviève turns to Pelléas, who has joined them, and sings quietly, 'Aie soin d'allumer la lampe dès ce soir' [See to it that the lamp is lighted from this night on]. It must be ever so soft and yet express the relief that her son will be accepted again and allowed to return home. Sometimes a phrase like this means weeks of work, for it seems like nothing and yet it is everything. I have often thought how many marvelous operatic scenes have been built around letters. Just think of the ones in *Eugene Onegin, Werther, Traviata* . . . and then this one.

"I sang a great deal with Karajan," she continued. "There is no way I can possibly remember the number of Beethoven Ninths and Missa Solemnises, Verdi Requiems and Bruckner Te Deums I performed under his direction. Actually, I sang more Beethoven Ninths and Bach Passions than any individual opera. Karajan chose me to appear as Gluck's Orfeo at the Salzburg Festival with him, and then later I repeated this marvelous role with Krips. From certain elegiac aspects, it is perhaps the most lovely opera ever written. In contrast to Geneviève, not only is Orfeo onstage from beginning to end, but on her shoulders rests the entire work. Amor, Euridice, and the Happy Shade flit in and out, but Orfeo is ever present. The recitatives are very

Elisabeth Höngen as Marina in *Boris Godunov*.

special, and how long I struggled to get them just right! Gluck does not employ the secco type, to the accompaniment of the harpsichord; he uses strings instead, and this makes a vast difference in how you enunciate your lines. Within its classical boundaries it is a highly emotional role, but what is so difficult, given the lovely text by Calzabigi, is to avoid ever being emphatic. It must all flow, and yet the strong, overwhelming feelings are there and changing all the time. One goes from the scene with the Furies, with the anguished cry 'Furie . . . larve . . . ombre sdegnose!' [Furies, ghosts, scornful shadows]; then on to the 'Che puro ciel' in the Elysian fields, a series of heavenly legatos; then to the celebrated 'Che farò senza Euridice?,' which is in the key of C, a noble outburst of powerless sorrow. What an assignment! Being so often alone on the stage with just the chorus, one must move so that it is never static, but the action always must respect the Greek motif and even the deepest despair must have its dignity.

"Krips had a lot of humor. When I repeated my Orfeo with him in Salzburg, my new Euridice was Jarmila Novotna. The previous one had been Maria Cebotari, who had died that very year—this was 1949—at the age of thirty-nine, a great loss. Novotna had been in the United States since the beginning of the war, and this was her return to Salzburg after a twelve-year absence. So in many ways, despite the fact that hers was not a long role, this was an event, for the public loved her deeply. Anyhow, at the first orchestra rehearsal, when lovely Jarmila (my goodness, how beautiful she was!) arose from the dead, the main theme of Lehár's *Giuditta* was played instead of Gluck's. For a moment I did not make the connection and thought I had gone quite mad. Not at all—it was Krips's enchanting way of welcoming Novotna back, for she had created *Giuditta* at the Staatsoper and it had become a smashing success.

"To go back to Karajan for a moment—when he asked me to undertake Kundry, I wavered. There was Martha Mödl at the time, and her Kundry was unforgettable. But he convinced me finally, for his was a very odd and ingenious innovation, though I discovered later that this was what Wagner had actually wanted all along: having two different singers for the role, one for the first and last acts and the Klingsor scene in the second and another for the garden scene. It proved such a popular success that we repeated it for several seasons at the Staatsoper, I being the bedraggled Kundry and Christa Ludwig the seductress.

"But you want me to start from the beginning—if one wants to accept that there is one. For me, it is all like an extraordinary tapestry that I wove with my two very own hands, with the help of so many extraordinarily talented people. For they still existed then." She sighed, then continued. "I was born in Gevelsberg, Westphalia, and my father was a builder. When I was six, my parents had already put a violin in my hands, and I studied both violin and piano for many years. In that era in Germany, it was a sort of blessed tradition that everyone played an instrument and that small ensembles existed in the homes; alas, it is no longer true. Not only did it build up the musical education of children, but it also helped to keep the family unit together. Nothing binds people together more than music, and I am firmly convinced that the reason today there are so few singers around of any quality is that the passion for music was not instilled in them when they were not even conscious of it.

"From an early age, I was determined to become a singer—the fire was already burning then—but my voice was small and ugly. I persisted, took singing lessons in nearby Wuppertal, and my voice did improve, but my parents would not hear of a singing career. So I went to Berlin for four years to study to become a singing teacher. In the meantime I studied with Hermann Weissenborn, who had been a very great lieder singer and much later became the teacher of Dietrich Fischer-Dieskau. He taught me how to absorb the essence of a score, where to save my vocal cords, and never, never to force. Although my instrument was not large, it was immensely pliable, and in fact I could sing anything and everything within the compass of my means. It took a lot of time and immense discipline, but where is one without that? I learned to suit my voice to the various styles, and despite some very heavy parts I undertook, I never lost my agility. I could confront boldly, in concert, Sesto's terrifying arias from *La clemenza di Tito,* an opera that has become fashionable again now, though, alas, it was not so in my time. When I showed my dear parents a two-year contract with the Wuppertal opera company—this was in 1933, and I was already twenty-seven years old—they accepted with sportsmanship that their battle had been lost and then did everything they could to encourage my efforts.

"I began, ironically, with Irmentraut in Lortzing's *Der Waffenschmied,* a meaty enough role with comic overtones. This was the first opera I had ever heard, at the age of six, when it charged me with the desire to become an opera singer. Lortzing's operas—he wrote so many—were tremendously popular in those days. Many assignments came rapidly in my direction, for I became known right away for the facility with which I could be transformed physically. I laugh today when there is so much talk that this is one of the great innovations of the modern lyric theatre—to make sure that the characters look believable. I assure you, this has always existed, but with one important difference: Previously they sought singers who looked the part *and* could sing it! Today all that matters is the way they look, just as in silent movies. I have often asked myself whether or not this face and figure of mine, which could be changed with such ease, has been a blessing. Anyhow, it did bring a huge variety of operatic foods to my kitchen. Had my face been less receptive to every sort of makeup, my repertoire would have been far less hazardous, but perhaps less interesting too.

"In Wuppertal they imported from Berlin all the top artists for a series of performances of the entire *Ring,* and I was the only member of the resident company singled out to take over the Frickas, Erdas, and Waltrautes, roles I was to sing very often during the next three decades. It was at this time that I first heard Maria Müller, who had returned to Germany after eleven years at the Metropolitan, and who impressed me enormously. Her Sieglinde was radiant and moving at the same time. She was also superb in Italian opera.

"The Düsseldorf Opera engaged me next, and I was very happy there from 1935 until 1940, enlarging my repertoire and making a name for myself. I hated to leave, but the offer from the Dresden Opera in 1940 was irresistible, as it and Berlin were then considered by the experts to be the most important opera houses in Germany. And I had the privilege there of appearing with so many fabulous artists the likes of which no longer exist. Marta Fuchs's Marschallin was in my estimation the greatest of them all, totally believable, a handsome woman with tremendous allure and a lovely voice. She came often from Berlin, and it fascinated me to know that she had started out as a mezzo. I sang Octavian with her, and every time she added a new touch. Another singer I admired greatly was Margarete Teschemacher, a wonderful actress too. As for Ursuleac's Empress in *Die Frau ohne Schatten*—I used to appear as the Nurse—she displayed a top that I don't believe has ever been equaled.

"But of all the women singers I appeared with—and she came into my life much later—the one I would say really stood in a class by herself was Kirsten Flagstad. I sang the entire *Ring* with her at La Scala under Furtwängler—fortunately, the recordings of these live performances are very good—and then again, in another season in the same theatre, a series of *Die Walküres*.

"She had—and she was fifty-five years old then—the most astonishing vocal force, and at the same time a profound tenderness. There were moments when the instrument gave the impression of almost breaking because of the emotion she felt—do not let anyone ever tell you that she was not a tremendously sensitive human being, for she was, even if she did eat sausages at breakfast!—and it never, never did. The fragility of that enormous voice could be heartbreaking and spine-chilling. She made very few gestures, but every move she made counted so very much, and I learned, without a doubt, more from watching her than from anyone else. It is easy to throw yourself around the stage; but it is supreme art to create an illusion the way she did, appearing almost remote and yet always spellbinding.

"Of all the outstanding conductors—and I believe that, with the exception of Toscanini, I did not miss any along my path, from Furtwängler to Jochum, from Walter to Böhm, from Cluytens to Kleiber, from Leitner to Karajan, and from Kempe to Krips—I recall with the greatest sympathy Krauss and Knappertsbusch, for they were most considerate to us performers. The latter was the most human of all. He rehearsed little, but this did not faze me. 'Elisabeth,' he used to say, 'just look at me and everything will be all right.' And it was, always. With Karajan I always felt terribly secure because of the endless rehearsals, but there never was an intimate contact between podium and stage.

"If I had not been called to the Vienna Opera in 1943, I would most probably not be here in front of you. The bombardments in Dresden not only destroyed the most beautiful theatre ever built but killed a great percentage of the population. Most of the friends I had there were, in a matter of few seconds, annihilated. One becomes fatalistic, but one can never quite be the same afterward. Of course, the Vienna Staatsoper was turned to ashes too, and until its reconstruction we appeared in the adorable Theater an der Wien, cozy to sing in. We all lived on starvation rations, but some of us survived. Although I made many guest appearances every year, from 1943 until 1971 the Vienna Opera was my home.

"From a numerical point of view, Fricka, Brangäne, Carmen, and Herodias were the roles I performed the most often—among the various hundreds. I appeared in all the Wagnerian roles, including Adriano in *Rienzi* in Wuppertal, Berlin, and Dresden. I was often asked to do Ortrud, including a production I had to sing in Italian at the Maggio Musicale Fiorentino, with Tebaldi as Elsa. She was magnificent in this part, really peerless, and I begged her to relearn it in German so that she could appear in this opera outside of Italy. I know that in Austria and Germany she would have made a sensation in it. But she was a shy person then, and kept saying that she could never master the language well enough.

"Ortrud is a difficult part, for she is really all evil, and she dominates the second act with her jealousy and falseness. Most interpreters end by shouting it, not only because of the heavy orchestration but also to denote the character. I was still under the spell of my teacher and refused to force my voice, so I found another way of expressing her tortured, wretched soul. The phrasing is essential if the audience is to understand what she is up to, for she plays a double game, and the voice must change color for the duet with Telramund, dark and foreboding, and then for the duet with Elsa, where she wishes to convince the girl that she is a victim. In the last act the acting is a great challenge, for as Ortrud cries out, 'Erfahrt, wie sich die Götter rächen, von deren Huld ihr euch gewandt!" [Learn how the gods take their revenge, the gods from whose grace you have turned!], Lohengrin kneels and the boy Gottfried makes his appearance as the swan sinks. She realizes then that she has lost the battle, her spells have been broken by the knight in shining armor, and, shrieking, she falls in a faint. Here the shrieking is essential, and it is far more effective if she has not done a lot of screaming before. It is a tremendously powerful scene, and one of the greatest *coups de scène* that Wagner created.

"Verdi's operas stayed with me through the years—Amneris, Ulrica, Azucena, Eboli, and Lady Macbeth. I recorded the latter under Karl Böhm's direction and in German. Piave's libretto translates very well; the sleepwalking scene, for instance, is marvelously striking in German too. While *Aida* loses a lot in the translation, *Macbeth* does not, in my opinion. Quickly I only did for television, but *Falstaff* is not often given in Central Europe.

"Of Mozart, apart from Marcellina and many Dorabellas, I did the Second Lady in *Die Zauberflöte* for five Salzburg Festivals as a favor to Furtwängler, who had always showed me so much esteem and affection. In the maestro's opinion, the Three Ladies are very important, and, in fact, when one looks at the casts of days gone by, they were always handed to leading prima donnas. Now they have a difficult time finding even a Pamina, so you can imagine what happens to these other roles.

"But the Strauss repertoire was often on my calendar. Apart from Octavian and the delicious Clairon in *Capriccio,* I was always much in demand for the Nurse in *Die Frau ohne Schatten,* Klytämnestra, and Herodias. The Nurse is a very tough vocal task, and difficult to make sympathetic. Klytämnestra demands a sort of declamation that is far from easy—again, the phrasing is essential—but it cannot compare to the demands made on the Nurse. The reason I sang only one season at the Metropolitan was that Mr. Bing could only envisage me as a Strauss specialist. I had a big success there as Klytämnestra and Herodias in 1952, but it did not lead me to anything else in that opera house. One of my credos in life has been never to argue with directors of lyric theatres. They are supposed to know what they are doing. The fact that I had well over seventy operas in my throat was ignored, but it did not really matter, for I had so many demands to fulfill in other theatres. But I would be lying if I were to say that I was not disappointed.

"One of the roles which became very dear to me was the Old Prioress in *Les Dialogues des carmélites,* and I sang it at its Vienna premiere and went on with it as long as it stayed in the repertoire. Again, it is not a very long part, but it is gripping, and the death scene holds the audience in a trance. I also very much enjoyed appearing in the lead of Britten's *The Rape of Lucretia* at the Salzburg Festival with Krips conducting."

Did she have any regrets?

With that wonderful serenity which emanates from her she answered, "Yes—one, although it is not in my nature to nourish grievances. I always wanted to sing Dalila, but the opportunity never came. Strangely enough, they don't give this opera in German opera houses, and when I was invited to foreign countries it was always for German roles.

"I never married, and I admire all my colleagues who were able to combine a private life with their artistic one. I became so engrossed in my work nothing else mattered. It is a little lonely now, but it is the logical price I must pay for a most rewarding life. After my retirement I agreed to give some courses, but I withdrew—I simply could not accept the lack of discipline that reigns today. They wish to burn their bridges behind them before they have even started building them, and this I cannot tolerate— I will not lend my name to this farce. The English and the Americans have now taken the lead, for they are more disposed to make the necessary sacrifices. Do you realize that we have hardly any outstanding singers coming up in Central Europe? It is simply appalling and very worrying. Where are the Welitsches, the Konetznis, the Jurinacs, the Guedens, the Bergers, the Lipps, to mention a few, of this new generation? And when Schwarzkopf really retires—she has been on the verge for some time—there will be no woman lieder singer of quality left.

"Just look at the program of the Staatsoper this week. Antigone Sgourda is Greek, Nilsson is Swedish, Roger Soyer is French, Gwyneth Jones is Welsh, Franco Bonisolli is Italian, and Judith Beckmann, Reri Grist, Carol Neblett, Jess Thomas, and James King are all American. Our veterans are still around, sixtyish or beyond: Anton Dermota, who still sings exquisitely, Waldemar Kmentt, Emmy Loose, Erich Kunz. I pray some Germans and Austrians come out of hiding, and not for nationalistic reasons. I firmly believe all art should be international, but if opera is to survive, every country must produce its own group. At first they explained this dearth as the result of the war, and this made sense. But now what is the justification? No one seems to be able to come up with any.

"I look at the future with misgivings, and not because I am a pessimist. I lived through the Hitler era, the destruction of our cities, and a long period when I did not have enough to eat. I recall that after a performance of *The Queen of Spades* in Vienna, I was invited by the high Russian command with the rest of the cast for supper, and we were all goggle-eyed at the sight of the elaborate buffet the conquerors offered us. So I am not talking about the political madness, which continues on a world scale, but about the total lack of dedication to my ever-beloved profession. So much amateurism has crept in, along with appalling materialism. So much nonsense is perpetrated in the name of art. I only hope that the German system, which no longer functions in the big cities, will go on as in the past in the provincial towns, for it is still best for a singer to be hired on an annual basis, learn ensemble work, and build up a repertoire. Every small city in Germany and Austria has its functioning opera house, despite heavy financial sacrifices, and this means a lot culturally.

"The Austrian public is wonderfully knowledgeable, and my heart is full of gratitude to the Viennese. They accepted me with open arms, made me a Kammersängerin in 1947, and until the end were touchingly and marvelously loyal. I love them."

KAMMERSÄNGERIN
JARMILA NOVOTNA

I doubt that anyone who heard Jarmila Novotna as Octavian in *Der Rosen-kavalier* will ever forget the final duet with Sophie. The way she sang von Hofmannsthal's beautiful phrase "Gehts all's sonst wie ein Traum dahin vor meinem Sinn" (All else passes like a dream through my mind) was one of those magical moments that happen all too rarely in opera. In the estimation of many, myself included, there never has been an Octavian to compare to hers for charm, distinction, utter credibility, and total involvement. Until the end of her career she looked a seventeen-year-old boy, an aristocrat with a sense of mischief and fun, who turned into a man right before one's eyes. Florence Page Kimball, for many years one of New York City's leading teachers and musical hostesses, used to say, "There have been far lovelier voices singing Octavian, but for me Jarmila and Octavian on the stage were all one. Now that she has retired, I simply cannot bear to see anyone else in the part." Lucrezia Bori, who was La Scala's first Octavian, concurred, and I remember her commenting, "Novotna's transformation into this young man is extraordinary, for she is never self-conscious about it. How this beautiful woman can accomplish this is true, great art."

I had not seen Novotna in two years when I went to call on her in June 1979, at her pretty, sophisticated house with its large garden in the Hietz-inger section of Vienna. She hardly went out then, spending all her time with her husband, Baron George Daubek, who was then past ninety and ailing. (He died in the winter of 1981.) With her inborn generosity and sense of duty, she considered this total dedication of hers the most natural thing in the world. Although she is seventy-four years old now, she still displays the wonderful bone structure that made her one of the loveliest women in the world for three decades, and as with all truly good people, her kindness and calmness are reflected in her serene face. In all the years I have known her—since 1935, to be exact—I have admired her seemingly effortless ability to combine an outstanding position in the music world with being an admirable wife, mother, and friend. She never played the operatic poker game, for all the cards came to her naturally, and so she kept away from cliques and intrigues. I don't believe anyone had a more varied, interesting span of activities than hers.

I recall being bowled over in 1934 when I attended a performance of *Giuditta,* Lehár's only opera, which he wrote for her and Richard Tauber, at the Vienna Staatsoper. I never saw Farrar or Cavalieri on the stage, but Novotna seemed to me the most beautiful creature imaginable. Hers was a classical type of beauty, with the most superbly proportioned head and body, and one could imagine her having walked out of a Greek frieze. But this was no mere beauty queen on parade; she was a consummate actress, with a natural command of the stage that made those around her appear artificial. From 1935 to 1937 I heard her at the Salzburg Festival in many roles; and it was in 1935, when she came to sing Cherubino (under Walter) at the Maggio Musicale Fiorentino, that my mother met her socially and invited her home for lunch. This was the beginning of an enduring friendship between us that never faltered. Here I was interviewing her forty-four years later to gather some information that I did not have at my fingertips. Much of her story I knew, but it amazed me how many details I was hearing for the first time.

"I was born in Prague, one of the most beautiful cities in the world, and until I die I shall be always enormously proud of having belonged to this once wonderful capital. My voice developed early, and I began studying in my teens. I started as a coloratura; everyone was convinced that that was what I was. But within a few years I had become a lyric, and so I remained; I never moved on to the spinto repertoire. Emmy Destinn was my main teacher, but as she came and went, whenever she was absent I took classes with Hilbert Vavia. Destinn was a very remarkable woman, with very clear ideas about the fundamentals of vocal training. It is from her that I first heard a lot about the Metropolitan Opera, where she had sung until 1921. She was amazingly versatile, having been Bayreuth's first Senta way back in 1901 and then the first Minnie in *La fanciulla del West* at the Metropolitan. She had succeeded equally in the German and Italian repertoire and had also taken on verismo parts. Two cats were always present at my lessons, but they were well behaved. Later I took classes in Milan with Tanaglia and Malatesta, and had the great privilege of being coached in some roles by none other than Antonio Guarnieri, a remarkable musician who had conducted at the Vienna Opera for some years and then, after Toscanini left Milan in 1929, went to La Scala and remained there until his death.

"When I think back, I cannot believe that I had enough nerve to make

Jarmila Novotna in the title role of *Manon*.

my debut at eighteen at the Prague Opera House as Marie in *The Bartered Bride*, which Destinn had sung at the Metropolitan. It is an opera with which I became very much identified for the rest of my professional life. Six days later, on July 3, 1925, I created a stir in *La traviata*. It all seems like a dream now, and what happened afterward. So many roles were assigned to me, including Rosina and the Queen of the Night. In January 1926 I became a regular member of the company and remained there for two years, increasing my responsibilities constantly with such roles as Nannetta in *Falstaff*, Ännchen in *Der Freischütz*, Karoline in Smetana's *Two Widows*, and ever so many others.

"In 1928 I started my international career with Gilda in the magnificent, huge spaces of the Arena in Verona, with Lauri-Volpi as the Duke, and then at the Staatsoper in Vienna, which later became so intimate a part of my life. In the city of Romeo and Juliet I became very frightened on opening night, for they came and asked me for money for the claque and I simply did not have it. I was told that they would revenge themselves by booing me. I sang 'Caro nome' trembling like a leaf, but I need not have worried. The acclaim was so general that I had to encore the aria, and Lauri-Volpi was very sweet to me. He said, *'Brava ciecoslovacchina, hai vinto'*—good for you, my little Czech, you have won. When I sang Gilda in Prague, my Rigoletto was someone everyone today has forgotten; his name was Georges Baklanoff, a Russian baritone of exceptional talent. His 'Si, vendetta' was much like a thunderstorm, and I was limp, standing beside him and trying to keep up with him. I was to sing again with him in Berlin in 1931— Antonia in *The Tales of Hoffmann* to his Dr. Miracle, and he was indeed a demoniacal, satanic figure, the like of which I have never heard since. The voice was not velvety in texture, but how infinitely expressive and chilling!

"Verona led to the San Carlo in Naples, and what a joy it was to sing in that exquisite theatre with the unique Tito Schipa in *L'elisir d'amore*. Then came several tempting Italian offers, but a contract was offered me by Berlin's Kroll Opera—a branch of the Staatsoper—to become a permanent member, and it was at the time considered the most exciting lyric theatre in Europe. Those were fantastic years, and my head spins as I recall some of the wonderful experiences I had there. My debut came on September 28, 1929, as Concepcion in Ravel's *L'Heure espagnole* under Zemlinsky—an interesting man, for he was also a successful opera composer and the brother-in-law of Schoenberg, who had been his pupil along with Korngold. Gustave Gründgens was the director, and he did a lot to improve my acting. Klemperer was the music director at the time, and he chose me to be his

Queen of the Night and Cherubino. He was a very stern conductor who worked incessantly to obtain a homogenous ensemble. We were all afraid of him, but I realized immediately that this was a tough but immensely profitable school. In those days he managed to unite an astonishing beauty of style with a burning intensity. I kept my old repertoire, but added new, heavier roles such as Butterfly (under Zemlinsky) and Manon Lescaut. I was also part of an all-Schoenberg evening conducted by Klemperer, and my assignment in *Die glückliche Hand*, which lasted only twenty minutes, was the most restful of my entire career: I did not have to sing a single note; my only responsibility was to look decorative.

"At this point, I believe it is necessary to explain the operatic situation in Berlin, which was somewhat confusing. The company I belonged to, the Kroll, with Klemperer and Zemlinsky, had existed only since 1927 and was a part of the Staatsoper, which was also known as Unter den Linden and had as principal conductors Erich Kleiber, Leo Blech, and George Szell. The other one, the Städtische or Municipal, was the responsibility of Bruno Walter. In July 1931 it was decided, for budgetary reasons, to close the Kroll, and they moved Klemperer, myself, and many others to the Staatsoper. It was here that I had the good fortune to do *La traviata* with Kleiber and appear as the Queen in a marvelous production of *Les Huguenots* under Blech. One night I received, in the intermission, a written message from Blech that I had not looked at him sufficiently during the previous act as he had instructed me. I sent back a note excusing myself but explaining that it was impossible, in order for the scene to be convincing, to keep my eyes on him as well as on my partner. Another note returned, and this proved he had a delicious sense of humor. It said he was going to disguise himself as Otto Klemperer, for he well knew how terrified all of us were of him. I also appeared as Madelon in the German premiere of the pleasant opera by Lattuada *Le preziose ridicole,* which I discussed much later with Lucrezia Bori, who had sung the American premiere at the Metropolitan at more or less the same time. Nineteen thirty-one was a year to remember, for I got married, and Max Reinhardt invited me to be his Helen of Troy in an unforgettable production of Offenbach's *La Belle Hélène* at the Theater am Kurfürstendamm. The difficulties of obtaining my release from the Staatsoper were considerable, but he managed. The spectacle was superb, and I learned a great deal from him, for I was later to appear in three other productions of his: *The Tales of Hoffmann,* the Calderón–von Hofmannsthal *Die grosse Welttheater,* and *Fledermaus.*

"Improvisation did not exist with Reinhardt. All was written down by him in a notebook before the rehearsals started. He explained with marvelous clarity the emotional reaction that a certain scene should produce, sometimes acting himself to show us the impressions he wanted us to convey. As soon as we had a clear concept of the meaning, he left it to our imagination and individual inspiration to create the character in our own personal way. This gave every performer a sense of freedom and spontaneity, and I am convinced that it is because of this manner of handling the artists that he obtained such miraculous results, from the leads to the comprimarios. He was the best audience ever, for he noticed everything. No detail of expression or posture escaped him. When he was pleased, he told us, and I cannot think of anything more exhilarating than one word of praise from him. In making a suggestion or correction, he never became impatient but was always helpful and constructive. With Gründgens it was quite different. He was a genius too, but while he had the ability to adjust himself to the artist's personality, with Reinhardt it was the other way around.

"For *La Belle Hélène* we had Erich Korngold as a conductor, and for *The Tales of Hoffmann* we had first Leo Blech, then George Szell. This is to give you an idea of the high musical quality of Reinhardt's productions. That my life was indeed full—and exhausting vocally—I don't need to tell you. For once or twice a week I had to sing at the Opera, and there was naturally an understudy for me with Reinhardt. In between, in 1933, I appeared at the Admiralpalast theatre in Jaromir Weinberger's *Frühlingsstürme* with Richard Tauber, the tenor who partnered me later so often at the Vienna Staatsoper, and one of the formidable bel canto artists of his generation. He was always searching for perfection, and he often achieved it. The fact that his instrument was immediately recognizable helped a lot, for he was one of the first singers to record extensively. It was a real joy to work with him, for he rehearsed and repeated innumerable times until the effect was just right.

"To go back to Reinhardt, in order to convince me to appear in *Welttheater,* a mystery play, with a huge cast which included his wife, the famous actress Helene Thimig, he had Mark Lothar write two arias for me, since I was afraid then to appear in a straight drama. He also tried to convince me to play in his version of Shakespeare's *A Midsummer Night's Dream,* but I was a singer and such I wished to remain. During all my years in Berlin I returned each season for guest performances in Prague.

"Dark clouds were already on the horizon, and the Calderón–von Hofmannsthal production was the last of Reinhardt, a veritable swan song; he left Germany because of the beginning of the persecution of the Jews. I was attacked too, by several newspapers, for having sung Beethoven's Ninth Symphony in Czech in Prague, at a concert honoring President Masaryk's birthday. I was also due to sing Mahler's Fourth Symphony in Berlin with Bruno Walter, who was advised to drop it since the composer had been Jewish. I soon realized that in this new atmosphere of manufactured hatred I did not wish to continue my activities in Berlin. I left in 1933, sang Butterfly in Vienna, and then appeared in an enchanting version of *Fledermaus* at the Théâtre Pigalle in Paris, and this was to be Reinhardt's farewell, on a professional level, to Europe. Korngold conducted, and it was a pleasure all the way around.

"In the meantime I had met Lehár in Vienna, who wanted me for his *Giuditta*, which he was writing. So in 1934 Tauber and I created this delicious, sparkling opera, which became such an extraordinary hit at the Vienna Staatsoper that we kept repeating it until 1938. The public never seemed to have enough of it. There is an aria in it, 'Meine Lippen, sie kussen so heiss' [My lips, they kiss so warmly], which begins in a memorable Spanish rhythm, then goes into a romantic vein, and finally becomes an irresistible waltz, and people literally hummed it on the streets. Whenever I went into a restaurant that had an orchestra—many did in those happier days—immediately the leader would strike this melody; and if my name became a household word in Austria, it is due to *Giuditta*.

"By then I had transferred myself to Vienna, and begun my very happy association with the Staatsoper, receiving also the title of Kammersängerin. I sang almost every role of my repertoire there, plus the four heroines in *The Tales of Hoffmann* (in Berlin I had only appeared as Antonia). Tauber often appeared with me in *The Bartered Bride* and *Butterfly,* and my Marschallins were usually either Lotte Lehmann or Anny Konetzni. I admired them both for different reasons. Certainly Lehmann's monologue was a great work of art. In America I greatly admired Traubel for her dignity and warmth, but since she is such a big woman, the scene in which she gets out of bed was not easy for her. So many Octavians move on to the Marschallin, but I never did. I do realize that I sang too many performances of this role, which lies so much in the middle of the voice and does not help the upper register; but I loved it, and the requests poured in.

"During all this time I was very busy appearing in motion pictures too. The first one I made in Prague back in 1925, and while in Berlin I made four, including *The Bartered Bride* with Max Ophuls as director. It is amazing that they made the film despite the fact that I was already six months pregnant with Jarmilina, but they arranged for me to wear bouffant skirts—Marie is a peasant, dressed in the Czech national costumes—so that my condition would not be noticed. One of my most successful films was *The Night of the Great Love,* with Gustave Frohlich, then a very big star in Germany. Then I made another picture in Prague, *The Song of the Nightingale,* in 1933; and then two in Vienna: one based on Lehár's *Frasquita* and the other *The Cossack and the Nightingale,* with another very well-known leading man, Ivan Petrovich. In Paris I made *The Last Waltz* with music by Oscar Straus. Ten years were to elapse before I made my next one, for MGM—*The Search* with Montgomery Clift, and although it was an unglamorous, nonsinging role, I loved the script and accepted Fred Zinnemann's offer right away. The last was *The Great Caruso* in 1950, but the role amounted to nothing, all the attention going, naturally, to Mario Lanza.

"So you see, there was little time to accept other engagements, with the exception of my Cherubino in Florence, where you and I first met, and then in 1937 when I appeared as Alice Ford in *Falstaff* at La Scala with de Sabata. That was a memorable experience, for he was an exceptional conductor, one of the greatest, in my opinion. But goodness! I was so lucky in this department. However, the conductor who played the decisive part in my life, as events proved, was Toscanini. Having heard me at Salzburg, he asked me to be his Pamina for the following season, when there was to be a new production of *Die Zauberflöte* especially mounted for him. It had always been an opera close to his heart, and the only one by Mozart he ever conducted at La Scala during his intermittent periods there. It was a switch for me to be singing the role of the sweet daughter after having appeared in the fiendishly difficult part of her mother, the sinister Queen of the Night. During those seasons in Salzburg I sang a lot of Mozart (Fiordiligi, the Countess, Cherubino) and in an interesting revival of *Der Corregidor,* the only opera Hugo Wolf ever wrote. It is based on the 'Three-Cornered Hat' story, but it moves somewhat slowly, and it has never caught on with the public. Toscanini and I became great friends." She pointed to a large mother-of-pearl box on the table in the corner of the drawing room. "There are the hundreds of letters that he wrote to me and which should be published someday. It is so fortunate that, with all that was lost in the war, none of them were destroyed. I really am tremendously obligated to the maestro, for he saved me and my family from a fate that would have been disastrous.

"That was to be the last Salzburg Festival before the Second World War for Toscanini and me," she affirmed, "as the Anschluss came the following winter and neither of us wished to return under the circumstances. Incredible to say, I was appearing as Tatiana in *Eugene Onegin* the night of March 12, 1938, at the Vienna Staatsoper when the Germans took over Austria in a matter of a few hours. Despite my binding contract with the Staatsoper, I had a valid excuse to absent myself, for I was expecting my second child, George Junior. I did not return to Vienna, and we retired to our castle of Liten in Bohemia, little realizing that this would have to be abandoned soon. Over the years, I had always gone back to Czechoslovakia—I even was given the honor of having my face put on the Czech kronen—to spend some time at our country place, to which I was very attached. My husband was a well-to-do gentleman farmer who had always come to see me in Vienna but never interfered with my professional life. He was a great connoisseur of music, and his judgment was sound.

"In the meantime," she went on, "Toscanini had invited me to sing *La traviata* and Alice in *Falstaff* at the opera season he had agreed to conduct at the forthcoming New York World's Fair. So it was fortunately decided that I would give birth to George Junior in England, and the last perform- ance I had sung during my early pregnancy had been in Dvořák's lovely *Rusalka* in Prague. After spending some time in England, I arrived in New York City on March 15, 1939, with the ghastly news greeting me that Czechoslovakia too had fallen prey to the Hitlerian folly. My husband and children were there, so you can imagine my state of mind when I began to rehearse Violetta with Toscanini. Although it was one of the operas I had sung most frequently, it was like reading a new score with him, a new revelation every day. But then came the realization that he simply could not conduct in a theatre that would be constantly disturbed by the noise of the planes taking off and landing nearby. He felt so bad that I had come over to the United States for nothing that he took me personally to Edward Johnson's office at the Metropolitan. This was quite a gallant gesture, since he had never returned there after 1915, when he left after a stormy disagree- ment. Johnson signed me immediately, my debut being fixed for January 1940, and I returned to Europe.

"It was odd how the United States had figured twice in my future and yet nothing had come out of the two initial proposals. The first one came way back in the Berlin days, from the Metropolitan, but I refused, for I was about to get married, and they offered me a long-term contract, the way they did in those days. Then the second came from Louis B. Mayer, whom I met at Max Reinhardt's magnificent country estate near Salzburg. He offered me a five-year contract at a thousand dollars a week, but again I turned it down. I had no intention of dropping my singing career, and I had seen too many persons signed by Hollywood film companies only to spend months collecting their checks with absolutely nothing happening.

"The third proposal proved to be the good one. I was singing *The Marriage of Figaro* in Scheveningen under Bruno Walter's direction the day before the Second World War was declared. The children, thank goodness, were with me in Holland, and our wonderful nurse too; and my husband, who had a sixth sense, managed to get us all out just in the nick of time. It was a formidable struggle to find passages for the United States, but we arrived there at the end of September, without a cent to our names.

"Fortunately for me, members of the Italian contingent who were to have sung in the fall season in San Francisco were unable to leave Italy—their passports had been literally confiscated—so I was rushed there and made my debut at the War Memorial Opera House on October 18 as Butterfly, a role that I regret I never sang at the Metropolitan. After Pearl Harbor it was taken out of the repertory, and later it became the property of the talented Licia Albanese. In San Francisco I also sang *La traviata,* and then in St. Louis *La Bohème,* which was to be the opera of my Metropolitan debut. New Yorkers heard me for the first time on December 2, 1939, when Toscanini introduced me to the Carnegie Hall audience with the NBC Symphony Orchestra in Beethoven's Ninth. He invited me later to sing with him in his Sunday afternoon broadcasts."

If her Mimi (with Jussi Bjoerling as her Rodolfo—she had sung with him in this same opera in Vienna) was greeted warmly, it was *La traviata,* which followed on February 7, 1940, that established her, according to all the critics, as the greatest singing actress of that period. Again, one might quarrel with the fact that she looked too aristocratic to be a courtesan, but her beauty left everyone breathless, and the way she walked backward in the second act to take a last, lingering look at Alfredo was heartbreaking. With impeccable Italian diction, she timed the significant phrases with a delicacy that was infinitely poignant. I never heard anyone sing the "Alfredo, Alfredo, di questo core, non puoi comprendere tutto l'amore" (Alfredo, Alfredo, you cannot understand all the love that is in this heart) as she did—beginning almost as a whisper (she is, in fact, really talking to herself) and then developing the following phrases to a crescendo. And at the end of the act, when she sings "Ah, io spenta ancora—pur t'amerò" (Even when I am dead I shall love you), the word "spenta," which in Italian means both dead and extinguished, was almost inaudible but still traveled throughout the auditorium.

It was Bruno Walter who persuaded her to take on Donna Elvira for the first time, and it became one of her most famous roles in the United States. "It is a treacherous part," she said, "for it is written very much in the middle of the voice, and finding the right interpretation is most problematic. She is a bore, complaining all the time to the sound of lovely melodies, and yet somehow one must make the public feel sorry for her. The way she pursues Don Giovanni is not dignified, and at the same time da Ponte has written that she is a noblewoman of great breeding." I remember Ezio Pinza, who often sang the Don with her, saying, "Casting Novotna as Elvira is a major mistake. She is so unbelievably beautiful that the audience simply cannot understand, and quite rightly so, why I am always running away from her."

In her seventeen seasons with the company—she retired from the operatic stage in 1956—she sang fifteen roles, and the three she was called upon to sing the most frequently were all trouser roles: Octavian, Cherubino, and Orlofsky. She was a ravishing Manon, a role she also sang at the Colón in Buenos Aires, the Municipal in Santiago, and many other theatres. Another role she sang for the first time at the Metropolitan was Mélisande. After the war she returned to Salzburg for *Orfeo ed Euridice* and *Der Rosenkavalier*. She became very much in demand for recitals and spent several months a year pursuing this activity. Later she gave lecture-recitals which became enormously popular, and she performed on numerous radio and television programs.

Needless to say, the moment the war ended, the Daubeks rushed back to Czechoslovakia and began rebuilding and refurnishing their castle, which had been devastated by the Russian troops. She sang recitals in all the principal cities and at a concert for the Red Cross (in the presence of President and Madame Beneš); and at the opera she sang in *Eugene Onegin* and *The Bartered Bride* to enthusiastic acclaim. This she received not only because of the worth of her performances but because everyone knew how generous she had been during the war years to all the Czech exiles in the United States and how much she had done to find them homes and jobs. When the communists took over, the Daubeks' property was nationalized, and not even her photograph albums were returned to her. Passionately attached to her country, she was never able to come to terms with the communist regime there. Nothing is more deeply moving than the record album entitled *Songs of Lidice,* which Novotna taped for RCA Victor with the late Jan Masaryk, the Daubeks' most intimate friend, providing the excellent piano accompaniment. His mysterious death—he was apparently murdered—has always haunted her. And if the Lehár aria had been her leitmotiv in Austria, Dvořák's "Songs My Mother Taught Me" became a fixture of all her American recitals, and with that simplicity which has always distinguished her, she brought to this song a pathos that moved audiences to tears.

In New York City, she continued her excursions away from the opera house. In 1944 she appeared on Broadway in a revival of *La Belle Hélène,* but this time in English, under the title *Helen of Troy.* Then in 1955 she played the part of Irene Adler in *Sherlock Holmes* with Basil Rathbone.

And what had been the most amusing experiences in her diversified career?

"There are two performances that stand out in my recollections. Once in Vienna, when I was singing the four heroines in *The Tales of Hoffmann,* they forgot to come to my dressing room to advise me that the second act was about to begin. As you undoubtedly recall, it starts almost immediately with the Barcarolle, and suddenly I heard the orchestra playing it. I rushed onto the stage, and so devastating was the hurry that, without thinking, I entered from the second wing, to the hilarity of the audience. I had forgotten that Venice's Grand Canal was located there, and so it looked as if I, in all my finery, were emerging from the water.

"Then in Baltimore, on tour with the Metropolitan, just as I was beginning Prince Orlofsky's famous 'Chacun à son gout,' there was an explosion of laughter in the theatre. I was stunned, for I could not imagine what was taking place. Was I losing my trousers or wig, or what? Then suddenly my eyes caught a real bat flying over my head. This story made all the front pages, but it was a coincidence of unusual interest for a bat to make his appearance in an opera that carries his name."

The fact that she is a linguist par excellence has not been mentioned, but the truth is that she sang most of her roles first in Czech, then in German, then some in Italian, some in French, and both *The Bartered Bride* and *Fledermaus* in perfect English. In all the years I saw the Daubeks socially in Manhattan, many people had no idea who the beautiful lady was, nor was she eager to inform them. As a matter of principle she never spoke of her career, for she always was able to keep her two lives on separate levels. Socially she was the Baroness Daubek, and that was that. The lack of ego in this truly noble creature was extraordinary, so totally unlike that erupting from many of her colleagues. Her tact was famous, and there are many stories of how she was able to placate artists whose sensibilities had created dramas. During a performance of *La Bohème* at the Metropolitan with Jan Kiepura as Rodolfo and Fausto Cleva in the pit, Kiepura, temperamental and unreasonable, was very rude to Cleva, and there was such tension that the fate of the performance was in doubt. Novotna went to Kiepura's dressing room for a few minutes, and the result of her visit was that he went and apologized to Cleva. But she never would tell what transpired. She never criticized other singers; anyone can have a bad night, she always said. When someone was in vocal trouble, I often heard her say, "Singing is so difficult, I wonder why anyone attempts it."

"Looking back," she said to me as I was preparing to leave, "I am ever thankful for all the privileges that I gained rather than regretful of the many that I lost. I am out of everything now, and it is just as well. The last time we went to the opera here, we were terribly disappointed. The spirit is gone; it's all routine, catch-as-catch-can, always in the dark—this seems the rule. And the new directors don't allow singers to develop as actors. You see the same production with a new cast two months later: the same gestures, every detail unchanged. This is not art; this is the factory system. And with opera it cannot work. Reinhardt showed me the way, and I know it was the right one. God bless him and all the others, wherever they are, for bringing so much light into my life."

KAMMERSÄNGERIN
LISA DELLA CASA

The last prima donna to combine outstanding vocal gifts, great personal beauty, a commanding stage presence, and acting ability was Lisa della Casa. Half Swiss and half Bavarian, she had exquisite dark looks which not only glowed across the footlights but expressed a tremendous voluptuousness. Her acting was subtle and never melodramatic, and I recall being vastly impressed with her handling of her two arias as the Countess in *Le nozze di Figaro*. Alone onstage on both occasions, she managed to appear as if she were having a dialogue with herself. The extraordinary legatos of the first aria, in the style of a larghetto, and the shift of mood in the second (from an andantino to an allegro that revealed her uncommon agility) proved what an accomplished Mozartian she was. No wonder that at the Metropolitan she sang a total of forty-seven performances of this role, for within my memory there never has been a lovelier Countess, with just the right mixture of self-pity and comedy.

Suddenly, after a career that lasted thirty-one years and with an instrument that gave little sign of wear and tear, she vanished without any farewells. Her last performance occurred in 1973 at the Vienna Staatsoper, where she had been one of the leading divas for twenty-eight consecutive years. The opera was *Arabella*, which had been considered her finest achievement. The public was not aware of the decision she had made that very morning; she had asked her husband, "Can I afford to quit?" and he had nodded yes. It meant making frantic calls all over the world to cancel engagements three years ahead.

When, during the waltz in the second act, Arabella utters to Lamoral, "Dann fahr ich fort von euch auf Nimmerwiedersehn" (Then I shall leave you, never to see you again), she sang it out to the audience, marking every word as she had never done before. "That was my way of saying goodbye," she explained to me when I visited her in her delightful castle on the romantic shores of Lake Constance. "But of course no one realized that I was bidding goodbye to my loyal public as well.

Lisa della Casa in the title role of *Arabella*.

"There were very serious reasons for my decision. Our one and only daughter was recovering from a terrible operation, and for a long time it was touch-and-go whether she would survive. It was all due to a neuritis that had suddenly afflicted her, and we knew the convalescence would be exceedingly complicated, long and delicate. Along with my husband, she was the most important person in my life, and I felt that I must dedicate all my time and efforts to try to reconstruct her life. It has been a major, protracted, uphill battle, but I think that finally we have partially won it. How could I go on singing under such tension?

"When I woke up that morning, after a restless night, and told my husband, there was no need to explain, for he knew the strain I was undergoing. He understood, for his devotion to the child equals mine. Apart from this personal drama, it was no longer a pleasure to sing and constantly to have arguments with stage directors who don't know their business and so-called leading conductors who simply do not learn their scores. I had had the best and was used to the highest standards. Since that night I have not sung a single note again, not even for my pleasure. 'Tis a long chapter that is finished. Can you understand?"

I said I did with all my heart; I had been deeply moved. In front of me sat this still divine-looking and yet delicate former prima donna; her handsome, sympathetic, gray-haired husband, Dragan Debeljevic (they were married in Zurich in 1947); and their daughter, so bright, and touching in her determination to overcome the many handicaps with which she had been burdened. I was deeply impressed with all three of them as human beings. But with the great know-how of a woman of the world, della Casa very naturally broke the emotionally charged atmosphere, and we plunged ahead with the interview.

"I was born in Burgdorf, a little town near Bern, in 1919," she recalled. "Although most people think mine is a made-up name, it is not. My father, della Casa, came from a family in the canton Ticino and had become an excellent eye doctor after his parents had forbidden him to become a singer. So when the moment came that I wished to dedicate myself to singing, he not only gave me every encouragement but provided me with sound and practical advice on all levels. My mother, a Bavarian, was a music enthusiast and also encouraged me.

"I started studying when I was fifteen, and for eight years my teacher was Margaret Haeser, who taught in both Bern and Zurich, so I followed her around. She instructed me in a mixture of bel canto and the Viennese school, and if I was able later to sing both repertoires, it is all due to her. I also studied piano at the conservatory and took all sorts of music courses.

"I finally made my debut, as Annina in *Der Rosenkavalier,* which of course is written for a mezzo. But the Zurich Opera House is small and very *gemütlich,* Europe was at war (my first appearance took place in 1943), and the reason I was given this part is very simple: they simply had no one else for it at the time. And they thought that with my jet-black hair I would at least look right for the Italian *intriguante.* Little did I know that three other parts in this opera would become so identified with me: Sophie, Octavian, and the Marschallin. Annina is in and out of the opera all the time, but she does not sing really much. However, she has the short letter aria, 'Herr Kavalier! Den morgigen Abend hatt'i frei' [Honored gentleman! Tomorrow evening I am free], which is accompanied by the waltz theme, and a lot can be done with this scene. And I did.

"The notices were all excellent, and next came a bigger assignment: Mimi. Then—my goodness!—came the Queen of the Night—in the original key, for I started out with a remarkable agility. I never transposed one tone during my entire professional life, and I am rather proud of this when I see what goes on around me today. I had a four-year contract, so I went on to Gilda, Nedda, Antonia, Marie in *The Bartered Bride,* Butterfly, Cleopatra in *Giulio Cesare,* both Donna Elvira and Donna Anna, Pamina, Ariadne, and then two parts written for mezzo—Dorabella and Marguerite in *La Damnation de Faust.* I was even assigned 'Summertime' in a production of *Porgy and Bess,* and naturally I wore blackface.

"But the two parts that brought me into real prominence were Sophie and Zdenka. Maria Cebotari came as a guest to sing Arabella, and I was enthralled with her. She had a sort of gypsy-sounding voice, but very cultivated, and a timbre that once heard was never forgotten. The personality on the stage was there, but it was the instrument that counted. Although I believe she was Russian born, she had an Italian approach, full of warmth, and yet under perfect control. Before her untimely death, the Viennese loved her so much that she sang as much as five times a week, including Turandot and Salome, both far too heavy for her. Anyhow, she was impressed with my Zdenka, and when the Salzburg Festival organizers were looking for one, she very kindly suggested me. To my utter amazement I was contracted without an audition. Naturally, I assumed that Cebotari would be singing Arabella, and she did too. Instead, because of those hard-to-understand intrigues that go on in the operatic world, it was Maria Reining. She was good too, but in my opinion she could not compare to Cebotari. Hans Hotter was Mandryka and Karl Böhm was in the pit. I was a smash hit, and suddenly there was a contract from the Vienna Staatsoper. All the managers were after me too, and I had no idea there existed so many of them.

"I knew I would have to be more careful in Vienna than in Zurich, for the latter's opera house is small, and there I could sing the heavier roles without forcing. Essentially I was always a strong lyric, although in the latter years I did make a few tactful and careful excursions into the spinto wing. In Vienna I began with Nedda, then the same week I sang Butterfly and Mimi. But where I made my mark was with Gilda, as I had no trouble with the high E. I had returned to my dressing room, but the applause would not cease, and against all artistic standards I was made to go out and take a bow.

"I did not leave Zurich, however, for four more years; I kept commuting backward and forward. I never had the time to remain in Vienna half of the season, and singing eight times a month was necessary to receive a pension. I was soon made a Kammersängerin there, and also in Munich a short time later. In 1948 I was back at the Salzburg Festival to sing Marzelline in *Fidelio* with Furtwängler, who took a great fancy to me. Today conductors are far more interested in the way one looks than in what kind of a voice one has to offer. So if you are not strong willed, you are in trouble, and it is enough to take a brief look around and see what is happening. This sort of crazy attitude began slowly after the Second World War and now has become part of the madness. Karajan saw me as Marzelline and, if you can believe it, immediately asked me to sing in *Tannhäuser* with him. He told me I had just the right kind of sexiness to make a splendid goddess of love. 'But what about the voice?' I asked. 'We will manage,' he replied without any concern. Can you imagine my taking on Venus, which is sung by both dramatic sopranos and mezzos with an easy upper register? I had the good sense to refuse, but he held a grudge for some time. Eventually he got over it. I sang Marzelline and Sophie with him at La Scala in 1952, and those were the days! Mödl was the Leonore, Schwarzkopf the Marschallin, and Seefried the charming Octavian. Then, after many Beethoven Ninths and the Brahms Requiem, I appeared with him as the Marschallin for the opening of the Salzburg Festival in 1960.

"The heaviest role I undertook was Chrysothemis, and it was Mitropoulos who talked me into doing it with him in Salzburg. He was an irresistible human being, goodness personified, and I simply found myself saying yes against my better judgment. He was really a great symphonic conductor, whose love for opera came in a second phase of his career, and he knew little about the limitations of the human voice. I repeated it in Vienna and San Francisco—those damned contracts and engagements signed a long time in advance—but then abandoned the part, which I hated from the very first day. My instinct had been correct about it, for it is a killer, and the crazed sister and neurotic mother walk away with the honors.

"I sang with all the prominent conductors of my era: both Erich and Carlos Kleiber, Clemens Krauss, Fritz Busch, Ormandy, Solti, and Knappertsbusch, besides those already mentioned. It was the last with whom I sang Sophie in Zurich, and this led me to Eva in *Meistersinger* with him in 1952 at the Bayreuth Festival. I did not like the atmosphere of this Wagnerian temple, stuffy and pretentious. I would never return there. But Eva did stay in my repertoire all along, and Elsa too. At the Metropolitan I appeared in *Lohengrin* with Schippers conducting and Brian Sullivan in the lead. It is terrible to think that these young men are now both dead, one because of cancer and the other a suicide. During my first broadcast of Elsa at the Thirty-ninth Street house, I received in one of the intermissions a telegram from Lauritz Melchior, whom I had never met, and all it said was 'Elsa, I love you.' What a very charming thing to do!

"I have kept count of my roles, and the three I sang the most were Countess Almaviva, Donna Elvira, and Arabella, close to two hundred performances each. Then Ariadne, Fiordiligi, Pamina, and the Marschallin —well over one hundred; and the Countess in *Capriccio*—about seventy. I particularly loved her, for it is a wonderfully refined score, like a subtle game of chess. It is a much-underestimated work, but it must be performed in a small house or all the nuances are lost.

"Sophie—and this will surprise you—was by far my favorite in *Der Rosenkavalier*. It made me feel like a race horse who wants to come out of the stables. Its tessitura was perfect for me, but I gave it up in 1953, for they always wanted me for Octavian or the Marschallin. Sophie is usually played as an ingenue, but there is much more to her than meets the eye. The wonderful Hofmannsthal text reveals her strong character, her humor, and at the same time her romantic nature. She knows what she wants from the beginning. What could be more entrancing than Sophie's phrase in the scene of the *coup de foudre*, when she falls in love with Octavian, who has presented her with the silver rose scented with a drop of Persian attar, 'Ich möchte mich bei Ihm verstecken und nichts mehr wissen von der Welt' [I want to hide myself in you and know no more of this world]? And then later, when she is singing to herself, commenting on what has happened, 'Ich verspür' nichts von Angst, ich verspür' nichts von Schmerz, nur das Feuer seinen Blicks durch und durch, bis ins Herz' [I feel nothing of fear, I feel nothing of pain, only the fire of his glance through and through to my heart!]—if expressed with deep emotion, this passage can be memorable. Her willpower is fantastic, for, after all, we are in the eighteenth century, and young people obeyed their parents without any discussion. But she sings out 'Heirat' den Herrn dort nicht lebendig und nicht tot! Sperr' mich zuvor in meine Kammer ein' [Neither living nor dead will I marry that man! Before that I shall lock myself in my room]. And in the last act the extreme sensibility of this girl comes to the fore, and one phrase in particular in the trio is so very tender and full of understanding: 'Weiss gar nicht, wie mir ist! Möcht' all's verstehen und möcht' auch nichts verstehen; möcht fragen und nicht fragen, wird mir heiss und kalt' [I don't know what I feel! I want to understand everything and want also not to understand; I want to ask and not ask, I feel hot and cold].

"Don't even ask me how I managed not to get mixed up with these three roles, for these characters have duets, and trios too, together." She laughed. "It was like pulling down a Venetian blind every time. My first Octavian was unveiled at the Salzburg Festival, under Clemens Krauss, the greatest Strauss expert ever. His was a very special interpretation, light and elegant, and it never surprised me that Strauss preferred him to all other conductors. The Marschallin I sang only once, in Vienna, before playing the role at the Metropolitan. I certainly enjoyed singing Octavian far more than the Marschallin, for he made me feel young and impetuous, and it was a challenge every time to be a woman playing the part of a man who disguises himself as a female. The score lies pretty low, particularly in the first part of the second act, and one must be careful. The Marschallin, in my estimation, despite some lovely passages and an interesting characterization, is depressing, and—just between you and me—almost a bore.

"My fifteen seasons at the Metropolitan were not happy ones. I started there in 1953 as Countess Almaviva and finished there in the same part. There lay the trouble, for in all those years at the Met I was assigned only eleven roles, and among them Butterfly for two nights and Mimi for one. It was the same fare over and over again. Mr. Bing would not have it any other way, for he kept repeating that I was indispensable to the Mozart and Strauss operas and that he had a surplus of sopranos for the Italian and French ones. So out of 174 performances I sang with the company, there were 47 of the Countess, 34 of Donna Elvira, 4 of Elsa, 23 of Eva, 17 of the Marschallin, 9 of Octavian, 4 of Ariadne, and 16 of Arabella. There were also 17 Saffis in *Gypsy Baron,* a far from felicitous production, but rendered agreeable by the charming director, Cyril Ritchard—the only one I did not have maddening arguments with. I argued with them at first with politeness and then with vigor. In the end I won out, but how much time and energy was lost in the meantime! I admired Tebaldi no end, for she was always having problems with them too, and she knew what suited her, I can assure you, far better than they did. She managed with far more tact than I did, always smiled and came to apparent compromises. Then at the time of the performance she did exactly as she wished. But I did not leave the Metropolitan for these reasons. They were purely economical, the taxes becoming astronomical. And as you well know, our careers are not like those of doctors or engineers. One must make good while it is still possible, but the American Internal Revenue does not seem to understand this.

"The only stage directors I really respected were Rudolf Hartmann and Herbert Graf. They knew how to deal with personalities and did not try to annihilate them, which is the system today. I remember in Munich when I was having some difficulties with *Ariadne,* Hartmann was so sensible and sensitive. The heroine's problem is that she must sing with a lot of expression but move very little. He used to say, 'Do what you think is right. If you do too much, I will tell you, and if you do not do enough, I will warn you of that too.' In Vienna they were wonderful to me, for they needed me, but I have always been a realist. They never were in the least considerate. From Arabella to Pamina back to Arabella and again Pamina in the space of a few days—do you realize what this means? Pamina must be all smooth legato, a crystalline sound, and Arabella is all sensuousness and temperament."

Why is it, I asked her, that some sopranos can sing Mozart and Strauss equally well while others cannot?

"To be able to sing Mozart the way it is written, not only a very solid technique is needed with a very even connection between the notes, but lots of agility too—and I don't mean only in the upper register but in all three. Donna Anna has often been sung very successfully by non–Mozartians, which would suggest that it is not as exacting as the others, provided the voice has dramatic impact and nimbleness upstairs. Ponselle, Giannini, Milanov, Welitsch, and Nilsson all did very well by it. Nilsson also sang Elettra in *Idomeneo,* another role that has often been confronted by non–Mozart specialists. On the other hand we have had such big names as Jeritza, Lotte Lehmann, and Rysanek who were not Mozartians but leading Strauss interpreters. The fact is that Strauss has many more patterns than Mozart, for his operas vary a lot in the scoring and the vocal demands. No fabulous technique is needed. A special instrument with a cutting edge in the throat is a prime necessity for *Elektra, Salome,* and *Die Frau ohne Schatten.* Octavian, the Marschallin, and the Composer do not present real problems, for they are all written very much in the middle of the voice. But when you come to Ariadne herself, Arabella and her sister, Zdenka, Aithra in *Die ägyptische Helena,* the Countess in *Capriccio,* or Sophie, an incandescent top is needed, and if you don't have it, you might as well forget them. Ursuleac, Grümmer, and Watson were three sopranos who could handle Mozart and Strauss with equal skill, because they were equipped with a superb technique and an enviable upper register. I was fortunate enough to be able to join them. Schwarzkopf, who was a real Mozartian, sang only the Marschallin and the Countess in *Capriccio,* which is written for a small orchestra. She recorded Ariadne but never sang the role onstage. In her early years she sang Zerbinetta, but that is a pure coloratura assignment, along with Fiakermilli; and, in fact, most sopranos with a fabulous agility can undertake both Zerbinetta and the Queen of the Night. I hope I have answered your difficult question!

"To return to the Vienna Staatsoper, it has always been—far more than Munich—a hotbed of intrigue. On the surface all is sweetness and light, but underneath there are many strange currents. I always kept away from them, for I knew that I had the best ally in the world: the public. Looking back, I wonder whether I did not commit a mistake in not canceling many engagements and following the wish of de Sabata, Ghiringhelli, and Graf, who wanted me to study *La traviata* and sing it at La Scala. I was there at the time for Beethoven's Ninth Symphony under de Sabata, and the offer was made in no uncertain terms. It was all very tempting, but I had so many signed contracts. They offered me Desdemona too; and, as so often happens, the opportunity never presented itself again. How to handle, dispose, save the voice—how to keep the top—all this was my anxiety from beginning to end. Every day I studied and tried to improve.

"I am happy that I came at the end of an era when there were still artists and personalities," she said plaintively. "There is no more authority or order. No one comes to the rehearsals. In my contracts I always demanded a full rehearsal, and in the last years no one turned up. I recall Karl Ridderbusch, singing his first Baron Ochs, having the impudence of going on without the benefit of a single rehearsal. He never said 'Good evening' or 'Good night.' Marvelous manners, *wirklich?*

"I sang in all the important opera houses: Covent Garden, the Paris Opéra, the Colón in Buenos Aires, and many others. I made many recordings, and two films—a *Don Giovanni* with Furtwängler and the incomparable Siepi as the Don, and then *Faust* with Gedda and, again, Siepi. The recording of *Orfeo,* with Stevens and Peters in the cast, was a delightful experience, for Pierre Monteux conducted, and he was an adorable old gentleman. I loved the role of Euridice, but it rarely came my way. I did a great deal of concertizing too, and Strauss's Four Last Songs are what I performed the most often; I sang them on all my appearances in Australia and Japan. Somehow I never got tired of them, for they have for me a sort of irresistible sorcery. They hold all the melancholy of a world that we are losing, and which perhaps is already lost.

"Everyone was most surprised when in 1961 I took on Salome in Munich under the powerful baton of Böhm. People believed it would prove too heavy for me, and many colleagues predicted that this would be my downfall. Actually, although the scoring for Donna Elvira is far less forceful, I found her far more tiring than the crazy princess, for Elvira's music lies very low, practically in the cellar. I was concertizing in Florida when a cable arrived from Munich begging me to replace Rysanek, who had canceled. I slept on it, and—to my husband's astonishment—next morning I sent back my acceptance. I made this wild decision without even looking at the score, and I must confess that it is the only part that got *me*. Usually it was the other way around: I got them. I did not think of Salome as a monster but as a very spoiled girl. After all, beheading in those days was quite normal, *wirklich*?

"Anyhow, it was a great hit, and even Rysanek and Leontyne Price were kind enough to come backstage and congratulate me. I had wanted to appear as Salome ever since I was eight, when my father had taken me to hear it in Bern. So in many ways it was a child's fantasy come true. My husband felt that my voice was too clear for it, but he had to admit that I was marvelously sexy in it. The trouble was that after my initial success, all the opera houses were after me to sing it, and this, of course, I realized was impossible. I did not want to wind up like that highly talented Bulgarian who had ruined her voice because she sang it too much. And so after two seasons, my vanity having been satisfied, I never went near it again. Now there are mezzos singing it too, so undoubtedly some brilliant metteur-en-scène will get the idea of casting a tenor in the part. Anything can happen now. In fact lyric theatres are so greedy today that immediately after my much publicized and applauded Salome, the Bavarian State Opera immediately wanted to cast me as the Empress in *Die Frau ohne Schatten*. That really would have been the mistake of all time. But you see what I mean? They simply don't care anymore. Squeeze the juice and then throw away the orange.

"The strange thing about a singer's destiny," she stated with infinite sadness, "is that you have to renounce everything for its sake, and then it's all over in a flash. One must then learn to dig into oneself and bring out the I, which for years has consisted of so many other, different persons." She pointed to the window; it was snowing outside. "The imprint we leave is like the snow you see falling this afternoon. Tomorrow it will be gone, and there will be nothing. Yes, a few people will remember, but only for a very short time."

THE GREAT INTERPRETERS OF VERISMO AND REALISMO

AUGUSTA OLTRABELLA

MARIA CARBONE

IRIS ADAMI CORRADETTI

The three sopranos whose conversations follow played a definitive part in the history not only of the verismo operas but also of those known as realismo—composers such as Malipiero, Lattuada, Lualdi, Petrassi, Pick-Mangiagalli, Allegra, and many others. Oltrabella's career was the longest —forty-four years; in fact, she saw all the others come and go. Carbone's endured a little more, and Adami Corradetti's a little less, than two decades, but both have become celebrated teachers. All were indefatigable, and their curricula vitae make one's head swim.

Oltrabella had one of those rare voices that could cope successfully with anything and everything; and as one reads the programs of La Scala, the Rome Opera, and the Comunale in Florence over several decades, one is staggered by the number of new operas she created. Tiny of stature, thin as a rail, with a most expressive face à la Giotto, she is intelligence personified. She was always good humored, disciplined, ready and eager for anything. At eighty, she looked forty. Her fame rests on her versatility and on her Suor Angelica, which everyone tells me was one of the most moving performances of that role.

Carbone and Adami Corradetti were almost contemporaries, but the latter's climb to fame was much slower. They were, like Oltrabella, known as great singing actresses and champions of new scores. Carbone started at the top and ended at the height of her fame, a prodigiously active woman, a forceful and intrepid spirit with a strong personality and the courage of her own convictions. Adami Corradetti, charming and feminine, very much a noble woman in looks and bearing, emerged from comprimario roles, like Simionato, with great determination and became the most admired Madama Butterfly and (after dalla Rizza's retirement) Francesca da Rimini in Italy.

AUGUSTA OLTRABELLA

Everyone who knew and had followed the long career of Augusta Oltrabella (her name means "more than beautiful") had told me she was one of
a kind, unique as both a singer and a human being. She was born in 1898,
and her career stretched from 1919 to 1963. When I met her she was already
past eighty, but physically and mentally she is ageless. I had heard her only
once, as Nannetta in *Falstaff* at the Salzburg Festival under Toscanini in the
mid-thirties, but she looked very much the same as I remembered her: small,
agile, thin, vibrant, with a long, narrow, expressive face and a lightning-
quick pair of eyes.

Oltrabella's repertoire was so enormous that it boggled my mind that she
was able to retain even a fraction of it. But she explained that her greatest
fortune had been to be born with a photographic memory; once she had read
a score, it remained impressed in her mind in every detail. As we talked,
she seemed to make the past come alive as she played her slightly uncanny
memory like a master organist playing a Bach fugue.

"I am sorry to receive you in a flat already packed up for the summer,"
she said, asking me to sit down on her Belle Epoque settee. "But my
husband, Dr. Paolo Asti, and I are off to our small house in San Remo. He
is eighty-seven, you know, and a real saint—imagine putting up with me
for almost fifty years! But you are in a hurry, I know; everyone is in a hurry
today. Life does slip by fast, but is it really necessary to rush so? Every day
can be our last, so what is the point? So I shall tell you, in disorderly fashion,
as fast as I can, what I remember that might interest you about Oltrabella.
(No one ever called me Augusta, you know, and probably the reason is that
my surname is amusing, particularly since I was never beautiful.)

"I was born in Savona, the town now made famous by Renata Scotto.
Have you heard her screaming in the new recording of *Nabucco*? She finds
people who pay her to scream, so she had better pocket the money quickly
while she can. In a singer's life tomorrow is not another day.

"Anyhow, I was born under the sign of Capricorn, and I don't need to

343

Augusta Oltrabella in the title role of *Suor Angelica*.

tell you how vigorous people born under this sign are. I was born impatient and strong willed. It is not only faith that can move mountains—will can too. I knew, ever since I can recall, that I wanted to be a singer, and my family had to learn to live with a stubborn child. At sixteen I knocked at the door of the conservatory in Milan, and they had the nerve to turn me down because I had not reached the proper age. So I went to a woman teacher—let her remain without a name, she is resting in the cemetery, she meant no harm—and instinctively I knew I was in the wrong hands. She kept telling me to sing *nella testa*—in the head—and did not seem interested in the rest of my vocal cords.

"Being very fresh, I pushed my way into the dressing room of Pertile, considered at that time the finest tenor of all, told him of my predicament, and asked for his advice. He had just come back from being beheaded in *Andrea Chenier* and was so helpful. For he suggested I go to Maestro Manlio Bavagnoli, the father of the famous conductor, and this was my salvation. This man had an extraordinary knack with voices and immediately discovered that I could go from a low A to a high D. I continued to go to him until he died, long after I had begun professionally, and he kept telling me that he had never encountered a voice quite like mine. As events were to prove, he was right. Despite the many impossible scores I sang, the resilience never failed, and the upper register remained intact. Among his pupils were Lina Bruna Rasa, the greatest Santuzza and Maddalena ever, and Lina Pagliughi, who—no one will ever believe this—was as thin as a rail when she arrived from the United States.

"Bavagnoli immediately recognized me as a spinto, but for four years he made me sing mainly lyric scores. Suddenly the chance came to make my debut as Leonora in *Il trovatore* in 1919, and as the theatre in Mondovì was small, he agreed. It was a trial balloon, but I never went near this part again, for I did not have a gorgeous enough voice for that branch of the Verdi repertoire, particularly since there were some really splendid voices then. I had to find my own way, and did. With several exceptions, I went on to verismo operas, which suited my temperament, and the strong edge in my voice could cut through any orchestra.

"Those first few years I received all my invaluable experience in provincial theatres. The rumor got around that I could sing everything, which was absolutely true, and I therefore became much in demand. I recall I was to appear in Venice in the same week as Margherita in *Mefistofele* and as Butterfly. That seemed plenty. The management came to me in despair, for the artist engaged for Elena in the Boito opera and Marina in *Boris* had been objected to by the conductor, and if I helped them out, they would give me the moon for the next season. Despite the fact that there were only two days before *Mefistofele* and four before *Boris,* I accepted—not because of the moon, but simply because I adored this type of challenge. And how could I resist taking on Elena, the most beautiful woman in the world, along with Margherita on the same evening? Only the outstanding prima donnas took on this double assignment. And Marina too was pretty irresistible, with her ambition to become tsarina of Russia. With my electric memory I stepped in, and for a long time no one knew of my tour de force, for naturally, out of consideration for the other soprano, it was announced that she was ill. But in operatic circles there is a lot of gossip, and the word was spread that Oltrabella was very valuable to have around.

"Much the same happened both in Lisbon and with a company with which I toured Brazil. Two sopranos canceled at the last minute, and I was singing everything, including Gilda in *Rigoletto* and Gomes's lovely opera *Guarany,* two scores I had never laid eyes upon before. Then in 1929 Gatti-Casazza engaged me for the Metropolitan, and I was given a contract for a year, with an option for two more if I made good. I only sang three Puccini roles, and the option was picked up immediately. But I was not happy there. It was all very casual, probably because my engagement was by the week. So one never knew what was in store. There were too many sopranos—Bori, the very fat Frances Alda, Easton, Moore, Queena Mario, and several others, all singing my parts. No rehearsals—one just jumped in. I did not come there as a star—in fact, I was not one at that time—and that may have also had something to do with it. It was a positive experience, however, for it gave me the chance to sing with major artists and to see how haphazardly this great theatre worked.

"When I returned to Italy, La Scala, which had until then ignored me —in those days they usually took their time accepting newcomers—came forward and offered me a rather spectacular debut as the Goose Girl in Humperdinck's *Königskinder.* It had not been on the boards since 1911, three decades exactly, when it had its premiere with Bori in the lead. Maestro Ghione thought I was perfect for the role, because of my size and my type of voice, which had just the right kind of incisiveness to cut through the forceful Wagnerian orchestration. At that time I also became engaged to Dr. Asti. So when Gatti-Casazza came to spend the summer in Europe, I went to see him and begged him to let me out of the Metropolitan contract, explaining the circumstances. The Metropolitan meant six months away from home, and what kind of marriage would that turn out to be? Also,

I told him that La Scala for me meant everything. He was most understanding and agreed. Anyhow, the Depression was on in full force, and I was one fewer person to be paid. Did I make a terrible mistake? I don't think so. Certainly, the United States would never have given me the absolutely incredible number of opportunities I had in Italy from then on.

"My success as the Goose Girl established me at La Scala, and the variety of roles was glorious. Suddenly in 1935 there was a telephone call from Toscanini, announcing that he wanted to hear me the following day in Nannetta's aria and the duet with Fenton from *Falstaff* at his home in the Via Durini. Just like that. I had never sung Nannetta, but I knew it incidentally, having already sung Alice many times, even during the last appearances of the fabulous Domenico Viglione Borghese. I stayed up that night and learned what had been requested, wondering what it could all be about. As you know, Nannetta is really for a light lyric, and what could the maestro want? But I went and did my audition, and all he said was 'Yes, that is the way I want it to sound. You will sing it with me at the Salzburg Festival.' 'But, Maestro, allow me to ask you a question. How did you even know of my existence, since you left for the United States before I came to La Scala?' 'First of all, Gatti-Casazza had told me about you, and the name stuck in my mind. How can one forget a name like Oltrabella? Then, the other night I listened to the radio when they performed *Jenůfa*, and the way you sang that prayer told me you would be just what I was looking for. I don't like a light Nannetta. I want one whose voice has a body and yet still can negotiate the agilities of the final aria. Do you know it is one of the most difficult Verdi ever wrote?' No, I did not, not having sung much Verdi. 'Well, it is,' he replied, 'not only because of the way it is written, but because it is atmospheric. It must smell of lilies and violets. You sang it with the right instinct—just study the words very carefully, for it is all a hymn to poetry and nature. And remember—I want the last phrase, 'Le fate hanno per cifre i fior' [Fairies have flowers for signatures] very, very ethereal, but every word must come out way in front.' And then, as I left, he added, 'Tell your coach I want more metronome in the approach.'

"That was my strange introduction to Toscanini, and I sang this part with him in Salzburg in 1936 and 1937. He rehired me for 1938 and 1939, but then the Anschluss came, and he refused to set foot in Austria. But I had a binding contract and went back. In 1938, however, Gui insisted I go back to Alice, while in 1939 Serafin gave me Nannetta again. From then on I continually alternated in these two roles. At La Scala I sang only Alice, but in Rome in two different seasons I went from one to the other—a far more difficult job than one might think, for they sing together a lot, but the mood, the expression, the approach are completely different.

"It was in 1935 that I sang for the first time at La Scala *Suor Angelica*, an opera I had already sung in other theatres. I was 'Pucciniana' all the way —I sang in all of his works—but for some reason this one-act opera became my glory. That first night in Milan, a frightening silence followed the bringing down of the curtain. I was utterly destroyed, as I always was when I played this role, but not enough not to ask myself what had gone wrong and why there was no applause. Then, suddenly, the biggest roar I have ever heard exploded, and when I came out to take my bow, it was a different kind of ovation from any I had received in the past. There was not a dry-eyed person in the audience, and, as if it had all been organized before-hand, they all began waving their handkerchiefs. I began to cry so much there was no stopping me. This was the first revival of *Il trittico* at La Scala since its premiere there in 1918. The amazing Elvira Casazza, who sang La Zia Principessa, had also appeared in the original production, and she told me there had been much applause the night of the premiere, but nothing comparable.

"If you will allow me, I would like to speak a little about this opera, so unjustly neglected, which La Scala revived for me for four different seasons. And the same sort of demonstration took place each time. Oltrabella and Suor Angelica became as one. I take no credit for this enthusiasm; it is the work that deserves it. But what I did—and, unfortunately, so many colleagues did not—was to understand the tremendous, overwhelming mys-ticism of this hapless nun and give it life. She is a simple soul, overcome by her cruel fate, unable to cope with the dramatic events of her cloistered life. Her love for her child—who was dragged away from her and whom she had seen and kissed only once—and her love for God become hopelessly entangled, and the strain is too much. The crescendo of her emotions and, in a sense, momentary derangement must be a mixture of hysteria and purity, and, vocally, these two phases must be indissoluble. From 'La grazia è discesa dal cielo, già tutta, già tutta m'accende' [Grace has descended from heaven, already, already it sets me aflame]—how very significant that repetition 'già tutta, già tutta' is, for it is the key to what comes later—onward to 'Ah! Son dannata' [I am damned] and 'Ho smarrita la ragione! . . . Non mi fare morire in dannazione . . . ' [I have lost my reason! . . . Do not make me die damned . . .], it must be a mixture of despair and helplessness, not shouted, but sung. Now they all scream it. It is in some ways like 'Vissi d'arte'—she is talking to herself and to God. The difficulty is to combine an intimate tragedy with a universal one. The Forzano text is absolutely superb, and the final scene of the miracle, when Angelica's suicide is forgiven, must be, and can be if properly handled, shattering. But if the interpreter does not feel this girl's tragedy deeply, it is no good. It becomes just a show of vocal histrionics. I was able to prove in Milan, and in ever so many other theatres, that *Suor Angelica* is a masterpiece. A great help for me was the fact that I am so small and looked young.

"It was because of the mystical side of my nature that Refice—in my estimation a very great composer—gave me the creation of his *Santa Margherita di Cortona* in Rome in 1939 and then in 1942 the revival of *Cecilia,* which he had written for Muzio, who has left us some unforgettable recordings of the two big scenes. It took courage to undertake this opera, for the memory of the divine Claudia was still very much present, but I gave my own individual interpretation."

And then, suddenly changing her mood completely, she went to a drawer and pulled out some photographs, which she handed over to me.

"These are to prove to you the esteem that surrounded me, and of which I am very proud. Look at this one. It is from old Charpentier, who heard my Louise on the radio. How kind of him to take the trouble to send this to an unknown!" The dedication read (I am translating from the French), "To a splendid Louise with my total and respectful admiration." Then she handed me one from Giordano (again I translate, from the Italian): "To Oltrabella, twice more than beautiful, for the perfect interpretation she gives to all my operas." There were so many that I could not possibly quote them all; but the one from Mascagni—known to be tough and not inclined to praise—struck me: "To the splendid Oltrabella, in memory of her magnificent—ideal really—interpretation of Maria in my *Guglielmo Ratcliff.*" Every composer of the period had written enthusiastically to her. Mario Peragallo, whose *Ginevra degli almieri* she had created in Rome in 1937 under Serafin's direction, declared that the splendid welcome his opera had received was entirely her doing.

"The most beautiful opera I created, out of several dozens," she said with some satisfaction, "was Rocca's *Dibuk,* first at La Scala in 1934 and then all over Italy. It is fascinating from every point of view, musically and dramatically. The role of Leah is tremendous, for she becomes possessed by the spirit of her dead fiancé and must be exorcised by the Torah. I had to utter some agonizing screams, and the public ate them up every time. But the composer did not and accused me of stealing the show from him. 'How would you feel if you had written a great score,' he asked me furiously, 'and the critics spent all their time raving over a singer's performance? My music is completely forgotten.'

"The most terrifying opera was Ghedini's *Le baccanti*." She laughed slyly. "I was not keen to take it on, but every soprano in Italy had turned it down. Knowing Ghedini's music, I had refused without asking to read the score. But when they came to me a second time in despair, I told them to go ahead and send me the score. I simply could not believe what I saw: there were high Ds jumping all over the pages. As I adored challenges on that level, I accepted. Oltrabella would show them—the world premiere was on February 21, 1948, a date I shall never forget—that with twenty-nine years of career behind her, she could still manage the upper regions with honor. Everyone was amazed, but I knew what I was doing. One critic called me 'the best mountain climber in the world.' What is the matter with these contemporary composers? What do they think vocal cords are made of?

"With so many years of professional life," she said with a smile, her eyes gleaming, "I was mixed up with various generations of singers, and I watched the old guard go, the second one come in and also disappear, and then the third one, which is already in deep trouble. I was ordered by the government, during the last war, to go to Athens, at the time occupied by the Italians, to sing a series of performances of *Adriana Lecouvreur* and a mass of recitals. Elvira de Hidalgo rang me up—she was teaching at the conservatory in the Greek capital at that time—wanting to see me. She came to my hotel and begged me to give the opportunity to a pupil of hers to sing a group in my concerts. Naturally, despite all my respect for Elvira, whom I knew well since our appearances together in Lisbon, I asked to hear the girl, and to my amazement, an enormous whale of flesh arrived, charmless, terribly nearsighted, looking desperately poor, with torn shoes. She revealed a stunning coloratura, and I was happy to have her share my programs. It was Maria Callas. Why oh why did she not stick to the coloratura repertoire? In that she was truly sensational, but the rest of the voice was simply manufactured.

"I sang the Marschallin in Trieste to Simionato's first Octavian, and I shall always recall my astonishment when she told me that she had been hanging around for almost fifteen years doing secondary roles. For this was one of her first big assignments, and the voice, personality, and musicianship of this mezzo were so extraordinary that I simply could not understand the blindness of the people in the métier. Thank goodness, she then came forward in the most spectacular manner, and deservedly so.

"Of Strauss I also undertook Salome at La Scala, with the ghosts of Giulia

Tess and Florica Cristoforeanu in the wings, who had been so exceptional in this part. It was during the war and the bombs were flying around. We rehearsed with Marinuzzi in a bomb shelter, and one afternoon I went home to find that my entire building had been completely destroyed. Thank God, my husband was at his office, and when we met on the street, we were confronted only with ashes. We were left without even a handkerchief. But the show must go on, and it did. A few weeks later I was to sing *Suor Angelica* with Marinuzzi for the last time. In August of that terrible year, 1945, he was killed in an uprising, and one of the great lights of the operatic world went out. I was shattered by his useless death, and ever so grateful that I had learned the role of Salome with him. I became quite fond of the bitch, and sang her a short time later at the Rome Opera with Santini, who gave a completely different reading of this masterpiece.

"One of the operas I was called upon to sing most often was *La traviata*, for many conductors resented—and I don't understand why—having to transpose the first act, and with me this was not necessary. I remember so well a series of performances of this opera at La Scala in 1938, again with Marinuzzi, when Caniglia and I shared Violetta. She sang it down a tone, like Tebaldi and so many others, and I as written. The orchestra went absolutely crazy with this constant changing. I have never been against transposing, for I think it is perfectly useless to sit there and suffer with singers who simply have to battle with certain notes. In my case it was different. My top remained unimpaired, despite all the modern works that were thrown at me, and I believe the reason is that Bavagnoli taught me a form of support in the lower and middle registers, which were like steel. One must know how to make the best of what has been given one. Cobelli, the most superb of all the artists I heard, had a sumptuous voice, the warmest timbre I can recall, with a splendid B-flat. But there it stopped. The C never came, despite every effort on her part. She was exceedingly intelligent and learned to live with it. And it could not have mattered less, for she never went near the roles that demanded it. The only time I had to sing *Traviata* transposed was in Parma, when Votto was conducting, and this time because of the tenor, who simply could not manage. He begged me, and after consulting with the maestro I agreed. But it is not as easy as it seems when you have another sound in your throat.

"Among the operas I was called upon to perform most often were *Tosca* and *Manon Lescaut*—many times with both Gigli and, later, del Monaco—and *Butterfly*. *Adriana*, which I also sang at La Scala and everywhere really, has a strange score, for the protagonist can be sung by any type of soprano since much of it lies in the middle, but gratefully. At La Scala there were Cobelli, a dramatic and in my opinion the greatest; Caniglia, Tebaldi, and myself, all spintos; Favero, a lyric; and then Clara Petrella and Olivero, whose range is hard to define. Magda, who is in her late sixties, sings the role still, and it has always been an attractive role which everyone wants. Before us the great ones had been Ersilde Cervi Cairoli and Carmen Melis. Cilea's orchestration is not too heavy, as he wanted the opera to have an eighteenth-century flavor to accompany the action. There seem to be no singing actresses left, with the exception of Raina Kabaivanska, who interprets the characters and, understandably, in the current desert, is much admired. Of the verismo operas—I became a specialist in verismo—those I favored were *Francesca da Rimini,* Alfano's *Risurrezione,* Giordano's inexplicably forgotten *Mese Mariano* (one of my most treasured successes at La Scala), along with his *Fedora* and *Chenier,* and also Mascagni's *Iris.* I sang them all at one time or another. And when Maria Labia and Giulia Tess retired, I took over the part of Felicia, in which they both had been incomparable, in Wolf-Ferrari's *I quattro rusteghi,* and when Saraceni stopped, I sang the title part in his adorable *La vedova scaltra."*

I interrupted her—it was not easy—and asked her whether she considered Wolf-Ferrari a *verista.*

"But naturally!" she replied, surprised at my question. "What is more *verista* than Goldoni, and most of the works of this delicious Venetian composer are based on Goldoni's plays. After all, as you well know, verismo is based on everyday life—the emotions or the problems of real people— and Goldoni revolutionized the legitimate stage, for he was the first to depict the Venetians of everyday life. Wolf-Ferrari is most definitely *verista.* Even *Il segreto di Susanna,* which I also sang at La Scala way back in 1934, is *verista.* It is a story of everyday life.

"I sang many Carmens too, in the second part of my career—before, I used to be Micaëla—and that is a different type of verismo. Toward the end, I undertook many Santuzzas too. But the great fun came in the last years: I went from the Countess in *The Queen of Spades* to Menotti's *The Medium* and *The Old Maid and the Thief* and de Banfield's *Colloquio col tango* and *Lord Byron's Love Letters.* My last performance was in Cremona in *La guerra,* an effective opera by Rossellini.

"But I never should have stopped. Look at Magda. I was loved too, you know; she is not the only one! I have more to tell you, but you are in a hurry. Goodbye."

Alas, I never saw her again. She passed away in the late spring of 1981.

MARIA CARBONE

Maria Carbone's activity as a voice teacher is simply prodigious, and obtaining an appointment with her was difficult, not because of unwillingness on her part, but simply because of the infernal schedule she faces daily. One of the most dynamic spinto sopranos of this century, she sang 176 operas during her twenty-three-year career, which began in 1930 at the San Carlo in Naples with Margherita in *Mefistofele* and ended in 1953. She became an essential part of the Italian lyric theatre.

"I am more than willing," she recalled in her small, crowded ground-floor apartment in Milan on a hot Saturday afternoon in July 1979, "to admit that I took on too much. But when I withdrew, it was not only because I was exhausted, but because since 1950 I had been teaching, and it was impossible to continue doing both. Already I was very much aware of what was happening to my beloved profession, and I decided that teaching was more important. I had accomplished for myself far more than I had anticipated when I began.

"It was Franco Alfano, who was then head of the conservatory in Pesaro, who talked me into holding classes there. He was a delightful man and, as you know, a great friend of Puccini. It was he who completed *Turandot*, and I sang all his works. Our deep friendship originated casually, simply because he admired how I performed his works. He always used to say that I gave another dimension to his feminine characters, and he felt I was the right person to support him in his effort to keep the Italian singing tradition going. Alas, most of it turned out to be in vain. I was born to be a teacher, and despite the fact that it has become a veritable nightmare, I am a fighter, and the more horrendous it gets, the fiercer the contest.

"I feel at times like a doctor must feel when he has saved a life. When I have managed to mend a voice, even if only temporarily, I am jubilant. I suppose I was also born with the inability to say no, and this is why, despite the wear and tear of the war years, I accepted the most incredible tasks, determined to get the better of them. And I did! The reason I was able to

Maria Carbone as Minnie in *La fanciulla del West*.

accomplish so much was the superb technical foundation that Agostino Roche gave me. He was also the teacher of Stignani and Caniglia. To satisfy my parents, I studied medicine for three years, for they were at first absolutely set against my going onto the operatic stage. (My father was the director of the naval stockyard at Castellamare di Stabia, just outside Naples.)

"I auditioned for Maestro Edoardo Vitale, then the music director of the San Carlo, who had conducted *La vestale* and the first Italian *Medea* for Mazzoleni at La Scala. He immediately gave me a contract to appear in *Mefistofele*. I signed it and then faced the family. I never returned to the university, and immediately my career took flight. Vitale liked me sufficiently to hand over to me in rapid succession Mimi, Micaëla, and Liù. Although I was a spinto, Roche felt it was wiser for me to begin with lyric parts. Then Vitale convinced me to appear as Romeo in Bellini's *I Capuleti ed i Montecchi,* a role that is written for mezzo, but he felt that the color of my voice, always on the darkish side, was right for it, and at that time my figure was right too. Heavenly music, but the classical repertoire did not suit my temperament. That is why I ended up as a *verista.*

"Conductors soon realized that, like Oltrabella, I had a photographic memory and was a very quick learner. I could even remember where a page of a score turned. If I went more and more into verismo and postverismo, it was because I was a serious student and knew how to phrase effectively. My Tosca, for instance, was always natural, the way Puccini wanted it. When she sings parlando 'Quanto? . . . Il prezzo!' [How much? . . . The price!] I did not yell it out the way most of them do; I delivered it with a voice trembling with emotion, but contained. 'E avanti a lui tremava tutta Roma' [And before him all Rome trembled] is a phrase Tosca mutters to herself; she is alone in his study—she must not scream it out to the public. In that manner it is *vero*—this is where verismo comes in. When you have killed a man, you don't cry out loudly for everyone to hear you. After all, he was the head of the Roman police; there are men in his antechamber. When Mimi appears in the last act of *Bohème,* fatigued from coming up the stairs to the garret, out of breath and close to death, I used the parlando so clearly indicated in the score, which is what a person in the last stages of consumption would do. And the commotion of the audience was because I brought *verità* to those touching phrases. The 'Sono andati' [They have gone] must be like a whisper—very difficult to do, because the public must hear you.

"I recall that in *Iris* when I sang that beautiful phrase 'In paradiso non si piange, ed io di lacrime ho pieni gli occhi' [In paradise one does not weep, and I have eyes full of tears]—it is all very central, no high notes— invariably the public burst into applause. My colleagues wondered why. It was because the audience could hear every word I uttered, and I was capable of projecting the deep perturbation that seized me every time. I sang this Mascagni opera on two different occasions at La Scala with Maestro Guarnieri, who after the first dress rehearsal came to my dressing room and in his very quiet way just said, 'You have understood the character. Very few do.' Coming from him, that meant a great deal. But again, the way I said it was an intimate revelation to myself, which I was fortunate enough to communicate to others. It rang true—a very simple secret.

"What I cannot tolerate today," she affirmed almost angrily, "is that in all opera houses the recitatives are all executed in exactly the same manner. But *Dio mio!* how can all these conductors be so ignorant? Why don't they take time out to study, the way we all did? I learned, in my intensive musical training, that in Monteverdi's works the recitative is declaimed; in Pergolesi, Paisiello, and Rossini it must be secco; in Bellini and Donizetti it is cantabile; and then in Verdi it is always dramatic, like the stunning 'È tardi, è tardi' in *La traviata*. And then there are many more types which I will not bore you with.

"As for stage directors, with the exception of Zeffirelli, Wallmann, and very few others, they have drained all personality from the singer. My first lamentable experience in this area came at La Fenice in Venice when I was to sing the Marschallin, with Pederzini as Octavian, and the famous Lothar Wallerstein was the régisseur. He had directed something like sixty operas in Vienna, and I cannot recall how many at the Salzburg Festival, and so I was looking forward to learning a lot from him. But at the very first rehearsal he began putting numbers in chalk around the stage. When you utter this sentence, he told me, you must be on number 10; when you say that, you are on number 15; and so forth. I let him go on until he had finished with his numbers, and then very calmly I said to him, 'Either you rub out all those numbers or Carbone does not sing the Marschallin. Find yourself a number-minded soprano. I happen to be a singer and not a numerologist. Perhaps they exist in Austria, but I think it will be difficult to find one in this country!' Other members of the cast applauded my remarks, and I won the battle. But today? No one dares to stand up to them, and the public often blames the singer for some idiotic thing he is made to do, not realizing that the responsibility lies elsewhere.

"To give you an idea of how my memory never faltered," she said, departing from a subject that I could see made her more and more indignant, "on one occasion I was singing the lovely role of Mariola in *Fra Gherardo* by Pizzetti and conducted by the composer, whose operas were all thrown at me in succession—*Debora e Jaele, Lo straniero, Fedra,* et cetera. After the leading lady is stabbed, she has a touching phrase, 'Per esserti più vicina nell'ora del supplizio' [To be closer to you in the hour of judgment]. After 'Per esserti' there is a big chord struck in the pit. I began and then stopped, waiting for the chord. It never came, despite my looking straight into Pizzetti's eyes, so then I went on. It was a matter of a few seconds, but the effect was ruined. Pizzetti came to my dressing room afterward and said, 'From an artist like you, Maria, I would not have expected such inattention.' I did not answer him, but took out the score, opened it at the right page, and without saying a thing I pointed out the passage in question. 'Do forgive me, please; it is inexcusable on my part,' he said plaintively. 'It is all right, Maestro—no harm done. It is your opera, you know!' And with this I gave him my most ravishing smile.

"But Mascagni was as great a conductor as Pizzetti was poor. Although his tempos slowed down increasingly with the years, he was with it every moment. I recall Gigli, during one of the intermissions of *Isabeau,* in which we were appearing together, coming to me, sitting down, and murmuring, 'That man will be the death of me!' I got to know Mascagni's operas intimately, for I sang them all; from *Lodoletta* (a trifle light for my voice) to Mariella in *Il piccolo Marat;* from *Pinotta,* which Favero created in San Remo, to *Le maschere,* a delightful and enchanting work that is bound to make a comeback; from the title trouser role of *Silvano* to *Guglielmo Ratcliff* and on to the really heavy ones, *Cavalleria* and *Parisina. Isabeau* is really for a dramatic soprano, but I found it quite congenial. It is an odd work, really for an arena sort of public, but immensely theatrical, and audiences loved it. Illica could not write a bad libretto if he tried, and the tragic version of the Lady Godiva story has some very effective moments. The problem was that she was supposed to be the most beautiful princess in the world, but I would not allow this to give me complexes! Mascagni's genius is that he never repeated himself. Every one of his operas has a different twist. And with what facility he wrote for the voice! *Iris,* which is coming back these days in many theatres, has one of the most lovely scores, with a true feeling for the Orient—one almost smells it—verismo again! Mascagni is *verista* all the way. Although the subject of *Iris* is not completely *verista* (the supernatural dominates the last act), the music is. *Lodoletta,* based on Ouida's novel *Two Little Wooden Shoes,* is romantic, but it deals with real human beings. It is a lovely part, as is Suzel in *L'amico Fritz*, which is so *verista* that it ends happily with the steward's daughter getting married.

"You want to know about my repertory, but I will wear you out"— she laughed—"and myself as well. Though it is absolutely true that I made my reputation as a *verista*, I sang some classical roles too. I was often given Donna Anna, the Countess in *Le nozze di Figaro* (one series at La Scala will be remembered for a long time; it had Marinuzzi conducting, Favero as Susanna, Simionato as Cherubino, Stabile as Figaro, and Pasero as the Count), and then Idamante in *Idomeneo*. Of the latter I remember a memorable production conducted by Gui at the Fenice in Venice. Many of the Wagnerian ladies came my way: Elisabeth, Elsa, Sieglinde, and—please believe it!—Isolde under Giulini's baton. He was a marvelous conductor even in the early days, and he gave a wonderfully lyrical and poetic reading of this masterpiece. Busoni's *Turandot*, idolized in Germany and ignored in Italy, finally appeared and was assigned to me, first in Florence and then in Rome and other cities. It is the opposite of Puccini's version (Busoni had premiered his in 1917), for it lies very much in the middle of the voice, with sudden high notes for which there is no buildup.

"One of the most harrowing experiences I had was when I was sitting at home one night, having just finished dinner, and I received a telephone call from La Scala to rush over as fast as possible, for Favero, who had started the performance of *Mefistofele*, had suddenly been taken ill and could not continue. Have you ever sung on a full stomach? I ended by singing all the performances, and the reward was that de Sabata conducted, one of those privileges that made life tremendously worth living. Giuseppe Lugo—what a beautiful voice, but how uninteresting!—was Faust, Sara Scuderi a stunning Elena, and Pasero the greatest Mefistofele after de Angelis. In Venice, where I was singing *Iris*, I also jumped in for Favero, who was there for *Manon Lescaut*. Again I had to sing all her performances, so I was on almost every night.

"Perhaps the opera I sang the most was *Fanciulla*, after my amazing success at La Scala in 1943. Lauri-Volpi was Dick Johnson, and his 'Ch'ella mi creda' was sung as a lament that tore one apart. I had never heard it done that way, and I suppose I never shall again. There never will be a tenor like him; he was a law unto himself, but blessed with flashes of magic. *Fanciulla* is just about the most *verista* of the Puccini operas, along with *Il tabarro*. All my colleagues found Minnie exhausting; I did not. One night after the performance, I sat down at the piano and began the cadenzas from *Lucia*. Suddenly there was a knock at my door; it was Votto, the conductor. 'What is the matter with you? Are your vocal cords made of steel?' he asked me incredulously. 'No,' I replied, 'but they were well reinforced by Maestro Roche. I am exercising, that's all.'

"Even Parisina, a killer, and Elektra, to which I graduated after appearing as Chrysothemis many times, did not leave any scars. Verdi did not suit me. I did not have the *morbidezza* [smoothness] necessary to do his works justice. After singing *La traviata* and Alice in *Falstaff* I knew there was no point. I sang a lot of Giordano (*Chenier, Fedora, Siberia*) and Zandonai (*Francesca da Rimini, Giulietta e Romeo*)—both were composers close to my temperament and in whose works I could show my mettle. I adored Respighi, for he knew how to write for the voice, and his operas—despite the fancy orchestrations—touch the heart. At La Scala, when Caniglia canceled in his *Lucrezia,* I took it over on the same night I was singing his *Maria Egiziaca,* one of his loveliest scores. (The two operas were given as a double bill.)"

"Do you consider Respighi a *verista*?" I asked her.

"A difficult question, for I feel he stood quite by himself. He was totally independent, impressionistic in some ways, like Debussy; but actually he found his own path. Perhaps it would be easier to call him post-*verista*. Certainly, the librettos by Claudio Guastalla, whom he always used, are a mixture of powerful drama and exquisite poetry. The words are terribly important. Lucrezia's chant after the rape has taken place is still so vivid in my memory—I can remember it all. She is shattered by the shame and by the desecration of her nuptial bed, which lead her to suicide. 'Luce, la livida luce . . . Ed io sono viva, ed il sole torna così come ieri. Soltanto in me questo orrore, nelle pupille, nel sangue . . . Fontana non c'è che mi lavi' [Light, the livid light. And I am still alive, and the sun returns like yesterday. Only within me this horror in my eyes, in my blood . . . there is no fountain which can wash me]. It is the prelude to the death that will wash away the dishonor—one of the most electrifying operatic scenes ever written. But again, the phrasing is everything; the audience must take in, drop by drop, the horror she feels at the assault on her fidelity. When I finished the scene, there was total silence, and then a hurricane of applause. . . . I also sang Magda in *La campana sommersa* and Silvana in *La fiamma,* a great score.

"One of the most interesting roles I took on at La Scala was Rosario in the first performance of Granados's *Goyescas* ever given in Italy, in 1937, with superb sets by José Maria Sert. To my surprise, for it holds the stage well, and the aria 'The lover and the nightingale' is irresistible, after only six performances it was never staged again. I would call this 'impressionismo' or postverismo. It is based on traditional Spanish folk tunes, but the handling of them is immensely sophisticated. It is a tragic story, a vignette of jealousy that leads to death. Another fascinating assignment was to sing in the hundredth anniversary celebrations of Pacini's *Saffo* at the beautiful Teatro Bellini in Catania. None of Pacini's seventy-three operas have really survived, and yet he was one of the most popular composers of the nineteenth century. I would have enjoyed sinking my teeth into another interesting opera, repeating it a few times; but the war came. I wonder what happened to those lovely sets and costumes. It was never mentioned anymore.

"But I spent my life creating operas that never saw the light again. It is discouraging to put so much effort and care into creating a work that is so short-lived. Malipiero fancied me, so for him I sang in the world premiere of his *Antonio e Cleopatra* at the Maggio Musicale Fiorentino in 1938; and, as luck would have it, Mussolini brought Hitler to Florence on a day's visit, and they came to one of the performances. Then in Rome I created Malipiero's *Ecuba*, which, again, fell into absolute obscurity. A curious composer, this Malipiero. He made an enormous international reputation for himself, and yet what has lasted? His scores are not easy to execute, for there is much declamation with strange rhythms. In Florence I also sang the local premiere of Porrino's *Gli Orazi*, premiered at La Scala a short time earlier with Pacetti singing my role, and because of Titus Livy's text it was not without interest.

"One of my favorite *verista* composers was Franco Alfano, perhaps the last really great composer of this series. I sang his *Cyrano de Bergerac*, *Madonna Imperia*, *La leggenda di Sakuntala*, and *Risurrezione*, based on the Tolstoy novel. The last scene, when Katiusha sings 'Vado ad espiare il male che ho fatto' [I am going to atone for the evil I have done], before going off to Siberia, is absolutely superb.

"I am not one of the enthusiasts of *Adriana*. There are some marvelous moments, such as the recitative in the third act, but actually the best role is for the mezzo—short and meaty. I much preferred Cilea's *Gloria*, but I sang both operas often. Catalani's *La Wally* and *Loreley* were also steadies in my repertoire; the first is far more demanding, for its length and its constant shifts from the middle to the top register and back. Despite the fact that there were so many Liùs around, it is a part I was entrusted with often, and in my opinion, the two most imposing Turandots with whom I appeared were Eva Turner and Clara Jacobo. Jacobo, who sang at the Metropolitan, was majestic and very musical. What a lovely human being, and what a sensible end! She is now a nun in a convent and is very happy there.

"I did not really have an international career. First I established my name in Italy, then came the war, and in 1940 I had married the architect Giuliano Rossini, so later I did not want to stay away for long periods. I was called to Germany on various occasions, mainly for the Puccini operas, and to Oslo for Butterfly and Tosca, both with Galliano Masini—in many ways the greatest tenor Italy had. And in South America I sang for the first and only time *L'amore dei tre re.* Then it was all over, as quick as lightning."

What was the most difficult score she had undertaken?

"Here I have no doubts," she laughed. "It was Krenek's *Karl V,* with Giulini conducting. In the scene with all the clocks, it was really almost comic, with what the composer, if I am not mistaken, called a twelve-tone technique. Giulini asked me, 'How can you manage this?' and I replied, 'Only by listening to the C inside of me.' It was an interesting experience, never to be repeated."

"And now how do you deal with all your students?" I asked, well aware that she is considered one of the finest vocal teachers in Europe.

"Now it is all ludicrous." She laughed again, but with a touch of bitterness. "With no agents allowed in this country, what are these young people to do? Agents are an absolute necessity. The youngsters go to sing at all these vocal competitions where not one thing happens, for the judges are chosen by the political parties and know nothing about voices. After the stand I took at La Scala some time ago, I have not been invited again to sit in on the jury, which now must include representatives from the various unions of the male and female choruses, the male and female comprimarios, and so forth. Before one girl presented herself to sing, I was told she had to be accepted because she was the member of a family very close to the mayor. 'Let us see what she can do' is all I answered, already boiling with rage. Well, a dog would have sung infinitely better. Everyone voted in her favor. I got up from my seat and said, controlling myself, 'Will someone kindly tell the mayor for me that as I do not interfere in how he runs this city, I cannot accept his interference in what has been my business for over fifty years.' To the amazement of those present, I walked out.'

"About the students, what can I say? The problems, alas, are not only vocal; they are general. But then there is no effort on their part to study a characterization. None of them know how to walk, for instance. I keep on repeating that Butterfly cannot come onstage like Nedda, and Aida has a different gait from Santuzza. Then they answer—at least some of them do—that Freni walks on the stage always in the same manner, with her head lowered, extended forward. And what can I say? She is now La Scala's national treasure. I recall that at a performance of *I puritani* in Rome I attended, a friend asked me, 'What is Freni looking for in the prompter's box?' And I replied, 'Arturo, no doubt. He must be in there!'

"These young people don't feel anymore, so how can they express pathos, joy, or humor? They are all miserable; they hate their parents, their families, the world. But I am stubborn and I do not give up. I have guided some who have made the grade, and among them are Maria Chiara, Renzo Casellato, Benito di Bella, and a Lebanese who has personality, merciful heavens!—Seta del Grande, whose real name is Palulian or something like that. This is not much, but it is already something. The fact that when they attend performances there is no one to inspire them is also very negative. I can remember the stimulus I used to receive from going to hear the divine Muzio and all the others.

"Now I must stop, for there is a singer who has problems and is coming here." And then, smiling: "He does not want to be seen. It is all very private."

There she stood, saying goodbye, a bundle of energy . . . sympathetic to a degree . . . small too, like Oltrabella, with burning eyes . . . and ageless, like so many others who became famous in this strange world of opera.

IRIS ADAMI CORRADETTI

When I went to visit Iris Adami Corradetti in her apartment in Padua, she had just returned from giving a three-week course in Mantua and was preparing to leave for Verona to be with her prize pupil, Katia Ricciarelli, during the rehearsals of *La traviata* at the Arena. It was a strangely cold, rainy morning in July 1979, and the most celebrated of all the Italian Butterflys, a very slender, delicate-looking elderly lady with crystal-like bone structure, received me with grace and not a touch of coquetry.

"Shall we begin with the present or the past?" she asked very directly. "I would rather, if you don't mind, mix the two, for one brings to mind the other and vice versa. The story of my career is interesting only because it was different from the others. Both my mother, Bice Adami, and my father, Ferruccio Corradetti, were singers of an established reputation. My mother, for instance, was chosen by Mascagni to sing in Rome the first performance of *Le maschere,* under his baton, the part of Colombina. But I had no intention of becoming a singer and wanted to be a pianist. So I studied at the conservatory in Milan, where I was born, and once I had graduated, I started the very hard climb of becoming a recitalist.

"At home I used to sing for my own pleasure, and then one night at a reception given by the Toeplitzes, a famous banking family, I was asked to play informally. A group of people—there were many guests on that particular occasion—surrounded the piano, and one thing led to another. I sang a couple of songs, and there was polite applause. A gentleman came up to me and asked me with whom I was studying voice. 'With no one,' I replied. 'I am not a singer.' 'It may interest you to know that Toscanini, who is at the other end of the room, thinks you have a nice voice and would like you to audition at La Scala.' 'You are joking,' I replied, all flushed. 'No, I am not. Call Toscanini's secretary and she will arrange it,' he said, and moved away. My mother was not in the least surprised, which infuriated me. 'I always told you that the timbre of your voice is most pleasing,' she said unconcernedly. She taught me, in a matter of days, a couple of arias,

Iris Adami Corradetti in the title role of *Madama Butterfly*.

and I recall that when I went, in a state of trepidation, for this amazing development in my life, I sang 'L'altra notte' from *Mefistofele* and then was asked to repeat it. *'E basta.* Thank you very much,' they said, and not one word more. I went home and became angrier and angrier with myself. How could I be so foolish as to put myself in such a situation, I who had not studied, and how could my mother, a real professional, allow me to do such a thing? I am telling you this to prove how little faith I had in my vocal abilities. Nothing happened, and the storm was calming down when Maestro Antonino Votto, at that time the répétiteur of Toscanini, called in person and made an appointment for me to go and see him. I went, and he told me that Toscanini wanted to sign me up for six months at twenty-five hundred lire per month and see how I developed. He realized I had no experience and thought I should start with small roles. I was in such a daze that I affixed my signature to the contract already prepared on his desk. Why ten days had elapsed between the audition and the telephone call I shall never know.

"I shall make it as brief as possible. It was on December 29, 1927, that I made my entry as the Page in that charming opera by Wolf-Ferrari, *Sly,* conducted by Panizza, and with Pertile, Mercedes Llopart (a Spanish soprano much in favor with Toscanini), and Luigi Rossi Morelli. It was a small part, but not insignificant. Some critics noticed me. Then followed, in rapid succession, the Page in *Rigoletto,* with Toti dal Monte, Stignani, Pertile, and Galeffi; the Milliner in *Der Rosenkavalier* and Barbarina in *Le nozze di Figaro,* both under Richard Strauss; a boy in the world premiere of Bianchini's Oriental opera *Thien-Hoa;* and finally, under Toscanini's direction, one of the Flower Maidens in *Parsifal.* It had been a positive experience. I had learned a lot just by being with the greatest singers of the period and the most fabulous conductors. But I suddenly got ambitious. I was re-engaged for the 1928–29 season, and I went from comprimario parts in *Hansel and Gretel, Louise,* and the Scala premiere of Respighi's *La campana sommersa,* to Fyodor in *Boris,* the cook in Rimsky-Korsakov's *Tsar Sultan,* and Jane in Franchetti's *Germania* conducted by Toscanini, to Biancofiore in *Francesca da Rimini* starring Gilda dalla Rizza. My contract with La Scala would not allow me to accept outside engagements.

"I was getting a little impatient, fully realizing what I was up against. These were spectacular artists, and I was most privileged to be among them. But how to push myself forward? My mother kept telling me to be patient. Then I became all pepped up because in 1930 I was assigned, along with some smaller parts, one Musetta in a *Bohème* co-starring Favero and Minghetti, the best-looking tenor in the business, and Liù in some performances of *Turandot* with Maria Nemeth, the leading soprano of the Vienna Opera, whom Lauri-Volpi considered one of the greatest dramatic sopranos he had sung with. When the season was over, I was invited to repeat Liù in Varese and Turin, and in the latter city I also sang my first Elsa, with the fabulous Ettore Parmeggiani, the greatest Lohengrin of those days. The notices were excellent, and a few more engagements in the provinces followed.

"At La Scala in 1931 I was assigned, amusingly enough, Colombina in Mascagni's *Le maschere,* the role my mother had created at the Costanzi in Rome; then a small part in Montemezzi's *La notte di Zoraima,* a world premiere; and then Arianna, the lead role in another novelty, *Bacco in Toscana* by Castelnuovo-Tedesco. But it all seemed to me a seesaw. I could not count on Toscanini's advice—he had left and gone to the United States for good—and I felt at a standstill. Every day I studied, and felt I had made considerable progress. But what exactly was my position in Italy's leading theatre? A step forward and then one backward.

"So in 1932 I agreed to sing only in six performances of *Fedora,* starring Cobelli and Pertile, with de Sabata conducting, in the second female lead of Olga—a silly sort of woman and a lightweight, but it gave me the opportunity to show that I could produce a characterization and could act. It worked. All the critics sat up and took notice—and, what was more important, the other important theatres did too. I made my debuts at the San Carlo in Naples and La Fenice in Venice, and then began working a lot for the EIAR (now RAI), the radio network, which produced a huge number of operas every year with the best possible casts. This was the best form of exposure, for it meant millions of listeners. Things were finally beginning to move. I was also showing my versatility, for I went from many contemporary operas—too many to enumerate—to Jaroslavna in *Prince Igor;* from Cherubino to Desdemona; from the trouser role of Paris in *La Belle Hélène,* with Pederzini in the title role, to *La traviata;* from Charlotte in *Werther* with Schipa to many productions of *Le maschere,* always conducted by Mascagni. For three years I stayed away from La Scala, maintaining cordial relations, but I kept refusing the bits and pieces offered.

"Then they finally sat up and took notice of my work in the other leading theatres, and in 1936 I returned with a bang. In quick succession I sang Elisetta in *Il matrimonio segreto,* Elsa, Lucieta in the world premiere of Wolf-Ferrari's delicious *Il campiello* with Favero and Tess, and then Giorgetta in *Il tabarro,* under Marinuzzi, with Merli and Franci absolutely marvelous as Luigi and Michele. This part established me as a real singing actress, and from then on every theatre wanted me, and I made up for lost time. I was blissful and accepted many interesting engagements. And because my personality came more and more to the fore, I was attracted by verista operas.

"It is a mistake to think that for verismo it is not necessary to have a solid base of bel canto. It is rather a question of learning how to express with more sensibility and dramatic power. Diction plays an essential part. One simply cannot put over a role without excellent diction. Toscanini taught me that one must respect what is written, within one's own possibilities.

"I will give you an example. In *La Bohème* there is an effect in 'Mi chiamano Mimi' in the passage between the F-sharp and the A-natural on the word 'primavera.' Puccini places a graphic mark to indicate that the note must be taken softly and with little voice, then amplified until it arrives at a fortissimo to conclude the word, which must express the joy of the coming of spring. No one does it anymore. Why? Does it mean nothing that it is written in the score? Certainly it's difficult; it means a lot of extra work. Today these sopranos sing Mimi as if it were Toselli's "Serenata." This little seamstress is not a character that dominates the stage, like Butterfly, and so the coloring of the voice must do a great deal. Some voices are born with a far wider palette of shades; the others must develop this ability. In some verismo operas, however, there are passages of pure bel canto. Take the love duet at the end of the first act of *Butterfly,* with the final high C. This is pure singing and demands a fine technique.

"But, alas, verismo today has become a joke. They think they can obtain the effects with sobs and ranting around. I heard all the fabulous divas of verismo and I believe I know what I am talking about. Cobelli, Pampanini (with her unbelievably beautiful instrument), Pederzini, Oltrabella, Cervi Cairoli, Bruna Rasa, Maria Farneti, dalla Rizza . . . I could go on and on. They knew how to squeeze out the juice of each characterization, and one left the theatre shaken by the depth of their involvement. In my opinion *La traviata* is really the first opera of verismo, for Violetta is the quintessence of a human being, and this is why so many sopranos who really did not have Verdian instruments made a great success of this opera. Even if some had their difficulties with the first act's tessitura, they were great in this role because of the particular sensitivity that a *verista* artist must have. Dalla Rizza and Favero are samples of what I am saying.

"Although *Manon Lescaut* is set in the eighteenth century, it is pure verismo, as all Puccini is. Did you happen to hear Sylvia Sass in this role at La Scala? You didn't? How very fortunate for you! I don't think she has any idea of what a *calamistro* [curling iron] is, but that scene with the hairdresser in the second act, when she sings out to him impatiently, 'Il calamistro, presto, presto' [The curling iron, quickly, quickly] became an intolerable joke. She simply did not know what she was saying, and she sat back calmly and indifferently. I am just giving this as an example of how unprepared she was for the entire opera. You cannot go out and just sing. So they must import Hungarians for this appalling disrespect to Puccini, to the public, to art in general! Before I went onstage, I knew the meaning of every word and its inflection, but this means work, work, and again work. Now they want to earn the money, that's all.

"There are different types of verismo," she went on. "All of Massenet's work belongs to this school, including *Thaïs* and *Werther*. What could be more true than Thaïs's heartbreaking death, despite its high poetical message, or Charlotte's marvelously delivered reading of the letter? There is also a considerable distinction between dynamic verismo such as *I gioielli della Madonna* and the stately verismo of *Francesca da Rimini* or *Parisina*.

"To return to me, I began singing Butterfly in 1936, but did not appear in the role at La Scala until January 12, 1938. It is a date I remember well, for on that night, despite the many satisfactions I had had, increasing my repertoire enormously, something happened. I became a star. I had de Sabata as a conductor, which was of course manna from heaven. His hypersensitive reading of this score gave it a transparency that seemed like gossamer.

"You want to know why, until I closed my career, I became so identified with Cio-Cio-San. I think it is because I had a different conception of her. I thought of her far more as a mother than as a wife abandoned by her husband. She kills herself not because Pinkerton has remarried, but because he demands the child, and she knows that he can give him a future she is unable to provide. Her suicide is prompted by her deep love for 'Dolore,' as the little boy is called, so that one day he will not be able to accuse his mother of having abandoned him. If one analyzes the masterful libretto of Giacosa and Illica, it is all there, written between the lines. There is no anger when she sees Kate Pinkerton walking in the garden and instinctively realizes who she is. 'There is no woman happier than you,' she says—but not one moment of resentment. But when she sings that heartrending phrase 'Fra mezz'ora salite la collina' [In half an hour climb the hill again], the idea of the suicide is already planted in her mind.

"I was the first to sing 'Un bel dì vedremo' in action. All the others sang it to the audience. I had a different gesture for every word, and this established a new precedent. The public did not exist; it was a dialogue between Butterfly and Suzuki, with the vision of the ship coming in and Pinkerton walking up the hill.

"As I have said, many parts of *Butterfly* are not verismo but pure bel canto. There is a passage from a G to a B-flat in the crystalline 'ed io col mio dolor' [and I with my sorrow] that, like the 'Vogliatemi bene' [Be affectionate with me] duet is all legato of the most exquisite texture. But *Fanciulla,* which I sang later, is all verismo, and in my estimation it is far less difficult than *Butterfly.* It needs above all an instrument that can pierce the heavy orchestration, a fine actress (particularly for the second act), and a conductor who realizes how far a voice can go. Butterfly I sang absolutely everywhere, and there was not the time to honor all the requests.

"Another opera that, after dalla Rizza retired, was given to me very often was *Francesca da Rimini,* which belongs to another type of verismo, the stately kind. Strangely enough, in my early Scala period I had sung both Biancofiore (the role of Toti dal Monte's debut in Milan's holy of holies) and Samaritana, always with dalla Rizza superb as the protagonist. Then in 1938 the opportunity came to move on to the lead in performances of this opera in Lisbon, and I accepted, particularly since the cast (I was always very careful of whom I sang with) promised well. Zandonai sent word to me that he thought I did not have sufficient vocal strength for the part and begged me to reconsider. Actually, it can be sung by either a dramatic or a spinto, but he had heard me only in a less demanding repertoire. I had signed my contract and went ahead. The triumph was so astounding—particularly for an opera that is not well known outside of Italy—that several extra performances had to be fitted in.

"In Italy, I sang it for the first time in Carpi that same year, and Zandonai arrived in person to beg me to desist. I had with me all the fantastic notices from Portugal and showed them to him. He was so afraid that he convinced the impresarios that I should not sing full out at the dress rehearsal, fearing my voice would tire. He behaved admirably, like the great gentleman he was. After the performance he came and told me that he had rarely been so moved, and that I had injected a tenderness into the role he himself had not known was possible. The next morning came a photograph"—and she pointed to it, in a silver frame on a table nearby—"that had the inscription 'To my very precious interpreter of yesterday, today, and tomorrow.' From then on he asked for me constantly when he was conducting his work.

"That year, 1938, was a big one for me, as I also undertook at the Carlo Felice in Genoa the fascinating *Feuersnot* by Richard Strauss, with the old gentleman—he was seventy-four years of age—conducting. The love scene is stunning, and Carlo Galeffi in the part of Conrad was amazing. How this baritone could go from pure bel canto—his *Orfeo* by Monteverdi at La Scala was memorable—to contemporary scores demonstrated what a solid technician he was. I told Strauss that I had twice before been honored to sing under his baton. He asked me when, and upon hearing that it had been ten years previously, in 1928, as the Milliner in *Rosenkavalier* and as Mozart's Barbarina, he was absolutely bewildered. *'Nicht möglich,'* he kept muttering! 'Maestro,' I answered, 'nothing is impossible.' "

Did she consider Strauss *verista*, I asked.

"Yes and no," she replied. "He is a unique phenomenon and stands alone. But some of his operas, like *Salome*, are *verista*, and so is *Arabella*. Bizet is completely *verista* in *Carmen* and not at all in *The Pearl Fishers*. In my opinion verismo comes more from the libretto than from the music. That is why I consider all of Wolf-Ferrari (I sang many of his operas and loved them all) *verista*, and Giordano too. Nothing is more so than *Sly*, with the dance of the bear. It is an opera that deserved better luck, for it is full of charm and wit. Mascagni is *verista* almost one hundred percent. I sang many *Piccolo Marat*s and *Lodoletta*s with him, and they too depend so much on the phrasing, which must be impeccable."

Then she turned to the present. "All my colleagues are down on Freni and Scotto, as you may have discovered. I deplore what they are doing, but I do not blame them individually. They are the victims of a system that has gone totally off balance. Freni has arrived because of all the concessions that she has made—totally wrong in my way of thinking, but they have made her a big name and, above all, a big recording artist. Karajan asked her to do *Aida* and she accepted. Serafin asked me to sing this opera and I refused. 'You are making a big mistake,' the wise and darling maestro said to me. 'Spintos can sing Aida. You have the sort of instrument Muzio had, and she handled it very well. You have the range for it.' 'Perhaps,' I replied—I who venerated Muzio like a Madonna. 'But there was only one Muzio. Desdemona and Violetta, yes; but one must know when to say no, even to a man like you who knows so much more than I do.' Scotto's is no *Norma*; it is a *Normina*. My pupil Margherita Rinaldi, a lyric-coloratura, sang Adalgisa with her in Florence. The fact is that this is an affront to tradition, and tradition is what they want to destroy today. It is very hard to follow, believe me, even for someone who is, like myself, in the operatic kitchen seven days a week and twenty-four hours per day. I was very pleased with the way Ricciarelli has progressed and matured, but now she is beginning to make some of the compromises that are constantly demanded of her. She has become a better actress, however; she moves with more assurance on the stage and is now very pretty indeed. Those who want to work in the lyric theatre today must learn to say yes, for none of the conductors seems to know that composers wrote for different types of voices. Now any voice will do.

"Pizzetti, so beloved by Toscanini, wrote some very lovely pages, but his operas are not vital. I can well see in his case why they are dropping by the wayside, while I cannot understand about others.

"It is not true that there are no voices today. They exist—and how! But they simply do not have the chance, even the serious ones, to come out of the quagmire we are in. No one is interested in them. This is the tragedy. Previously, the provincial impresarios were on the lookout. Now there is no one. Can you imagine that for the tour La Scala is planning this fall in Switzerland, Belgium, and the United States they have Verrett—as a soprano!—Obraztsova, Domingo, and van Dam for the Verdi Requiem. Not one Italian among them. Why? There aren't any, and all these great theatres hire the established foreigners and make no effort to look for what exists in the backyard. I see it every day with my students, even those who are willing to listen to advice—and there are few—the difficulty that exists in just obtaining an audition for them!

"Actually, what worries me the most in the sorry situation of the lyric theatre these days is a side issue: the recording industry. People listen to records, and obviously buy a great many, and they never hear anymore anything that is really spontaneous. The enlargement or diminution of the sound is child's play for the technicians. It is the triumph of science over art, but it is much like the sculpted jewel as against the synthetic one. A voice can no longer be judged, neither its size nor its timbre—only the way of singing. The leveling is frightening, and inevitably it follows from the recording studio to the stage. The old ones may have been defective, but heavens! you can tell whether it is Capsir or dal Monte or Saraceni singing. Now it is all the same, except for some who are obliged to scream their notes. That is the only time I recognize them.

"More about me?" she asked, smiling. "I was born in 1903, and it seems like yesterday except when I look at the list of roles. Like Oltrabella and Carbone, I was a quick learner, and so many new works—roughly thirty-five—were assigned to me. And I believed strongly in giving new composers a chance to be heard. But in all, between the smaller roles at the beginning and the leading ones, I sang well over one hundred roles. I closed my career officially at La Scala as Butterfly in 1945, with del Monaco as

Pinkerton and beloved Guarnieri on the podium, because I was terribly tired after the strain of singing throughout the war years, in impossible conditions, and also because I married a man who did not wish me to continue. Both were mistakes. I should not have stopped when I did, for when I came out of retirement in 1951 for an overdue commemoration of Zandonai— I sang Francesca again—my voice was mellow and the top unimpaired. And the man I married was not the person I expected him to be.

"Then I began my teaching career. When I attend some of the performances of my pupils and go backstage at the end, I am always surprised at how their costumes are never stained by mascara, the way mine always were from all the tears I shed. They assure me that they cried, but I wonder. Has mascara made that much progress?"

THE LATE BLOOMERS

GIULIETTA SIMIONATO

GERMANA DI GIULIO

CLAIRE WATSON

There is no set time when a voice is, or should be, ready to enter the operatic sweepstakes, but it has been unusual for singers to get started after the age of thirty. In the past, women actually began their vocal training earlier than they do today, and many of them were already well on their way to fame at the age of seventeen or eighteen: Maria Malibran, for instance, and her sister, Pauline Viardot; and later Emma Carelli, Kirsten Flagstad, Gilda dalla Rizza, Lina Bruna Rasa, Geraldine Farrar, and Milka Ternina. Yet here are three (Martha Mödl and Elisabeth Grümmer are discussed elsewhere) who began late, each for a different reason.

In the German and Austrian opera houses, comprimarias have a fairly good chance of eventually graduating to leading roles. Nor is this unheard of in the United States. Although Alma Gluck sang various minor assignments and only three major roles at the Metropolitan (such was the case also for Elisabeth Schumann), more recently Lucine Amara, Mignon Dunn, and Teresa Stratas went up the ladder fairly rapidly. But this situation rarely occurs in Italy, and so the case of Giulietta Simionato is particularly interesting. She went on doing minor roles at La Scala for a long time until finally she became the world's leading mezzo (a situation that is not complimentary to the judgment of those running the opera house). Germana di Giulio, who began late for a variety of reasons, immediately became much in demand in the leading opera houses because of an increasing dearth of dramatic sopranos. Claire Watson's problem consisted of a husband and four children, and Dr. Watson took a dim view of his wife's ambitions. Eventually she broke away, and she rapidly made a great position for herself in Europe.

GIULIETTA SIMIONATO

In 1966 Giulietta Simionato abandoned the lyric theatre to become the happy wife of Italy's most celebrated physician, Dr. Cesare Frugoni, who recently died at the age of ninety-seven. Her decision had been maturing for some time, since the mezzo had made up her mind that once all the complications (and there were many, since at that time in Italy there was no divorce, and Frugoni's wife had been for years in a clinic for nervous disorders) were swept aside completely and she married him, she would quit the stage. When Signora Frugoni died and the way was finally clear, Simionato decided to retire on February 1, 1966, the approximate anniversary of her debut at La Scala thirty years before as one of the Flower Maidens in *Parsifal*.

So she asked Luigi Oldani, at the time artistic director, what was on the calendar, and he replied that it was to be *La clemenza di Tito* at the Piccola Scala. "I must sing in it," she told him. "But all the roles have been assigned," he replied. "Never mind," she retorted. "I don't need an important part. I want to sing on that date for nostalgia's sake. Please do me this favor." Surprised at her request, never imagining what was in the making, he assigned her the role of Servilia for just that one performance, and she learned it in a few days. No one had been let in on the secret, but when the makeup artist was at work on her face in her dressing room, she casually said to him, "Please do a good job, for this is the last time I shall appear on this or any other stage." The news spread like wildfire among the stage personnel and then reached the public. No one could believe it, and the performance ended with the audience stomping and in tears.

"It was the only way of doing it. I could not have gone through a prepared farewell; I'm a very emotional person. I slipped out of my career almost as quietly as I entered it.

"I've never looked back," she reflected, her beautiful white hair framing that unforgettably clever and youthfully cheerful face, in her large apartment overlooking the gardens of Villa Savoia in Rome. "If I hadn't married,

Giulietta Simionato as Amneris in *Aida*.

I would have gone on singing—the voice was still in good condition. But my husband was many years older than me, and I wanted to enjoy to the fullest his stimulating company. He was a phenomenon really, of a species that no longer exists. And I believe I quit at just the right time. Standards have gone down so fast these last ten years, and I cannot fathom what we are heading for, except total decadence. From time to time I still accept 'jury duty' at vocal competitions, and my colleagues are amazed with me at how many small voices we hear, and all off key—so much so that one begins to think that one's hearing has been impaired. And then suddenly a singer comes along who is on key, and one knows that the situation, alas, is what it is.

"I don't believe, as many others do, that it's the lack of good teachers. Something mystifying has happened, and I'm at a loss to put my finger on it. Is it that the food we eat is no longer healthy, that the air we breathe is totally polluted? Is it something from outer space? Or is it the sacred flame that is extinguished? There's less discipline and too much hurry, on this I agree; but it goes way beyond that. The mechanics of singing have been dealt an unexplainable blow. What has happened to the contralto species? It appears to have vanished. It went two octaves from F to F. Now all mezzos are taking on the contralto repertory, but they must resort to chest tones. Is it because all the orchestras today have a much higher diapason? There's no doubt that Americans and Britishers are way ahead of us now, but even among the better-trained voices there is no magic.

"Mario del Monaco declared on television the other night that young people love opera and the theatres are full. Only part of what he said was true. First of all, most of the provincial opera houses, which were the backbone of Italian lyric life, give very few, if any, performances a year. Private impresarios have disappeared—there's no way they can pay an orchestra and chorus without government or city subsidy. And the state, along with every single province, is in total bankruptcy. The important opera houses, which used to have a repertory of anywhere between twenty and thirty operas a year, are down to eight or ten. Even after the war, when the country was totally ravaged and half destroyed, opera's prestige was untouched. Now what used to be a weekly custom for the citizen—a night at the opera—has become a rare event.

"My father came from Sardinia," she explained, "and he was in the employ of the state, so it was pure chance that I was born in Forlì. My mother was a Venetian. I began singing at school with the nuns, and then in Rovigo I took lessons with the local bandmaster, a most talented man who played all the instruments. My voice was already placed, however, and the agility was completely natural. He taught me how to take advantage of what God had given me, with more know-how, and when and where to save. When we moved to Padua, I studied with Maestro Palumbo.

"One day an impresario walked in to see if there was any fresh talent he could pick up for a few lire, so I agreed to sing Maddalena in *Rigoletto* in Padua and Lola in *Cavalleria* in Montagnana. Then in 1933 I presented myself at the first competition launched by the Maggio Musicale Fiorentino, and there were 385 contestants, with 18 mezzos. The jury was enough to induce a stroke—Tullio Serafin, the legendary tenors Amedeo Bassi and Alessandro Bonci, the eminent Rosina Storchio, and the ever-fascinating Salomea Krusceniski, who brought *Butterfly* to its triumph in Brescia after the Scala flop and later became a memorable Salome and Elektra. I won with selections from *La favorita* and *Mignon,* was patted on the back, handed five thousand lire and a tiny role in Pizzetti's *Orsèolo.* I was convinced that after winning such an imposing competition I'd be swamped with offers, but absolutely nothing happened.

"In 1936 I was handed a contract by La Scala, the likes of which I don't think ever existed. I had to be ready with every role, comprimario and otherwise. I was assigned, among other roles," she recalled with a hearty laugh, "to be the maid in the second act of *Manon* in a glittering production starring Gigli and Favero. All I had to do was to bring in the coffee on a tray and utter a brief sentence. Well, I upset the pot and remained completely silent. I got to sing a string of secondary roles—Beppe in *L'amico Fritz* on various occasions, Ciesca in *Schicchi* practically every year, Fyodor in *Boris,* Smaragdi in *Francesca da Rimini,* Maddalena in *Rigoletto,* Berta in *Barbiere*—but nothing positive was really moving. In 1942 I was finally given Hansel, in which I did very well, but it led nowhere.

"Just as I was beginning to have great doubts, Marisa Morel—whose real name was Merlo and who sang at the Metropolitan a few seasons—came backstage one evening. She too had won a prize at the Maggio, and developed into a charming artist; she explained that with the war having washed away all her savings, she was trying her luck as a manager, organizing several operatic seasons in Switzerland. She had faith in me; would I sing leading roles with her company, accepting small fees at first? I went to La Scala's management and explained my predicament. They granted me enough freedom to accept Morel's offer. With her I sang Cherubino, Dorabella, and Fidalma in *Il matrimonio segreto.* The notices were marvelous, and the news traveled back to Italy, and in April 1947 I finally was assigned Dorabella at La Scala. With the exception of Hansel five years earlier, this was my first real leading role there. Then Trieste followed with Octavian, and finally *Mignon,* conducted by Gavazzeni, in Genoa.

"It is difficult to explain, but the Thomas heroine for me was like a figure out of my own past. It was as if I had been Mignon in some previous existence. I performed it in a state of rapture—and, I might add, of grace. The reception was so overwhelming that La Scala immediately assigned me for the month of October to a series of *Mignons* with di Stefano—I believe this was the second opera he sang there—and Siepi. The mezzo who had been singing the role season after season went to the management when she heard that I had been assigned 'her' opera. Were they out of their minds to give a comprimaria such a responsibility? After she was shown the Genoa clippings, she quieted down, offering to come to the rescue of the house if I was unable to finish the performance. She did not need to, for the same thing happened at La Scala as in Genoa, and I was a star overnight. Serafin came up to me and said, 'This is not progress but a real somersault.' He then went on to offer me Carmen under his own direction, with Lauri-Volpi as Don José, the following summer for RAI. I stalled—that jump seemed a little too steep for Giulietta—but he cajoled me into accepting, and Carmen became one of the heroines most identified with me.

"From then on, every leading mezzo role was thrown at me, not only at La Scala, but all over Italy and abroad. Cinderella became a hard-working princess. During the following nineteen years I made up for lost time, for I sang sometimes even more than ninety performances per season, and this does not include all the recording sessions. Looking back, I don't really know how I managed, except that I used a kind of radar of my own invention to control my instrument. I lived on a razor's edge—watching myself like a hawk—and didn't even drink a glass of wine, fearing the acidity might hurt my vocal cords. I led a spartan existence. My personal life vanished, and I learned to sing through colds and sore throats. In fact, I can count the number of performances I canceled.

"I was a mezzo, but with a very generous extension, and there were some soprano roles I could undertake without fear of damage. In fact, I sang Ännchen in *Der Freischütz* and Donna Elvira, which lies very much in the middle of the voice. I also sang Valentine in the famous Scala production of *Les Huguenots* with Corelli and Sutherland; it had not been performed there for sixty-three years, and the last time it had been the celebrated Hariclea Darclée who had been entrusted with the role. In that same year, 1962, twenty days later, I created the part of Pirene in the world premiere of Falla's opera *Atlántida*, completed posthumously by Ernesto Halffter, but despite the mise-en-scène of Margherita Wallmann and the brilliant conducting of Thomas Schippers, it proved a bore, too static and untheatrical. I also sang in the first performance ever at La Scala of *Les Troyens*, under Kubelik, and Dido appealed to me immensely. Her last apostrophe, her farewell to the city and her subjects before killing herself—'Dieux immortels' [Immortal gods], ending with 'Adieu, beau ciel d'Afrique, astres que j'admirais' [Goodbye, fair African sky, stars I marveled at]—is extraordinarily moving and tender, and it left me quite limp, so noble and contained are the text, adapted from Virgil by the composer himself, and the admirable music. Mario del Monaco was ideally cast as Aeneas. In the classical repertoire both *Orfeo* and *Ifigenia in Aulide* gave me great satisfaction, the first one being, I think, the supreme test for eighteenth-century bel canto singing. I also enjoyed my excursions into verismo and sang many Fedoras and Santuzzas. The Mascagni heroine is in my opinion more suited to a mezzo, provided she has an easy top—most of those devastating thirty minutes lie in the middle of the voice, and a soprano must make a tremendous effort in that section, so when the top notes come along she is tired. For a mezzo it comes more naturally.

"I was offered many more soprano roles, which I turned down. I had accepted Leonora in *Il trovatore* and was most pleased with the way I was able to handle 'D'amor sull'ali rosee.' Most conductors give one the wrong advice, so greedy are they for performers at any cost or price. But Antonino Votto was the exception: when he heard of my new undertaking, he dissuaded me, and I have always been most grateful. He told me that he knew I could handle the role, but that the consequences in the next few years might be troublesome—if I pushed up the voice, a hole would develop in the middle. 'The voice is like a rubber band,' he reminded me. 'Pull it one way and it gives way elsewhere. You are a superb Azucena; be satisfied. A Leonora at this point of your career is not going to mean that much.' He was right, and that is why I kept turning down offers to appear as Norma instead of Adalgisa. As for Lady Macbeth, I could not see myself being such a malevolent character. Minnie was very tempting, but knowing how emotional I am, I knew I could never hold back, and it would have meant soaring with my voice in the upper regions for three intense acts, over a very heavy orchestration.

"There were four parallel roads I followed, and I loved them all. There was the coloratura repertoire, consisting of the Rossini operas *(Cenerentola, Italiana, Tancredi, Barbiere,* Arsace in *Semiramide)* along with Bellini's

I Capuleti ed i Montecchi, Handel's *Giulio Cesare,* Giovanna Seymour in *Anna Bolena,* and Preziosilla in *Forza.* Then the heavy dramatic repertory: Ulrica in *Ballo,* Amneris, Azucena, Eboli, Marfa in *Khovanshchina,* Dalila, *La favorita,* and the Princess in *Adriana.* And the many lyric parts, such as Adalgisa, Charlotte in *Werther,* Mignon, Dorabella, Cherubino, Hansel, Octavian, Orfeo, Ifigenia, Fenena in *Nabucco,* Neris in *Medea.* And then the verismo roles like Santuzza, Fedora, Carmen, Zanetto, and many others.

"When I exploded at last and quickly gained recognition, everything came my way, for Stignani, Nicolai, and Pederzini were singing less, and then eventually stopped. I became a regular member of the Vienna Staatsoper and appeared regularly at the Salzburg Festival. Along with the Metropolitan (where I appeared in only four roles, and then as Dalila on tour), I sang everywhere, including London, Mexico City, Tokyo—what a fantastic public!—Chicago, Hamburg, Rio de Janeiro, and . . . the world. But somehow it was never possible to make dates coincide with the Teatro Colón in Buenos Aires.

"I've always been against jumping in for ailing colleagues, simply because I dislike unprepared performances, but on one occasion I found myself trapped. I was singing *La Cenerentola* at the San Carlo in Naples and, having two days between performances, went to Rome to attend to some personal business. There the manager of the San Carlo, a great personal friend, rang me up, absolutely frantic. At the dress rehearsal of *Carmen,* Artur Rodzinski had objected to Inge Borkh, and he begged me on his knees to take over. This was Friday, with the premiere the next night, and *Cenerentola* scheduled for Sunday matinee. I took the plunge, much against my wishes. By the time I arrived at the final rondo on Sunday afternoon, I was so tired I didn't know how I would ever get through all those treacherous passages. But God was with me, and my determination to succeed was such that I had one of the biggest ovations of my life, as if Don José had not stabbed me to death the night before. Standing on its own, the 'Nacqui all'affanno' is in many ways the most demanding in agility of any mezzo aria that I know of. And coming as it does at the very end of the opera, it is really sadistic on the part of my beloved Rossini, particularly since it is very exposed. I went on alternating these two operas, so totally different in style and vocal demands —one all sensuality which ends in tragedy, and the other pathos which instead has a sparklingly happy ending.

"I have admired many artists, but it is impossible to think of all of them. There is no doubt that Callas brought something new to the profession— another dimension, so to speak. Not only did Maria behave perfectly with me, but she was very fair. When we sang *Norma* together, I always sang, as was my custom, the C in the duet, without having it transposed as so many do. In an interview Maria expressed surprise that the critics never gave me credit for this. She was a prima donna through and through and could be most difficult, yet could also be sensible and reasonable. I recall that during a rehearsal of the second act of *Norma* the tenor walked behind her. Since she was seated, he did not dare obstruct her from the audience's view, but this was not a natural thing to do. Maria became conscious of this and told him to go ahead and pass in front of her—an unheard-of thing for someone with her temperament to allow. The *Anna Bolena* at La Scala in the 1956–57 season was such a triumph that we repeated it the following year. There was a certain movement in the scene with Percy that Maria did not do again, and as it was marvelously effective—a sort of stalling—I brought it to her attention. 'I had quite forgotten it,' she said, thanking me. But however hard she tried, she could never obtain the same effect again. I always found her interpretations immensely dramatic, but never moving.

"But Mafalda Favero, with that curiously diaphanous voice of hers, brought tears to my eyes. There was an animal sensuality about her that was spellbinding, despite the very limited means at her disposal, and she gave of herself—even too much for her own good. But the result was heartbreaking. Cesare Siepi was for me the king of bassos, a *grand seigneur* on the stage, a rare thing these days. His voice was pure gold, so effortless and all-enveloping. Ettore Bastianini, whose untimely death upset me deeply, was the greatest baritone of my generation. His instrument was a mixture of bronze and velvet. And he was a great human being.

"As for tenors, my choice would go to di Stefano and del Monaco. The first was unfortunately as generous with his instrument as he was with his purse. His career could have lasted ever so much longer, but how much we had to treasure during his great period! Del Monaco—in my opinion the last heroic tenor we've had—was the opposite. Despite his blowups, he was a calculator and knew exactly how much he could expend on all levels.

"Now, with the famine of sopranos, there is a group of mezzos making the journey. They have not had a maestro like Votto, who held me back. We will see what happens to them. For me the greatest living singer is Caballé. Not only is the instrument superb in quality, but the technique is prodigious. Some criticize her for not having enough temperament, but don't they realize she wouldn't be so astoundingly perfect if she had that too? Anyhow, one must readjust one's way of thinking and judging. I have sung with the best conductors, from Toscanini (I had the honor of appearing with him in 1948 in one act from *Nerone*) to Karajan. But it is obvious what is happening. The conductor, always important, is now the shining star, with the stage director a close second. I had the best, and don't envy those who must make their path into the jungle today."

Since Simionato was celebrated for never quarreling and for her scintillating good humor—her imitations of her colleagues would provide a marvelous one-woman show—I brought up the question of her row with Antonio Ghiringhelli, then head of La Scala, in connection with the company's first visit to the Bolshoi in Moscow. "I protested vehemently over what had been done to my distinguished colleagues," she said calmly, "more than to myself, as I knew that within a short time I'd be retiring. There were two young divas who were being interviewed and photographed exclusively, as if the company in its entirety had consisted only of them. I was not questioning their worth, only the appalling injustice to the others. Politics should never interfere with art—never, never."

As I left her, I recalled the words of Gilda dalla Rizza shortly before her death: "There have been many great singers, but few will leave a permanent place for themselves in the history of opera. Of the group who came after me, I would put Simionato on top of the list, not Callas. They talk about Callas singing everything; yes, but how? With three voices, and only the coloratura was, for a few years, impressive. But Simionato sang everything, and with only one wonderful voice. She became a luminous star not through publicity, but through exceptional merit."

GERMANA DI GIULIO

One of the most beautiful dramatic soprano voices, velvety and sensuous, belonged to Germana di Giulio, whose career lasted less than two decades. She started when she was almost thirty, and retired in 1958 when she became the wife of the banker Achille Dalmasso. When I went to call on her (she is now a widow) in early July 1979 at her apartment in Milan, I was not prepared to meet a woman so knowledgeable about the art of singing and so cognizant of its problems. In fact, she was so enlightening and gifted in explaining some of the mysteries of the vanishing bel canto technique that we ended by talking relatively little of her accomplishments. Not in the least didactic, she kept going to the piano to illustrate her theories, which appeared eminently sensible.

A handsome woman with a Gothic appearance, her face dominated by huge, almond-shaped eyes, she impressed me by her innate dignity and authentic grand manner. She was particularly famous for her Aida (the role of her bow at La Scala), Gioconda, Tosca, Thaïs, Maddalena in *Chenier,* Leonora in both *Trovatore* and *Forza,* and Norma. She was the last important Italian to do full justice to Turandot and Isabeau.

"I came from an intrepid family," di Giulio stated, "a sort of clan that no longer exists in our day and age. The Consalez tribe, of Spanish origin, started out in the last century by being a legitimate stage touring company. Then, later, they went on to operetta and, eventually, opera. It was a unique traveling company with which they toured the world. It functioned from around 1890 until 1933, and they were undaunted, immensely courageous pioneers, for they took Italian opera to Greece and Russia, including its most distant provinces. Giulia Tess stayed with them for one year, when she sang as a mezzo under the name of Tessaroli. They also went to China, Japan, Australia, and South Africa. It was a spectacular undertaking, for they took their own orchestra, which in those days was limited to about thirty instruments, the chorus, the sets, costumes, stagehands, and of course the singers. My mother, who was a Consalez, acted on the stage, but later retired when she married my father, Salvatore di Giulio, a well-known basso who traveled with the company. So I was brought up among singers, and I can still recall instructive conversations my father had with artists of the stature of Pasquale Amato and Giuseppe Danise.

"No one in the family was anxious for me to follow in their footsteps, but the lyric theatre was in my blood—everything about it intrigued me. That is why I began late, for I had to break down a lot of resistance, and in those days we were brought up very strictly. The discipline I had at home helped me later, and I believe one of the reasons that today singing teachers have such difficulties with their pupils is that they are undisciplined to a degree.

"I studied vocalises for four years with Ernestina Consalez, and then repertoire for two. Everyone was convinced that having started with so much delay, I would never be able to get going in time. But when I commenced, my preparation and foundations were solid, and within a year I was already appearing in important theatres. I was born a dramatic soprano in timbre and temperament, but possessed the agility to cope with a score such as *Norma*.

"When I first entered the operatic gates, the system was different, and far more sensible. Nowadays singing teachers give lessons that last forty minutes each, and are paid accordingly. Previously a student made a contract with the instructor for a minimum of four years, and all the necessary time was allotted to him. The identification of the teacher with the voice he must train is completely nonexistent now. What is forty minutes two or three times a week? A drop in the ocean. It takes a lot of patience, willpower, and exercise to learn how to compose legatos and polish one's tones.

"The legato is the base, and one must learn to use it even when there is portamento—a delay on certain notes or words in order to obtain more pathos or passion. As this demands a certain amount of extra rehearsing, conductors today tend to minimize it, which is a grave error. If used with care and intelligence, it makes all the difference to the expression of a phrase. Cilea and Giordano, with whom I had long conversations, both were of the same opinion: the artist must learn how to interpret, for the composer cannot do it all.

"I remember when I sang Thaïs for the first time, with Gabriele Santini, a marvelous operatic conductor, he spent one entire hour with me working on one phrase: 'Dis-moi que je suis belle.' Quite rightly, as I was to discover over and over again singing in this opera, he wanted to obtain the expression by expanding the first note slowly and then hurrying ever so subtly, by

Germana di Giulio in the title role of *Aida*.

degrees, to the last ones. This aria establishes an important side of the courtesan's nature. She is talking to her mirror and becomes somewhat impatient, waiting for an answer that she will never obtain from an inanimate object.

"When I began studying, there were three qualities a voice had to produce: the so-called chest tones, the *voix mixte,* and the head tones with the two extremes almost touching one another. For instance, in the 'Invan la pace,' the last part of the aria 'Pace, pace' in *Forza,* one must get one's support down and then come up. There is no other possible way to obtain that magical, eerie effect required. A little portamento there, just a touch of it, makes all the difference. Caballé is one who won't let conductors rule it out, and she is one thousand percent right. I am not trying to take away from her what she has—a superb voice—but she makes it even more exciting by using these nuances, which create all the difference. Have these conductors never read the exercises written by two of the world's leading singing teachers, Manuel Garcia and Barbara Marchisio, who were very great singers themselves? After all, Garcia is responsible for the teaching of his daughters, Maria Malibran and Pauline Viardot, and the tenor Nourrit, among many others. And Marchisio had to her credit Rosa Raisa and Toti dal Monte. Well, their exercises have portamentos all the way through. Actually, portamento does a lot for the flexibility of the instrument too.

"Leopoldo Mugnone, who conducted *Cavalleria* and *Tosca* at their world premieres, used to say to me when he came to visit the family and I was a student: 'Give me an interpretation—it does not matter which, but an interpretation.' The vocal focus is obtained by supporting a certain note, either low or in the middle, to bring it up to the top of the same vibration. What mystifies me is that currently vibrations are ignored, and for this recording companies are partially responsible, since vibrating voices do not record well. But the emotion of the voice is obtained by vibrations. No wonder all these recordings sound the same. The other night I was utterly astonished to find myself, at dinner, seated next to one of our foremost young conductors and discover that he did not know that between one semitone and the next, there are seven fractions of sound. Each and every one of them must be utilized to obtain the vibration of a sound." Upon making this statement, she went to the piano and managed miraculously (she never told me her age, but I would guess from certain dates she mentioned that she was born around 1910) to produce these fractions.

"The study of singing," she went on, "involves an enormous amount of research. In order to find the beautiful tones, one must also produce ugly ones and learn what is necessary in order to discard them. Without vibrations, the sound has no dimension, and that is why today monotony reigns supreme. To spin a note one must learn to pull it from the combination of the openings of the nose, larynx, windpipe, but the passage must never cease to be pliable and soft."

Again she went to the piano, and while playing and singing, she demonstrated what she had just said by having me place my fingers on her face. "When I first began," she informed me, "I arrived at a B-flat and no further. Eventually I reached the D with security, and I always sang *La traviata* in its original key. They always talk today about how difficult Turandot is, but no one mentions the concertato in the second act of *Aida,* which must sound like a horn, and then the singer must go on to all the pianissimos of the third act. The truth is that no one any longer hears Aida in the big ensemble.

"Some people think that some Bs and high Cs are more difficult than B-flats. Not true! There is a B-flat in 'Pace, pace' and one in *La Gioconda* (in the phrase 'Ah, come t'amo') that are placed in such a manner that a C in *Turandot* is child's play in comparison. What so many people forget is that the voice came into being long before the instruments, and that during the course of the evening, as the instruments get warmer and warmer, they add certain fractions of a note. I recall my teacher passing on to me some invaluable advice. 'You have excellent intonation,' she used to say, 'but you must sharp a tiny bit or they will say you sing out of tune.' This is because of the distance of the stage from the orchestra and the augmentation of the diapason. This, of course, is fraught with danger too, unless one's hearing is infallible. Many teachers today tend to push the voices up, fearing that the upper register will not maintain itself.

"What is also fast disappearing from performing in these strange times we live in is the use of the so-called *corona,* or crown. There is no doubt that some singers have exaggerated this trick, but to do away with it is sheer insanity. The *corona*—in which one holds a note a little longer in order to build the next one—is a must to obtain the desired effect in certain phrases. Take, for instance, the passage in *Butterfly* when she sings 'Noi siamo gente avvezza alle piccole cose' [We are people accustomed to small things]—how are you going to give the proper, touching meaning to 'piccole cose' without a crown? Impossible. The crown is a sort of device, for at a certain moment the diaphragm must drop and then build up once more."

She finally spoke of her career, which began in the form of a tryout in the little town of Felonica, as Santuzza. The reviews were so enthusiastic that she was engaged right away at the Teatro Petruzelli in Bari, at that time one of the leading opera houses in Italy, for *Forza,* and at the Teatro Grande of Brescia for *Guglielmo Tell* with Francesco Merli and Mario Basiola. Then came the opportunity to create Jenůfa in Italy, the first performance being at the Fenice in Venice. She was engaged for Leonora in Verdi's rarely performed *Oberto* in his hometown of Busseto as part of a festival held there. Norma soon entered her repertoire, and she first sang it in Catania, Bellini's birthplace. In Trieste she had Ebe Stignani as her Adalgisa, "and the Olympian serenity of this woman with so staggering a technique was in itself an unforgettable lesson." She went to Turin for some performances of *Faust* —she also took on lyric and spinto roles—and it was then that she heard for the first time Magda Olivero, who was appearing in the same season as Francesca da Rimini.

"Many of my former colleagues tend to underevaluate her," she said. "I am not quite sure why—they envy her perhaps, because she is still going and they are not. I was enormously impressed with her then, and I am still. I made it my business to discover why this woman, with a relatively unimportant instrument and timbre, could and can hold an audience spellbound. After attending several performances, I knew why. It is her mastery of vocalization. Now they all close their vowels, thinking that this keeps up the tone, but she knows better. It is not the voice for which people go to hear Olivero, still successful as she is nearing seventy. It is her incredibly clear enunciation, the value of each word, which all the others have forgotten in this so-called marriage of the vocal instrument to the orchestra. The public, who are instinctive, hunger for it. Then, of course, there is the personality—another lost item. She has the gift of making the audience feel privileged to be in her presence, and the way she has of taking the curtain calls, walking the entire area of the footlights, makes everyone present feel she is thanking him personally. Despite a worn voice, she is never off key and still manages to produce a messa di voce that does not seem to belong to an earthly instrument. Her manners are those of a great lady, and, again, even in a chaotic democracy, this is appreciated.

"I made my debut at La Scala as Aida," she went on, "in 1945, with Merli again, and Pasero, a magnificent Ramfis. Then the next assignment was *Tosca,* and then *Andrea Chenier* with Serafin."

Had she sung *Norma* at La Scala? I asked.

"No, I didn't. But the performances of the Bellini opera in this theatre have a curious background. Even the divine Mazzoleni never sang it there, while Burzio did one series and Russ another immediately preceding the

First World War. Then it disappeared from the repertoire until 1932, when Scacciati was entrusted with the lead and Stignani was Adalgisa. Then there was another long hiatus, until 1947, when Caniglia received the coveted assignment—and did not do too well with it. But the very great Normas of the period between the two world wars—such as Raisa, Pacetti, and Cigna, not to speak of Muzio—never sang it there. Then the next one was Callas in the 1950s. Toscanini, incredible to say, never conducted *Norma* there. He had it in rehearsal and, I believe, had reached the final phase when he felt that Ines de Frate—this was the 1898–99 season—was not suitable. It created quite a to-do. And then, as far as I know, he never went near it again. He did conduct it in Turin in 1898, and that, I believe, was the last time.

"I was both fortunate and unfortunate to have started on the eve of the Second World War, an immense handicap, for so much important activity came to a stop, and nothing functioned the way it should. The immediate postwar years were difficult too, although there was an almost frantic desire for opera and good music after the nightmares people had gone through. But I was lucky in having been able to perform with some of the giants in the tenor department before their exit from the scene. Some of them were way beyond fifty, and they still sounded superb. This was an invaluable experience. To appear with Pertile, then close to sixty, was a memorable lesson in true art. Boito's *Nerone* is not in any way as eminent a score as *Mefistofele,* which I sang often, but with him it became a revelation in characterization. This man, so simple and truly modest, became the Roman emperor onstage and was fascinating. The role of Asteria is not one to afford many satisfactions, but I was happy to appear with him. I sang Desdemona to his Otello too, and, again, he became the Moor, raging, impetuous, and touching. With Gigli it was the complete opposite. Dramatically he never became the character at all, but I remember some *Cheniers* with him at La Scala where the bewitchment of the voice was such that he became the poet, and he was then fifty-seven. With Lauri-Volpi, who was to become my frequent partner at the Liceo in Barcelona and the Zarzuela in Madrid, where I returned for many seasons, again it was a totally different form of art. I have never known anyone who worked so seriously and with such love on his vocal production, even in the later years, when he became a sort of myth; and the continual new effects he was able to produce were riveting. Being so deeply interested in vocal production myself, I formed a very close relationship with him.

"With the retirement of Cigna and Pacetti, I was called upon to sing

Turandot everywhere, and I had Lauri-Volpi as a partner in this work very often. His Calaf was no longer a voice but a trumpet because of the formidable vibrations he was able to produce, and yet when he sang Verdi he used a completely different approach. I have read all his books on singing, and although he wrote pompously, there is a lot of good sense and some very acute observations. His *Voci parallele* is undoubtedly the best. Calaf was a very sore point with him, for he had been sure that he would be called to sing it at its world premiere at La Scala; he was acutely hurt when Toscanini gave it instead to Fleta. But he did have the satisfaction of singing its first performance at the Metropolitan a few months later.

"Merli, at fifty-six, his age when he sang Radames with me at La Scala, was still a miracle of sound technique. With del Monaco I sang on a tour of the Sicilian provinces and in Cairo, when we were both beginners. Like Lauri-Volpi, he was always in search of perfection. And as a colleague kind, considerate, and helpful.

"I did not have many chances to sing verismo roles, not only because fewer and fewer of those operas were being given after the war, but also because with the dearth of dramatic sopranos I was always entrusted with heavy roles like Gioconda, Isabeau, and even Brünnhilde in *Die Walküre* the few times Wagner still appeared on the Italian horizon. But I did sing *Fanciulla, Fedora, Cavalleria,* and *Adriana.* It is fashionable today to underestimate this last opera. The critics call it saccharine, but they have never bothered to do their homework. For Cilea (a great friend of mine, and often hurt by the comments) wanted to re-create as much as possible the rococo atmosphere surrounding the Comédie-Française tragedian. I think, finally, it is the public who are always right, and at the end of this opera the audience invariably dissolves in tears. Cilea's *Gloria* and *L'arlesiana* are totally different. But one cannot give *Arlesiana* today unless one has a mezzo with a tremendous presence and dramatic guts.

"Now darkness is descending. The Comunale in Bologna has just spent a fortune to produce an opera by Ligeti entitled *Le Grand Macabre.* The composer has called it an 'anti-opera.' Then why give it in an opera house? The stage was full, so I was informed by friends who went, of phallic symbols, and the two main characters were called Clitoria and Spermando. The text is obscene from beginning to end—and this is what they call avant-garde art! I find it a tragedy of epic proportions, and the truth is that a definite form of terrorism has made its entry into the lyric theatre."

Germana di Giulio died in February 1981.

KAMMERSÄNGERIN
CLAIRE WATSON

The former tsarina of the Bavarian State Opera in Munich, Claire Watson is an intelligent, alert woman with very clear and precise ideas on the operatic past and present. My conversation with her in Munich, where we met for lunch in June 1979, was most stimulating. Since her retirement in 1976, she has been living in the lake district near the Bavarian capital. From the mid-fifties to the mid-seventies no other American singer enjoyed the kind of prestige in Central Europe that surrounded Claire Watson.

"I started late," she said, laughing in her unaffected manner, "but I did catch up. I was born Claire McLamore in New York City and went to the Eastman School of Music in Rochester to study voice. But I fell in love with Michael Watson and was so impressed with his being young and already a brilliant doctor of biophysics. Our families had known each other, and he was very attentive to me during 1942, my first year there. And so I ended by becoming a housewife. I heard him say one day, 'The best way to keep a woman out of trouble is to keep her pregnant.' And this is what happened, one child after the other.

"But my love for singing had not been burned out, and in 1948 I began to go to New York to take lieder lessons with Elisabeth Schumann. She was a very special person, and I owe a great deal to her. How lucky I was to have her guidance for those few years, as she died in 1952. One day she looked me straight in the eyes and suddenly said, 'Do you realize that you have a real operatic voice? Lieder are all very well, but you should really be in the lyric theatre.' Then she talked to me about learning Octavian, but my heart had always been set on the Marschallin.

"At that time Schumann was still an intimate friend of Otto Klemperer. You probably have heard that they had a very passionate love affair."

I interrupted her to ask if it was true that, many years previously, Schumann's husband had walked down the aisle of the opera house in Cologne while Klemperer was conducting and had knocked him down off the podium. The scandal had been such that both the maestro and the soprano had been barred from singing in all German theatres for one year, and the rumor was that the heavy fall Klemperer had suffered caused the brain tumor that later killed him.

"Of course I heard of it," she replied. "I am not sure that it was Cologne, but I believe it is unfortunately correct. As I came to love them both a lot, it saddens me, for they were both highly respectable and nice people, and it must have hurt them deeply.

"Anyhow, I auditioned for him in New York, and he was of the same opinion. So it was arranged that I accompany the maestro, who was going to Europe, so that he could coach me in three roles: Agathe, Elsa, and Donna Anna. They both had agreed that I was a *jugendlich dramatisch* soprano, or what the Italians call a spinto. My husband took a dim view of all of this, but more about that later.

"In Vienna Klemperer took me to a party, and the hostess asked me to sing. The conductor, who had suffered a stroke, accompanied me with one hand as I sang Donna Anna's 'Or sai chi l'onore' and Elsa's Dream. The basso Emanuel List, who was present, came up to me and, in his inimitably jolly way, introduced himself. 'How would you like to come to Graz with me?' he asked. 'I know the director there is looking for a soprano like you.'

"I naturally asked Klemperer's permission, and he gave his assent, for he knew that that provincial opera house had high standards. It turned out to be a most complicated trip due to the fact that Austria was still partly occupied by the Russians. The audition was arranged ipso facto, and I was invited to open the season in six weeks' time as Desdemona. After accepting the engagement—I was rather thrilled, I must admit—I flew back to the United States and immediately called Schumann to tell her what had transpired. She berated me and said, 'You are mad—you are not ready yet! And how can you prepare this difficult role in so short a time?' I went on to Rochester and had to face my husband with the news, which he accepted with grim humor. 'If you are going to do this,' he declared whimsically, 'I hope you will use my name.' The problem of finding a score of *Otello* in German became an absolute nightmare. I tried everywhere with no success. But Schumann was able to locate a libretto of the opera in German which belonged to Baroness Clarissa de Rothschild, who lived in New York. By this time Schumann had quieted down and agreed to coach me in the role.

"I returned to Graz, and it all luckily went so well—this took place in 1951—that they offered me a contract to remain for Micaëla in *Carmen*, Freia in *Das Rheingold,* and the Countess in *Le nozze di Figaro.* In the

Claire Watson as the Countess in *Capriccio*.

meantime, a cable came from Dr. Watson that it was imperative I return home for Christmas. Although I had not signed any agreement with the opera house, the management was furious, threatening to blacklist me and stop me from singing in every opera house on the continent.

"You can imagine my state of mind, to be so near the goal and then have to withdraw. I flew home, and naturally became pregnant again. The fourth child was born in 1953. But I simply could not get singing out of my system, fully realizing that time was slipping by. The chance came suddenly to sing Butterfly in the summer in a local al fresco performance, and it was a triumph. Even my husband had to admit that everyone in Rochester was very impressed with Mrs. Watson. In 1954, through the grapevine, I heard that the Juilliard School was putting on Mozart's *Idomeneo* and was desperately looking for a soprano to sing the part of Elettra, which needs a real spinto. I rushed to Manhattan, auditioned, got the job, and again I succeeded. Then I took an agent in New York, and he arranged for three auditions: one in Zurich, one in Frankfurt, and the other in Düsseldorf.

"They were all a success," she said with a grin, her vivacious and sparkling eyes lighting up, "but I decided on Solti, who was the music director in Frankfurt and was to remain there until 1961. I knew right away this was an extraordinary talent and that under his guidance I could learn a lot. I sang Desdemona with him, and, incredibly enough, my husband agreed to come and spend a year with me in Europe. But after a few months he changed his mind and ordered me to return home with him. Solti hit the ceiling— and quite rightly so—and so we reached a compromise. I would be given a contract to sing twice a year for two periods of three months each. The first year in Frankfurt I took on eleven roles, and among them were Aida, Elsa, Elisabeth, and Tatiana in *Eugene Onegin*. This was to be my first really big affirmation.

"Germany was still licking its wounds from the horrors of the war, and, miraculously, because of their passion for opera and music in general, all the theatres were resuming at full speed. But because an entire generation had been destroyed, there was a considerable lack at that time of German singers coming to the fore, and this was the moment that so many Americans found employment—and, may I add, they still are. So despite my having wasted so much time and coming onto the scene late, I burned the bridges rapidly. I was quick to learn the language well, and the critics were always complimentary on my diction. And then I had the type of voice that fitted into various wings of the repertoire.

"Nineteen fifty-eight was a very significant year for me, for Munich's

Cuvilliés, the most beautiful rococo theatre in the world, was going to reopen. Very wisely, the Bavarians had taken the precaution, when the bombs began to rain on the city, of dismounting the marvelous *boiseries* [wooden panels], chandeliers, and everything else, and put them away in a safe place. Ferenc Fricsay, the music director, was looking for a Countess, as *Le nozze di Figaro* had been chosen for the grand reopening in June, and I was handed the much-sought-after task. With Fricsay conducting and a major cast, the production was a smash, a night of infinite nostalgia, and I did so well as the Countess that I was given a contract that would enable me to appear in both Munich and Frankfurt. The ovation I received after 'Dove sono' is what really made me in Munich. Because of Schumann's training, the Mozartian line and style suited me, and the Countess was one of the roles I sang the most often. At every performance in Munich the reception became more and more enthusiastic, so I moved there for good in 1959. That was also the year of the inevitable divorce from Dr. Watson.

"It is difficult to describe what happened with me and Munich; it was love at first sight on both sides. Although I sang all over the world later, Munich remained, and will always be, my spiritual home.

"I learned a lot from Solti, and enjoyed him. He is precise and a perfectionist; one knows exactly where one is with him. No temperament—just a lot of hard and well-justified work. I appeared too with Carlos Kleiber, who is now by many considered the great rising star. There is no doubt that he is a genius, and it is very rare, as you know, that a son should become, in the same métier, as prestigious as his father. But he is neurotic, difficult; one never knows what he wants, and one is completely at his mercy. He walked out, for good, of a recording session—at least, so it came out in the papers—because a singer who had arrived one day late because of an airplane strike did not wish, understandably, to begin the session at nine in the morning. But he is a master at uncovering details in a score, and his shading from one tone to the other is extraordinary. I realized certain particulars in the phrasing of Desdemona and the Marschallin thanks to his fantastic intuition."

"The most obvious sign of the esteem in which I was held in Munich was when I was asked to sing Eva in *Meistersinger* on November 23, 1963, when the reconstructed Nationaltheater—the job done was fantastic, for it was the exact replica of the old one bombed during the war—reopened with a festive gala. That I, an American, who had been made the previous year a Kammersängerin, should receive this great honor was thrilling and moving in the extreme. It was the day after President Kennedy had been murdered, and it was touch-and-go whether we would have the opening as scheduled.

A compromise was reached and the gala went on, but many tears were shed when 'The Star-Spangled Banner' was played in his memory.

"In Munich I had begun at the Prinzregententheater, which functioned as the main opera house until the National was rebuilt, as Elsa, and later went on to Fiordiligi and Elisabeth. I have never stopped to count all the roles I sang there, but they included, apart from Wagner and Strauss, all the leading Mozart heroines—in *Don Giovanni* I sang both Donna Anna and Donna Elvira; a lot of Verdi, including Elisabetta in *Don Carlo*, Amelia in *Ballo*, Alice in *Falstaff*, and Aida; and then Tatiana in *Onegin*, Handel's Cleopatra, and Giulietta in *Hoffmann*.

"In Vienna I made my debut in 1957 as Aida, and there I remained until the end as a yearly guest artist, with anywhere between ten and twenty performances a year. In Vienna I often alternated Elvira and Anna with Jurinac, who also sang both roles. I recall Klemperer asking me once in connection with Donna Anna, 'Miss Watson, what do you think happened before the first act? I think the rape has taken place and she hates the Don because, in a Freudian manner, subconsciously she enjoyed it.' The matter is open to many interpretations. Certainly 'Or sai chi l'onore' is underlined by passion embroidered with revenge. As a singing actress I much preferred Anna to Elvira. They are both difficult to interpret for they must sing with a lot of style and yet they are both deeply emotional.

"Klemperer, incidentally, was a superb conductor. He was very demanding, but never put on any airs and was totally natural. When I look around and see the conductors of today, I feel that singing with him was very much like looking at a landscape from an airplane. His reading of the score was all-embracing and luminous.

"I never had trouble with Fiordiligi," she remarked, speaking of her Mozart repertoire, "and even the big jump in 'Come scoglio,' which worries so many sopranos, I could handle without worry, for I had the extension. But I was never comfortable with Pamina. That G-minor aria of hers is hell, and you live or die with it. Unless you feel absolutely at home in it—it is so plaintive, the mood is so somber, the legatos interminable—somehow it interferes with the rest. Vitellia in *La clemenza di Tito* is effective and presents no problems. The Countess, however, remained my favorite. Her music is sublime, and she is a woman with many facets. Her first aria, 'Porgi amor,' is all a series of legatos too, subdued and difficult, but I sailed through it effortlessly. I sang her even at the Salzburg Festival, the Holland Festival, and in San Francisco.

"The Countess was also one of the many roles I sang at Covent Garden, where I first started as the Marschallin way back in 1958. Then later came

Ellen in *Peter Grimes*, Sieglinde (it was my first anywhere), Eva, Elisabetta di Valois, and Elvira. In 1960 I also sang *Der Rosenkavalier* at the Glyndebourne Festival. I had actually recorded *Peter Grimes* in 1958 before singing it at Covent Garden. It was an exciting experience, for it was conducted by Britten himself and had Peter Pears, a tremendous artist, in the lead. With Klemperer I recorded Donna Anna. I was a free-lance, so I accepted recordings that interested me. With Solti I taped Freia and Gutrune for his complete *Ring*, and also the last act of *Walküre* with the sublime Flagstad as Brünnhilde. With Matačić I did Agathe in *Freischütz*, a part I loved musically very much.

"In Italy—at La Scala, in Florence, Rome, and the Fenice in Venice, one of the most enchanting theatres ever conceived—I was always called for Wagner. In Venice I sang Senta, which was the last of my Wagnerian roles. I tried it for the first time in Stuttgart, as a trial balloon, but I did not find it as heavy as I had anticipated. There are many lyrical passages in it, but one must be very careful with the ballad and start it very softly, otherwise one arrives at the end exhausted. It must be a slow crescendo, and then it is all right. I remember Jurinac telling me that she had not found it congenial and eliminated it. But this wonderful artist is very emotional, and it is easy to get carried away with Senta. In Rome I also appeared in *Fidelio*, which I took on toward the end—I sang it for the first time in 1971 in Nuremberg.

"Everyone asks me why I never sang at the Metropolitan," she laughed, "because most Americans consider it a must. As a matter of fact, I was invited various times to appear there, but it never worked out. I won the Auditions of the Air there in 1956, but had in the meantime already accepted Frankfurt. Then I was asked to do Sieglinde, and I did not feel ready for such a responsibility in so large a house, having only sung it once before. Then Mr. Bing wanted me for the Italian wing, and this I did not feel was right for me. In Munich and Vienna, where I was established, it was one thing; at the Metropolitan it was another, with a group of sopranos like Tebaldi, Milanov, and Leontyne Price who were specialists in that repertoire.

"But I did sing some opera in the United States. As I recall, it was *Don Carlo* and *Le nozze di Figaro* in San Francisco in 1966; Pamina and Donna Anna in Chicago; Elsa, Ariadne, and Arabella in New Orleans; and Senta and Elisabeth in Pittsburgh. With the Boston Symphony, under Erich Leinsdorf, I sang in concert form the original version of *Ariadne*, and my Zerbinetta was Beverly Sills, who had not yet become quite so famous. But to close the Metropolitan chapter, which never opened, I knew that, at least in those days, the choice of a debut role was of capital importance. Just think for a minute: della Casa came in with Countess Almaviva, Tebaldi with

Desdemona, Nilsson with Isolde, and Sutherland with Lucia, just to mention a few, each one in a role for which she was world-famous. So why should I agree to make my bow in a role I felt did not show me off at my best?

"I never enjoyed dressing up like a man, so I kept away from the Octavians, Cherubinos, Composers, and the others. My adoration for the music of Richard Strauss started off in Frankfurt when I first took on the Marschallin. She became so close to my heart that when I bade adieu to opera I sang her for the last time. My problem with her, when I first sang her in Vienna in 1964—for the Viennese are most particular about accents, and, after all, she is a local princess—was to sound Viennese, and I worked incessantly at it. The easiest simile that comes to mind is what would happen in New Orleans if an actress playing a Tennessee Williams Southern lady used a Northern accent. I passed the test, but believe me, it was like singing this part for the first time.

"Ariadne, the Countess in *Capriccio,* and Arabella followed in the sixties, and I was particularly concerned about the Arabella, for della Casa was so absolutely perfect in it. But I discovered that the important thing is to study the character and find one's own interpretation. My instrument was undoubtedly very suited to Strauss: it had that phosphorescent—as one critic called it—top register and those pianos and pianissimos that could be heard over the orchestra. I loved all three of them, and I could not really make a choice between them. To have sung *Capriccio* as often as I did at the Cuvilliés is an unforgettable privilege, for the action onstage seemed part of the baroque house, since it all takes place in the eighteenth century. The opera will never be a favorite of the masses; it is strictly for the connoisseurs. Krauss's text is a delight from beginning to end, and so is the delicate score, which underlines every phrase and word. Is the text or the music the most important item in an opera? This is the subject, and each character has his opinion. In the end, as so often in life, there is no solution. In my estimation, it is the most sophisticated opera ever written.

"Ariadne is as static and noble as the Countess is active and busy. But what heavenly music! Every time I undertook 'Es gibt ein Reich, wo alles rein ist' [There is a land where everything is pure]—a tender-hearted monologue, accompanied by a rapturous marchlike melody—I felt transported to that island myself. Is there anything more heavenly than when Ariadne is awakened by the sound of the quiet trio, a sequence of two chords that manages to express all her anguish?

"I could discuss *Arabella* for hours," she went on radiantly, "as I love every moment of it. But I don't believe there is a more emotionally disturbing and lovely moment in all of Strauss's operas than when at the end Arabella sings, 'Nein, mich erfrischt schon das Gefühl von meinem Glück, und diesen unberührten Trunk kredenz' ich meinem Freund den Abend, wo die Mädchenzeit zu Ende ist für mich' [No, the feeling of my good fortune has already refreshed me, and I offer this untouched drink to my friend on the evening when my maidenhood is to end]. The Hofmannsthal text is a masterpiece, and so is the way he has built the character of the protagonist. I could follow every thought and feeling she had. I only took on Chrysothemis in 1972—a tremendously difficult role because of the tessitura, and emotionally too. Her 'Kinder will ich haben' [I want to have children] is the most riveting passage in the opera.

"In this desert that is spreading around us, it is a consolation to know that Dietrich Fischer-Dieskau is still working. He is an intellectual, and no one knows more about singing and the scores than he does. I sang often with him and found him a marvelous colleague.

"Certainly, vocal production today is in a state of revolution. They are doing away with the vibrato; the sound must be concentrated and smooth. The recording companies now rule, and, unfortunately, singers use the same technique before the public that they do in front of the microphones. The more like an instrument, the better chance the voice has to record well. Take Schwarzkopf and Streich—they are perfect for recordings. But Gwyneth Jones has too much vibrato, and as a result she records far less than others who cannot compare to her vocally. I remember singing the Countess with Carlo Maria Giulini, a marvelous musician and conductor. He kept saying, 'Signora, il timbro, il timbro!' And I knew exactly what he meant; but today very few do. Timbre is the pureness of sound, without the tone picking up additional vibrato in the vocal cord area. The trend today is toward a growing monotony of sound. Too much vibrato can be dangerous, but none does away with all emotional impact."

Claire Watson is not a classic beauty, but she always looked absolutely ravishing in the theatre. She had an innate sense of the stage, and one could not help but watch what she was doing every minute. There was never an empty or meaningless gesture on her part, and she had a natural, winning smile that conquered the public.

She told me that she felt like a statue molded by four sculptors: Elisabeth Schumann, Otto Klemperer, Georg Solti, and her second husband, David Thaw, whom she married in 1960. He was then—and is still—a tenor at the Bavarian State Opera, and he has been of great help and assistance to her, understanding well the various problems she had to face.

Years ago I was told that Claire Watson was the only active prima donna in the New York social register. I checked, and she was. Her husband's father, Lawrence Copley Thaw, was a well-known figure in Manhattan society. (Also in the blue book was Anna Case, the Metropolitan's first Sophie in *Der Rosenkavalier,* through her marriage to Clarence Mackay.)

As we left the restaurant, the various members of the staff bowed to her, just like old times, and one of them said, "Frau Kammersängerin, since we no longer can come and applaud you on the stage, do come back soon to visit. We all love you."

"Do you see?" She turned to me with that lovely smile of hers. "Didn't I tell you that Munich and I have a love affair? You know, they made me a star, and this is not so easy to forget."

THE MONEY MAKERS

GLADYS SWARTHOUT

GRACE MOORE

LILY PONS

In the thirties, when the new medium the talkies came into its own, the film studios began searching for photogenic opera singers to appear in their musical productions. This was true not only in the United States but in Europe as well. Among those I remember making a deep impression abroad were Jarmila Novotna, Richard Tauber, Maria Cebotari, Jan Kiepura, Beniamino Gigli, Gino Bechi, and Margherita Carosio. In the United States, the three who for a certain period of time were most in demand were Gladys Swarthout, Grace Moore, and Lily Pons—signed by Paramount, Columbia, and RKO, respectively. And there were others too: Nino Martini, Lawrence Tibbett, Miliza Korjus. The beautiful Ilona Massey, who went on to regular dramatic parts, had been a member of the Vienna Staatsoper under the name Halmassy. Jeanette MacDonald and Nelson Eddy were a case in reverse: from films they went into opera, and although they had little time for it, so busy were they at MGM, I recall an excellent performance by Eddy as Wolfram in *Tannhäuser* in San Francisco in 1934.

Grace Moore was the first to be highly successful and, as far as I can recall, was the first Metropolitan Opera star to be lured by the new medium (Geraldine Farrar, long before her, had made several silent films). Swarthout and Pons followed. Eventually, scripts that gave opera stars the opportunity to perform became more and more difficult to find. But in the meantime the publicity for Swarthout, Moore, and Pons had been enormous, and this brought up their fees in opera, concert, and radio, turning them into big money-makers.

GLADYS SWARTHOUT

When I first met Gladys Swarthout in Venice in the summer of 1938, she was not only a star of the Metropolitan Opera, with fourteen years behind her at the Chicago Opera (where she had made her debut in 1924 as the Shepherd Boy in *Tosca*), but a much-publicized motion picture star. Those were the years when musical films were immensely popular. None of her films for Paramount—the most famous was *The Rose of the Rancho*—ever gained the popularity of Grace Moore's *One Night of Love* or *New Moon*, but Swarthout had nevertheless earned a nationwide fame and was often heard on important radio programs.

Her face was lovely, for she had classical features with superbly photogenic cheekbones and large brown eyes. She was always impeccably and exclusively dressed by Valentina, who knew how to drape her body wisely, which was not an easy task, for she had a long waist and short legs. Her hands were tiny, and she was self-conscious about them. Her hair, parted in the middle, framed her serene face, like an angel's in a Ghirlandaio painting.

We immediately became friends, and for thirty years, except during wartime, she and her husband, Frank Chapman, were very much part of my life. It is not because she was dear to me as a person that I include her in this series, but because she represented a certain period of America's musical life that was quite special and should not be ignored. Like Dorothy Kirsten, she was an American who made her entire career in the United States, and although she spent her years of retirement in a villa near Florence, she rarely spoke Italian. But both her Italian and French were idiomatic, and her pronunciation was excellent.

Born in Missouri, supposedly in 1904, she was a small-town girl who drew attention while singing in a church choir with her lovely, smooth, evenly placed mezzo-soprano voice. She was sent to Chicago to study and later was coached by conductor Leopoldo Mugnone. She always told me she owed him a great deal, for he had taught her what she had become

Gladys Swarthout in the title role of *Carmen*.

famous for: the legatos and the lack of forcing even when the voice needed to swell. She also used to express much gratitude toward Giorgio Polacco, who was for a long time chief conductor of the Chicago Opera. He drew her out, step by step, from comprimario roles to more important ones.

Her debut at the Metropolitan came in 1929, at a moment when two other Americans, Marion Telva and Carmela Ponselle, were its leading mezzos, soon to be joined by the Italian Bruna Castagna. Being small and svelte, she was assigned many trouser roles at the Met: Frédéric in *Mignon,* Siebel in *Faust,* and Pierotto in *Linda di Chamounix;* but her first really great success came as La Cieca in *La Gioconda.*

"I always considered myself a lyric mezzo," she told me one day at her farm in Connecticut, "and only undertook Cieca because it is a short, effective role. But, actually, the part should be sung by a contralto, for then there is far more contrast with Laura, which is written for a dramatic mezzo. I really came into my own with Preziosilla in *La forza del destino* and Adalgisa in *Norma.* I had the extension for both, and they were both immensely grateful scores for my type of instrument. Later I undertook the two roles that were to become so closely identified with me, Mignon and Carmen.

"I never was one who wished to experiment, and although there were many opportunities offered to me to sing roles such as Amneris and Santuzza, I always declined. Anyhow, I did not have either the chest tones or the temperament for them. One must know one's own limitations, and in that era far more singers did. Look at both Grace Moore and Lily Pons. They never strayed from the kind of repertoire that suited them to the hilt. Castagna was, for instance, an Amneris to the marrow of her bones, and I never could have been. There were two admirable Scandinavian Wagnerian mezzos, Kerstin Thorborg and Karin Branzell, who undertook the role, but they were simply not right for this part. Many mezzos—as a matter of fact, a number of sopranos do it too—manufacture their chest tones, but I was adamant not to do it, for if you are a musician, you are always aware of the break that occurs.

"Although at first I undertook many roles, even taking part in the premieres of Hanson's *Merry Mount* and Taylor's *Peter Ibbetson* with Bori and Tibbett, I then began to limit my operatic appearances and dedicated many months of the year to recitals and concerts. That is where the real money was—a factor not to be ignored, for a singer's career is terribly short —and where I also felt free and independent. I was particularly suited to the music of Bach, Purcell, and Handel; and in those days the operatic repertoire was not too varied, because of the Depression first and then the war.

"As time wore on, I sang less and less at the Metropolitan and only did guest performances as Carmen and Mignon. There simply was no repertoire for me. I stayed on until 1945, then accepted a few operatic performances with other American companies and stuck to the recital field. In all, I sang 162 performances at the Metropolitan. One of my great regrets is that I never had the chance to appear as Marguerite in *La Damnation de Faust,* for that is a score that enchanted me. But at that time it was never given."

For over thirty years she sang, limiting the number of her appearances and always taking four months off to rest. At the time of her retirement, the voice still poured out fresh and untired. She had a loyal and faithful public who knew it could count on a gracious performer, exquisitely turned out and in excellent voice. What she lacked was temperament, and she knew it. This was particularly strange, for she had plenty of it offstage and felt very strongly about people and ideas. But it did not project across the footlights. Although she looked wonderful as Carmen and had definite sex appeal, she was rather demure. Virgil Thomson wrote in his *Herald Tribune* review of her performance that her gypsy "never left the country club." Her fans were incensed; and, as is often the case, the criticism helped her in the long run. And in the provinces, the fact that she was incapable of being sluttish or common was enormously appreciated.

How hurt she was by the Thomson notice I never knew. But a short time later, when discussing another performer in this role, she remarked to me, "You know, I don't think that some of our leading critics have ever taken the trouble to read either Prosper Mérimée's novel or Halévy and Meilhac's libretto. Gypsies have their own brand of dignity, and Carmen is not a tramp. If she had been one, she would have carried on with both Escamillo and Don José. The fourth act tells her attitude very clearly. At one point she says to Don José, 'Jamais je n'ai menti, entre nous tout est fini' [I have never lied, between us all is finished] and then again 'Jamais Carmen cédera; libre elle est née et libre elle mourra' [Never will Carmen give in; free she was born and free she will die]. She knows all the time that unless she gives in to Don José, he will kill her, and yet she refuses, knowing it will be her end. Actually, a woman who is willing to die not to betray her man is heroic. And she is no hussy, believe me. Not for one moment. Read the entire text of the last act and then tell me what you think." I did that very night, and Gladys was perfectly right. She had done her homework most conscientiously.

She was, in my estimation, the most ideal Mignon one could hope for. She looked the part, had both the lusciousness of tone and the sweetness of demeanor for the Thomas heroine, and she infused it with tremendous romantic appeal.

Her husband, Frank Chapman, a singer who never made it and who later became a major during the war, took charge of her with an iron hand, and I often wondered whether he was not the reason for her not daring to experiment and branch out more in the realm of opera. He was very commercially minded and undoubtedly managed her career wisely from a financial point of view, for she was one of the highest-paid singers in the United States. (Once, while singing *Carmen* in Pittsburgh, impetuous and talented David Poleri, the tenor whose career was unfortunately so brief, wounded her with a knife by mistake in the grand finale. The wound was only superficial, but her husband milked it for all the publicity it was worth.) I always felt that if there had been a sacred fire in Gladys, it had been put out long ago. Being a quiet, unassuming, and traditionally feminine person, she just allowed him to take over, and she depended on him for everything. I never could detect any real ambition in her, and if it was there, she hid it most cleverly.

She belonged to the era of Bori, Tibbett, Moore, Pons (and Kostelanetz), and Novotna (who came in a little later), and they formed a very special elite. When they sang, all the smart people, who rarely attended musical events, were there, for they had that very special type of Hollywood glamour which is hard to understand today. Being socially minded, they were happy to accept invitations to the best houses. But Gladys was very disciplined and took good care of herself. She was never one to overdo.

"Actually," she said to me, "even when I don't work, I must keep terribly fit, do my vocal exercises every day, watch my figure, and get plenty of sleep. You cannot imagine how draining recitals are, even if they are more satisfactory than opera. You stand for two hours alone on the stage with no orchestra to sustain you; any slightly off note is immediately more noticeable. You have to be on guard every moment—and don't believe for a minute that audiences in small towns are not highly demanding. They may not be as sophisticated as to the choice of the music you sing, but they know instinctively. They don't want to be taken for granted. God help you if you should be so stupid. I always have managed to introduce some new musical material and have been amazed, for instance, at how popular the folk songs from Auvergne, which first were introduced by the splendid Madeleine Grey, have become. Now everyone has recorded them."

I asked her once who were the singers she had admired most. "A hard question—there have been so many," she replied pensively. "But I suppose the one who impressed me most consistently was Flagstad. She had everything—a spectacular technique, dignity, sensitivity—and in her own dimension I thought her a very remarkable actress. Ponselle's instrument was unbelievably beautiful, and I recall the emotion she imbued me with every time I sang with her. Of the coloraturas, I would put Pagliughi first, despite my tremendous admiration for Lily Pons's admirable technique and discipline. I sang many Mallikas to Pons's Lakmé, and she was the greatest perfectionist. But Pagliughi combined a marvelous purity with a warm timbre, which is miraculous. Marjorie Lawrence, alas, lasted only a short time, because of the polio which paralyzed her legs, but she had an overwhelming personality, and there was a wild quality in her voice that electrified me. I was always very impressed by the total sincerity of Grace Moore. She was not a musician, but what a sensuous, stirring voice!

"Of the tenors, Gigli gave me the most pleasure. The timbre was incredible, and he is the only lyric I know of who became first a spinto and then a dramatic without hurting his instrument in the least. He knew what he was doing every minute. Of the baritones I would give the palm to de Luca and Tibbett, the first one for his smoothness and bewitching artistry and the second for his tremendous temperament and insight into the characters he undertook. I shall never forget de Luca returning to the Met, opposite Novotna, as Germont in 1940. He was sixty-six years old and could still spin a phrase like no one else. Tibbett did not have the beauty of timbre that Leonard Warren possessed, but in my opinion his Iago was the greatest of all. Of the bassos, Virgilio Lazzari was perhaps number one on an artistic level—his Archibaldo in *L'amore dei tre re* was an unforgettable achievement —but I would put Pinza and Siepi ahead of all the others for beauty of vocal production."

I once asked her whether it had not been difficult to switch, even if temporarily, from the lyric theatre to the cinema. "Yes, I hated every moment of it," she replied, "for there never was any continuity of any sort. The retakes were interminable, and it is difficult to sing with those tremendous spotlights on you. When you appear in a theatre, you don't have to worry how your mouth looks, but on the screen it is of the greatest importance. As there was absolutely no knowledge on the part of the directors and producers of a classical singer's limited resistance, there was never any consideration for the vocal cords.

"Every experience is fruitful, and I know that my work in Hollywood gave an incredible push to my career. Offers did come from European opera houses, as in the cases of Grace Moore and Tibbett, following the showing of my films. But while they accepted and did sing abroad, I was Cinderella and stayed home. Somehow, I was shy and never felt international, although the musical world is. Few people realize that despite all the hoopla, I am a retiring person and have remained a little girl from Missouri. Looking back, perhaps it was a mistake, but no one really pushed me—certainly not my managers, who could make better contracts for me in the U.S.A."

I knew that every word she said was true. For with her husband's direction and support, she was for a long time one of the most glamorous figures of the American musical world. But there was never the brazenness of a Moore or the determination of a Pons. She never went after anything, just allowing things to come to her. It is this aspect that, although seemingly contradictory, has given her a permanent place in the hall of fame. Nor did she ever brag about her appearances with conductors of the stature of Toscanini.

That she felt completely lost after her husband's death, all her friends can testify. She was like clay in his hands, and shortly after the sculptor died, she followed him. I remember that the last time I saw her in Florence I felt deeply, deeply sorry for her. "Life without Frank," she said, "just does not have any meaning for me. The villa, which he loved so deeply, is like a haunted house for me. The world has changed so much, and I just cannot seem to find the strength to face the endless daily chores and problems. I know I should pull myself together, but what for? The best is all behind, and I have had a great deal from life. There is no home to go back to. This should be my home, but without Frank I feel almost like a stranger." A few months later, in 1969, she joined him.

GRACE MOORE

When I was sent by *The New York Times*'s radio department to interview Grace Moore in 1940, I had recently heard her Louise at the Metropolitan and had changed my mind about her. While I had enjoyed her film *One Night of Love* (and a couple of others) immensely, I had not taken her very seriously as an opera star until she undertook Charpentier's heroine. Though the quality of the voice was sumptuous and velvety, her lack of artistry had disturbed me, and I had found her acting totally unconvincing. But with Louise, which she had prepared with old Charpentier himself, and a year later with Fiora in *L'amore dei tre re,* in which she had been coached by its composer, Montemezzi, she came into her own. Her singular energies had finally been channeled into the right direction, and her temperament—she had lots of it—controlled intelligently.

By the time I came away from my encounter with her, she had won me over completely, and those two hours led to a warm friendship which lasted until she was killed in a brutal plane accident in 1947.

The last time I heard her sing was in Seattle during the war. I was in the army, stationed at Fort Lewis, and when I read the announcement of her recital, I managed with great difficulty to get to the city that evening. I had not written to her in advance, as I was not quite sure whether I would be on duty that night. The moment she came on the stage, or rather swept in, in a pale-blue dress and wearing her diamond necklace, she spotted me sitting on the stage and blew me a kiss. During the intermission I went to see her, and she immediately suggested I have supper afterward at her hotel.

I like to remember her the way she was that night: natural, thoughtful, beguiling. Grace Moore was a marvelously warm and alive human being, one who could put anyone at ease within a matter of a few seconds. The recital had been a revelation, for it was in this type of provincial appearance that she was at her best. She knew how to communicate with an audience in the most appealing way and how to hold it in the palm of her hand. She was folksy to the extreme, while remaining at all times a prima donna; and the wonderful humanity that she was seldom able to project in opera came across in this setting. She talked to the audience, explaining the foreign songs, and at the end she dedicated one to her mother, "sitting by the fireside in her home in Tennessee," and one "to this dear boy"—pointing at me— "who is doing his duty to the United States although he is not an American." All the tricks of the trade were there, and she sang all the favorites: from "Un bel dì" to "Ciribiribin." No one sang this Italian ditty the way she did; it was like a joy ride, bursting with fun, life, and love. It was all very corny and yet totally endearing.

This was the real Grace, a mixture of so many elements, the very grand and the very simple. I recall so vividly that night her telling me that she had been scheduled to fly into Seattle and that her husband, Valentine Parera, had begged her not to. "He was so insistent, I gave in to him," she said. "And do you know—you must have read it in the papers yesterday—it was that very plane which exploded over Wyoming. I am a fatalist; it just was not my moment yet." And then she explained how her husband had always been very nervous about her flying. But Valentine's instinct had been all too correct. That was to be her death, over the city of Copenhagen, as she set off to sing in Stockholm, on an airliner that also had onboard the crown prince of Sweden.

She was not beautiful, but she created the illusion of beauty. Her face was irregular, her nose too big, her blue eyes not particularly expressive, and her figure was that of a healthy but not sophisticated woman. She tended to be slightly overdressed, overbejeweled, and overcoiffed. But when she walked into a room, she radiated, strangely enough, far more than she did on the stage. Although she had made a big name for herself in operettas on Broadway and later in the Hollywood film industry, one felt that she was never completely comfortable with her operatic heroines. Somehow her great femininity did not project, and one usually felt that her action was calculated and did not flow.

In the interview she gave me in the fall of 1940 in her Park Avenue apartment, she confessed that she was no longer ambitious. "I have made a major place for myself, and now I can sit back and reap the benefits. I started out in musical comedy, but I was anxious to make the switch into opera and succeeded. I was the first opera star to have my own radio program and the first to make a real hit in motion pictures. So now I can take time out and enjoy the art of living. The tours I have made in so many out-of-the-way places, the summers I have spent in Europe, the many friends I have acquired, are all a part of gaining experience, which is important. There is,

Grace Moore as Mimi in *La bohème*.

of course, far more that I could have done, but I became very wary of filmmaking. A good picture can be your doing and a bad one your undoing. It is not like singing an opera or a concert when your voice is not in its best condition. There will be three thousand people who will say, 'Well, she was not at her top tonight,' but that's it. If a film is poor, you are confronted with bad notices the world over. You cannot imagine the number of bad scripts I have been sent and turned down despite fabulous sums of money offered. Also, I refused to have another radio program, for this would mean giving up so many other interesting things. If you appear regularly on the air, you have to get all your activities centered around it. It becomes quite stagnant after a while, and monotonous. I loathe routine, and that is why I was happy to get away from musical comedies, for it meant the same thing night after night.

"I am very much involved at the moment in fighting to keep politics out of the world of art. Already the concert halls are beginning to show signs of boycott; already there is talk of not performing this and that opera. It is utterly ridiculous, but people do not reason, and this war hysteria should not concern music, which is above nationalities and races. In art we must all be totally neutral, and I feel very strongly about this point. We are living in an era that has induced people to abandon all hope, and most feel that there is nothing to look forward to. I don't agree with this attitude. All that we have worked for must not be destroyed. What is the use of the present if we have no belief in the future? We must fight for what we believe in. We must do something to protect fragile heroines like Butterfly and many others from the war. Why should they be crushed when the people who created them are not in the least responsible for what is happening today? I don't sing *Butterfly*, but I find it utterly uncivilized for opera houses to refuse to perform this Puccini opera.

"One new role a year is a lot," she went on. "Now I have prepared Fiora in *L'amore dei tre re* and will sing it in Chicago first, then at the Metropolitan under the composer Montemezzi's direction. There is no doubt that *Louise* was a turning point in my career. Critics up until then never took me very seriously, simply because of the Hollywood background. But after the enormous success of the Charpentier opera I am encouraged to take on new assignments, and on the Met's spring tour there will also be *Tosca*.

"I am very concerned about American artists. They should be given every opportunity, but at the moment they are facing one of the worst crises ever, the reason being that all the great talent from Europe who could escape is here. The competition is simply terrific."

Her repertoire was small, and she was frank in admitting that learning a new role was a considerable effort, for her musical memory was not quick on the uptake. She earned fortunes with her recitals, which sold out everywhere in a few hours; opera was really a sideline. She sang only a very limited number of performances at the Metropolitan and very few outside the New York scene. She sang Mimi, the role of her Metropolitan Opera debut in 1928, and Tosca, but no other Puccini heroine. She considered herself too tall for Butterfly and felt that her voice was not dramatic enough for Manon Lescaut. This last omission is interesting, since Dorothy Kirsten (who was her protégée) and Licia Albanese, whose voices were not as big as hers, sang the role at the Metropolitan for years. Gounod's Juliette and Marguerite, along with Massenet's Manon, represented her excursions into French repertoire, but she never attempted the Cours-la-Reine scene in *Manon*: the coloratura bits scared her. During her initial years at the Metropolitan, she also sang two Giuliettas in *The Tales of Hoffmann* and three Micaëlas. In *Tosca* she used to have Thelma Votipka, a talented and famous comprimaria, sing for her the high notes of the cantata Scarpia listens to from the window.

No one could upstage her, as Jan Kiepura soon found out when he appeared as Rodolfo opposite her Mimi at the Thirty-ninth Street house. As she started "Mi chiamano Mimi," he put himself into a position that practically obscured her from view, and all those present that night (myself included) will never forget how she forcefully pushed him out of the way.

Regarding her performances of *La Bohème* at Covent Garden in London in 1936, Lady Cunard and Sir Thomas Beecham resigned from the board when they learned that she was being paid at least double the fee of any of the other great artists appearing there. Lady Cunard felt so strongly about it that she even refused to meet her socially, which is a pity, because the wittiest woman in England would have liked Grace. I tried to arrange it in New York a few years later, but London's number-one music patron would never hear of it. "It's all absolutely nonsensical," Grace said to me, commenting on this episode. "I am worth what they are willing to pay me." If it disturbed her, she never showed it.

Grace was not one to let anyone get away with anything that she did not consider respectful. There is the famous story of when Garbo went up to the Pareras' country house in Connecticut for a weekend, and on Sunday before lunch Grace asked the various guests to write their signatures in the house's guest book. The Swedish actress, who always had a complex about giving her autograph, refused. "If my home is not good enough for you to let others know you have been here, I think you had better leave immediately. I shall have the car ready to take you back to New York in fifteen minutes," she calmly said; and within the amount of time Grace had specified, Garbo was on her way to the city.

Grace lived exceedingly well and spent money like someone who had always had it. And she had. Contrary to what so many have written, the Moore family in Tennessee was very wealthy, for they owned among other things an important department store in Chattanooga. She was generous with her friends, and I never heard her speak unkindly about her colleagues. She looked and acted like a prima donna, and when she made her entrances and exits as part of an audience at the opera or in a concert hall, everyone knew she was there. She was devoted to her Spanish husband, who looked and always acted like a gentleman. During the war years, after Seattle, she never forgot me and took time out to write me letters in her beautiful, round, well-schooled handwriting.

Grace succeeded in establishing herself as an interpreter in two roles— Louise and Fiora in *L'amore dei tre re*—which would always be identified with her. It proved that with study and concentration she could achieve real artistry. Gustave Charpentier was already a very old man when she went to Paris to study Louise (he was born in 1860), but, as she was to tell me on various occasions, a very special rapport was established between them from the first day. He was intrigued by this healthy, enthusiastic American celebrity and flattered that she allowed him to instruct her like a schoolgirl. "How I wish," I recall her saying to me one day, "that I had met more Charpentiers in my life. He was not only a tremendous perfectionist, but he relived his score so intensely that one could not help but be deeply moved by him and wish to please him in every way. It was the hardest work I ever had to put up with, but, you know, I never regretted it. By the time he finished, I really felt I was no longer Grace but Louise."

Temperamentally, this heroine suited her all the way: vibrant, passionate, in love with love and life; and vocally, her luscious instrument was able to bring out all the sensuousness of the beautiful score. The jump from Tennessee to Montmartre was a big one, but the earthiness was there to start with. If her "Depuis le jour" did not have the exquisite roundness of a Dorothy Maynor or the crystalline quality of a Dorothy Kirsten, it possessed a sexiness that I have never heard since. The extraordinary warmth of her voice also suited the erotic appeal of Fiora, loved by three men; and under Montemezzi's guidance she was restrained enough to suggest a royal personage.

But as Tosca, somehow, she was never totally convincing, although vocally the part should have been ideal for her. For she was unable to impart the correct Italian accents demanded by the drama, and she overacted and gestured. She was overly impetuous and never sophisticated. And yet I believe that she loved this part more than any other. Thaïs was a role she discussed with me often—it was at that time in the repertoire of the Metropolitan—but she never got to do it, because she never took the time to learn it. It is a pity: I think she would have been just right for it. But Grace Moore remains a unique phenomenon, for she was equally successful in three different mediums: musical comedy, films, and opera.

LILY PONS

The French word *"chic"* has become part of the English language, but in French *"avoir du chic"* means something more. It is difficult to translate, for it implies a combination of several very positive traits: character, courage, correct behavior, and style. And the best description of Lily Pons is just that: she had *"du chic."* Everyone loved her, from her secretary, Margherita Tirindelli, to her manager, Humphrey Doolens, from her colleagues to the stagehands and the CBS men with whom she made many recordings. She was a professional through and through. She accepted no nonsense from anyone, but she never expected people, even at the height of her fame, to accept any nonsense from her. Thus she won everyone's respect during her long time before the public. Although she stopped singing at the Metropolitan Opera in 1959, after twenty-eight years on the roster, this did not mark her retirement. She went on, singing less and less, until the mid-sixties. Then, at the age of sixty-eight, she made a most unexpected appearance at Philharmonic Hall in New York City, under the baton of her ex-husband, André Kostelanetz. She sang six arias to delirious acclaim, and the concert became part of a television documentary dedicated to her.

Thoroughly French, she was always aware of how to earn money, keep it, and enjoy it. For control was the secret of her long career and her lack of errors in judgment. "I started really earning some cash," she once told me, "when I was approaching the age of thirty, and I knew that the time ahead for a coloratura was not long. Actually, because I treasured and protected what God had entrusted to me, the silver flute in my throat, it lasted much longer than I could ever have hoped or anticipated."

She was a very special phenomenon and fitted into no category. When she became an overnight star in January 1931 with a matinee performance of *Lucia di Lammermoor* at the Metropolitan, she had almost no background to speak of; her only experience was in minor provincial theatres in France. Galli-Curci's forced withdrawal from the United States's leading opera house (due to the inexorable advancement of a goiter) had left the coloratura throne vacant, and Gatti-Casazza was desperately searching for someone to

Lily Pons in the title role of *Lakmé*.

replace the crippled Italian nightingale. Toti dal Monte was still smarting from the manner in which she had been treated, because of Galli-Curci's jealousy, by the management at the Met during the 1924–25 season; Lina Pagliughi's figure was considered impossible for the standards of such a sophisticated audience; and Mercedes Capsir was no longer in her prime.

Giovanni Zenatello and his wife, Maria Gay, two former great singers who ran the summer seasons in the Arena at Verona and had become prominent agents, took a big chance and brought Pons to America to audition. Her credentials were so unimpressive that it took a great deal of patience to persuade Gatti-Casazza to listen to her. The famous general manager thought the French soprano represented a considerable gamble, but he decided to take it. The voice was tiny, and after the solid coloraturas of Sembrich, Barrientos, and Galli-Curci, he wondered how the public would respond. But in her favor were her dark looks, small waist, a piquant charm, and very assured high Es and Fs. He saw to it that she came on with no fanfare whatsoever; the press department was ordered not even to send any advance photos of the new singer to the newspapers. His acuteness brought unhoped-for results. The public, totally unprepared, was dazzled by the purity and daring acrobatics of the diminutive voice, which, because of infallible schooling (she had studied in Paris with Alberto di Goristiaga), always managed to reach the last row of the gallery, however big the theatre. The mad scene was a triumph, and in the excitement no one could recall how many curtain calls there were.

Despite the drama of the Depression, lines formed at the box office of the theatre where the new nightingale would sing. Pons had come at just the right psychological moment, as she herself admitted with total frankness. Those were the days when films had been revolutionized by sound, and being so personable and attractive, she was immediately signed up for several motion pictures. *I Dream Too Much* and *This Girl from Paris,* among others, were not artistic successes, but they helped enormously to project her unknown name all over the world. With her keen intelligence and shrewdness, she became the darling of all the women's pages. Her large, spectacular apartment on Gracie Square and her country house in Connecticut were eminently suited for photograph sessions, and with her unfailing taste she became one of the world's best-dressed women. She started collecting paintings by Renoir, Matisse, Braque, and Chagall, among many others, when the prices were still fairly reasonable. She was so well known that a town in Maryland was named for her and for many years her Christmas cards carried the postmark "Lilypons, Md."

Her every appearance, on- and offstage, was eagerly anticipated because of her innate elegance and the glamour she projected. She learned to keep her figure trim—for most of her career she weighed around 104 pounds, and she was a little less than five feet tall—and make the best of a really not well-proportioned figure (she had a long waist too, and rather short legs) by wearing just the right kind of clothes. She became part of the society circuit, but when she worked she rarely attended parties. Her marriage to André Kostelanetz, the conductor, always remained a mystery even to her close friends. Was it a love match? Most people near her did not think so but suspected it was a sensible union between two persons who had many interests in common and whose joint appearances brought in very high fees. This was particularly true of the summer al fresco concerts, such as those held at the Hollywood Bowl, Philadelphia's Robin Hood Dell, and New York City's Lewisohn Stadium, where year after year Pons was heard by tens of thousands. After their divorce she and Kostelanetz remained on excellent terms, and while he remarried, she never did. Like Moore and Swarthout, Pons never had any children, and in later years she did not regret it. "When I look around and see the despair of so many of my friends who have been so disillusioned and deceived by their sons and daughters," she once said to me, "I realize that I have been lucky."

Because she was so deeply admired by her friends, the gossip of her love affair with a Texan whom she could not marry was always discussed sotto voce. But no one was surprised when she left New York and took an apartment in Dallas. She suffered terribly from nausea before every performance; and as singing in public held little pleasure for her, the more financially independent she became (she was one of the highest-paid singers of the century) the more she curtailed the number of her appearances. With the Metropolitan, where she sang from 1931 to 1959, she appeared 198 times in only ten different operas, and 85 times on tour with the company. So in the space of twenty-eight years she sang an average of only ten times per season. In the latter period of her career she was determined to spend the three winter months in her desert home in Palm Springs, California. And though she also sang for twenty-seven years with the San Francisco Opera, whose seasons were always in the early fall, she wanted to remain at the Metropolitan because of the prestige the name gave for her concert tours. Several coloraturas came, some went, others stayed; but her star kept shining, for she was a special case, the Lily whom everyone had learned to love and could not do without.

Everyone in her large entourage knew the terrible nervous ordeal she went through before performances. She told me that she had been to see many specialists and no remedy had ever been found to soothe her stomach, which never stopped being affected by her public appearances. But with the enormous discipline she imposed upon herself, she went on bravely, knowing that the torture must be endured silently. As she became increasingly famous, she concentrated on fewer roles, until in the second part of her career they were reduced to five. In the first years at the Metropolitan she undertook Olympia in *The Tales of Hoffmann*, Philine in *Mignon*, the title role in *Linda di Chamounix*, Amina in *La sonnambula*, and the Queen in *Le Coq d'or*, which she and Ezio Pinza, as King Dodon, turned into a huge commercial success. Then she stuck to Rosina, Gilda, Lucia, Lakmé, and Marie in *La Fille du régiment*. These last two were her crowning glory, for somehow even her acting seemed more spontaneous, and in the Donizetti part she showed humor and spirit. It was she who, with conductor Gennaro Papi, convinced Edward Johnson to stage this long-neglected opera, and it became a smash hit.

She never attempted the Queen of the Night, for she knew she did not possess the lower range to do it justice, and she abandoned Violetta in *La traviata* after trying it out in San Francisco, for she realized that her instrument was too limited in scope for the drama of the role. While the first act was right for her, the rest demanded a larger, more expressive type of voice. She also spoke to me about Mélisande, but later told me that after going over the score, she had found it lay too much in the middle.

Her career, with few exceptions (she sang at Covent Garden in London in 1935, at the Paris Opéra, at the Colón in Buenos Aires, and at the Bellas Artes in Mexico City), was mainly American. And during the war she braved the stifling summer heat in Burma, China, and India—and always dressed in beautiful evening gowns—to sing for the GIs. Being intelligent and a realist, she knew that the American public was exceedingly loyal and that in the United States she had become an institution. Abroad, it was a different story: competition was intense, and the smallness of the voice was a drawback. It was crystal clear, delicate, somewhat colorless, and she had an effective way of hitting the high Es and Fs that made one realize what a feat she had accomplished. And although she usually had no trouble with her pitch, the expression was practically nonexistent given the lack of palette in the sound. I attended several of her Carnegie Hall recitals and was always impressed by the choice of her selections, keeping her programs on the highbrow side. Despite the meticulousness of the preparation and the musicianship, though, the general impression I received was one of monotony.

But she was a musician to her fingertips; she was a pianist before she turned to singing. In fact, Darius Milhaud, whom she asked to coach her in his Chansons de Ronsard, declared how surprised he had been at how beautifully she could sight-read. Limited as an actress, she relied on her personality, which always came to her aid.

In an interview she gave me for *The New York Times* in 1941 when she became an American citizen, she spoke at length about how she was finally satisfied with the way her type of voice sounded in the numerous radio broadcasts she made. "Before they perfected the system," she declared, "the vibrations of the upper register were terrible, and any note above a high C sounded metallic. People never get tired of listening to vocal acrobatics, and radio audiences are no exception. So I have had to include over and over again the mad scene from *Lucia*, the Shadow Song from *Dinorah*, 'Una voce poco fa' from *The Barber of Seville*, and the Bell Song from *Lakmé*. For three years I went on once a week, and of course this was commercially excellent, as it brings your voice and name into millions of homes. The sale of the recordings also increased astonishingly. I have always felt, however, that the standard of the selections could be improved upon and always had discussions about them with the sponsors. The public is more hip than it is given credit for. I had avalanches of mail from both Americans and Canadians after the broadcast of *La Fille du régiment*, all congratulating me for taking on a new opera and giving them the opportunity to get acquainted with a delicious, forgotten score."

In 1946 I interviewed her again, for *Opera News*, and the occasion was her assuming the title role of *Lakmé* for the opening night of the season, having reworked her conception of the part after her stay in India. It was interesting that her predecessor Galli-Curci had told me, ten years before, how she had hated the Delibes opera and how trashy she thought the music was. But Pons's point of view was entirely different. "This is the first time I will be singing the Hindu priestess in New York City since my having visited India. I must confess that although I had been singing the part since the beginning of my career, I was never very clear as to the very intricate patterns of Brahmanism. The simple love story of 'East and West can't meet' always appealed to me, but I had never looked into any hidden significance behind Lakmé's and Nilakantha's motives."

During her long wanderings around India while she sang for the American troops in 1944, she explained, she became terribly aware of the curse of the caste system. The hopelessness hovering over all Hindus derives from the fact that they know from birth that theirs is a narrow path from which it is impossible to deviate. Lakmé's tragedy, therefore, is in the best Greek tradition. Fate is against her from the very minute the curtain rises on the first act, and although in her youthful emotion she tries to counteract it, she is doomed from the start.

"There is little evolution in Lakmé's soul and heart," she continued, "during the course of the opera, and that is how my interpretation differs now. From the first moment she appears with Mallika in the flower duet to the dying scene, she is a willowy instrument in the hands of her gods. Formerly I built up her character to a series of climaxes. But that was wrong and not according to the Hindu mentality. While death to us of the West is an important step, to Easterners it is not. When Lakmé drinks the juice of the poisonous exotic flower, she is only facing karma and reincarnation. I am underplaying her now emotionally, keeping in mind her closing sentence: 'Love, you have given me beauteous dreams.'

"The opera should be visualized and interpreted as a series of vignettes in the Persian-Hindu miniature style of the eighteenth century. It should be stylized and never leave the dream world. From the temple of the first act to the square of the second and the jungle of the third, the three different Eastern moods should always be underlined. There should be no attempt at desperate histrionics or heavy dramatic accents on the part of anyone, even the infatuated hero, Gerald. He is never deeply in love. In fact, in the end he is quite willing to leave the priestess who has sacrificed everything for his welfare and go back to his garrison.

"As for the costuming, it is one of the most difficult I have ever faced, for the heroine belongs to one of the highest castes, and she must at the same time convey a great simplicity of line. Heroines can be visualized in most cases as color or as emotion. While Gilda's shade is pastel, Rosina's is a Goya red or yellow, and Lucia is white and black. But in the case of Lakmé, there is no definite color that can be applied to her. Her motive is one that escapes definition, for she is like a flower, whose span of life is very brief indeed. The mood is one of mist and tenderness, of delicacy and withering ecstasy. Lakmé is, strangely enough, best known for the Bell Song, but to an interpreter that is not really the most important part. I don't mean vocally, of course. Its fireworks are extremely difficult, but they do not reveal anything of her character. The 'Pourquoi dans les grands bois' is infinitely more revealing and poetic, for in this lyrical outburst the young priestess gives vent to her delight in nature. And throughout the third act there are pages of haunting loveliness."

The last time I saw Pons was in New York City in 1972, and I never dreamed that she had so short a time ahead to live. She had come from out west, where she divided her time between the house in the desert in Palm Springs and the apartment in Dallas, and was on her way to spend her usual two months in France, visiting her sister in Normandy and spending some time at her flat in Cannes, where she had been born in 1904. It had been a long time since we met, but I was not surprised to find her looking beguilingly petite as ever, not an extra pound in sight, her hair dyed blond and superbly coiffed, and dressed in a becoming blue *tailleur*. We always spoke French together, for despite all her years in the United States, English did not come easily to her; nor did Italian, which I always found surprising, since her mother had been Italian. What she said to me that day impressed me enough that I wrote it down in my diary that night.

"You and I know," she said, "that the best is behind us. We are fortunate to have lived when there was still a certain amount of style and manners, and people still had a heart." In saying this she pointed to her own. "Now it's all so cheap, tawdry, shoddy, and people do not seem to have any feelings left.

"As for the world of opera, I cringe. Everyone is singing what is not suited to their voices; they all look like unkempt gypsies. That is why I am happy to live in the desert many months of the year, in contact with the sun and nature. The air is pure, and Westerners are rough but nice people. Come and see me there and we will talk about the old times."

Alas, I never went, and in February 1976, at the age of seventy-two, she died in Dallas, quite suddenly, of cancer of the pancreas. I was told that from the time the cancer was discovered until she passed away, barely a month had elapsed. If she had to go, I am happy that she could go quickly and, I hope, with as little pain as possible. For a nightingale who had given such infinite pleasure to so many people deserved not to be caged, but to fly away into the beyond, leaving behind only pleasant memories.

THE GRAND MADEMOISELLE OF THE METROPOLITAN OPERA

LUCREZIA BORI

LUCREZIA BORI

The reason Lucrezia Bori is given a section to herself is that she does not really fit into any one category. A major star during her career, she remained after her retirement one of the leading figures in the musical life of the United States, receiving more publicity than any other retired opera star, with the later exception of Callas. But while the Greek soprano's constant press appeal was caused by her tempestuous life, Bori's was due to her gigantic efforts in behalf of her beloved Metropolitan Opera House and many other musical projects. As much as Callas was criticized for one reason or another, Bori was admired and deeply respected by all. She became a leading figure in the most exclusive international society. She took on the mantle of a good fairy, and hardly a day passed that she did not make news for her admirable deeds. After she died on May 14, 1960, at the age of seventy-three, her funeral was as imposing a demonstration of universal regret and affection as any outstanding political or civic figure might have received. People instinctively knew that with her passing a very special person had gone—a woman whom the Spanish ambassador to the United States so aptly described as "the symbol of art and diplomacy combined in one."

Bori once had a French maid who always called her Mademoiselle. I began to call her "la grande Mademoiselle," like Louis XIV's first cousin, and there were obvious similarities. Just as Mademoiselle de Montpensier was the most important lady at Versailles (the queen led a very secluded life), Bori was the major female figure, after her retirement, at the Metropolitan. This despite the formidable presence of Mrs. August Belmont, who as Eleanor Robson had been a famous Broadway actress.

Lucrezia Bori was a very complex character, and I wonder whether anyone was ever able to get really close to her. She was affable, friendly, and warm, and yet I shared the feeling with others that she was never completely spontaneous, always slightly on guard, even with persons who she knew loved her and in whom she could trust. She was, as the Spanish ambassador said, a diplomat through and through, and her extraordinary ability to take a positive point of view and never offend anyone seemed second nature to her. I learned to detect her opinions, in certain instances,

Lucrezia Bori as Giulietta in *Les Contes d'Hoffmann*.

by what she left unsaid rather than by any positive statements that she made. Her silences were most eloquent.

But perhaps I should start with the beginning of my acquaintance with her, which eventually turned into a close relationship. I first met her in the very early fall of 1934. When I arrived, at the age of nineteen, at the University of California, as an exchange student from Italy, I learned of a very important opera season that was to begin the following month at the War Memorial Opera House: the imposing casts included such stars as Elisabeth Rethberg, Lotte Lehmann, Ninon Vallin, Lauritz Melchior, Richard Crooks, Dino Borgioli, Ezio Pinza, and Lucrezia Bori. Although season tickets were sold out, Maestro Gaetano Merola (general manager, artistic director, and chief conductor of the company) arranged for me to become an usher. In this way I was able to enjoy all the various treats of the season, not least of which was hearing the legendary Bori at long last.

Bori's name, of course, was very familiar to me, but that season I was to hear her for the first and last time (she bade farewell to the stage a year and a half later, in 1936, at a gala in her honor at the Metropolitan) in four of her most celebrated roles: Manon, Mignon, Magda in *La rondine,* and Violetta. When I met her at a Sunday lunch at the house of mutual friends, I told her of the affection with which she was still regarded in Italy, despite her absence from Italian stages since before the First World War; she seemed highly pleased. She kindly invited me, despite her full schedule of rehearsals, to have lunch with her in the city the following Saturday; and, overcoming the considerable gap in our ages, we quickly became friends. I recall her telling me that of all the operas in her repertoire, *La traviata* worried her most, especially the first act. "There is nothing trickier than that word 'Gioir,' is there?" she said. "It is enough to give one a stroke—not only the tessitura, but the way that one word changes mood. It occurs three times in the recitative and then twice again in the 'Sempre libera,' and it is really the key to Violetta's state of mind." But it was really after the war (although I had seen her many times in New York in the interim) that I saw more and more of her and on many occasions functioned as her escort at the opera and at other musical events.

Bori had been born in Valencia. Originally the family name was Borja, which translates into Italian as Borgia; and she claimed that hers was the branch of that notorious family that had remained in Spain and fallen into obscurity. She is believed to have been born in 1887, but some dictionaries tell a different story. She was educated at first in a convent—she was very religious—and then took courses at the conservatory in Valencia. She then traveled to Milan, where she took singing lessons with Maestro Vidal, and her debut at the Teatro Adriano in Rome as Micaëla followed in 1908. She took on Nedda in *Pagliacci* in Piacenza and Varese and then *Butterfly* in Naples.

She had a stroke of great luck when the Metropolitan Opera visited Paris in 1910: Lina Cavalieri, who was to have appeared in the title role of *Manon Lescaut,* canceled, and a quick replacement had to be found. Tito Ricordi, the famous music publisher, recommended Bori, and she auditioned for a select group that consisted of Puccini, Toscanini, and Gatti-Casazza. She received unanimous approval, and soon Paris was at her feet. With Caruso as her partner and Toscanini in the pit, this young unknown, the delicate and charming Spanish girl with her relatively small but impeccably trained voice, won her battle.

The Metropolitan would have liked her services right away, but in the meantime La Scala had signed her to a contract. In Milan's holy of holies she appeared during three seasons as Nannetta in *Falstaff,* Carolina in *Il matrimonio segreto,* Gounod's Juliette, and Frau Fluth in *The Merry Wives of Windsor,* and then created Octavian in *Der Rosenkavalier* and the Goose Girl in Humperdinck's *Königskinder* in the Italian premieres of these two operas, both conducted by Serafin. She reached American shores in 1912, making her debut at the Metropolitan in the same role she had sung with the company in Paris: Manon Lescaut. She immediately became a favorite, although at first critics found her instrument somewhat limited. Eventually she became one of the opera house's leading stars.

It was therefore a considerable treat for me to be able to hear her in San Francisco in four different roles, each of which showed off her particular gifts as an interpreter. She conveyed fragility like no one else I have ever heard, not even Sayão. If Kirsten Flagstad expressed, in a singular manner, dignity and regality, and Callas smoldered with internal fire, Bori was a master in projecting a beguiling femininity and a need for protection. Everything she did on the stage was calculated to the last infinitesimal degree, but the projection of a never-ending series of minute details produced a devastatingly natural effect. None of her recordings do her justice, for the voice was in no way exceptional, and in those days the microphones were unable to pick up the nuances of which her art was made. The heroines she portrayed in San Francisco in 1934 were four distinct characters, but to each one of them she brought a dimension of irresistible charm and gentleness.

Not really beautiful, she was immensely appealing with her intensely expressive face, transparent white skin, typically sad Spanish eyes, and raven-black hair. She had a good enough figure, and, unlike so many of her colleagues, she managed to disguise a somewhat short and stocky neck. Her head was a bit too large for her body, but this flaw was subtly corrected by costumes especially designed for her by the best couturiers abroad. Exceedingly well (and discreetly) turned out over the years, always immaculately groomed, coquettish in an old-fashioned manner, she looked like the lady that she was.

Her voice was neither velvety nor rich; it was inclined to be metallic, as so many Iberian voices are, and lacked sensuousness. But it was most artfully and expressively maneuvered, and she had an uncanny knowledge of its limitations and exemplary diction. She ably created all-engrossing moods and aptly built them slowly and affectingly, scene by scene. In *Manon*'s Saint-Sulpice scene the action can seem absurd; the heroine must convincingly entice her former lover from his newfound vocation in the Church. The duet is the most dramatic in the opera, full of pitfalls, and the singers must keep their eyes on the conductor. I shall never forget the way Bori ran her beautiful hands over des Grieux's chest from the sides; the seduction was utterly believable. The Meilhac and Gille libretto is very poetical at moments, and how she took advantage of the text! Shivers went through the audience as she sang, demurely and yet so convincingly, the "Hélas! Hélas! l'oiseau qui fuit ce qu'il croit l'esclavage le plus souvent, la nuit, d'un vol désespéré revient battre au vitrage! Pardonne moi!" (Alas! Alas! the bird that flies from what it believes to be slavery most often, in the night, in a desperate flight, returns to beat against the window! Forgive me!) while, ever so discreetly, she imitated with her hands the flight of a bird. At the end, when Manon is dying on the road to Le Havre—it is with this phrase that the opera ends—she has an unenviable task for she must sing "Ah, je meurs. . . ." and then immediately afterward "Il le faut . . . il le faut. . . . Et c'est là . . . l'histoire . . . de Manon Lescaut" (I am dying. It must be, it must be. . . . And that is the story of Manon Lescaut). It is dramatically effective, as Bori said to me, but completely unnatural for a young countrygirl-turned-courtesan to mention her own name as she dies. Bori sang it in a whisper, as if life had already left her, as if she were already on the other side, and it was devastating.

In *La traviata* she wore fresh camellias with every costume, and in the last act Doctor Grenvil brought her a bouquet of these flowers, which he handed over silently to Annina, the maid, who placed them in an empty vase. When Bori as Violetta pulled herself up from the chaise longue just before dying, singing "Cessarono gli spasimi del dolore" (The spasms of pain have ceased), she grabbed the camellias from the container, and as she dropped lifeless to the floor, she let go of them so that they spread all around her. It was an unforgettable moment, and she told me that she had worked this stage effect out after several other attempts to resolve the opera's finale in a romantic manner. (One must remember that those were the days when an artist had complete leeway on the stage to do as she pleased, with the metteur-en-scène standing in the background, mainly preoccupied with the chorus.)

Many times in later years I begged her to write her memoirs, or at least to dictate to someone all that she remembered. But her reply never varied: "To tell the truth would hurt too many persons, both alive and dead. And not to tell it—what is the point?" This was her philosophy, and while there were many people who thought her insincere, I was never among them. She was immensely reserved and disciplined; and under a veneer of bubbling vivacity—she was the life of every party—she dominated herself one hundred percent. Obviously, she had made up her mind never to say anything unpleasant, and she never did, even when discussing colleagues with whom it was known she had experienced some differences. She annoyed some of her friends by finding excuses for everyone and always finding positive qualities. Many times, to my criticism of a singer's performance, she would reply: "It will be better next time. Everyone can have an off night."

Once, attending a performance of *Pelléas et Mélisande* with Bori, I remarked that the beautiful Helen Jepson, who sang the title role, had poor French diction. And Bori, who had sung Mélisande at the Metropolitan over thirty times, came to Jepson's defense. "If you think it is easy to enunciate French clearly while singing, just try it. Give her a chance; I feel sure that she will improve."

Speaking of this opera, which everyone agreed had become one of her most memorable achievements, she told me what a soul-searching decision it had meant for her to agree to sing it for the first time in 1925. "There comes a moment when an artist must take a very significant big step," she said, "and the responsibility is his alone. Mary Garden had been everyone's idea of what Mélisande should be like. She had created it in 1902 in Paris and was still singing it very successfully. In a way it really belonged to her. But she had never sung it at the Metropolitan, which in many ways made a big difference to me. When Gatti-Casazza asked me to undertake it, I studied the score for several days and then decided to attempt it. I felt that the music was right for me and that I could do justice to this ethereal, mysterious creature. But Garden's ghost haunted me for some time. Then, suddenly, one day I felt quite free of it. I never would have undertaken it at the beginning of my Metropolitan career, but by 1925 I felt I was established enough to take the risk of a comparison. I never compare artists —this has always been my philosophy—but the public does. So I took the plunge, and the Holy Virgin of Montserrat was with me."

One evening we discussed *L'amore dei tre re,* which she had created at the Metropolitan under Toscanini's direction in January 1914. The occasion of this conversation was the revival of the Montemezzi opera in the winter of 1941 with Grace Moore as Fiora. Bori sang the role over thirty times at the Metropolitan. Muzio inherited the part during Bori's six-year leave from the Met, and later Ponselle sang it for two performances; but otherwise Fiora was all hers, and I had always been told that this had been Bori's greatest role. In this opera devoid of arias and written in a semi-verismo vein, the heroine is trapped between her loyalty to Manfredo, whom she was forced to marry, and her passion for Avito, the great love of her youth. When Bori sang "Ah tortura! Indicibile contrasto!" (Ah torture! Unspeakable conflict!), her anguished cry literally sent shivers through the audience.

"I loved this score and the libretto by Sem Benelli," she explained to me, "the moment I laid eyes on it. It made a sensation at the time, but now it becomes increasingly difficult to perform. Four exceptional singing actors are needed, for Fiora and the three kings—Archibaldo, Avito, and Manfredo —are creatures of flesh and blood. The text is marvelously poetic, a crescendo of breathless intensity, but the words are so important. You saw what happened tonight: much of it was unintelligible. Fiora is a complex woman, and she does try, like Isolde, to resist the temptation that Avito represents. Could anything be more tender and desperate than when she sings, at the moment when her passion has overcome her, 'Ahimè! Si piega il voto mio, come all'albero pietoso a chi muore di sete' [Alas! I bow down before you like a merciful tree over one who is dying of thirst]? And then when her father-in-law seizes her and, strangling her, demands to know her lover's name: 'Si chiama dolce morte'—his name is sweet death. What marvelous theatre! You cannot imagine how superb our first cast was. Edoardo Ferrari-Fontana sang Avito, Pasquale Amato was Manfredo, and the Polish basso Adamo Didur was a splendid Archibaldo. In some ways it is a sort of Italian version of *Tristan und Isolde,* particularly in the marvelous scene where Fiora begins, but never ends, waving the veil from the top of the tower— reminiscences of Brangäne! Each one of the four principals is superbly delineated in both text and score, which is contemporary in a sense, and yet never leaves the path of harmony and counterpoint. Fiora is a relatively short part—she lies dead in the chapel in the last act—and yet I found it far more tiring than many other, longer ones which demanded greater effort from the voice. It is because of the tension, which never lets go—the succession of rapid changes in the coloring of the voice. And when Archibaldo drags Fiora's dead body over his shoulders, across the stage, this may seem easy to the public seated comfortably in the orchestra, but it is nerve-racking to the singers. Being blind, he must give the impression that he does not quite know where he is putting his feet, and Fiora that she is no longer of this world."

I asked her what she thought of Grace's performance. Always kind, she answered: "She looked lovely and she has temperament, but the aching strain of this young woman torn between conflicting emotions was not quite there. Perhaps it will come with time."

I asked her once why she had forsaken *Butterfly* and had taken on *Iris* for its American premiere, under Toscanini's direction, in 1915; I had been told by many sopranos that the Mascagni scoring was even heavier than the Puccini.

"First of all, I only agreed to sing it a few times; in fact, I believe it amounted to four performances. Toscanini adored this opera and thought I was just right for it. And he could be most persuasive. But I do not agree that it is more grueling than Cio-Cio-San. First of all, it is much briefer, and it does not require that ever-increasing depth of feeling and heartbreak which the other does. I was always a lyric soprano and very careful as to what I undertook, particularly after those four soul-searching years when I did not know whether I would ever be able to sing again. When nodes appeared on my vocal cords in 1915—not too long, as a matter of fact, after *Iris* had come and gone—I began to look at every score through different eyes. For four years I sat and waited, and they seemed eternal. For one solid year I never spoke a word to anyone; I just disappeared from sight, and no one knew where I was. Why do these nodes appear suddenly? There are so many different explanations, and it is impossible for even a specialist to determine the cause. Overstress, overfatigue, singing through a bad cold—it could be so many reasons. Anyhow, I do not like to relate all this, except for the sake of colleagues who may be suddenly faced with this problem. I never lost faith, for I perceived that singing was the fountain of being of my life, and I could not even conjecture what I would do if I could never begin again.

"My trial run took place in 1919 in the adorable Garnier opera house in

Monte Carlo. I wanted a small theatre to gauge my resources, and the instrument was back in shape. But I did not return to the Metropolitan until 1921, for I wanted to make absolutely sure that I could really resume my career in full.

"You talked about mistakes before. Well, I think every artist makes them. I know that I committed an error when I went back to Gilda—fortunately not at the Metropolitan. I got through the evening, but I felt out of sorts all the time. When I had gone over it with the coach at the piano, it all had seemed fine, but in the theatre it can be very different."

Bori admired Licia Albanese and befriended her. On one occasion I asked whether she did not think that Albanese was singing too many Madama Butterflys, a role Bori herself had eliminated early in her career, considering it too strenuous for her instrument. "No," came the reply, "I think it's all right. Licia is very smart and never forces. When the orchestra covers her, particularly in the first act, she just lets it and does not try to overcome it. She is an emotional person, but the role does not destroy her the way it does others. Every artist has her own brand of sensibility; and that is what, unfortunately, many of the conductors coming up now do not seem to take into consideration."

When Albanese undertook *Tosca* for the first time in 1952, again I expressed concern. "I have faith in Licia's judgment," Bori answered, "and she will manage, for she knows how to husband what limited and beautiful resources she has. The voice is lovely, as we all know, and small, which we all know too. For Tosca we are undoubtedly used to far bigger voices. Hers will be a cameo Tosca, but with temperament—she has lots of it—and different. You know, I never would have approved of her doing it at the beginning—but not now, when not only is she well established, but the public loves her. This makes all the difference!" And she was right, for although the part suited her neither physically nor vocally, Albanese did make a living person out of the Puccini prima donna, and there were moments that proved most affecting.

I asked Bori which were the most beautiful voices among the women singers she had heard. The answer was quick in coming. "Ponselle and Rethberg, in their own different ways, had the most gorgeous instruments of all. Muzio was a case apart: you cannot classify her, for in the end you had been so emotionally destroyed by her performance, you did not even know anymore what kind of an instrument she had. As a complete performer, I would say Flagstad. In fact, I have never missed a single performance of hers unless humanly impossible. The glorious instrument, the presence, the majesty—all seemed so natural and true.

"But for versatility—and I would like to tell you about her—there never was anyone like Florence Easton. She retired the same year I did, and I asked her, 'Florence, why do you stop? Your voice has never been in better shape.' And she replied, 'Lucrezia, I am tired. I deserve a rest after thirty-three years.' I am amazed at how rapidly this phenomenon has been forgotten. It is perhaps because she was gifted with a large voice of no particular color, but with such an even, easy extension at the top that she could handle such light lyrical parts as Lauretta in *Schicchi*—she created this role at the Metropolitan in 1918—along with *Cavalleria, La Gioconda, Carmen, Andrea Chenier,* the Marschallin, even *Fedora,* and many contemporary works, including *Turandot.* I kept saying to Gatti-Casazza first, and to Edward Johnson later, 'Your gold mine is called Florence Easton.' I remember that when I came back, *L'oracolo* by Leoni, which I had created at the Metropolitan in 1915, had in the intervening years been sung by Easton. She came up to me and said ever so charmingly, 'You are far more suited to Ah-Joe than I am. I hope she becomes all yours again.' Actually, this one-act opera was pretty enough, but what made it was the absolutely marvelous performance of Antonio Scotti as Chim-Fen. Even when his voice was almost gone, he managed to continue being sensational in this part."

Bori always asserted that she had no favorite role, but she was particularly proud that she brought Puccini's *La rondine* into the Metropolitan Opera repertoire on March 10, 1928, and that it remained until her retirement. I discussed this opera with her on various occasions, for I could not comprehend why it had been so underrated. "I agree with you one hundred percent," she said, "and how I wish poor Puccini could see how New Yorkers took it to their hearts. The score is delicious, far more difficult than at a first glance, but the libretto is the weakest of his operas. One must work hard to give Magda a real characterization; the text does not really define her very well." She told me an amusing story of when she sang *Manon Lescaut* in Paris with the Metropolitan Opera in 1910. She had spent a lot of money on the costumes; but Puccini, present at all the rehearsals, felt that the one she wore in the last act did not make her look bedraggled enough for a refugee stranded in the deserted countryside of Louisiana. So he threw a cup of coffee on it. "It came as a shock," she related, "but actually he was right."

A point Bori often made was the tremendous importance of balance between the voices. "I know that it is difficult for the general manager to obtain the right singers together for the same evening," she used to say, "but the success of a performance depends on just this. A tenor with a very large voice and a soprano with a smaller one, or vice versa, cannot, however well they sing, do justice to the score. Caruso and Ponselle, for instance, were wonderfully paired, and so were Rethberg and Martinelli. One of the partners with whom I was always at my best was Edward Johnson. There was a total understanding between us, and vocally, we were most comfortably paired together. Now we have Flagstad and Melchior, a union made in heaven." (Because Flagstad had arrived at the worst moment of the Metropolitan Opera's financial crisis and sold out every performance, Bori called her "*la nostra salvatrice*," our savior).

Bori spoke Italian and French to perfection; and although her spoken English was heavily accented, when she sang it her pronunciation was excellent. She mentioned, to my surprise, that her greatest professional regret had been not to have learned German so as to be able to have sung Eva in *Die Meistersinger*. "Don't you consider it a somewhat dull part?" I asked. "Dull? did you say *dull?*" she asked incredulously. "I find her absolutely delightful from start to finish. From the very first scene with Magdalene and Walther, when she cannot find the scarf or the brooch—she has misplaced them—to the scene with Hans Sachs when she discusses the shoes she has not worn yet, to the heavenly quintet (she starts the act by complaining about the shoes being too tight!), she is a humorous, willful, adorable creature. The trouble is that most sopranos just sing her and do not interpret her."

Bori found the French operas particularly suited to her type of voice; she sang, with relish, Micaëla, Juliette, Manon, Mignon, both Antonia and Giulietta in *The Tales of Hoffmann,* Louise, and Mélisande. She brought *Mignon* (the title role is usually sung by a mezzo) back to the Met repertory with enormous success and sang a total of forty performances. In the United States she also created Concepcion in *L'Heure espagnole,* Vittadini's *Anima allegra,* Falla's *La vida breve,* and Lattuada's *Le preziose ridicole.* With the exception of Gilda in the early days, her Verdian excursions consisted only of *Falstaff* and *La traviata.* She had considered Desdemona, but decided that her voice could never cut through the concertato in the third act. I pointed out to her that Albanese had sung the role, and tactfully she replied, "Now it's all different. In my epoch the big phrase in the concertato was considered essential, and the soprano must sing it against all the other voices and the orchestra. Rethberg was superb in this dramatic moment, her voice soaring. Now times have changed, and this matters less. Licia banked everything on the fourth act, and there she was wonderful."

Bori always spoke with great pride of having been a pioneer in furthering

American opera and claimed that she had greatly enjoyed appearing in Deems Taylor's *Peter Ibbetson* as the Duchess of Towers. "Not great music," she observed to me one night, "but very agreeable to the ears, and Deems has a real sense of the theatre. The public liked it, for we gave over twenty performances of this work, unheard of for a contemporary work in full Depression time." When I went with her to the revival of *Le nozze di Figaro*, which became a tremendous hit at the Met only after 1940, she expressed regret that so little Mozart had been performed during her years in the theatre and that she had been cheated out of one of her favorite composers. (She sang only Despina in New York.)

Her love for the Metropolitan was overwhelming, and after her withdrawal from the stage she never stopped channeling all her energies into obtaining much-needed financial aid for its preservation. No singer has ever shown more loyalty to the Met than its grande Mademoiselle. She never sang in Europe again after her return to New York; and she remained there throughout the season, except for occasional appearances with the other American opera companies and her very successful concert tours. She was a close friend of Edward Johnson, who, like her, belonged to another class of singers. They were, to use words unfashionable in today's world, a lady and a gentleman. Although one came from the warmest province of Spain and the other from freezing Canada, they understood each other on all levels. Johnson became general manager of the theatre the year before she retired and remained in the saddle for fifteen years, until 1950, when Rudolf Bing took over. Johnson realized her value as a public relations officer and a fund raiser—no one could resist that smile of hers—and asked for her assistance more and more until she became invaluable.

When Bing took over, her role in the affairs of the Metropolitan continued, but in a minor key. It was clear to everyone that the new manager wanted to create his own kingdom with its own court. Bori's position was so strong, though, that she remained at the palace, even if her influence had diminished. One could sense that she was not on Bing's side, but one had to know her very well to detect it. It was, once more, what she did not say that told more than what she said. She was deeply concerned about the new wave of stage directors the Bing management brought in, admitting from time to time how shocked she was at their lack of respect for scores and librettos. "If this continues," she said to me one day at a performance that had particularly annoyed her, "where will we end? Alfred Lunt is a wonderful actor, but what knowledge does he have of how to direct *Così fan tutte*? Experiments of this sort can be made in a provincial theatre, not at the Metropolitan."

Bori was a perfectionist, and I was told that she had always rehearsed more than anyone else—all the people who sang with her said so. She was not simply content that the music be firmly embedded in her throat; every gesture and nuance of the character had to become a part of her. Of the twenty-nine roles she sang at the Metropolitan, Mimi came first with a total of seventy-five performances, *La traviata* second with sixty-one, and Nedda third with forty-four. She claimed she enjoyed singing the Leoncavallo heroine, for it gave her the chance to show her temperament and acting ability without wearing herself out. "The aria is grateful and well written for the voice. It climbs steadily but evenly, and the words are so beautiful. The trick is to imitate, as well as possible, the sound of the birds; then the romantic nature of this passionate woman—but a woman with a particular sensitivity—comes forward. She is not just a sexpot; she is looking for love. When she sings 'Oh! che volo d'augelli, e quante strida! Che chiedon? Dove van? Chissà?' [Oh! what a flight of birds, and such cries! What are they seeking? Where are they going? Who knows?], and then later when she talks of her clairvoyant mother, who understood their language, and used to tell her as a child, 'Lanciati a vol come frecce, gli augel disfidano le nubi e il sol cocente, e vanno, e vanno per le vie del ciel' [Hurled in flight like arrows, the birds defy the clouds and the burning sun, and wander, and wander through the heavens], this is real lyricism, and very tender. So often it is sung without evaluating the text, and then it just becomes a vocal exercise. I resent the Neddas who ignore the composer's words and play her like a slut. She does try to resist Silvio's advances—it is all there in that phrase 'Non mi tentar! Vuoi tu perder la vita mia?' [Don't tempt me! Do you want me to lose my life?]."

Bori took between two and three months' rest each year. "Every season I went to sing in Ravinia Park, and then to Europe to see my friends until the fall. After what happened to me, I knew I had to preserve my energies and not overdo. It is essential for every singer to give time for the vocal cords to rest. Then, after I retired, I played it by ear but never failed to go and see my friends abroad. Not having ever married—and therefore with no children—I am as free as one of those birds Nedda sings about. But when I look around and see the results of some of my friends' marriages, I think perhaps I was wise to remain wed to my profession. My heroines never let me down, nor did my public. I shall never forget my tearful farewell before that wildly cheering audience, bringing down the curtain on 429 performances—yes, I kept count—in the same house. And the fame my modest contribution to opera brought me did enable me to do so many helpful and useful things for music."

For many years she was president of the Bagby Music Lovers Foundation, which offered anonymous help to retired artists, whatever their past importance, and she looked into each case, bringing her smile and the donations that kept these people alive. Often I would call her at nine in the morning only to find that Mademoiselle had already departed for a nine-thirty board meeting. After the smashing success of a benefit she staged in 1958 for the victims of the terrible flood that had hit her hometown of Valencia (she had raised well over fifty thousand dollars, which in those days was a lot of money), she said to me, "This is the sort of occasion when it is worthwhile to be a celebrity, for one can really be of some help." At the Metropolitan, where she attended several performances a week, she was welcomed by every usher and member of the staff like an old friend. To all of them she would flash her lovely, slightly sad, irresistible smile.

THE ITALIAN BEAUTIES

BIANCA STAGNO BELLINCIONI

GEMMA BOSINI STABILE

SARA SCUDERI

It is a curious coincidence that three of the four most beautiful sopranos Italy has produced are all penniless and living free of charge in the Casa Verdi in Milan. (The fourth, Lina Cavalieri—the most staggering beauty of them all—died in an air raid in Florence in 1944.) I went to see them on different occasions, and the resignation and dignity of these ladies made these perhaps the most touching of all my interviews. While none of the three had exceptional voices, they had a special musical sensitivity and a formidable stage presence. They were remarkable singing actresses and had great sex appeal—and the public adored them. Scuderi was entirely self-made, but Stagno Bellincioni began with a magical name, her parents having been among the most sensational opera stars of their time, and Bosini was the wife of the prestigious baritone Mariano Stabile.

BIANCA STAGNO BELLINCIONI

When I interviewed her in 1979, Bianca Stagno Bellincioni, one of the legendary figures of D'Annunzio's Italy, was past ninety years of age (she was born in 1888), yet she was stylish and superbly coiffed, and traces of her famous beauty were still in evidence. At the Casa Verdi in Milan, where she had been living for some years in a small, immaculately kept bed-sitting-room, she was dressed in black with a purple scarf thrown over one of her frail shoulders, flashing the luminous smile that had both opera and cinema fans at her feet in the days when stars were truly stars. Her manner was of a chatelaine receiving in a superb drawing room; the modesty of the surroundings ceased to exist through the sheer authority she emanated.

"There is nothing left of the former glories," she said, pointing with slender hands to the walls and the sticks of furniture, "the wonderful paintings and sculptures, the silver, the houses, the jewels, the furs, even the possessions I valued most, letters and photographs of the great I have known —all blown up in the last war. Even Massenet's moving message to my mother, all gone up in smoke. There are a very few left, saved by a miracle," and she indicated an autograph of Verdi to her mother, Gemma Bellincioni, "alla grandissima Violetta," and others of d'Annunzio, Marconi, and Mascagni addressed in glowing terms to her. "It is a great pity, and not for snobbish reasons," she continued, "but for historical ones. My parents were so loved by the tsar and tsarina of Russia, the emperor and empress of Germany, the emperor of Austria, not to speak of all the other rulers, that they received gifts, telegrams, and handwritten notes from them. They have all gone with the wind, and I shall soon be gone too, and I don't care. The ideals for which we worked have crumbled in the dust; there are only memories."

In a fascinating conversation that lasted two and a half hours but seemed only five minutes long, the word she used most frequently was *"rispetto"* —respect—and she used it when speaking of her parents, whom she idolized, of her fellow artists, and of her art. Never had I met one so modest

451

Bianca Stagno Bellincioni in the title role of *Thaïs*.

yet so acutely aware of the heavy responsibilities she felt toward her family name. And at the same time, because of her aristocratic heritage (the Bellincionis were the clan to which Dante Alighieri's mother belonged) and her musical lineage, I kept sensing the pride that still surged within her.

"All children of famous persons," she declared, "are born with the terrible handicap of how to live up to their reputation, while at the same time finding doors automatically open because of their name. I don't mean to be Pirandellian when I say that often what you are is not necessarily what you should be. Particularly in my case, when my mother insisted I follow in my parents' luminous footsteps. On my mother's side I am the third generation of singers. My grandfather, Cesare Bellincioni, was a great basso comico, and his wife, Carlotta, a mezzo-soprano, was celebrated for her Rosina. My mother, Gemma, stunning looking, with a divine figure and truly classical features, started at age sixteen in Naples. In 1882 things began to move fast for her when the aging but still remarkable Enrico Tamberlik signed her to sing all the coloratura roles opposite him in a six-month tour of Spain and Portugal. Then came *La traviata* at the Costanzi in Rome, which made her reputation overnight: she demonstrated a real tragedienne's temperament, and the public was all in tears. She repeated the triumph at La Scala and then was engaged for a long period in South America.

"Accompanied by her mother, on the ship she met Roberto Stagno, Italy's leading tenor, who was at the height of his fame and was unsurpassed in *Robert le diable*. It was more than love at first sight. An overwhelming passion engulfed the young girl—she was twenty-one at the time, and the great Sicilian star in his forties. Though he was married, with children, nothing—not even my grandmother's anguished disapproval—could stop their romance, which lasted, vibrant and delirious, until his death in 1897. During those twelve years they often teamed up, and their appearances as the ill-starred lovers in Gounod's *Roméo et Juliette* were heartbreaking.

"They sang all over Europe, and every possible honor was heaped on them in Russia, Germany, and Austria (where my mother was made a Kammersängerin by order of Emperor Franz Josef, despite the fact that she was not a member of the Vienna Opera). What is so incredible is that in those years they sang everything. My mother was equally successful as Gilda, Lucia, Carmen, Zazà, and Lucrezia Borgia. My father went from Almaviva (which he often sang to Patti's Rosina) to Turiddu, which became his great warhorse. When Bellincioni and Stagno sang together in the world premiere in Rome of *Cavalleria rusticana,* all hell broke loose, and they became the symbols of the verismo school. From then on there was no contemporary composer who did not prevail on them to launch his operas, many of which are now forgotten, including Giordano's *Mala vita,* in which they won another triumph. My father died of heart trouble, and my mother went on like the trouper she was, not to let down an entire company built around her.

"In 1898 Giordano chose her to create *Fedora* in Milan, and she suggested Caruso as Loris. Again it was a memorable occasion, and every opera house wanted Bellincioni in this opera. She also became a great Salome, the first to refuse to have a dancer take over the Dance of the Seven Veils. It was as this Strauss heroine that she said farewell to the stage in 1911. Then my mother agreed to teach singing in Berlin, at the request of the imperial family, but the war soon came and she lost everything, for Italy entered the war against Germany. And the house in Berlin, which I recall so well, was fabulous. She went on teaching, first at the Santa Cecilia in Rome, then at the Accademia Chigiana in Siena, in Vienna, and at the conservatory in Naples. When she had to retire from there, she opened her own school. Both she and my father were extravagant. Money came in and went right out again. They lived like matinee idols.

"I was born in Budapest, where my mother was worshiped. As a child I lived like a gypsy, but a luxurious one, with music as my daily bread. I was taught the piano very thoroughly, and this came in handy later on, for I could read scores without anyone's help. And I sang for my own pleasure. At age sixteen I fell in love with a member of the Ricordi family; since this was considered a proper marriage, my mother made no objection, and in 1905, before my seventeenth birthday, I became a bride. Two boys were born from this union, which proved a great fiasco. After five years we separated, and I was down and out and at loose ends. My mother took me in hand and convinced me to follow her into the opera labyrinth. She put all her vigor and ability into preparing me, and I studied very much in earnest.

"In 1913 I was ready and took the plunge in Graz, Austria, as Cio-Cio-San. In my dreams I had always thought how wonderful it would be to become a prima donna, but I had never dared to follow through because of the respect I had for my parents. 'Your voice is not extraordinary,' my mother said, 'but you are very musical, and you have personality. You can make a success if you discipline yourself, and your heroines will never let you down, even if others do.' Three years of coaching showed results, and the Austrian audience responded so well that my contract was extended for the entire season, during which I took on Mimi, Nedda, and Massenet's Manon. A *Faust* in Prague followed, and my career took wing.

"I never accepted too many engagements, as I was a devoted mother and didn't want to stay away from my sons for too long. I have always been honest with myself, and I know what my limitations were. My voice was not large, but it had an easy and agreeable top, and my mother taught me how to float the notes so that they reached the last row of the balcony, even in big theatres. Somehow to me that art seems lost today. It may be due to the orchestras, which have increased in size, and the conductors, who no longer show consideration toward the singers, wishing only to assert themselves.

"I never had great agility, yet I managed comfortably to sing *La Fille du régiment.* The first act of *La traviata,* which became with *Madama Butterfly* one of the operas I sang most, put the fear of God in me every time—tricky, ungrateful, and wretched! When I took on Violetta, a role so identified with my mother, I felt it was almost a disservice to her, but she encouraged and cajoled me, and I succeeded way beyond my expectations. I never sang in the summer months, as I became a successful movie star and managed the two careers for many years, one complementing the other. Geraldine Farrar was doing the same in America. I do not even remember the number of silent movies I made.

"It was my privilege to sing with some great artists, and I always approached them with respect. In 1914 I found myself singing *Manon Lescaut* at Covent Garden with Martinelli. How handsome he was, and what a virile, exciting voice! You may not know that my parents were asked by Puccini to create *Manon Lescaut,* and my father, who wore a black beard, refused to shave it for des Grieux. Puccini, understandably enough, could not conceive of the chevalier with a beard and refused point blank. My mother would not accept without Stagno. Many letters went back and forth between them. While at Covent Garden I was asked to replace Emmy Destinn in *Madama Butterfly,* and what a challenge that was! The Pinkerton was Caruso, who owed so much to my mother, and the gentleness and kindness of the man were unbelievable. The sensuousness of the voice was overwhelming, and his 'Addio, fiorito asil' was emotional beyond belief.

"At Covent Garden one night a Baroness Cederstrom was announced in my dressing room. A formidable-looking woman swept in, embraced me forcefully, and said, 'You have real talent, but it is understandable, being the daughter of the sublime Stagno. How I treasure the memories of my appearances with him!' I had no idea who she was and asked her. 'I am Adelina Patti,' she replied, amazed at my ignorance. I was acutely embarrassed and could not have been more surprised at her graciousness, particularly since I had always heard at home what a difficult partner she had been.

"Another Pinkerton, of a very different nature, I had the luck to sing with was Tito Schipa at the San Carlo in Naples. His was the true art of bel canto, and I remember how he spun the notes in the love duet in such a manner as I've never heard since. I had the good fortune to appear with Battistini, considered Italy's baritone, in both *Thaïs* and *Maria di Rohan* at the Rome Opera. He was so powerful a personality that it was most understandable why a sinner like Thaïs should want to repent to please him. And in *Maria* he had the audience spellbound when he dragged me across the stage. Gigli sang with me in many performances of *Lodoletta* conducted by Mascagni himself, and his tone was pure honey. I cannot understand why this opera is now shelved, for we always had sold-out houses. Another tenor who made an impression on me for his musical instinct, aristocratic style, and admirable diction was Edward Johnson, known in Italy as Eduardo di Giovanni. He was often my Pelléas.

"One of the experiences I remember with the most pleasure was appearing as Liù in the French premiere in Monte Carlo of *Turandot*. My great friend Gilda dalla Rizza sang the title role for the first time, and the production was a real fairy tale in spirit; there was no big staircase, and the action was so fluid and attractive, as it must have been in Gozzi's eighteenth-century fairy tale. I loved trouser roles, and if I may be so immodest, I liked to show my shapely legs. Octavian, curiously enough, suited my voice, though I believe a mezzo is better for the role, and Mascagni's *Zanetto,* an adorable one-act opera that takes place on a terrace overlooking Florence, became very much identified with me. Mascagni thought I was just right for it. If he had not been so great a composer—one day he will be re-evaluated as he deserves—he could have made a great place for himself as a conductor. What a clear beat he had, and what a deep feeling and understanding for the voices! I never attempted any Verdi roles besides Violetta, and I soon dropped Tosca from my repertoire. I just was not right for it physically— she must be tall and commanding—and vocally I found it even more fatiguing than Salome, which I sang up to the end of my career. Mélisande, Marguerite, Manon, and the heroine of Rabaud's *Marouf* were my favorite French roles, and another opera I found stimulating was Zandonai's *Conchita.*

"I never sang in America," she said with sadness, "and I was disappointed. Oscar Hammerstein had signed me to a five-year contract, and along with Maria Barrientos and many others I found myself stranded in Paris for weeks. It is rather confused in my mind, but I think what happened was that the Metropolitan Opera prevented him legally from producing opera at the Lexington Theatre, and we were caught in the dispute and never got paid.

"In my era there were touring companies with big stars and good ensembles. I did some very satisfactory work in Portugal—a divine theatre, the San Carlos in Lisbon—Spain, and Egypt. *Tutto finito!* It's all ended. Now the unions have a stranglehold; managers can't do anything anymore. The demands of the chorus, orchestra, ballet, and stagehands are outrageous, and the singers have become money-mad, rushing around, singing sometimes as many as three roles in three different cities at the same time. Now I ask you!

"I stopped when my son, an ensign in the navy, was killed rescuing some sailors in the China Sea." She gestured toward a big medal set in a gilded frame. "That's for valor—little consolation to a broken heart. I simply could not continue singing. For several years I thought I would go mad, had no desire or wish for anything. My mother managed to snap me out of it. I helped her with her teaching until 1950, the year she died. The atmosphere was already different, and pupils in Italy no longer serious, so I decided to close the school in Naples—a mistake, perhaps.

"I have no regrets except one: I never sang at La Scala. Several opportunities came, but they were never the right ones; I was offered roles I did not feel suitable. When Max Reinhardt chose me for Rosalinda in an Italian version of *Die Fledermaus,* we opened in San Remo and played to packed houses. Then we were due to move to the Teatro Lirico in Milan, a very respectable house which La Scala still often uses when its schedule becomes too intense. Instead, at the very last minute, because of some contractual dispute, the engagement was moved to the Odeon, a music-hall theatre. I refused to go on. A Stagno Bellincioni does not, cannot, appear in such surroundings. They sued me, but I won. In those days judges were honorable, and he knew I was right. You see, respect for the name of my parents, which blazed a trail of glory in the world, always guided me. And as far as I know, I never faltered."

Despite all the crosses she had to bear, she remained a true diva until her death in the summer of 1981.

GEMMA BOSINI STABILE

The snow was falling so heavily in Milan that all traffic had come to a stop, and I had an appointment that I did not want to miss with Gemma Bosini, widow of Mariano Stabile, considered by many to be the greatest singing actor of this century. There was no other way but to walk—perilously, for the ground under the snow was pure ice, and all around me people were falling. The set was certainly appropriate for my meeting with one of Italy's celebrated Mimis.

Although I had been at the Casa Verdi several times before, never had it appeared so severe and austere as it did on that bleak day. I confess I was unaware that I was about to encounter a really stoic and heroic woman. Following the instructions of the man at the front desk, I walked and walked until I found her door. In a tiny room, with no telephone or private bath, stood smiling a very old lady almost totally blind and crippled with arthritis. "I am Gemma Bosini Stabile," she greeted me, inviting me in.

In a few feet of space, surrounded by boxes filled with clippings attesting to the former glories of her husband and herself, the ex–prima donna expressed her gratitude at having a roof over her head. "But for how long?" she asked without expecting an answer. "You have read of course how Casa Verdi risks being shut down because of a disgraceful argument between the city, the region, and the political parties. They have had the audacity to call it a useless institution! What is going to happen to us all, living here with nowhere else to go? Is it because we are old and helpless that this great institution which Verdi created and endowed has itself become useless? I am ninety years old—I was born in 1890—so the time ahead of me is getting shorter and shorter. Maybe I will live out these outrageous quarrels and manage to die right there." And she pointed to an exceedingly narrow bed. She confessed that hers was a lonely life, but that great artists such as Gina Cigna, Elena Nicolai, and Giacinto Prandelli and his wife were kind enough to remember her and came to see her from time to time. She referred to her colleagues as "Signor" and "Signora"—an insight into the dignity she gave to her former profession.

Suddenly I thought of all the photographs I had seen of her, when she was acknowledged as one of Italy's most beautiful women, wrapped in furs and jewels; photographs of her sophisticated home, of the deluxe hotel suites she and her husband had occupied all over the world; of the Isotta Fraschini they had driven around Europe. And now? A room far smaller than the garret in which Mimi meets Rodolfo for the first time. Not a word of complaint was uttered by her, and no mention of all that had been lost in the Second World War; of the properties destroyed; or of the savings put away for a safe old age wiped away by the ever-increasing inflation. All she was interested in telling me was what a wonderful fate hers had been, to be married to the greatest artist of his era and a true gentleman.

"You know that Sicilians are very special," she explained, "for if they are from top stock there are none finer. And you know, naturally, that the Stabiles were one of Palermo's most distinguished families. Most people take it for granted that the street in the center of Palermo named Mariano Stabile was the result of his fame, but this is not so. It was in honor of my husband's uncle, a great patriot who helped a lot in creating a united Italy. Poor, wretched man, how overcome with grief he would be if he saw the results today!

"My husband, who was born in 1888, died on January 11, 1968, at the age of eighty: I believe his was one of the longest careers on record, for he made his debut in 1911, and although he officially retired in 1961, he did sing on here and there until 1963."

At first she did not want to talk about herself. "Not interesting," she kept repeating. But I insisted—I knew that she had had an important career in her own right—and so she finally got going, and all that she said was punctuated with dry humor.

"I was born in Belgioioso, near Pavia," she reminisced, "and my father handled the administration of the large estates of the Visconti family. My brother, who had very poor eyesight, became a celebrated organist and, until his death, was the soloist at the cathedral in Milan. I was a terribly poor student at school and only wished to sing. My parents were very much annoyed with me and decided to give me a lesson. They talked to Baroness Airoldi, who knew Tito Ricordi very well. Could she arrange an audition? they begged her. And then when this impossible child heard from so great an authority that she would never amount to anything, then perhaps she would forget it and turn to something else. The kind baroness consented. 'What will you sing?' Ricordi asked me pompously, after exchanging the usual phrases of welcome. ' "Di quella pira," ' I replied. There were explosions of laughter from the various persons in the room—his staff was present

Gemma Bosini Stabile as Desdemona in *Otello*.

—but not from him. 'Let us leave that aria to the tenors! Anything else?' he said. ' "Ebben, ne andrò lontana" from *La Wally,*' I ventured. He went to the piano and played it for me by heart. At the end he asked me to repeat it, suggesting I give a little less voice. Then, without saying a word to me or my mother, who was standing trembling nearby, he asked his secretary to put in a telephone call to Maestro Messina. He spoke loud enough so that we all heard him. 'I am sending you a girl by the name of Bosini. Teach her *Bohème* and *Faust,* and remember that every two months I want to hear how she is progressing. I believe she has possibilities.' My mother was overcome, and so was my father. I was exactly sixteen years old, and the consensus was that I had good looks.

"In those days," she continued, "impresarios used to roam around the teachers' studios always on the lookout for new talent for provincial theatres —they were regular factories where artists were made. And so one came along and offered me a series of Mimis in Genoa. Absolutely thrilled, I was foolish enough to accept, but then I did many foolish things in my life. By doing this I made a mortal enemy of Ricordi, who never forgave me. He was absolutely right, and I do not blame him one bit, for it was unpardonable on my part not to ask for his advice and permission. If I had just waited, as he had enormous influence at La Scala, I would probably have landed there, for he had been very pleased with my progress.

"Anyhow, from Genoa the innocent Bosini went everywhere, spreading like wildfire. In Milan I was engaged at the Lirico, which often had first-class operatic seasons, for fifteen Toscas; and Umberto Giordano, who came one night, insisted I immediately learn his *Fedora*. He undertook the job himself, something I will always be very proud of, and on March 23, 1918, I made my first appearance as the Russian princess in an opera that was to be very closely identified with me in the future. On that occasion I sang thirty performances—but that was the way in those days. If an opera was good box office, the impresarios continued the run, and engagements were less binding than they became later. That was also the year I recorded with Gigli the duet 'Lontano, lontano' from *Mefistofele*. Actually, I was born for verismo roles, since I had a bite in my voice that was completely natural. I never had to force, and I was an impulsive and compulsive actress. I threw myself into the various parts and gave all of myself.

"Then came the San Carlo in Naples, where I was given Manon Lescaut, Margherita in *Mefistofele,* Micaëla, and Alice Ford. Little did I know that this last role would be the one I would sing the most—over four hundred performances certainly, and maybe more. It is not a showy part—she does not have a single aria—but one that musically demands much care and attention. I became a specialist in it, the way Ilva Ligabue is today, and I sang it all over, from the Colón in Buenos Aires to the royal theatres in Cairo, Alexandria, and Malta, which in those days signed up all the top artists.

"But it was as Micaëla that I first sang opposite Stabile, the Escamillo, in Trieste. Immediately I found him irresistible as an artist—I found it very natural that Carmen should prefer him to Don José—and as a man. He was married then, and I tried to shut him out of my thoughts. But it was not easy, as fate brought us together over and over again on the stage. And eventually, after his wife died, we got married.

"I recall vividly my first *Tosca* with him and the many that followed. I loved the part and was used to stealing the show. But when he was Scarpia, this was never the case. He had such magnetism that eventually I gave up any idea of competing with him; I knew that I was beaten before the curtain went up. I only really came into my own during the third act, when he was already dead. Everyone knows how difficult it is to stage 'Vissi d'arte.' Is she really singing to herself, or is she praying to the Madonna, or is she addressing, in a sort of haze, the head of the Roman police? There are many different ways of interpreting it. Jeritza chose to do it all from the floor, Olivero slouched on the couch, and so on. With Stabile, who was a mixture of infinite elegance and insidiousness, one never knew what to expect from him during the aria. He told me many times that he himself had to follow his impulses at the time. Sometimes he went to the window and stood there, or he went back to his desk signing papers, or he came and stood quite near me. I was self-conscious, for while I realized that this scene should have been the high point of the evening for me, I knew that the audience was galvanized by him. He played constantly with his expressive hands wherever he was, and I caught myself at different times looking at him. When I sang Alice Ford to his Falstaff I felt freer, for on the stage I was far less exposed to him than in *Tosca*.

"I became a great favorite of Marinuzzi, a wonderful maestro, and sang *Iris* and *Lohengrin* with him at the Massimo in Palermo, the San Carlo in Naples, and other opera houses. He wanted me for an opera at La Scala, but the rule there was very strict: no matter how well one had made out elsewhere, one had to audition for Toscanini and his staff. It was *the* temple, and one had to enter it on one's knees. Somehow I was paralyzed with fear and did my best, when the moment came, to wriggle out of it. But there was no way. Was it my guilt feelings toward Ricordi that had put me in such a state? I really don't know. The fact is that I stood there with my mouth wide open, and not a sound came out. It was as if my vocal cords were completely torn to pieces. I don't know who was more embarrassed, Marinuzzi or me. 'You have disgraced me,' he said, walking out, and what could I reply? He was absolutely right. Somehow, despite the scandal—everyone in Milan knew about it five minutes later—my career went on busily, although, of course, I never got to sing in the holy of holies. As a matter of fact, I recall that shortly afterward I, who was not a Mozartian, made a big success as Elvira in *Don Giovanni* at the Liceo in Barcelona. Battistini, on the wane, was the Don, and he was still an artist to his fingertips, and Graziella Pareto was a Zerlina to be treasured. She was grace personified. And then, suddenly, out of the blue came another role, Maria in Mascagni's *Guglielmo Ratcliff,* which was particularly suited to me and for which I became much in demand.

"But now, *basta* about myself," she said with finality. "Let us talk about Mariano. After studying in Palermo, he went to Santa Cecilia in Rome to perfect his technique with the famous Antonio Cotogni, responsible for Lauri-Volpi and Gigli. My husband always told me that he had great faith in Cotogni's judgment, and for the rest of his life he tried to follow it. 'I am no prophet,' Cotogni had said to him, 'and of course with time your voice may become darker and larger, but I think this is highly improbable. Remain in the lyric domain, and stray only when the interpretation is more important than the vocalizing.' He gave him a long list of roles to be avoided. And Mariano was strong enough not to allow himself to be tempted. He did become a great Iago and, of course, the greatest Falstaff of all, because in these two Verdi roles it was not the volume that counted, but the refinement of the technique.

"The first great sensation he made was in Rome, in *La favorita;* and the impresarios of the theatre, Emma Carelli and Walter Mocchi, signed him to a long contract. He became the first Klingsor in Italy when *Parsifal* was given in Rome for the first time and also sang the role at the Colón in Buenos Aires. He never, wisely, tackled the heavy Wagner parts, but he was a fabulous Beckmesser. He did not make him ridiculous, as so many artists do, for he was incapable of any kind of exaggeration. He brought out the pathos and the humor, but always within certain limits of good taste.

"In Milan he sang for the first time at the dal Verme in *Manon Lescaut* with Muzio and Martinelli. He had sung Ford several times when in 1921 Toscanini approached him about switching to the role of Falstaff himself. He studied the part with Ferruccio Calusio, and by the time the rehearsals began at La Scala, he was so deep in the character that Toscanini predicted he would be a smash. And he was. On the night of December 26, 1921, ten years after the beginning of his career, the premiere of the last opera Verdi ever wrote was a sensation, and Mariano was turned into an international star overnight.

"Toscanini used him later on many occasions, and I remember particularly his Scarpia, Iago, and Gerard under the maestro's baton. Later too he sang many Falstaffs with him at the Salzburg Festival. Respighi chose him in 1923 to create his difficult and demanding opera *Belfagor* at La Scala and then refused to let any theatre give it unless Mariano sang it. And Richard Strauss requested him for the Barber in the Italian premiere of *Die schweigsame Frau* in 1938. He was also to sing often under Strauss's direction the Mozart operas *Don Giovanni, Le nozze di Figaro,* and *Così fan tutte.* Bruno Walter also considered him an exceptional singer of these operas and often used him in Salzburg and elsewhere. Glyndebourne latched on to him too, and Mr. Christie became a great admirer. Actually, Mariano loved the part of Don Alfonso in *Così,* which suited his natural sense of elegance and wisdom. I remember him saying to me, 'It is perhaps the most complete role Mozart and Da Ponte conceived together. He is, in a way, superficially, a figure of contradictions, but actually it all makes sense.'

"Mariano's artistry, somehow, was on such a high level that I never heard of any colleague resenting him. Everyone realized he was someone apart, and he could go with ease from the brooding tragedy of Thomas's *Hamlet* to the comedy of Dr. Malatesta in *Don Pasquale.* I recall some exceptional performances of *Don Giovanni* at the Théâtre des Champs-Elysées in Paris in 1928. At the premiere the public became hysterical and kept shouting at the end, *'Stabile, Stabile, nous voulons Stabile.'* They wanted, of course, for him to take a curtain call alone, but even when the management insisted, he refused. I remonstrated with him afterward, and he asked me, 'Are you crazy?' Very quietly he explained to me that with such world-famous artists at his side as Frida Leider, Gabrielle Ritter-Ciampi (an unforgettable Elvira), Alexander Kipnis, and René Maison, a solo bow would have been very disrespectful toward them. Either each one gets his curtain call or no one—this was always his motto, even when the other singers were much inferior to him.

"He never spoke of retirement," she continued, "for the stage was his life. His voice was still in perfect condition, even if smaller, and offers kept pouring in. But in 1961, after he sang a very successful *Falstaff*—he also did the mise-en-scène—at the Accademia Chigiana in Siena, with Franco

Capuana conducting, he said to me, '*E adesso basta, voglio chiudere in bellezza*' —enough now, I want to finish in beauty. I knew that after fifty years he was tired of having to fight so many battles with all the ignorant new conductors and stage directors who had the temerity to want to change this and that. While I was unnerved by them, he was only saddened. He saw that all the experience that had enriched him so did not interest them. All they wanted was to find a new angle, to destroy all that had been built through blood, sweat, and tears. He simply no longer had the strength to fight them as he had until then, and despite the unimpaired freshness of his voice, he announced his retirement.

"When the final curtain came down and he died in 1968, it was the end of everything for me. But God has willed it that I stay on and do my purgatory. As endlessly as I admire Verdi and Boito, I cannot agree with them when they say in *Falstaff* that 'tutto nel mondo è burla'—everything in this world is a joke. Life is not like that—at least not for me."

As I went out again into the blizzard, I felt invigorated, for I had spent two hours with a brave human being who staunchly accepted having lived too long when life no longer had anything to offer her.

She finally closed her eyes forever in the spring of 1982 at the Casa Verdi.

SARA SCUDERI

In 1977, when the door of Room 26 at Casa Verdi opened, standing there was Sara Scuderi, whom I recalled as the most dazzling and convincing Tosca of my youth. The room was tiny, modest, quite cold, and very neat, but the occupant transcended it with her authority and serenity. Everything around her seemed to disappear, and she dominated the space as if she were alone on a large, empty stage.

Laurette Taylor once said to me, during the original New York run of *The Glass Menagerie,* "Many factors help to build a star, but when all is said and done, one has magic or one does not. It is something that cannot be learned." Sara Scuderi, so simply dressed, was born with it, and even now, with all the glory of her career behind her, living in a rest home for musicians, she was as commanding as she was profoundly touching. There were moments too when her beauty came to the fore, her sculpted features kindled by large, dark, passionate eyes.

"Don't you think I am exceedingly fortunate," she asked, "in having this cozy little room all to myself? It's quiet, it looks out on the courtyard, and there is not a sound, except when these sweet nuns come to praise the Lord in the nearby chapel. They are there now. Can you hear them? I am so deeply grateful to Verdi"—and she pointed to a large portrait of the composer, wearing a large black hat, hanging on the wall—"for it was he who made this possible. We are wonderfully looked after, you know. Breakfast is brought to our rooms every morning at eight, and for lunch and dinner we are well fed in the big dining room. The conversation is stimulating.

"The present defeats me. They are all protesting about something, killing each other, allowing this wonderful gift of life to slip through their hands. At night this city is so full of violence one cannot go out unless one is fetched in a private car and brought back. Materially speaking, I have nothing, but I am so rich in memories, and that is the kind of wealth no one can take away from you. If I were to start again, I would follow exactly the same path. It was a tremendous honor to serve the muse of music, and

I am immensely obliged to all those who helped me on the way up and then after I arrived. Like so many colleagues, I was never interested in the financial aspects of my career. Anyhow, with the last world war, my savings went up in smoke, because of the terrible inflation."

Sara Scuderi was born in Catania of a Sicilian father and a Bolognese mother. "Mine was not a well-to-do family, but we lived with dignity within our means. I sang for my own pleasure, and all those who heard me complimented my parents. Finally, one day my mother took me to Maestro Matteo Adorno to find out if my wanting to take singing lessons was warranted. He listened to me warbling away some arias and then asked my mother to tell him the truth: it was obvious I had been studying, he said, so why make a mystery of it? My mother and I vehemently denied I had ever taken a lesson. 'It happens very rarely,' he said, 'but I have known a few cases like hers. Her voice is perfectly placed, and the texture is lovely. She takes the high Cs as if she had been working at them for years. She is giving too much, has not yet learned to spare herself. The mezza voce is practically nonexistent, and there is room for improvement in parts of the range; but in my estimation, with two years' concentrated training, she'll be ready to sing in public. This voice is a true lirico spinto, and never let anyone tell you she is a dramatic soprano—that would be a fatal mistake.' I left the studio walking on air, and within a week I had started working with him. I never had any other teacher. True to his prediction, two years later I made my debut at the Coccia in Novara as Desdemona, which I followed with Leonora in *Il trovatore*.

"Modesty aside, I was good-looking," she went on, "and had a shapely figure. This, added to a good-sized voice and dependability—I never canceled unless absolutely necessary—facilitated my entrance into the lyric theatre, and engagements rained down on me. My mother went everywhere with me and was very strict, and she was absolutely right: singing is a lifetime's dedication, and one's private emotions must not interfere. I emoted a lot on the stage, but that was it. I never married, and men were never important in my life. I saw around me what an impediment husbands and lovers could be to a truly dedicated artist, and for me a career was more important than eating. What if a husband insisted after a while that I quit? What if he insisted on having children?

"One of my only regrets is that I never recorded an entire opera, only arias. But I want you to hear me again."

She got up from her chair, took a record from the table, and put it on the turntable. It was an all-Puccini album, and I was startled by her voice: the exemplary diction, every word not only intelligible but full of meaning,

Sara Scuderi in the title role of *Tosca*.

combined with the velvet roundness of the instrument, the finely detailed yet emotional phrasing, the swelling of the sound, and then the diminuendo.

"I never forgot my maestro's advice," she continued, "and refused real dramatic roles. My debut at La Scala came with Fiora in *L'amore dei tre re,* and following in the footsteps of Gilda dalla Rizza was no joke—she was worshiped, and I an unknown. But I won my battle; and when La Scala in 1937 decided to revive the Montemezzi opera, I was again the heroine. Because of my knack for learning new roles, I was handed the premieres of Mulè's *Dafni,* Alfano's *Madonna Imperia,* and Camussi's *Volto della Vergine.* A role I sang often at La Scala was Elvira in *Don Giovanni,* and I had the fortune of having Schipa as Ottavio and Stabile as the Don. Vocally there have been greater Dons, but the roguishness he emanated, combined with the humor, the toughness balanced by irresistible charm, have never been equaled. The ever-complaining Elvira, despite the beautiful music, was not my favorite part, but I never refused it when I knew Stabile was in the cast. I often sang Alice to his Falstaff and Tosca to his Scarpia.

"The second act of *Tosca* leaves any soprano limp, but with him it became pure joy—he was totally dependable, yet never quite the same. There was always the element of surprise, yet the assurance that he would never try to steal the action from you. He was as fine a colleague as Beniamino Gigli, with whom I sang many times in *La Bohème, Manon Lescaut,* and *Andrea Chenier.* Gigli had a generous nature and always wanted to share his success with one. There was never any nonsense. Obviously, he could not touch Stabile as an actor, but the voice never failed to bring a lump to my throat, despite his not having quite the tear that Caruso had. How musically intelligent he was, always refusing, even at the end of his career, to take on the superdramatic roles such as Otello and Samson. They knew their limitations then."

The soprano also sang a great deal with Lauri-Volpi, particularly in *Il trovatore* and *Otello.* "I always made it my business to get along with my fellow artists, and despite Giacomo's underhanded tricks—such as holding on to a note forever but never in the same place—I never argued with him. It was always exciting, much like a gymkhana. It may not have been very artistic, but on his good nights he was unique—the strength, the color of his instrument, and the temperament. Now the tables have turned. You don't sit wondering whether a note will be held too long but whether it will be reached successfully. It was more thrilling in the old days. Where has the breath support gone today?"

In her room there were photographs of Zandonai and Mascagni with enthusiastic dedications. "I sang their operas a lot," she explained, "and often with them conducting. Of all the Mascagni works, the one I love the best is *Amica,* now forgotten. It's great theatre, and the soprano has a most agreeable part. Mascagni's tempos were the slowest on record, but we all knew it and had to be prepared for long breaths. I sang *Isabeau* with him and also many Santuzzas. Her forty minutes onstage are a killer, and no one who has not attempted the role can imagine what she is in for. In my opinion my voice was neither dark nor opulent enough, according to the tradition established by some of the divas, but Mascagni thought I was just right for it. Often composers get carried away by the way one looks, and a good figure is really needed for *Isabeau,* which is effective but so tiring. I had to keep turning down impresarios for performances of *Cavalleria* and *Madama Butterfly.* Cio-Cio-San is also a dangerous part for an emotional singer, which I was. Tosca is not onstage the whole time, the way Butterfly is, and there is less legato and gentleness. It's easier, you know, to be angry and jealous over a big orchestra than it is to be tender, and the orchestration of *Butterfly* is heavy, unless the maestro is not out to kill you.

"In the non-Italian department, I was stuck constantly with Eva. In those days all Italian opera houses had *Die Meistersinger* in their repertory, and my mother used to say, 'Go ahead and accept it. It's a leading role, very gratifying vocally, and you don't have much to do. You're saving yourself for heavier operas.' I followed her advice, and, with Tosca, it was one of the parts I sang most frequently. I also appeared as Elsa, which appealed to me musically, and I understood her—except for the cyclone that hits her toward the end, she is as serene a person as I am. I never could make up my mind to accept Sieglinde, as much as I was tempted, for it lies so heavily in the middle of the voice. I made a success at La Scala as Jaroslavna in *Prince Igor.* It was a glorious production, and I was pleased when the duke of Aosta came backstage to congratulate me. 'Who taught you to be so regal?' he asked. 'You should have been born to a crown.' In those days, gentlemen knew how to be gallant.

"At La Scala I performed Elena in *Mefistofele,* but in many other opera houses I sang Margherita, which suited me very well—not a long role, but effective and vibrant. For ten years I was re-engaged in Holland, and there I often sang the other Marguerite, by Gounod. In the second half of my career I accepted Violetta; and for six months before my debut, I went over that terrifying first-act finale every day to lighten my voice. Of Respighi I sang Magda in *La campana sommersa* in Rome and *Lucrezia* at the Carlo Felice in Genoa.

"I retired after twenty-eight years, and it was a hard decision. My mother became a total invalid and could no longer travel with me and needed constant care. I felt I owed a great debt to her and did not feel I could leave her in a clinic. One must be willing to pay the price for graces received, and I did the right thing."

When asked what she thought of the situation today, she sighed deeply. "Look at La Scala," she said, "and its miserably tiny repertoire. They used to put on seven or eight new productions every year, plus anywhere from fifteen to twenty operas from the repertoire. All the Italian opera houses are falling apart, because of the unions' absurd demands and the politically chosen managers. Voices? There are a few lovely ones—who could be better than Caballé or Sutherland? But one cannot understand a word they're saying. I was brought up to give great importance to the word, and I never sacrificed diction to sound. Today there are a few great singers but not great artists.

"When I look back, I'm staggered by the involvement of the divas with their roles. Giuseppina Cobelli's Tosca paralyzed me with admiration, and so did Gina Cigna's Gioconda. Adelaide Saraceni was one of the most intelligent sopranos, and Giannina Arangi-Lombardi's Verdi heroines were superb. I learned something from each one. When people came backstage in tears to see me, I knew I had won not only my personal battle but that of the composer. And we had conductors who knew us, liked us, helped us. They didn't arrive two days before the general rehearsal, but were there every day, knowing our limitations in depth. Where are the de Sabatas, the Serafins, the Vottos today? We have distinguished conductors, but they want to be the stars, hugging the spotlight for themselves.

"Every cycle must wear out its course. I will not be here to see it, but someday there will again be people like those whose lives I share in this building, who will understand that the muse comes first. The lyric theatre is a temple, not a football field. If one does not approach it humbly and religiously, it just cannot work. I have no regrets, and serenity is my passport. I was asked to teach and gave it up after a short while, for I have a lot of patience, but not with presumptuous people. Young singers today are so arrogant, and there's no way of making them understand that there's one candle, only one, and once it's burned, there's no replacement. For myself, I'm still ready to learn, particularly from those who are worse off than I am and yet never complain."

The nuns were still singing as I walked toward the exit along those icy corridors, but I no longer felt cold.

THE OPERA AND LIEDER SINGERS

LOTTE LEHMANN

SENA JURINAC

IRMGARD SEEFRIED

In this chapter I have grouped Lotte Lehmann—in a conversation that occurred way back in 1936—with Sena Jurinac and Irmgard Seefried, both of whom I interviewed in the spring of 1979. Each of these sopranos faced the same challenge: a lovely instrument, sumptuous and generous in the middle, but short on top. With the passage of time the upper register became increasingly problematic. Intelligently, all three turned more and more to *Liederabende*—lieder evenings—where transpositions are easier and the choice of songs that avoided uncomfortable notes was most abundant. Each started giving recitals early in her career, and this explains why they became so appreciated in this area. A lieder singer needs a special expressive ability to establish the rapid changes of mood, and superb diction to underline the subtle meaning of each phrase. Audiences are far more likely to accept vocal deficiencies in recitals than in opera, provided the interpretation is out of the ordinary. A recital singer, alone on the stage, can produce an emotional impact that is more difficult to achieve in the lyric theatre. The charm of a performer—and each of these women was extraordinarily charming— plays a vital part, for it establishes a close rapport with the audience, making any wrong notes seem unimportant.

Lehmann remains a giant among this century's prima donnas. A difficult woman who suffered from strong jealousies, and whose quarrels with Elisabeth Schumann, Maria Jeritza, and Viorica Ursuleac are a matter of public domain, she later became a teacher who could be very hard on her pupils (as Marilyn Horne can attest). Nevertheless, she emanated an irresistible personal warmth that went straight to the heart of her audience.

Jurinac, like Lehmann, was the fortunate possessor of a very special color in her voice that could always be recognized in broadcasts and recordings. But she was among the forerunners of the new breed of singer who doesn't realize her limitations: her Donna Elvira was superb, but her Leonore in *Fidelio* was a major mistake.

Seefried, in the opinion of many experts, did not possess a very solid vocal technique and, like Jurinac, began professionally during the Second World War after a relatively short period of preparation. It is common knowledge that she did not allow a sufficient time to elapse after having two cesarean-section births, and her voice did not entirely regain its sheen. Unlike Lehmann and Jurinac, she stuck to a relatively small repertoire, and her Marzelline, Composer, and Susanna were unsurpassed in their spontaneity and vivacity. When her instrument began to produce warning signals, she undertook modern operas, where her deficiencies were less noticeable; but these did not help her vocal condition.

Wisely, these three women remained loyal to the Vienna Staatsoper— Lehmann eventually left for political reasons—where they had built their fame, and their loyal public continued to love them long after the sun had started to set.

KAMMERSÄNGERIN
LOTTE LEHMANN

When I was sent to interview Lotte Lehmann in the fall of 1936 in her hotel suite in New York City, the German diva had already celebrated her forty-eighth birthday. And yet she went on singing in opera for ten more years and in concerts for fifteen. She had the kind of solid good looks, combined with an irresistible warmth and outgoingness, that made age seem unimportant. With wavy brown hair, a fine complexion, and bright-blue eyes, she was vivacity and frankness personified. At her Town Hall farewell in 1951, at the age of sixty-three, she looked pretty much the same.

This prima donna, whose standing in Europe was assured, had been asked to join the Metropolitan Opera only after her longtime rival Maria Jeritza had left, and the timing was wrong. Although she remained there, for a limited number of performances, until 1945 (there were sixty-nine in all, and only six roles), she never really became a big attraction, and it was as a lieder singer that she became one of the most winning and beloved figures of the American musical scene. When she first came to the Met in 1934, another German soprano, Elisabeth Rethberg, was firmly entrenched and equally successful in the German and Italian wings. Then, a year later, Kirsten Flagstad, an unknown Norwegian, burst onto the Met stage like a clap of thunder, singing many of the Lehmann roles. Intelligent and honest, Lehmann talked about this predicament, but she never mentioned names.

"Everything in life, in a musical career as in any other, depends on being in the right place at the right time," she remarked. "Sometimes we can help this sort of thing along, but then there are, at times, circumstances that take the situation out of our hands. When the wind blows against one, there is nothing to do but to take cognizance of it and accept it. I have been exceedingly fortunate during most of my life, with so many fantastic opportunities coming in my direction, that something was bound to go wrong somewhere. The Metropolitan does not have much to offer me in terms of repertoire, and so while I am in the United States, I give lieder evenings, which are very rewarding and afford me the chance to visit this great country."

Lotte Lehmann as Leonore in *Fidelio*.

She did not refer to her disappointment that her first New York appearance as the Marschallin—a role closely identified with her and for which, the world over, she was considered the ideal interpreter—had not won the delirious acclaim that she had expected. Eventually, however, it was recognized to the extent that *Time* magazine gave Lehmann a cover story, picturing her as the Strauss heroine.

The greatest mistake Lehmann made at the Thirty-ninth Street house was to appear as Tosca, a role closely identified with the glamorous Jeritza—and Lehmann was in no way glamorous. She had sung the role often in Germany and Austria, but that was a different story, for there she had been deeply esteemed for years. From an international viewpoint, her interpretation was far too Germanic. The temperament and the passion were very much there, but she could not help turning the Roman prima donna into a provincial character. I had heard her sing Tosca as well as a most unfortunate Butterfly at the San Francisco Opera and recalled the unflattering criticisms of her Puccini appearances there, and so I could not understand why she had allowed Edward Johnson to talk her into repeating her error in New York. In Vienna she had sung most of the Italian repertoire in German, and her Italian diction left much to be desired. And by this time her top showed signs of increasing strain. At the Met she sang a total of fifty-four performances in the house and fifteen on tour.

"I am an inexact artist," she confessed most candidly. "When I go out on the stage, I live the music, and this is what counts for me. Technique has never concerned me, for I am a creature of instinct. So what if I hit a wrong note? For certain perfectionists this is not acceptable, but in my estimation it is the expression in an artist that counts. People can take me or leave me, for that is the way I am. Phrasing, for me, is the clue to an interpretation, and the knowing audience has always appreciated very much the fact that it never misses what I am saying. Inaccuracy in the notes here and there—that they can accuse me of; but of betraying the text, never. I have given of my voice with no restraint, and I am fully aware that this has to be paid for dearly. But I cannot restrain myself, for I become tremendously involved with a characterization or a song, and the reason for my success has always been that the public knows I am handing it all I have. Actually, considering how much of my vocal resources I have squandered away, it is a miracle that I still have an instrument in fairly good shape."

The honesty of this statement did disarm me, for I knew how great conductors like Toscanini, totally won over by her art, had agreed to lower for her the "Abscheulicher" in *Fidelio*, which had become the best-seller at the Salzburg Festival. She sang this opera for eleven years in succession there, from 1927 until 1937.

There are sundry stories of her flaming temperament: of her celebrated row with Elisabeth Schumann when the latter was assigned the first Sophie in the Hamburg premiere of *Der Rosenkavalier* in 1911, an honor Lehmann felt should have been hers (the two women were later to become good friends); of her lifelong resentment of Jeritza, with whom she shared the stage in *Ariadne auf Naxos, Die Walküre, Die Frau ohne Schatten,* and other operas; of her profound ill feeling toward Viorica Ursuleac, who she felt had usurped several of her operas in Vienna. At the time of my conversation with her, the *Fidelio* drama at the Met had not yet occurred: when the role was assigned to Flagstad, very much against Lehmann's protests, such was Lehmann's pique that even after the Norwegian diva returned home, she refused to take on the role that along with Sieglinde and the Marschallin was one of her most unforgettable achievements.

"Although everyone thinks I am Austrian," she told me, "because of my long-standing connection with Vienna and Salzburg, I was born in Perleberg, a small town in Germany, in 1888. I have never made a mystery of my age as so many of my colleagues do. My father, a civil servant, had no ambitions for me, but thought that my studying to become a schoolteacher might be a sound and practical idea in case I did not find a husband. I followed his advice, but having always been irresistibly attracted to music, I studied the piano, and this led me on to singing. My first vocal teacher was discouraging; she just did not think I had either the goods in my vocal cords or the discipline needed. But being terribly stubborn, I did not give up. I tried the Berlin Imperial Opera School and was accepted. Eventually Mathilde Mallinger, who had been the first Eva in *Die Meistersinger* in 1868, took me under her powerful wing, and my hopes soared. My debut took place in Hamburg in the very unimportant part of the Third Boy—and a big boy I was!—in *Die Zauberflöte,* and for a while I bided my time between the Flower Maidens in *Parsifal* and the Rhinemaidens. Then Freia in *Das Rheingold* came up, and this goddess, actually not in the least interesting, somehow called attention to my potentials. Anyhow, I was no longer one of a group. I was never beautiful in the true sense of the word, but I did possess a certain type of sensuality that came over the footlights.

"Things began to happen," she continued, "including the thrill of having some of my poems published by *Der Tag,* a newspaper in Berlin. I always enjoyed writing, and after my retirement I will do more, in real earnest. Then Vienna offered me a contract, and this was to become my permanent home from 1914 onward. The five years in Hamburg had not been wasted, for I had the time to measure my pulse and learn my possibilities. In Vienna I began as Eva, and at first it was all very far from being easy. The competition was fierce, and I was not sophisticated enough to cope with the hidden intrigues of this very wordly opera house. I have always called a spade a spade, and my talent for playing games is nil.

"My break came when the revised version of *Ariadne auf Naxos* had its premiere in Vienna on October 4, 1916. Franz Schalk was the conductor, and Jeritza, who had sung in the first version in Stuttgart in 1912, was again the Ariadne. I had been entrusted with the Composer for the second cast, but as the famous Marie Gutheil-Schoder did not turn up at the rehearsals, I filled in every time. Strauss's music was not new to me; I had already sung both Sophie and Octavian. The maestro, who came to all the rehearsals, became impressed with my work and increasingly annoyed at the diva's casual attitude. One day Strauss snapped and insisted with the management that I be moved up for opening night. For the first time, both the critics and the public not only took notice of me but raved.

"Goodness knows, it was tough going, since Jeritza was a big star and always received all the attention. That night I also got considerable competition from Selma Kurz, who was a splendid Zerbinetta. From that night on the Viennese took me to their hearts, and this is a love affair that has continued unabated. My voice was always difficult to pigeonhole, for I started as a lyric and then moved on to halfway between a spinto and a dramatic. Of the latter repertoire I sang, for instance, Charlotte in *Werther*, also often done by a mezzo; the Dyer's Wife in *Die Frau ohne Schatten*, which I created in Vienna in 1919, again with Jeritza, who was the Empress; and then Turandot, which I was the first to perform in the Austrian capital in 1926. Now this is a real *hochdramatisch* part—no getting away from that fact. I had also been the first Suor Angelica in Vienna in 1920, and this is a score that can be undertaken by both a lyric and a spinto.

"Of the Wagner heroines, I have never dared go beyond Elisabeth, Elsa, Sieglinde, and Eva. I did sing Gutrune at one time, but left her behind, for she never appealed to me. Along with Franz Schalk, Bruno Walter, who was always a very close friend and adviser, convinced me to take on Isolde, and I learned the entire score. But, however engrossed and fascinated I was with the role, I never felt sure that Isolde was right for me. I could handle the emotional side of her character, but the tessitura was uncomfortable. I got cold feet and canceled it, the only time I can recall having done this sort of thing. But I feel sure that it was the right decision. The voice has grown darker and darker in color, but its strength has not grown in the same proportion. And for Isolde one needs terrific stamina. In fact, now Eva has begun to be too light for me.

"I have always turned down modernistic scores, as they are ungrateful to the vocal cords and often can be immensely dangerous. Alban Berg could never persuade me to take on Marie in his *Wozzeck,* an opera that, incidentally, I have always thought to be most overrated. But I agreed to sing Marietta in Korngold's *Die tote Stadt,* which lies very comfortably for the voice. It is not superlative music by any means, but attractive to the ear and grateful. Perhaps I never should have accepted Turandot, for it is a voice wrecker, although musically most fascinating and imaginative; my alternate in Vienna, Maria Nemeth, had a far more suitable instrument for this type of tessitura than mine."

She made no mention of the fact that she would no longer be singing Eva in the Toscanini production of *Die Meistersinger* at the Salzburg Festival the following summer, or that Maria Reining would be taking her place as Hans Sachs's daughter. (She had implied earlier that the role was no longer really right for her.) But she did talk freely about her relationship with Richard Strauss, which at the time was far less close than it had been. She was Vienna's first Arabella, and she sang a great number of Ariadnes, a role to which she had graduated from the Composer. She created the part of Christine in *Intermezzo* in Dresden in 1924; and the Dyer's Wife and, of course, the Marschallin were also much identified with her.

"I don't really know myself what happened," she said with total naturalness. "Perhaps nothing. Certainly not in any way anything that is tangible. He is well aware that there is no greater champion of his operas than I, for I happen to love them all and know they will live forever. No one sings his lieder more often than I do, and this he also knows. But he considers Clemens Krauss to be the greatest conductor of his works, and of course the latter admires Ursuleac. People drift away from one another, and it is sad."

It occurred to me that the high tessitura Strauss wrote for all his heroines no longer suited Lehmann's voice. In fact, it was impossible at that stage of her career to imagine this great artist coping with the incandescent top registers of Ariadne and Arabella. Strauss was to compose several more operas after my meeting with Lehmann, and all required a soprano with a brilliant upper range. It was well known that Lehmann had considerable trouble with the end of the trio in the last act of *Der Rosenkavalier,* and this only increased in the following years. She was too wise and shrewd not to realize all this, but she simply did not discuss this aspect, which undoubtedly must have saddened her.

"I never was a Mozartian," she told me, "although during the first part of my career I often sang Pamina, Donna Elvira, and the Countess. The emotionally charged instrument I have is not suited to that pure, flawless style of singing. In fact, these operas were sung in my own special way. I have appeared, and still do, in several Italian operas in Vienna, and Desdemona is the role I love the best. It was a wonderful experience for me to sing it again last spring under Victor de Sabata, one of the most sensitive musicians I ever came in contact with. He was surprised that I had never sung at La Scala, and I replied that I was too. But the year is only made up of twelve months, and one simply cannot be everywhere. Tatiana in *Eugene Onegin* is very much my cup of tea, and I sang it a short time ago, before coming here, along with Elsa, Elisabeth, and Leonore. In Salzburg next summer I will sing Leonore once more, but in the new Festspielhaus, which I pray will have good acoustics. Salzburg for me is like home, very much like Vienna, and I love to bathe in the cool, fresh waters of the nearby lakes.

"Toscanini gave me real hell when he heard—he always knows everything somehow—that before the premiere of *Meistersinger* I had been swimming in St. Wolfgang Sea. He was absolutely right, for I might have caught cold and developed a sore throat. He loves this opera more than any other by Wagner, and in fact it is the one he has conducted most often. His photographic memory is fantastic; he knows where every pause or comma is. I had sung Eva very often and found I had to develop another approach. You know how that first act can be somewhat boring, with that long scene with all the guild members carrying on. Well, he infuses into it such vivacity and so many different shades, marking the character of each one, that it seems almost short."

The horror of what was to come soon after our conversation was not in the air as yet: the Anschluss and the precipitous abandonment of her beloved home and the Staatsoper in Vienna. But she would return in triumph in 1955 when the new opera house, modeled on the old, was inaugurated. Her reception that night, by all those who remembered not only her unique contribution to music but her firm and outspoken denunciation of the Nazis, was tremendous. The entire audience stood in tribute to her.

Lehmann's stand against the Hitler regime had been made very clear from the beginning. She told me that when the Nazis came to power, Hermann Göring wired her in Southern Germany, where she was singing a recital, to fly to Berlin right away, as he had matters of the most vital importance to discuss with her. Curious, she went to the German capital; and her surprise and subsequent shock were considerable when she was offered the title of Nationalsängerin. It was an exceptional tribute to her art and included a spectacular contract at the Berlin Staatsoper; but it also entailed a pledge never to sing outside the fatherland again. Göring—who received her in one of his most dazzling white uniforms, with two lion cubs at his feet—was a rabid opera fan and appeared to have unlimited authority in the musical domain. Apparently he had never taken into consideration the possibility that she might not accept, and upon her blank refusal he shouted that she would never be able to sing in Germany again. Trembling with rage, she walked out.

Lehmann's husband, Otto Krause, was Austrian, and until his death he never missed one of his wife's performances. An insurance salesman, he eventually gave up his job to manage her career, and he became completely indispensable to her. Not socially minded, she was a law unto herself. Protocol played no part in the prima donna's independent ways, and in Vienna she created a furor by leaving, without excusing herself, a luncheon in honor of Austrian Chancellor Schuschnigg. Later, after she retired to Santa Barbara, California, she divided her time between writing (she published several books, including her autobiography, *Anfang und Aufstieg*), painting, and giving classes. When she died in August 1976, she had reached her eighty-eighth birthday.

Unlike the passing of so many of her colleagues, her death not only did not go unnoticed, but it revived a decades-old controversy regarding her work; and she had been a controversial singer from the very beginning. No one ever questioned the fact that she was a great lieder singer, following in the legendary tradition of Elena Gerhardt, bringing a very special insight into each and every song, with a special feeling for words that none of her successors were able to achieve. (Her memory was far from outstanding; she always carried a booklet with her during her recitals, and from time to time she referred to the texts.) No one could ever deny that her timbre was of the kind that once heard could never be forgotten. But her operatic heroines will be discussed for a long time by those who recall them. There were many who thought her Marschallin was not all it was trumpeted to be, for she did not possess the allure necessary to portray this Viennese princess; only in the first-act monologue before the mirror, when she sings "Wo ist die jetzt? Ja, such' dir den Schnee von vergangenen Jahr!" (Where is she now? Yes, seek the snows of yesteryear!) did she achieve a very special pathos. Certainly no one put such overwhelming emotion into the phrase "Die alte Frau, die alte Marschallin" (The old woman, the old Marschallin) quite like she did. Others felt very strongly that her excursions in the Italian repertoire were ill-advised.

It was as Sieglinde and Leonore that I shall always treasure Lehmann. As Hunding's wife, she conveyed like no one else the intense, almost unbearable drama of a woman caught by a fate she cannot control. Her "Du bist der Lenz" was overpowering in its sensuousness and almost mystical joy; and her arrival with Brünnhilde after her escape through the mountains and forests was nearly unendurable in the despair and sense of overwhelming fatigue she was able to convey. When she sang "Nicht sehre dich Sorge um mich; einzig taugt mir der Tod!" (Do not trouble yourself with worry over me; truly death were now best), I found that chills were going down my spine. As Leonore, despite the obvious difficulties in the upper range, she created so believable a character that the tragedy came to life in the most natural way. The fact that she was so big a woman and that it was difficult to accept that she was portraying a man was soon forgotten, so sincere was her interpretation and so moving her projection of the duress and tension to which Leonore was exposed. Will we ever again hear Leonore's declaration in the second-act trio "Die hehre bange Stunde winkt, die Tod mir oder Rettung bringt" (The sublime and fearful hour beckons, which brings me death or salvation) sung so expressively, a mixture of terror and faith? There have been many more perfect singers, but few have been more intense and honest than Lotte Lehmann.

KAMMERSÄNGERIN
SENA JURINAC

At the end of the Second World War two lyric sopranos exploded onto the Viennese musical scene with their lovely voices and their interpretative gifts. They were Sena Jurinac and Irmgard Seefried. The first, nearing sixty when I interviewed her in May 1979, is still a radiantly attractive woman, her silver hair framing a mobile face dominated by intense round eyes, which have an odd, disquieting way of expressing surprise and sadness at the same time—the look of someone who has not entirely come to terms with herself. She projects total assurance, and yet there were moments during our meeting when I felt that perhaps it was not as complete as it appeared on the surface. Of all the divas I met with, she was the one whose conversation—smooth, elegant, ingratiating—was the most baffling: statements were often contradictory, and terms were not always explicit. She received me in her Paris hotel the morning after she had sung a *Liederabend* to tumultuous applause, despite faulty intonation.

"I keep thinking of retiring," she declared, "and then when one is greeted by enthusiasm like that of last night, it is all the more difficult to let go. Actually I have cut down my activity now to a very few recitals a year, and I still sing the Kostelnička in *Jenůfa*, in Vienna, where I have appeared uninterruptedly since 1944. I no longer live in the Austrian capital, having moved to Augsburg to be with my second husband, Dr. Josef Lederle, a well-known surgeon there. I commute to Zurich, where I give classes, and in the summer I do the same in Lenk, near Bern. I am getting increasingly interested in teaching, for I am fully conscious of what a tremendous need there is for it, and in all probability, by the time your book is published I will have pulled down the curtain on what has been an interesting life marked by ever so many adventures. I have lasted longer than most people predicted when I started singing heavier roles which demand a lot of endurance and where one cannot cheat. But at a certain moment my temperament demanded them, and I took the plunge.

"Singing is a constant risk, and I learned a bitter lesson in 1958 when some nodes formed on my vocal cords. Were they a result of strain, fatigue, or nerves? One never knows. What is certain is that I had sung much too much. My laryngologist warned me that I must stop even speaking for two months or he could not guarantee what might happen. It could easily be that I would never be in a condition to sing again. I obeyed him to the letter, and then, when I went back to see him, he found that the nodes had miraculously vanished. But for the next six months, he announced, I must sing only very light roles, and never more than once a week. Again I obeyed him to the letter and came out of the impasse, but it taught me a lesson I shall never forget. During that period I limited my activities to Ighino in *Palestrina* and several operettas. When I was faced with a tonsil operation at one point, I was terrified. It was a long time before I dared emit a sound again, and then only daintily. Along with the joy of singing, there is always lurking the fear that something may happen to one's voice. One can never be sufficiently careful, and yet one is human—sometimes one does get carried away.

"Many people believe that I started out as a mezzo," she explained, "because at first, in Vienna, I began with Dorabella and Cherubino. Actually, as you know, the latter can also be sung by a soprano, but Dorabella usually is not, for it lies very much in the middle of the voice. But the fact is that as the war ended, the Vienna Opera simply did not have a mezzo for this part, and I was given three days to learn it. Since we were appearing in the Theater an der Wien, smaller than the Staatsoper, which was still in ruins, I could manage it without forcing, and I enjoyed this assignment so much that I later repeated it in Glyndebourne. This Neapolitan girl is full of wit and charm, and the da Ponte text is bubbling. There is a phrase in the second act that gives the key to both her superficiality and her pragmatism. She sings to Fiordiligi about the possibility of their two swains' not returning from the war and shrewdly declares, 'E allora? Entrambe resterem colle man piene di mosche. Tra un ben certo e un incerto c'è sempre gran divario'—we'll both be left empty-handed; there's still a big difference between a bird in the hand and one in the bush. It is an instrumental role, for the voice must always be in unison with the wind instruments, and this is the reason why so many interpreters of the role have problems with pitch.

"My first year in Vienna I did over a hundred and fifty performances, which was of course totally irresponsible on the part of those in charge, but I was not as yet in a position to argue with them. With Austria and Germany utterly destroyed, it was a miracle that opera was being given every night, and one was thankful to have a job and manage to keep hunger—which I had experienced often earlier—away from one's door.

"I was always labeled a Mozart and Strauss specialist, but only part of

Sena Jurinac as Donna Elvira in *Don Giovanni*.

this is true. As far as Mozart is concerned, it is very much so, but with Strauss this is not the case. I sang very often three roles: the Composer in *Ariadne* and Octavian and then the Marschallin in *Der Rosenkavalier.* But there I stopped. I never possessed the high, floating range to do justice to Ariadne herself, Arabella, the Countess in *Capriccio,* or some of the others. I spent all of my life turning down Chrysothemis, and I cannot understand why important sopranos are so enthusiastic about this wretched young woman, who is totally overshadowed by her sister and mother. Octavian is a danger-ous undertaking if one resorts—and many do—to chest tones, and one must not sing it too frequently. The Marschallin too lies in the center, but the role is shorter, and she is less impetuous, so it is not necessary to underline the phrasing quite so much. The Composer—I began to sing the role way back in 1947, for again, as in the case of Dorabella, there was no mezzo to undertake it—is tougher than Octavian, but appears only in the Prologue.

"So much depends too on how one approaches these roles—the temper-ament of the artist. As I always had too much from the very start, I had to be doubly careful about protecting my top. Being a passionate admirer of Strauss's song literature, I often include some of his lieder. Could anything be more heartwarming than 'All mein Gedanken' or 'Traum durch die Dämmerung'?

"Mozart, on the other hand," she said, laughing, "has been my daily bread all along. I sang all his major operas, and in four of them I alternated in two parts. In *Le nozze di Figaro* I went from Cherubino to the Countess, in *Idomeneo* from Ilia to Elettra, in *Don Giovanni* from Donna Elvira to Donna Anna, and in *Così fan tutte* from Dorabella to Fiordiligi. The latter I sang only at the Glyndebourne and Edinburgh festivals, and this is disap-pointing, for she is one of the most compelling creations of this composer. Although I kept hearing from all sides how powerful I had become at the Vienna Opera, this is not so. They had Schwarzkopf, della Casa, and Seefried do it and always found excuses not to assign it to me. I also often sang Pamina, but in those days no one could compete with Seefried in this part.

"There was a considerable amount of Wagner in my fare. At first Furt-wängler entrusted to me one of the Rhinemaidens and the Norns, along with Gutrune, one of the most dismal ladies conceived by the great Richard. I eliminated her from the list as soon as was feasible. But at the beginning there was no way I could refuse the formidable maestro, and there were actually colleagues who were envious that I had been assigned the role. She is *antipatica* as a person, and none of her music is endearing. Then I went on successfully to Eva, Elsa, and Elisabeth. But Senta was not right for me, and after singing her in Strasbourg, I eliminated her. Vocally, it is a hard-to-define role, for it lies halfway between a *jugendlich dramatisch* and *hoch-dramatisch* soprano.

"I found much to admire in these Wagner heroines, but for my nature they are too contemplative: the fire smoldering but never exploding really in the open. Sieglinde would have appealed to me, but it never came my way. It is utterly astonishing how rapidly a career goes by, with certain wishes left unfulfilled. One goes from one assignment to the other, thinking that next season or the next the chance will come for a certain role. And it doesn't. In the meantime one is so busy with bookings, one keeps putting it off until it is suddenly too late.

"I was at the Salzburg Festival in 1947 and 1948, but there was a long interval before I went back, for from 1949 to 1956 I was engaged at the Glyndebourne Festival, where I was exceedingly happy. A pleasant, relaxed atmosphere prevails there, and so much good will, with intrigues rarely coming to the fore—at least in my day this was so. Among the roles I sang there were Donna Elvira, Donna Anna, the Countess, the Composer, Ilia in *Idomeneo,* and Leonora in *Forza.* Later Karajan called me to Salzburg to appear as Marina in *Boris,* a role usually sung by a mezzo—it appealed to me because of the stunning duet with Rangoni and the polonaise—and Elisabetta in his first production of *Don Carlo.* His productions are always such a hit that they are apt to be repeated for several seasons. Karajan always gave much importance to how an artist looked, and I am sure he chose me for these two princesses because he felt I had the *physique du rôle.* I have worked a lot with Karajan over the years. His prominence, fully deserved, has now put him on a distant pedestal, but this is not his fault. He always showed me consideration, and singing with him did not represent an effort, for he has a very clear baton and knows exactly what he wants. I recall with pleasure singing with him a variety of roles, including Marzelline, Amor and Euridice in *Orfeo,* and Desdemona. At La Scala I appeared twice with him as Cherubino, in 1948 and again in 1953, and as the Countess in 1960.

"I appeared a lot in Italy, for at La Scala I also sang Octavian, Suor Angelica, and Butterfly. In Naples, at the San Carlo, one of the most beautiful theatres in Europe, I appeared as Mimi, Micaëla, Marie in *The Bartered Bride* (in Italian they call it *La sposa venduta*), Pamina, and the delightful opera by Wolf-Ferrari *Le donne curiose,* based on a ravishing play by Goldoni. By the same composer is *La vedova scaltra,* which I sang at the Volksoper. I also was married for a time to Italy's great baritone Sesto Bruscantini, from 1953 to 1957.

"I waited until 1966 to sing Tosca, and I believe it was a wise decision, for this needs a darker type of instrument than I had in the earlier years. Desdemona suited me, and so did Leonora in *Forza;* but I did not venture further into Verdi. A work I added in the latter part of my career was *L'incoronazione di Poppea,* and it was an exceptionally interesting experience, for it really is the skeleton of what opera was to become later. Every time I sang it, I found an increasing richness to its apparently simple but actually very subtle structure.

"I first became a recitalist in order to increase my income, and it developed into a very essential part of my activities. It is hard to understand why there are so few lieder singers today. Now with Ludwig cutting down and Schwarzkopf having eased out of the picture, who is there among the women? With the men we are better off, having Prey, Fischer-Dieskau, and Schreier. Caballé and Horne sing lieder exquisitely, but as correct as their German is, they are not true lieder singers. I always dedicated much time to this form of art and believe I have contributed something to it. Brahms and Schumann were particularly suited to my timbre."

I asked her about her early life. "I was born in 1921," she replied, "in Travnik, Bosnia, which had been for a long time under the Turks and then became, until 1918, part of the Austrian empire. This is why I was born bilingual and learned German as a matter of course. My grandfather was the mayor of the town and my father a doctor employed by the Solvay company in Bosnia. First I studied voice privately in Zagreb, then later went to the conservatory, where I dedicated a lot of time to the piano. My debut came, in full wartime, at the Zagreb Opera in 1942 as Mimi. Immediately I was cast as one of the Flower Maidens in *Parsifal,* an inevitable must for any soprano in Central Europe, and then Marguerite, Nedda, Marie in *The Bartered Bride,* and several Yugoslav operas of which I remember very little. I auditioned for Vienna two years later, with little hope, but I was given a contract. Because of the constant bombings, it was six months before I had the chance to begin there. I started out as a lyric but moved on fairly rapidly to some *jugendlich dramatisch* roles, while not abandoning the original ones.

"The first period in Vienna was no joke—no clothes available, no heating, not enough food. We did not look like divas but like homeless persons. Somehow I got around to having a personal life too, which consisted of two marriages. After my divorce from Bruscantini, Professor Lederle became my husband in 1965.

"The conductor who most influenced my early years was Erich Kleiber, perhaps the most cultivated man I ever worked with. Recording *Der Rosen-*

kavalier with him is an experience I shall never forget. I sang often with him in Stuttgart, where I was contracted for a yearly number of guest appearances, and much of the insight I was able to bring to some of my interpretations I owe to him. He had a lot of patience, and no question one asked him was ever answered hastily. This is the striking difference with those who hold the batons today. The old-timers found the time and were anxious for one to give one's best. I liked Mitropoulos as a person very much, but he was more suited to the symphonic repertoire. Although admirably conceived, his *Butterfly* was definitely very loud and quite a strain for the voice. Klemperer, who had a tremendous reputation, was a major disappointment to me. He led my first Leonore in *Fidelio* at Covent Garden, and with his heavy, pedestrian tempos he nearly drove me up the wall. With Zubin Mehta at the Maggio Musicale Fiorentino it was a different story. He approached the Beethoven opera romantically and not with the exaggerated heroics of Klemperer." (It is strange that in his biography of the late Sir David Webster, longtime manager of Covent Garden, entitled *The Quiet Showman,* Montague Haltrecht claims that "her terms were not easy; they included a new production and either Klemperer or Karajan as a conductor." Never did she mention that the German maestro had been her choice.)

I inquired about Seefried, whom she had praised so extravagantly as Pamina. "A most delightful woman," she answered, "and a very personal artist. Nothing she ever did was routine. When in form, she created a distinctive glow on the stage which always seemed, unlike that of the very talented Schwarzkopf, entirely natural. After the birth of her two daughters, the voice was never quite the same.

"But singing is such a difficult business. I was not born with a facile top and managed to reach a C but no further. Since I had a large and generous middle, I had to keep constantly on the alert not to take too much advantage of it. I never resorted to chest tones, as more and more singers tend to do nowadays; I achieved the same effect by relaxing the throat and obtaining the resonance in that manner. In my opinion, chest tones must originate in the head. One flats when the sound is not properly set in the mask of the face. It is a question of focus, as in photography. Now that I am so involved with lessons, all these problems come to the fore all the time, and when I listen to auditions, I try to imagine how that particular instrument would sound when corrected."

In regard to her failure to appear at the Metropolitan, she denied vehemently that she did not want to sing in the United States, calling these reports "absolute nonsense." In fact she sang several roles at the San Francisco

Opera in 1959, 1971, and 1980. "I was in Australia on a concert tour in 1956," she explained, "when I was offered the title role in the creation of *Vanessa* at the Metropolitan. My English was no problem, but the opera was not as yet finished, and I insisted on reading the final version. Menotti came to see me in Europe, and, frankly, despite the admiration I have for him and for Samuel Barber's music, I disliked the role of this frustrated woman; I considered Erika by far the more interesting of the two. I simply did not enjoy the idea of having to sing 'Find something better than that!' and 'Sick of pheasant . . . canard' and 'Too many sauces.' If they announced my name before I had agreed, this is no fault of mine. Later I was offered some performances of Donna Elvira, but they did not fit into my calendar. Then, finally, it seemed all set for me to appear as Butterfly and Donna Anna. But a long strike took place in the first part of the year, and there was no guarantee that the season would take place. Once it was settled, I could not change my European dates. I believe in destiny; it evidently was not meant to be, and I am indeed very sorry." (According to Samuel Barber, Jurinac not only had accepted the part but had already been studying it, amazing everyone with her excellent English diction. Then a cable came, pleading illness, followed by a doctor's certificate. Sir Rudolf Bing, with his unfailing sarcasm, was heard to say that the reason Jurinac never appeared at the Metropolitan was that she was either too happily in love or too unhappily.)

What opera had afforded her the greatest emotion?

Without a moment of indecision, she answered, "*Iphigénie en Tauride*! I sang it in both German and French. It has the most moving second act I know. To give it all the necessary pathos and yet remain within the classical frame imposed by Gluck is the sort of challenge that makes being an opera singer a very considerable privilege.

"Do you know the lovely song by Schubert 'Der Einsame'? The last words are 'Wenn euer Lied das Schweigen bricht, bin ich nicht ganz allein' —when your song breaks the silence, I am no longer all alone. They are poetic but ever so true: a song is the best company in the world."

KAMMERSÄNGERIN IRMGARD SEEFRIED

She was enchanting on the stage, and she is equally so in person. Unlike so many of her colleagues, whose private and public images are so different, Seefried's are very much the same. When I went to call on her in the late spring of 1979 and sat in the lovely, spacious garden that surrounds her cottage in the Viennese suburb of Grinzing, she was sparkling and smiling; the sun's rays played on the lustrous gray streaks in her hair.

"I feel happy today because I heard a nightingale," she said, "and I immediately thought of Brahms's 'Nachtigall': 'O Nachtigall, dein süsser Schall, er dringet mir durch Mark und Bein' [O nightingale, your sweet sound pierces through all of my being]. Composers were once in touch with nature; her influence is in all their songs. I often take refuge in them, for today the world is sick, and so is humanity. So why shouldn't the lyric theatre be seriously ill too? It is a deadly virus, and only the very strong will survive. The composers are safe, and that is all that matters. Tradition, alas, dies very rapidly, in a generation or two; but somehow, somewhere, it will be rediscovered. I came just before the end, and I consider myself very privileged that I have known greatness and have worked with giants. Now, suddenly, there are only gnomes around, with a few rare exceptions."

"Weren't you very close to Karajan?" I asked her.

"Yes, I was," she replied, her dimples evident even when her puckish face was in repose. "For it is with him that I started. He was not celebrated then. Fame often changes people, but I don't think this happened to me, for I was never able to take myself too seriously. I always felt that I was the bearer of a gift that I must handle with care. But Karajan—an extraordinary man —is no longer the person I knew when he signed me at the age of nineteen for the opera in Aachen, of which he was then the director. Now he has become an institution and a legend in his own time, which is quite a weight to bear.

"I made my first appearance under his direction as the Priestess in *Aida,* and my mother had to sign the contract, for I was underage. I was also onstage in some of the other scenes as a member of the chorus, and he scolded me later for having moved too much. 'Do you want people to notice you to such an extent?' he asked me. 'No,' I replied—and this was true—'I was not aware of it.' Next came Nuri in *Tiefland,* which gave me a better chance to assert myself, and then suddenly there was Donna Anna.

"When he asked me if I knew the score," she recalled, "I was stunned. No, I replied; since I was a lyric soprano, it had never occurred to me to learn it. 'I need a Donna Anna,' he said, with total lack of concern, 'so you had better prepare it fast.' I was overcome with fear, for I knew that this was sheer madness and could be the rapid beginning of my end. That much I was sure of; I had heard *Don Giovanni* many times and knew the insidiousness of this role, with its dramatic range. Goodness, the 'Or sai chi l'onore,' the first aria, puts the fear of God even in very experienced prima donnas. And the second, 'Non mi dir,' demands much agility. In fact, a soprano who does well by the first one is usually less satisfactory in the second, and vice versa.

"But even then Karajan never thought of anything but the orchestra. Singers are there to be used, and from the early days he loved to experiment with them. None of this has changed; it's still very true today. I don't believe, as many persons claim, that he does not know voices. He simply employs them as if they were members of the orchestra. He is full of contradictions, for when you sing with him he is very considerate of your limitations; but why then does he so often cast performers in the wrong roles?

"In the meantime, for me it was sink or swim. I swore to myself that if I ever got through those performances without losing too much face, I would never go near Donna Anna again. And I stuck to my word. I got away with it, first of all because the theatre was not large. And then I sang a totally lyrical Donna Anna—which of course was not right.

"I have seen Karajan get enthusiastic over certain artists to whom he hands over all the plums, even when they are absolutely unsuited. Now he is all worked up about the very gifted Hildegard Behrens. I sincerely hope that she does not end up like Helga Dernesch, whom he used for all the *hochdramatisch* Wagner roles. Now she has become a mezzo. For Behrens I feel it is too soon to take on roles like Isolde and Leonore, and it is a pity, for hers is a fine talent. I wish her well.

"Anyhow, in Aachen I managed not to repeat that type of dangerous experiment again, and long after I left that theatre, I sang with Karajan on many different occasions, including two productions at La Scala, in 1949 and 1953, of *Le nozze di Figaro.*

"I was born in Köngetried in Bavaria in 1919, and studied voice at the

Irmgard Seefried as Susanna in *Le nozze di Figaro*.

conservatory in Augsburg. My father wanted me to have a musical degree in case I needed to earn a living, but when it was discovered that I had a voice, I began my vocal training. After spending three years in Aachen, I moved to Vienna in 1943, before the tragedy of the opera house's destruction. How we got through those ghastly years I am not quite sure. There was no transportation, and I had to walk to the theatre from Grinzing and back, a very long way, for rehearsals and performances. I was permanently hungry and never knew whether my small room would still be there when I returned, because of the contant bombardments. In both Aachen and Vienna, we artists had to follow the audience—as we were, all made up and in costume—into the cellar during the air raids. My father died during the war, and my mother was prostrate with grief. I needed tranquility to concentrate and study, but this proved impossible to find. Anyhow, in Vienna I made my debut as Eva in *Die Meistersinger* under Karl Böhm, and found my way into what was to become my limited repertoire.

"Then I made a great success as Pamina, and this made me happy, for there is no greater test for the production of a smooth legato. Some of my colleagues find her dull; I never did. On the contrary, she is a woman of character—she stands up to her mother, and in discovering love she learns her true self under very trying circumstances. It is a symbolic fable, but, alas, in our epoch the stage directors exaggerate in their often grotesque interpretation of what is basically a struggle between good and evil. For me Pamina is one of Mozart's most interesting female characters. I had the pleasure of singing it in Salzburg, at the Festival, under Furtwängler, and it was a joy to hear the score as it is written. With this enlightened conductor I was honored to sing many orchestral concerts, including Haydn's *The Creation,* the Bach St. Matthew Passion, and Beethoven's Ninth Symphony.

"From Donna Anna I went to Zerlina, which suited my voice and sense of comedy. She is really the audience's key to understanding what the Don is like. Neither with Donna Anna nor with Donna Elvira does he have the chance to show his character, for they are either running away from him or after him. I remained with Zerlina through the years. Another big success came with Susanna in *Le nozze di Figaro,* the role of my Metropolitan Opera debut and the one I sang the most often of all. In the early part of my career I was confronted with Fiordiligi. She is hard to sing, but in my estimation one must think of her as a violin. Although many people think the role is ideal for an Italian soprano, that is not true. Name me one Italian who has become outstanding in this assignment! There is a very subtle sense of fun, but one cannot overdo it either, the way directors seem to be inclined to depict her today, because she takes herself more seriously than her sister, Dorabella. She is very close to the characters of the commedia dell'arte—but again not quite; she is ambiguous in some ways, but never to be underestimated. When *Così* was first performed in 1790, the role was sung by da Ponte's mistress, who specialized in fioritura passages and was gifted with a strong lower register. This is why 'Come scoglio' has such a dangerous leap at the very beginning, which sopranos often simplify nowadays.

"I was the Composer in a memorable production of *Ariadne* under Böhm, with my beloved Max Lorenz as Bacchus, Maria Reining, and Alda Noni, a Zerbinetta whom even Strauss admired very much. This was the part that marked my debut with the Chicago Opera. My first Octavian came in the early sixties, and recording it for Deutsche Grammophon in the unheated bombed cathedral in Dresden in December was a chilling experience difficult to forget. Marianne Schech was the Marschallin, Streich an adorable Sophie, and, if you can imagine, Fischer-Dieskau played the marginal role of Faninal. I sang a lot with this baritone, who was to become so famous and is undoubtedly the busiest classical recording star in existence. Is there anything he has not taped? He was the first person with whom I ever interpreted Hugo Wolf's Italienische Liederbuch."

"What is he like?" I inquired.

"I am not sure," she answered spontaneously. "He is not a colleague—he is just Fischer-Dieskau! Not unpleasant—goodness no!—just very much the *vedette.*"

"And of all the fine Marschallins you appeared with, who was the most appealing?" I asked.

"What a question!" she laughed. "There were so many! But I suppose Claire Watson was the most human and natural, and Schwarzkopf the most stylish. I sang a great deal with Elisabeth and was fortunate—not everyone was—in establishing an excellent rapport with her. You could always feel a sense of rivalry with her, but this is very positive for the public. Every time I appeared with her I knew I had to be on my toes. I can't think of anyone who has worked harder than she has, with her husband always in the front line giving endless suggestions, and perhaps this is the reason that she sometimes gave the impression of being very affected.

"I sang relatively little Italian repertoire, except for Puccini: Butterfly, Mimi, and Liù. When Grob-Prandl sang Turandot, the walls shook. What an immense voice she had—it just poured out. There are none today that I know of that size and power. I was very partial to *The Bartered Bride*—such a cheerful opera. But more and more I loved *Liederabende* and concentrated in that direction. In 1948 I married the talented violinist Wolfgang

Schneiderhan, and we began soon afterward to do concerts together. I had to interrupt my activities twice because of the births of two daughters, Barbara Maria and Monica Maria. The latter is now an actress in Hamburg.

"After adding the touching Blanche in *Les Dialogues des carmélites* and Handel's Cleopatra, I went on to Marie in *Wozzeck* in a very intelligent production directed by the late Günther Rennert in Stuttgart, with Carlos Kleiber conducting. As I adore roles that afford the opportunity to really act, I did not regret this step, and I also repeated the role at the Edinburgh Festival. Then I took on Bartók's *Bluebeard's Castle* in Vienna and later at the Colón in Buenos Aires. My farewell at the Staatsoper was in 1976 in *Káta Kabanová,* and then at the Volksoper I did a few character parts. Now I teach, which is a hell of a job, because most young people who are sent to me have already received the wrong technical advice. I was always so conscious of new technical problems facing me that every year I took time off to study with Paola Novikova, who helped me a lot."

And whose was the most impressive voice she had ever heard?

"Here," she quickly replied, "I have no doubts: Flagstad's. I had the honor of appearing as Marzelline, under Furtwängler, to her Leonore in *Fidelio* at the Salzburg Festival. Hers was the voice to end all voices; the grandeur, nobility, security—all were awe inspiring, and these qualities were reflected in her as a human being. We had six weeks of rehearsals. One day, when the stage was very dark, I did not see a step and I fell. I screamed, for I thought I was in a thousand pieces. Before I realized what was happening, Flagstad rushed forward, picked me up in her strong arms, and took me to lie down in her dressing room. She didn't leave until the doctor had been called to ascertain the damage—thank God, nothing was broken, but the shock stayed with me for days. But that was the way this admirable woman behaved—affectionate and real.

"No voice has impressed me more for beauty of timbre than Ljuba Welitsch's at a certain stage of her career. When she sang Donna Anna with me, I was overwhelmed by the velvet sound. But she gave too much of herself, and nature is fierce, for the price to be paid is high. But I believe that with all of us, most things are predestined. We are what we are meant to be. I gave too much of myself too at times, and I don't regret it. With my impulsive nature, it could not have been different."

As I bid my adieu, she picked up a small rose from the garden and, handing it to me, said, "Denkt an die Rose nur, wie klein sie ist, und duftet doch so lieblich, wie ihr wisst'—just think of the rose, how small it is; and yet it smells so lovely, as you know. These pretty words are from 'Auch kleine Dinge' by Hugo Wolf, but how I wish I could take credit for them!"

THE SMALL
VOICES THAT
TRAVELED FAR

BIDÚ SAYÃO

MAFALDA FAVERO

RITA STREICH

There once existed small voices that were so expertly focused that they were able to cut through large orchestras and be heard despite the limitations of their size. The Italians called them *"voci che corrono"*—voices that run; and they would be particularly welcome today, when voices are so reduced in volume. The three of this vanishing species with whom I spoke were Bidú Sayão, Mafalda Favero, and Rita Streich.

These three ladies, who made an impression and became world celebrities despite their limited natural resources, all shared a presence that communicated itself to the public even before they had uttered a note. Petite and well proportioned, they possessed a particular brand of personal charm that came strongly over the footlights. I recall vividly the occasions when I first heard Favero, as Zerlina in Florence; Sayão, as Carolina in Rome; and Streich, as Zerbinetta in Salzburg. They exploded like firecrackers. However studied their performances may have been, they seemed as fresh as champagne bubbles.

Sayão's and Streich's careers stretched over three decades; their voices became slightly smaller in the later years, yet not too noticeably so. But Favero, as she so honestly admits, was unable to check her strong temperament and took on assignments too heavy for her delicate instrument. In less than a quarter of a century the beautiful fountain of her sound was in serious trouble. When I heard her after the war at La Scala in *Manon,* which had been her most acclaimed interpretation, she could no longer sustain long phrases.

BIDÚ SAYÃO

The very special gifts of Bidú Sayão—whose real full name is Baldovina de Oliveira Sayão—singled her out and made her one of a kind: the fragility of her instrument, crystal clear, which cut like a diamond across a large orchestra; the exquisite delicacy of her phrasing; her innate sense of the stage, which created a thousand and one nuances; and a feminine pertness that was totally irresistible. When she received me in the spring of 1979 in her New York apartment on West Fifty-seventh Street (she spends several months a year in her house in Maine), I noticed that she had changed very little over the past twenty years. She was much as I recalled her: the piquant appearance; the dyed red hair parted in the middle, with a chignon; the smiling eyes; the tiny nose; the sensual mouth; and a firmness of the jaw that the years cannot impair.

Time seemed to have come to a standstill for Sayão. She was born in 1902; her career, which ended in 1957, spanned just a bit over thirty years. (She came out of retirement briefly in 1959, to record the *Floresta Amazonica* for her great friend Heitor Villa-Lobos; she had been one of the supreme interpreters of his Bachianas Brasileiras No. 5.) Sayão's second husband, the famous baritone Giuseppe Danise, died in 1963, and her mother followed in 1966; since then, she has lived alone. But their names cropped up constantly during our long conversation, and their presence was deeply felt.

No one could have made such a dazzling place for herself in the lyric pantheon had she not been unusually bright, and as I talked to Sayão, the cleverness, the sense of measure, and the quick repartee offered proof of that brightness. After more than fifty years of constant operagoing I still feel that she was the best Adina, Norina, Rosina, Zerlina, and Susanna. My memory of her at the Metropolitan Opera in the last act of *Le nozze di Figaro*— she sang "Deh vieni, non tardar" while cutting the roses in the garden— will never be obliterated. It was total, intoxicating enchantment. As Manon, Mimi, Violetta—the lyric roles she added in the second phase of her career, and which she herself much preferred to the others—she won her battle through that peculiar magic of hers. But it is in the lighter repertoire that

Bidú Sayão as Mélisande in *Pelléas et Mélisande*.

she had no equals. As Mélisande, she was perfectly cast, for she conveyed the evanescent mystery of this lost creature with a voice that was like gossamer.

"Life, as we all discover," she explained, "is a series of compromises, and sometimes they are for the best. Becoming a singer was not what I really wished, but I had to come to terms with an adorable but formidable mother. Like all Brazilians, I am a mixture of several bloods, for on my father's side they were all Portuguese, but on my mother's they were French, Swiss, and Italian. My brother—sixteen years my senior—and I lived with our mother, who was widowed when I was four. Intent on her duties and determined to bring us up with no outside interferences, she refused to remarry.

"While my brother studied law and never gave any trouble, I was difficult to manage. I was determined to become an actress, and in Rio de Janeiro at that time going on the stage was absolutely out of the question for a girl born in a respectable family. Rio, in those days, had a fine musical life, and the Teatro Municipal imported the best singers in the world. Ask the old-timers and they will tell you. So a substitute was found for my ambitions: I would study voice.

"Stubborn and spoiled, I insisted on having the best teacher available. But Elena Teodorini, the great Rumanian soprano who had sung at La Scala and was settled in Rio giving lessons, she had no intention of taking me as a pupil. I was too young, in the first place, and the voice much too small. I pleaded and pleaded, and managed to make myself such a nuisance that I broke down her resistance and she accepted me. Eventually she became impressed by my willpower and discipline. I soon realized that there was no way to become a singer without a solid musical background, and so I trained in all areas. By my third year it was obvious that I was a coloratura; I hit a G with facility, and the *picchettati* came without effort.

"Then, suddenly, a major problem arose. Madame Teodorini had decided that the time had come for her to return to her native Rumania, and I would not hear of changing teachers. So, after many discussions at home, I followed her to Rumania, where dreams began to come true. The stunning Queen Marie was an indefatigable patroness of music and, after hearing me, chose me to be the soloist with the orchestra at a concert given in the palace for the official visit of Hirohito, at that time crown prince of Japan. Despite being extremely nervous, I made out very well.

"There had never been any question of my becoming an opera singer, since my mother frowned on this idea. I was to work toward becoming a recitalist. After my success at the palace, on the queen's advice, I was sent to Vichy to audition for Jean de Reszke so that he could prepare me for

a concert career. I was tremendously fortunate not only that he accepted me
—"*une ravissante petite voix*" was the verdict—but that I had his enlightened
guidance for two years; he died in 1925, and in fact I was one of his very
last students. I settled in Nice for two years and took classes every day.

"It is difficult to describe today the awe and respect surrounding his
person. He had been one of the greatest tenors of all time, his brother
Edouard a magnificent basso, and his sister Josephine an outstanding soprano.
With what skill he put me through the cadenzas that developed and steadied
the highest notes in the upper range! I shall never forget some of the
exercises. There was one, which he put me through over and over again,
to eliminate the break from chest to head: a sequence of four notes consisting
of F, F-sharp, G, and G-sharp. He instructed me to obtain a high palate by
the sensation of surprise and not to pull the muscles of the throat up. Only
the soft palate should be raised.

"De Reszke had an extraordinary ability to evaluate the text, integrating
it to the music until they became one. This was to be of enormous help to
me when I took on many of the Debussy scores. I never sang the role of
Ophelia in *Hamlet* by Thomas, but her dazzling mad scene, which became
a must on my concert programs, became a real part of me, so many were
the times he made me go over it, concentrating on the words' essence and
producing sounds that would enhance them. I was also immensely fortunate
in having Reynaldo Hahn accompany me on the piano in the school and
teach me some of his enchanting songs. The time element was never considered until the right effect had been reached. The struggle was to make it
all sound spontaneous while actually it was the fruit of much work. Hahn
made me go over and over again 'Si mes vers avaient des ailes' until the
airiness of the text was duly conveyed on the breath.

"As time went by, my mother adjusted herself to the fact that there was
no real stigma attached to opera singers, having met many charming ones.
So she agreed that I could go to Rome to audition for the famous Emma
Carelli, who had been one of the most important Italian sopranos and since
1912 had been running the Teatro Costanzi. (To Carelli's distress, it was soon
to be taken away from her, when the decision was made to transform it into
the Teatro Reale, to be run by the city.) She had been married to Walter
Mocchi, who later became my husband and who was responsible for the
seasons at the Colón in Buenos Aires as well as having a hand in many Italian
opera houses. Carelli was a formidable organizer, despite the limited means
at her disposal, and had a knack for discovering voices. It was she who
discovered Lauri-Volpi and gave him his first big chance. When I auditioned
for her, I was terrified, for she sat there with her vibrant, unforgettable blue

eyes never leaving me for one second. Immediately she decided that I had possibilities and confided me to the care of Maestro Luigi Ricci to learn repertoire. 'The voice is limited,' she said, 'but sometimes it is the tiny birds who fly the greater distances and for the longest time.'

"My debut came unexpectedly, as Rosina in *Il barbiere di Siviglia*, with an all-star cast consisting of Carlo Galeffi, Nino Ederle, and Nazzareno de Angelis, under the baton of Edoardo Vitale. There were no orchestra or stage rehearsals, and I had rapidly to get my own costumes. My mother and I decided to splurge and went to Caramba, who rapidly made some lovely ones in the Goya style. It was a leap in the dark, but I landed safely, for the notices were uniformly excellent. Carelli showed her faith in me by giving me the opportunity to sing Gilda to Carlo Galeffi's fabulous Rigoletto and then Carolina in an adorable revival of *Il matrimonio segreto*, the role that made me famous and opened the doors of the Municipal Theatres in São Paulo and my native Rio, where I always sang in the summer months. Carelli died a short time later, victim of a tragic automobile accident in 1928.

"Rome became my base for several years, and I was afforded the honor of singing at the royal gala in *Don Pasquale* in January 1930 when Umberto, the crown prince of Italy, married the Princess Marie José, daughter of the king of the Belgians. Every box was covered with flowers, and all the women wore tiaras. I went on to *Lucia di Lammermoor*, *I puritani*, which I even sang at the Bellini celebrations in Catania, and *La sonnambula*. I don't really know which of these two Bellini operas presents the greater difficulties. Technically, perhaps Elvira was the more demanding, but Amina's recitatives are very tricky, and to keep the voice expressive in the midst of all the acrobatics is a tremendous challenge.

"Giordano chose me to sing in his new opera *Il re*, which has a devilish tessitura. Toscanini believed in it and conducted its premiere in Milan with Toti dal Monte, and I did it in Rome. Without a doubt the most harrowing role I ever undertook was Zerbinetta, which I sang in Italian in Genoa, San Remo, the Colón, and Rio's Municipal.

"I appeared with all the leading tenors, Gigli and Pertile included, but the one from whom I learned the most artistically was Schipa, for he chiseled phrases like a goldsmith. He lowered many of his roles one tone, but no one noticed it, so consummate was his art. My first *Lakmé* was at the Comique in Paris, and my first *Roméo et Juliette* at the Paris Opéra with Georges Thill, who sang with the most lovely Italianate sound. In fact he had studied in Naples with de Lucia. I also sang with him in *Guarany*, Brazil's national opera, in both Rio and São Paulo. He was the last of the great French tenors—another tradition gone down the drain.

"Gradually I moved away from the straight coloratura parts, with the exception of Gilda and Rosina, and went into the leggero and then some of the lyric roles. The reason I never agreed to appear as Lucia at the Metropolitan was the presence of Lily Pons, whose range was so high that she had the part transposed upstairs. I felt that the public at that time was so accustomed to hearing Lucia's music pushed up that it would probably think I had transposed it down! It is ironical that I always loathed the repertoire my instrument was suited for, as my instinct drove me to crave dramatic and pathetic parts. It is very much like a painter gifted at executing miniatures whose ambition is to do huge frescoes. So I always was in a state of frustration." And she laughed.

"My marriage to Mocchi lasted from 1927 until 1934, with the divorce coming later. In the meantime Danise—with whom I sang often, particularly in South America, and who was at the end of his career, for he retired in 1935—took me in hand to steer me gradually into some of the lyric roles. He was fantastic as a teacher and tremendously strict. Look at the marvels he accomplished with Regina Resnik, transforming her from a soprano into a mezzo. Watching me like a hawk, he ignored my pleas to take on Desdemona, Fiora, and Butterfly. He allowed me to try Violetta, which I sang first in Brazil and then at the Colón, and then Mimi, Mélisande, and Manon. I had sung Marguerite in *Faust* at the Opéra in Paris, but Danise did not approve, for he considered the church scene too heavy, so I dropped it. At the end of my career I appeared in San Francisco as Margherita in *Mefistofele* and as Nedda, but by then I was willing to take risks, for I was about to put an end to my activities.

"It was Danise who was totally responsible for my American career. He knew his way around, for he had appeared over four hundred times at the Metropolitan. In 1936 he persuaded me to accompany him to New York, and he introduced me to Bruno Zirato, who was very influential at the Philharmonic. As Toscanini was just at that precise moment looking for a soloist to sing Debussy's *La Damoiselle élue*, he arranged for me to audition. My prayers were answered: the famous maestro engaged me, and I made my New York debut at Carnegie Hall, to considerable acclaim, in this cantata. Danise knew what he was doing. Bori had just retired, and the Metropolitan needed someone to take over some of her roles. My debut there as Manon on February 13, 1937, led me to a happy association with the Thirty-ninth Street theatre that lasted until 1952. It was as Mimi, with di Stefano as my Rodolfo, that I said goodbye to this building, which had become a second home for me."

Actually, when Rudolf Bing took over the management in 1950, with a few exceptions he wished to clear the Metropolitan of singers brought in by his predecessor, Edward Johnson. In some cases he simply did not re-engage them; in others, the deal offered was such that they preferred to bow out. In the 1950–51 and 1951–52 seasons all Sayão was offered was a few performances of *La Bohème,* and although she did not wish to discuss this particular situation with me ("What has been, has been," she said), everyone knew that Danise (whom she had married in 1947) advised her to leave the Met and concentrate on recitals, for which she was much in demand. There was also a question of a revival of *Pelléas,* closely identified with her, which Bing wished to assign to another soprano. Partly because of the war and then the postwar conditions, and also because the United States had become home to her, she never returned to sing abroad, with the exception of her engagements in South America in the summer.

"If the Metropolitan became my permanent base for all those years," she stated, "the San Francisco Opera came a close second. In 1957 I was asked to perform *La Damoiselle élue* with André Cluytens, and it seemed right that I should end my activity in the United States with the music that had opened its doors to me. There were still engagements to fulfill, but I canceled them. It is always a hard decision to part with one's raison d'être; but I saw too many of my colleagues who did not know when to call a halt, and I was not going to be one of them.

"I don't have the teaching gift—it is an inborn ability—and I am sorry, for the wonderful de Reszke method should have been passed on. Now many former prima donnas have eagerly turned to giving master classes. But what use are they if the students are not fully prepared technically? When I went to Gemma Bellincioni to instruct me in the pitfalls of *La traviata,* and to Rosina Storchio for her precious advice on *La sonnambula,* it was not for singing problems, since I was already well launched, but to try to seize their musical characterization from the inside.

"There are good voices today, but there is no depth in any profession anymore, not only in mine. It's all superficial and leaves one untouched. To convey love, which is essential in most operas and songs, is not a matter of phonetics. If you don't feel it, you cannot transmit it. Looking back dispassionately, the fragility of my instrument was my curse and at the same time my treasure. Pathos can be of many dimensions, and frequently the frail one is even more affecting than the big one. I would have given happily ten years of my life to be able to appear as Butterfly. When she sings 'Vogliatemi bene, un bene piccolino,' she goes straight to the heart, for a small love can be stronger than many others. It is the intensity that counts, not the size."

MAFALDA FAVERO

When Mafalda Favero opened the door of her elegantly furnished apartment in Milan in 1977, I was struck by the enormous eyes that dominated her wide, sensitive face, just as I was struck later by her utter candor. Bright, enthusiastic, and impulsive, she created the kind of electric current that had made her so celebrated during her distinguished career. Her vivacity is captivating; her moods mercurial.

Born in 1905 near Ferrara, she studied in Bologna with the intention of becoming a recitalist. "Instead," she reminisced, "the chance presented itself to sing Liù in *Turandot* at the Regio in Parma—the most terrifying stage in Europe, because of its capricious public, which is very knowledgeable but also terribly rowdy. So I was thrown to the wolves from the start, and perhaps it is better to know the worst from the beginning. But sometimes fortune smiles on the fearless. Not only was I praised by the critics, but I received ovations after both 'Signore ascolta' and 'Tu che di gel sei cinta.' What is more, I was re-engaged immediately for Margherita in *Mefistofele*, a short role, but with an aria really more suited to a spinto. My professors were astounded, for they had always claimed that with so small a voice my only hope was as a recitalist. But they had not realized that I was a born actress. For the next two years I divided my time between concerts and opera, but every operatic engagement became more and more successful. As I was fascinated by the theatre, I decided to throw in my lot with opera. My voice remained small, but the public was never aware of it. Only the real connoisseurs knew. The explanation is that I learned to use emotion and expression as a means to cover vocal deficiencies.

"For me," she continued, using her delicate hands to underline some of the phrases, "emotion was the most vital aspect of any heroine I undertook. What did she really feel and think? I dug and dug into the character until it became totally mine. Though I was infinitely more attracted to tragic roles, I was a great success in comedy and was constantly in demand for Carolina in *Il matrimonio segreto*, Susanna and Zerlina (I often sang these under Bruno Walter), Adina, and Norina. Critics singled me out as the best in Italy for this repertoire, because I approached these parts not as soubrettes but as human beings. I loved all of them, though Norina the least, for she is a scheming person, and this went against my open nature. Of Mozart I also sang Pamina at the happy time in Italy when there existed singers who knew this composer's particular style. Today they must all be imported—*che vergogna!*

"It was on December 26, 1929," she said, smiling happily, "that I made my debut at La Scala as Eva in *Die Meistersinger* with Toscanini—and I remained there twenty-six years, singing at least five or six different operas every season. The Toscanini experience was thrilling, and what a marvelous stage director he was! I remember Angelica Cravcenco, who had to enter at a certain moment carrying a basket, and he wanted to obtain from her a certain effect that she could not quite grasp. He rapidly jumped onto the stage and showed her. Magdalene, as we all know, is not a leading role, but she was such a fine artist she made it seem important. *Meistersinger* was Toscanini's favorite Wagner opera, and in the years of his return at La Scala from the end of 1921 until the late spring of 1929 he conducted it for five different seasons. How lucky I was, for this was the last time he ever led it in Italy! He then left La Scala, and I did not sing with him again until May 11, 1946, when the opera house reopened after its reconstruction in the teariest atmosphere imaginable. I sang the third act of *Manon Lescaut,* one of the most memorable events in my life. (After La Scala was destroyed by bombs, the company had moved to the Lirico, and there we continued until the main house was ready again.)

"If memory does not betray me, I sang twenty-seven operas in all in Milan, including *La Bohème* for six different seasons and the Massenet *Manon* for seven. Although La Scala was my permanent home, I was always given time to do guest appearances in Rome, in Naples, at the Maggio Musicale Fiorentino, and in other theatres. I went to Covent Garden in 1937 and 1939. Success at the San Francisco Opera as Mimi, Martha, and Norina brought me to the Met in 1939 for *La Bohème.* I was re-engaged for the following year, but I was unable to honor my commitment because of the war. When the government took my passport away in 1940, along with those of Cigna, Stignani, Caniglia, Masini, and others, claiming that if we left Italy the opera houses would be bereft of stars, I was absolutely livid with rage and disappointment.

"It was in this state of mind that I came to *La traviata,* an opera I had never considered suited to me vocally and therefore had put aside. What

Mafalda Favero as Juliette in *Roméo et Juliette*.

the hell, I thought, why not try it? And I succeeded with it to such an extent in Bologna that every theatre in Italy demanded it.

"Actually," she admitted with her total candor, "it took me a very long time to find my own interpretation, for I was haunted by Claudia Muzio in this role. When she sang it at the Colón in Buenos Aires in 1933, I went to each rehearsal, worshiping her, and it took a superhuman effort for me to finally obtain my personal approach. My Violetta was on a far more intimate scale, not only because of my voice but because of the helplessness I felt this character suffered from her fate. I recall a performance of Muzio's in Refice's *Cecilia,* an opera she created in Rome in 1934 which deals with the saint's martyrdom. She had been so sublime in it that I went backstage to express my admiration at the end and impulsively dropped to my knees. 'Now, really, my child!' she said with those sad eyes which haunted me. 'What are you doing?' Her Norma was also an unforgettable creation. She had the quality I consider so essential in an artist: to make the public suffer along with her. If a singer doesn't make the audience cry at certain passages, in my estimation she has failed in her job. Callas was a phenomenon, but she had no femininity, and she never produced chills down my spine. She was theatrical to a degree, but never touching. Giuseppina Cobelli's Isolde and Katiusha in *Risurrezione* absolutely always tore me apart, and I was grateful for the pain she had made me suffer, a sort of cleansing and purification.

"I have always been more impressed by a singer's temperament than by the voice. Galliano Masini was one of the few who had both. His Don José was one of the greatest interpretations I ever witnessed, and his fourth act let out such a stream of emotions I became limp. Gino Bechi's Athanaël was magnificent, and somehow a current existed between us—I sang Thaïs with him on many occasions—that electrified the public. I never actually studied scores with anyone, but once I had the part in my throat I often went to Carmen Melis, an artist I admired without reservation, whose Manon was a masterpiece. She gave me some very valuable pointers. Today I would put Renata Scotto at the head of all the Italians. Too often she tackles the wrong assignments, but she never fails to stir me.

"Butterfly was my undoing," she said pensively. "I adored the part and allowed myself to be tempted into singing it much too often. To sing it the way I did, giving everything I had, took a tremendous toll. The first time I appeared as Cio-Cio-San at La Scala, under Antonio Guarnieri's magical direction, so light and yet so meaningful, it didn't seem quite so heavy; but he very intelligently allowed no intermission between the second and third acts, and this was far less exhausting, for the interruption, emotionally speaking, necessitates recreating the tension all over again. I went one night to hear Raina Kabaivanska in this opera, and I found her backstage at the end, perfectly composed, not a bead of perspiration anywhere! After a performance of Cio-Cio-San I was literally undone, and it took me a couple of days to regain my composure and strength. But that was the only way I could approach a role—unsparing and dedicated. I am fully aware that Butterfly shortened my career by at least five years.

"Now I will show you what I mean about dedication." She went to the phonograph and searched nearby for one of her records, and I recognized the aria right away: "Flammen, perdonami" from Mascagni's *Lodoletta*. There it was, that exquisite voice, almost flagrant, infinitely fragile, utterly overwhelming in its total simplicity and heartbreak, the words dropping like pearls in a pool of clear water. "This was another role I gave my whole being to. I am an ardent Mascagni fan, and one of these days he'll be rediscovered. I often sang Suzel in *L'amico Fritz* and also Iris—undoubtedly the heaviest assignment I undertook, but I found the way to give body to the accents, substituting them for the volume I did not possess."

Vocally and temperamentally, she was eminently suited to the French repertoire, and *Manon* is the opera she sang most often. "I was also very partial to Louise and Juliette. The coloratura in the first act of *Roméo* scared me, but once I mastered it I found Juliette a very rewarding part. When the opera reappeared on the boards of La Scala in 1934, after an absence of twenty-four years, the last soprano to have sung it in the previous production had been Bori. Gigli was my partner, and I had to work hard with my fantasy to imagine that he was young, handsome, and worth dying for. Then I found the solution: I had fallen in love with his voice, and that was worth any great passion. How he phrased 'Ah, lève-toi, soleil'—enthralling and memorable! I also appeared often as Micaëla and particularly enjoyed Gianna Pederzini as Carmen. She was simply fabulous, and the contrast between us made Don José's dilemma seem quite real. I also sang Saamsceddina (what a name! it took me weeks to get used to it) in the revival of *Marouf* at La Scala in 1938, and I fell in love with Charlotte in *Werther* after having sung the ingenue Sophie earlier. The color of my voice was not dark enough, but, again, through the emotion I gave to the music it suited me. Thaïs brought out my sexiness, and as I had a good figure, I looked the part of the courtesan."

In the verismo repertoire, she recalled, Zazà and Adriana Lecouvreur suited her temperament, and she was partial to both, "for they offer a singing actress ever so many opportunities. I also enjoyed doing Magda in *La rondine,* which is no joke vocally, one of Puccini's most treacherous under its false simplicity. Because I was quick in learning new scores, they kept throwing heaps of them at me. There were so many, both tragic and comic, that I cannot mention them all; but one I recall with much pleasure was the world premiere at La Scala of Lattuada's *Le preziose ridicole.* It is fascinating to think that this opera was considered so important in those days—1929 to be exact—that at almost the same time the Berlin Staatsoper presented it with Novotna taking on Madelon (my role) and the Metropolitan Opera too, with Bori. La Scala gave it a beautiful production, and I had as my colleagues Jan Kiepura, Stignani, and Baccaloni. It was such a hit that we repeated it the following season. And then total silence. It has always been said that all operas based on Molière's plays inevitably failed, and it must be true that there is some sort of a curse.

"At La Scala I also created two enchanting operas by Wolf-Ferrari, again gone into limbo, *La dama boba* and *Il campiello;* the latter lasted four seasons before its eclipse. In San Remo I created Mascagni's *Pinotta,* a delectable one-act opera; in Rome, Zandonai's *La farsa amorosa;* and in Naples, Alfano's *L'ultimo lord*—a difficult assignment dramatically, as I had to impersonate a young boy. At La Scala I also appeared in the local premiere of Milhaud's *Le Pauvre Matelot,* which turned out to be my farewell to that theatre in 1949. Now this is one opera that I can understand is forgotten.

"I think stage directors are doing a great disservice to the lyric theatre," she said with passion. "They are often pretentious, ignorant, and worry too much about innovations they can bring to the text and the score. The improvisation that is a part of the instinct of every real artist has been eliminated. I never did quite the same thing twice. What seemed natural one night did not appear so three days later. Instinct is most essential in an opera singer, and very often it is right. I was happy to listen to suggestions, but in the end it was always I who decided what was right for me—and, believe me, it should not be any other way. Today a director instructs a certain singer in a certain role and then supposes that the one who takes over a few performances later should do the same gestures and poses. It won't work.

"There are no great singing actors today, and for this very reason. Why, please tell me, should an artist obey a director the way a soldier must obey a general? It's the singer the public is interested in, not the director. The reason I became a favorite is that I developed my characters the way I felt them. The public was interested in hearing my Butterfly because it knew mine was totally different from Pampanini's, Adami Corradetti's, or Oltrabella's. Directors should be there to coordinate, of course, but not to stifle the interpreter in his own creative moment.

"Actually, for the past few years we have been faced with a total change in values. Up until some time ago we were not merely singers, but artists in the creative sense. Now today singers are considered almost members of the chorus, and I do not mean this disrespectfully, for I have always had tremendous respect for members of this profession. Conductors no longer have the time, rushing here and there, to take an active interest in what goes on. Rehearsals for a new production can go on and on, but there are hardly any for a revival. Overrehearsing can be as bad as underrehearsing, and between the two I'd take the latter. So many singers today, who have practiced an opera for hours with the orchestra, arrive on opening night with no voice left.

"Like Mimi (the Italian role I sang most often), as you see, *vivo sola, soletta* —I live all alone. My husband, Mario Giacomo Signorelli, a doctor, died some years ago. I have a tiny country place in Brianza, where I spend the hot season, and I often agree to be a judge at singing competitions, for I like to be in touch with what goes on, despite the fact that most of the time I am quite appalled. So many promising voices are exploited too soon, disappearing after so short a time. The lack of judgment of those in charge is most discouraging, and it makes one wonder where we go from here. Anyhow, after a conversation like ours, I feel that so little has remained of what I was, and the words of Adriana Lecouvreur in the fourth act come to mind: 'La mia corona è solo d'erbe intessuta'—my crown is only made of grass. And grass, as we all know, soon becomes straw."

Mafalda Favero died in 1981.

KAMMERSÄNGERIN
RITA STREICH

No other coloratura soprano recorded more in her era than Rita Streich, for her small, pure, and perfect instrument was ideally suited to this medium. That she had a remarkable career in opera as well as in concert is because she belongs to that disappearing elite who learned to project what little volume they had over large orchestras in large theatres with astonishing results. A musician to her fingertips, she could cope brilliantly with both the coloratura roles and the leggero and soubrette repertoire. After her teacher Erna Berger went into retirement, few could compete with Streich as the Queen of the Night in *Die Zauberflöte,* not only for the precision of the staccatos and the phenomenal breath control, but also for her ability, despite her vocal limitations, to infuse her own brand of drama into the infernal tessitura.

When I met her for lunch at the Hotel Imperial in Vienna in the spring of 1979, I had no difficulty in recognizing her. There she was, looking every inch a diva of times gone by, in a becoming pink bouffant skirt with matching blouse and a large garden-party-style straw hat. Mischievous and adorable, she did not seem a day over forty, but when I asked her the date of her birth, she skirted the question ably, replying only that she had been born in Siberia. Although she told me that she had left Russia with her parents (an Austrian father and a Russian mother) in 1920, she did not specify her age. They settled first in Essen, then in Jena, but it was in Augsburg that she first began taking singing lessons. Later, in Berlin, she studied with Erna Berger, who was still active at that time. After her debut at the Berlin Staatsoper in 1946, she studied Zerbinetta with Maria Ivogün, the celebrated Hungarian soprano who had excelled in this role, and later returned to Ivogün and her husband, Michel Rauch-Eisen, to take classes in coloratura lieder singing.

"There never had been any question that I was anything but a coloratura from the very start," she told me in her warm, cheerful manner, "and I never changed range. In a way I consider this very fortunate, for I did not have to go through the stress and the indecision that so many others do. When I first started at the Staatsoper, I also made guest appearances at Walter Felsenstein's so-called Komische Oper in East Berlin. It was only in 1950

Rita Streich as Zerbinetta in *Ariadne auf Naxos*.

that the demarcation line between West and East Berlin became so decisive, and then I never went back. My first real affirmation came with Blondchen in *Die Entführung,* with my fabulous teacher Berger as Konstanze and the unequaled Mozartian tenor, Peter Anders, as Belmonte. Then I scored heavily as Olympia in *The Tales of Hoffmann.*

"From the very beginning I was determined to play the cards in my pack wisely and without haste, for I kept my eyes wide open and took stock of what happened to some of those around me. I recall with surprise my vehemence and courage when I stood up to the great Frida Leider, who had retired from singing but had been put in charge in Berlin of a new production of *Die Zauberflöte.* She asked me to take on the Queen of the Night, and until then I had always sung one of the Three Boys. Berger was away on a concert tour, and I did not feel ready to be exposed to this colossal assignment without the proper preparation. She became nastily furious and claimed there was no one else. I was determined not to give in, since, after all, it was my reputation I was risking and not hers. At one moment I even feared that my contract might be annulled for insubordination. It became a regular tug of war, but eventually Berger returned, intervened with great tact, and the storm blew over.

"After ten years I moved to the Vienna Staatsoper, and there I remained. My Salzburg debut came as Ännchen in a production of *Der Freischütz* with Furtwängler, and the following year came the Queen of the Night under Solti, and this role, along with Zerbinetta, made my international reputation. I sang it everywhere, including the Colón of Buenos Aires under Sir Thomas Beecham's very personal baton. The difficulty that every coloratura encounters is to be expressive with a voice of restricted size and color, and both Berger and Ivogün helped me extensively with this. I found the Queen of the Night far more taxing than Zerbinetta, for she is always placed way upstage on a platform and in so limited a space she can hardly move. The first aria has a troublesome recitative, and then the aria itself is marked by a sort of pulsation, a combination of force and elasticity. How to put over the dark side of the Queen's cry for help to Tamino is perplexing, for it is hard to enunciate the text forcefully and clearly amidst all the trills. What could be more desperate than when she exclaims, 'Ihr ängstliches Beben, ihr schüchternes Streben'. [What fearful trembling, what timid striving] or 'Du wirst der Tochter Retter sein' [You will be my daughter's savior]? But these cries lose much of their anguish if the words do not ring out.

"While the second aria, 'Der Hölle Rache kocht in meinem Herzen' [The wrath of hell rages in my heart], is technically very hard, there is the advantage that by then the Queen has established her character. But there is a lot of needling in the score, and the finale—'Hört, Rachegötter! Hört der Mutter Schwur' [Hear, gods of vengeance, hear a mother's cry]—must be shattering to the audience. I believe that the reason I became for many years the virtuosa of this relatively short but staggeringly demanding role is that the public understood what I was saying. I owe this to Berger, who was a perfectionist and would not allow even half a syllable to be lost in the pyrotechnics. 'The Queen of the Night is a fighter,' she used to say to me. 'You must learn to push this force through to the auditorium. To color the voice is the art of singing.'

"Some people are born with a special timbre—take, for instance, Callas, Tebaldi, Jurinac, and Leontyne Price—and it is unmistakable even on recordings, which, as we all know, are very much manipulated. I had the good luck that I too possessed a certain color in my cords, but the battle was always to hold on to it despite the endless cadenzas my roles required. Gilda was more relaxing, since she has many lyrical passages where you can express pathos; but to inject some humanity into some of the other roles is a constant challenge.

"Specialists who have analyzed my voice," she continued in her perky manner, "tell me that my timbre is a mixture of Slavic and Germanic elements. I have always been conscious that I possess the spontaneity of the Slavs and the almost cruel self-analysis of the Germans. If my voice could travel far despite its miniature size, the explanation is that it was always in perfect focus. The scales I went through before singing in public and then afterward daily account for it. Every day I practiced over and over again just as if I were a beginner.

"The coloratura parts I sang most frequently, apart from those already mentioned, were Sophie in *Der Rosenkavalier*, Rosina in *Il barbiere di Siviglia*, Adele in *Fledermaus*, Oscar in *Un ballo in maschera*, and the Forest Bird in *Siegfried*. Among the leggero roles were Mozart's *Zaïde*, *La finta giardiniera*, and *Der Schauspieldirektor*, along with Susanna, Despina, and Zerlina, Amor in *Orfeo*, Norina in *Don Pasquale*, Adina in *L'elisir d'amore*, and Nuri in *Tiefland*. Other Strauss roles were Fiakermilli in *Arabella* and the Italian Singer in *Capriccio*. The Bird in the *Ring* I also sang in Bayreuth under Clemens Krauss and then later with Keilberth. Knappertsbusch made me very happy, for he used to tell me that my bird was not a vocalise, the way it is often performed, but the perfect imitation of a nightingale. In fact, I had listened as often as possible to this heavenly sound in the forest, and I did everything in my power to imitate its flutelike sound. The words are so well impressed in my memory—goodness, they are so beautiful! And how to do justice to the text within a scale that must not be really human took months of study and reflection. The 'Lustig in Leid, sing' ich von Liebe' [Happy in sorrow, I sing of love] passage keeps on haunting me."

Had she ever married? I asked her.

"Yes," she replied, "to Dieter Berger, and I had a child. But my private life is of no interest."

And why had she not sung at the Metropolitan?

"There were already several coloraturas at the Met, and the repertoire for my heroines was limited. But I did sing in San Francisco as Sophie, Despina, and Zerbinetta, while in Chicago it was the turn of Amor and Susanna. If you can imagine such a thing, with my small voice I sang at the Hollywood Bowl, but then so did Lily Pons. I made many recital tours of the United States, and in the last two decades I returned to Australia six times, to New Zealand seven, and to Japan three. Every year I spent a lot of time recording, and among the complete operas I am satisfied with are *Die Entführung, Die Zauberflöte, Rigoletto, Hänsel und Gretel,* and *Der Rosenkavalier.* But then there are so many albums—lieder, folk songs, anything else you can name.

"I believe I am one of the last Mozart specialists," she said with obvious pride. "Mozart wrote some fifty-six concert arias, and I believe I have sung them all. They are really concertos in miniature, and the voice is used as an instrument more than by any other composer. Perhaps the most stirring for me is 'Vorrei spiegarvi o Dio'—potentially dangerous vocally, for it is at the same time very contained and yet so heartrending.

"I went on with my operatic appearances here and there, always keeping Vienna as my base until I retired from the Staatsoper in 1973 to dedicate myself to recitals.

"The current system, with all this coming and going of singers from one opera house to another, and no one really belonging anywhere, is turning into a major disaster. There are no more real ensembles. Performances are not properly rehearsed—half the artists are elsewhere—and the result is often fifth-rate. Can you imagine appearing as Zerbinetta, where it is all a question of intricate trios and quartets—I even was able to stand on my toes, giving the illusion I was a ballerina—without the necessary practice? During my long career I was a member of only two opera houses, Berlin and Vienna, and during the months I was engaged I stayed put. Now it has become a vicious circle. Very few new singers appear on the horizon, because those already established manage to be in four or five different cities the same week. They don't last long, but while they do every theatre wants them.

"Since I have become passionately interested in teaching, these problems affect me deeply. Not only do I give courses at the Academy here in Vienna but also in Essen and in the summer at the Salzburg Mozarteum. Elisabeth

Schwarzkopf was stunned when she heard that I was actually teaching instead of giving master classes, which she manages to squeeze in between her recitals. 'Why do you reveal your secrets?' she asked me incredulously. There could be no answer on my part, for obviously we were poles apart on this question.

"I have known her since the early years, when she was a pupil of Maria Ivogün. She was always a very stylish singer, but she varied very much from role to role. While she was a lovely Countess in *Capriccio,* for instance, marvelously sophisticated and subtle, I never cared for her Pamina—she was too artificial and lacked spontaneity, which is one of the musts of this character."

I asked her about conductors.

"I was so spoiled, for I sang with Leo Blech, Krips, Furtwängler, Fricsay, Mitropoulos, Böhm, Klemperer, Solti, Knappertsbusch, Karajan, Leinsdorf ... the list goes on. Shortly before his death I sang with Richard Strauss. I was at the very beginning and he at the end; it was such a touching experience, for he was still very much with it and yet had reached another dimension. None of these conductors—with one exception!—were egomaniacs, but now they are interested only in themselves. As a result, singers have lost their beam and no longer know where they are going. Even here in Vienna, where common sense used to prevail—even if at times over these last twenty years there were not really enough first-rate artists—one now witnesses some astonishing casting. When you try to find out who is responsible, you discover that no one is—or at least so it would appear. Everyone passes the buck.

"I tell my students that no one is going to save you from drowning unless you learn to swim for yourself. People who heard me at the beginning never believed that with my small frame and voice I could become a diva in my own right. But they did not know that I had such a strong will and sense of discipline. When I began appearing in recitals and with orchestras, I believed in being as glamorous as possible. I always wore a ball gown, white gloves, and jewelry. I know that even today the public does not want to pay the price of admission to see a waif come out on the stage. The era of prima donnas is finished, we all agree; but I am scandalized by how some of these performers appear in private life and on the concert stage. They have already lost part of the battle before they have opened their mouths. I tell my pupils daily all of this and more, hoping that the victories I won for myself will not be entirely lost on the new generations. But I also say to them what Sophie declares to Marianne at the very beginning of *Rosenkavalier*'s second act: 'Die Demut in mir zu erwecken, muss ich mich demütigen' —to awaken humility in myself, I must humble myself."

THE
SWITCHERS

GIULIA TESS

MARTHA MÖDL

ESTHER RETHY

The lyric theatre has seen cases of baritones who have successfully turned into tenors (the reverse also occurs, but less frequently). The same applies to women singers in the various ranges. A little less than a hundred years ago, Gemma Bellincioni started out as a coloratura and then swept into heavy verismo roles, becoming an unforgettable Santuzza, Salome, and Fedora. Selma Kurz is a case in reverse. Well established as Elisabeth and Elsa at the time of Gustav Mahler's celebrated regime at the Vienna Staatsoper, she later became a ,dazzling Zerbinetta and Lucia. Her trill, which lasted twenty seconds, has never been equaled. In our own time, Joan Sutherland went from the spinto to the coloratura repertoire with fabulous results. Regina Resnik was exceedingly fortunate in changing registers with success, going from dramatic soprano to dramatic mezzo.

For this chapter I have chosen three prima donnas who switched in midstream and conquered their new territory with laurels. Giulia Tess, whom I interviewed a year before her death in 1977, had established herself with distinction as a mezzo-contralto. Her rise to dramatic soprano—with a change of name to avoid confusion—led her into the verismo repertoire and made her a great favorite of Toscanini and Richard Strauss.

Martha Mödl is a particularly fascinating case, for she went from mezzo to dramatic soprano and then on to contralto. Although her mezzo and contralto repertoires were huge, as a dramatic she stuck to the heavy Wagner heroines and Leonore in *Fidelio*. She lacked the ringing high notes of Flagstad and Nilsson, but she impressed critics and public alike with the gripping intensity of her characterizations and her overwhelming vocal warmth. When she turned to contralto parts, the very critical and important English monthly *Opera* wrote of a performance of *Elektra*: "The great feature of this revival was Mödl's shattering Klytämnestra, a truly great piece of singing-acting that can rarely have been equalled."

Up until the Second World War, opera and operetta casts were often interchangeable, particularly in Austria and Germany. Since operettas had scores that demanded first-class voices, there were artists—Jeritza, Novotna, Tauber, Kiepura, and, later, Anneliese Rothenberger—who were very much in demand in both fields, though their main base always remained the operatic. Maggie Teyte did a balancing act between opera and operetta, finally returning to opera for good. And there were those who crossed the Rubicon and never returned: Mary Lewis and Grace Moore left Broadway for the Metropolitan, and Fritzi Scheff abandoned opera to become a highly applauded musical comedy star. Mimi Benzell and, incredibly, Helen Traubel left the Metropolitan for the nightclub circuit.

Today, not only have light operas such as *La Périchole, La Grande Duchesse de Gérolstein,* and *The Merry Widow* become common fare for opera companies, but also Cole Porter's *Kiss Me Kate* and Lerner and Loewe's *My Fair Lady.* So I chose as my third switcher Esther Rethy, one of the most beautiful and most admired sopranos of the Vienna Staatsoper, who became the number-one operetta star in the Austrian capital, although she never cut her operatic ties.

GIULIA TESS

Italy's most celebrated Salome and Elektra, Giulia Tess, was still going strong at eighty-seven when I visited her in 1976 in her pleasant apartment in Milan. Every day her gracious and cozy drawing room, dominated by a Steinway, was the mecca for young singers who came to vocalize, learn roles, and receive advice on stage deportment and to listen to her words of wisdom. For apart from her reputation as one of the great singing actresses of our century, she was considered gifted with a creative form of intelligence.

It was difficult to believe, when I was ushered into her presence, that the petite woman standing in front of me, small-boned, birdlike, with piercing blue eyes and the profile of a *grande dame,* had dominated the stages of the leading opera houses in the most taxing roles of the repertoire. But the moment she began speaking and telling me her story, it was obvious that she had a bright flame burning within. With an astonishing memory for details and the simplicity of a truly great person, she went to the core of every question, and always was generous toward colleagues.

"My life is a play divided in four acts," she began. "But do you think anyone is interested in such a prolific one? My name was Giulia Tessaroli and I was born in Verona, the daughter of a notary. My family was very proper middle-class and did not share my ardor for music and opera. So as not to bother them, I sang to my heart's content in the attic, aping the voices I had heard in the theatre. One day Rabbi Basevi, who lived in the same building, heard me from the stairs and asked whose voice it was. After listening to me on several occasions, he stopped my father and asked if I was studying to become a singer. 'Of course not,' he replied, 'she has no such idea.' 'Well, she should,' replied the rabbi. 'I know talent when I hear it. She has untold possibilities.' He then spoke to my mother. After his insistence, which encouraged me, my parents agreed to have me audition for Bottagisio, a well-known coach in the city, and obtain his opinion. He agreed with the rabbi, and to my great joy I began studying all the mezzo-soprano parts with him. I was entirely self-taught, having been born with

Giulia Tess in the title role of *Salome*.

an instrument that was naturally placed. The idea of a teacher seemed superfluous.

"In those days there were some very serious and honest agents who went around and scouted for new talent. My turn came, and I was chosen to make my debut in the title role of *Mignon* at the Teatro Rossini in Venice. I was terribly annoyed at Antonio Guarnieri, the eminent conductor, who upon meeting me at the first rehearsal declared, 'I do not like dealing with members of a kindergarten.' 'It will be my pleasure,' I replied, cut to the quick, 'to prove to you that I left that establishment long ago.' He mellowed, and actually was most helpful. I looked the part and made a success.

"Then came an offer to do Carmen in Saluzzo, and for that I really looked too young. But I adored the gypsy and did well by her. Other engagements followed. My big chance came two years later, when Arturo Vigna, whose reputation abroad as a conductor was considerable, heard me and signed me to appear as Leonora in *La favorita* in Prague. The cast was fabulous, for the tenor Giuseppe Anselmi was bel canto personified, and I still shiver when I think of his 'Spirito gentil.' Then there were Vittorio Arimondi, a magnificent bass, and Mattia Battistini, the number-one baritone of his era. This was a big challenge, and it came off so well that I was immediately signed for Amneris too. Prague in those days rivaled Vienna, where I was also called for guest performances.

"There followed one of the most exhausting and interesting episodes in my life: I undertook a year's tour with the famous Consalez company in Russia, and after a long stay in Moscow we went deep into Georgia and Turkestan. In those days operatic groups were formed for long journeys, and it meant a big organization, over two hundred people. It was a wonderful experience, not only because of the enthusiastic audiences, but for the chance it afforded me to sing a variety of roles—Adalgisa, Preziosilla, Maddalena, Charlotte in *Werther,* Azucena, Amneris, Carmen. We sang for the imperial family on several occasions—sweet, shy people who adored music. I treasured a letter from the tsar, but it was destroyed during the last war, with so many other precious possessions.

"Mezzo roles were ideal for displaying my temperament—and there was always a lot of it to display! So it came as quite a shock when the great Battistini, who had followed my progress with paternal kindness, asked to speak to me one day on a private matter. 'What I am about to say will upset you,' he said, 'and perhaps surprise you, but I feel it is my duty to do so. You are not a mezzo. I thought so from the beginning, but now I am convinced. You are such a clever minx that you imitate mezzos to perfection, but your low notes are all manufactured; they are not really there. And you have a glorious top. We need sopranos more than mezzos; do make the transition.' I was nonplussed. But my confidence in his judgment was so complete that the next day I canceled all my engagements, including a very profitable one in South America. For six months I studied soprano parts, again without calling a teacher for help. Then I asked Battistini to hear me, and he gave me his blessing: 'Go ahead; you are ready.' And he added, 'My advice is for you to change your name. If you continue to sing as Giulia Tessaroli, everyone—including the unimaginative critics—will be confused and start making comparisons.' Again I obeyed him and with his help decided to cut the last letters from my name. 'Giulia Tess,' he said, 'sounds exotic, but it is a name one remembers.'

"Engagements followed in a flurry. I could not get over how rapidly this second phase went happily into gear. I was busy, busy, busy, going from Mimi to Butterfly and Tosca, from Adriana to Francesca da Rimini and Loreley, from Maliella in *I gioielli della Madonna* to Santuzza. There were exciting events such as a series of *Francesca da Rimini*s in Florence under Zandonai (he drew magic from his score that no one else did); *Fedora* in Naples with Fernando de Lucia—old, fat, and ungainly looking as Loris, but he enraptured me with his 'Amor ti vieta'; and eleven performances of *La fanciulla del West* in Viareggio. These were part of a Puccini festival— Viareggio is a few miles from Puccini's home at Torre del Lago—and the composer wrote another love duet for the second act, which I had to learn in haste. I found it highly dramatic and convincing, but the maestro decided later to eliminate it, as he thought it made the action stretch out too much. I believe I'm the only soprano who had the exceptional opportunity to sing it.

"It was at this time that I began to realize that I was in some sort of vocal trouble. Some of the passages were no longer smooth. Since I was not quite thirty, I became very worried. Puccini's intimate friend Carlo Redaelli, who had always taken an interest in me, sent me to the famous Adelina Stehle Garbin, whom Verdi had chosen to be his first Nannetta in *Falstaff* and Leoncavallo, his first Nedda in *Pagliacci*. 'You have no reason for anxiety,' she said, so tenderly and protectingly. 'But you have neglected your breathing for too long. You must learn to sustain your diaphragm far more and to give less of yourself. Voices are not inexhaustible fountains. So much ardor! It's exciting for the public, but don't burn yourself up too quickly.' The next day I went to her for a class, and as long as she lived, whenever I was in Milan I went to her for advice. She was so levelheaded, sensible, and good.

"The third and most significant phase of my artistic achievements began when Toscanini chose me to create Jaele in the world premiere of Pizzetti's *Debora e Jaele* in 1922. All hell broke loose on opening night, and Toscanini, Elvira Casazza (a superlative Debora), and I were called out on the stage endlessly. The opera became so popular that La Scala included it in its repertory for several seasons running with the same cast. The public simply could not hear it enough, and then, inexplicably, it fell into oblivion. I adored the role, and it was real meat for my teeth. I was also grateful to it, for on that day I became a big star. There has always been a great indecision as to whether Pizzetti was *verista*. In my opinion perhaps some of his operas are—he wrote masses of them, and for thirty years Italy was inundated with them—but by no means all, since some of them included a sort of recitative chanting base on syllabic articulations. But he followed his own set of harmonic laws, and his way of writing for the voice was never natural to me.

"*Salome,* in Italian, followed; and Toscanini, then the music director of La Scala, came to every single rehearsal, unlike those of today who are always absent and earning big money elsewhere. Ettore Panizza was the conductor. Ernest Lert, the renowned stage director, and I did not see eye to eye on several aspects of the protagonist's behavior. I was stubborn, and Toscanini sided with me. 'She knows what is right for her,' he calmly told Lert. 'She has worked with me often and is nobody's fool. You can trust her instinct.' I shall always recall vividly how Toscanini insisted on my pronouncing the word '*terribile*' in a special way—*terrrriiiibiiiile*—and how right he was, for it had a bloodcurdling effect. I knew what the word 'triumph' meant on that opening night, and on the many that followed, for La Scala brought this opera back several times. But it did not turn my head. On the contrary, I suddenly became very conscious of my immense responsibilities as a new reigning prima donna. In those days, *Salome* was rarely performed alone, since it is a one-act opera. Now it always is.

"When Richard Strauss heard my Salome, he insisted I take on Elektra at La Scala, and that again was a memorable experience. I threw myself into the part so completely that I always fell in a dead faint at the end and had to be revived. Strauss was very insistent that I learn Salome and Elektra in German, for he wanted me to sing them with him in Vienna. 'You have the Latin temperament for these roles,' he used to say, 'and the authentic thrust of the German voice, which is a must for them.' But I never considered my German good enough. Of all the Salomes I sang, those that satisfied me the most were at La Scala in a production that Victor de Sabata conducted. He gave a very individual reading of the score, bringing out a translucent sensuousness that was pure magic. Though I also often sang

Octavian, it was Salome and Elektra that I was called upon to sing the most often, and of the over seventy roles I undertook, Elektra was the most thrilling of all.

"At La Scala I took on all sorts of operas, including the delightful *Spinning Room* of Kodály and Wolf-Ferrari's *I quattro rusteghi*. Though I had sung Marina in the latter, it was Felicia with whom I became identified —to such an extent that I sang this role more than any other. It was a total change from Strauss, for Felicia is a lady of the world, wise and sophisticated, with much humor. The long discourse with which she brings all the problems to a sensible solution is one of Wolf-Ferrari's most acute and able musical pages. During the twenties and thirties *I quattro rusteghi* was one of the most popular operas in Italy, and in Germany too, under the name *Die vier Grobiane*. One of these days, like *Debora e Jaele,* it will be brought out of mothballs, and people will realize what a masterpiece it is. I also sang at La Scala in the world premiere of Wolf-Ferrari's adorable *Il campiello* in 1936, with Carosio, Adami Corradetti, and Favero—all outstanding; and toward the end of my career I took on another very rewarding comic role, Fidalma in *Il matrimonio segreto.*

"All the conductors with whom I worked wanted me to tackle the Wagner heroines, and the one I set my heart on was Isolde. I learned it very diligently; but it moved me so deeply, stirred my emotions to such an extent, that I knew I could never reach the Liebestod with enough strength left. My temperament got in the way again.

"Had it not been for World War II, I would have gone on singing; but in the meantime I got myself involved with teaching, in Bologna, at the school of the Maggio Musicale Fiorentino, and later at the conservatory in Milan. Then they retired me, and I have gone on privately. Maria Caniglia studied with me—one of the world's most beautiful voices, but she took on too heavy roles too soon. Fedora Barbieri, Ettore Bastianini, Enzo Mascherini all gave me satisfaction, and more recently Atsuko Azuma. The Japanese are very studious; they ask advice and then take it. Alas, this is not the case with most of ours. Discipline does not exist, and the fire that must burn in every artist's heart is not there. Several of my ex-colleagues have become so discouraged with teaching that they have given up, even at the sacrifice of cutting down their already dwindling incomes. I am a fighter and so I continue, hoping always that I can save someone from suicide.

"Singing must be a form of total dedication. It's like a nun of another epoch entering a convent. We all gave up so much to succeed . . . but these youngsters are unwilling to do so."

KAMMERSÄNGERIN
MARTHA MÖDL

Meeting Martha Mödl for the first time, in a hotel hall in Munich on a late June afternoon in 1979, was no ordinary experience. The moment she walked in I recognized that extraordinary face which, across the footlights, could express such anguish and despair. Here I had before me the Brünnhilde (I had heard her in the entire *Ring*) who had touched me profoundly, not so much along heroic lines but along the human. Was there ever a more moving and distressing "War es so schmählich?" at the end of *Die Walküre* than hers?

After she had gone, I tried to sum up my impressions of her—a difficult task. They were very mixed, and I wondered which of them corresponded to the real Mödl. Perhaps all of them—or none! Of all the divas I interviewed, she turned out to be the most elusive; and yet I know it was not deliberate evasion on her part. There exists a sphinxlike quality about her. Small, impeccably dressed in black, with jet-black hair, a most significant face without a single wrinkle and ruled by two gigantic eyes, a ready but slightly mechanical smile—she could have been a prime minister or a captain of industry at a board meeting, such were the authority and assurance emanating from her. As the talk progressed, I sensed her iron will and total self-control. But never could I perceive the emotional temperament that had made her such a star: according to some, the greatest of her kind. She produced an impressive litany of her accomplishments, staggering in number and clearly etched in her memory, but she never boasted or acted superior. The facts spoke for themselves; her tenacity had brought her to the summit and kept her there for almost four decades.

There was no small talk, no gossip, no deviation from the main subject —Mödl. With all the others I had found it hard not to digress. But when I asked Mödl for an opinion, it was expressed in telegraphic terms—not one extra word!

"My private life is of no interest," she emphasized right away, "since I dedicated all my time and energies to my profession. Some people are able

Martha Mödl as Isolde in *Tristan und Isolde*.

to scatter them; I was not. It has been an unusual course that I followed, for there have been numerous aspects, too many to go into at length. It is hard for me to determine whether these various phases have been dictated by circumstances or simply by survival. My starting very late partly explains why I lasted such a long time. Those crucial years between the ages of twenty and thirty, when so many voices encounter trouble, did not find me in the rat race. When I made my debut in 1942, at thirty, in Ramscheid, I started out as a light mezzo. I began with Cherubino and then went on to Hänsel and Mignon. I was born in Nuremberg, and I studied voice there for a very long time, and also the piano so I could accompany myself. I came from an artistic milieu; my father was an art professor. When I moved to Düsseldorf in 1945, I took on Nicklausse in *The Tales of Hoffmann,* along with Dorabella and Carmen. Since I had a svelte figure, I was constantly cast in trouser roles. As for Carmen, she remained with me even after I had changed range and become a soprano. The role suited me, and I even sang it in English at Covent Garden, a daring thing to do. Just think of it—a German having the nerve to interpret an Andalusian tigress in the language of Shakespeare! But fear is something that never existed in my character.

"They needed an Azucena in Düsseldorf, so I came to grips with her, in German, but *Il trovatore* is not an opera I went on with. But Eboli, Marina in *Boris Godunov,* and Klytämnestra, which I undertook in this same theatre, along with the Composer and Octavian, remained with me. The conductor Heinrich Hollreiser, who believed in me and gave me many opportunities, also offered me Marie in *Wozzeck,* which I accepted, as it afforded me the chance to prove that I could be a tragic actress. It is a role written for a darkish-sounding soprano, and the very favorable reception accorded me began to generate the idea that I could undertake a certain species of dramatic soprano parts. In the meantime I was invited for some guest appearances at the Vienna Staatsoper, performing at that time in the Theater an der Wien, as Carmen and Octavian under Josef Krips. This was indeed fortunate, for he knew more about the texture and possibilities of voices than any of his colleagues. A turning point was in sight.

"My appearances in Vienna in 1950 as Lady Macbeth convinced more and more people in the profession that I could move on to some *hochdramatisch* scores, for already at that time this type of instrument was beginning to be very scarce. Apart from the wonderful Flagstad, who was near the end but still very stirring, and the huge-voiced Grob-Prandl, the field was there to be conquered. A short period elapsed before the glorious talent of Nilsson was discovered, but even then she could not meet all the demands for her services. At the Nuremberg conservatory my teacher, Frau Klinck-Schneider, always told me that she had never come across a type of voice quite like mine. I recall her exclaiming one day in despair, 'There are more colors in your voice than in the rainbow. One day I am convinced that you belong to a certain category, and the next day to another.' As events were to prove, she was right.

"The fact that my C became sturdy and sure, along with the passages in the upper range, convinced me to make the change, by degrees, and so I did. Unlike others who switched from mezzo to soprano, ceasing for a certain period and then beginning again, I never stopped; I simply dropped certain operas. In 1950 I began to take on assignments such as Magda Sorel in Menotti's *The Consul* and then Kundry at La Scala with Furtwängler.

"Kundry opened all the doors for me, and it was with her that I made my debut, under Knappertsbusch's direction, at the reopening of Bayreuth after the war, beginning my long association with the Festival, which was to last until 1967. Shortly before that, in the spring of 1951, when told of my engagement, Frida Leider, who had reigned in the Wagnerian temple for ten years, wished me good luck, and then added, 'Beware. Unless it is much changed, I know by experience that vipers abound there.' Her warning was useful. I kept out of trouble by avoiding local politics, and I was also in the very advantageous position that Wieland Wagner from the very start enjoyed working with me. Our connection lasted a very long time, for apart from the Festival he directed me in many other theatres.

"I owe a great deal to Wieland Wagner," she admitted boldly, "for it is he who really built me into an international prima donna by showing unlimited faith in my possibilities. Although I did not always agree with some of his visual conceptions, I understood what he was trying to achieve: the universality of his grandfather's masterpieces rather than the traditional romanticism and the old-fashioned painted decors. For seven different seasons I portrayed Kundry at Bayreuth, always under Knappertsbusch, and Wieland's mise-en-scène, particularly that first year, created a big scandal. Today he would appear almost a traditionalist, with Ponnelle plunging ahead with his mysterious symbolism. Thrice I undertook Isolde, with Karajan, Eugen Jochum, and Karl Böhm, and five times between 1953 and 1958 I sang the entire *Ring*, some with Keilberth and others with Knappertsbusch. I also assumed Sieglinde there in 1954, and then later, after I returned to the mezzo-contralto wing, Waltraute and Fricka in both *Rheingold* and *Walküre*. I do not know of any other singer who undertook all three female leads in this opera.

"I enjoyed Bayreuth, which became my summer home. Although the productions there have become more and unnecessarily revolutionary, the town has changed relatively little and is still somewhat special. No big hotels have been built, and people either sleep in private homes or commute from other cities. There existed, at least during the period I was there, an enormous respect for the music, and although some of the wishes of the composer have been altered, the loyalty to his genius never wavered.

"Of the Brünnhildes, which I sang incessantly for over fifteen years, the most taxing for me was the shortest—the one in *Siegfried*. Its tessitura lies much higher than the others. The one in *Götterdämmerung*, considered by most the toughest written for a Wagnerian prima donna, represented less effort for me than Isolde, since the lyrical passages in *Tristan*'s second act do require an almost *jugendlich dramatisch* soprano.

"My first Leonore in *Fidelio*, which was to become one of the roles with which my name became so intimately associated, took place in Hamburg, where I sang for eighteen years and where the late Günther Rennert, a metteur-en-scène in the grand tradition, directed me countless times. I was fortunate in having him for my debut in the Beethoven work, for it is a treacherous part unless you are able to completely identify yourself with this courageous, anguished, and clever woman, and he showed me the right way. Leopold Ludwig, with his sure hand, conducted me, and it was a most happy occasion. The following year I sang the role with Karajan at La Scala, and then in Vienna in 1953 with Furtwängler. His *Fidelio* was a cleansing experience, a symphonic poem of love and justice triumphant. The way he accompanied Leonore's stupendous phrase at the end of the opera, 'Liebe führte mein Bestreben, wahre Liebe fürchtet nicht' [Love directed my endeavor, true love is not afraid], was a moment to cherish.

"It was a stroke of luck," she said, her eyes shining, "that I sang the entire *Ring* with Furtwängler in Rome at the RAI, in concert form, and that all of it was recorded and is now available to the public. For this wonderful maestro and human being died one year later. There will be other great *Ring*s, but none like his for the grandeur, the sweeping passion; and at the same time there were moments in the dialogue between Wotan, the father, and Brünnhilde, the daughter, that were infinitely delicate and intimate. The year of his death, 1954, I recorded *Die Walküre* with him in the Musikvereinsaal with the Vienna Philharmonic, and with all due respect to the excellent Italian orchestra, nothing can compare to the Vienna strings.

"One of the most memorable moments of my life"—her voice trembled with emotion—"came when I was asked to reopen the Vienna Staatsoper in 1955, entirely reconstructed according to its original plan, with *Fidelio*. It was a historic occasion. I have always managed to control myself on the stage—one must arrive at the end in one piece, if possible—but on that night I was overcome with tears. I knew how much this theatre meant, not only to the Viennese but to the entire civilized world.

"I had many satisfactions in the rebuilt house, and among other roles I was assigned Jocasta in *Oedipus Rex,* led at first by Stravinsky himself and then by Karajan, who also conducted me as Isolde and as Brünnhilde in both *Walküre* and *Siegfried.* Since I was in Bayreuth every summer, I could not perform at the Salzburg Festival because of conflicting dates, except for two series of *Elektras* under Karajan, who chose me to be his Klytämnestra. This is another part I kept singing throughout my career. If sung cautiously, it is not as dangerous for the vocal cords as it might seem, because much of it is declaimed. And it is a very satisfying acting assignment. My interpretation differed from the others, for I saw her as a sad, pathetic woman, and not at all a sinister character. She is a weak person, dominated by angst. I also tried Elektra herself four times, and then I gave her up, for the role is very dangerous, at least for my sort of instrument.

"I was able to sing some contemporary operas: Orff's *Antigonae,* Schoeck's *Penthesilea,* Britten's *Albert Herring,* and Fortner's *Die Bluthochzeit.* The Fortner premiere was in Stuttgart, with Ferdinand Leitner in the pit and Rennert directing, and it was such a hit that we went with it to Berlin and to the Théâtre des Nations in Paris. It is based on Garcia Lorca's *Blood Wedding,* and the role of the Mother gave me a tremendous scope as a tragedian.

"I became an indefatigable traveler. I went back to Covent Garden, first for the *Ring* and then later for Klytämnestra; to La Scala, again with Karajan, for Ortrud, with a very delicately voiced Elsa in the person of Elisabeth Schwarzkopf, and also for *Die Walküre.* At the Colón in Buenos Aires I appeared as Venus, and then in more *Walküres,* with Leitner, who had been my conductor in Stuttgart for ten years and also at the Paris Opéra for Kundry and Isolde. But for the *Ring* in Paris I had Knappertsbusch instead. At the Maggio Musicale Fiorentino came my first opportunity to sing with Mitropoulos, in *Elektra* with Anny Konetzni in the lead. I found the Greek conductor again at the Metropolitan, where I sang for three seasons. In New York I appeared with him in *Die Walküre,* but I much preferred him in Strauss—far more vibrant and exciting, even if it was much too loud. For the *Ring, Tristan,* and *Parsifal,* I always had Fritz Stiedry, a solid but not terribly inspiring conductor.

"Rudolf Bing amused me. I remember him discussing the hiring of a famous soprano, who had been for a long time persona non grata to him because of her reported Nazi sympathies. With his dry wit he said, 'I can forgive her for having worn a Nazi uniform and for taking an American colonel as boyfriend right after the war, but I cannot swallow the fact that she then married a Jew.' Wagner came and went with the Bing regime at the Met, but, as he admitted frankly, finding the right casts was becoming increasingly difficult.

"Later I went back to some of my mezzo parts, and then took on even contralto roles. I added the Nurse in *Die Frau ohne Schatten,* a most difficult and interesting part, first in Munich and then everywhere; Herodias; the Countess in *The Queen of Spades,* which has one of the greatest scenes ever written for a singing actress; the Widow Begbick in *Mahagonny;* the Kostelnička in *Jenůfa;* and Gräfin Geschwitz in *Lulu,* an opera I never learned to appreciate. Have you ever tried playing the score on the piano? A Chinese puzzle is far less demanding. But if I closed with opera after thirty-seven years, this does not at all mean that I am through. I recently completed a series of performances of Lorca's *The House of Bernarda Alba,* and I am now rehearsing for a Zurich production of *Fiddler on the Roof.* The legitimate stage has opened its arms to me, and I have taken this challenge too. I am not the sort of person who can stand still and become panicky as to what is in store for us all. Better to keep busy."

I asked her about her recordings.

"There are some, among the many," she said, "that I think do give an idea of what Mödl was like, such as the Bayreuth *Parsifal;* the *Frau ohne Schatten* with Ingrid Bjoner as a fabulous Empress, Inge Borkh, and Fischer-Dieskau, under Keilberth's direction; the *Oedipus Rex* conducted by Stravinsky; and Henze's *Elegy for Young Lovers,* again with Fischer-Dieskau. I was recording before the era of the revolutionary changes. We still sang with expression and feeling. Now, because of the increasing demands of the electronic monsters, it must all be subdued and expressionless. This is science's gift to art. What about this as a commentary on today's technical advancements? No matter, as far as I am concerned, for I am among the privileged who have been to Valhalla and back. And it was a wonderful trip.

"But to close, as I am late for a rehearsal, let me repeat what Wolfgang Windgassen's father, a celebrated tenor himself, once said to me: 'Martha, when you have fifty percent of the love of the public with you, you are made.' He was absolutely right. It is the public's love that over the long years has made me what I am. Please, please write this. But also say that it has been totally reciprocal, all the way until the end."

KAMMERSÄNGERIN
ESTHER RETHY

Esther Rethy was a perfectly beautiful Hungarian soprano who burst upon the lyric theatres of Central Europe in the mid-thirties. Later she would forsake the world of opera to become the undisputed queen of the operetta stage in Vienna. When I went to call on her in the late spring of 1979, in her small and comfortable house in the outskirts of Vienna, I found that she had maintained her celebrated classical beauty and her excellent figure. A pale blonde with a creamy complexion, she is utterly feminine and gentle, handing out her opinions in a totally detached manner and speaking of her achievements with a modesty rare among the members of her profession. I remember her so well at the Salzburg Festival in 1937 as a mischievous Susanna in *Le nozze di Figaro,* where her gaiety was infectious and her sense of timing outstanding. The voice was supple and tender, with a delicious silvery timbre.

"I was born in Budapest," she recalled, "to an unmusical family. But I knew from an early age what I wanted to become, and for six years I studied at the Musical Academy with Magda Rigo, who had been a dramatic soprano of note at the Budapest Opera and a guest at the Vienna Staatsoper. When she thought I was ready, she arranged for me to audition at the opera house, and I was given a contract. Wisely, I began with minor roles. In my case at least, it was the right way, for I was shy and had to obtain my own identity by degrees. Establishing a contact with the public is an urgent necessity, and this is lacking more and more today. There are some good singers, but they are no longer able to build that essential bridge of sympathy and communication with the audience. Maneuvered by directors, they have become automatons.

"Anyhow, I began with the delicate cameo part of the Shepherd in *Tannhäuser.* It is very short, yet essential in establishing the atmosphere of that picturesque scene, giving it a romantic and nostalgic tinge. I still recall the lovely words I had to sing (Wagner was a real poet): 'Da träumt' ich manchen holden Traum, und als mein Aug' erschlossen kaum, da strahlte warm die Sonnen, der Mai, der Mai war kommen' [There I dreamed many a fair dream, and scarcely had I opened my eyes when the sun was shining warm, and May had come].

"Then I took on Ortlinde, one of the Valkyries, and considered it a most valuable experience, for it necessitated learning how to work in a team. Then came Micaëla and the First Lady in *Die Zauberflöte,* which used to be considered a major role. Now they assign it to almost anyone. I kept adding new roles, which afforded me the chance to polish my style and stage presence. My big chance came when I was chosen to appear as Marzelline in a special performance of *Fidelio* in the unique setting of the superb Esterhazy castle. Bruno Walter, Knappertsbusch, and Erwin Kebert, régisseur at the Staatsoper, all traveled from Vienna to attend this performance and, from then on, mine became a blitz race. To my astonishment, they all came to my dressing room and offered me a contract with the Staatsoper. I made my debut there as Marguerite in *Faust* at Eastertime in 1937. It was a fabulous cast consisting of Bjoerling, perhaps the greatest tenor of all, Alexander Sved, Alexander Kipnis, and Rosette Anday, conducted by Krips, and I knew only too well the gigantic tasks I was facing. But it is the right role in which to be thrown to the lions, for she is a demure creature, a little afraid of everything. I confess that I was utterly terrified. But despite the confusion in my head—I had been obliged to relearn the role in German, as in Budapest we sang everything in Hungarian—the critics hailed me as a revelation. If this is good for the ego, it is extremely perilous too, for one must live up to the sudden fame.

"Marzelline followed, again under Krips and also under Clemens Krauss, along with Sophie, Lauretta in *Schicchi,* Micaëla and Ighino in Pfitzner's *Palestrina* under Walter, both Nannetta and Alice in *Falstaff,* Pamina (with Erna Berger a spectacular Queen of the Night), Euridice (with the imposing Margarete Klose as Orfeo), Mimi, Violetta, Eva, Desdemona, Orff's *Carmina Burana,* and others. I was flattered, but also overcome by this deluge of performances.

"My first appearance on the international scene was not long in coming for in the summer of 1937 Bruno Walter cast me as Susanna in a splendid production of *Le nozze di Figaro* at the Salzburg Festival. The Finnish soprano Aulikki Rautawaara was a ravishing Countess, Novotna a delectable Cherubino, Pinza a formidable Figaro, and Stabile a sophisticated Count. It was a performance people are still talking about. I was to continue in Salzburg for seven years, singing, among other roles, Donna Elvira and Sophie. My Marschallins included the two Konetzni sisters, who at the time

Esther Rethy as the Countess in *Le nozze di Figaro*.

were the undisputed sovereigns of the Vienna Staatsoper, prima donnas to their fingertips. When they came into a room, there was a moment of silence, such was the respect they commanded. Personally, I was always more partial to Hilde's interpretation of the role, for she had more warmth, and the voice, while lighter, had some radiant, magical tones.

"Furtwängler, who conducted *Don Giovanni,* had a different approach to the Mozart score. His reading had a far greater tension; it was much less baroque, but fascinating nevertheless. I preferred him in Wagner and orchestral concerts. But the conductor I lost my heart to was de Sabata. There was a controlled, almost suppressed feeling of a fire that was about to ignite that I found almost hypnotic. When I sang the Verdi Requiem with him, I did not recognize my voice, for he brought out sensuous sounds I did not know I possessed. But such was the ability of the conductors of my generation. Today all this is over and done with. The orchestras sound beautiful, but the singers are ignored or simply tolerated. They have become part of the production.

"I also began to sing guest appearances in Munich at the request of Clemens Krauss, who was general director there from 1937 until 1942; and I feel, looking back, that perhaps he was the greatest of them all. I recall singing Eva and Mimi with him, and so light was the *Meistersinger* quintet, so clear and almost vulnerable, that no one had to strain one bit. The death of Mimi was memorable too, for this man, who could stir one to profound depths with his Wagner and Strauss, knew how to underline those soft passages like no one else could. I was unable to hold back my tears, when he started, with a delicacy that was not of this world, the 'Sono andati? Fingevo di dormire' [Have they gone? I was pretending to be asleep].

"Krauss chose me for the much-awaited revival of Humperdinck's *Königskinder,* and I became very attached to the Goose Girl, one of the most puzzling characters I ever had to grapple with. The scoring is far from easy, for unlike *Hänsel und Gretel* it is very Wagnerian—a series of themes, leitmotivs really, that follow one another and create an invisible chain. It is a children's tale, but with all sorts of symbolic meanings. There is a marvelous scene where the Goose Girl, refusing to admit that she is ill, dances in the snow until she falls into a faint. Then, later, after the Witch has poisoned the bread that the Goose Girl and the Prince eat to calm their hunger, there is an extraordinary aria-pantomime before she dies, when she mistakes the snowflakes for linden blossoms. A singing actress of infinite sensibility is needed, to touch the audience and yet keep it in a world of make-believe; and the singer must look almost like a child. It is not surprising that so lovely an opera is so rarely given, for the demands on the protagonist are on so many different levels. What a time I had keeping the geese in order! I rehearsed those episodes over and over again—I could never foresee what they would do next!

"After the war I sang Strauss's *Die Liebe der Danae* to do Krauss a service; but I did not care for the score—very ungrateful to the vocal cords and, unlike *Königskinder*, not very satisfactory dramatically. I was called to Berlin for many guest performances, and also to Dresden, which had the most exquisite theatre in the world. When it was destroyed, I wept. But all those war years were a constant nightmare. In Berlin I had the singular experience of singing Sophie to the Marschallin of Tiana Lemnitz, an artist who was revered as a goddess. She used to be a famous Octavian, then in later years she changed roles. She had great presence, but in my opinion she did not have the *Gemütlichkeit* of Hilde Konetzni, or that special haunting timbre that Ursuleac's instrument had. I kept singing with Karl Böhm in all the various cities—he is really indestructible—but, those days, he was not taken into such consideration. His great fame came later. He was very precise, but cold as ice. The snows would never have melted with him: not a very sympathetic person. I recall appearing in a revival of *Rodelinda* in Vienna that he conducted. Handel wrote this lovely opera in 1725, and it was a wonderful form of escape from the miseries of a torn and divided Europe.

"I became much in demand for oratorios and big orchestral concerts. I have not kept count of the number of times I was called upon to sing Beethoven's Ninth Symphony and his Missa Solemnis. For these two chefs d'oeuvre I much preferred Bruno Walter's renditions to all the others, for his sensibility was extreme, and no matter how many times he had to repeat them, there was never that element of routine which so often creeps in. One knew he was inspired every time. Then came many lieder recitals, and I became particularly known for my Schubert.

"Two productions I luckily escaped because of the war were a *Butterfly* with Krips and a *Trovatore* with Karajan. I knew I was not suited to either, but the transformation was already in progress, although in an embryonic state. The production was becoming far more important than the individual artists, and whether or not a singer was right for the part was beginning to be secondary.

"In Berlin I was always cast as Pamina, and at first following in the footsteps of Lemnitz—who had been considered for two decades the ideal interpreter of this role—did not put me at ease. Interestingly, my mother, the Queen of the Night, was Elisabeth Schwarzkopf, who at that time was a coloratura. She was not right for it; the agility was there, but not the dazzling staccatos that Berger used to have, and then later Rita Streich, despite her tiny voice. Streich was also ideal as Adele in *Fledermaus,* and we often sang this work together, having great fun. The way she tossed off the 'Mein Herr Marquis' was a pure mischievous delight. As for Schwarzkopf, she was very clever, and her ambition, combined with an iron will, put her very rapidly in the front ranks. I never found her performances moving—too cerebral for my Hungarian nature—but they were perfect, not a comma missing.

"My going into operetta did not happen all at once. It was a slow process. With the Staatsoper destroyed, we worked at the Theater an der Wien and at the Volksoper. It all started with my singing Rosalinda in a *Fledermaus* conducted by Karajan, and Krips used to affirm that I reminded him of Jeritza—also a Hungarian—for I could dance my head off and possessed a lot of *entrain.* The czardas of the second act was ideally suited to my voice, and it stopped the show. When Hermann Juch, the Volksoper's director, decided to rebuild the operetta repertoire, he insisted on assembling first-rate artists. With Erich Kunz, Anton Dermota, Waldemar Kmentt, and Rosette Anday, I began appearing in *Der Zigeunerbaron, Boccaccio, Eine Nacht in Venedig, Die lustige Witwe, Orpheus in the Underworld,* and many others. The main problem for me was producing, in the spoken dialogue, the authentic and very special Viennese accent which the public demanded. At that time I kept on singing at the opera: roles such as Nedda, Agathe in *Freischütz,* and the Countess in a new production of *Figaro,* with Böhm conducting and Hilde Gueden as Susanna. I also sang many Maries in a new production of *The Bartered Bride* and Frau Fluth in *Die lustigen Weiber von Windsor,* that perfectly delightful opera by Nicolai. It annoys me no end that it is falling into oblivion. The pity is that the advent of *Falstaff* has overshadowed it more and more, until now it is considered a museum piece. And it is not! There are three operas dealing with Goethe's *Faust,* and they are all successful; so I cannot see the problem.

"I also undertook new operas such as Orff's *Die Kluge,* Franz Schmidt's *Notre Dame,* and Franz Salmhofer's *Das Werbekleid,* which was an outstanding success. But with time, to my enormous surprise, my popularity in operetta grew to such an extent that my name automatically sold out all performances featuring me. So the management of the opera pushed me more and more into this field. Until 1968, when I retired after thirty-three years, I was almost totally involved in that lighter make-believe world, and

I must admit I enjoyed it hugely. I had never really studied dancing, but I was completely at home in it, even though many of the numbers I had to do were with professional dancers. I believe that my success was because the audience knew that it was all utterly spontaneous on my part, and that I was having fun too.

"You have heard the same story from the others: the war wiped us all out financially, and the postwar years were very hard too, for we were paid pittance salaries. So despite the pension we all get after twenty-five years' service—and on which we must pay taxes—one cannot rest on one's laurels. So I too give courses at the Academy, to students who are forever tired in a world filled with vitamins. They are sick all the time, or pretend to be. But at my age, snow and blizzards notwithstanding, I am there every day. I live alone, for my husband, Dr. Vincent Imre, died in 1968. My son Lazlo is a conductor at the Dortmund Opera, so the musical atmosphere in which he grew up has borne fruit."

I asked her when she had become a Kammersängerin. "Only in 1952," she replied. "They took their time in those days! It was a real honor then, for the president of the Republic had to approve it personally. It is a tradition that goes way back to when there were only court theatres; actually, a Kammersänger was an imperial performer. But even when, later, the theatres became public, it was a very sought-after honor, as it was almost like a title bestowed by the emperor. It became so rooted a tradition that it went on even after both empires, in Austria and in Germany, disappeared. Now, like everything else, it has less importance, and yet there is still quite a to-do about it. I was also given the Order of the Golden Cross."

I asked her about the new crop of singers. Were there any about whom she had hopes?

"You are bringing up a very painful subject," she said, with a sad smile. "There are two here in Vienna who are promising—a coloratura and a light mezzo. But the latter is already singing roles that are too heavy for her, so what will be her future? The reason why, in the preceding generations, once in a while artists could take over roles a little too heavy for their means was their reserve, based on a solid technique that taught them to use the dividends and not the capital. Now they spend all they have got, and their vocal savings are soon gone. But I prefer Figaro's famous sentence: 'Molto onore, pochi contanti'—much honor, little cash. To have been honored has its rewards."

THE
METEORS

STELLA ROMAN

ROSANNA CARTERI

ANITA CERQUETTI

There have been many prima donnas whose careers were relatively short but who left an unforgettable mark on opera because of the exceptional quality of their voices and their interpretative powers. I have chosen three: Stella Roman, who retired officially after nineteen years (but who sang very few performances in the last two); Rosanna Carteri, who withdrew after seventeen years; and Anita Cerquetti, after twelve. While Roman unfortunately made hardly any recordings, the other two have left behind them quite a number, which help to explain why they were considered leading exponents of the lyric theatre in their respective repertoires.

Two others come to mind who established great reputations despite the very short periods in which they performed. Margaret Sheridan, the Irish soprano, sang only from 1919 to 1931, and Gerda Lammers, a fabulous Kundry and Elektra, turned to opera at the age of forty after a career as a lieder singer. Today, alas, the lyric theatre is filled with meteors. They came yesterday and will be gone tomorrow because of the hasty preparation, the overly large number of engagements, and the totally inappropriate repertoires with which they are confronted.

STELLA ROMAN

Stella Roman was always a woman of wit, warmth, and charm; I first met her in 1941, and the years have enhanced these qualities. With great humor she has come to terms with aging, and one is never quite sure whether or not she is taking herself seriously. And now that her name has been inscribed in the Olympus of great singers—were there ever more ethereal pianissimos than hers outside of heaven?—this quality is particularly striking and attractive. Living again in Manhattan after twenty-five years in California (she had been married to a Californian—an experience she prefers not to discuss), she dedicates much of her time to painting. "It has a lot in common with singing," she asserted in her comfortable apartment, showing me various vividly colored pictures of hers when I went to call on her in April 1979, "for both of them deal with coloring, one of the vocal cords and the other of the canvases."

Small and stouter than previously, Roman still sparkles, with her flaming red hair, her wise brown eyes set wide apart, and her impish smile. As she talks, she often uses her hands to accompany her words. She was born in Kluj, Transylvania, and still feels passionately rooted to that beautiful, verdant land. Hers was a distinguished family whose men all chose the army to defend their country and their king; her father rose to be a general. "Those men used to dream, have ideals, fight for them," she sighed, showing me portraits of her grandparents and parents. "Now who cares?

"I came from a musical background. My mother was an excellent amateur pianist, and our cousin, Madame Cosma, a lady-in-waiting to the beautiful Queen Marie, had studied with the famous Marchesi. In those happier days many people studied singing just for their own pleasure, and that is why they knew so much. But I wanted a career, and my parents agreed to my becoming a concert singer. Opera was never mentioned, for it was considered—how shall I say?—just a bit wicked. I studied singing for eight years before I felt ready to take the plunge before the public—first in Kluj, then in Bucharest, and it is here that I won a scholarship to continue my training in Milan, at that time considered the capital of the vocal arts. Actually, my

Stella Roman as the Marschallin in *Der Rosenkavalier*.

technique was more or less ready, but I had neither the polish nor the repertoire. I studied with Giuseppina Baldassare Tedeschi, who was Albanese's teacher, but her style did not quite suit me. She had been a superb verismo interpreter, but I felt I needed someone with a greater sense of style and sensitivity.

"I was tremendously fortunate, for living in Milan, in the most precarious conditions—a member of her family had completely ruined her—was that great compatriot of mine, Hariclea Darclée, who was over seventy and whose vocal production was still miraculous. Everything I became I owe to her, for not only did she accept me to work with her, but with enormous patience and inspiration she taught me the value of every word and phrase, and revealed to me how deeply she had delved into the psyche of every character she had sung. She was an exquisite woman, and as the poet Ezra Pound wrote, 'They will come no more' like her. If I indulge in talking about her, it is because I feel that she more than deserves it. The fact that Catalani chose her to be his first Wally, Mascagni for his first Suzel in *L'amico Fritz* and Iris, and Puccini for his initial Tosca, indicates the high regard the composers of that era had for her. She was also the first Italian Elisabeth in *Tannhäuser* and Marschallin. Gounod said of her that she reminded him of a Stradivarius, and he was right. If I was able to handle heavy roles, it is all because of the advice she gave me on how to produce the dramatic effects without ever forcing. Sometimes we would work six months just on one passage. When I first sang for her 'La mamma morta' from *Chenier,* she allowed me to finish and then said, 'No, it is all wrong. You must begin pianissimo, almost a whisper. After all, your heart is broken because of the very recent death of your mother. But then, when you begin to discuss the awakening of love, then you begin to swell the voice and give it an increasingly sensuous quality. Always sit at the beginning of an aria, whenever it is possible, and then rise. It is more effective that way, more natural.'

"For an unknown in Italy, which was jammed with excellent sopranos, beginning was far from easy. At first I was offered roles the others refused, but I refused them too, for I knew the dangers these scores would represent for my instrument. Finally an offer came for me to make my debut in Bologna in 1934 as Maddalena in *Chenier,* which would mark the comeback of the tenor Bernardo de Muro, who had been a great celebrity—a huge voice, but not much artistry—who had gotten bored being retired. He was most unhappy at having an unknown as a partner and only changed his mind when he heard me. '*Molto carina, mi piace,*' I remember him saying.

"He was less happy with the success I made and the public's insistence that I repeat the aria. I was ready for everything on that fateful day, but not for an encore. Before I had time to pull myself together, the conductor made a gesture and started again 'La mamma morta.' Not only was I terrified of not being able to do it as well the second time, but I did not see myself going back to sit at the table and start again in the same way. It did not make sense. So I just followed my instinct and worked out a different type of action altogether. Since then, I have rarely repeated myself. As many times as I sang Tosca, I don't believe I ever did the 'Vissi d'arte' the same way. I am happy that I am not having my career now, in an epoch when directors regiment singers as if they were soldiers on a drill.

"Anyhow, my initial appearance did create a stir, and following Darclée's wise advice, I accepted all the engagements that came in from the provincial theatres, a marvelous training. 'You build your experience in small theatres,' Darclée used to say, 'and you find out for yourself what is suitable and what is not. You risk little, for the houses and the orchestras are not large enough to harm you.' I sang Brünnhilde in *Siegfried* in Como, which was an error, for although the top rang out, I did have to push the middle. There were many offers to repeat it, for even then Wagnerian singers were not in abundance. I never did. Instead I sang many Elsas, Sieglindes, and Elisabeths, the latter even in San Francisco and at the Metropolitan. I also attempted Turandot—Albanese was my Liù—but immediately realized that in a larger theatre I would have had to scream, since I did not have the lungs of a whale.

"The San Carlos in Lisbon was one of the first great theatres that engaged me for *Tosca,* with Lauri-Volpi, and little did I realize that he would be my partner over and over again during the next few years. I was scared of him, for his reputation was that of a very capricious man who often amused himself at the expense of his partners. But this was not the case. He always behaved perfectly with me, protected me, and once in Rome gave me a good laugh when he suggested while we were singing *La Bohème* together that I sing 'lauri e fiori' instead of 'gigli e fiori.' I changed the text to satisfy him, and he was as pleased as a child. My Desdemona in Florence made a big splash, and Francesco Merli, in my opinion the greatest Moor I ever appeared with—and I have sung it with giants such as Pertile, Martinelli, and Vinay—advised me never to miss any part of the rehearsals, even when the heroine was not involved. I shall always be grateful to him for this, as it taught me a great lesson. One is part of the entire opera even when one actually is not appearing, and one should always be present.

"Then Tullio Serafin offered me a three-year contract with the Rome

Opera, and then I was in the big time, for under his direction the capital's opera house was superb. I was all set to make my debut there in 1937 in a new opera, *Re Lear* by Ghislanzoni, when suddenly, four months early, I was called to jump in for an ailing soprano at a Sunday-afternoon performance of *Aida* with an all-star cast. Serafin went over the entire score with me at the piano and at the end made only one comment: 'You will become very rich singing this opera.' Being a firm believer, I rushed to Santa Maria Maggiore to pray and ran into a black cat and a hunchbacked woman. To a superstitious person like myself this spelled disaster. I bought every single candle available, and that huge church was ablaze with all my savings. But those candles accomplished a miracle. People cheered and cheered.

"Luckily, I had already sung this very tricky Verdian princess—she was to become my warhorse—a short time earlier in Cairo. The gold-and-white theatre, later destroyed by fire, was one of the prettiest I have ever seen, and the sets, too exquisite for words, were the original ones of the 1871 production. I recall a live leopard and also an elephant, all part of an Arabian Nights–like dream. Queen Nazli came, asked that I be presented to her, and invited me to the palace several times during my stay with wonderful warmth and grace. Little could I have foreseen that after I had stopped singing, I would be able to repay her hospitality very modestly in California, where she lived as an almost penniless exile. She was a very gallant lady, and fate was most unkind to her. It was in Cairo that one night I collected some water from the Nile, and this was to be the beginning of a large collection of waters I have gathered from rivers all over the world.

"Speaking of *Aida*, once at Caracalla the after-midnight breezes uncovered my legs as I lay dying in the temple cellar. It was a split skirt, and there was not much I could do about it. As I was walking back to my dressing room, the angry wife of the tenor came up and said unpleasantly, 'So you think you can steal my husband by exposing your legs to him!' 'No, Signora,' I replied, 'I uncovered them to give pleasure to the ten thousand men in the audience.' But the wife of a tenor is a very special breed. I have run into many of them just like her. Tenors appear to attract a particular type of insanely jealous woman. I have never understood jealousy, and on a professional level it makes me laugh. We all had our good and bad nights, so what does it matter? When Olin Downes wrote a really incredible number of superlative adjectives in *The New York Times* to describe my first Mimi at the Metropolitan, all the other sopranos who sang the part— and there were many—were perfectly furious, and there was a lot of intrigue so that I wouldn't get the opportunity to sing it again.

"But to go back to Rome, I sang so many operas, including contemporary scores—the world premiere of *Re Lear* and the Rome premieres of Mulè's *La monacella della fontana* and Riccitelli's *Madonna Oretta*. In Berlin, when I sang there with Lauri-Volpi, I was re-engaged for twelve Aidas. They wanted to sign me to a long contract, but I refused. Though I was always politically uninvolved, I had an uneasy feeling there. And so I continued to sing all over Italy, including some memorable *Cheniers* in Palermo with Gigli, who was in a real state of grace. There had been approaches from La Scala, but nothing they offered me, including *La Gioconda,* seemed appropriate for a debut in this major house. And then, suddenly, an incredible opportunity presented itself. Richard Strauss was looking for an Empress for his *Frau ohne Schatten,* which was about to be premiered in Italy at La Scala. Gino Marinuzzi proposed that he audition me, assuring him I had the high, soaring tessitura necessary for this assignment, and I got the part. Strauss came to every rehearsal and taught me the fiendish role from A to Z."

"What makes the part so difficult?" I asked her.

"One swims in the stratosphere all the time. It is not that one has a series of difficult high notes; it's all terribly high, and therefore immensely tiring for the vocal cords—although not risky, because one is never asked to force. Strauss and I got on very well together, for I liked his patience, his old-world manners and consideration. He wanted me to follow him to Germany, for he considered my voice eminently suitable for most of his operas. It was all very tempting, for he was then the major composer alive. But the war was advancing, and, fortunately, an offer came from the Metropolitan Opera, which I eagerly accepted, as a terrible sense of doom had begun to haunt me. It was a stroke of luck, for I got out just in time. Naturally, I lost track of Strauss for several years, but in 1948 I went to spend the summer in Pontresina to study the Four Last Songs and the Marschallin with him. We reminisced for a long time about the *Frau* at La Scala, which he had enjoyed so much, having nothing but praise for Marinuzzi and for Benvenuto Franci and Iva Pacetti, who had sung the Dyer and his wife. He had often thought of it during the tragic, long war years as a last ray of sunshine before the holocaust.

"Every day I went to his home," she declared, her eyes shining brighter and brighter, "and he sat down at the piano, never looking at his watch, indicating the inflection of every word, the coloring of each sentence, and, above all, the pauses. I was amazed at the importance he gave to the pauses, but later, when I sang *Der Rosenkavalier,* I realized how essential they are.

He kept stressing that it was ridiculous to assume that the princess was a tragic figure. Octavian had been her young lover, yes; but there had been many others, and one could sense that he would not be the last. He then gave me a clue, for when in the third act she sees the Police Commissioner, she says, Er kennt mich? 'Kenn' ich ihn nicht auch?'—don't we know each other?—a very subtle way of indicating that he probably had been at one point one of her bed companions. Alas, I never got to sing the Marschallin at the Metropolitan, but I did in other cities, and closed my career with it at the San Carlo in Naples, singing it in Italian with Giulietta Simionato as Octavian.

"I regret terribly that I never had the opportunity to sing under Strauss's baton, for he was a first-class conductor. And I did appear, in Italy, with all the important composers of that era. Zandonai was the best of all of them, and I loved appearing in his *Giulietta e Romeo* with him in the pit. I sang in Cilea's revised edition of his *Gloria* with Gigli, and in *Lo straniero* by Pizzetti. But the one I appeared with the most often was Giordano, especially on radio broadcasts, which were very well done in Italy in those days, bringing opera to all the homes. I sang *Chénier, Madame Sans-Gêne, Fedora,* and *Siberia* under his elegant direction. He was so soigné, wore the most marvelously well-cut suits and silk shirts and a monocle. A man from another epoch—a blessed one, in my opinion.

"At the Metropolitan I was engaged mainly as a spinto, and I got little opportunity to do the lyric parts, with the exception of Mimi and Butterfly. I have always deeply regretted I never was given the chance to appear as Violetta, but there were some very valid ones under contract—Albanese, Novotna, Sayão. I did a lot of Verdi, Donna Anna, Santuzza, Manon Lescaut, Tosca, and Elisabeth. I never sang the Countess in *Figaro* either, though I did it in San Francisco, where I appeared almost every season. I added *La Gioconda*—actually I had tried it out in a small house in Italy— at the Metropolitan, and despite my not being a dramatic, I managed quite well, keeping in mind Madame Darclée's advice. I also sang a lot in Mexico City and in São Paulo and Rio de Janeiro. I never sang Norma in the United States, and I believe the last time I appeared as the Druid priestess—a role I loved passionately—was in Rio. Somehow, during those years, *Norma* was not given often. Now it's in every opera house's repertoire, and literally everyone sings it. I think there are more Normas"—and she laughed heartily —"than Micaëlas!

"How the world of opera has changed! But don't ask me if it's for the better. Anyhow, I am not a pessimist. A lot of work needs to be done, and

now. Many voices can still be saved. A repair job can be done if there is
the willpower and the right teacher can be found for the student in trouble.
I have participated as a judge in many vocal competitions. There are some
very good voices, but the trouble is that they don't know the power of
expression; most of the time they simply don't know what they are saying."

I asked her why she had left the Metropolitan in 1951.

"It's very simple," she replied calmly. "Mr. Bing came in and had all his
own group of singers. He did not need me. Edward Johnson had been a great
artist himself and knew voices and how to treat singers. His successor was
another story. I stopped in 1953 because I had married for the second time
—my first husband went out of my life long before—and thought at the
time I wanted a rest. It was a mistake, for I still had a lot to give; actually,
I sang for only nineteen years. Now it is very satisfactory to have my four
grandsons continue the traditions of the family. They have formed a quartet
in Boston called Romanul and successfully appeared with the Boston Pops
and other important musical organizations. God bless them. I was rewarded
by having a wonderful son who has given me satisfaction and tenderness and
also am deeply grateful that this little Transylvanian has brought honor to
her country, even if that is lost for the time being.

"My compatriot Georges Enesco, as great a human being as he was a
musician, was very close to me until he died. And I hope the recordings that
we made together of Rumanian folk songs will one day be released. He used
to say to me, 'Stella, God must love you very much, for He has blessed you
with a golden throat,' and, all modesty apart, I like to think that wonderful,
dear Georges was right."

ROSANNA CARTERI

For seventeen years Rosanna Carteri was among the most versatile and applauded prima donnas of the lyric soprano repertoire, both at La Scala, which was her main base of operations, and elsewhere in the world. Gifted with a delicious voice—very evenly produced and yet capable of much expression—she had the good fortune to be very beautiful; her face was that of a Renaissance Madonna, and her figure was that of a model. And she possessed a capacity to communicate with the public that was particularly rare. *La traviata, La Bohème, Faust, Manon,* and *Otello* were the operas she sang most often, but she went with equal facility from Zerlina and Susanna to Elsa and Euridice, from Gounod's Juliette and Bellini's Giulietta to Micaëla and Blanche in *Les Dialogues des carmélites,* from Matilda in *Guglielmo Tell* to Adina and Norina, from Suor Angelica and Liù to Natasha in Prokofiev's *War and Peace.* She became famous for her ability to infuse life into long-neglected operas of the bel canto school, such as Piccinni's *La buona figliuola* (which marked her Scala debut), Cherubini's *L'osteria portoghese,* and Handel's *Orlando,* and also for the ease with which she could negotiate coloratura in scores demanding great agility. Among them were Donizetti's *Linda di Chamounix* and Rossini's *La donna del lago;* the Rossini opera was reintroduced by her after a fifty-year absence from the repertoire.

Carteri retired after the birth of her second child. The first, a daughter, was born in 1960, and this was followed by a miscarriage. She promised her husband, Franco Grosoli, an important industrialist from Padua, that she would present him with a son, and when she became pregnant again in 1966, she canceled all her contracts in order to avoid any risks. Having kept her promise, she decided to dedicate all her time to her husband and children.

"I don't know how my former colleagues are able to maintain a career and dedicate enough time to the raising of a family," she explained to me, still ravishing and wonderfully groomed, in her spacious flat in Monte Carlo during an afternoon in May 1978. "After my marriage in 1959, I soon discovered that being a valid mother and wife is difficult to reconcile with

Rosanna Carteri as Giulietta in *I Capuleti ed i Montecchi.*

a profession that keeps one moving all the time. Singers today, unlike those of former times, no longer belong to one theatre for the greater part of the year but are constantly honoring engagements here and there. Singing is a very difficult undertaking which demands enormous concentration and continual sacrifices. One cannot fool the public, you know. One must give one's all, and as one's name becomes increasingly known, the responsibilities augment daily. And that is why I decided to shut the door—much to my regret, for I was passionately attached to my work—and like Violetta say 'Addio del passato.' I realized that as much as I loved the lyric theatre, I considered my husband and children even more important, and so I did not have a choice. I have occasionally given a few recitals, but it just does not work that way. You are either in the profession or out of it. The consolation I have is that I stopped when I was at the very top, and at a moment when the signs of the profound malaise that is affecting the operatic world were becoming increasingly worrisome.

"But you have come here to discuss whatever contribution I was able to make to opera, and I shall try to be brief, despite the fact that, as I look back, I cannot believe I accomplished as much as I did.

"I was born in Verona, and when I was fourteen my voice was already in order, two full octaves with no break, and Maestro Ferruccio Cusinati, who was at the time the director of the chorus of the Arena, began teaching me roles. I kept studying the piano, which was always to help me immensely, and I cannot understand why many singers don't realize this. It is as important to the voice as water is to keep plants and flowers alive. To be able to accompany oneself while studying a new score or when one wants to rehearse is of vital importance, for it gives one a sense of measure and balance.

"A great piece of luck was the fact that I had an unusually musical and intelligent mother. She functioned as both an adviser and a guardian, for even in those days they asked me to sing just about everything. With great tact she would make me answer, 'Let us wait a little while.' Looking back, if I had to start all over again, I would limit my repertoire, which was much too vast and so demanded a tremendous effort on my part. It was absolutely insane to study for a long time an absolutely charming new opera such as Castelnuovo-Tedesco's *The Merchant of Venice,* which received its world premiere at the Maggio Musicale Fiorentino, rehearse it for an entire month, and then only sing it twice. As far as I know, it was never performed again. I will not even begin to speak of the folly of spending a fortune on sumptuous sets and costumes for so ridiculously brief a run.

"I was always being called to sing in world premieres. As a matter of fact, there were so many I simply cannot recall them all. But among those I have not forgotten are *Proserpina e lo straniero* by Castro and *Il calzare d'argento* by Pizzetti, both at La Scala; *I misteri gloriosi* by Cattozzo at the Fenice of Venice; and Prokofiev's *War and Peace* in Florence (it had already been given in concert form) under the magical baton of the late Artur Rodzinski. I also sang, at the San Carlo in Naples, *Vivi* by Mannino, and it is in this same theatre that I appeared as Blanche in *Les Dialogues des carmélites,* which I repeated in many theatres in the glorious production of Margherita Wallmann.

"It is in Naples that Poulenc heard me and asked me to create his Gloria at the Théâtre des Champs-Elysées in Paris in 1961. I sang this work many times at the request of the composer, who was very insistent that I also perform his *La Voix humaine.* But I got cold feet because of the diction. While my French is quite good—in fact, in Paris I created Gilbert Bécaud's *Opéra d'Aran,* again with the outstanding Wallmann as director—this particular Poulenc work hinges so much on the superb Cocteau text, and the protagonist is alone onstage for a little over an hour. It also lies very much in the middle of the voice, which is fatiguing for a lyric soprano. Among all the composers I worked with, Poulenc was the gentlest and most considerate, the most vulnerable. He was a most sensitive man, and I believe *Les Dialogues* to be one of the great masterpieces of the twentieth century. In some ways I regret not having given Poulenc the pleasure of my performing his one-act opera; but, on the other hand, I always allowed my instinct to guide me.

"At La Scala I also created Rossellini's *Il linguaggio dei fiori,* which we later repeated here in Monte Carlo for Prince Rainier and Princess Grace. One of the contemporary operas I found congenial and sang often was Pizzetti's *Ifigenia,* now put on the shelf; and I enjoyed appearing as Monica in *The Medium* by Menotti, an outstanding man of the theatre. The time element is more precious than gold; and the hundreds of hours I spent learning new works, often never performed again—were they well employed? I often ask myself that question.

"I was eighteen when I made my debut in 1949. Just how wise it was to appear in a sophisticated role like Elsa in *Lohengrin* in the open air at the Terme di Caracalla in Rome before ten thousand people is debatable. But the opportunity suddenly presented itself, and my mother decided to accept it. My instrument carried, even in the pianissimos, to the outer spaces; and despite the total lack of publicity—we had decided that this would be a form of trial balloon—the success was undeniable, and everything came my way at once.

"Of the Verdi scores I sang many *Falstaff*s, alternating as Alice and Nannetta. The latter is more attractive musically—her aria 'Sul fil d'un soffio etesio' is pure witchcraft—but Alice is more interesting as a person. I was fortunate in singing a production of this opera at La Scala conducted by de Sabata at his best, with Tebaldi a superb Alice and Stabile, despite his age, a spectacular Sir John. I felt I was floating on air. No one who ever heard Stabile in this part could forget him.

"I sang many Desdemonas, but the Verdi role with which I was most identified was Violetta. I had the ingredients, both physical and vocal, to make this gentle creature my very own, and the first act never presented any problems. But Gilda was another story. It is very odd how secure my E-flat was when I practiced or sang in a room, but on the stage it frightened me. I reached the D-flat with total assurance, but from then on I became nervous. And those were still the days when the Italian public expected the E-flat at the end of the 'Caro nome.' I agreed to sing this role in a memorable production at La Scala with Leonard Warren and Giuseppe di Stefano, and I must confess that I was ever so happy each time that ordeal was over. I never sang *Rigoletto* again, and singing it was the only error of judgment that I made. Never mind the fact that Verdi did not write the E-flat; the audience was used to it, and that's that.

"With Desdemona I had a terrible disappointment, and I think of it with great sadness. Furtwängler heard me at La Scala and chose me for his production of *Otello*, starring Ramón Vinay, at the Salzburg Festival in 1952. We went through some very inspiring rehearsals, and then suddenly he suffered a bad heart attack, which was the prelude to his end; he died in 1954. Naturally, the performances could not be canceled, and we proceeded with another maestro, who did his best; but he could bring no excitement into the performances. I sang with Karajan and Bruno Walter, with whom I participated in a superb rendition of Brahms's Requiem. But as far as I am concerned, in the operatic medium no one could be superior to Tullio Serafin. He sustained the singers like no one else, and his knowledge of the voice—what it could do, and how far it could go without forcing—was so miraculous, one felt absolutely secure and protected.

"Puccini was very close to me on a temperamental level," she asserted. "But I was very careful in the choice of his heroines, knowing that I would be carried away by their intensity and dramatic upsurge. I appeared often in *Suor Angelica,* a highly intense work, but fortunately very short, and as Liù,

Mimi, and Magda in *La rondine,* an opera that has never become popular despite a delightful and very sophisticated score. But I stayed away from Butterfly, Tosca, and Manon Lescaut. The Massenet *Manon* suited me ideally, and it was among the operas that established me as a favorite in San Francisco, where I returned, as I did in Chicago. The only important American opera house I never sang in was the Metropolitan. But the explanation is not hard to find. They had a huge number of lyric sopranos at the time—I can think of Tebaldi, Albanese, Kirsten, Steber, Moffo, and Rigal, among others. And sopranos specializing in the German wing, like Hilde Gueden and Lisa della Casa, were also given Italian assignments from time to time.

"I was always deeply attracted to Mozart, but only Zerlina and Susanna came my way often. A *Don Giovanni* I shall never forget was the one in 1956 at La Scala with Siepi, an unsurpassed Don, and Elisabeth Schwarzkopf, whose Elvira was so divine in looks and delivery it made no sense that the Don was always running away from her. I understand perfectly why Patti insisted on singing Zerlina in all the lyric theatres. It is an exquisite role, and one written in so expert a manner that she wins over the public from her very entrance. I adored Euridice, ever so touching, and the Palermo production under Serafin, with Margherita Wallmann giving one of the best displays of what she could do with her double talent of director and choreographer. It was a challenge to undertake the two Marguerites, Boito's and Gounod's, poles apart musically and dramatically. The French one afforded me enormous satisfactions, for not only was the scoring absolutely right for my type of voice, but the development of the character, spurred on by the drama in which she becomes entangled, does give one, particularly in the church scene, great opportunities to act. How so many sopranos can consider this part dull is something I was never able to understand.

"To sing with artists of a certain class," she stated very emphatically, "is essential in order to give the best of oneself. A second-class cast affects one's own chances of giving the best. I always wanted to know who my partners would be before signing a contract, but you cannot begin to imagine how many times it happened to me to have several if not all of them changed. Then one is stuck; one must make the best of it. To have Nilsson as the rival of my affections for Corelli in *Turandot* was most inspiring, and the sort of competition that is eminently healthy and positive. The privilege of singing Micaëla to Simionato's Carmen was tremendous and made all the difference. When I sang with her in *Zanetto,* the adorable one-act opera by Mascagni, how much we laughed together, for she has a wonderful sense of humor. She sang a trouser role and was quite a bit smaller than me, and so we kept inventing ruses so that our love scene should not become ridiculous. She was a genius—everything she touched became pure gold—and I have never encountered anyone who had a finer sense of discipline and responsibility. Such was the mastery of this mezzo over her fabulous instrument that she could give an astonishing performance even when suffering from a bad cold or influenza. On the other hand, mediocrity is, unfortunately, difficult to counteract, and it can easily become contagious.

"Today I sit and watch from the outside, and it is as if everything were out of phase. Seasons are planned with certain operas, and then the search is begun for the singers—the same system used in motion pictures. They buy a novel and then the hunt starts for the actors. But opera is not like a film; it makes very definite requirements which only a determined instrument and technique can fulfill. It is an error that everyone is paying for very dearly. Voices crack up in no time for the lack of knowledge of what responsibilities certain roles entail. The public is disoriented, and no wonder. It has become used to so many small voices that when a large one turns up and a lot of shouting goes on, this is now considered thrilling. The enormous market for recordings, with the great favorites all singing everything, has not helped any to set things right.

"Personally, I am not satisfied with several of my recordings, above all *Suor Angelica* and *Guglielmo Tell;* even *Falstaff* could have been better. But all of these originated as concert versions of operas prepared for radio broadcasts. But the *Traviata* with Warren and Valletti and the *Elisir* with Alva, the *Bohème,* the Poulenc Gloria, the Bécaud *Opéra d'Aran,* the *Roméo et Juliette* highlights with Gedda, and the duets with di Stefano—these do give one an idea of what my voice was like. It is not for me to pass judgment, but I only hope that those who listen today will realize that I was totally dedicated to my responsibilities and deeply involved with the joys and the sorrows of my heroines, who always were my best friends."

I asked her why she was living in Monte Carlo.

"We have two children, and with the situation what it is in Italy," she explained, "we feel more secure here. It is agonizing to have to leave one's own country because of these constant kidnappings, but we feel we must do everything we can to protect them. My husband has a hard time, for he must commute all the time between Padua, where he has his business, and here; but he would rather do that than live in anguish all the time. I don't even touch the piano anymore; I have simply lost interest. How I envy those who can rise above the terrors and horrors of the present, the complete dehumanization. I continue the routine of my life every day; one must. But the disintegration of all I have loved, which has meant so much to me, haunts me, particularly because I am so helpless in trying to stop it."

ANITA CERQUETTI

In 1961 Anita Cerquetti, considered at that time the foremost dramatic soprano of the Italian repertoire, vanished; she disappeared as if she had been kidnapped. The music world is still full of speculation about what actually happened. The loss of her voice . . . a serious heart condition . . . some incurable hormone dysfunction . . . a sudden call to some religious order —all these reasons were circulated. I made it my business to investigate, and after one year's search I finally located her right in Rome. At first the former prima donna was not eager to see me, but eventually she received me in the most cordial manner. With her were her husband, handsome Edo Ferretti, and her beautiful daughter, Gioia.

A large, tall woman with ash-blond hair and a superb Junoesque face that seems to have been sculpted out of white marble in ancient Greece, she is strangely self-conscious and totally sincere. She soon realized, however, that I had taken an immediate liking to her, and she spoke about why and how she had withdrawn from the operatic world just when every important international opera house was clamoring for her.

"I have known about all the talk and gossip," she declared, "and the more it developed, the less I wanted to discuss my retirement. But you broke down my resistance. Actually, none of the rumors were true, but often reality is difficult to explain. When my father got hopelessly ill, I canceled all my performances so that I could be with him, as I loved him with all my heart. After the shock of his death came another terrible blow. My beloved maestro Mario Rossini, to whom I owed everything, passed away unexpectedly, and I was plunged into despair. I kept postponing the signing of contracts, and then I found myself pregnant. After the birth of Gioia— a perfect name, for she has given me and my husband every possible satisfaction—once more I could not make up my mind to resume. She needed care, attention, and love, and who was going to give it to her with a mother always on the go?

"So I waited and waited, and in the meantime precious time had flown. The more I thought about it, the less I wanted to begin again. The conditions

of the lyric theatre kept changing for the worse, and the level of performances had taken a nasty nose dive. In my estimation this was caused by the
increasing infiltration of politics and the rising influence of stage directors
with their preposterous ignorance. I became disenchanted.

"I had been blessed with twelve wonderful years, and I finally decided
that they had been sufficient. Why was I not willing to discuss all of this
until today? I don't know, unless it is that being immensely sensitive, I feared
that in the increasingly inhuman world we live in, people could not understand. Don't think for a moment that it was easy to close the doors on what
had been my life's motivation and for which I had worked so hard. But I
am a highly emotional person, and that is perhaps why I was able to stir
audiences when I sang. One pays for everything in life, and had I been more
rational and less impulsive, I would not have sung the way I did."

As she spoke, I recalled the deep impression she had made on me as
Abigaille in *Nabucco* at La Scala and as Norma at the Arena in Verona. She
had sent shivers down my back, not only with the immensity of her
instrument—a cascade of sound—and the warmth of its color, but with the
solid technique, innate taste, and enormous dignity she brought to these
murderous roles. As I sat there, I could only deeply deplore the chain of
circumstances that had cheated so many listeners out of hearing so unique
an instrument.

"I was born in the small village of Monte Cosaro in the Marche," she
recalled, "a province of Italy to which we owe the voices of Gigli, Corelli,
and Tebaldi. When I was in my teens, though, my parents moved to Città
di Castello, a very pretty town in Umbria. I studied the violin for eight years
but always sang for my own pleasure. At the wedding of a friend, when
I was not yet sixteen, I was asked to sing Gounod's 'Ave Maria,' and as we
left the church a stranger came up to me and said, 'Are you aware that there
is a treasure in your throat?' I replied that he must be joking. 'No,' he replied
seriously, 'I really mean it.' He turned out to be a member of the faculty
of the Conservatorio Morlacchi in Perugia. He persuaded my family to send
me there for an audition, and I was immediately accepted into the classes
of the third year by Maestro Zeetti. My instrument was naturally placed,
and all it needed was polishing up and breath control. There were no
discrepancies in my voice, and I had such facility in the top that, until I
stopped, for exercises I always sang the Queen of the Night's arias from
The Magic Flute in the original key. In concert I always sang the first-act
aria of *La traviata* with great ease and never had it transposed.

"When I was ready, I began going from one vocal competition to the
other, winning every single one, including the very important one of 'Voci

Anita Cerquetti as Abigaille in *Nabucco*.

Nuove' for the RAI on television; this led to performances of *Il trovatore* in Modena. And after I won the Spoleto first prize and appeared as Aida there, all the cards fell into place. Every opera house showed interest in me, and my career exploded like a meteor.

"But when Tullio Serafin, who was not only a very great conductor but a remarkable connoisseur of voices (which is not always the case, unfortunately), expressed interest in me to sing Abigaille under his direction, I was undecided. I knew that in many ways it was Verdi's toughest heroine. My maestro, however, who stopped me from singing many operas, thought I could tackle this particular score. I went to Rome and spent one afternoon with Serafin playing the entire opera on the piano, and the walls shook with the vibrations of my voice. Fortunately, I had learned every note. 'You have been prepared most beautifully,' he said in dismissing me, 'and you must congratulate the person who is responsible. It is as if you had been singing Abigaille for many years.' And then, just as I was about to leave, he added, 'And your voice is one that will go as far as you want it to.'

"When I sang this very arduous role under his direction a few weeks later, I became famous overnight. But I was sparing with the number of performances I sang of this part. It has an unbelievable tessitura, and, as you know, it ruined forever the voice of Giuseppina Strepponi, who later became Verdi's wife. But I was made for Verdi's music and sang practically all of his operas, with the exception of *Macbeth* and *La traviata*. I did not have the figure for Violetta, but Caballé, who is bigger than I am, has made a great success with it. I learned it, but the opportunity never came, as there were many Violettas around but hardly any dramatic sopranos. For ten years I was asked to sing *Norma* everywhere, and it will forever remain the opera closest to my heart. It combines bel canto at its purest, the stylish elegance of those happier days, and deep, overwhelming emotion.

"I was a great admirer of Callas, despite her vocal shortcomings. She was very clever too. I shall never forget when in an interview they asked her how she compared herself with Tebaldi. 'I am built by an unknown artisan,' she replied, 'but my instrument is played by Paganini. She, instead, is a Stradivarius played by an amateur.' Basically, she was completely right— just as she was when she compared herself to French champagne and Tebaldi to beer.

"In 1956 when I was appearing in Florence in *Don Carlo,* Callas was appearing as Violetta at La Scala amid ovations, and Tebaldi was singing the same role at the Comunale. I felt so sorry for Tebaldi, seeing how nervous and uncomfortable the opera made her, and I kept thinking, But

why do you do it? Who obliges you, when there are so many other operas
that are so right for you and in which you have no equal? I have never
understood why an artist of her tremendous stature should be afraid to admit
that something is not right for her. Puccini was not for me, and every year
I turned down innumerable offers to do *Turandot, Tosca, Fanciulla,* and
Manon Lescaut. My maestro always warned me against verismo roles; in fact,
I never even accepted Santuzza, though the actual singing is only about half
an hour. I did sing *Loreley,* which suited me, but that is about all.

"Another opera I was constantly in demand for was *La Gioconda,* and,
like Abigaille, I would accept only a few performances from time to time.
I loved the role, but every time I was aware that my voice had dropped,
and this meant time to recover and pull it up again. Serafin advised me never
to sing it in the open air, and I obeyed him. Year after year the Arena of
Verona asked me to do them this great favor, but I never complied. Every
time I undertook Ponchielli's heroine, Serafin would say *'Attenta, attenta.'*
He knew what he was talking about.

"I sang relatively little at La Scala because of Callas. She was the reigning
lady there, and I was always being asked to take on her roles after she had
finished a certain number of performances. But in that I was a diva: first,
yes; second, never—despite my high esteem for the Greek prima donna. At
one point, after agreeing to sing *Ballo,* she insisted they change it to some
other opera, and—amazingly enough, for her word was law—they refused.
So then they offered Amelia to me, and I accepted. When Callas learned
this, she changed her mind again and decided to sing it after all. I was not
in the least angry; on the contrary, I was most flattered. The reason I never
sang at the Metropolitan was that Mr. Bing not only wanted to sign me
to a long contract, which meant my having to be in New York for very
long periods, but he wanted me to be available for roles such as Tosca and
Santuzza, which I refused to sing. So I sang in Chicago and Philadelphia
and had my satisfactions there.

"I had the great fortune of singing with fabulous partners—from Gigli
to the unsurpassed Simionato, from Bjoerling to del Monaco, from Gobbi
and Bastianini to Siepi and Christoff—and the privilege of singing with
conductors of the stature of the late Dimitri Mitropoulos (I sang many
Ernanis with him) and Carlo Maria Giulini. I always sang bel canto operas.
I was particularly fond of Rossini's *Mosè,* I also enjoyed resurrecting an
interesting Cherubini opera, *Gli abenceragi.* I was also considering taking on
Medea. When I sang at the Concertgebouw in Amsterdam in a gala concert,
I had no idea that this would be the last time I would sing in public.

"I never accepted contemporary works, and it is my conviction that today's composers—Berio, Nono, Stockhausen, and a number of others—loathe singers and are hell-bent on wrecking their voices. It is a form of sadism which perhaps is unconscious. Those who take on their works are insane, for in no time they tear their instruments into shreds. Have you ever looked at one of their scores? They might as well be written by a machine. The most extraordinary aspect of this phenomenon is that they find lambs to immolate, so one can only conclude that some singers today are masochists.

"It is extraordinary too how many colleagues who started with me have fallen by the wayside. The only one left is Carlo Bergonzi. His was a beautiful lyric tenor—I sang with him when he had just made the switch from baritone—but despite a good technique, the heavy roles he has undertaken have, alas, taken away the bloom.

"Not only do I have no advice for those who are beginning, but I feel deeply sorry for them. I would not like being in their shoes. It is not bitterness—you do understand, don't you?—but great sadness at seeing the operatic ship sinking, sinking, sinking."

No greater compliment has been paid to Cerquetti than by the tenor Mirto Picchi, a remarkable singing actor who for twenty-eight years was considered Italy's greatest interpreter of difficult contemporary operas. In his fascinating autobiography, *Un trono vicino al sol* (published in Italy in 1979), he writes, "I was Anita Cerquetti's Ismaele in her debut in *Nabucco* at the Arena of Verona in 1956, and that same year we sang in a triumphant *Norma* at the Liceo in Barcelona and in 1957 *Oberon* at the RAI. To sing with her was a joy, for she was simple, genuine, open, and without any sort of dissimulation. Her triumph in *Norma* in Barcelona was the greatest of all I have experienced in this opera, and there were more than a few. [He had sung Pollione frequently to the Normas of Callas, Caniglia, Caterina Mancini, and Maria Pedrini.] This voice so full of light and velvet created such hysteria that at the stage exit the crowd around this soprano was so dense that the police had to be called. One looked at her, quite rightly, in those years as the last great dramatic voice, never to be replaced—she is remembered by everyone, and justly so."

But the mystery of Cerquetti's retirement lingers on. In Tito Gobbi's autobiography, *My Life* (published in England in 1979), he states that "she had a beautiful 'stage' face, and her voice was absolutely stunning. . . . Hers was a splendid talent, and it was indeed a tragedy that ill health cut short her career before she arrived at her full powers."

Whatever the truth, her withdrawal from the lyric theatre meant the loss of the greatest dramatic soprano of the time.

THE ONE AND ONLY

MARIA CALLAS

MARIA CALLAS

There has never been a more contradictory singing actress—one who fought like a tigress to arrive at an exalted position, only to throw it all away—than Maria Callas. Like many of the heroines of the ancient Greek tragedies (and this artist, whose real name was Kalogeropoulos, had all the characteristics of her fiery race), she was immensely self-destructive. She died, suddenly, on September 16, 1977, under circumstances that are still far from clear. So many books have already been written about her—with more in the works—that I have decided to omit as much biography as possible and concentrate on artistic issues. I use the word "possible" because much of the time her private life was so entangled with her career that they are almost impossible to separate.

I never actually held a formal interview with Callas, but she was in and out of my life between 1955, the year of her Metropolitan Opera debut, and 1976, the year before her death. Many were our conversations, but as I look back none seems satisfactory, for despite the witchery that so many people have called her magic, she was basically a rather simple and uninformed woman. Had she been truly intelligent, her few luminous years might have stretched out over a longer period, for she had the world at her feet.

What is fascinating about her, in my opinion, is that she was totally a creature of deep instinct. What she achieved in her character portrayals was the result not of profound study and reflection but of an innate ability to identify with each character. Musically, she was always superbly prepared, and everyone was amazed at the hours and days she dedicated to rehearsals without a word of complaint or a sign of impatience. But there it stopped. Other singers, including Beverly Sills when preparing the three Donizetti operas *Maria Stuarda, Roberto Devereux,* and *Anna Bolena,* have been known to read everything in sight to become acquainted with the historical backgrounds of their characterizations. Callas never did. When I asked her, for instance, about her approach to *Anna Bolena*—in my estimation her finest accomplishment—she told me that she considered it a nineteenth-century melodrama set to lovely music, and that the Donizetti heroine and the real Anne Boleyn had little in common. Nor did she know how many other wives Henry VIII had had; they did not interest her. It was the music alone that gave her the proper insight into the part she was to perform. Not having

Maria Callas in the title role of *Anna Bolena*.

heard her in the early part of her career, when she was overweight and, apparently, ungraceful and untidy, I had believed what many of her former colleagues had told me: that she did not then appear to possess the qualities of an actress. The great opera connoisseur Gerald Fitzgerald, who knew her exceedingly well and has written most interestingly about her, does not agree. He has shown me old photographs of Callas in which some of the imposing gestures that were later to become permanent elements of her performances were already evident. In Fitzgerald's opinion, it was only her enormous weight and unattractive appearance that prevented her from revealing all of which she was capable.

I recall one night in December 1956 at a dinner in the Waldorf Towers, shortly after Callas's appearance at the Metropolitan in *Lucia di Lammermoor,* when she explained that she had not read Sir Walter Scott's *The Bride of Lammermoor.* "It's not important," she said in that delightful Venetian accent which underlined her perfect Italian, "for it is the music that matters. The mad scene is a result of Donizetti's genius and not of the novel. These literary works are the springboard, but what really matters is what the composer does with them. There is nothing Scottish about the way Donizetti interprets her. She becomes a universal character. Try to translate 'Ardono gli incensi' [The incense is burning] into English, and much of the gripping drama is gone."

As well as she could peruse a score and learn it with amazing rapidity, Callas was not a reader. I was also amazed to discover that she had not acquainted herself with Alexander Dumas *fils*'s *La Dame aux camélias,* from which *La traviata* was adapted. *Traviata* and *Norma* were her favorite operas because, she told friends, she could identify herself totally with these two heroines. This gives one considerable insight into her unpredictable makeup, for there could not be two more different characters. The Bellini priestess, thirsty for vengeance, causes the death of her lover and father of her two children, and her own immolation. The Verdi heroine on the other hand, vulnerable and feminine, is capable of any sacrifice for the man she loves. Here again it was the music and not the literature that interested her.

One night, in February 1958, I listened to Callas's grievances about the *Traviata* production at the Metropolitan, and I could only agree with her. At La Scala in 1955 she had been given a fabulous production directed by Luchino Visconti, with sets and costumes by the incomparable Lila de Nobili; the conductor had been Carlo Maria Giulini, and the superlative cast had included Giuseppe di Stefano—then at the height of his vocal powers —and Ettore Bastianini. The various innovations in Visconti's direction— such as having Violetta throw off her shoes at the end of the first act—did not meet with an enthusiastic reception from the very conservative Milanese public. However, the following year, when the production was revived, it became a great hit. At the Met she was faced with uninteresting sets by Rolf Gerard, uninspiring direction by Tyrone Guthrie, and a third-class tenor, Daniele Barioni, as Alfredo.

"One can only give one's best when everything around one is just right," she said that evening. "For years I have been spoiled by La Scala, which has always presented me with top-notch casts and directors. Here in New York there are hardly any rehearsals because they are too expensive, and then one steps into a production which was never top-notch even when first staged. Opera is make-believe, and the visual part is very important. I have told the management exactly how I feel, and yet I fear that with the system that prevails here, the situation will not improve." The Greek soprano never went near this opera again after performing it in Dallas in 1958, knowing that her voice was no longer up to it (unlike Tebaldi and others, Callas always sang Violetta in the original key), but she always hoped to be able once again to meet its demands successfully and wanted very much to record it with Giulini. She confided to me that she had preferred the Zeffirelli production in Dallas to Visconti's because "the costumes were so ravishing." But by then Visconti no longer met with her favor.

On another occasion she complained to me bitterly of being given Eugenio Fernandi as her partner in *Lucia* at the Metropolitan, for she did not feel—and rightly so—that he could honorably handle the role of Edgardo. Yet despite what has often been written, she rarely had rows with her colleagues. I believe that, in most cases, she felt she was simply above all that. There was her famous quarrel with Boris Christoff, which keeps turning up in her biographies—after the Bulgarian bass supposedly ex-pressed his displeasure at her taking a solo bow at a performance of *Medea* in Rome, she never sang with him again—but this was the exception to the rule. Her admiration for Christoff's brother-in-law, Tito Gobbi, was uncon-ditional, and she told me in February 1965, at the time of the performances of *Tosca* at the Paris Opéra, that she did not know of a baritone who projected the role of Scarpia more effectively.

Callas did have a contretemps with Mario del Monaco (who, however, always spoke glowingly of her) at a Saturday-afternoon performance of *Norma* at the Metropolitan in 1956. She was not in good voice and was undecided as to whether to cancel or not. Finally she decided to continue. She called the Italian tenor to her dressing room and asked him not to take the B-flat in the finale, as she was convinced that she could not make it herself, and, of course, he obliged her, understanding her predicament. But when the moment came she suddenly found the strength to take the high note, leaving the celebrated tenor high and dry. When the artists came out to take their bows and del Monaco was not among them, a deluge of vegetables was thrown onto the stage, perhaps marking the first time that such a dubious homage had been paid to a diva. (Being so nearsighted, Callas did not realize at first that the turnips and cauliflowers were not posies.) The public was convinced that del Monaco did not appear to take his curtain call along with the others because he was aware that a cabal against her existed that would take advantage of the fact that she had sung poorly. But the truth is that he did not come out because he was so angry that she had taken the B-flat, making it appear as if he did not have it.

Callas's relations with Corelli, di Stefano, and del Monaco (the above incident notwithstanding), the leading tenors of their time, were always friendly, except during the rehearsals of *La traviata* at La Scala, when she became very annoyed with di Stefano for always arriving late. Later, after her turbulent period with Onassis was over (the shipping tycoon had walked out on her to marry Jacqueline Kennedy, apparently informing Callas of his intentions only twenty-four hours before), she became very close to di Stefano. He persuaded her to give joint recitals with him on a worldwide concert tour, but it turned out to be an unfortunate venture. The money (which she did not need) poured in, but both singers were in disastrous vocal condition. One critic referred to them as "dogs who barked at one another."

Callas's relationship with Tebaldi was an extraordinary one, and one in which I, as Tebaldi's press representative, was much involved. Trouble had started early on in South America, where they both appeared in São Paulo and Rio de Janeiro; but the resentment was always on the part of Callas. In all truth, I can state that Tebaldi never spoke unkindly about her so-called rival. In fact, she was deeply upset when Elsa Maxwell eulogized her at Callas's expense, fearing that the readers of the column might think that she was behind these ferocious attacks. But when Maxwell began praising Callas to the skies, ignoring Tebaldi, the latter never said a word about it to me.

Tebaldi is a quiet woman who has always known her worth, and any kind of intrigue is foreign to her serene nature. In fact, she went on record as saying that she would not dare attempt Norma since Callas was so extraordinary in this role. But the Greek soprano resented Tebaldi; whether it was a reaction—conscious or subconscious—against Tebaldi's finer instrument I never knew. Whenever Callas ran into me, she never failed to ask in a condescending manner how was *"povera* Renata." Whether the *"povera"* referred to Tebaldi's life (she never married and there was never much talk of a beau) or to something else remained a question mark. It is well known that once, while listening to a radio broadcast in Venice of one of Tebaldi's records, Callas turned to Dorle Soria and said, "What a lovely voice! But who cares?" She was also annoyed by the deep affection that Tebaldi felt for her mother; Callas's relationship with her own mother was extremely tempestuous.

Callas never failed to appear in a proscenium box at La Scala when Tebaldi sang *La forza del destino,* and she attended many of Tebaldi's *Aidas* at the Chicago Opera. At one of these performances, just as Tebaldi began to sing the fiendishly difficult "O patria mia," Callas created quite a stir by summoning an usher with a flashlight to find a bracelet she had dropped by her seat. One wonders why someone who so respected art would stoop to such a cheap trick to disturb a fellow artist. I have heard the story from many people but never from Tebaldi, who often stated that if opera were to continue, there must be a number of first-class sopranos.

Antonietta Stella was an excellent singer, and though she never became a runner-up in the Tebaldi-Callas sweepstakes, she was the cause of one of Callas's unexplainable actions. The Greek soprano owed a great deal to Tullio Serafin—considered by all of the divas I interviewed to know more about voices than any other conductor—but she exploded in a rage when she heard that the venerable maestro was recording *La traviata* with Stella for EMI. The reason for his choosing Stella was logical: Callas had already recorded the role for Cetra, and her contract had stipulated that a certain number of years had to go by before she could rerecord it. She broke off relations with Serafin over this; but he took it all very philosophically, claiming that she was *"un poco pazza"* (a little crazy), and eventually she forgave him, recording two more operas with him before his death. Logic never seemed to play a part in Callas's makeup and one could not reason with her.

Of the old-timers, she most admired Ponselle and Muzio and often played their records. She told me that when preparing for Spontini's *La vestale,* she had listened with infinite care to Ponselle's renditions of "Tu che invoco" and "O nume tutelar." She plied me with questions, since I had heard Ponselle sing this opera in Florence at the Maggio Musicale Fiorentino (her one and only appearance in Italy), but Callas's performance was very different. The miracle of Ponselle's instrument, apart from its timbre, was the evenness of registers, and Callas's one great weakness was her obvious switch from one register to the other.

Being so highly musical, Callas usually got on well with conductors. To me she spoke with perhaps more enthusiasm for Giulini than for the others, including Karajan, with whom she sang a celebrated *Lucia.* At one point her favorite among the metteurs-en-scène was Luchino Visconti, who was largely responsible for developing her personality on the stage, but she eventually turned against him; somehow it had been repeated to her that he had claimed, "I have made her." Franco Zeffirelli, who had been swept aside by Callas after the very successful *Il turco in Italia* (the only comic opera in which she had a big success), returned to her favor: she was delighted with his 1959 *Traviata* in Dallas, conceived in a series of flashbacks. Later he did a splendid production of *Norma* at the Paris Opéra and stood by like the rock of Gibraltar when she was cruelly booed; the audience had paid outrageous prices, not knowing, of course, that they would hear her in sad vocal condition. She never followed Zeffirelli's wise advice to change her repertoire and take on certain operas in which her acting powers could overcome her growing vocal deficiencies. She should have made a film with him, who worshiped her, instead of with Pier Paolo Pasolini, with whom she made the disastrous *Medea*.

In 1955 Callas appeared at the Chicago Opera for her only performances of *Madama Butterfly*. It was after the last of these that she was served papers in a lawsuit by Robert Bagarozy, who claimed she owed him 10 percent of all the money she had earned since the beginning of her career. Some people thought that it was because of this incident that she refused to sing Cio-Cio-San again. But when I had seen her in Chicago before this incident had occurred, she had said to me, "I don't think the geisha is right for me. I'm too tall, and all those small, mincing, miniature gestures don't really suit my style. The music is lovely, but so sentimental, and I prefer roles that I can really get my teeth into." But why then had she gone to all the effort of learning and undertaking the role? She knew the opera well and realized exactly what it would entail. She had even gone to the trouble of learning, from a famous Japanese Butterfly, Hizi Koyke, how to unwind the complicated coiffure and let her hair fall suddenly at the moment of the suicide.

Indeed, I was continually intrigued by the fact that, unlike most other singers, Callas undertook many new roles for a very few performances and then never went back to them. This meant a tremendous investment of time, money, and energy. For example, in her entire career she sang only two performances of Gilda in *Rigoletto;* three each of Abigaille in *Nabucco*, Margherita in *Mefistofele*, the title role in Rossini's *Armida*, Euridice in Haydn's *Orfeo*, and *Butterfly;* four of Alceste, *Iphigénie en Tauride*, and Konstanze in *Entführung* (the only Mozart opera she ever sang); five of Kundry in *Parsifal*, Paolina in *Poliuto*, Amelia in *Ballo*, Rosina in *Il barbiere*, Elisabetta in *Don Carlo*, Giulia in *La vestale*, Leonora in *Forza*, and Lady Macbeth in *Macbeth;* six of Brünnhilde in *Die Walküre*, *Fedora*, and Maddalena in *Andrea Chenier;* seven of Imogene in *Il pirata;* nine of Fiorilla in *Il turco in Italia;* eleven of Elena in *I ves-*

pri siciliani; twelve of *La Gioconda;* and thirteen of Elvira in *I puritani.*

At the beginning of her career, in Athens, she appeared in various operettas, sometimes only once or twice, and sang Leonore in *Fidelio* and Santuzza in *Cavalleria* (which she later recorded), two heroines she never returned to onstage. The only operas she sang twenty times or more were *Il trovatore* (20), *La sonnambula* (21), *Turandot* (23), *Aida* and *Medea* (31 each), *Lucia* (43), *Tosca* (52), *La traviata* (58), and *Norma* (84). She also recorded *Pagliacci, La Bohème, Manon Lescaut,* and *Carmen,* operas in which she never appeared on the stage.

I could never get Callas to talk about her teacher, Elvira de Hidalgo; every time I would ask about her, Callas would say *"È tanto cara"* (She is so dear) and quickly change the subject. When I tried to obtain an interview with de Hidalgo in Milan in 1977 (she has since died), she screamed at me on the telephone that she refused to discuss Callas and asked me what fee I would pay for the privilege of conversing with her. She sounded so unappealing that I gave up. It is a matter of common knowledge that the Spanish coloratura was very proud of her pupil's success at first, but later became jealous when she was no longer referred to as the incomparable de Hidalgo but as Callas's teacher. Curiously, one of the few roles in which Callas failed was Rosina, the one role in which everyone agrees that de Hidalgo had excelled. But Callas was a tragedienne; comedy was not her forte. The relationship between de Hidalgo and Callas was never really interrupted, from the early days in Athens up to the time when the former Spanish nightingale was called by her ex-pupil to Paris to help her with her performances of *Tosca* and *Norma* at the Opéra.

Most musical experts agree that Callas's greatest accomplishment was *Medea.* Here she could combine effectively her Greek heritage—which became more and more overt as time went on—and the overwhelming sense of fury that she was so expert at projecting and whose drama the stridency of some of her notes was so useful in underlining. Why she failed in verismo operas such as *Andrea Chenier* and *Fedora,* which require a very strong personality, was hard for me to understand. I questioned Augusta Oltrabella, one of the greatest exponents of verismo, about this. "Verismo was not for her," she explained, "because despite what everyone says, she was an actress in the expression of the music, and not vice versa. In verismo the music is often secondary, and one must know how to create an atmosphere apart from the score."

It was the coloratura technique that de Hidalgo had taught Callas that was eventually to be her "open sesame." In the first years of her career Callas was stuck with *Turandot* and the Wagnerian repertoire. When Tullio Serafin had her audition for Francesco Siciliani, then director of the Comunale in Florence, he asked her with whom she had studied. When she mentioned de Hidalgo, she was immediately asked if she could tackle coloratura roles. She replied affirmatively; Serafin played "Qui la voce" from *I puritani*, and Siciliani knew immediately that he had found the Norma he was looking for. If her first excursion into this opera was a revelation to the Florentines, it was what followed shortly after in Venice that helped to turn the tide completely.

Callas had been engaged at the Fenice for *Die Walküre* at the same time that Carosio was to have sung *I puritani*. When Carosio fell ill, Serafin, recalling how well Callas had managed the aria from this opera, persuaded her to jump in for the celebrated Italian coloratura, even though she did not know the score in its entirety. It was a gamble from which Callas emerged with flying colors, and the bel canto repertoire opened up for her—something that might never have happened otherwise. It would never, for instance, have occurred to Artur Bodanzky to ask Flagstad to substitute for Lily Pons; but Serafin had already heard the proof of the latent agility in Callas's voice.

Many critics have claimed that this going from the heavy repertoire to the light one, along with the rapid loss of weight, prepared the way for Callas's vocal undoing, and I am inclined to agree with them. But others insist that she always sang with three voices and that the instrument was fractured from the very beginning. It is immensely sad that this soprano who created such a worldwide commotion lasted so short a time. Her career went strong for just over a decade, and then—with interruptions caused by her happy, then unhappy, relationship with Onassis—lamely for five more years. There is no doubt that the scandals helped her legend; they followed each other rapidly, making her front-page news everywhere. Her cancellations—which in the case of other singers would not have created such a fuss —became international events. Her refusal to appear at the last performance of *La sonnambula* at the Edinburgh Festival in 1957 would not have attracted so much attention had it not been that she refused to appear in order to attend Elsa Maxwell's ball in Venice. Her withdrawing from the San Francisco Opera season that September at the very last minute made the management irate, since it was discovered that the "nervous exhaustion" which had prevented her honoring her engagement with the opera house had not stopped her from recording *Medea* from September 12 to 19 in Italy. At the Rome Opera, on January 2, 1958, she withdrew from the opening night of *Norma* after the first act, abandoning the president of the Republic and an elegant audience to their fate; later she blamed the management for not having had an understudy. This was absolutely true, but having known it all along, she should have canceled that morning. The consensus was that she was not in good voice that night and had been incensed at the hissing coming from the gallery.

She became so controversial that eventually no one knew what to expect from her. The night in the spring of 1958 at La Scala when she vented her wrath at manager Antonio Ghiringhelli will forever remain in the annals of the theatre. In the wonderful finale of Bellini's *Il pirata,* as Imogene cries out "Là . . . vedete . . . il palco funesto" (There . . . you see . . . the accursed scaffold), Callas moved downstage, pointing with an angry gesture to Ghiringhelli's box (*palco* also means theatre box). Everyone got the message, pandemonium broke out, and there was wild cheering for her courage in defying this powerful man. But she did not sing again at La Scala until December 1960, in *Poliuto.*

Her memory seemed always to be working to her own advantage. She claimed that she had sung only in the greatest opera houses, forgetting that she had appeared in provincial theatres in Rovigo, Ravenna, Reggio Calabria, Udine, Cagliari, Brescia, and Bergamo. Before she realized that Meneghini was rich she disliked him, but when it was pointed out to her how his money could help her career, she changed her mind and found him *"adorabile."* She sang his praises for years, but later she could not find enough vituperative adjectives to describe him. Many believe that their marriage was never consummated and that the relationship was on the level of father and daughter.

Callas fascinated, but did not inspire affection. The only colleagues who were truly fond of her were Simionato and Graziella Sciutti. To conservative prima donnas, the unevenness of Callas's voice was not acceptable. Amelita Galli-Curci made an interesting statement, claiming that Callas's instrument was "tortured." Ester Mazzoleni, like so many others, felt that Callas's mania to sing everything was a fever that has spread to others, ruining the current crop of voices.

It is a matter of mystery that this singer who worked so hard to reach perfection did not know when it was time to stop and leave the opera world gracefully. Even her attempt to direct an opera failed miserably. When the new opera house in Turin was inaugurated, she and di Stefano directed *I vespri siciliani,* a score that had been one of her most admired interpretations. But as Zeffirelli wisely said, "She never knew what was going on onstage, for she was too involved with what she herself was doing." The few people who saw or talked to Callas toward the end of her life felt that her death was a welcome release to a tortured soul unable to find any other form of serenity or peace. Until the end she was a figure out of a Greek tragedy.

EPILOGUE

We have heard from these prima donnas how operatic tradition has been thrown to the winds, and an undertone of sadness and helplessness comes through strongly when they speak of the precarious condition of the opera world today. Not all these women were perfect singers—or artists, as they preferred to be called—but each and every one of them was a personality in her own right, having reached this state through strict discipline, hard work, and uncanny instinct. They are a vivid part of the fascinating tapestry of twentieth-century opera, and they are still remembered and loved. I wonder whether, years from now, we will be able to say the same of today's singers. I was present recently when Gianna Pederzini walked into the Teatro dell'Opera in Rome, and the applause that greeted her was far more marked than the ovations later received by the singers onstage. In May 1981 I was with Renata Tebaldi at a recital by Katia Ricciarelli at the Théâtre de l'Athénée in Paris. Tebaldi's presence in the hall was announced by the director of the theatre, and there was a long standing ovation. This amazed me, since half of the audience was made up of very young people, and Tebaldi has not sung for some time. She was actually much embarrassed, for she was greeted with far more enthusiasm than the charming recitalist. But Tebaldi and the other prima donnas interviewed here were stars, and they became stars through their search for perfection and their never-ending sacrifices. They seemed to have followed the precept of Adriana Lecouvreur's famous aria "Io sono l'umile ancella," in which the legendary French actress sings that she is but a humble servant totally dedicated to her art.

Contrary to popular belief, it is not the fan-club business, the personally addressed Christmas cards, or the various receptions held for adoring admirers that can prolong a career. When a voice is gone for good, no amount of promotion can help. Those who have been able to stretch out their professional lives way beyond the normal course of events are possessors of a very special technique combined with unusually durable vocal cords. Apart from those already discussed, there are several divas whose careers lasted for unusually long periods of time. Ernestine Schumann-Heink seemed to have topped them all: the leading contralto of her day, she sang from 1878 until 1932, making her farewell at the Metropolitan as Fricka at the age of seventy-two. Gatti-Casazza described her as "a true vocal miracle, for, past seventy, she could still command style and quality of voice." Lilli Lehmann went on for forty-two years, Elvira Casazza for forty, Nellie Melba for thirty-nine, Emma Calvé and Zinka Milanov for thirty-eight. And there were situations such as Frida Leider's: her career was cut *short* after thirty years by the traumas of the war.

On the other hand, two famous Americans had relatively short careers, for different reasons. Franca Somigli, whose real name was Marian Clarke, was a sensation abroad, but she never made good either in Chicago, where she was born, or at the Metropolitan Opera, where she made the mistake of appearing in two roles utterly uncongenial to her quality of voice: Mimi and Cio-Cio-San. Toscanini admired her and used her at the Salzburg Festival, and at La Scala she sang in fifteen different operas within a decade. She had enormous personality, but it is perhaps because she took on such heavy roles as Minnie, Kundry, and Salome (along with an impressive number of contemporary works) that she lasted less than two decades. Helen Traubel began in opera when she was in her thirties, and while Flagstad was away during wartime and after, she became the leading Wagnerian diva at the Metropolitan. When the Norwegian soprano returned and was offered Wagner's *Ring* for the 1950–51 season, she accepted only on condition that Traubel be given another series. "She is a very great singer," Flagstad announced, "and kept Wagner going during my absence. I could not possibly consider being the cause of her being pushed aside." Needless to say, Miss Traubel remained. But in 1953 she argued with Rudolf Bing over her appearances in Las Vegas, which Bing would not tolerate, and that was the end of her operatic career.

Many prima donnas had long and successful careers on the strength of a handful of roles. Schwarzkopf, in the second half of her professional operatic life, cut her repertoire to six roles. Teresa Berganza became a celebrity with a very limited number of Mozart and Rossini roles, and now she has added Carmen. The Bizet role became so identified with Risë Stevens that for well over two decades no one in America could have believed that there existed any other Spanish gypsy. With the Metropolitan Opera Stevens repeated it seventy-five times at the House and forty-nine times on tour. It is a staggering record. Emma Calvé, considered the greatest Carmen of all, outdid Stevens by only seventeen performances, having sung at the

Met and on tour a total of 141 times. Ina Souez, who has become a mythical figure, was a perfectly wonderful Donna Anna and Fiordiligi; but did she ever sing anything else? And for the last fifteen years Graziella Sciutti has been the indispensable Despina in productions of *Così fan tutte*—everywhere.

But, more and more, sopranos and mezzos simply vanish—here today, gone tomorrow. In the past, gala farewells were virtually required when a singer decided to retire; today, not only are they considered old-fashioned, but often the artist is no longer in sufficiently good vocal condition to face this sort of ordeal. One could fill pages with the names of those who have simply disappeared. Two American protégées of Toscanini—Teresa Stich-Randall, who sang the High Priestess in *Aida* and Nannetta in *Falstaff* in two of his famous NBC productions, and Ann McKnight, who was Musetta in his *La Bohème*—left no traces. Stich-Randall won the important Lausanne singing competition in 1951 and became a favorite at the Aix-en-Provence Festival and a permanent member of the Vienna Staatsoper, where her Mozart was considered of the highest quality. She became a fine recitalist too. And then silence. I asked after her in Vienna, but to no avail. McKnight, who went to Italy and changed her name to Anna de Cavalieri, began taking on heavy assignments, and her Turandot was in demand for some years in important theatres. Then, almost overnight, she made a rapid exit. Delia Rigal, an Argentine find of Rudolf Bing, was assigned every important spinto role during the first years of his regime, and then unfortunately (for there was no nicer woman) she had to retire permanently, her instrument having gone to pieces. Other Americans who showed so much promise (all were talented and had good basic vocal resources) only to go into limbo were the delightful coloratura Gianna d'Angelo, Irene Jordan (who went from the dramatic soprano into the mezzo range), Lucy Kelston (who made a lovely recording of *Luisa Miller* for Cetra), Laurel Hurley, Jean Fenn, Camilla Williams, Frances Greer, and Mattiwilda Dobbs. I recall the Italo-American Florence Quartararo bursting onto the Metropolitan stage, a great new find, but she too was gone almost immediately. The gifted black soprano Felicia Weathers is another one who made an immediate success, took on roles that were too heavy for her delicate instrument, and was gone with the wind.

Sometimes this sort of disappearance occurs not long after the debut. Nothing is more dangerous than making a debut that has been preceded by a great deal of publicity; it has proved fatal on many occasions. One famous case is that of Marion Talley, a newcomer to the Met from Kansas City.

The newspapers were all full of reports of her exceptional merits two weeks preceding her bow, but she simply was not ready for the vast spaces and responsibilities of the Metropolitan Opera House. I recall Lauritz Melchior telling me that he was making his debut in *Tannhäuser* in a Saturday matinee on February 17, 1926, and was absolutely thrilled upon arriving at the theatre to see long lines of people clamoring for tickets and standing room. He was most disappointed to discover that they were all there hoping to catch Miss Talley's debut in *Rigoletto* in that evening's performance. Melchior lasted twenty-four years in the Thirty-ninth Street theatre; Talley lasted three. In 1962 there was the case of another American, Margherita Roberti (whose real name was Margaret Roberts), who came to the Metropolitan preceded by a very fine reputation as a dramatic soprano in Italy, where she had sung in all the leading houses. New York critics, annoyed by the overenthusiasm of the people who had traveled from her hometown to New York to hear her debut in *Tosca,* gave her poor reviews. Mr. Bing did not give her another chance, and there was no re-engagement; she too has vanished from the operatic profession.

Triumphant recital debuts have been known to be perilous to a singer's operatic career. I recall vividly the New York concert debut of the Greek mezzo Elena Nikolaidi (no relation to the Bulgarian mezzo Elena Nicolai). The critics spewed forth so many superlatives for her that the Metropolitan Opera felt something must be done about this new wonder. So she was signed up and given the honor of opening the 1951–52 season as Amneris in *Aida* along with Milanov and del Monaco. She made little impression and was eased out of the picture. A success in a concert hall can mean very little in an opera house, and vice versa.

Then there are those who reach a specific opera house too late to make a real career there. The exquisite Norwegian lyric coloratura Eidé Norena arrived at the Metropolitan for the 1933–34 season at the age of fifty, after twenty-six years of professional singing. Then there was Erna Berger, also a coloratura, who came to the Met in 1949 at the age of forty-nine, stupefying audiences and critics alike with the youthful agility with which she negotiated the Queen of the Night, Gilda, and Sophie. But three years later she left, and in 1955 she drew the curtain on her singing activities.

Choosing the right role for a debut in an important opera house has always been a tricky decision for singers, and it is fascinating to observe how many of them have miscalculated their resources. The first appearance by a singer in a major part in a leading theatre is bound to cause nervous tension, and even the most assured artist is rarely at his best. And so it is essential to pick a gratifying assignment, vocally and dramatically, and at the same time one that does not present unusual vocal hurdles or complicated acting problems. This was not so true in the past, when a singer was signed for a certain number of roles in one season, and consequently there were more opportunities. Now, very often a new artist is engaged for one role only, and if that is not an immediate success, there is no follow-up.

I recall the bow of Ilva Ligabue in 1963 at Carnegie Hall in New York in the concert version of Donizetti's *Maria di Rohan*. This fine soprano, with a very handsome presence—certainly the best Alice Ford today, and a superb Francesca da Rimini and Maddalena in *Andrea Chenier*—is a versatile artist, but the bel canto repertoire of the mid-nineteenth century is not suited to either her voice or her temperament. She undermined her future in New York by this appearance, as it provoked neither interest nor excitement. Marcella Pobbé, a beautiful woman who was the best Desdemona and Tosca in Italy after Tebaldi left for the United States, came to the Metropolitan for performances of *La Bohème* and *Faust*. She went on—it was a Saturday night—with not a single rehearsal, rushing around between the acts in a state of agitation to see where her entrances and exits were. She was too tall for Mimi, and it had never been a role to which she was particularly suited. For her Marguerite, a role she had never sung in French, she faced the same problems: no stage or orchestra rehearsals. So while she was in no way a flop, she did not make the impression that could have led her to a permanent position with the company. When I asked Pobbé why she had not asked for a better deal, she replied that she had not been given a choice—it was a take-it-or-leave-it offer.

Many years later Pobbé was announced for a series of *Aidas* at the open-air Terme di Caracalla in Rome. I asked her why she had accepted an assignment which I felt was so unsuited to her essentially lyric voice—and doubly dangerous because of the large outdoor amphitheatre her voice would have to fill. Her answer was significant; in a few words it depicted clearly, and put into tragic focus, what goes on in the operatic world today: "There are no dramatic or spinto sopranos left, and all we lyrics are forced, if we want to survive, to accept these offers. Look at Virginia Zeani and Gabriella Tucci, who are in the same boat. There are plenty of very small-voiced lyrics, and these directors think that we, with the experience of years, can cope with our little more know-how. It is crazy, I know—but I must pay my bills at the end of each month. If one wants to work in the summer, all the opera seasons are out of doors, and they only go in for spectacular works. Only rarely is there a Micaëla or a Liù. Even Tosca is a far tougher proposition for me under the stars. But one must live." Shortly after, Pobbé fell into oblivion. As for Gabriella Tucci, a charming lyric, the dramatic roles she undertook caused her downfall too.

Gundula Janowitz also made the unwise decision to make her debut at the Metropolitan under Karajan's direction as Sieglinde, a role uncongenial to her cool, unimpassioned instrument. She never returned. Lou Ann Wyckoff, essentially a lyric, made her bow at La Scala as Amelia in *Un ballo in maschera* a few years ago, and Italians, used to bigger voices in this part, simply did not respond; she was not re-engaged. A debut in the United States is far riskier than one in Europe, since music critics play a far greater part in establishing and consolidating the careers of singers in America. Many Europeans are not aware of this and are surprised to find themselves suffering at the hands of these reviewers.

Still, there are singers who, through sheer perseverance and enormous toughness, can bounce back from seeming defeat and come out on top. No one has lost more battles than Mirella Freni at La Scala, where her *Traviata*, under Karajan, was so poorly received that she was immediately replaced by Anna Moffo, at the time a charming lyric in full possession of her instrument. Then Freni did Gilda, drawing violent protests—Italians are used to coloraturas in this part; and more recently, when she abandoned her adorable Susanna to take over the Countess in *Le nozze di Figaro,* she was heavily criticized. Karajan has an elephant's memory, and he never forgave the Milanese for questioning his choice of Violetta; by booing her, they ruined his performance, and, in fact, he withdrew too. But he has continued to use her in Vienna and Salzburg in both spinto and dramatic roles. Then Abbado too took her under his powerful wing. Despite her frail, beguiling face, Freni is made of steel; she survived all these storms and emerged triumphant, with masses of recordings and engagements. What Iris Adami Corradetti said about her (and Scotto) has a lot of truth: it is not they who are to blame, but the system, which has gone off course. But although, unlike Scotto, Freni never forces, the tone has become far more metallic, causing her voice to lose that wonderful freshness it once had, and she cannot project the drama of the spinto repertoire that she has now undertaken, because of the instrument's limitations.

Why are certain artists tremendously successful in some theatres and not in others? It is very difficult to answer this riddle satisfactorily. One thinks of the cases of Anny Konetzni and Gertrud Rünger, who appeared two years apart at the Metropolitan and made virtually no impression there, while in most leading European opera houses they were—and continue to be—

considered among the finest of the Wagnerian heroic sopranos. The late English soprano Amy Shuard, considered everywhere to be one of the finest Turandots, appeared in this opera at the San Carlo in Naples, and the protests were so loud that the event became international news.

But audiences have always been unpredictable, and this is one factor in opera that has not changed. Hissing and booing in opera houses has always occurred, but in the past it was contained within certain limits, and most of it seemed to come from the balconies and the standees. Then, for a while, it seemed to quiet down. Now it is happening again, and with such frequency and ferocity that opera houses seem more like sports arenas. And the interesting development is that these outbursts are no longer the privilege of those occupying the less expensive seats; the members of the audience who have paid dearly for their seats have adopted this distasteful behavior. On several occasions recently I heard protests from the entire audience at the Paris Opéra that were so prolonged the conductor had difficulty continuing. On June 4, 1977, after Edda Moser's delivery of the Queen of the Night's first aria, the booing—coming even from the boxes—shook the rafters.

Sometimes, however infrequently, this total lack of manners is a manifestation of the audience's avid thirst for one of the few remaining great stars. An example of this occurred at La Scala during the 1981–82 season. As one of the few important events of the season, a revival of the famous Visconti-Benois production of *Anna Bolena* was planned for February. In 1957 Callas and Simionato had sung the leads; the revival would have Caballé and Obraztsova. Tickets for the entire series of performances were sold out; they were not even available at black-market prices.

The day before the premiere, Caballé came down with stomatitis, gastroenteritis, and nausea, and she immediately informed the management. As her condition worsened, it became obvious to her that she would not be able to perform. According to Caballé (every newspaper carried a different version of the story), the only person from the management of La Scala she could find the morning of the performance was Francesco Siciliani, the artistic director. She advised him of her inability to perform, and her understudy, Ruth Falcon, was notified. But instead of announcing the change in cast on the radio and television, and changing the advertisements posted at the opera house, no one did anything.

When, at eight o'clock on the night of the performance, an anonymous voice announced over the theatre's loudspeaker that Caballé would not appear, a fury unlike anything in the history of this theatre exploded. The announcement that Ruth Falcon would be replacing the Spanish soprano could not be heard. The conductor, Giuseppe Patané, stepped onto the podium, but instead of starting to conduct, he walked off as the booing increased. Insults directed at the Indendant, Ernesto Badini, reached such a level that he withdrew quickly from his box. The audience seemed to have gone mad. In the midst of the storm, Siciliani begged Giulietta Simionato, who was in the audience, to go onstage and try to calm the house down. But even though she is so deeply beloved, she was unable to utter a word, and all that could be heard was a shout from the audience: "Let that clown Badini come and speak to us himself!" The imprecations—even from bejeweled ladies in the boxes—continued at such a hysterical pitch that at 8:30 the anonymous loudspeaker voice announced that the performance was canceled and reimbursements would be made. But the pandemonium only increased; it was quite a while before the angry spectators left.

The repercussions of this incident went on and on, and it became headline news in all the Italian newspapers, with *Anna Bolena* taking precedence even over terrorists. For the next few days there were endless stories speculating on what would happen, as Caballé's indisposition continued and several more performances were canceled. Finally it was announced that she would sing. But what is so extraordinary is that at this performance, Caballé—who did show some signs of vocal stress, but whose mezze voci were as beautiful as ever—was booed, as were Obraztsova, Paul Plishka, and the other principals, by some members of the audience. Critics were divided but, on the whole, unkind. Caballé was a marvelous sport in the various interviews she gave afterward, speaking highly of Ruth Falcon (who had herself in the meantime become ill, and no wonder). Finally, after that single performance Caballé left for Spain, and Cecilia Gasdia—only twenty-one years old but the winner in 1980 of the first prize in the Callas competition—got the job, and apparently came out of it with honors and an ocean of publicity.

Marilyn Horne and *Les Troyens* recently kept the Italian press busy as well. The American mezzo had signed a contract with La Scala to sing *L'italiana* during the 1981–82 season, with the understanding that should the Berlioz opera be performed (there were some unsettled questions at the time, as is often the case with this opera house), she would be assigned the role of Cassandra. When she learned secondhand that *Les Troyens* was indeed scheduled, but with Elena Obraztsova engaged to sing both Cassandra and Dido, Horne, who knows her worth and will not stand for any foolishness, considered La Scala's behavior inexcusable and canceled her contract for *L'italiana*. *Il Giornale,* one of Italy's most authoritative newspapers, declared that la Horne is a truly professional singer and sided with her one hundred percent, insisting that La Scala had shown a total lack of courtesy toward a great artist. The subscribers, already deprived of Caballé, were incensed, and the opera house, for lack of an available valid protagonist, had to cancel *L'italiana.*

A lot of nonsense has been written in recent years about the streamlining of prima donnas and how the public will no longer accept singers who because of their size do not lend credibility to their characterizations. Nothing could be less true: the two biggest moneymakers before the public today are Montserrat Caballé and Luciano Pavarotti. Announce Caballé anywhere and within twenty-four hours the house is sold out. Marilyn Horne, Rita Orlandi Malaspina, Margaret Price, and Rita Hunter are large ladies who have all the engagements they want. A lesson that many people have forgotten is how much better the heavy Callas sang than the thin, glamorous diva who eventually lost her voice completely. No one is less physically suited to Carmen or Tancredi than Marilyn Horne—short and stocky—but she sells out every time. More than ever the public wants to hear great voices, particularly now when there are so few; and the directors who continue to think that forty or fifty pounds more or less make a big difference could not be more mistaken.

Since there are so few artists with big names, the demand for those who exist—and the fees they command—are spectacular. They travel incessantly, and so their voices are constantly deteriorating. Yet such is the public's hunger for names that houses go wild at the performances of Birgit Nilsson, for example, who, at sixty-four, should probably be in retirement or only concertizing. Her off-pitch and strident singing of the Dyer's Wife in *Die Frau ohne Schatten* at the Metropolitan in 1981 saddened me greatly, for this had been one of the great voices of all time. Many of the divas I interviewed predicted the vocal problems that Renata Scotto was to encounter when she opened the Met season as Norma in September 1981. And these problems are not limited to women. In November 1981, Luciano Pavarotti sang Radames in *Aida* with the San Francisco Opera. It was his first time in this role, which is far too heavy for him, and it was a fiasco. Neither the press nor Pavarotti's usually adoring audience hid its extreme disappointment. Yet Pavarotti and Scotto are vivid personalities with a great command of the stage, and they stand out because so many of those around them are not.

Go to the Metropolitan, whose prices have risen alarmingly, when a major singer is appearing, and it is sold out. I attended performances of *Siegfried* and *La traviata* in October 1981, with third-rate casts, and the number of empty seats was disturbing. What is the answer? We eagerly look to the young singers, but in a world where all standards are slipping and falling, it stands to reason that most of them—despite talent, schooling, and promise—will fully realize only a fraction of their potential. Many of the prima donnas stated that they sang with the dividends of their vocal instruments and never with their capital. Today it's capital all the way, and in a period of galloping inflation the capital soon vanishes, leaving nothing.

It is no wonder that the former prima donnas I spent so many hours conversing with should be not only disoriented but frightened that the entire operatic structure is coming apart. The liberties taken with scores and librettos are assuming scandalous proportions. Once upon a time (as in the cases of Toscanini, de Sabata, Giulini, Klemperer, Kleiber, and so many others) conductors started with opera, learning the repertoire and the vocal equipment of each singer, and then went on to the symphony orchestras. Now the opposite is true. Today distinguished maestros are fascinated by opera and make excursions into the field without real basic preparation for it, nor with the proper respect. In the course of these talks a mezzo pointed out to me that at La Scala, Georges Prêtre, one of France's leading conductors, had taken it upon himself to switch the role of Siebel in *Faust* from a mezzo to a tenor. "I was shocked," she said to me, "not only because this is not respecting the score, but because it changes musically every scene in which the young man appears. If Gounod wrote it for a light mezzo, there was a musical reason. He wanted a particular sound for the part of the young man deeply in love with Marguerite. The enchanting aria 'Faites-lui mes aveux' is intended to express the adoration of an almost sexless youth. If it is given to a tenor, the sensuous element comes in and the meaning is gone."

There was much surprise when Zubin Mehta, for a new production of *Die Fledermaus* at Covent Garden, insisted on having a man sing Orlofsky. Strauss had wanted a woman to sing the part because the prince is only eighteen years old and he felt that not even a light tenor could handle the particular sound he had in mind. It was amusing to read Rodney Milnes in *The Spectator* commenting on this very fact: "Mehta says he cannot stand female Orlofskys. Well, of course, composers will keep making these elementary mistakes, and how lucky we are with musicians like Mr. Mehta who knows better and can tidy them up. I look forward to hearing a tenor Octavian and bass-baritone Cherubino when he gets around to giving us his *Rosenkavalier* and *Le nozze di Figaro*."

Yniold in *Pelléas et Mélisande* is a boy, but Debussy specified he wanted a soprano for this part. Granted that she is not easy to locate, for she must be small and graceful; but somehow opera companies have always found the right performer. Gian Carlo Menotti, also a respected stage director, always chooses a boy for his Yniold. On the three different occasions that I have been present, the voice could not be heard over the orchestra. "After all," the late Gilda dalla Rizza protested, "Debussy is not Palestrina, who wrote for the white voices of children, with no orchestra to bother him. Menotti is one of the few operatic composers of the new wave I admire, but he has no right to do this."

When La Scala in 1966 used a tenor Romeo instead of a coloratura mezzo in Bellini's *I Capuleti ed i Montecchi,* purists were scandalized. Despite his good intentions, Giacomo Aragall could not sound like Marilyn Horne, Tatiana Troyanos, or Agnes Baltsa, who sing Romeo so admirably, much less like Giulietta Simionato, who was overwhelming in this part. The experiment was lamentable. Bellini had written Romeo and Giulietta for the Grisi sisters, Giuditta and Giulia, but conductor Claudio Abbado ignored Bellini and made this foolish change, upsetting the entire balance of the score.

The same deviations from original intent are being made by directors and set designers. With the exception of Franco Zeffirelli, Filippo Sanjust, and a few others, they all seem to ignore the scores and librettos, looking for nonexistent symbolic connotation. Managements, afraid not to be "with it," accept all of this, even when catcalls break out during performances.

At La Scala *Madama Butterfly* as conceived by Jorge Lavelli (the production was taken later to the Paris Opéra) had a nylon tent descend from the ceiling "to express loneliness." Maria Caniglia was indignant: "How can a conductor with the reputation of Georges Prêtre agree to conduct such a travesty?" she cried. "Are sopranos like Mauti Nunziata [who appeared in it at La Scala] and Zylis-Gara [at the Paris Opéra] so hungry for money that they will lend their names and persons to these shenanigans? As if the music by Puccini and the libretto by Illica and Giacosa did not express Cio-Cio-San's loneliness sufficiently? Are they all mad? Please tell me! So the production was booed at La Scala—I don't know what happened in Paris —but they went right on with it. People protest about everything today, but there are no picket lines around La Scala, and this is a great pity, for they deserve it. And can you imagine having to sing through the nylon?"

Wolfgang Sawallisch, music director of the Bavarian State Opera in Munich—one of the most in-demand conductors in Europe—accompanied

Luca Ronconi's vision of *Die Walküre* at La Scala, with the Valkyries dressed as schoolgirls and Wotan's favorite daughter falling asleep on a kitchen stove. It is still talked about with amazement in Milan. The Ronconi series of the *Ring* did not reach its conclusion but continued with shocking results, in Florence.

Pierre Boulez found it perfectly natural in his Bayreuth *Walküre* for Sieglinde and Siegmund to meet for the first time not in the forest but in a cement power house. Patrice Chéreau's entire *Ring* cycle left the public goggle-eyed, but its absurd innovations received a lot of publicity. In a new production of *Walküre* at the Paris Opéra, Hunding's lodge in the woods consisted of a modern room with a wall made of an endless series of coat hangers, and a large white modern table and two white chairs in center stage. Sieglinde was garbed in a white evening dress, which remained immaculate throughout the opera, even after she had escaped across the mountains on foot. There is no need to dwell on the rest, for it was all in the same lunatic spirit. After the Bayreuth Festival's new *Lohengrin* in 1979, the review by Martin Bernheimer in the *International Herald Tribune* described "a lumber-yard-like forestage that provided a primitive private haven for the forces of evil; a huge bridal bed that resembled nothing so much as a misplaced birthday cake; a tiny robot-like figure in gold who appeared at the denouement and conjured up instant images of R2-D2 rather than the noble Gottfried, savior of Brabant." And about the performance he wrote: "In the title role a slender, youthful tenor, Peter Hofmann, looked like a blond superman and sang like a somewhat strained mortal. Karan Armstrong, who used to be a lyric-coloratura in Los Angeles, introduced a wobbly middle-weight soprano as Elsa. . . . Ruth Hesse played Ortrud like a mini-Elektra and did her share of screaming." All this for eighty-three dollars a ticket in the orchestra!

The baritone Thomas Stewart told me that even the highest-paid artists don't dare argue too strongly with stage directors—so powerful have they become—for fear of being replaced. But there have been two isolated exceptions to this pattern recently which show that finally something is changing. During the rehearsals of *Tristan* in Bayreuth in July 1981, the director, Jean-Pierre Ponnelle, told Johanna Meier—the first American ever to sing Isolde in the Wagnerian temple—that during the third act he wanted her to sing from the orchestra pit while an actress mimed the "Liebestod" text on stage. The reason behind this innovation was that the director envisaged the finale as a figment of Tristan's imagination. Running the risk of being fired, Meier refused to accept this absurd notion. But she won her battle and performed the death scene herself. One can only applaud her for standing up for tradition.

Another singer who made headlines in the Italian papers for ten days was the tenor René Kollo. He protested the direction of Giorgio Strehler for the new production of *Lohengrin* on the opening night of La Scala's 1981–82 season, December 7. Part of the problem was a tremendously heavy armor and helmet, designed by Ezio Frigerio, which did not allow Kollo to move about freely or breathe easily. But more than that, he strongly disapproved of Strehler's conception of the protagonist as a political warrior instead of a Christian knight, which is what Wagner intended. Kollo left Milan but was called back when no replacement with equal prestige could be located —and his costume was changed. According to the singer, in a long interview given to the prestigious weekly *Gente,* Strehler did not show up in the theatre for the last days' rehearsals. Kollo sang at the premiere and then another tenor took his place.

When the Metropolitan Opera presented in 1979 the production of *Der fliegende Holländer* directed by Jean-Pierre Ponnelle, imported from the San Francisco Opera, everyone was outraged, and there was a great deal of booing. The program presented Mr. Ponnelle's explanation: "I wanted to tell the story on a different level than the primitive legend, so I decided to turn the entire opera into a dream of the Steersman. . . . In this production the Steersman and Erik the Huntsman are the same person, the latter being the former's fantasy of himself. Like the modern soldier or astronaut, the Steersman and all the men on Daland's ship have been compelled to leave home without women. This dream, therefore, reflects the young sailor's loneliness and jealousies." "The trouble with that idea," wrote the acute Andrew Porter in *The New Yorker,*

> is that Wagner didn't write an opera about a hysterical, sex-starved little sailor in love with the boss's daughter. It would make as much sense to present *Salome* as Narraboth's dream, *Tosca* as the Sacristan's dream, and *La traviata* as Dr. Grenvil's dream. Narraboth could be doubled with Herod, the Sacristan with Scarpia, and Dr. Grenvil with Giorgio Germont. . . . At the end of the respective operas, Narraboth, the Sacristan, and Doctor would wake up to discover that nothing had really happened—they had imagined it all. . . .

All the action is made to take place on Daland's ship, which seems to be a tramp steamer. Its helm also serves as a giant spinning wheel. The Dutchman's vessel is represented by some spectral shrouds, in which bodies are tangled, and a suggestion of red sails in the backdrop. The Steersman is present throughout, writhing in his heated dream, sometimes mopping and mowing and dancing about. (The role is shared by the tenor who sings the Steersman's and Erik's music— William Lewis on the first night—and a smaller-size, mute double. During one episode, the pair dance a mirror pas de deux.) This staging is not merely silly, willful, and pointless. Besides destroying the large drama of the opera, it renders ineffective theatrical passages that one thought were surefire.

Porter, one of the most erudite among the music critics, is worth quoting again in another context. In his review of a 1978 Metropolitan Opera production of *La favorita* he described Patrick Tavernia's stage direction as "weak and characterless" and added, "The director is positively perverse only when he has Fernando blindfolded at precisely the point where the plot and stage directions require him to take a blindfold off."

Filippo Sanjust (one of today's most talented and imaginative set designers and directors) said to me in an interview which appeared in *Opera News:*

> I am talking against my own interests, but today too much importance is being given to production. The emphasis is more and more away from what opera is all about; my philosophy is that one should not spit into the dish one eats from. I cannot begin to understand why in a recent German production of *Die Zauberflöte* a Lesbian element was underlined. You can reread the libretto a hundred times and you won't find it. In Verdi's *Macbeth* in Frankfurt there were two doubles playing the lead, bumping into one another. Lady Macbeth was always in bed with three people, extras actually, and this is all wrong—she was interested in power, not sex. The witches were dressed like Floradora girls, and the men at court like musketeers with colossal behinds. Banquo was killed and put into a plastic bag, and during the second act there was a cancan. Lady Macbeth was made to look like a madam from a brothel, and Duncan was wheeled in by nurses on a bed covered with lilies. At the end a sign was flashed across a screen saying *"Lady Macbeth,* a fairy tale by Verdi." While the audience roared its disapproval, critics raved.

Cases such as these become more and more frequent. John Ardoin wrote of a *Norma* given in Houston in 1978, "The sets looked like an Indian trading post in the winter." It is not very comforting to know that millions of people watched this performance of the Bellini masterpiece on national television. The new production of *Parsifal* at the Grand Théâtre in Geneva in January 1982, directed by Rolf Liebermann and designed by Petrika Ionesco, attracted a lot of attention, and no wonder. For if the first act pretends to be a state of mind which has lived through Hiroshima, the second act takes place in an atomic center to show the opposite side of the coin. In his witty review in *La Suisse* Jean Delor wrote that "Wagner's music seemed out of phase, and one wondered whether there should not have been a re-reading of the score, suggesting electronic additions."

Opera, in my estimation, should be illusion and should transport one into a world of dreams. Now it has become in most cases a hideous spectacle. In a *Tristan* in Rio de Janeiro in August 1981, Tristan (Jon Vickers) and Isolde (Janice Yoes) wore identical silver tunics during the love duet, and in the ensuing obscurity that now appears to be a must for all Wagner productions it was impossible to tell them apart. Is this what Wagner wanted? Of course not. Nor did the public, who were incensed.

Today there are no more operatic ensembles; repertoires are chosen and then singers must be found to meet the requirements of the roles. In the past it was, logically, the other way around, and every repertory house had a permanent ensemble of singers capable of handling a variety of roles. They were there to jump in at emergencies and were often given their own performances as payment for their good will. Throughout the Johnson regime at the Metropolitan there was Irene Jessner, the Austrian soprano, who was at home in both the German and the Italian repertoires. During the Bing regime there were Lucine Amara and, for a long time, Mary Curtis-Verna. Now there seems to be no one comparable to these singers at the Met. When Leontyne Price canceled her *Ariadne* in the winter of 1979, no replacement was available, and the performance had to be changed to *Don Carlo*, which, being much longer and lasting until after midnight, came to cost considerably more because of union rules. It seems that no singer wants to be tied to any one house; in fact, all of the divas interviewed lamented the lack of permanent ensembles. The managements of the opera houses don't seem to be able to foresee the immensely varied and complicated problems facing repertory companies; nor do young singers seem ready to wait and learn their craft while covering for the more established artists. These young singers are no longer protected or guided; they are thrown— or throw themselves—to the wolves.

At many of the productions I see today—distorted by the whims of the directors or designers, performed by singers either not ready for their roles or not good enough for them—I watch and listen with pain and a sense of rebellion. I often think of Agathe's cry in the third act of *Freischütz:* "Where am I?" And also of Andrew Porter's term "malinscenation," a brilliant summing-up of the current situation.

It is frightening to think that many people hear and see opera for the first time in these distorted productions, and it is a great pity when someone must hear a production in which the voices themselves are distorted. I was present at La Scala at a performance of *Macbeth* that was being taped for television, and so, of course, there were recording microphones onstage. The voices of the singers—Shirley Verrett, Piero Cappuccilli, Veriano Luchetti, and Nicolai Ghiaurov—sounded enormous when they sang close to where the microphones were positioned but were practically inaudible when the singers moved to the back. To make matters worse, Strehler, who was in charge of this production, had dressed Macbeth and Lady Macbeth like twins, and so I wonder whether they could be differentiated on a small television screen. They were made to rush about from one end of the stage to the other, and their increasingly labored breathing was fully amplified and recorded. In my opinion, these televised performances should be taped with no audience present; there is an enormous difference between the way a work is presented to an audience of three thousand and to one of twenty million.

The wealth of available recordings has contributed vastly to the confusion in the minds of operagoers. Small voices are made to seem larger, and every possible trick is used to minimize vocal deficiencies, to the point where certain notes are literally split and respliced together. Sometimes a passage is recorded a dozen times until either the right one is chosen or various elements from each "take" are pieced together. On records singers take on scores they could never handle in an opera house, and one can only conclude that the reasons are purely commercial. The miscasting before the microphones is not really new—it started over two decades ago—but in recent years it has increased by leaps and bounds. Why did both Joan Sutherland and Katia Ricciarelli record the title role in *Turandot,* for which they are both unsuited and which would wreck their voices if they sang it in public? Seiji Ozawa's choice of a soubrette like Edith Mathis for the dramatic impact of Marguerite in Berlioz's *La Damnation de Faust* on Deutsche Grammophon is a veritable puzzle. Now Margaret Price, a spinto, and René Kollo, a light Wagnerian, have recorded *Tristan und Isolde* under Carlos

Kleiber, who is reportedly unhappy with the result and has not as yet given his go-ahead for the release. Undoubtedly, some compromise will be reached, for too much money is at stake.

Callas, Tebaldi, Sills, and Moffo in the past, and now Caballé, Sutherland, Scotto, and Freni (with Cotrubas trailing behind), have recorded just about everything, including many works they never sang onstage. Caballé has even treated us to a *Lucia di Lammermoor* that, according to the liner notes, is sung in the original key. And so it may be, but the fact remains that Donizetti wrote the opera for Fanny Persiani, who was famous for her range (she apparently could reach high F). So Caballé's fans rush to buy a *Lucia* without the pyrotechnics for which the original interpreter was so celebrated. As Claire Watson in particular and other former prima donnas have discussed throughout this book, modern recording has engendered a new vocal technique, eliminating the vibrato that provides the emotional base to the music and creating a monochromatic sound.

Transposing is as old as opera itself; it was taken for granted, and no one gave it much thought until Verdi came along. His contracts with singers usually specified heavy penalties should this happen. Now it is a constant habit, and particularly so in recordings. For some reason (in the past it was never even mentioned that such famous sopranos as Ponselle, Caniglia, and Tebaldi had the first act of *La traviata* transposed) critics now often go into long disquisitions about this relatively matter-of-fact habit. When in 1979 Marilyn Horne transposed "O don fatale" in the Met *Don Carlo,* there was a big fuss about it, all the more strange since it has been done many times in the past without anyone's even noticing it. The aria, written in the key of A-flat, was transposed to F to suit the American mezzo. I asked Miss Horne about it, and this is what she replied: "I have appeared as Eboli before, and, as everyone knows who has sung it, the tessitura is tricky. It is not the top note that in my particular case presents any problems, but simply the way the scoring is worked out. Verdi actually wrote several cadenzas, and I chose the one that suited me the best, which happens to be in F."

But Miss Horne, along with Caballé, is a welcome reason why so many long-forgotten works have been resurrected recently, for they are real exponents of bel canto and can do full justice to these scores. Their *Semiramide* together in Paris in November and December 1981 was one of the most gorgeous experiences I have ever enjoyed. Iris Adami Corradetti discussed the problem of revivals with me at length: "There are some of the Bellini, Donizetti, and Rossini scores that never should have left the repertoire, and I am one hundred percent for them. But throwing away so much public money on Vivaldi's operas is totally unwarranted. They are simply not suited to the stage: too long, too static, too many recitatives. *Tito Manlio* has no fewer than thirty-six arias. Only a very special type of audience can sit through them, and now, because of the success of the *Orlando Furioso,* repeated for two seasons in Verona, everyone thinks Vivaldi must be brought back at all costs. But let us not forget that Marilyn Horne sang the *Orlando,* and she is a colossal draw. The Monteverdi operas are another kettle of fish. Some of them are fairly theatrical, but they were written for small court theatres, and transforming them into big productions in large theatres is part of today's total dementia. The balance is all wrong; the orchestration (the composer barely marked the essentials) is elaborated by this one and that one, with each one thinking he is on the right track, and becomes a travesty of the original, which was written for a handful of instruments. There is a terrible mix-up, with tenors sometimes taking the roles written for the castratos; then sometimes it's the sopranos. Does anyone really know what a castrato sounded like anyhow? It's all pretty much a world of fantasy." I knew exactly what she meant, for I had just heard at the Spoleto Festival in July 1979 *L'incoronazione di Poppea* in a version by Alan Curtis. Sopranos took castrato roles, mezzos high tenor parts, and the Nurse was assigned to a tenor. But in the Paris Opéra *Poppea* the soprano role of Nero was interpreted by none other than Jon Vickers. So where are we?

The progress made in the last twenty-five years by American singers is amazing: they now hold very important positions around the world in the lyric theatre. "Where would most opera houses be today without them?" Lisa della Casa commented. "They would all have to close." Although the following list reads like a catalogue, it gives an idea of how tremendously impressive the American contribution to the world of opera is today. Among those who are now considered veterans, there are Beverly Wolff, Annabelle Bernard, Carmen Balthrop, Helen Donath, Gwendolyn Killebrew, Olivia Stapp, Johanna Meier, Leona Mitchell, Diana Soviero, Barbara Hendricks, Judith Beckmann, Lucy Peacock, Patricia Wise, Florence Quivar, Ruth Welting, Faye Robinson, Nancy Shade, Jeanette Scovotti, Arleen Auger, Gianna Rolandi, Gwynn Cornell, Carol Vaness, Catherine Malfitano, Julia Migenes-Johnson, Joy McIntyre, Ruth Falcon, Lynn Strow, Catherine Gayer, Ashley Putnam, Linda Zoghby, Constanza Cuccaro, Sandra Browne, Lella Cuberli, Kathleen Battle, Gail Robinson, Ellen Shade, and Faith Esham. It is far easier for Americans to get started in the Central European opera houses than in Italy, where there exists a strange law that allows foreigners to appear only in the few opera houses labeled Class A —except in emergencies.

"But if they are not very, very careful—and, again, *terribly* careful—" Claire Watson remarked to me, "how many of these wonderful young singers will still be singing ten years from now? In my generation I already saw it coming—this reckless desire to sing everything."

"The old system," Germaine Lubin remarked, "very much resembled that of the film studios. Opera houses signed actors to long-term contracts, and it was a big investment they were making. There was very definite guidance, and great care was taken to protect them. At the Opéra, for all its faults and rigidity, we were led, we were made to take one step at a time, we were protected. Monsieur Rouché always discussed each new assignment with me, explained why he thought I could take it on. But he never imposed anything on me. Don't do what may make you nervous. That was good, common sense. Where do you find this today?"

Madame Lubin was of course right. The craze of contemporary singers for cash knows no limits. On June 17, 1979, the Teatro Municipal in Rio de Janeiro was giving its last performance of *Tosca*. As the curtain rose on Scarpia's study in the Palazzo Farnese, Orianna Santunione and Nunzio Todisco, the Tosca and Cavaradossi, to the astonishment of the audience advanced toward the footlights, gestured to the conductor to stop the orchestra, and announced that they would not finish the performance since they had not been paid in full. Then they calmly walked out. One minute later a spokesman for the opera house came onstage and begged the public to be patient; the performance would continue with two Brazilian singers. The contracts with both Santunione and Todisco were for $4,500 a performance, it was reported, but the artists did not want to have the money deposited in Italy; they wanted it immediately so that they could change the dollars on the black market. Both singers were then sued for breach of contract.

Recently, at a performance of *Die Meistersinger* I attended in Geneva, the address of Hans Sachs in the last act stood out, and I think that if singers, conductors, set designers, directors, opera house managements, and audiences would mull over his words, opera could straighten itself out. He simply states that no art can exist ignoring classicism and tradition. Alas, this is just what everyone is doing today.

INDEX

PHOTO CREDITS

A NOTE ON THE TYPE

The text of this book was set in film in a typeface named Bembo. The roman is a copy of a letter cut for the celebrated Venetian printer Aldus Manutius by Francesco Griffo. It was first used in Cardinal Bembo's DE AETNA *of 1495—hence the name of the revival. Griffo's type is now generally recognized, thanks to the research of Stanley Morison, to be the first of the old-face group of types. The companion italic is an adaption of the chancery script type designed by the Roman calligrapher and printer Lodovico degli Arrighi, called Vincentino, and used by him during the 1520's.*

Composed by The Haddon Craftsmen, Inc.,
Scranton, Pennsylvania.

Design by Dorothy Schmiderer